Microsoft Pow
Cookbook

Second Edition

Gain expertise in Power BI with over 90 hands-on recipes, tips, and use cases

Greg Deckler
Brett Powell

BIRMINGHAM—MUMBAI

Microsoft Power BI Cookbook

Second Edition

Producer: Suman Sen

Acquisition Editor – Peer Reviews: Saby Dsilva

Project Editor: Parvathy Nair

Content Development Editor: Alex Patterson

Copy Editor: Safis Editor

Technical Editor: Aditya Sawant

Proofreader: Safis Editor

Indexer: Manju Arasan

Presentation Designer: Ganesh Bhadwalkar

First published: September 2017
Second edition: September 2021

Production reference: 2141022

Published by Packt Publishing Ltd.
Livery Place
35 Livery Street
Birmingham
B3 2PB, UK.

ISBN 978-1-80181-304-4

www.packt.com

Contributors

About the authors

Greg Deckler is a Vice President at Fusion Alliance and has been a professional of consulting services for over 27 years. Recognized as an expert in Power BI, Greg is a six-time Microsoft MVP for the Data Platform and an active member of the Power BI Community site with over 5,000 solutions authored and hundreds of Quick Measure Gallery submissions. Greg founded the Columbus Azure ML and Power BI User Group in Columbus, OH in 2016 and continues to hold regularly monthly meetings.

I would like to thank the dynamic and vibrant Power BI community as a whole and especially all of the Super Users and my User Group members. Finally, I'd like to thank my son, Rocket, for keeping me supplied with excellent graphics and videos!

Brett Powell owns Frontline Analytics LLC, a data and analytics consultancy specializing in the Microsoft data platform. Brett has over ten years of experience in business intelligence and data warehouse projects as both a developer and technical architect. In addition to project engagements, Brett shares technical tips and examples via his popular *Insights Quest* blog and has authored two commercially successful books – *Mastering Microsoft Power BI* and *Microsoft Power BI Cookbook*.

I'd first like to acknowledge and praise Jesus Christ, my Lord and Savior, for blessing me with these opportunities and for loving me and guiding me each day. I'd also like to thank my mother, Cathy, and brother Dustin, for their endless support and encouragement. Finally, I'd like to thank Packt for their efforts to produce quality, valuable content.

About the reviewer

David R. Eldersveld is a Technical Specialist at Microsoft currently focused on Power BI. Prior to joining Microsoft, he was a Data Platform MVP and spent nearly ten years as a data and analytics consultant with CapstoneBI and BlueGranite. David has contributed to technical communities as a blogger, speaker, and contributor to *Workout Wednesday*'s Power BI challenges.

Table of Contents

Preface

Microsoft Power BI is a collection of business intelligence and analytics applications and services designed to work in coordination with each other to provide visual, interactive insights into data.

This book provides detailed, step-by-step technical examples of using all the primary Power BI tools and features and also demonstrates end-to-end solutions that leverage and integrate with Power BI technologies and services. You will become familiar with Power BI development tools and services; go deep into data connectivity and transformation, modeling, visualization and analytical capabilities of Power BI; and see Power BI's functional programming languages of DAX and M come alive to deliver powerful solutions that address challenging scenarios common to business intelligence.

This book is designed to excite and empower you to get more out of Power BI via detailed, step-by-step recipes, advanced design and development tips, and guidance on enhancing existing Power BI projects.

The second edition of this book includes even more recipes covering the latest enhancements and integrations to Power BI. All other recipes have been updated and revised to make the recipes more detailed, easier to follow, and entirely based on the stock Adventure Works DW database.

Who this book is for

This book is for business intelligence professionals that want to enhance their knowledge of Power BI design and development while increasing the value of the Power BI solutions they deliver. Those interested in quick resolutions to common challenges and a reference guide to Power BI features and design patterns are certain to find this book a useful resource.

What this book covers

Chapter 1, Configuring Power BI Tools, covers the installation and configuration of the primary tools and services that BI professionals utilize to design and develop Power BI content, including Power BI Desktop, the On-Premises Data Gateway, Analyze in Excel, DAX Studio, Tabular Editor, and ALM Toolkit.

Chapter 2, Accessing and Retrieving Data, dives into Power BI Desktop's Get Data experience and walks through the process of establishing and managing data source connections and queries.

Chapter 3, Building a Power BI Data Model, explores the primary processes of designing and developing robust data models.

Chapter 4, Authoring Power BI Reports, develops and describes the most fundamental report visualizations and design concepts. Additionally, guidance is provided to enhance and control the user experience when consuming and interacting with Power BI reports in the Power BI service as well as on mobile devices.

Chapter 5, Working in the Service, covers Power BI dashboards constructed to provide simple, at-a-glance monitoring of critical measures and high-impact business activities.

Chapter 6, Getting Serious with Date Intelligence, contains recipes for preparing a data model to support robust date intelligence as well as recipes for authoring custom date intelligence measures.

Chapter 7, Parameterizing Power BI Solutions, covers both standard parameterization features and techniques in Power BI as well as more advanced custom implementations.

Chapter 8, Implementing Dynamic User-Based Visibility in Power BI, contains detailed examples of building and deploying dynamic, user-based security for both import and DirectQuery models as well as developing dynamic filter context functionality to enhance the user experience.

Chapter 9, Applying Advanced Analytics and Custom Visuals, contains a broad mix of recipes highlighting many of the latest and most popular custom visualizations and advanced analytics features of Power BI.

Chapter 10, Administering and Monitoring Power BI, highlights the most common and impactful administration data sources including Windows Performance Monitor, SQL Server Query Store, the Microsoft On-Premises Data Gateway, the MSDB system database, Extended Events, Office 365 audit log, and Power BI REST API.

Chapter 11, Enhancing and Optimizing Existing Power BI Solutions, contains top data modeling, DAX measure, and M query patterns to enhance the performance, scalability, and reliability of Power BI datasets.

Chapter 12, Deploying and Distributing Power BI Content, contains detailed examples and considerations for deploying and distributing Power BI content via the Power BI service and Power BI mobile applications.

Chapter 13, Integrating Power BI with Other Applications, highlights new and powerful integrations between Power BI, SSAS, SSRS, Excel, PowerPoint, PowerApps, Power Automate, and Dynamics 365.

To get the most out of this book

- Some prior knowledge of Power BI is recommended.
- A Power BI Desktop and Power BI service account (both free).
- Tabular Editor 2.x (free).
- DAX Studio (free).
- SQL Server (any edition, including Express and Developer, which are free) with the **AdventureWorksDW2019** database installed. This database is a free download and instructions for installing are available here: `http://bit.ly/2OVQfG7`.

Download the example code files

The code bundle for the book is hosted on GitHub at `https://github.com/PacktPublishing/Microsoft-Power-BI-Cookbook-Second-Edition`. We also have other code bundles from our rich catalog of books and videos available at `https://github.com/PacktPublishing/`. Check them out!

Download the color images

We also provide a PDF file that has color images of the screenshots/diagrams used in this book. You can download it here: `https://static.packt-cdn.com/downloads/9781801813044_ColorImages.pdf`.

Conventions used

There are a number of text conventions used throughout this book.

`CodeInText`: Indicates code words in text, database table names, folder names, filenames, file extensions, pathnames, dummy URLs, user input, and Twitter handles. For example; "After completing these steps, the reports all have a live connection back to the dataset, `CH5_R1_SalesAndFinanceDataset`."

A block of code is set as follows:

```
let
    Source = AdWorksDW,
    Data = Source{[Schema="dbo",Item="vCH3R2_Products"]}[Data]
in
    Data
```

When we wish to draw your attention to a particular part of a code block, the relevant lines or items are set in bold:

```
Products Rows (Sales) = CALCULATE(COUNTROWS('Products'),'Internet Sales')
```

Bold: Indicates a new term, an important word, or words that you see on the screen, for example, in menus or dialog boxes, also appear in the text like this. For example: "The **Manage roles** dialog box includes the ability to set **Precedence**."

Warnings or important notes appear like this.

Tips and tricks appear like this.

Get in touch

Feedback from our readers is always welcome.

General feedback: Email feedback@packtpub.com, and mention the book's title in the subject of your message. If you have questions about any aspect of this book, please email us at questions@packtpub.com.

Errata: Although we have taken every care to ensure the accuracy of our content, mistakes do happen. If you have found a mistake in this book we would be grateful if you would report this to us. Please visit, http://www.packtpub.com/submit-errata, selecting your book, clicking on the Errata Submission Form link, and entering the details.

Piracy: If you come across any illegal copies of our works in any form on the Internet, we would be grateful if you would provide us with the location address or website name. Please contact us at copyright@packtpub.com with a link to the material.

If you are interested in becoming an author: If there is a topic that you have expertise in and you are interested in either writing or contributing to a book, please visit `http://authors.packtpub.com`.

Share Your Thoughts

Once you've read *Microsoft Power BI Cookbook, Second Edition*, we'd love to hear your thoughts! Scan the QR code below to go straight to the Amazon review page for this book and share your feedback.

`https://packt.link/r/1801813043`

Your review is important to us and the tech community and will help us make sure we're delivering excellent quality content.

Download a free PDF copy of this book

Thanks for purchasing this book!

Do you like to read on the go but are unable to carry your print books everywhere?
Is your eBook purchase not compatible with the device of your choice?

Don't worry, now with every Packt book you get a DRM-free PDF version of that book at no cost.

Read anywhere, any place, on any device. Search, copy, and paste code from your favorite technical books directly into your application.

The perks don't stop there, you can get exclusive access to discounts, newsletters, and great free content in your inbox daily

Follow these simple steps to get the benefits:

1. Scan the QR code or visit the link below

`https://packt.link/free-ebook/9781801813044`

2. Submit your proof of purchase
3. That's it! We'll send your free PDF and other benefits to your email directly

1
Configuring Power BI Tools

Power BI is a suite of business analytics tools and services that work together to access data sources, shape, analyze, and visualize data, and share insights. Although not all tools are required for all projects or deployments of Power BI, synergies are available by utilizing the unique features of multiple tools as part of integrated solutions encompassing diverse data sources and visualization types.

In this chapter, we walk through the installation and configuration of the primary tools and services **business intelligence** (**BI**) professionals utilize to design and develop Power BI content. This includes official Microsoft tools such as Power BI Desktop, the on-premises data gateway, and Analyze in Excel, as well as third-party tools such as DAX Studio, the ALM Toolkit, and Tabular Editor. Since Power BI tools and services are regularly updated with new features and enhancements, resources are identified to stay up to date and to best take advantage of these tools for your projects.

The recipes in this chapter are as follows:

- Installing and Configuring Power BI Desktop
- Creating an On-Premises Data Gateway
- Installing Analyze in Excel from the Power BI Service
- Installing and Configuring Additional Tools

Technical Requirements

It is assumed that the reader has access to a Power BI Pro license, rights to download and install the development tools on their machine, and has the necessary access and rights to deploy and manage content in the Power BI service and utilize the Power BI mobile applications.

Power BI licensing options and assigning and managing these rights are outside the scope of this book. In addition, the following are required to complete the recipes in this chapter:

- A Windows PC running Windows 10 version 14393 or higher. There is no Power BI Desktop for Apple computers or operating systems.
- Microsoft Excel.
- Ensure that you have at least 10 GB of disk space available; the Power BI Desktop download is up to 600 MB in size and the installed application is over 1.5 GB.
- A Power BI login for the Power BI service.

Additionally, the Microsoft on-premises data gateway requires the following:

- .NET Framework 4.7.2 (Gateway release December 2020 and earlier)
- .NET Framework 4.8 (Gateway release February 2021 and later)
- A 64-bit version of Windows 8 or later or a 64-bit version of Windows Server 2012 R2 or later with current TLS 1.2 and cipher suites
- 4 GB disk space for performance monitoring logs (in the default configuration)

Installing and Configuring Power BI Desktop

Power BI Desktop is the primary tool used to develop the visual and analytical content that is then deployed and collaborated on in the Power BI service, embedded in other applications and portals, or even shared on the public internet. Although Power BI Desktop runs as a single application, it includes three tightly integrated components with their own options and settings:

- The Power Query and Power Query Editor experience, with its underlying M language and data mashup engine.
- The Analysis Services tabular data modeling engine and its DAX analytical language.
- The interactive reporting and visualization engine.

Configuring and leveraging these capabilities, in addition to advanced analytics and customization features such as R, Python, mobile layout, and natural language queries, makes it possible to build robust and elegant BI and analytics solutions.

Getting ready

Most organizations restrict the ability of employees to install software such as Power BI Desktop onto their corporate devices. These organizations typically define a policy and process for pushing a particular version of Power BI Desktop to all user devices or to certain groups of users thus avoiding compatibility issues and ensuring users have access to recent features.

How to install and configure Power BI Desktop

There are actually three different versions of the Power BI Desktop application, as follows:

- Power BI Desktop (Microsoft Store app)
- Power BI Desktop (Microsoft Installer)
- Power BI Desktop RS (Report Server Edition)

The preferred method of installation is by using the Microsoft Store app. In order to install Power BI Desktop from the Microsoft Store, execute the following:

1. Open the Microsoft Store app and search for Power BI Desktop. Alternatively, you can enter `https://aka.ms/pbidesktop` into any browser bar and the Microsoft Store app will automatically open to the Power BI Desktop app, as shown in *Figure 1.1*.
2. **It is important to make sure that you are getting the Power BI Desktop app and not just the Power BI app. The Power BI app is for viewing reports published to the Power BI service only.**

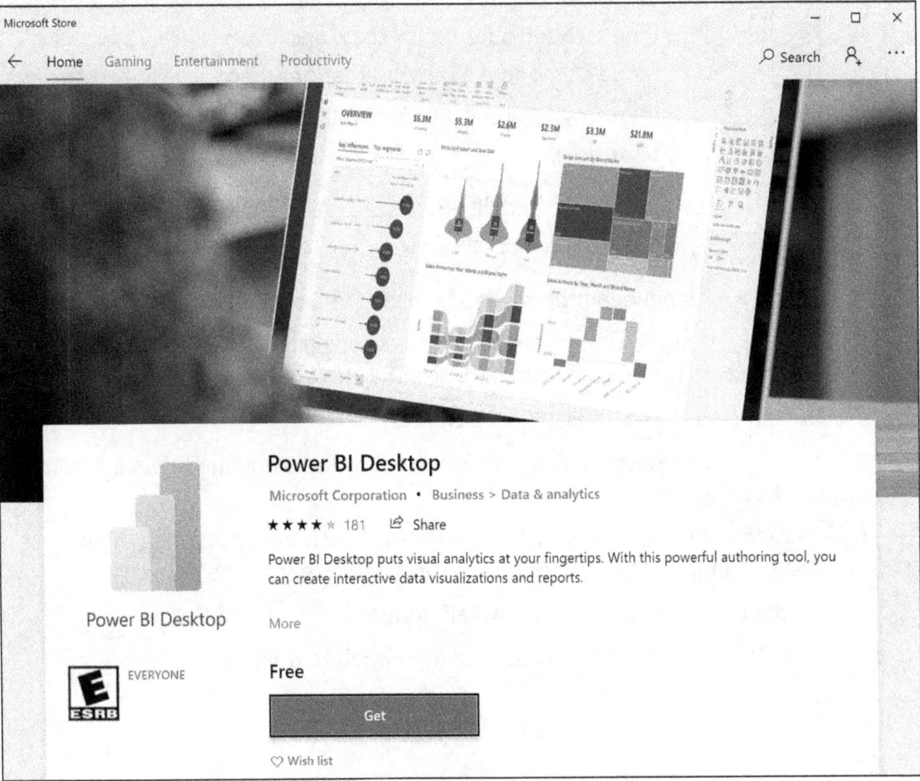

Figure 1.1: The Power BI Desktop app in the Microsoft Store

3. Click the **Get** button.
4. Once the download and installation is complete, click the **Launch** button.

For a variety of reasons, it may not be possible to install the Microsoft Store app version of Power BI Desktop. This may be because of running an older version of Windows, corporate policies, or a desire to use the 32-bit version of Power BI Desktop (the Microsoft Store app is 64-bit only). In this case, you can install the **Microsoft Installer** (**MSI**) version. To install the MSI version, follow these steps:

1. The **Microsoft Installer** (**MSI**) version of Power BI Desktop can be downloaded on the Power BI downloads page: `https://powerbi.microsoft.com/downloads`.
2. Under **Microsoft Power BI Desktop**, choose **Advanced download options**.

Figure 1.2: Download the MSI version using Advanced download options

3. Select your language preference and click the **Download** button.
4. Choose either the 64-bit version (`PBIDesktopSetup_x64.exe`) or the 32-bit version (`PBIDesktopSetup.exe`) and then click the **Next** button.
5. Once the file downloads, click **Open file**.
6. The Microsoft Power BI Desktop Setup Wizard will launch. Select a language and click the **Next** button.
7. Complete the rest of the installation wizard, including accepting the license terms and destination folder, clicking the **Next** button each time.
8. On the final screen, click the **Install** button.
9. Once the installation finishes, click the **Finish** button.

Figure 1.3: Successful installation of Power BI Desktop (MSI)

If you are using Power BI Report Server (on-premises) you need to download the corresponding version of Power BI Desktop optimized for Report Server (RS version). Updates for Power BI Report Server come out quarterly and there is a specific version of Power BI Desktop released simultaneously that is optimized to work with each quarterly version. The installation is the same as the MSI version. However, to find the download for the RS version, follow these steps:

1. Use a browser to navigate to `https://powerbi.microsoft.com/report-server`.
2. Use the **Advanced download options** link directly under the **DOWNLOAD FREE TRIAL** button.

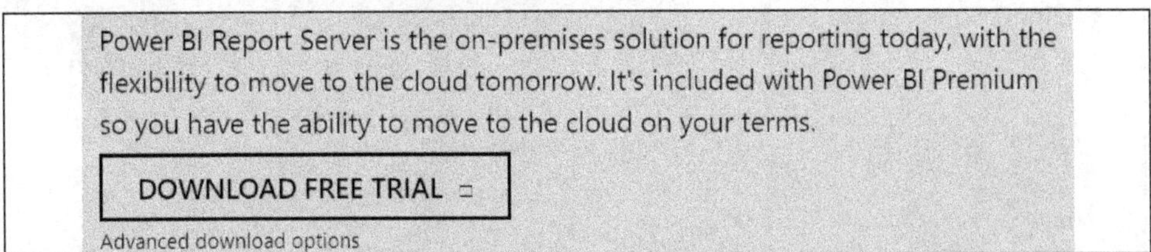

Figure 1.4: Download the RS version using Advanced download options

How it works

Power BI Desktop supports a rich set of configuration options both for the currently open file and for all instances of Power BI Desktop on the given device. These options control the availability of preview and end user features and define default behaviors resource usage, security, and privacy/isolation of data sources.

Regardless of the version of Power BI Desktop that is installed, these options are available by using the **File** menu in the ribbon and then selecting **Options and settings**, and then **Options**, as shown in *Figure 1.5*.

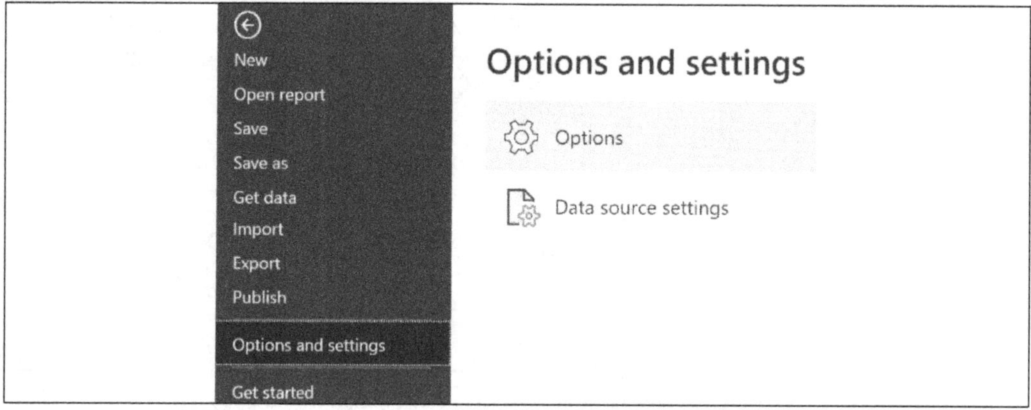

Figure 1.5: Power BI Desktop Options and settings

Selecting **Options** brings up the **Options** window, displayed in *Figure 1.6*.

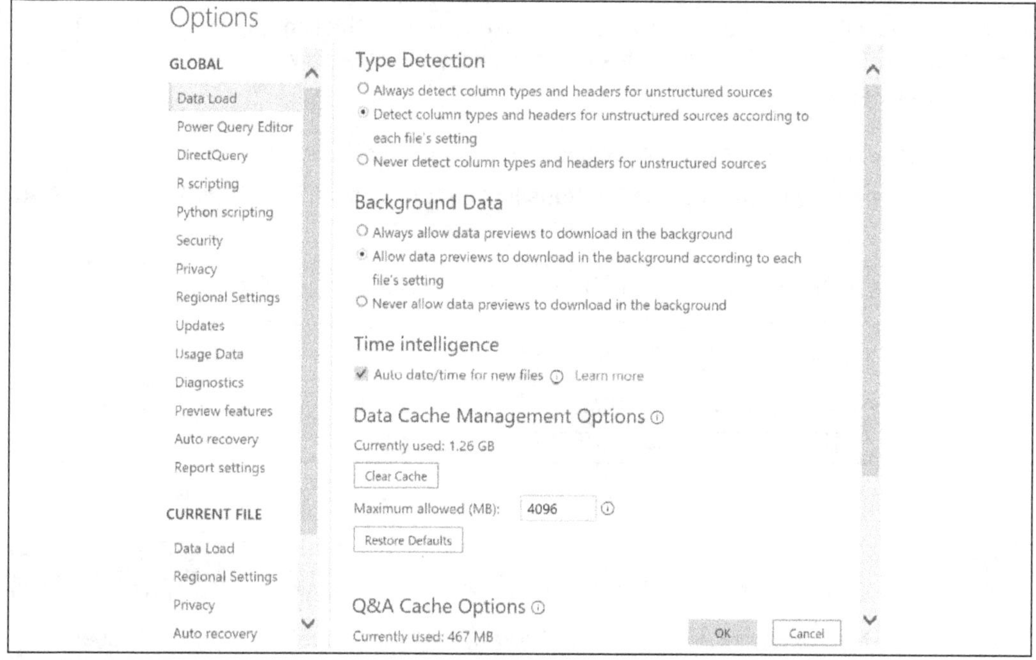

Figure 1.6: Power BI Desktop Options (February 2021)

GLOBAL options are applied to all Power BI Desktop files created or accessed by the user, while **CURRENT FILE** options must be defined for each Power BI Desktop file. The following steps are recommended for **GLOBAL** options:

1. On the **Data Load** tab, under **Data Cache Management Options**, confirm that the currently used data cache is below the **Maximum allowed (MB)** setting. If it is near the limit and local disk space is available, increase the value of **Maximum allowed (MB)**. Do not clear the cache unless local disk space is unavailable as this will require additional, often unnecessary, queries to be executed.

Time intelligence

Auto date/time for new files Learn more

Data Cache Management Options

Currently used: 1.26 GB

Clear Cache

Maximum allowed (MB): 4096

Restore Defaults

Figure 1.7: Global Data Load options

In addition, under the **Time intelligence** heading, consider turning off **Auto date/time for new files**. While its convenient to have out-of-the-box calendar hierarchy functionality for date columns, this can also significantly increase the size of a data model and its strongly recommended to utilize a common date dimension table, preferably from an corporate data warehouse source. Finally, under the **Type Detection** heading, it is recommended that you choose the option to **Never detect column types and headers for unstructured sources**. The default detection of column types from unstructured sources such as text or Excel files will create a hardcoded dependency on the column names in the source file. Additionally, this default transformation will be applied prior to any filter expression and thus can require more time and resources to perform the refresh.

2. On the **Power Query Editor** tab, under the **Layout** header, ensure that **Display the Query Settings pane** and **Display the Formula Bar** are both checked, as seen in *Figure 1.8*.

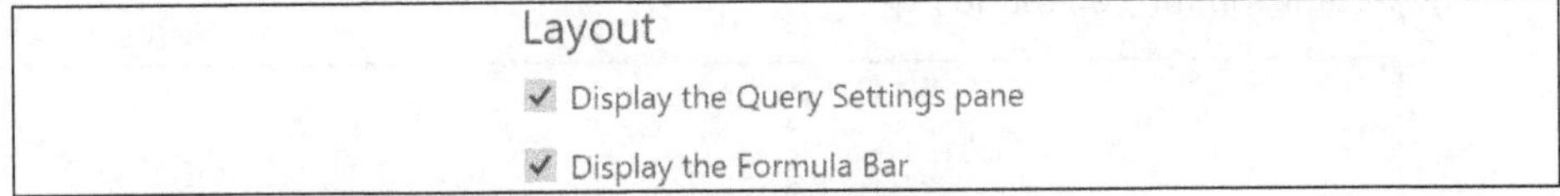

Figure 1.8: Power Query Editor Layout settings

3. On the **Security** tab, under the **Native Database Queries** header, select the option to **Require user approval for new native database queries**. Native queries are the user-specified SQL statements passed to data sources as opposed to the queries Power BI generates internally.

Figure 1.9: Security option for Native Database Queries

Optionally, set **Show security warning when adding a custom visual to a report** as well. Custom visuals can be divided into three categories as follows:

- Certified for Power BI (only on AppSource)
- Uncertified but available in AppSource
- Third-party, not available in AppSource

Certified custom visuals have been thoroughly tested for safety to ensure that the visuals do not access external services or resources and that they follow secure coding practices. Uncertified visuals available in AppSource have been through a validation process, though there is no guarantee that all code paths have been tested or that no external services or resources are accessed. Third-party visuals not available in AppSource should be used with caution, and it is recommended that organizations establish policies and procedures regarding their use.

4. On the **Privacy** tab, under the **Privacy Levels** heading, configure the privacy levels for all data sources and enable the option to **Always combine data according to your Privacy Level settings for each source**. Use the **Learn more about Privacy Levels** link for details on these settings.

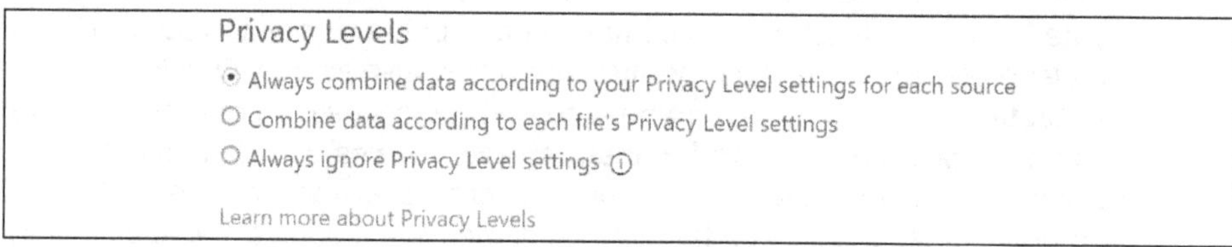

Figure 1.10: Global Privacy Level options

5. Use the **Diagnostics** tab to provide version information and diagnostics options if there is a need to troubleshoot a particular problem with Power BI Desktop. The **Enable tracing** option under the **Diagnostic Options** header writes out detailed trace event data to the local hard drive and thus should only be activated for complex troubleshooting scenarios.

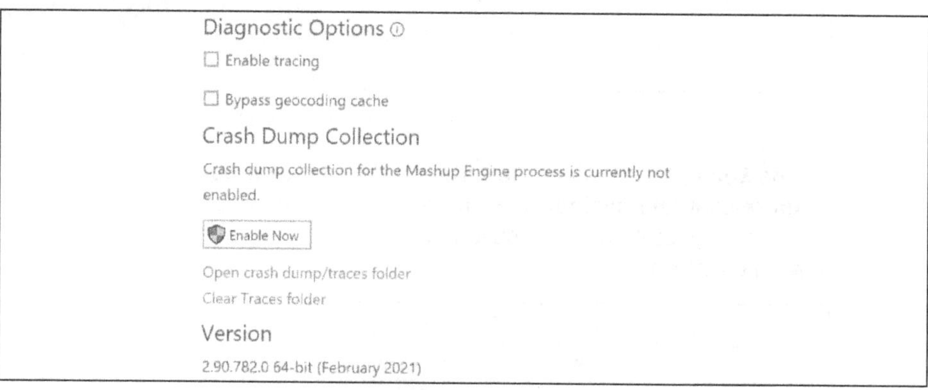

Figure 1.11: Diagnostics Options in Power BI Desktop

6. Use the **Preview features** tab to enable preview features for evaluation purposes. The options under **Preview features** change with new versions as some previous options become generally available and new preview features are introduced. The monthly Power BI Desktop update video and blog post (see `https://powerbi.microsoft.com/en-us/blog/`) provide details and examples of these new features.
7. Usually a restart of the Power BI Desktop application is required once a new preview option has been activated.

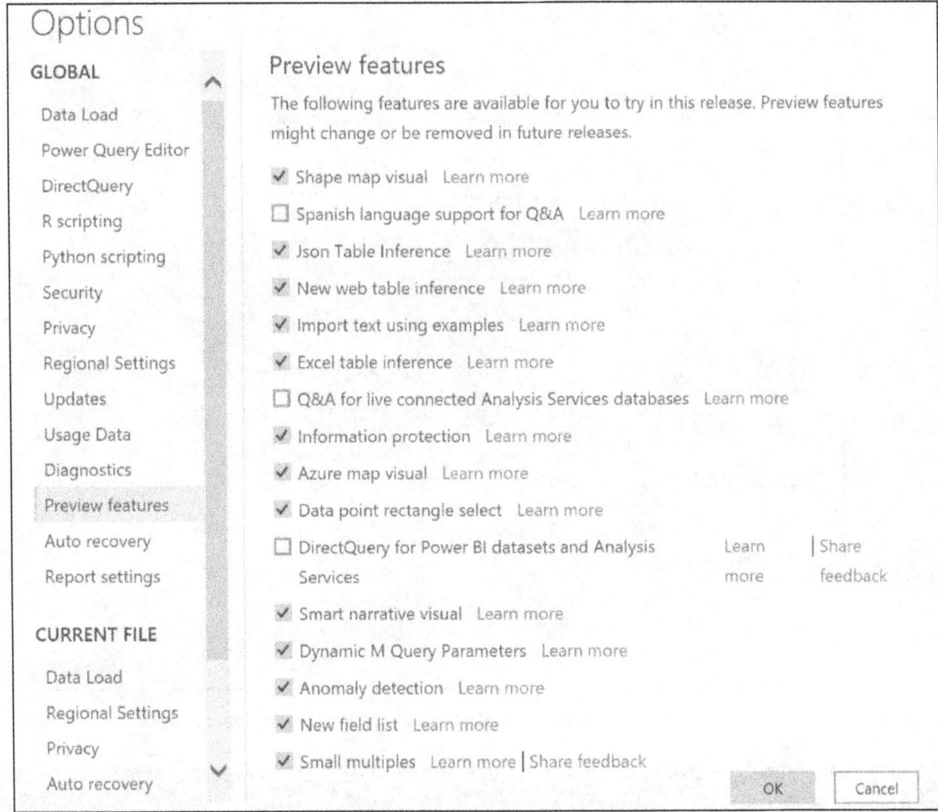

Figure 1.12: Preview features available with the February 2021 release of Power BI Desktop

8. On the **Data Load** tab under **CURRENT FILE**, more experienced users should disable all of the options under the **Type Detection** and **Relationships** headings; these model design decisions should be implemented explicitly by the Power BI developer with knowledge of the source data.

Also note that you can disable **Auto date/time** here on an individual file basis if you did not disable this option at a **GLOBAL** level.

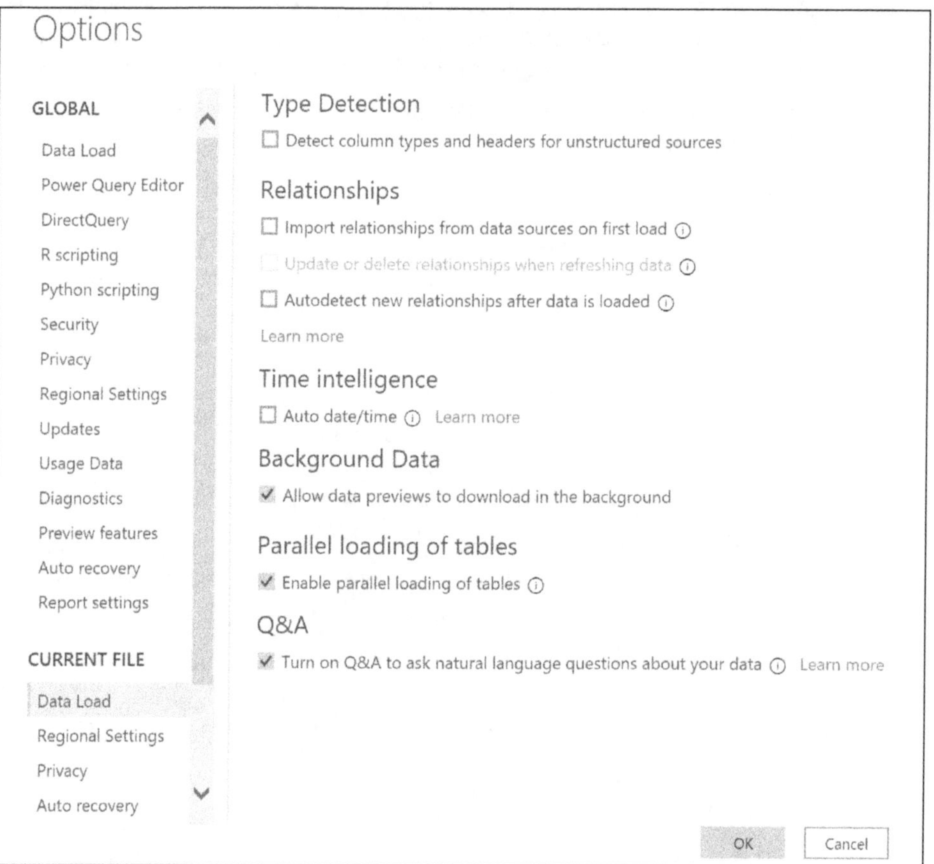

Figure 1.13: Current File Data Load Options

There's more...

As a modern cloud and service-oriented analytics platform, Power BI delivers new and improved features across its toolset on a monthly basis. These scheduled releases and updates for Power BI Desktop, the Power BI service, the on-premises data gateway, Power BI mobile applications, and more reflect customer feedback, industry trends, and the Power BI team's internal ideas and product roadmap.

BI professionals responsible for developing and managing Power BI content can both stay informed of these updates as well as review detailed documentation and guidance on implementing the features via the Microsoft Power BI blog (`http://bit.ly/20bcQb4`), Power BI documentation (`http://bit.ly/2o22qi4`), and the Power BI Community (`http:/bit.ly/2mqiuxP`).

Figure 1.14: Blog post and supporting video for February 2021 update to Power BI Desktop

The Power BI Community portal provides a robust, searchable hub of information across common topics as well as an active, moderated forum of user experiences and troubleshooting. The community also maintains its own blog featuring examples and use cases from top community contributors, and links to local **Power BI User Groups** (**PUGs**), relevant events such as **Microsoft Business Applications Summit** (**MBAS**), along with various galleries such as a Themes Gallery, Data Stories Gallery, R Script Showcase, and Quick Measures Gallery.

The Power BI Ideas forum (`https://ideas.powerbi.com`) is a valuable source for identifying requested features and enhancements, and their status relative to future releases. Ideas are provided a status, such as "Planned," "Under Review," or "Needs Votes." The search functionality allows for filtering by these status details. Filtering for **Planned** ideas, particularly those with higher community vote counts, provides a sense of impactful updates to be released over a longer time horizon.

See also

For additional information on topics covered in this recipe, refer to the following links:

- Power BI Security white paper: `http://bit.ly/22NHzRS`
- Data source privacy levels: `http://bit.ly/2nC0Lmx`
- Power BI Auto date/time: `http://bit.ly/3bH59cn`
- Change settings for Power BI reports: `http://bit.ly/2OP8m0F`

Creating an On-Premises Data Gateway

The Microsoft on-premises data gateway (or simply gateway) is a Windows service that runs in on-premises environments or in **infrastructure-as-a-service** (**IaaS**) data sources running in the cloud, such as virtual machines running SQL Server databases. The sole purpose of the gateway is to support secure (encrypted) and efficient data transfer between on-premises and IaaS data sources and Microsoft Azure services such as Power BI, Power Apps, Power Automate, and Azure Logic Apps, via an outbound connection to Azure Service Bus. It is important to note that if all data sources used in Power BI reports are in the cloud (and so not on-premises) and accessible by the Power BI service, then the Microsoft on-premises data gateway is not required, as the Power BI service will use native cloud gateways to access native cloud data sources; this could be something such as Azure SQL Database or Azure SQL Managed Instances.

Once installed, a gateway can be used to schedule data refreshes of imported Power BI datasets, to support Power BI reports and dashboards built with DirectQuery, plus live connections to **Analysis Services** databases.

A single on-premises data gateway can support the refresh and query activity for multiple data sources, and permission to use the gateway can be shared with multiple users. Currently, the gateway supports all common data sources via scheduled imports, including **Open Database Connectivity** (**ODBC**) connections, and many of the most common sources via Live Connection and DirectQuery.

Getting ready

The hardware resources required by the gateway vary based on the type of connection (import versus live connection), the usage of the reports, and dashboards in the Power BI service, and the proportion of data volume handled by the gateway versus the on-premises source systems. It is recommended to start with 8-core CPUs, 8 GB of RAM server, and Windows 2012 R2 or later for the operating system. This machine cannot be a domain controller, and to maintain the availability of Power BI content, the gateway server should always be on and connected to the internet.

Another top consideration for the gateway is the location of the gateway server in relation to the Power BI tenant and the data sources to be supported by the gateway. For example, if a SQL Server database is the primary gateway source and it runs on a server in the Western United States, and the Power BI Tenant for the organization is in the West US Azure region, then the gateway should be installed on a server or potentially an Azure **virtual machine** (**VM**) in the West US Azure region or a location in the Western United States.

Based on an analysis of current and projected workloads, the gateway resources can be scaled up or down and, optionally, additional gateways can be installed on separate servers to distribute the overall Power BI refresh and query deployment workload.

For example, one gateway server can be dedicated to scheduled refresh/import workloads, thus isolating this activity from a separate gateway server responsible for DirectQuery and Live Connection queries.

The gateway does not require inbound ports to be opened and defaults to HTTPS but can be forced to use TCP. For the default communication mode, it is recommended to whitelist the IP addresses in your data region in your firewall. This list is updated weekly and is available via the Microsoft Azure Datacenter IP list (`http://bit.ly/2oeAQyd`).

How to create the Gateway

The gateway has two modes, the Standard mode and the Personal mode. The Personal mode is intended for personal use, and thus cannot be shared among users within an enterprise. We will focus on the Standard mode, as the installation and configuration are essentially the same for the Personal mode:

1. Download the latest Microsoft on-premises data gateway from `https://powerbi.microsoft.com/downloads/`

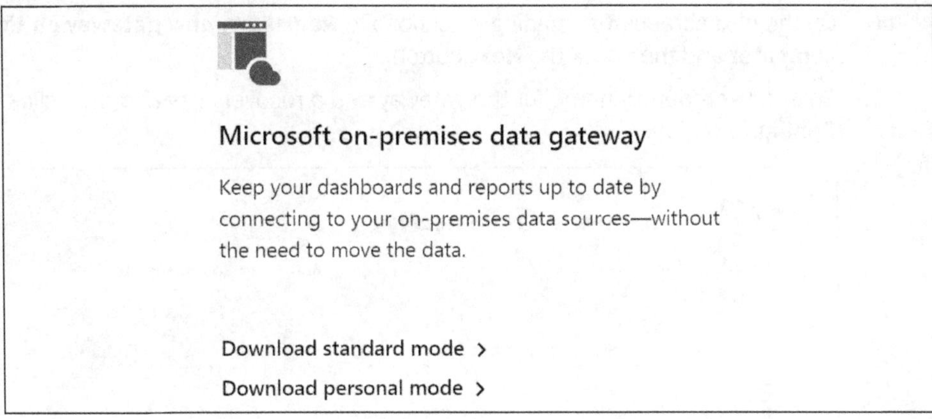

Figure 1.15: Download the Microsoft on-premises data gateway

2. Select the **Download standard mode** link.
3. Once downloaded, choose **Open file** to run **GatewayInstall.exe**.

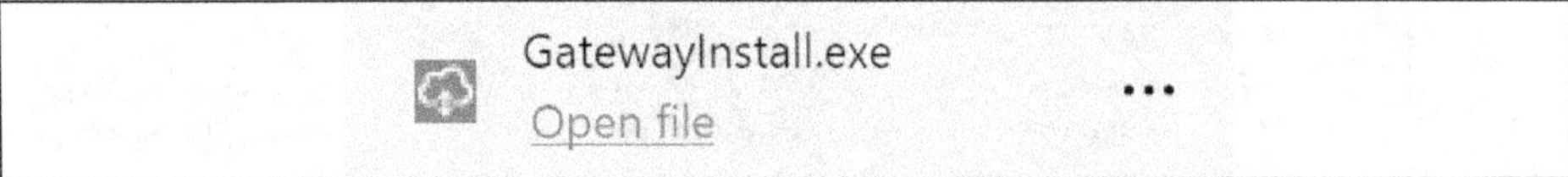

Figure 1.16: GatewayInstall.exe

4. Choose the file directory for the installation, accept the terms of use and privacy agreement, and then click the **Install** button.

5. Sign in to the Power BI service to register the gateway:

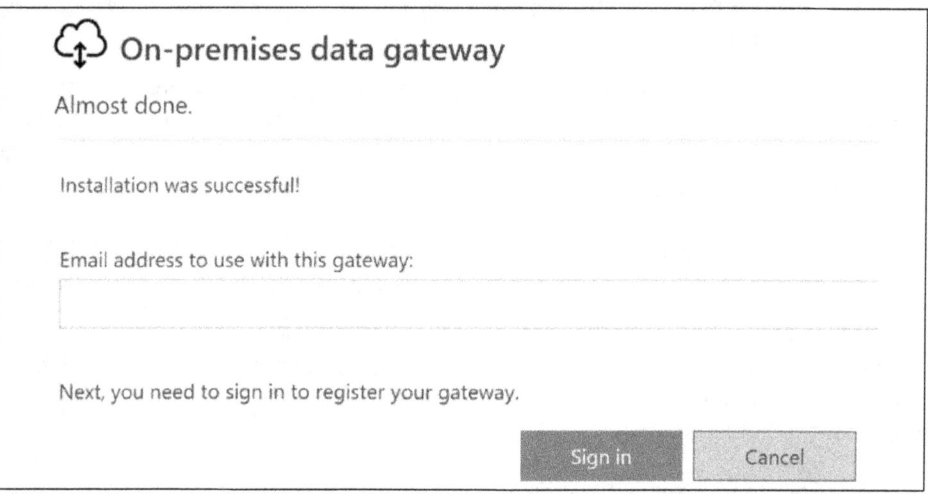

Figure 1.17: Registering the gateway

6. On the next screen after signing in, choose to **Register a new gateway on this computer** and then click the **Next** button.
7. Enter a user-friendly name for the gateway and a recovery key and then click the **Configure** button.

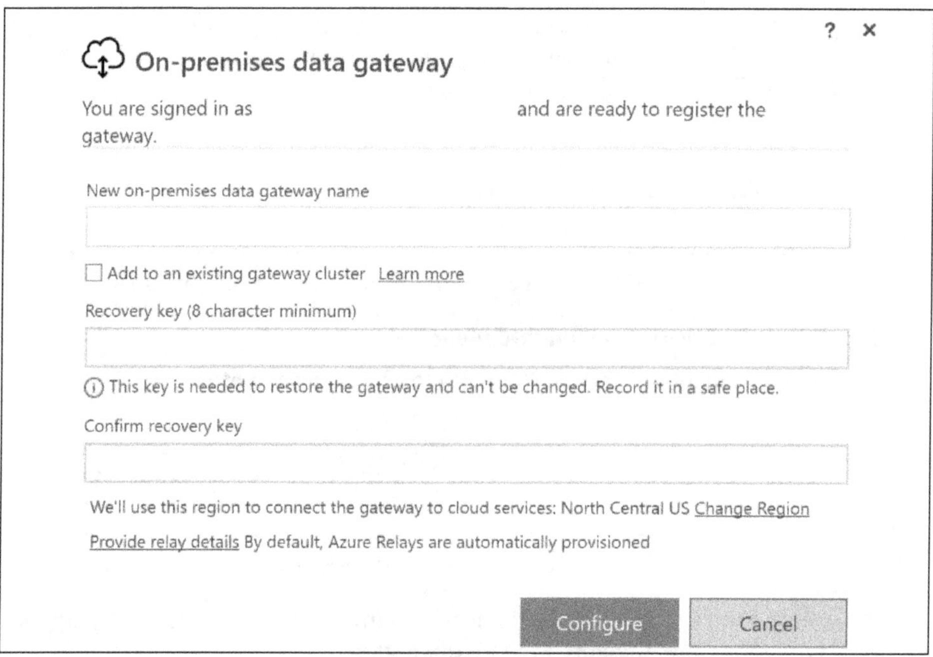

Figure 1.18: Final configuration information for the gateway

With the gateway installed and registered, data sources, gateway admins, and authorized data source users can be added to the Power BI service. A **Manage Gateways** option will be available under the gear icon in the Power BI service. See the Configuring On-Premises Gateway Data Connections recipe of *Chapter 12, Deploying and Distributing Power BI Content*, for details on this process.

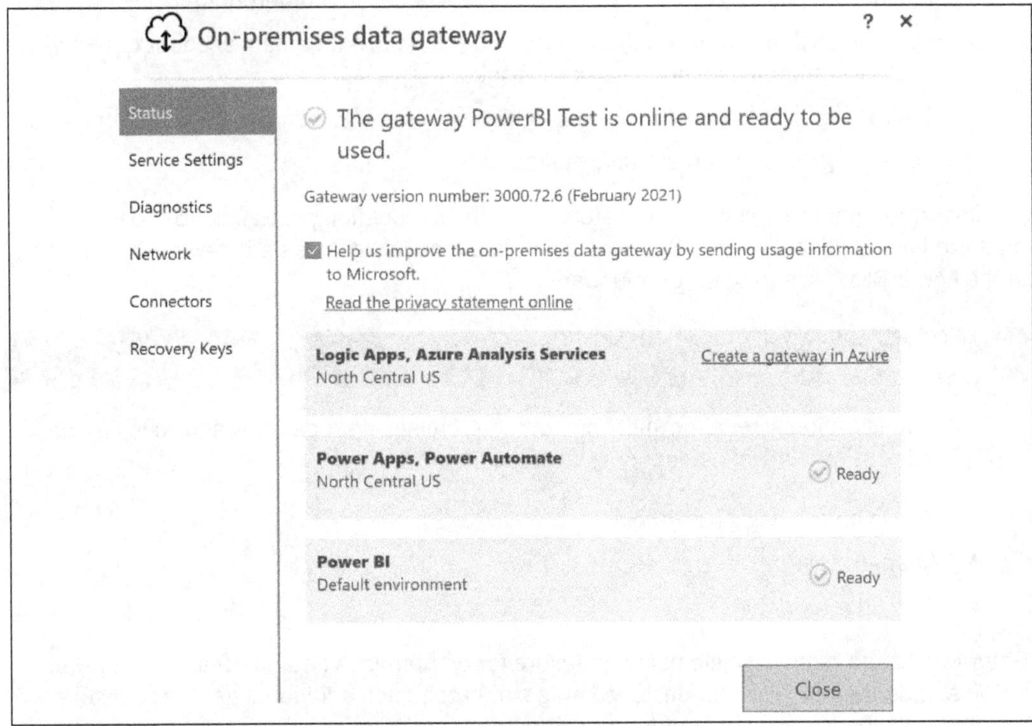

Figure 1.19: Successfully installed gateway

How it works

As new versions of the gateway become available, a notification is made available in the **Status** tab of the on-premises data gateway UI, as per *Figure 1.19*. The Power BI gateway team recommends that updates should be installed as they become available.

The Standard mode on-premises data gateway, rather than the personal mode gateway, is required for the DirectQuery datasets created in this book and the use of other Azure services in the Microsoft business application platform.

The Power BI service uses read-only connections to on-premises sources, but the other services (for example, Power Apps) can use the gateway to write, update, and delete these sources.

The recovery key is used to generate both a symmetric and an asymmetric key, which encrypts data source credentials and stores them in the cloud. The credentials area is only decrypted by the gateway machine in response to a refresh or query request. The recovery key will be needed in the following scenarios:

- Migrating a gateway and its configured data sources to a different machine.
- Restoring a gateway to run the service under a different domain account or restoring a gateway from a machine that has crashed.
- Taking over ownership of an existing gateway from an existing gateway administrator.
- Adding a gateway to an existing cluster.

It is important that the recovery key is stored in a secure location accessible to the BI/IT organization. Additionally, more than one user should be assigned as a gateway administrator in the Power BI service to provide redundancy.

There's more...

The final configuration screen for the Microsoft on-premises data gateway shown in *Figure 1.18* provides several advanced options, including the following:

- Add to an existing gateway cluster
- Change region
- Provide relay details

Gateway clusters remove single points of failure for on-premises data access. Since only a single standard gateway can be installed on a computer, each additional gateway cluster member must be installed on a different computer. If the primary gateway is not available, data refresh requests are routed to other gateway cluster members. When using gateway clusters, it is important that all gateway cluster members run the same gateway version and that offline gateway members are removed or disabled—offline gateway members will negatively impact performance.

By default, the gateway is installed in the same Azure region as your Power BI tenant in the Power BI service. In almost all cases, this setting should not be changed. However, with multi-geo support in Power BI Premium, it may be necessary to install gateways in different Azure regions. The **Change Region** option provides this flexibility.

Azure relays are automatically provisioned for installed gateways at the time of installation. However, the **Provide relay details** option allows you to provide your own relay details if you wish to associate the relay with your Azure subscription and manage the sender and listener keys for the relay. This is a very advanced option and you should fully understand Azure relays and what you are trying to accomplish before attempting this configuration. It is important to note that only WCF relays with NetTcp are supported for this feature.

See also

- Details of configuring and managing data sources through the on-premises gateway are covered in *Chapter 12, Deploying and Distributing Power BI Content*
- Set the Azure relay for on-premises data gateway: `http://bit.ly/3rMJMvP`

Installing Analyze in Excel from the Power BI Service

Excel-based data analysis and reporting artifacts, such as PivotTables, charts, and cell range formula expressions with custom formatting, remain pervasive in organizations. Although a significant portion of this content and its supporting processes can be migrated to Power BI, and despite the many additional features and benefits this migration could provide, Power BI is not intended as a replacement for all Excel-based reporting. Organizations, and in particular those departments that use Excel extensively (such as Finance and Accounting), may prefer to leverage these existing assets and quickly derive value from Power BI by both deploying Excel content to Power BI and analyzing Power BI-hosted data from within Excel.

The Power BI service's Analyze in Excel feature replaces the deprecated Microsoft Power BI Publisher for Excel. The Analyze in Excel feature allows you to use Power BI datasets in Excel and use Excel features like PivotTables, charts, and slicers to interact with the datasets.

Getting ready

To get ready to install and use the Power BI service's Analyze in Excel feature, make sure that Microsoft Excel is installed on your computer and then sign in to the Power BI service.

How to install Analyze

1. In the upper-right corner of any Power BI service page, click the ellipsis and then choose **Download** and then **Analyze in Excel updates**.

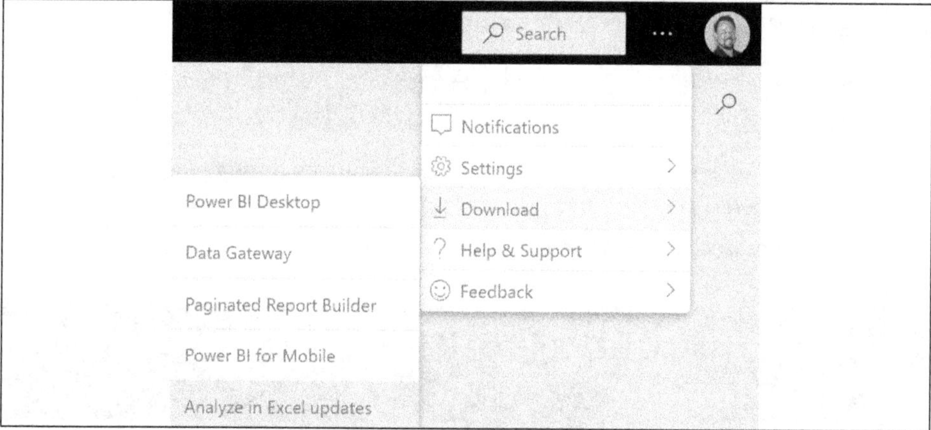

Figure 1.20: Downloading Analyze in Excel

2. On the splash screen that appears, choose the **Download** button.
3. Once the file downloads, choose the **Open file** link or run the file from your **Downloads** folder.

Figure 1.21: Analyze in Excel installer

4. The installation wizard for **Microsoft Analysis Services OLE DB Provider Setup** launches. Click the **Next** button.
5. Accept the licensing terms and click the **Next** button.

6. Click the **Install** button to begin the installation.
7. Once the installation finishes, click the **Finish** button.

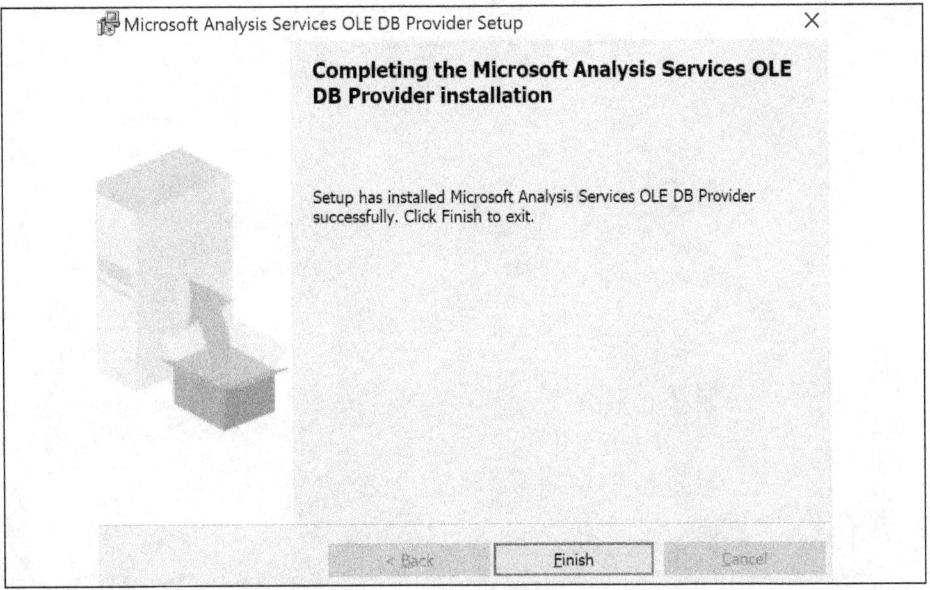

Figure 1.22: Successful installation of the Analyze in Excel feature

How it works

Now that the Microsoft Analysis Services OLE DB provider is installed locally on your computer, you can use the **Analyze in Excel** feature for reports. To use **Analyze in Excel**, follow these steps:

1. Click on any workspace to see the dashboards, reports, and datasets available in that workspace.

2. Hover over a report or dataset, click the "more" menu (three vertical dots), and then choose **Analyze in Excel**.

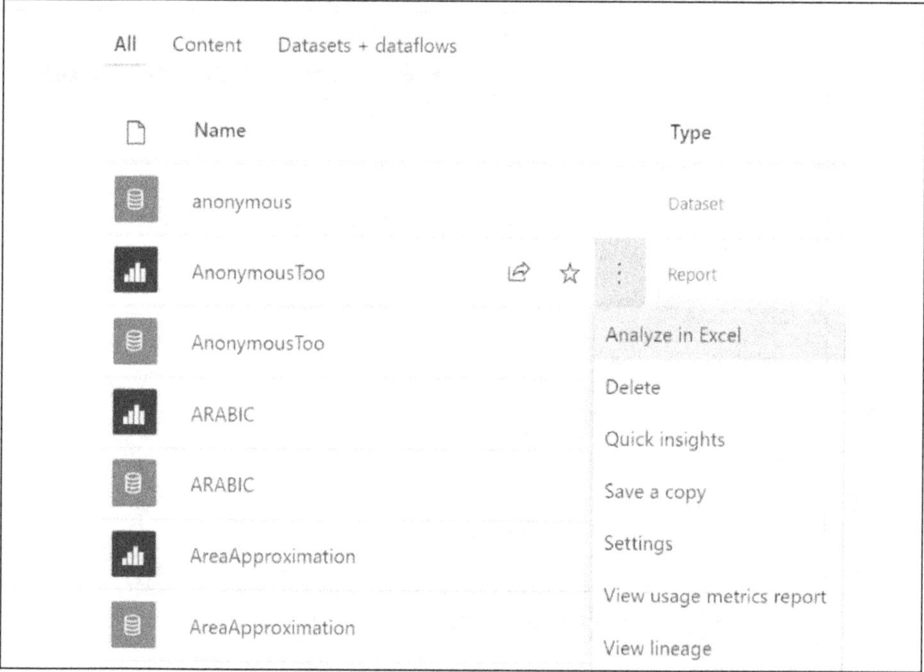

Figure 1.23: Analyze in Excel

3. If you receive a splash screen informing you that you need some Excel updates, click the **I've already installed these updates** link.
4. The Power BI service creates and downloads an Excel file that is designed and structured for use with **Analyze in Excel**. The name of the Excel file will match the name of the Power BI report or dataset from which the Excel file was created.
5. Open the Excel file using the **Open file** link, or open the file from your **Downloads** folder.
6. Make sure to click the **Enable Editing** button in Excel, as the file will open in **PROTECTED VIEW**.
7. Finally, click the **Enable Content** button to activate external data connections.

   The Excel file contains a single page/tab with the same name as the report or dataset from which the report/dataset was created. This page contains a PivotTable called **PivotTable1** that is tied to the Power BI dataset in the Power BI service. Clicking on the PivotTable presents the dataset tables, columns, and measures in the PivotTable **Fields** pane.

There's more...

Depending on the Office license, users can also connect to Power BI datasets from the **Insert PivotTable** option and from **Data - Get Data experience** in Excel.

Table 1.1 lists blogs that contain many articles and examples on Power BI's tools and features.

Blogger(s)	Blog	URL
Michael Carlo Seth Bauer	PowerBI.Tips	http://powerbi.tips
Chris Webb	Crossjoin	https://blog.crossjoin.co.uk
Rob Collie and others	P3 Adaptive	https://powerpivotpro.com
Alberto Ferrari Marco Russo	SQL BI	http://www.sqlbi.com
Kasper De Jonge	Kasper On BI	https://www.kasperonbi.com
Matt Allington	ExceleratorBI	http://exceleratorbi.com.au/blog
Ruth Martinez	Curbal	https://curbal.com/blog
Reza Rad	RADACAD	http://radacad.com/blog
Imke Feldman	The BIccountant	http://www.thebiccountant.com
Brett Powell	Insight Quest	https://insightsquest.com
Gilbert Quevauvilliers	Fourmoo	https://www.fourmoo.com/blog
Tom Martens	Mincing Data	https://www.minceddata.info/blog
Nicky van Vroenhoven	Power BI, Power Platform, Data Platform	https://www.nickyvv.com/
Debbie Edwards	Debbie's Microsoft Power BI, SQL and Azure Blog	http://bit.ly/3eQsb2G
Zoe Douglas	DataZoe	https://www.datazoepowerbi.com/blog
Ibarrau	LaDataWeb (Spanish)	https://blog.ladataweb.com.ar/
Various	Power BI Community Blog	http://bit.ly/3qIoDl9
Various	Power BI Weekly	https://powerbiweekly.info/

Table 1.1: A list of blogs that detail Power BI features and tools, with examples on how to use them

With the exception of *Kasper On BI*, all of these blogs are from non-Microsoft employees and thus do not necessarily reflect the views of Microsoft or recommended practices with its products. Additionally, several of these blogs are not exclusive to Power BI; they may also include coverage of other MSBI, Azure, SQL Server, and Office 365 tools and services.

An additional resource for learning and deploying Power BI is Adam Saxton's and Patrick LeBlanc's *Guy in a Cube* video channel (`http://bit.ly/2o21RqU`). These videos feature concise, hands-on reviews and resolutions to common issues and scenarios. They also have high-level summaries of recent Power BI updates and releases. As members of Microsoft, Adam and Patrick can incorporate specific guidance from Microsoft product and technical teams, and they regularly identify recent blog posts from the wider Power BI community. It is highly recommended that you subscribe to this channel so that you are always aware of new posts!

See also

- Analyze in Excel: `http://bit.ly/3bIMSeM`
- Analyze in Excel – the Advanced Method: `https://bit.ly/3bLbpzG`

Installing and Configuring Additional Tools

Power BI professionals responsible for the development of semantic models (datasets) routinely utilize additional tools beyond Power BI Desktop to create and manage their models. For example, they use Tabular Editor to quickly implement changes to measures or add new objects, such as perspectives and calculation groups. Likewise, the ALM Toolkit is routinely used to deploy incremental and metadata-only changes to Power BI.

Another such tool is DAX Studio, a third-party tool used to query data models, edit and format code, browse the structure and metadata of data models, and analyze the performance and execution characteristics of DAX queries. For larger and more complex data models and expressions, as well as projects involving multiple models, DAX Studio becomes an essential supplement to the development and performance-tuning processes.

DAX (**Data Analysis Expressions**) is the "language of Power BI," as it is used to create the measures and queries visualized in Power BI reports and dashboards. Power BI generates and submits DAX queries to the source data model based on the structure of the visualization, user selections, and filters—just as other tools such as Excel generate MDX queries based on the selections and structure of pivot tables and slicers from workbooks. DAX expressions are also used to define security roles and can optionally be used to create columns and tables in data models based on other tables and columns in the model, which can be refreshed at processing time and used by measures and queries. DAX serves the same function in Azure Analysis Services (AAS) and SQL Server Analysis Services (SSAS) tabular models as well as Power Pivot for Excel models, it's essential that BI professionals have a robust tool for developing and analyzing DAX code and the data models containing these expressions.

How to Install and Configure Additional Tools

1. Download the latest version from the DAX Studio website: `https://daxstudio.org/downloads/`. The installer version is a single file that provides a wizard-based installation and setup, while the portable version is a ZIP file that does not provide a wizard-based installation.
2. Use the **Open file** link or run the file from your **Downloads** folder.

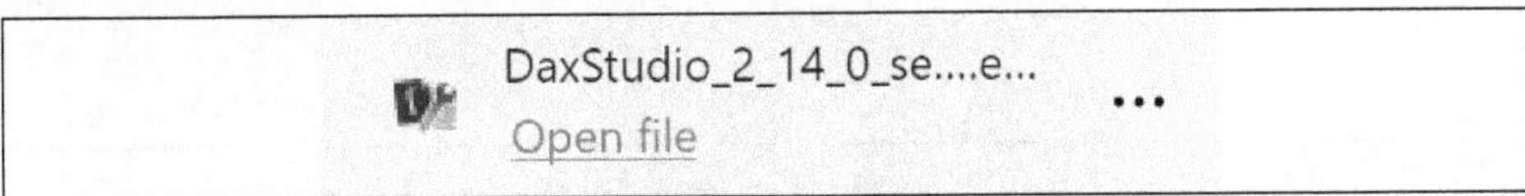

Figure 1.24: DAX Studio installation file

3. Once the installation starts, select the option to **Install for all users (recommended)**.
4. Accept the license agreement and click the **Next** button.
5. Choose a folder path to install the tool and click the **Next** button.
6. Choose whether the DAX Studio add-in for Excel will also be installed. Click the **Next** button. Note that:
   - The add-in for Excel is required to connect to Power Pivot for Excel data models.
   - Additionally, when DAX Studio is opened from Excel, query results can be exported directly to Excel tables.
7. Select the **Start menu** folder (the default is DAX Studio) and then click the **Next** button.
8. Check the box to **Create a desktop shortcut** and then click the **Next** button.
9. Finally, click the **Install** button.

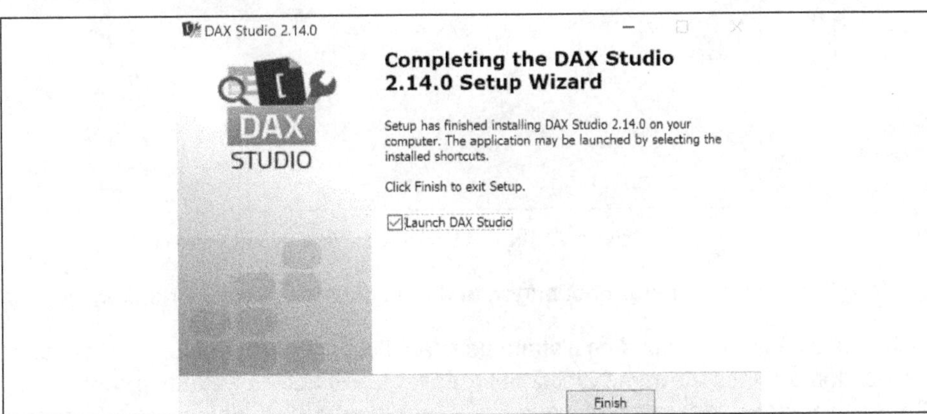

Figure 1.25: Successful installation of DAX Studio

How it works

Upon full installation, including the add-in for Excel, a DAX Studio icon will appear on the **Add-Ins** tab in the Excel ribbon, like the one shown in *Figure 1.26*.

Figure 1.26: DAX Studio in the Add-Ins ribbon in Excel

The full installation with the Excel add-in is recommended, as this enables direct output of DAX query results to Excel workbook tables and is required for connecting to Power Pivot data models. For Power Pivot to be available, you must enable the **Microsoft Power Pivot for Excel COM Add-in** using the **File** menu in Excel, and then choose **Options**. Click on the **Add-Ins** tab. Select **COM Add-ins** from the drop-down control at the bottom of the dialog box and then select the **Go...** button. The DAX Studio add-in can be deactivated using this same interface. To demonstrate how this works in Excel, follow these steps:

1. Open an Excel workbook.
2. Open a Power BI Desktop file.
3. From the **Add-Ins** tab of the Excel toolbar, activate DAX Studio.

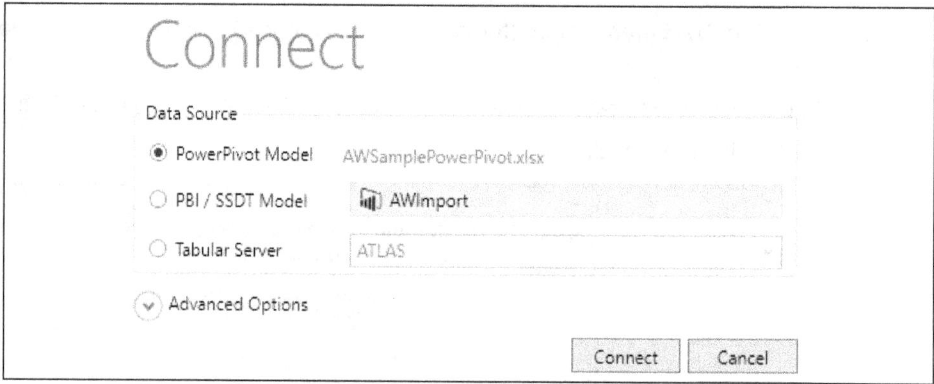

Figure 1.27: The DAX Studio add-in for the Excel Connect dialog

4. For now, click the **Cancel** button and then close the Excel workbook.

DAX Studio can also be used as a standalone application outside of Excel. The standalone application provides the same functionality as the Excel add-in, excluding connectivity to Power Pivot for Excel data models and Excel output options. To demonstrate this, follow these steps:

5. Launch the DAX Studio standalone Windows application.
6. Connect to a Power BI Desktop file or SSAS tabular instance.

   The **Advanced Options** settings of the **Connect** dialog box allow you to control exactly how DAX Studio connects to the model, such as the ability to specify a security role, effective user name identity, and **locale** when defining connections to data models and when analyzing trace events associated with DirectQuery data models (that is, the SQL statements generated and passed to sources).

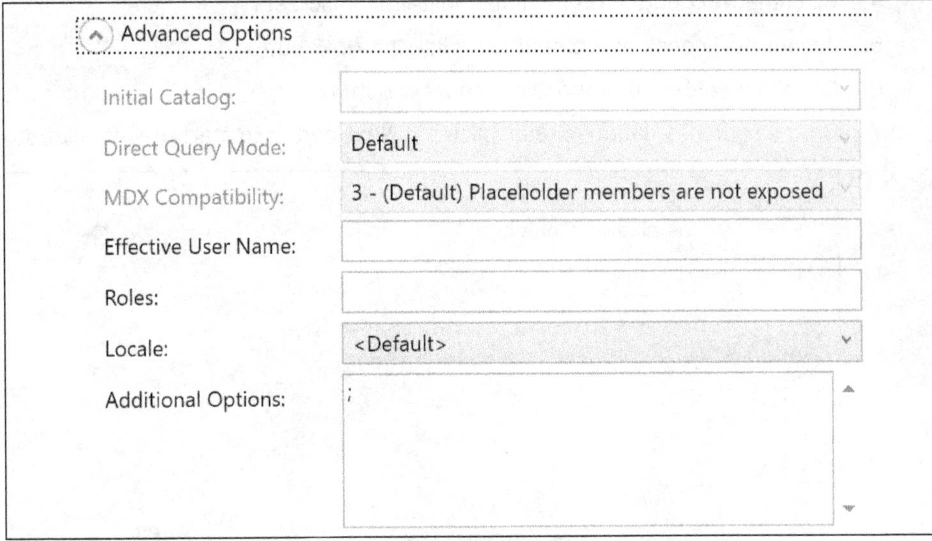

Figure 1.28: DAX Studio advanced connection options

There's more...

There are two additional tools that are useful for Power BI. Namely:

- ALM Toolkit
- Tabular Editor

The ALM Toolkit is a third-party tool from MAQ Software that provides advanced features such as Power BI dataset comparison, code merging, partial deployments and bug fixes, source control integration for dataset metadata, and definition reuse between tabular models. To download and install the ALM Toolkit, follow these steps:

1. In a browser, navigate to `http://alm-toolkit.com`.
2. Near the top of the page, click the **DOWNLOAD LATEST VERSION** button.

3. Use the **Open file** link to launch `AlmToolkitSetup.msi` or open the file from your **Downloads** folder.

Figure 1.29: ALM Toolkit installer

4. Click the **Next** button on the initial installation screen.
5. Accept the license agreement and click the **Next** button.
6. Choose a **Folder** path and click the **Next** button.
7. On the final installation screen, click the **Next** button to start the installation.

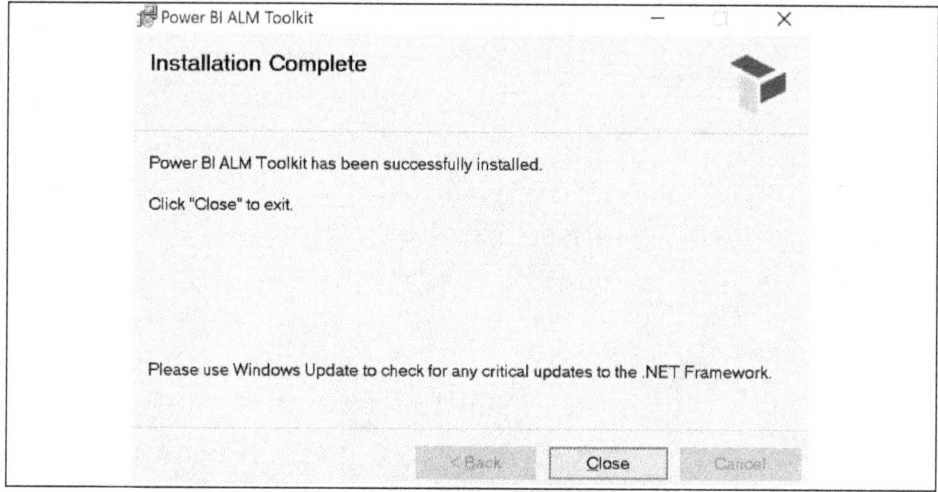

Figure 1.30: Successfully installed ALM Toolkit

The Power BI ALM Toolkit can now be launched from the Windows Start menu.

Another powerful tool is Tabular Editor. At the time of this book being published, Tabular Editor comes in two versions, the free, open source version 2 and the commercial version 3. Tabular Editor is an alternative to **SQL Server Data Tools** (**SSDT**) for authoring and editing tabular models for Analysis Services. Tabular Editor provides a hierarchical view of the objects in your tabular model metadata, such as columns, measures, and hierarchies. Tabular Editor integrates with Power BI Desktop, allowing batch changes to DAX measures and enabling advanced capabilities such as calculation groups and perspectives. Finally, Tabular Editor also enables offline editing capabilities by allowing you to open the tabular model directly from `Model.bim` files. To install and use Tabular Editor, follow these steps:

1. Download the latest Tabular Editor from here: `https://bit.ly/3bJFBvl`.
2. Scroll to the bottom of the page and click the link for **TabularEditor.Installer.msi**.

3. Once the file downloads, use the **Open file** link or open the file from your **Downloads** folder.

Figure 1.31: Tabular Editor installer

4. Click the **Next** button on the initial installation screen.
5. Accept the license agreement and click the **Next** button.
6. Choose a **Folder** path and click the **Next** button.
7. Check the boxes **Create Desktop shortcut** and **Create Program Menu shortcut**, and then click the **Next** button.
8. On the final installation screen, click the **Next** button to start the installation.

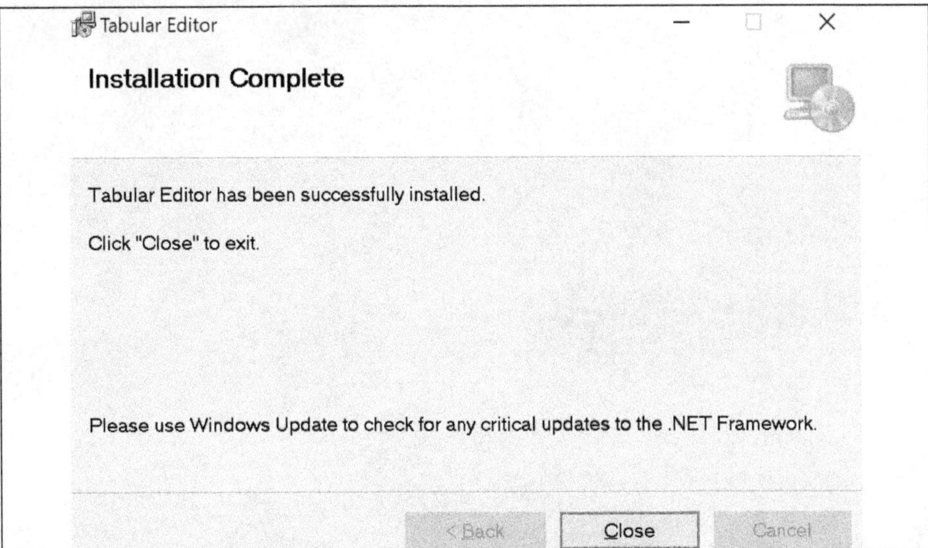

Figure 1.32: Successfully installed Tabular Editor

Tabular Editor can now be launched from the Windows Start menu.

See also

- DAX Studio tutorials and documentation: `https://daxstudio.org`
- ALM Toolkit documentation: `http://alm-toolkit.com/HowToUse`
- Tabular Editor documentation: `https://docs.tabulareditor.com/`

Conclusion

In this chapter, we walked through the installation and configuration of the primary tools that BI professionals utilize to design and develop Power BI content, including official Microsoft tools such as Power BI Desktop, the On-premises data gateway, and Analyze in Excel, as well as third-party tools such as DAX Studio, the ALM Toolkit, and Tabular Editor. These tools, coupled with the Power BI service, are the primary resources needed by BI professionals to be productive with Power BI. Later chapters of this book explore the use of these tools in developing and enhancing Power BI solutions.

2

Accessing and Retrieving Data

Power BI Desktop contains a rich set of connectors and transformation capabilities that support the integration and enhancement of data from many different sources. These features are all driven by a powerful functional language and query engine, M, which leverages source system resources when possible and can greatly extend the scope and robustness of the data retrieval process beyond what's possible via the standard query editor interface alone. As with almost all BI projects, the design and development of the data access and retrieval process has significant implications for the analytical value, scalability, and sustainability of the overall Power BI solution.

In this chapter, we dive into Power BI Desktop's Get Data experience and walk through the process of establishing and managing data source connections and queries. Examples are provided of using the Power Query Editor interface and the M language directly, to construct and refine queries to meet common data transformation and cleansing needs. In practice and as per the examples, a combination of both tools is recommended to aid the query development process.

A full explanation of the M language and its implementation in Power BI is outside the scope of this book, but additional resources and documentation are included in the sections titled *There's more...* and *See also*.

The recipes included in this chapter are as follows:

- Viewing and Analyzing M Functions
- Managing Queries and Data Sources
- Using DirectQuery
- Importing Data

- Applying Multiple Filters
- Selecting and Renaming Columns
- Transforming and Cleansing Source Data
- Creating Custom Columns
- Combining and Merging Queries
- Selecting Column Data Types
- Visualizing the M Library
- Profile Source Data
- Diagnosing Queries

Technical Requirements

The following are required to complete the recipes in this chapter:

- Power BI Desktop
- SQL Server 2019 or newer with the **AdventureWorksDW2019** database installed. This database and instructions for installing it are available here: `http://bit.ly/2OVQfG7`

Viewing and Analyzing M Functions

Every time you click on a button to connect to any of Power BI Desktop's supported data sources or apply any transformation to a data source object, such as changing a column's data type, one or multiple M expressions are created reflecting your choices. These M expressions are automatically written to dedicated M documents and, if saved, are stored within the Power BI Desktop file as Queries. M is a functional programming language like F#, and it is important that Power BI developers become familiar with analyzing, understanding, and later, writing and enhancing the M code that supports their queries.

Getting ready

To prepare for this recipe, we will first build a query through the user interface that connects to the **AdventureWorksDW2019** SQL Server database, retrieves the **DimGeography** table, and then filters this table to a single country, such as the United States:

1. Open Power BI Desktop and click on **Get Data** from the **Home** tab of the ribbon. Select **SQL Server** from the list of database sources. For future reference, if the data source is not listed in **Common data sources**, more data sources are available by clicking **More...** at the bottom of the list.

2. A dialog window is displayed asking for connectivity information. Ensure that **Data Connectivity mode** is set to **Import**. Enter the name of your SQL server as well as the **AdventureWorksDW2019** database. In *Figure 2.1*, my SQL server is installed locally and running under the instance **MSSQLSERVERDEV**. Thus, I set the server to be **localhost\MSSQLSERVERDEV** to specify both the server (localhost) and the instance. If you leave the **Database** field blank, this will simply result in an extra navigation step to select the desired database.

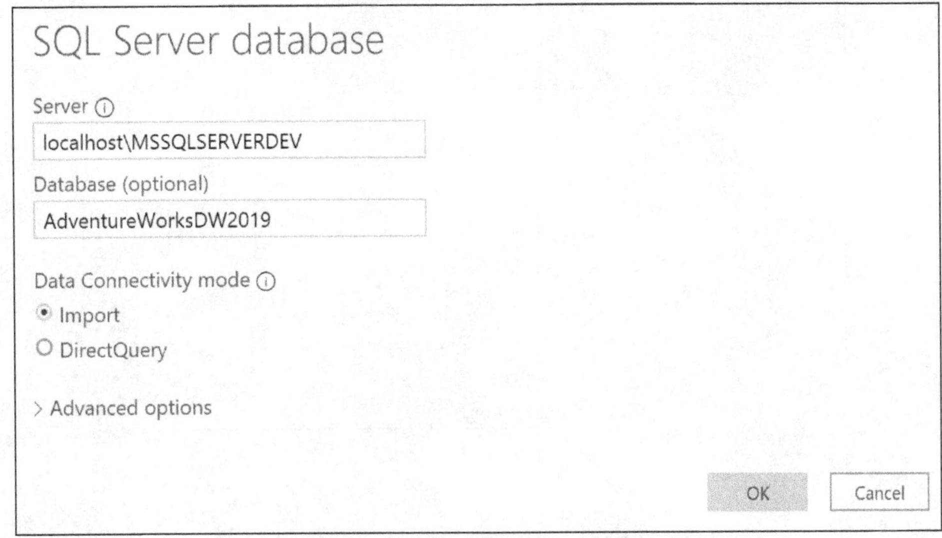

Figure 2.1: SQL Server Get Data dialog

3. If this is the first time connecting to this database from Power BI, you may be prompted for some credentials. In addition, you may also be warned that an encrypted connection cannot be made to the server. Simply enter the correct credentials for connecting and click the **Connect** button. For the encryption warning, simply click the **OK** button to continue.
4. A navigation window will appear, with the different objects and schemas of the database. Select the **DimGeography** table from the **Navigator** window and click the **Transform Data** button.
5. The Power Query Editor launches in a new window with a query called **DimGeography**; preview data from that table is displayed in the center of the window. In the Power Query Editor window, use the scroll bar at the bottom of the central display area to find the column called **EnglishCountryRegionName**. You can also select a column and then click **Go to Column** in the ribbon of the **View** menu to search for and navigate to a column quickly. Click the small button in the column header next to this column to display a sorting and filtering drop-down menu.

Uncheck the **(Select All)** option to deselect all values and then check the box next to a country, such as the **United States,** before clicking the **OK** button.

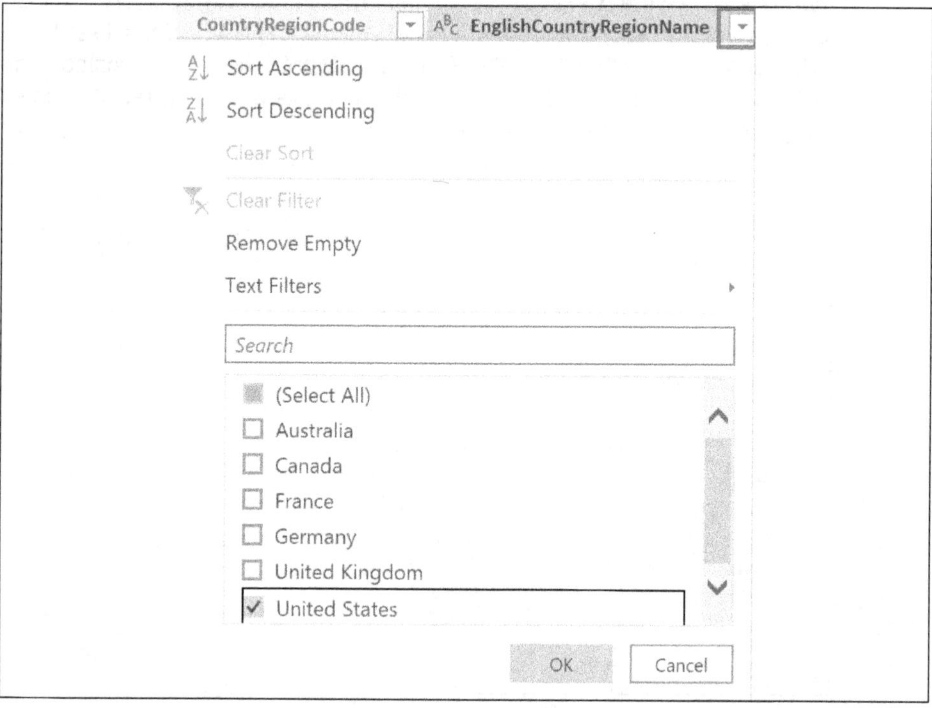

Figure 2.2: Filtering for United States only in the Query Editor

Note that the button for the **EnglishCountryRegionName** column changes to display a funnel icon. Also notice that, in the **Query Settings** pane on the right side of the window, a new option under **APPLIED STEPS** has appeared called **Filtered Rows**.

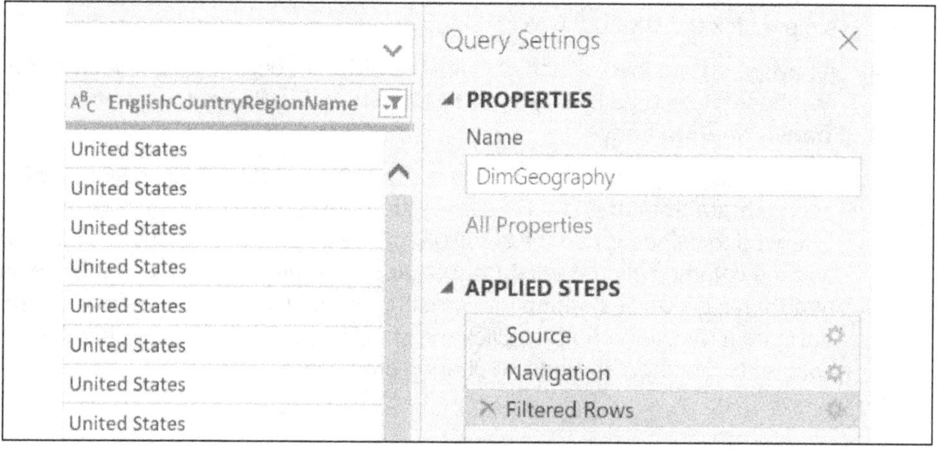

Figure 2.3: The Query Settings pane in the Query Editor

How to View and Analyze M Functions

There are two methods for viewing and analyzing the M functions comprising a query; they are as follows:

- Formula bar
- Advanced Editor

The formula bar exposes the M function for the current step only. This formula bar appears just above the column headers for the preview data in the central part of the window. If you do not see this formula bar, click the **View** tab and check the box next to **Formula Bar** in the **Layout** section of the ribbon. All such areas of interest are boxed in red in *Figure 2.4*.

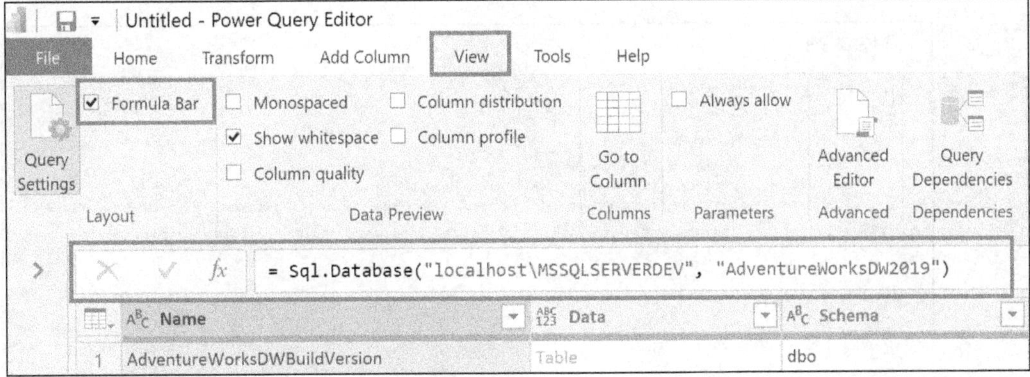

Figure 2.4: The Power Query Editor formula bar

When the **Source** step is selected under **APPLIED STEPS** in the **Query Settings** pane, as seen in *Figure 2.3*, we see the connection information specified on the initial dialog after selecting **Get Data** and then **SQL Server**. The M function being used is `Sql.Database`. This function is accepting two parameters: the server name, `localhost\MSSQLSERVERDEV`, and the database name, `AdventureWorksDW2019`. Clicking on other steps under **APPLIED STEPS** exposes the formulas for those steps, which are technically individual M expressions.

The formula bar is useful to quickly understand the M code behind a particular query step. However, it is more convenient and often essential to view and edit all the expressions in a centralized window. This is the purpose of the **Advanced Editor**. To launch the **Advanced Editor**, follow these steps:

1. Click on the **Home** tab and then select **Advanced Editor** from the **Query** section of the ribbon, as shown in *Figure 2.5*. Alternatively, the **Advanced Editor** can also be accessed from the **View** tab, shown in *Figure 2.4*.

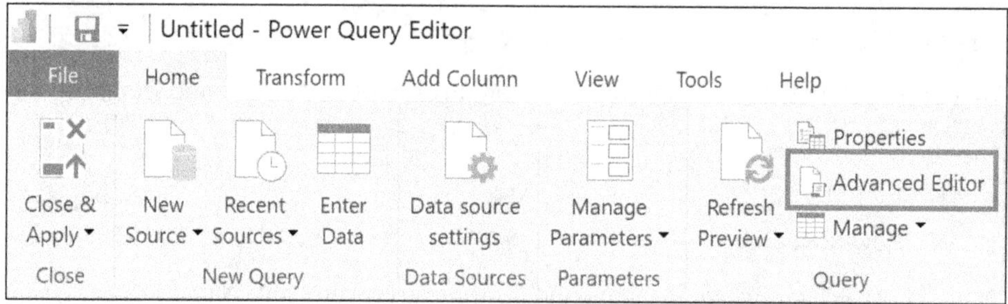

Figure 2.5: Advanced Editor on the Home tab of the Query Editor

2. The **Advanced Editor** dialog is displayed, exposing all M functions and comments that comprise the query. The M code can be directly edited from within this dialog.

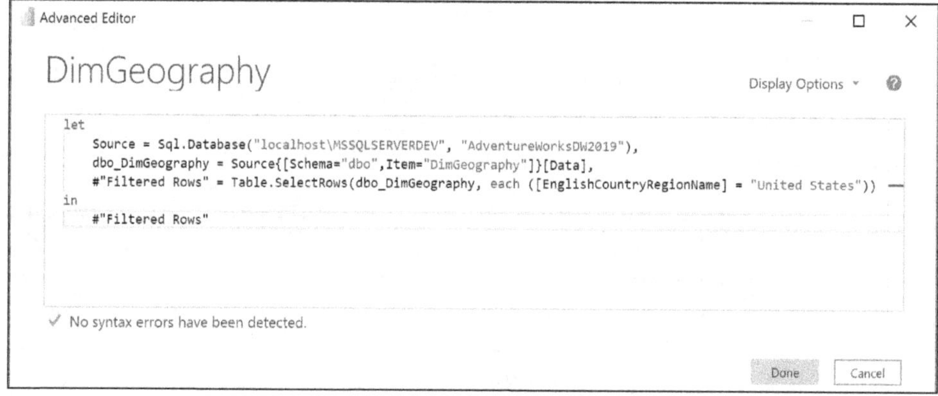

Figure 2.6: The Advanced Editor view of the DimGeography query

As shown in *Figure 2.6*, using the **Advanced Editor** will mean that all of the Power Query code that comprises the query can be viewed in one place.

How it works

The majority of queries created for Power BI follow the `let...in` structure, as per this recipe. Within the `let` block, there are multiple steps with dependencies among those steps. For example, the second step, **dbo_DimGeography**, references the previous step, **Source**. Individual expressions are separated by commas, and the expression referred to following the `in` keyword is the expression returned by the query. The individual step expressions are technically known as "variables".

Variable names in M expressions cannot have spaces without being preceded by a hash sign and enclosed in double quotes. When the Query Editor graphical interface is used to create M queries, this syntax is applied automatically, along with a name describing the M transformation applied. This behavior can be seen in the **Filtered Rows** step in *Figure 2.6*. Applying short, descriptive variable names (with no spaces) improves the readability of M queries.

Note the three lines below the `let` statement. These three lines correspond to the three **APPLIED STEPS** in our query: **Source**, **Navigation**, and **Filtered Rows**. The query returns the information from the last step of the query, **Filtered Rows**. As more steps are applied, these steps will be inserted above the `in` statement and the line below this will change to reference the final step in the query.

M is a case-sensitive language. This includes referencing variables in M expressions (`RenameColumns` versus `Renamecolumns`) as well as the values in M queries. For example, the values "Apple" and "apple" are considered unique values in an M query.

It is recommended to use the Power Query Editor user interface when getting started with a new query and when learning the M language. After several steps have been applied, use **Advanced Editor** to review and optionally enhance or customize the M query. As a rich, functional programming language, there are many M functions and optional parameters not exposed via the Power Query Editor's graphical user interface. Going beyond the limits of the Power Query Editor enables more robust data retrieval, integration, and data mashup processes.

The M engine also has powerful "lazy evaluation" logic for ignoring any redundant or unnecessary variables, as well as short-circuiting evaluation (computation) once a result is determinate, such as when one side (operand) of an `OR` logical operator is computed as `True`. Lazy evaluation allows the M query engine to reduce the required resources for a given query by ignoring any unnecessary or redundant steps (variables). The order of evaluation of the expressions is determined at runtime—it doesn't have to be sequential from top to bottom.

In the following example, presented in *Figure 2.7*, a step for retrieving `Canada` was added and the `"Filtered Rows"` step for filtering the results for the `United States` was ignored. Since the `CanadaOnly` variable satisfies the overall `let` expression of the query, only the `Canada` query is issued to the server as if the `"Filtered Rows"` step were commented out or omitted.

```
let
    Source = Sql.Database("localhost\MSSQLSERVERDEV", "AdventureWorksDW2019"),
    dbo_DimGeography = Source{[Schema="dbo",Item="DimGeography"]}[Data],
    CanadaOnly = Table.SelectRows(dbo_DimGeography, each ([EnglishCountryRegionName] = "Canada")),
    #"Filtered Rows" = Table.SelectRows(dbo_DimGeography, each ([EnglishCountryRegionName] = "United States"))
in
    CanadaOnly
```

Figure 2.7: Revised query that ignores the "Filtered Rows" step to evaluate Canada only

As a review of the concepts covered thus far and for future reference, *Table 2.1* presents a glossary of the main concepts of the M language utilized in this book.

Concept	**Definition**
Expression	Formulas evaluated to yield a single value. Expressions can reference other values, such as functions, and may include operators.
Value	The result of evaluating an expression. Values can be categorized into types which are either primitive, such as text ("abc"), or structured kinds, such as tables and lists.

Function	A value that produces a new one based on the mapping of input values to the parameters of the function. Functions can be invoked by passing parameter values.
Type	A value that classifies other values. The structure and behavior of values are restricted based on the classification of their type, such as Record, List, or Table.
`let`	An expression that allows a set of unique expressions to be assigned names (variables) and evaluated (if necessary) when evaluating the expression following the in expression in a let...in construct.
Variable	A unique, named expression within an environment to be conditionally evaluated. Variables are represented as Applied Steps in the Query Editor.
Environment	A set of variables to be evaluated. The global environment containing the M library is exposed to root expressions.
Evaluation	The computation of expressions. Lazy evaluation is applied to expressions defined within let expressions; evaluation occurs only if needed.
Operators	A set of symbols used in expressions to define the computation. The evaluation of operators depends on the values to be operated on.

Table 2.1: M Language elements

There's more...

M queries are not intended as a substitute for the data loading and transformation workloads typically handled by enterprise data integration and orchestration tools such as **Azure Data Factory** (**ADF**), Azure Databricks, or **SQL Server Integration Services** (**SSIS**). However, just as BI professionals carefully review the logic and test the performance of SQL stored procedures and ETL packages supporting their various cubes and reporting environments, they should also review the M queries created to support Power BI models and reports. When developing retrieval processes for Power BI models, consider these common ETL questions:

- How are queries impacting the source systems?
- Can we make our queries more resilient to changes in source data so that they avoid failure?
- Are our queries efficient and simple to follow and support, or are there unnecessary steps and queries?
- Are our queries delivering sufficient performance to the BI application?
- Is our process flexible, such that we can quickly apply changes to data sources and logic?
- Can some or all of the required transformation logic be implemented in a source system such as the loading process for a data warehouse table or a SQL view?

One of the top performance and scalability features of M's query engine is called Query Folding. If possible, the M queries developed in Power BI Desktop are converted ("folded") into SQL statements and passed to source systems for processing.

If we use the original version of the query from this recipe, as shown in *Figure 2.6*, we can see Query Folding in action. The query from this recipe was folded into the following SQL statement and sent to the server for processing, as opposed to the M query engine performing the processing locally. To see how this works, perform the following:

1. Right-click on the **Filtered Rows** step in the **APPLIED STEPS** section of the **Query Settings** pane, and select **View Native Query**.

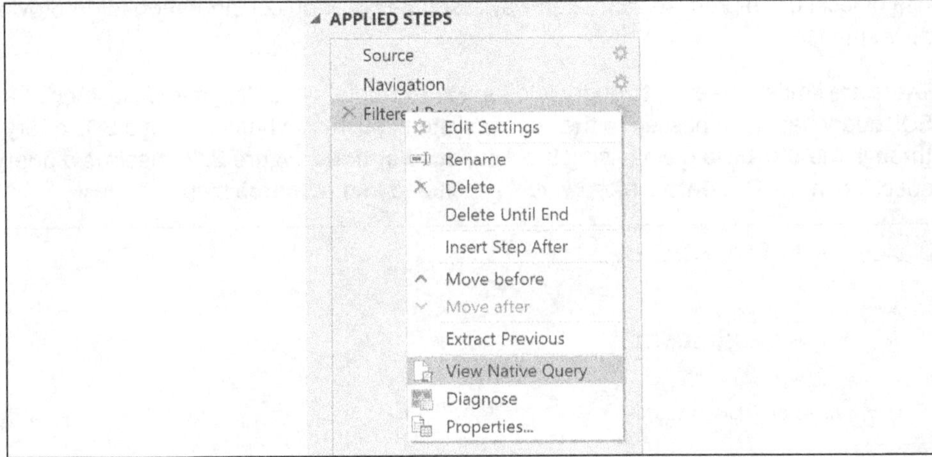

Figure 2.8: View Native Query in Query Settings

2. The **Native Query** dialog is then displayed, as shown in *Figure 2.9*.

Native Query

```
select [_].[GeographyKey],
    [_].[City],
    [_].[StateProvinceCode],
    [_].[StateProvinceName],
    [_].[CountryRegionCode],
    [_].[EnglishCountryRegionName],
    [_].[SpanishCountryRegionName],
    [_].[FrenchCountryRegionName],
    [_].[PostalCode],
    [_].[SalesTerritoryKey],
    [_].[IpAddressLocator]
from [dbo].[DimGeography] as [_]
where [_].[EnglishCountryRegionName] = 'United States' and [_].[EnglishCountryRegionName] is not null
```

OK

Figure 2.9: The SQL statement generated from the DimGeography M query

Finding and revising queries that are not being folded to source systems is a top technique for enhancing large Power BI datasets. See the *Pushing Query Processing Back to Source Systems* recipe of *Chapter 11, Enhancing and Optimizing Existing Power BI Solutions*, for an example of this process.

The M query engine also supports partial query folding. A query can be "partially folded", in which a SQL statement is created resolving only part of an overall query. The results of this SQL statement would be returned to Power BI Desktop (or the on-premises data gateway) and the remaining logic would be computed using M's in-memory engine with local resources. M queries can be designed to maximize the use of the source system resources, by using standard expressions supported by query folding early in the query process. Minimizing the use of local or on-premises data gateway resources is a top consideration for improving query performance.

There are limits, however, to query folding. For example, no folding takes place once a native SQL query has been passed to the source system, such as when passing a SQL query directly through the **Get Data** dialog using the **Advanced options**. *Figure 2.10* displays a query specified in the **Get Data** dialog, which is included in the **Source** step.

SQL Server database

Server ⓘ

localhost\MSSQLSERVERDEV

Database (optional)

AdventureWorksDW2019

◢ Advanced options

Command timeout in minutes (optional)

SQL statement (optional, requires database)

```
SELECT
  [GoegraphyKey],
  [City],
  [StateProvideCope]
FROM [AdventureWorksDW2019].[dbo].[DimGeography]
```

☑ Include relationship columns

☐ Navigate using full hierarchy

☐ Enable SQL Server Failover support

OK Cancel

Figure 2.10: Providing a user-defined native SQL query

Any transformations applied after this native query will use local system resources. Therefore, the general implication for query development with native or user-defined SQL queries is that if they are used, try to include all required transformations (that is, joins and derived columns), or use them to utilize an important feature of the source database that is not being utilized by the folded query, such as an index.

Some other things to keep in mind regarding Query Folding are the following:

- Not all data sources support Query Folding, such as text and Excel files.
- Not all transformations available in the Query Editor or via M functions are directly supported by some data sources.
- The privacy levels defined for the data sources will also impact whether folding is used or not.
- SQL statements are not parsed before they are sent to the source system.
- The `Table.Buffer` function can be used to avoid query folding. The table output of this function is loaded into local memory, and transformations against it will remain local.

See also

- Power Query M language specification: `http://bit.ly/2oaJWwv`
- Power Query M Function reference: `http://bit.ly/3bLKJ1M`

Managing Queries and Data Sources

There are two primary components of queries in Power BI: the data source and the query logic executed against this source. The data source includes the connection method (**DirectQuery** or **Import**), a privacy setting, and the authentication credentials. The query logic consists of the M expressions represented as queries in the Query Editor and stored internally as M documents.

In a typical corporate BI tool, such as **SQL Server Reporting Services** (**SSRS**), the properties of a data source such as the server and database name are defined separately from the queries that reference them. In Power BI Desktop, however, by default, each individual query created explicitly references a given data source (for example, server A and database B). This creates an onerous, manual process of revising each query if it becomes necessary to change the source environment or database.

This issue is addressed in the following steps by using dedicated M queries to centralize and isolate the data source information from the individual queries. Additionally, detail and reference information is provided on managing source credentials and data source privacy levels.

Getting ready

To prepare for this recipe, we will create a query from a database, which will serve as the source for other queries via the standard **Get Data** and Power Query Editor experience described in the previous recipe. To create this query, perform the following steps:

1. Open Power BI Desktop.
2. If you have already connected to your SQL Server, you can find the connection under **Recent sources** on the **Home** tab. Otherwise, on the **Home** tab, select **Get Data** from the ribbon, and choose **SQL Server**.
3. Select a table or view, and click on **Transform Data** to import the data.
4. The **Power Query Editor** window will launch and a preview of the data will appear. In this example, we have chosen the `DimEmployee` table from the **AdventureWorksDW2019** database on our local SQL Server instance **MSSQLSERVERDEV**. The full code of the query can be viewed in the **Advanced Editor** window but is also shown below.

```
let
    Source = Sql.Database("localhost\MSSQLSERVERDEV",
"AdventureWorksDW2019"),
    dbo_DimEmployee = Source{[Schema="dbo",Item="DimEmployee"]}[Data]
in
    dbo_DimEmployee
```

5. Copy just the **Source** line (in bold in the previous step).
6. Close the **Advanced Editor** window by clicking the **Cancel** button.
7. Remain in the **Power Query Editor** window.

How to Manage Queries and Data Sources

In this example, a separate data source connection query is created and utilized by individual queries. By associating many individual queries with a single (or a few) data source queries, it is easy to change the source system or environment, such as when switching from a **Development** environment to a **User Acceptance Testing** (**UAT**) environment. We will then further separate out our data source queries and our data load queries using query groups. To start isolating our data source queries from our data load queries, follow these steps:

1. Create a new, blank query by selecting **New Source** from the ribbon of the **Home** tab and then select **Blank Query**.

2. Open the **Advanced Editor** and replace the **Source** line with the line copied from the query created in **Getting ready**. Be certain to remove the comma (,) at the end of the line. The line prior to the `in` keyword should never have a comma at the end of it. Your query should look like the following:

```
let
    Source = Sql.Database("localhost\MSSQLSERVERDEV",
"AdventureWorksDW2019")
in
    Source
```

3. Click the **Done** button to close the **Advanced Editor** window.
4. Rename the query by clicking on the query and editing the **Name** in the **Query Settings** pane. Alternatively, in the **Queries** pane, right-click the query and choose **Rename**. Give the source query an intuitive name, such as `AdWorksDW`.
5. Now click on the original query created in the *Getting ready* section above. Open the **Advanced Editor**. Replace the **Source** step expression of the query with the name of the new query. As you type the name of the query, **AdWorksDW**, you will notice that IntelliSense will suggest possible values. The query should now look like the following:

```
let
    Source = AdWorksDW,
    dbo_DimEmployee = Source{[Schema="dbo",Item="DimEmployee"]}[Data]
in
    dbo_DimEmployee
```

6. Click the **Done** button to come out of **Advanced Editor**. The preview data refreshes but continues to display the same data as before.

We can take this concept of isolating our data source queries from data loading queries further by organizing our queries into query groups. You should also use query groups to help isolate data source and staging queries from queries loaded to the dataset. To see how query groups work, follow these steps:

1. Duplicate the revised data loading query that loads the **DimEmployee** table, created in **Getting ready**. Simply right-click the query in the **Queries** pane and choose **Duplicate**.
2. With the new query selected in the **Queries** pane, click the gear icon next to the **Navigation** step in the **APPLIED STEPS** area of the **Query Settings** pane.
3. Choose a different dimension table or view, such as **DimAccount**, and then click the **OK** button. Dimension tables and views start with "Dim".

4. Rename this new query to reflect the new table or view being loaded.
5. Create a new group by right-clicking in a blank area in the **Queries** window and then selecting **New Group...**
6. In the **New Group** dialog, name the group **Data Sources** and click the **OK** button.
7. Create another new group and name this group **Dimensions**.
8. Move the **AdWorksDW** query to the **Data Sources** group by either dragging and dropping in the **Queries** pane or right-clicking the query and choosing **Move To Group...**, and then select the group.
9. Move the other queries to the **Dimensions** group.
10. Finally, ensure that the query in the **Data Source** group is not actually loaded as a separate table in the data model. Right-click on the query and uncheck the **Enable Load** option. This makes the query available to support data retrieval queries but makes the query invisible to the model and report layers. The query name will now be italicized in the **Queries** pane.

Your **Queries** pane should now look similar to that in *Figure 2.11*:

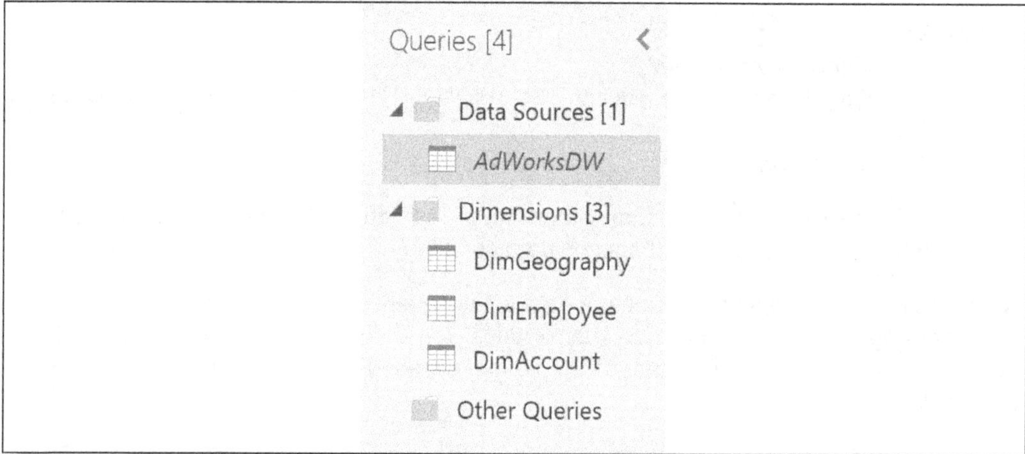

Figure 2.11: Queries organized into query groups

How it works

The **Query Dependencies** view in Power Query provides a visual representation of the relationships between the various queries. You can access this dialog by using the **View** tab and then selecting **Query Dependencies** in the ribbon.

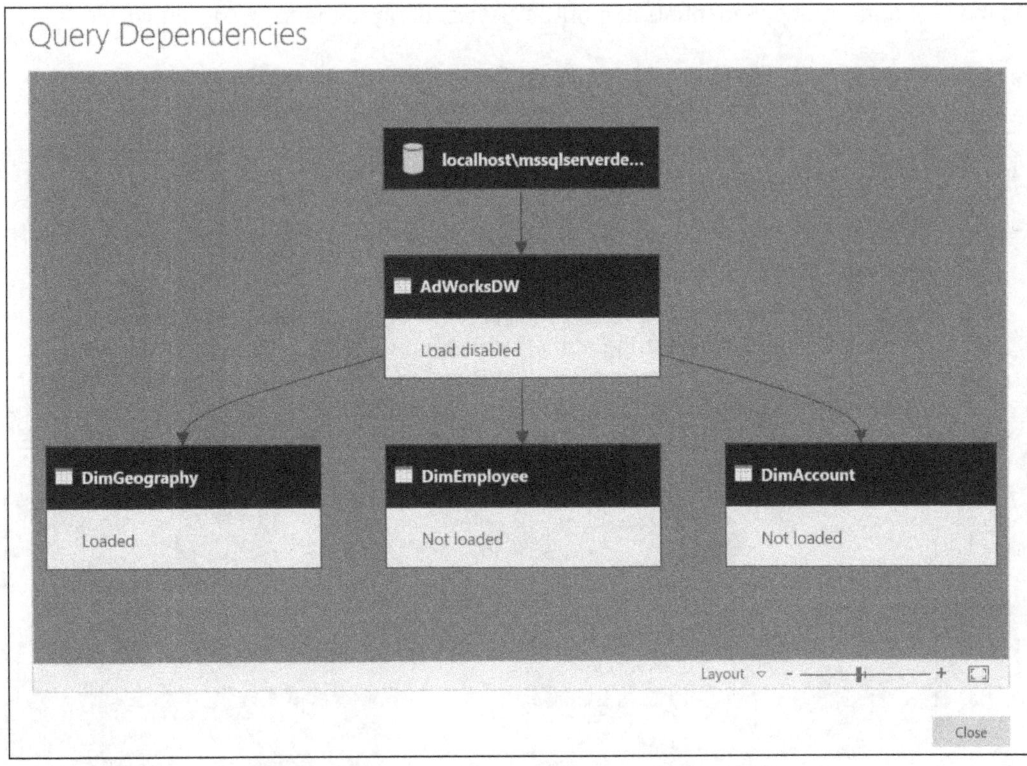

Figure 2.12: The Query Dependencies View in Query Editor

In this example, a single query with only one expression is used by multiple queries, but more complex interdependencies can be designed to manage the behavior and functionality of the retrieval and analytical queries. This recipe illustrates the broader concept used in later recipes called "composability", where functions call other functions; this is one of the primary strengths of functional programming languages such as M, DAX, R, and F#.

There's more...

Power BI Desktop saves data source credentials for each data source defined, as well as a privacy level for that source. It is often necessary to modify these credentials as passwords change. In addition, setting privacy levels on data sources helps prevent confidential information from being exposed to external sources during the Query Folding process. Data source credentials and settings are not stored in the PBIX file, but rather on the computer of the installed application.

To manage data source credentials and privacy levels, perform the following steps:

1. From Power BI Desktop (not the Power Query Editor), click on **File** in the menu, then click **Options and settings**, and finally click **Data source settings**.
2. Click on the **Global Permissions** radio button such that your settings are persisted into other Power BI Desktop reports.
3. Select a data source.
4. Click the **Edit Permissions** button.
5. From the **Edit Permissions** dialog, you can click the **Edit** button under the **Credentials** heading to set the authentication credentials for the data source. In addition, you can set the privacy level for the data source using the drop-down under the **Privacy Level** heading. Click **OK** to save your settings.

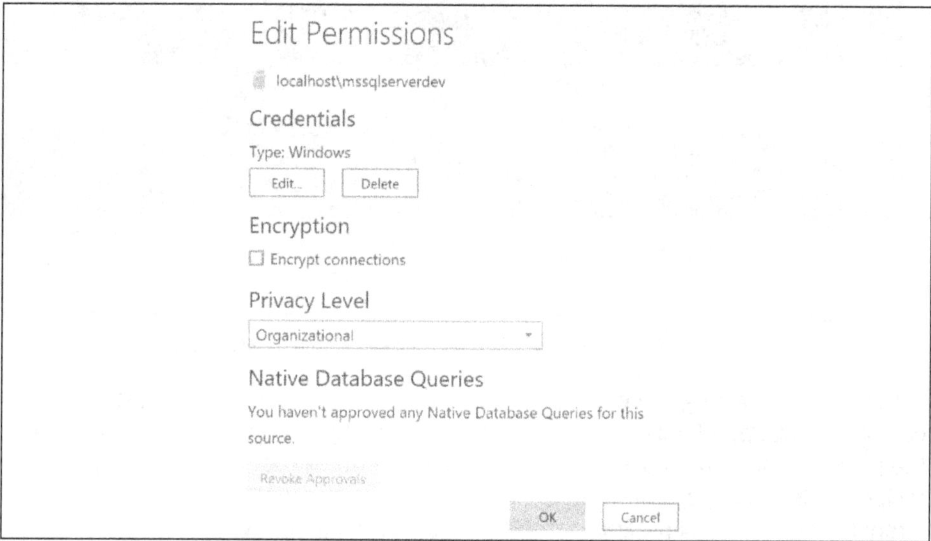

Figure 2.13: Edit credentials and privacy level for a data source

Definitions of the available **Privacy Level** settings are provided in *Table 2.2*.

Privacy Setting	Description
None	No privacy level defined.
Private	A Private data source is completely isolated from other data sources during query retrieval. For example, marking a text file Private would prevent that data from being processed on an external server.
Organizational	An Organizational data source is isolated from all public data sources but is visible to other organizational data sources during retrieval.

Public	A Public data source is visible to other sources. Only files, internet sources, and workbook data can be marked as Public.

Table 2.2: Privacy Level Settings

Just as relational databases such as SQL Server consider many potential query plans, the M engine also searches for the most efficient methods of executing queries, given that the data sources and query logic are defined. In the absence of data source privacy settings, the M engine is allowed to consider plans that merge disparate data sources. For example, a local text file of customer names can be merged with an external or third-party server, given the better performance of the server. Defining privacy settings isolates data sources from these operations thus increasing the likelihood of local resource usage, and hence query performance may be reduced.

See also

- Authentication with a data source: `http://bit.ly/30It2tV`
- Power BI Desktop privacy levels: `http://bit.ly/29blFBR`

Using DirectQuery

One of the most valuable features of Power BI is its deep support for real-time and streaming datasets, with the ability to provide immediate visibility to business processes and events as this data is created or updated. As Power BI Desktop's data modeling engine reflects the latest **Analysis Services** features, it becomes feasible to design DirectQuery models or composite models (DirectQuery and import) in Power BI Desktop, and thus avoid the scalability limitations and scheduled refresh requirements of models based on importing data.

The three most common candidates for DirectQuery or composite model projects are as follows:

- The data model would consume an exorbitant amount of memory if all tables were fully loaded into memory. Even if the memory size is technically supported by large Power BI Premium capacity nodes, this would be a very inefficient and expensive use of company resources as most BI queries only access aggregated data representing a fraction of the size. Composite models which mix DirectQuery and Dual storage mode tables with in-memory aggregation tables is the recommended architecture for large models going forward.
- Access to near-real-time data is of actionable or required value to users or other applications, such as is the case with notifications. For example, an updateable Nonclustered Columnstore index could be created on OLTP disk-based tables or memory-optimized tables in SQL Server to provide near-real-time access to database transactions.

- A high-performance and/or read-optimized system is available to service report queries, such as a SQL Server or Azure SQL Database, with the Clustered Columnstore index applied to fact tables.

This recipe walks through the primary steps in designing the data access layer that supports a DirectQuery model in Power BI Desktop. As these models are not cached into memory and dynamically convert the DAX queries from report visualizations to SQL statements, guidance is provided to maintain performance. Additional details, resources, and documentation on DirectQuery's current limitations and comparisons with the default import mode are also included to aid your design decision.

Getting ready

1. Choose a database to serve as the source for the DirectQuery data model.
2. Create a logical and physical design of the fact and dimension tables of the model including the relationship keys and granularity of the facts. The AdventureWorksDW database is a good example of data designed in this manner.
3. Determine or confirm that each fact-to-dimension relationship has referential integrity. Providing this information to the DirectQuery model allows for more performant inner join queries.
4. Create view objects in the source database to provide efficient access to the dimensions and facts defined in the physical design.

Be aware that DirectQuery models are limited to a single source database and not all databases are supported for DirectQuery. If multiple data sources are needed, such as SQL Server and Oracle, or Teradata and Excel, then the default Import mode model, with a scheduled refresh to the Power BI Service, will be the only option.

How to use DirectQuery

For this recipe, we will use the **AdventureWorksDW2019** database that has been used thus far in this chapter. To implement this recipe, follow these steps:

1. Create a new Power BI Desktop file.
2. From the **Home** tab, click on **Get Data** in the ribbon and then **SQL Server**.
3. In the **Data Connectivity mode** section, choose the **DirectQuery** radio option.

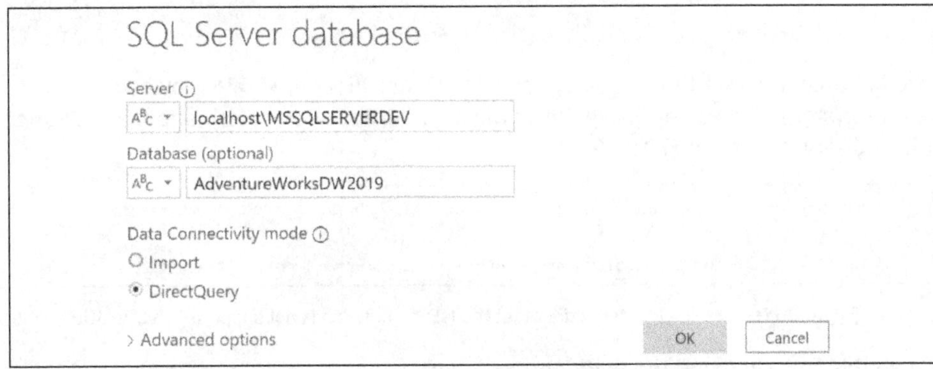

Figure 2.14: Creating a DirectQuery data source

4. Select a table or view to be used by the model via the **Navigator** dialog, such as the **FactResellerSales** table, and then click the **Transform Data** button.
5. Duplicate the initial query and revise the **Navigation** step to reference an additional view supporting the model, such as the **DimReseller**. This can be done by editing the `Item` in the formula bar or by clicking on the gear icon next to the **Navigation** step under **APPLIED STEPS** in the **Query Settings** pane. Also, rename this query to reflect the data being referenced.

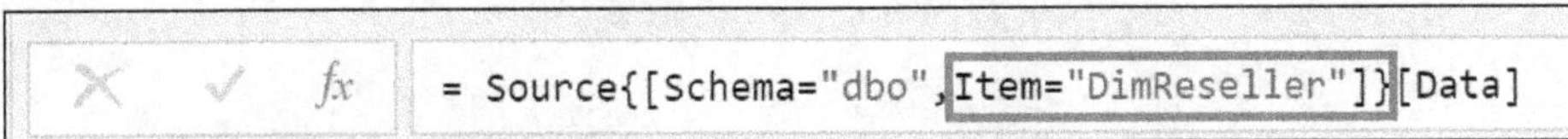

Figure 2.15: Editing the Navigation step in the formula bar

6. Repeat *step 5* for all required facts and dimensions. For example:
   - `DimEmployee`
   - `DimPromotion`
   - `DimCurrency`
   - `DimSalesTerritory`
7. Click the **Close and Apply** button.

The **Report Canvas** view will confirm that the model is in **DirectQuery** mode via the status bar at the bottom right (see *Figure 2.16*). In addition, the **Data** view in the left-hand pane, which is visible for import models, will not be visible.

Storage Mode: DirectQuery (click to change)

Figure 2.16: DirectQuery Status in Power BI Desktop

How it works

The M transformation functions supported in DirectQuery are limited by compatibility with the source system. The Power Query Editor will advise when a transformation is not supported in **DirectQuery** mode, per *Figure 2.17*.

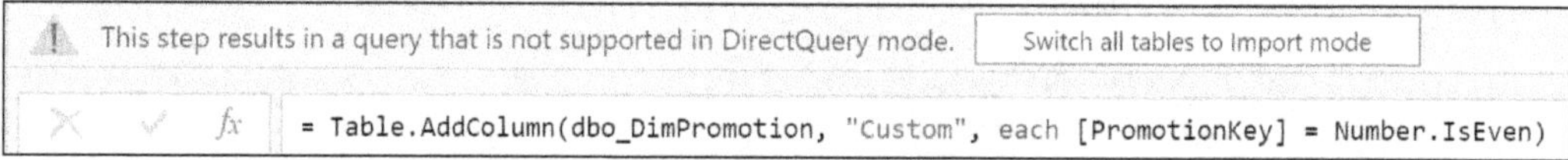

Figure 2.17: A warning in Query Editor that the IsEven function is not supported in DirectQuery mode

Given this limitation and the additional complexity the M-based transforms would add to the solution, it is recommended that you embed all the necessary logic and transforms in the source relational layer. Ideally, the base tables in the source database themselves would reflect these needs. As a secondary option, a layer of views can be created to support the DirectQuery model.

If the database objects themselves cannot be revised, the `Value.Native` M function can be used to directly pass the SQL statement from Power BI Desktop to the source database, as per *Figure 2.18*.

ProductNativeQry

```
let
    Source = AdWorksDW,
    ProductNativeQuery = Value.NativeQuery(Source,
"SELECT
        P.ProductKey
,       P.Class AS 'Product Class'
,       p.Color as 'Product Color'
,       p.EnglishProductName as 'Product Name'
,       p.ListPrice as 'List Price'
,       p.ModelName as 'Product Model'
,       p.Weight as 'Product Weight'
,       p.Style as 'Product Style'
,       p.StandardCost as 'Standard Cost'
,       p.ProductLine as 'Product line'
,       p.Status as 'Product Status'
,       S.EnglishProductSubcategoryName AS 'Product Subcategory'
,       C.EnglishProductCategoryName AS 'Product Category'
FROM
DBO.DimProduct AS P
LEFT JOIN DBO.DimProductSubcategory AS S
ON P.ProductSubcategoryKey = S.ProductSubcategoryKey
LEFT JOIN DBO.DimProductCategory AS C
ON S.ProductCategoryKey = C.ProductCategoryKey")
in
    ProductNativeQuery
```

Figure 2.18: The Value.Native function used to pass a SQL statement to a source system

As report visualizations are refreshed or interacted with in Power BI, the DAX queries from each visualization are translated into SQL statements, utilizing the source SQL statements to return the results. Be aware that Power BI does cache query results with DirectQuery models. Therefore, when accessing a recently utilized visual, a local cache may be used rather than a new query sent to the source.

The SQL statements passed from Power BI to the DirectQuery data source include all columns from the tables referenced by the visual.

For example, a Power BI visual with **SalesAmount** from the **FactResellerSales** table grouped by **ResellerName** from **DimReseller** would result in a SQL statement that selects the columns from both tables and implements the join defined in the model. However, as the SQL statement passed embeds these source views as derived tables, the relational engine is able to generate a query plan that only scans the required columns to support the join and aggregation.

There's more...

The performance and scalability of DirectQuery models are primarily driven by the relational data source. A denormalized star schema with referential integrity and a system that is isolated from OLTP workloads is recommended if near real-time visibility is not required. Additionally, in-memory and columnar features available to supported DirectQuery sources are recommended for reporting and analytical queries.

By default, DirectQuery models generate outer join SQL queries to ensure that measures return the correct value even if there's not a related dimension. However, you can configure DirectQuery models to send inner join queries. This is done by editing the relationship between tables in the modeling view by checking the **Assume referential integrity** setting (see *Figure 2.19*). Along with source system resources, this is one of the top factors contributing to the DirectQuery model's performance.

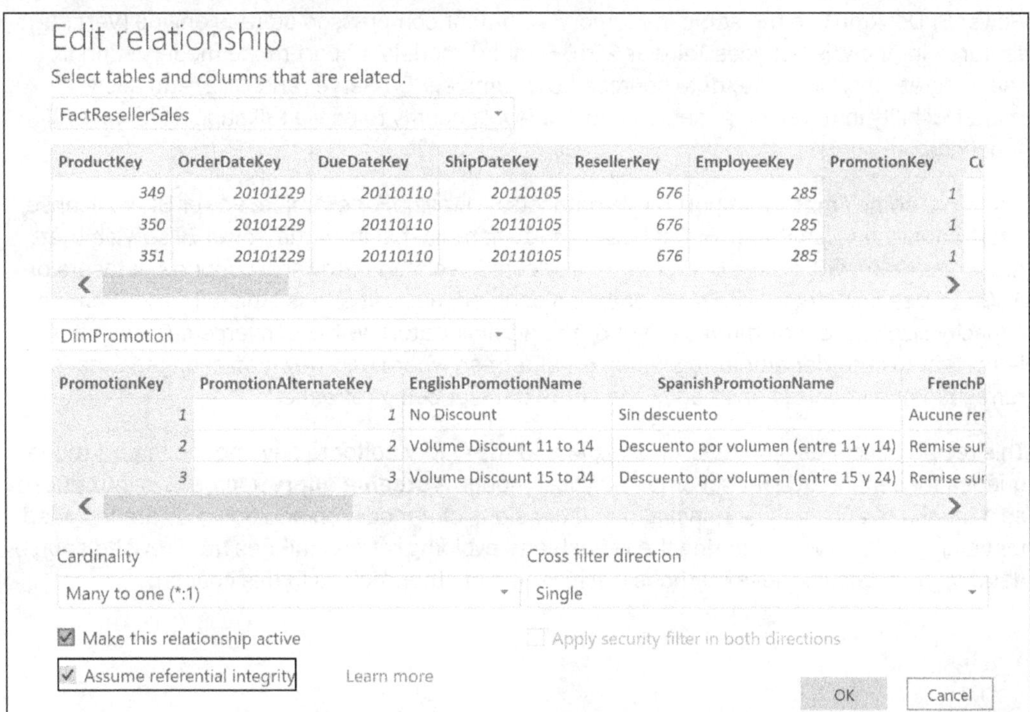

Figure 2.19: Activating referential integrity assumption in relationships

Of course, you should ensure that there is referential integrity in the source before enabling this setting; otherwise, incorrect results could be returned.

The design of the source relational schema and the hardware resources of this system can, of course, greatly impact the performance of DirectQuery models.

A classic star-schema design with denormalized tables is recommended to reduce the required join operations at query time. Optimizing relational fact tables with column store technologies such as the Clustered Columnstore Index for SQL Server and table partitions will also significantly benefit DirectQuery models.

See also

- Power BI Desktop DirectQuery documentation: `http://bit.ly/2nUoLOG`
- The *Power BI data sources* documentation provides a detailed list of data sources broken down by the connectivity options supported: `http://bit.ly/30N5ofG`

Importing Data

Import is the default data connectivity mode for Power BI Desktop. Import models created in Power BI Desktop use the same in-memory, columnar compressed storage engine (VertiPaq) featured in Analysis Services Tabular 2016+ import models. Import mode models support the integration of disparate data sources (for example, SQL Server and DB2) and allow more flexibility in developing metrics and row-level security roles via full support for all DAX functions.

There are some limits for Import mode datasets, however. For example, Power BI Pro license users cannot publish Power BI Desktop files to shared capacity in the Power BI service that are larger than 1GB. Power BI Premium (dedicated, isolated hardware) supports datasets of 10GB in size and larger (with large datasets enabled, dataset size is limited by the Premium capacity size or the maximum size set by the administrator). With such large datasets, it is important to consider employing incremental refresh where only new and changed data is refreshed and imported, instead of the entire dataset being refreshed.

This recipe describes a process of using M and the Query Editor to develop the Import mode queries for a standard star-schema analytical model. A **staging query** approach is introduced as a means of efficiently enhancing the dimensions of a model. In addition, tips are included for using fewer resources during the refresh and avoiding refresh failures from revised source data. More details of these methods are included in other recipes in this chapter.

Getting ready

In this example, the **DimProduct**, **DimProductSubcategory**, and **DimProductCategory** tables from the **AdventureWorksDW2019** database are integrated into a single import query. This query includes all product rows, only the English language columns, and user-friendly names. Many-to-one relationships have been defined in the source database.

To prepare for this recipe, do the following:

1. Open Power BI Desktop.
2. Create an Import mode data source query called **AdWorksDW**. This query should be similar to the following:

   ```
   let
       Source = Sql.Database("localhost\MSSQLSERVERDEV",
   "AdventureWorksDW2019")
   in
       Source
   ```

3. Isolate this query in a query group called **Data Sources**.
4. Disable loading of this query.

For additional details on performing these steps, see the *Managing Queries and Data Sources* recipe in this chapter.

How to import data

To implement this recipe, perform the following steps:

1. Right-click **AdWorksDW** and choose **Reference**. This creates a new query that references the **AdWorksDW** query as its source.
2. Select this new query and, in the preview data, find the **DimProduct** table in the **Name** column. Click on the **Table** link in the **Data** column for this row.
3. Rename this query **DimProduct**.
4. Repeat *steps 1 - 3* for the **DimProductCategory** and **DimProductSubcategory** tables.
5. Create a new query group called **Staging Queries**.
6. Move the **DimProduct**, **DimProductCategory**, and **DimProductSubcategory** queries to the **Staging Queries** group.

7. Disable loading for all queries in the **Staging Queries** group. Your finished set of queries should look similar to *Figure 2.20*.

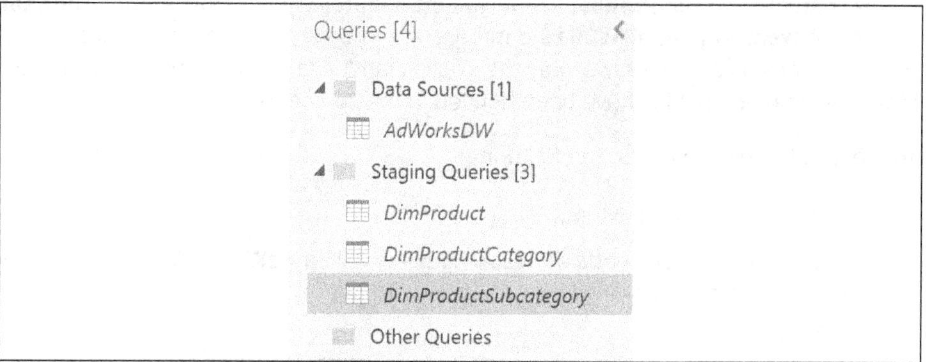

Figure 2.20: Staging Queries

The italics indicate that the queries will not be loaded into the model.

8. Create a new **Blank Query** and name this query **Products**.
9. Open the **Advanced Editor** for the **Products** query.
10. In the **Products** query, use the `Table.NestedJoin` function to join the `DimProduct` and `DimProductSubcategory` queries. This is the same function that is used if you were to select the **Merge Queries** option in the ribbon of the **Home** tab. A left outer join is required to preserve all `DimProduct` rows, since the foreign key column to `DimProductCategory` allows null values.
11. Add a `Table.ExpandColumns` expression to retrieve the necessary columns from the `DimProductSubcategory` table. The **Products** query should now have the following code:

```
let
    ProductSubCatJoin =
        Table.NestedJoin(
            DimProduct,"ProductSubcategoryKey",
            DimProductSubcategory,"ProductSubcategoryKey",
            "SubCatColumn",JoinKind.LeftOuter
        ),

    ProductSubCatColumns =
        Table.ExpandTableColumn(
            ProductSubCatJoin,"SubCatColumn",
            {"EnglishProductSubcategoryName","ProductCategoryKey"},
            {"Product Subcategory", "ProductCategoryKey"}
        )
in
    ProductSubCatColumns
```

The `NestedJoin` function inserts the results of the join into a column (`SubCatColumn`) as table values. The second expression converts these table values into the necessary columns from the **DimProductSubcategory** query and provides the simple `Product Subcategory` column name, as shown in *Figure 2.21*.

Product Subcategory	ProductCategoryKey
Helmets	4
Helmets	4
Helmets	4
Helmets	4
Helmets	4
Helmets	4
Socks	3
Socks	3

Figure 2.21: Product Subcategory Columns Added

The query preview in the **Power Query Editor** will expose the new columns at the far right of the preview data.

12. Add another expression beneath the `ProductSubCatColumns` expression with a `Table.NestedJoin` function that joins the previous expression (the **Product to Subcategory** join) with the `DimProductCategory` query.
13. Just like *step 8*, use a `Table.ExpandTableColumn` function in a new expression to expose the required **Product Category** columns.

```
        ),

    ProductCatJoin =
        Table.NestedJoin(
            ProductSubCatColumns,"ProductCategoryKey",
            DimProductCategory,"ProductCategoryKey",
            "ProdCatColumn",JoinKind.LeftOuter
        ),

    ProductCatColumns =
        Table.ExpandTableColumn(
            ProductCatJoin,"ProdCatColumn",
            {"EnglishProductCategoryName"}, {"Product Category"}
        )
in
    ProductCatColumns
```

Be certain to add a comma after the `ProductSubCatColumns` expression. In addition, be sure to change the line beneath the `in` keyword to `ProductCatColumns`.

The expression `ProductCatJoin` adds the results of the join to `DimProductCategory` (the right table) to the new column (`ProdCatColumn`). The next expression, `ProductCatColumns` adds the required **Product Category** columns and revises the `EnglishProductCategoryName` column to `Product Category`. A left outer join was necessary with this join operation as well since the product category foreign key column on `DimProductSubcategory` allows null values.

14. Add an expression after the `ProductCatColumns` expression that selects the columns needed for the load to the data model with a `Table.SelectColumns` function.
15. In addition, add a final expression to rename these columns via `Table.RenameColumns` to eliminate references to the English language and provide spaces between words.

```
        ),

    SelectProductColumns =
        Table.SelectColumns(ProductCatColumns,
            {
                "ProductKey", "EnglishDescription",
                "EnglishProductName", "Product Subcategory", "Product
Category"
            }
        ),
    RenameProductColumns =
        Table.RenameColumns(SelectProductColumns,
            {
                {"EnglishDescription", "Product Description"},
                {"EnglishProductName", "Product Name"}
            }
        )
in
    RenameProductColumns
```

Be certain to add a comma after the `ProductCatColumns` expression. In addition, change the line beneath the `in` keyword to `RenameProductColumns`.

The preview in the **Power Query Editor** for the **Products** query should now be similar to that shown in *Figure 2.22*.

	ProductKey	Product Description	Product Name	Product Subcategory	Product Category
212	212	Universal fit, well-vented, light...	Sport-100 Helmet, Red	Helmets	Accessories
213	213	Universal fit, well-vented, light...	Sport-100 Helmet, Red	Helmets	Accessories
214	214	Universal fit, well-vented, light...	Sport-100 Helmet, Red	Helmets	Accessories
215	215	Universal fit, well-vented, light...	Sport-100 Helmet, Black	Helmets	Accessories
216	216	Universal fit, well-vented, light...	Sport-100 Helmet, Black	Helmets	Accessories
217	217	Universal fit, well-vented, light...	Sport-100 Helmet, Black	Helmets	Accessories

Figure 2.22: Product Query Results

It is not necessary to rename the `ProductKey` column since this column will be hidden from the reporting layer. In practice, the product dimension would include many more columns. Closing and applying the changes results in only the **Products** table being loaded into the model.

The denormalized `Products` table now supports a three-level hierarchy in the Power BI Desktop model to significantly benefit reporting and analysis.

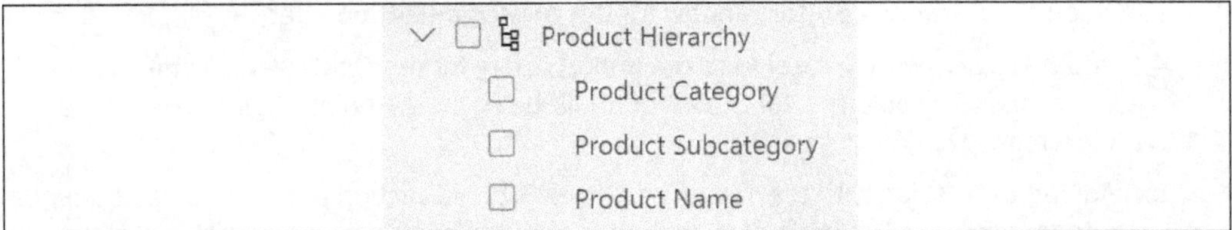

Figure 2.23: Product Hierarchy

How it works

The default join kind for `Table.NestedJoin` is a left outer join. However, as other join kinds are supported (for example, inner, anti, and full outer), explicitly specifying this parameter in expressions is recommended. Left outer joins are required in the **Products** table example, as the foreign key columns on `DimProduct` and `DimProductSubcategory` both allow null values. Inner joins implemented either via `Table.NestedJoin` or `Table.Join` functions are recommended for performance purposes otherwise. Additional details on the joining functions as well as tips on designing inline queries as an alternative to staging queries are covered in the *Combining and Merging Queries* recipe in this chapter.

When a query joins two tables via a `Table.NestedJoin` or `Table.Join` function, a column is added to the first table containing a **Table** object that contains the joined rows from the second table. This column must be expanded using a `Table.ExpandTableColumn` function, which generates additional rows as specified by the join operation.

Once all rows are generated by the join and column expansion operations, the specific columns desired in the end result can be specified by the `Table.SelectColumns` operation; these columns can then be renamed as desired using the `Table.RenameColumns` function.

There's more...

Using **Import** mode, we can do many things to enhance our queries to aid in report development and display. One such example is that we can add additional columns to provide automatic sorting of an attribute in report visuals. Specifically, suppose that we wish for the United States regional organizations to appear next to one another by default in visualizations. By default, since the **Organization** column in the **DimOrganization** table in **AdventureWorksDW2019** is a text column, the Central Division (a part of the USA), appears between Canada and France based upon the default alphabetical sorting of text columns. We can modify a simple query that pulls the **DimOrganization** table to add a numeric sorting column. To see how this works, follow these steps:

1. Using the same Power BI file used for this recipe, open the **Power Query Editor**, right-click the **AdWorksDW** query, and select **Reference**.
2. Choose the **DimOrganization** table and rename the query to **DimOrganization**.
3. Open the **Advanced Editor** window for the **DimOrganization** query.
4. Add a `Table.Sort` expression to the import query for the **DimOrganization** dimension. The columns for the sort should be at the parent or higher level of the hierarchy.
5. Add an expression with the `Table.AddIndexColumn` function that will add a sequential integer based on the table sort applied in the previous step. The completed query should look something like the following:

```
let
    Source = AdWorksDW,
    dbo_DimOrganization =
        Source{[Schema="dbo",Item="DimOrganization"]}[Data],
    OrgSorted =
        Table.Sort(
            dbo_DimOrganization,
            {
                {"ParentOrganizationKey", Order.Ascending},
                {"CurrencyKey", Order.Ascending}
            }
        ),
    OrgSortIndex = Table.AddIndexColumn(OrgSorted,"OrgSortIndex",1,1)
in
    OrgSortIndex
```

6. Finally, with the Ctrl key pressed, select the **OrganizationKey**, **OrganizationName**, and **OrgSortIndex** columns by clicking their column headers. Right-click on the **OrgSortIndex** column and choose to **Remove Other Columns**. The preview data should now show as presented in *Figure 2.24*.

	OrganizationKey	OrganizationName	OrgSortIndex
1	1	AdventureWorks Cycle	1
2	10	Pacific Operations	2
3	9	European Operations	3
4	2	North America Operations	4
5	8	Canadian Division	5
6	14	USA Operations	6
7	11	France	7
8	12	Germany	8
9	13	Australia	9
10	3	Northeast Division	10
11	4	Northwest Division	11
12	5	Central Division	12
13	6	Southeast Division	13
14	7	Southwest Division	14

Figure 2.24: Modified Organization Dimension Query

With this expression, the table is first sorted by the `ParentOrganizationKey` column and then by the `CurrencyKey` column. The new index column starts at the first row of this sorted table with an incremental growth of one per row. The net effect is that all of the US divisions are grouped together at the end of the table.

We can now use this new index column to adjust the default alphanumeric sorting behavior of the **OrganizationName** column. To see how this works, perform the following steps:

1. Choose **Close & Apply** to exit Power Query Editor to load the **DimOrganization** table.
2. In the **Data View**, select the `OrganizationName` column.
3. From the **Column tools** tab, set the **Sort by column** drop-down to the **OrgSortIndex** column.

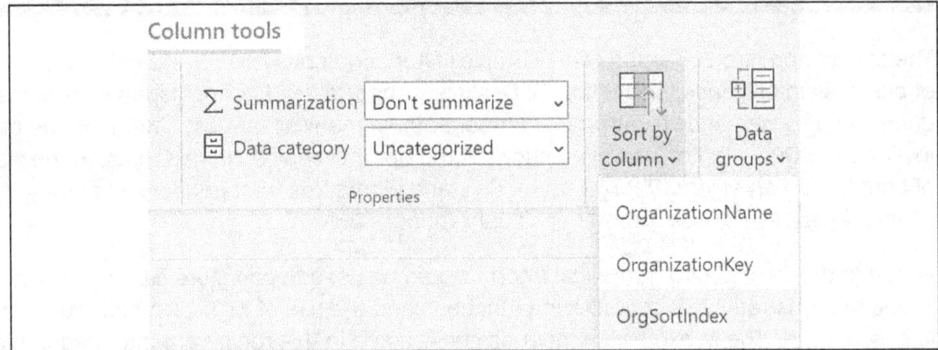

Figure 2.25: Sort By in Data View

4. Finally, right-click on the **OrgSortIndex** column and select **Hide in report view**.

Visuals using the `OrganizationName` column will now sort the values by their parent organization such that the USA organizations appear together (but not alphabetically).

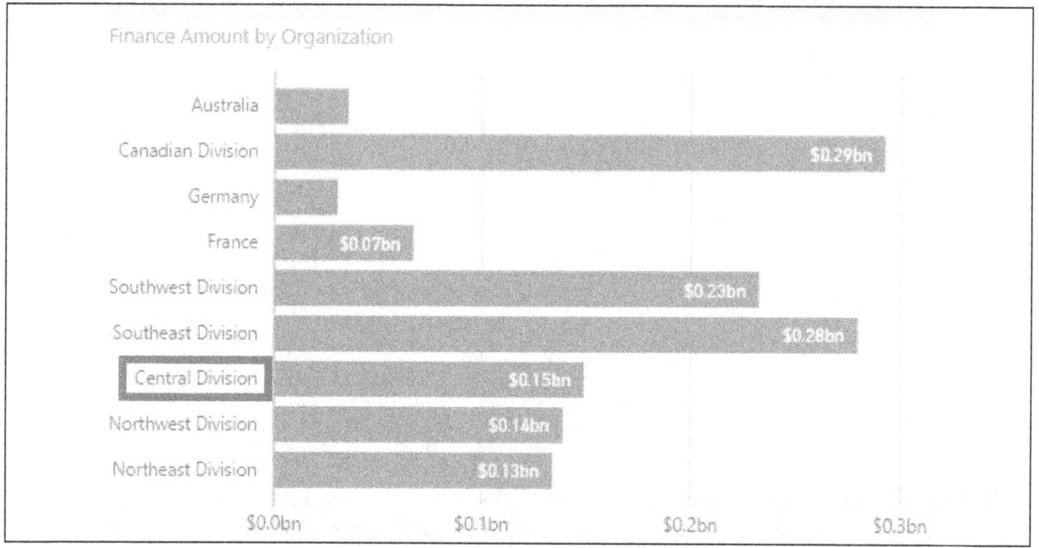

Figure 2.26: Organization automatically sorted

See also

- Dataset modes in the Power BI service: `http://bit.ly/30P2HKF`
- Data reduction techniques for Import modeling: `http://bit.ly/30RsMZI`

Applying Multiple Filters

The application of precise and often complex filter conditions has always been at the heart of business intelligence, and Power BI Desktop supports rich filtering capabilities across its query, data model, and visualization components. In many scenarios, filtering at the query level via the Query Editor and M functions is the optimal choice, as this reduces the workload of both Import and DirectQuery data models and eliminates the need for re-applying the same filter logic across multiple reports or visualizations.

Although the Query Editor graphical interface can be used to configure filtering conditions, this recipe demonstrates M's core filtering functions and the use of M in common multi-condition filter scenarios. The M expression queries constructed in this recipe are intended to highlight some of the most common filtering use cases.

Note that applying data transformations as part of a data warehouse ETL (extract-transform-load) or ELT (extract-load-transform) process is generally preferable to using Power Query (M). BI teams and developers should be careful to avoid creating Power BI datasets that significantly deviate from existing "sources of truth".

The following eight filtering queries will be developed in this recipe:

- United States customers only
- Customers with three or more children
- Customers with null values for either the middle name or title columns
- Customers with first purchase dates between 2012 and 2013
- Customers in management with the female gender or a bachelor's education
- The top 100 customers based on income
- A list of distinct sales territory countries
- Dates less than or equal to the current date and more than ten years prior to the current date

Getting ready

To prepare for this recipe, import the `DimCustomer` and **DimDate** tables from the **AdventureWorksDW2019** database by doing the following:

1. Open Power BI Desktop and choose **Transform data** from the ribbon of the **Home** tab to open the **Power Query Editor**.
2. Create an **Import** mode data source query called `AdWorksDW`. This query should be similar to the following:

```
let
    Source = Sql.Database("localhost\MSSQLSERVERDEV",
"AdventureWorksDW2019")
in
    Source
```

3. Isolate this query in a query group called **Data Sources**.
4. Right-click `AdWorksDW` and choose **Reference**.
5. Choose the `DimCustomer` table and rename the query `DimCustomer`.
6. Repeat *steps 4* and 5 for the `DimDate` table.
7. Group the dimension queries into a query group called **Base Queries**.
8. Disable the loading of all queries.

9. For the `DimCustomer` query, find the `DimGeography` column. In the column header, click the diverging arrows icon, uncheck **(Select All Columns)**, and then check the box next to `CountryRegionCode` and **DimSalesTerritory** before clicking the **OK** button.

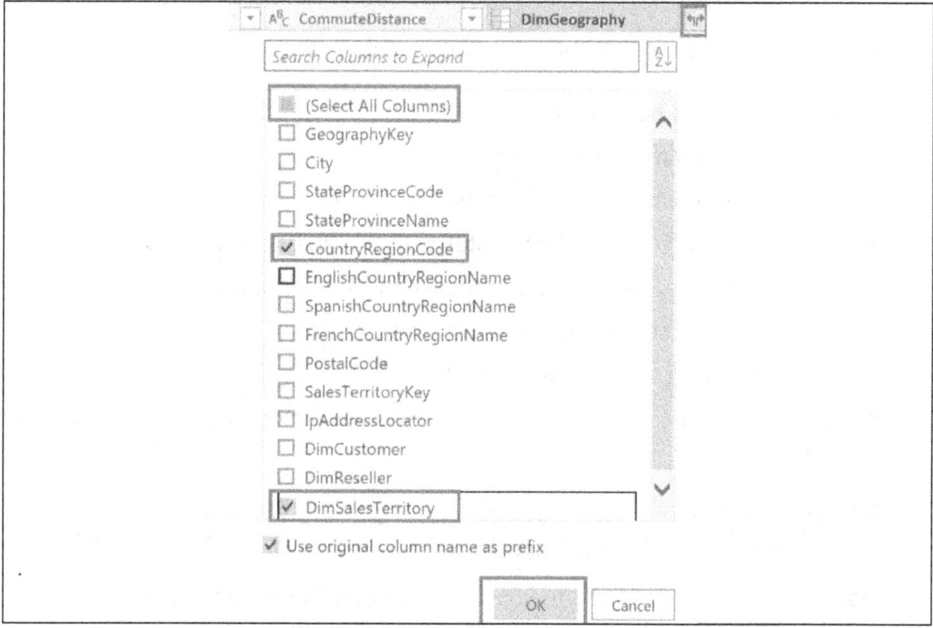

Figure 2.27: Expanding DimGeography to Include CountryRegionCode and DimSalesTerritory

10. Now expand **DimGeography.DimSalesTerritory** and only select the **SalesTerritoryCountry** column.
11. Rename the **DimGeography.CountryRegionCode** column to **CountryCode** and the **DimGeography.DimSalesTerritory.SalesTerritoryCountry** column to **SalesTerritoryCountry**.

For additional details on performing these steps, see the *Managing Queries and Data Sources* recipe in this chapter.

How to Apply Multiple Functions

To implement this recipe, use the following steps:

1. Right-click the **DimCustomer** query, choose **Reference**, and then open the **Advanced Editor** window for this query. Use the `Table.SelectRows` function to apply the US query predicate and rename the query **United States Customers**. The finished query should appear the same as the following:

```
let
    Source = DimCustomer,
    USCustomers = Table.SelectRows(Source, each [CountryCode] = "US")
in
    USCustomers
```

2. Repeat *step 1*, but this time filter on the `TotalChildren` column for `>=` **3** and rename this query **Customers w3+ Children**:

```
let
    Source = DimCustomer,
    ThreePlusChildFamilies = Table.SelectRows(Source, each
[TotalChildren] >=3)
in
    ThreePlusChildFamilies
```

3. Repeat *step 1*, but this time use the conditional logic operator `or` to define the filter condition for blank values in the `MiddleName` or `Title` columns. Use lowercase literal `null` to represent blank values. Name this query **Missing Titles or Middle Names**:

```
let
    Source = DimCustomer,
    MissingTitleorMiddleName =
        Table.SelectRows(
            Source, each [MiddleName] = null or [Title] = null
        )
in
    MissingTitleorMiddleName
```

4. Repeat *step 1*, but this time use the `#date` literal to apply the **2012-2013** filter on the `DateFirstPurchase` column. Rename this query **2012-2013 First Purchase Customers**:

```
let
    Source = DimCustomer,
    BetweenDates =
        Table.SelectRows(
            Source,
            each [DateFirstPurchase] >= #date(2012,01,01) and
                [DateFirstPurchase] <= #date(2013,12,31)
        )
in
    BetweenDates
```

5. Repeat *step 1*, but this time use parentheses to define the filter conditions for an `EnglishOccupation` of `Management`, and either the female gender (`F`), or `Bachelors` education. The parentheses ensure that the `or` condition filters are isolated from the filter on `Occupation`. Rename this query **Management and Female or Bachelors**:

```
let
    Source = DimCustomer,
    MgmtAndFemaleOrBachelors =
        Table.SelectRows(
            Source,
            each [EnglishOccupation] = "Management" and
            ([Gender] = "F" or [EnglishEducation] = "Bachelors")
        )
in
    MgmtAndFemaleOrBachelors
```

6. Right-click the `United States Customers` query, select **Reference**, and open the **Advanced Editor**. This time, use the `Table.Sort` function to order this table by the `YearlyIncome` column. Finally, use the `Table.FirstN` function to retrieve the top 100 rows. Rename this query to **Top US Customers by Income**.

```
let
    Source = #"United States Customers",
    SortedByIncome =
        Table.Sort(
            Source,
            {{"YearlyIncome", Order.Descending}}
        ),
    TopUSIncomeCustomers = Table.FirstN(SortedByIncome,100)
in
    TopUSIncomeCustomers
```

7. Repeat *step 1*, but this time use the `List.Distinct` and `List.Sort` functions to retrieve a distinct list of values from the `SalesTerritoryCountry` column. Rename this query **Customer Sales Territory List**.

```
let
    Source = DimCustomer,
    SalesTerritoryCountryList = List.Distinct(Source[SalesTerritoryCount
ry]),
    OrderedList = List.Sort(SalesTerritoryCountryList,Order.Ascending)
in
    OrderedList
```

8. Group the queries created thus far into a **Customer Filter Queries** query group.

9. Create a new query by referencing **DimDate** and open the **Advanced Editor**. Use the `DateTime.LocalNow`, `DateTime.Date`, and `Date.Year` functions to retrieve the trailing ten years from the current date. Rename this query **Trailing Ten Years from Today** and place this query in its own group, **Date Filter Queries**.

```
let
    Source = DimDate,
    TrailingTenYearsFromToday =
        Table.SelectRows(
            Source,
            each
                [FullDateAlternateKey] <= DateTime.Date(DateTime.
LocalNow) and
                [CalendarYear] >= Date.Year(DateTime.LocalNow) - 10
        )
in
    TrailingTenYearsFromToday
```

How it works

The `Table.SelectRows` function is the primary table-filtering function in the M language, and is functionally aligned with the `FROM` and `WHERE` clauses of SQL. Observe that variable names are used as inputs to M functions, such as the `Source` line being used as the first parameter to the `Table.SelectRows` function.

Readers should not be concerned with the `each` syntax of the `Table.SelectRows` function. In many languages, this would suggest row-by-row iteration, but when possible, the M engine *folds* the function into the `WHERE` clause of the SQL query submitted to the source system.

In the queries **United States Customers**, **Customers w3+ Children**, **Missing Titles or Middle Names**, and **Management and Female or Bachelors**, notice the various forms of the `each` selection condition. The syntax supports multiple comparison operators as well as complex logic, including the use of parenthesis to isolate logical tests.

In the **2012-2013 First Purchase Customers** query, the `#date` literal function is used to generate the comparison values. Literals are also available for `DateTime (#datetime)`, `Duration (#duration)`, `Time (#time)`, and `DateTimeZone (#datetimezone)`.

In the **Top US Customers by Income** query, the `Table.Sort` function is used to sort the rows by a specified column and sort order. The `Table.Sort` function also supports multiple columns as per the *Importing Data* recipe in this chapter. The `Table.FirstN` function is then used to return 100 rows starting from the very top of the sorted table. In this example, the set returned is not deterministic due to ties in income.

The **Customer Sales Territory List** query returns a list instead of a table. This is evident from the different icon present in the **Queries** pane for this query versus the others. Lists are distinct from tables in M, and one must use a different set of functions when dealing with lists rather than tables. A list of distinct values can be used in multiple ways, such as a dynamic source of available input values to parameters.

Finally, in the **Trailing 10 Yrs from Today** query, the current date and year are retrieved from the `DateTime.LocalNow` function and then compared to columns from the date dimension with these values.

There's more...

With simple filtering conditions, as well as in proof-of-concept projects, using the UI to develop filter conditions may be helpful to expedite query development. However, the developer should review the M expressions generated by these interfaces, as they are only based on the previews of data available at design time, and logical filter assumptions can be made under certain conditions.

To access the **Filter Rows** dialog, click on the drop-down button in a column header and then choose the **Text Filters** option, before specifying a starting filtering condition.

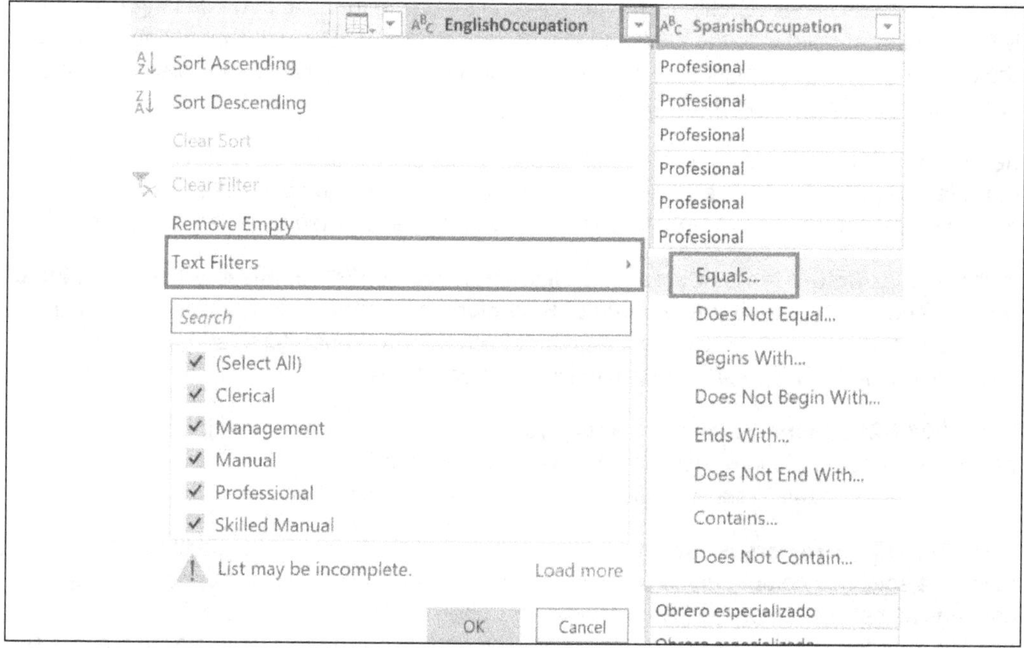

Figure 2.28: Accessing the Filter Rows dialog

The **Basic** option of the **Filter Rows** dialog only allows you to work with the currently selected column. However, by clicking on the **Advanced** radio button, you can work with any column in the table.

And/Or	Column	Operator	Value
	EnglishOccupation	equals	Management
And	Gender	equals	F
Or	EnglishEducation	equals	Bachelors

Figure 2.29: Advanced Filter Rows dialog in the Query Editor

Despite this, even the **Advanced** version of the **Filter Rows** dialog does not provide the ability to group logical filtering criteria. While the dialog in *Figure 2.29* looks like it recreates the query for **Management and Female or Bachelors**, the generated M code does not include the parenthesis that groups the **Gender** and **EnglishEducation** clauses. Thus, the code generated would have to be edited manually in the **Advanced Editor** to return the same results as the original **Management and Female or Bachelors** query. The M code generated by the **Filter Rows** dialog shown in *Figure 2.29* generates the following code:

```
Table.SelectRows(
    Source,
    each
        [EnglishOccupation] = "Management" and
        [Gender] = "F" or
        [EnglishEducation] = "Bachelors"
)
```

See also

- Table.SelectRows: http://bit.ly/3bSkEyj
- Table.Sort: http://bit.ly/3qPaeUo
- Table.FirstN: http://bit.ly/3ttb0In
- List.Distinct: http://bit.ly/3lnCqwq

- `List.Sort`: `http://bit.ly/30QLEb1`
- *10 Common Mistakes You Do In #PowerBI #PowerQuery – Pitfall #3*: `http://bit.ly/2nLX6QW`

Selecting and Renaming Columns

The columns selected in data retrieval queries impact the performance and scalability of both import and DirectQuery data models. For Import models, the resources required by the refresh process and the size of the compressed data model are directly impacted by column selection. Specifically, the cardinality of columns drives their individual memory footprint and memory per column. This correlates closely to query duration when these columns are referenced in measures and report visuals. For DirectQuery models, the performance of report queries is directly affected. Regardless of the model type, the way in which this selection is implemented also impacts the robustness of the retrieval process. Additionally, the names assigned to columns (or accepted from the source) directly impact the Q&A or natural language query experience.

This recipe identifies columns to include or exclude in a data retrieval process and demonstrates how to select those columns as well as the impact of those choices on the data model. In addition, examples are provided for applying user-friendly names and other considerations for choosing to retrieve or eliminate columns of data for retrieval.

Getting ready

To get ready for this recipe, import the **DimCustomer** table from the **AdventureWorksDW2019** database by doing the following:

1. Open Power BI Desktop and choose **Transform data** from the ribbon of the **Home** tab to open the **Power Query Editor**.
2. Create an **Import** mode data source query called `AdWorksDW`. This query should be similar to the following:

   ```
   let
       Source = Sql.Database("localhost\MSSQLSERVERDEV",
   "AdventureWorksDW2019")
   in
       Source
   ```

3. Isolate this query in a query group called **Data Sources**.
4. Right-click `AdWorksDW` and choose **Reference**.
5. Select the `DimCustomer` table in the data preview area and rename this query `DimCustomer`.

For additional details on performing these steps, see the *Managing Queries and Data Sources* recipe in this chapter.

How to Select and Rename Columns

To implement this recipe, use the following steps in Advanced Editor:

1. Create a name column from the first and last names via the `Table.AddColumn` function.

```
CustomerNameAdd =
    Table.AddColumn(
        dbo_DimCustomer, "Customer Name",
        each [FirstName] & " " & [LastName],
        type text
    )
```

2. Use the `Table.SelectColumns` function to select 10 of the 30 available columns now available in the **DimCustomer** table.

```
SelectCustCols =
    Table.SelectColumns(CustomerNameAdd,
        {
            "CustomerKey", "Customer Name", "Annual Income",
            "Customer Gender", "Customer Education",
"MaritalStatus",
            "Customer Phone Number", "CommuteDistance",
"AddressLine1",
            "TotalChildren"
        }, MissingField.UseNull
    )
```

Note that some of the column names specified do not actually exist. This is on purpose and will be fixed in the next step. But note that instead of generating an error, `null` values are displayed for those columns.

Customer Name	Annual Income	Customer Gender	Customer Education
Jon Yang	null	null	null
Eugene Huang	null	null	null
Ruben Torres	null	null	null
Christy Zhu	null	null	null
Elizabeth Johnson	null	null	null

Figure 30: Non-existent columns return null instead of error

Use the `Table.RenameColumns` function to apply intuitive names for users and benefit the Q&A engine for natural language queries. Insert this statement above your `SelectCustCols` statement and adjust as appropriate. The full query should now be similar to the following:

```
let
    Source = AdWorksDW,
    dbo_DimCustomer = Source{[Schema="dbo",Item="DimCustomer"]}[Data],
    CustomerNameAdd =
        Table.AddColumn(
            dbo_DimCustomer, "Customer Name",
            each [FirstName] & " " & [LastName],
            type text
        ),
    #"Renamed Columns" =
        Table.RenameColumns(CustomerNameAdd,
            {
                {"YearlyIncome", "Annual Income"},
                {"Gender", "Customer Gender"},
                {"EnglishEducation", "Customer Education"},
                {"Phone", "Customer Phone Number"}
            }
        ),
    SelectCustCols =
        Table.SelectColumns(#"Renamed Columns",
            {
                "CustomerKey", "Customer Name", "Annual Income",
                "Customer Gender", "Customer Education",
"MaritalStatus",
                "Customer Phone Number", "CommuteDistance",
"AddressLine1",
                "TotalChildren"
            }, MissingField.UseNull
        )
in
    SelectCustCols
```

How it works

The `Table.AddColumn` function concatenates the `FirstName` and `LastName` columns and includes an optional final parameter that specifies the column type as `text`.

The `Table.SelectColumns` function specifies the columns to retrieve from the data source. Columns not specified are excluded from retrieval.

A different method of accomplishing this same effect would be to use the `Table.RemoveColumns` function. However, in this case, 20 columns would need to be removed versus explicitly defining 10 columns to keep. To avoid query failure if one of the source columns changes or is missing, it is better to specify and name 10 than 20 columns. Query resilience can further be improved by using the optional parameter for `Table.SelectColumns`, `MissingField.UseNull`. Using this parameter, if the column selected is not available, the query still succeeds and simply inserts `null` values for this column for all rows.

Another advantage of using the `Table.SelectColumns` function is that columns can be reordered as selected columns are retrieved and presented in the order specified. This can be helpful for the query design process and avoids the need for an additional expression with a `Table.ReorderColumns` function. The initial column order of a query loaded to the data model is respected in the **Data** view. However, the field list exposed in the **Fields** pane in both the **Report** and **Data** views of Power BI Desktop is automatically alphabetized.

For import data models, you might consider removing a column that represents a simple expression of other columns from the same table. For example, if the `Extended Amount` column is equal to the multiplication of the `Unit Price` and `Order Quantity` columns, you can choose to only import these latter two columns. A DAX measure can instead compute the `Extended Amount` value. This might be done to keep model sizes smaller. This technique is not recommended for DirectQuery models, however.

Use the `Table.RenameColumns` function to rename columns in order to remove any source system indicators, add a space between words for non-key columns, and apply dimension-specific names such as `Customer Gender` rather than `Gender`. The `Table.RenameColumns` function also offers the `MissingField.UseNull` option.

There's more...

Import models are internally stored in a columnar compressed format. The compressed data for each column contributes to the total disk size of the file. The primary factor of data size is a column's cardinality. Columns with many unique values do not compress well and thus consume more space. Eliminating columns with high cardinality can reduce the size of the data model and thus the overall file size of a PBIX file. However, it is the size of the individual columns being accessed by queries that, among other factors, drives query performance for import models.

See also

- `Table.SelectColumns`: `http://bit.ly/38Qk7Lt`
- `Table.RenameColumns`: `http://bit.ly/3rTVfd4`
- `Table.RemoveColumns`: `http://bit.ly/3cJju7p`
- `Table.ReorderColumns`: `http://bit.ly/3cEoOJg`

- `Table.AddColumn`: `http://bit.ly/3vGJZ6b`
- Power BI Documentation on preparing data for Q&A: `http://bit.ly/2nBLAGc`

Transforming and Cleansing Data

The transformations applied within Power BI's M queries serve to protect the integrity of the data model and to support enhanced analysis and visualization. The specific transformations to implement varies based on data quality, integration needs, and the goals of the overall solution. However, at a minimum, developers should look to protect the integrity of the model's relationships and to simplify the user experience via denormalization and standardization. Additionally, developers should check with owners of the data source to determine whether certain required transformations can be implemented in the source, or perhaps made available via SQL view objects such that Power Query (M) expressions are not necessary.

This recipe demonstrates how to protect a model from duplicate values within the source data that can prevent forming proper relationships within the data model, which may even result in query failures. While a simple scenario is used, this recipe demonstrates scenarios you may run into while attempting to merge multiple data sources and eliminating duplicates.

Getting ready

To prepare, start by importing the **DimProduct** and **FactResellerSales** tables from the **AdventureWorksDW2019** database by doing the following:

1. Open Power BI Desktop and choose **Transform data** from the ribbon of the **Home** tab to open the **Power Query Editor**.
2. Create an **Import** mode data source query called **AdWorksDW**. This query should be similar to the following:

```
let
    Source = Sql.Database("localhost\MSSQLSERVERDEV",
"AdventureWorksDW2019")
in
    Source
```

3. Isolate this query in a query group called **Data Sources**.
4. Right-click **AdWorksDW** and choose **Reference**, select the **DimProduct** table in the data preview area, and rename this query **DimProduct**. Right-click the **EnglishProductName** column and select **Remove Other Columns**.
5. Repeat the previous step, but this time choose **FactResellerSales**. Expand the **DimProduct** column and only choose **EnglishProductName**. Rename this column to **EnglishProductName**.

6. Drag the **DimProduct** and **FactResellerSales** queries into the **Other Queries** group and apply the queries to the data model.
7. In the **Model** view of Power BI Desktop, attempt to form a relationship between the tables using the **EnglishProductName** columns from both tables. Note the warning that is displayed.

> ! This relationship has cardinality Many-Many. This should only be used if it is expected that neither column (EnglishProductName and EnglishProductName) contains unique values, and that the significantly different behavior of Many-many relationships is understood. Learn more

Figure 2.31: Many-Many relationship cardinality warning

For additional details on performing these steps, see the *Managing Queries and Data Sources* recipe in this chapter.

How to Transform and Cleanse Data

We wish to remove duplicates from the **EnglishProductName** column in our **DimProduct** query. To implement this recipe, use the following steps:

1. Remove any leading and trailing empty spaces in the `EnglishProductName` column with a `Text.Trim` function.
2. Create a duplicate column of the `EnglishProductName` key column with the `Table.DuplicateColumn` function and name this new column `Product Name`.
3. Add an expression to force uppercase on the `EnglishProductName` column via the `Table.TransformColumns` function. This new expression must be applied before the duplicate removal expressions are applied.
4. Add an expression to the **DimProduct** query with the `Table.Distinct` function to remove duplicate rows.
5. Add another `Table.Distinct` expression to specifically remove duplicate values from the `EnglishProductName` column.
6. Drop the capitalized `EnglishProductName` column via `Table.RemoveColumns`.

   The final query should resemble the following:

```
let
    Source = AdWorksDW,
    dbo_DimProduct = Source{[Schema="dbo",Item="DimProduct"]}[Data],
    RemoveColumns = Table.SelectColumns(dbo_DimProduct,{"EnglishProductN
ame"}),
    TrimText =
        Table.TransformColumns(
            RemoveColumns,{"EnglishProductName",Text.Trim}
        ),
```

```
        DuplicateKey =
            Table.DuplicateColumn(
                TrimText,"EnglishProductName","Product Name"
            ),
        UpperCase =
            Table.TransformColumns(
                DuplicateKey,{{"EnglishProductName", Text.Upper}}
            ),
        DistinctProductRows = Table.Distinct(UpperCase),
        DistinctProductNames =
            Table.Distinct(
                DistinctProductRows, {"EnglishProductName"}
            ),
        RemoveEnglishProductName =
            Table.RemoveColumns(
                DistinctProductNames,"EnglishProductName"
            )
    in
        RemoveEnglishProductName
```

How it works

In the `TrimText` expression, the `Trim.Text` function removes white space from the beginning and end of a column. Different amounts of empty space make those rows distinct within the query engine, but not necessarily distinct within the model. Therefore, it is always a good idea to use `Trim.Text` first and then remove duplicate rows and values.

In the next expression, `DuplicateKey`, the `Table.DuplicateColumn` function is used to duplicate the column where we will be removing duplicate values. We give this new column the name that we desire for our final column. This is done because we will need to transform the values in the column we are removing duplicates from, in order to account for mixed cases such as "Fender Set" and "Fender set". Thus, we wish to preserve the original values and casing by using this duplicate column.

In order to eliminate mixed casing issues, the `UpperCase` expression changes all values in the `EnglishProductName` column to uppercase using the `Table.TransformColumns` function, and specifying `Text.Upper`. The M engine considers mixed casing values unique, but the data model engine does not.

The next two expressions, `DistinctProductRows` and `DistinctProductNames`, simply demonstrate two different methods of using the `Table.Distinct` function. The first, `DistinctProductRows`, eliminates rows where the entire row (all column values) are identical. The second version looks only at the values in a single column when determining whether or not the row is a duplicate.

At this point, the query is now resilient to duplicate values and rows, mixed cases, and spaces. However, the `EnglishProductName` column is now in the uppercase format. Since we preserved a copy of the original values and casing in our `Product Name` column, we can simply drop the `EnglishProductName` column using the `Table.RemoveColumns` function.

We can now form a one-to-many relationship between our **DimProduct** and **FactResellerSales** tables.

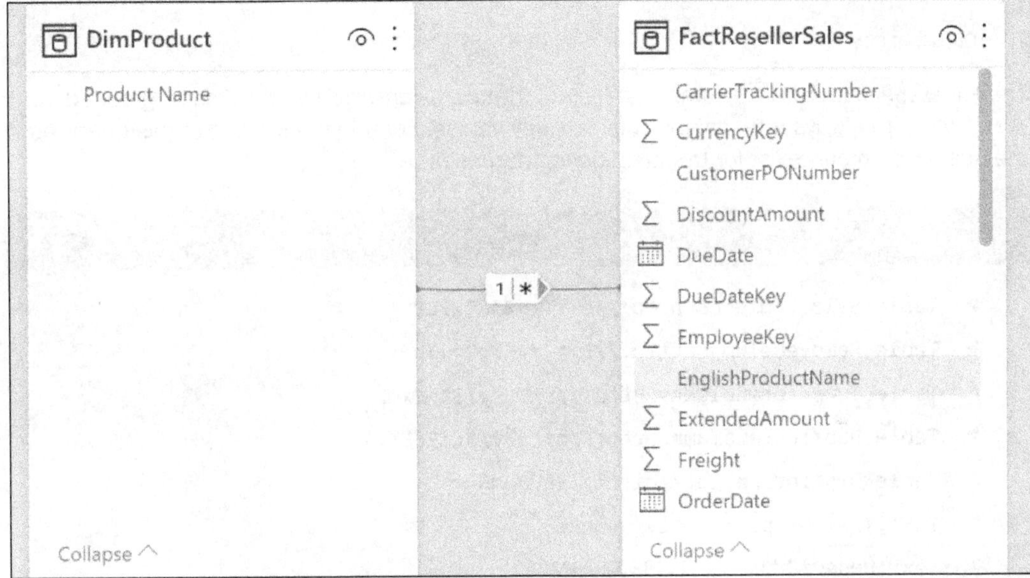

Figure 2.32: Simple one-to-many relationship model

There's more...

To support troubleshooting, create a query that accesses the same source table and retrieves the values from the `EnglishProductName` column with more than one row.

```
let
    Source = AdWorksDW,
    dbo_DimProduct = Source{[Schema="dbo",Item="DimProduct"]}[Data],
    RemoveColumns = Table.SelectColumns(dbo_DimProduct,{"EnglishProductName"}),
    TrimText =
        Table.TransformColumns(
            RemoveColumns,{"EnglishProductName",Text.Trim}
        ),
    UpperCase =
        Table.TransformColumns(
            TrimText,{{"EnglishProductName", Text.Upper}}
```

```
        ),
    GroupedRows =
        Table.Group(
            UpperCase, {"EnglishProductName"},
            {{"Rows", each Table.RowCount(_), Int64.Type}}
        ),
    Duplicates = Table.SelectRows(GroupedRows, each [Rows] > 1)
in
    Duplicates
```

The `EnglishProductName` column is selected, trimmed, converted to uppercase, grouped, and then filtered to always retrieve any duplicate key values. Disable the loading of this query, as the query would only exist for troubleshooting purposes.

See also

- `Table.SelectColumns`: `http://bit.ly/38Qk7Lt`
- `Table.RemoveColumns`: `http://bit.ly/3cJju7p`
- `Table.TransformColumns`: `http://bit.ly/3tsdxm2`
- `Table.DuplicateColumn`: `http://bit.ly/3cIF63X`
- `Table.Distinct`: `http://bit.ly/38V8mmN`
- `Text.Trim`: `http://bit.ly/3eUmAZ0`
- `Text.Upper`: `http://bit.ly/3vFW2R6`
- M functions reference for text: `http://bit.ly/2nUYjnw`

Creating Custom Columns

Business users often extend the outputs of existing reports and data models with additional columns to help them analyze and present data. The logic of these columns is generally implemented through Excel formulas or as calculated DAX columns. A superior solution, particularly if the logic cannot quickly be migrated to a data warehouse or IT resource, is to create the columns via the Power Query Editor and M language.

Developing custom columns can also significantly enhance the ease of use and analytical power of data models and the visualizations they support. In this recipe, columns are created to apply a custom naming format and simplify the analysis of a customer dimension via existing columns.

Getting ready

To get ready for this recipe, import the `DimCustomer` table from the **AdventureWorksDW2019** database by doing the following:

1. Open Power BI Desktop and choose **Transform data** from the ribbon of the **Home** tab to open the **Power Query Editor**.
2. Create an Import mode data source query called `AdWorksDW`. This query should be similar to the following:

```
let
    Source = Sql.Database("localhost\MSSQLSERVERDEV",
"AdventureWorksDW2019")
in
    Source
```

3. Isolate this query in a query group called **Data Sources**.
4. Right-click `AdWorksDW` and choose **Reference**, select the `DimCustomer` table in the data preview area, and rename this query `DimCustomer`.

For additional details on performing these steps, see the *Managing Queries and Data Sources* recipe in this chapter.

How to Create Custom Columns

To implement this recipe, perform the following steps:

1. Use `Table.SelectColumns` to retrieve the required source columns from the `DimCustomer` table, `FirstName`, `LastName`, `MiddleName`, `Title` and `BirthDate`.

```
let
    Source = AdWorksDW,
    dbo_DimCustomer = Source{[Schema="dbo",Item="DimCustomer"]}[Data],
    SelectColumns =
        Table.SelectColumns(dbo_DimCustomer,
            {"FirstName", "LastName", "MiddleName", "Title",
"BirthDate"}
        )
in
    SelectColumns
```

2. Write a `Table.AddColumns` function with an `if...then` expression that accounts for the different scenarios given a target format of `Mr. John A. Doe`:

```
    NameFormatTble =
        Table.AddColumn(
            SelectColumns,"Formatted Name", each
```

```
                if [Title] = null and [MiddleName] = null
                    then [FirstName] & " " & [LastName]
                else if [Title] = null
                    then [FirstName] & " " & Text.
Range([MiddleName],0,1)
                            & ". " & [LastName]
                else
                    [Title] & " " & [FirstName] & " "
                        & Text.Range([MiddleName],0,1) & ". " &
[LastName]
        )
```

3. Add variables that allow the expression to support the comparison between the current system date and the `BirthDate` column.

```
let
    CurrentDate = DateTime.Date(DateTime.LocalNow()),
    CurrentYear = Date.Year(CurrentDate),
    CurrentMonth = Date.Month(CurrentDate),
    CurrentDay = Date.Day(CurrentDate),

    Source = AdWorksDW,
```

4. Use the `Table.AddColumn` function to create `Customer Year`, `Customer Month`, and `Customer Day` columns based upon the `BirthDate` column.

```
    AddCustomerYear =
        Table.AddColumn(
            NameFormatTble, "Customer Year", each Date.
Year([BirthDate]),
            Int64.Type
        ),
    AddCustomerMonth =
        Table.AddColumn(
            AddCustomerYear, "Customer Month", each Date.
Month([BirthDate]),
            Int64.Type
        ),
    AddCustomerDay =
        Table.AddColumn(
            AddCustomerMonth, "Customer Day", each Date.
Day([BirthDate]),
            Int64.Type
        )
```

5. Add an Age column via an `if...then` expression.

```
CustomerAge =
    Table.AddColumn(
        AddCustomerDay,"Customer Age", each
        if [Customer Month] < CurrentMonth
            then CurrentYear - [Customer Year]
        else if [Customer Month] > CurrentMonth
            then CurrentYear - [Customer Year] - 1
        else if [Customer Day] < CurrentDay
            then CurrentYear - [Customer Year]
        else CurrentYear - [Customer Year] - 1
    )
```

6. Add a `Customer Age Segment` column via the column computed in *step 4*.

```
CustomerSegment =
    Table.AddColumn(
        CustomerAge, "Customer Age Segment", each
        if [Customer Age] < 30 then "Less than 30"
        else if [Customer Age] < 40 then "30 to 39"
        else if [Customer Age] < 50 then "40 to 49"
        else if [Customer Age] < 60 then "50 to 59"
        else "60 or Older"
    )
```

How it works

In the `NameFormatTble` expression the `Table.AddColumn` function is used, coupled with an `if...then` expression. M is a case-sensitive language, so writing `IF` instead of `if` or `Table.Addcolumn` instead of `Table.AddColumn` will return an error. `if...then` expressions follow the following structure:

```
if <condition1> then <result1> else <result2>
```

All three inputs (`condition1`, `result1`, and `result2`) accept M expressions. `if` expressions can be nested together with the following structure:

```
if <condition1> then <result1> else if <condition2> then <result2> else
<result3>
```

The equivalent of a SQL CASE expression is not available in M. However, the order of conditions specified in `if...then` expressions drives the evaluation process. Multiple conditions could be true but the second and later conditions will be discarded and not evaluated. If the value produced by the `if` condition is not a logical value, an error is raised.

The three `if...then` conditions in the `NameFormatTble` expression account for all scenarios to return the formatted name, since the query must account for nulls in the `Middle Name` and `Title` columns, as well as different values in the `Middle Name` column. `Text.Range` is used to extract the first character of the middle name.

For the variables `CurrentDate`, `CurrentYear`, `CurrentMonth`, and `CurrentDay`, the `DateTime.LocalNow` function is used as the source for the current date; it is then used for year, month, and day.

For the `AddCustomerYear`, `AddCustomerMonth`, and `AddCustomerDay` expressions, the `Int64.Type` value is passed to the optional type parameter of `Table.AddColumn` to set the new columns as whole numbers.

For the `CustomerAge` and `CustomerSegment` expressions, nested `if…then` expressions are used. This method is used because, currently, the equivalent of a `DATEDIFF` function (T-SQL, DAX) with date intervals like `Year`, `Month`, `Week`, and so on, are not available in M. A `Duration.Days` function can be used for day intervals and additional duration functions are available for hour, minute, and second intervals.

The `CustomerAge` expression compares the `CurrentMonth` and `CurrentDay` variables against the values of the customer columns created in the `AddCustomerMonth` and `AddCustomerDay` expressions in order to compute the age of the customer using the `CurrentYear` variable and the column created by the `AddCustomerYear` expression. The column created by the `CustomerAge` column is then used in the `CustomerSegement` expression to derive the age segmentation column. The new custom columns can be used to support various visualizations based upon the ages and segmentation of customers.

There's more...

The Power Query Editor provides graphical user interfaces for adding columns. These interfaces provide mechanisms for adding columns that are an alternative to writing out the code manually. In essence, the M code for the added columns is generated as an output from these interfaces.

One such interface is the **Column From Examples** feature, which allows users to simply type examples of a desired column's output. The engine determines which M functions and series of steps to add to the query that return results consistent with the examples provided. To explore this feature, follow these steps:

1. Create a new query referencing the **AdWorksDW** query.
2. Select the **DimCustomer** table.
3. Select the **Title**, **FirstName**, **MiddleName**, **LastName**, and **BirthDate** columns and remove all other columns.

4. Select the **Add Column** tab and then choose the **Column From Examples** button in the ribbon.

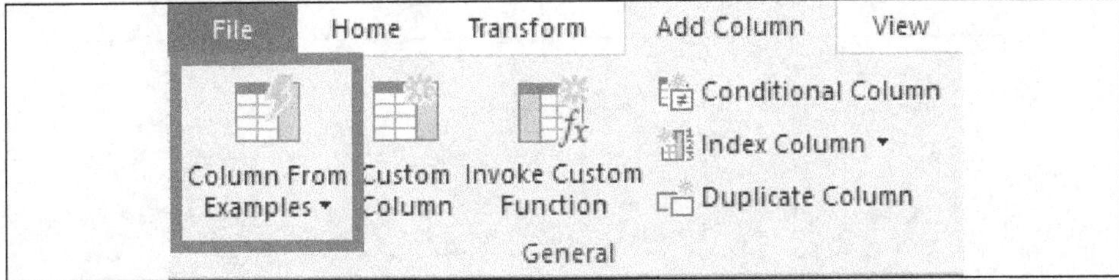

Figure 2.33: Column From Examples feature

5. Type the customer's `FirstName`, `MiddleName`, and `LastName` values into the first row and hit the **Enter** key. Notice that the rest of the rows are automatically calculated based upon this first row.

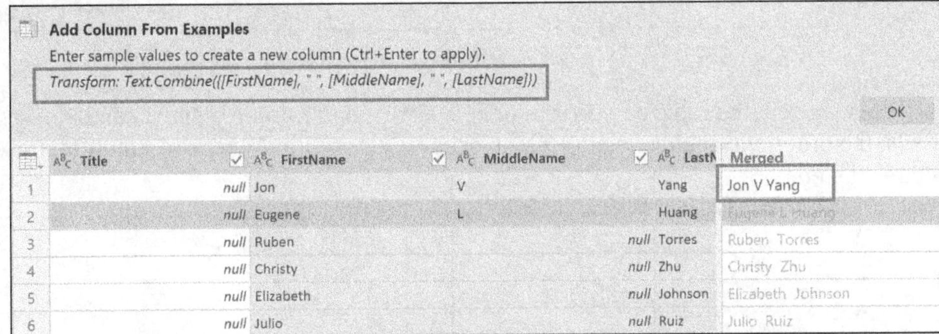

Figure 2.34: Column From Examples interface

6. Click the **OK** button to accept the transformation.

Another interface for adding columns is the **Condition Column** feature. This feature provides a method of creating conditional columns as an alternative to writing out the `if...then` expressions. To see how this feature operates, follow these steps:

1. Select the **Add Column** tab and then select **Conditional Column** from the ribbon.

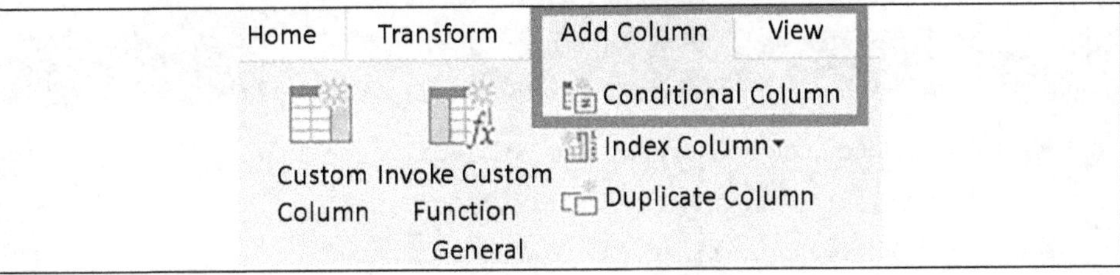

Figure 2.35: Conditional Column feature

2. Fill in the fields on the **Add Conditional Column** dialog, using the **Add Clause** button to add additional `else if` statements; click the **OK** button to exit the dialog and create the new column.

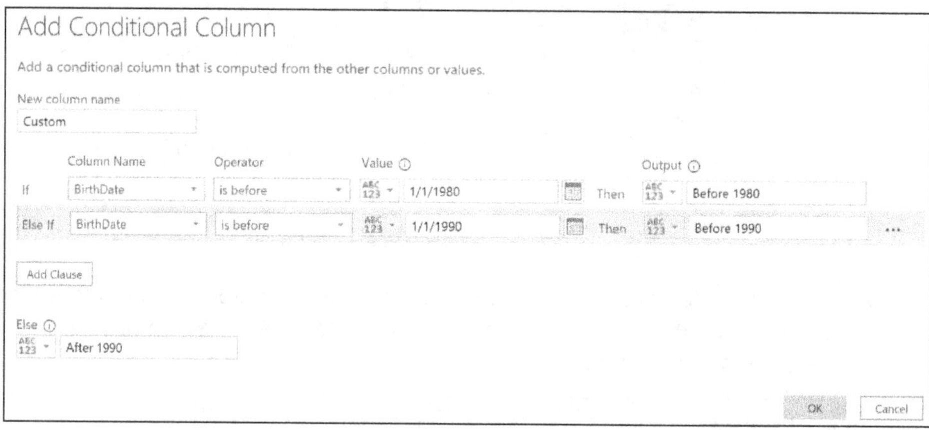

Figure 2.36: Add Conditional Column dialog

Any column from the table can be referenced, and multiple created steps can be moved up or down the order of evaluation using the ellipses (...). Open the **Advanced Editor** to inspect the code created.

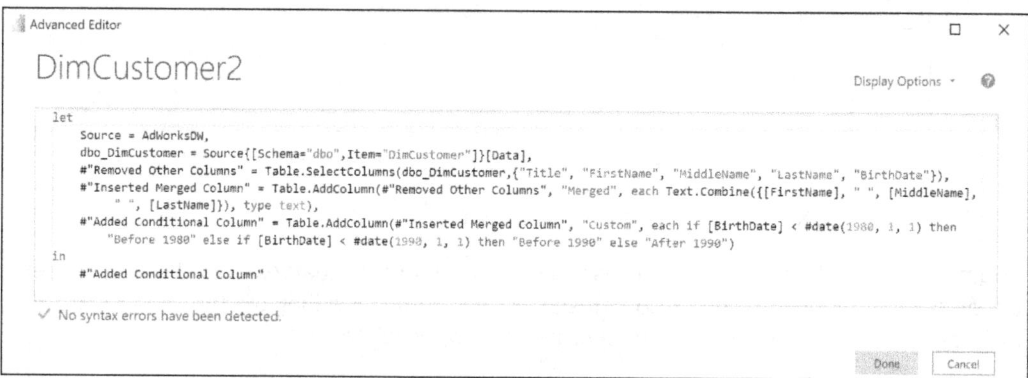

Figure 2.37: Added conditional column M code

See also

- `Table.AddColumn`: `http://bit.ly/3vGJZ6b`
- `Table.SelectColumns`: `http://bit.ly/38Qk7Lt`
- `DateTime` functions: `http://bit.ly/3tPtKlJ`
- **Add Column From** examples: `http://bit.ly/3eWTLv6`

Combining and Merging Queries

The full power of Power BI's querying capabilities is in the integration of distinct queries representing different data sources via its merge and append transformations. Retrieval processes that consolidate files from multiple network locations or integrate data from multiple data sources can be developed efficiently and securely. Additionally, the same join types and data transformation patterns SQL and ETL developers are familiar with can be achieved with the M language. This recipe provides examples of combining sources into a single query and leveraging the table join functions of M to support common transformation scenarios.

Getting ready

To follow along with this recipe, you can use the **Merge Queries** and **Append Queries** icons on the **Home** tab of the Power Query Editor to generate the join expressions used in this recipe. However, as joining queries is fundamental to the retrieval process, it is recommended to learn how to use the `Table.Join`, `Table.NestedJoin`, and `Table.Combine` functions.

To get ready for this recipe, import the `DimCustomer` and `FactCallCenter` tables from the **AdventureWorksDW2019** database by doing the following:

1. Open Power BI Desktop and choose **Transform data** from the ribbon of the **Home** tab to open the **Power Query Editor**.
2. Create an Import mode data source query called `AdWorksDW`. This query should be similar to the following:

   ```
   let
       Source = Sql.Database("localhost\MSSQLSERVERDEV",
   "AdventureWorksDW2019")
   in
       Source
   ```

3. Isolate this query in a query group called **Data Sources**.
4. Right-click `AdWorksDW` and choose **Reference**, select the `DimEmployee` table in the data preview area, and rename this query `DimEmployee`.
5. Repeat *step 4* but choose the **FactInternetSales** table and name this query **Sales2011**. Filter the **OrderDate** column to be between January 1, 2011 and December 31, 2011.

   ```
   Let
       Source = AdWorksDW,
       dbo_FactInternetSales = Source{[Schema="dbo",Item="FactInternetSal
   es"]}[Data],
       #"Filtered Rows" =
           Table.SelectRows(
   ```

```
                dbo_FactInternetSales, each
                    [OrderDate] >= #datetime(2011, 1, 1, 0, 0, 0) and
                    [OrderDate] <= #datetime(2011, 12, 31, 0, 0, 0))
in
    #"Filtered Rows"
```

6. Right-click the **Sales2011** query and choose **Duplicate**. Name this query **Sales2012**. Edit the `Table.SelectRows` expression to filter dates between January 1, 2012 and December 31, 2012.
7. Repeat *step 6*, naming this new query **Sales2013** and filtering for dates between January 1, 2013 and December 31, 2013.

For additional details on performing these steps, see the *Managing Queries and Data Sources* recipe in this chapter.

How to Combine Queries

The goal of this example is to produce an integrated table based on three "Sales" queries. While in this example the three queries come from the same data source, it is important to realize that the three queries could point to completely different data sources, such as three text files or even a text file, an Excel spreadsheet, and a SQL database. What is important is that the three queries have the same column names and number of columns. To implement this recipe, perform the following steps:

1. Move the **Sales2011**, **Sales2012**, and **Sales2013** queries to a new query group called **Staging Queries**.
2. Disable the load for the **Sales2011**, **Sales2012**, and **Sales2013** queries.
3. Create a new **Blank** query in the **Other Queries** group and call this query **FactInternetSales2011to2012**.
4. Open the **FactInternetSales2011to2012** query in **Advanced Editor**.
5. Use the `Table.Combine` (or **Append Queries** feature in the ribbon) function to return a single table based on the rows of the **Sales2011**, **Sales2012**, and **Sales2013** queries.

```
Let
    Source = Table.Combine( {Sales2011, Sales2012, Sales2013} )
in
    Source
```

6. Move the **DimEmployees** query to the **Staging Queries** group and disable loading.

7. Duplicate the **DimEmployees** query and call this new query **Managers**.
8. Disable loading for the **Managers** query.
9. Open the **Managers** query in the **Advanced Editor**.
10. Add a **Manager Name** column using the `Table.AddColumn` function.

```
ManagerName =
    Table.AddColumn(
        dbo_DimEmployee,
        "Manager Name", each [FirstName] & " " & [LastName]
    )
```

11. Select only the **EmployeeKey**, **Manager Name**, and **Title** columns using the `Table.SelectColumns` function.

```
SelectCols =
    Table.SelectColumns(
        ManagerName,
        { "EmployeeKey", "Manager Name", "Title" }
    )
```

12. Create a new **Blank** query in the **Other Queries** group and call this query **Employees**.
13. Open the **Employees** query in **Advanced Editor**.
14. Join the `Managers` query and `DimEmployee` query using the `Table.NestedJoin` function or the **Merge Queries** feature in the ribbon.

```
Let
    Source =
        Table.NestedJoin(
            DimEmployee, "ParentEmployeeKey", Managers, "EmployeeKey",
            "ManagerColumn", JoinKind.LeftOuter
        )
in
    Source
```

15. Use the `Table.ExpandTableColumn` function to add the `Manager Name` and `Manager Title` columns.

```
ManagerColumns =
    Table.ExpandTableColumn(
        Source, "ManagerColumn",
        { "Manager Name", "Title" },
        { "Manager Name", "Manager Title" }
    )
```

16. Add an **Employee Name** column.

```
EmployeeName =
    Table.AddColumn(
        ManagerColumns,
        "Employee Name", each [FirstName] & " " & [LastName]
    )
```

17. Rename the **Title** column to **Employee Title**.

```
RenameTitle =
    Table.RenameColumns(
        EmployeeName,
        { "Title", "Employee Title" }
    )
```

18. Select the `EmployeeKey`, `Employee Name`, `Employee Title`, `Manager Name`, and `Manager Title` columns.

```
SelectCols =
    Table.SelectColumns(
        RenameTitle,
        {
            "EmployeeKey", "Employee Name", "Employee Title",
            "Manager Name", "Manager Title"
        }
    )
```

How it works

For the **FactInternetSales2011to2013** query, only a single expression is required using the `Table.Combine` function. No other expressions are necessary in this example given that the staging queries have identical column names and the same number of columns. The `Table.Combine` function performs an append operation and does not remove duplicate rows similar to a SQL UNION statement.

Any columns which are unique to one of the input tables in a `Table.Combine` function will be added to the result set with null values for the rows from the other tables. Depending on the scenario, the developer could apply the `Table.Distinct` function to avoid any duplicate rows from reaching the data model.

The **Employees** query references the **DimEmployees** query as the left table in a `Table.NestedJoin` function, and is joined to the `Managers` query via a left outer join. The left join is required to retain all employee rows in this scenario, as the `DimEmployees` table includes one employee that does not have a parent employee key, the `Chief Executive Officer`.

The join is performed on the `ParentEmployeeKey` column in the **DimEmployees** query to the `EmployeeKey` column in the **Managers** query. After this step, all of the rows from the matching **Managers** table are stored within the row as a `Table` object in the column **ManagerColumn**. When expanding the **ManagerColumn** column using the `Table.ExpandTableColumn` function, the **Manager Name** column can retain the same name, but the **Title** column is renamed to **Manager Title** in order to avoid conflicting with the **Title** column in the **DimEmployees** query.

In implementing the table joins, you can choose to use the `Table.Join` and `Table.NestedJoin` functions. All six join types—inner, left outer, right outer, full outer, left anti, and right anti—are supported by both functions. The `Table.NestedJoin` function enters the results of the join (the right or second table) into a new column of table values and will use local resources to execute the join operation, unless the `Table.ExpandTableColumn` function is used to replace this new column with columns from the right table. A left outer join type is the default if the `JoinKind` parameter is not specified. For performance reasons, `Table.NestedJoin` should not be used without a `Table.ExpandTableColumn` function removing the column of tables.

Conversely, the `Table.Join` function automatically expands the left table with the columns from the right table input (a flat join) and defaults to an inner join if the `JoinKind` parameter is not specified. The `Table.Join` function gets folded to the source without any additional functions but requires that there are no matching column names between the joined tables for a `JoinKind` other than inner join. For inner joins, the matching column names from both tables must be specified in the join key parameters. A `Table.SelectColumns` function is required to exclude any columns from the right table added with the join.

Whether implemented via `Table.NestedJoin` or `Table.Join`, developers should look to use inner joins if the source tables have referential integrity, such as with foreign key constraints and whether this meets requirements. For joins against larger tables, developers should confirm that query folding is occurring and can evaluate the different query plans generated by alternative retrieval designs in terms of performance.

Note that the two rows for Rob Walters are due to a **Slowly Changing Dimension** (**SCD**) Type 2 process applied in the source database. For more information on SCDs, refer to this Wikipedia article: `https://bit.ly/3yIQeI5`.

There's more...

Rather than creating separate lookup/join staging queries, it is possible to consolidate these expressions into a single `let...in` M expression. For example, the following single query returns the exact same results as the **Sales2011**, **Sales2012**, **Sales2013**, and **FactInternetSales2011to2013** queries:

```
let
    Source = AdWorksDW,
    Sales = Source{[Sche"a=""bo",It"m="FactInternetSa"es"]}[Data],
    Sales2011Rows =
```

```
        Table.SelectRows(
            Sales, each
                [OrderDate] >= #datetime(2011, 1, 1, 0, 0, 0) and
                [OrderDate] <= #datetime(2011, 12, 31, 0, 0, 0)
        ),
    Sales2012Rows =
        Table.SelectRows(
            Sales, each
                [OrderDate] >= #datetime(2012, 1, 1, 0, 0, 0) and
                [OrderDate] <= #datetime(2012, 12, 31, 0, 0, 0)
        ),
    Sales2013Rows =
        Table.SelectRows(
            Sales, each
                [OrderDate] >= #datetime(2013, 1, 1, 0, 0, 0) and
                [OrderDate] <= #datetime(2013, 12, 31, 0, 0, 0)
        ),
    Append = Table.Combine( {Sales2011Rows, Sales2012Rows, Sales2013Rows} )
in
    Append
```

Inline query approaches are helpful in limiting the volume of queries, but you lose the management benefits provided by group folders and the **Query Dependencies** view. The graphical support makes it easier to explain and quickly troubleshoot a data retrieval process over a single but complex M expression. Staging queries are recommended for all but the most trivial projects and retrieval processes. Staging queries should generally never be loaded to the data model, as staging tables could both confuse the user and would require the data model to use additional resources to process and store the additional data.

Similarly, merge queries can also be combined into a single query. The following table breaks down the six different join types that can be specified in both the `Table.NestedJoin` and `Table.Join` functions. Both the **Parameter** and **Parameter Value** can be used, though the recipes in this book use **Parameter** as this makes the expressions easier to follow.

Join type	**Parameter**	**Parameter value**
Inner	`JoinKind.Inner`	0
Left Outer	`JoinKind.LeftOuter`	1
Right Outer	`JoinKind.RightOuter`	2
Full Outer	`JoinKind.FullOuter`	3
Left Anti	`JoinKind.LeftAnti`	4
Right Anti	`JoinKind.RightAnti`	5

Table 2.3: Power Query (M) join types, parameters, and parameter values

One final note is that, for data source files with the same structure stored in the same network directory folder, Power BI offers the **Combine Binaries** transformation, which can be used with text, CSV, Excel, JSON, and other file formats. This feature can be used when creating a **Folder** query. The **Combine Binaries** feature automatically creates an example query and a function linked to this query, such that any required modification to the source files can be applied to all files, and the source location of the files can be easily revised.

See also

- `Table.Combine`: `http://bit.ly/3c6L2o0`
- `Table.NestedJoin`: `http://bit.ly/30ZO3jZ`
- `Table.Join`: `http://bit.ly/3lxMRh7`
- `Table.ExpandTableColumn`: `http://bit.ly/3eY6u0z`
- `Table.AddColumn`: `http://bit.ly/3vGJZ6b`
- `Table.SelectColumns`: `http://bit.ly/38Qk7Lt`
- `Table.RenameColumns`: `http://bit.ly/3rTVfd4`
- M table function reference: `http://bit.ly/2oj0k0I`
- Combining binaries in Power BI Desktop: `http://bit.ly/2oL2nM4`

Selecting Column Data Types

Setting the data types of columns in Power BI Desktop is usually the final step of data retrieval queries, and has great implications for all layers of the solution, including data refresh, data modeling, and visualization. Choosing appropriate data types reduces the risk of refresh failures, ensures consistent report results, and provides analytical flexibility to the data model and visualization layers.

This recipe demonstrates how to choose and define data types to load to Power BI Desktop. Additional details on data types and the implications of data types for Power BI development are contained in the sections following these examples.

Getting ready

In preparation for this recipe, import the `FactCallCenter` table from the **AdventureWorksDW2019** database by doing the following:

1. Open Power BI Desktop and choose **Transform data** from the ribbon of the **Home** tab to open the **Power Query Editor**.

2. Create an Import mode data source query called `AdWorksDW`. This query should be similar to the following:

```
let
    Source = Sql.Database("localhost\MSSQLSERVERDEV",
"AdventureWorksDW2019")
in
    Source
```

3. Isolate this query in a query group called **Data Sources**.
4. Right-click `AdWorksDW` and choose **Reference**, select the **FactFinance** table in the data preview area, and rename this query **FactFinance**.
5. Move the **FactFinance** query to the **Other Queries** group.

For additional details on performing these steps, see the *Managing Queries and Data Sources* recipe in this chapter.

How to Select Column Data Types

To implement this recipe, perform the following steps:

1. Use the `Table.TransformColumnTypes` function to revise the type of the numeric integer **FinanceKey** column to text. Note that the column header for the **FinanceKey** column is initially prefaced with a **123** icon and changes to an **ABC** icon. Also, note that the row values are initially left justified and italicized and after transformation to text are aligned to the right and not italicized.

```
let
    Source = AdWorksDW,
    dbo_FactFinance = Source{[Schema="dbo",Item="FactFinance"]}[Data],
    FinanceKeyText =
        Table.TransformColumnTypes(
            dbo_FactFinance, {{"FinanceKey", Text.Type}}
        )
in
    FinanceKeyText
```

2. Add a numeric column from a source column stored as text using the `Number.FromText` and `Table.AddColumn` functions.

```
    FinanceKeyNum =
        Table.AddColumn(
            FinanceKeyText, "FinanceKeyNum",
            each Number.FromText([FinanceKey]),Int64.Type
        )
```

3. Change the fixed decimal **Amount** column to currency using the `Table.TransformColumnTypes` function. Note that the column header icon changes from **1.2** initially to a dollar sign, **$**.

```
Currency =
    Table.TransformColumnTypes(
        FinanceKeyNum,{{"Amount", Currency.Type}}
    )
```

How it works

For the `FinanceKeyText` expression, the `Table.TransformColumnTypes` function takes two parameters. The first parameter is the table to operate upon; the second is a list of list pairs that include the column name to transform and then the transformation data type. Multiple pairs can be included in the form:

```
{ { "Column1", type }, { "Column2", type } }
```

Additional valid values for the type parameter include the following:

- `Currency.Type` sets the column as a **Fixed Decimal Number** to two decimal places.
- `Decimal.Type` or `type number` sets the new column as a **Decimal Number**.
- `Percentage.Type` sets the column as a **Percentage** data type. Unlike **Whole Number**, **Fixed Decimal Number**, and **Decimal Number**, this type does not have a corresponding type in the data model. When loaded to the data model, the **Percentage** data type is represented as a **Decimal Number** type.
- `Text.Type` or `type text` sets the column to a **Text** data type.
- `Date.Type` or `type date` sets the column to a **Date** data type.
- `DateTime.Type` or `type datetime` sets the column to a **Date Time** data type.
- `DateTimeZone.Type` or `type datetimezone` sets the column to a **Date/Time/Timezone** data type.
- `Time.Type` or `type time` sets the column to a **Time** data type.
- `Duration.Type` or `type duration` sets the column to a **Duration** data type.
- `Logical.Type` or `type logical` sets the column to a **True/False** data type.
- `Binary.Type` or `type binary` sets the column to a **Binary** data type.

Like all M expressions, data type declarations are case-sensitive.

For the `FinanceKeyNum` expression, the type parameter for the `Table.AddColumn` function is optional. Leaving this parameter blank results in an **Any** data type, which would be loaded into the data model as a **Text** data type. By specifying `Int64.Type` as the optional type parameter to `Table.AddColumn`, the new column stores whole numbers instead of text.

Great care should be taken when choosing data types. For example, convert **Decimal Number** to **Fixed Decimal Number** data types if consistent rounding results are required. Also, converting from **Decimal Number** to **Fixed Decimal Number** can marginally improve data compression and query performance. A **Decimal** data type is approximate and can produce inconsistent reporting results due to rounding. **Decimal Number** data types are floating-point (approximate) data types with 15 digits of precision. **Fixed Decimal Number** data types store 19 digits of precision and four significant digits after the decimal. **Whole Number** data types store up to 19 digits of precision.

Revising **Text** data types to **Numeric** data types impacts the DAX metrics that can be written. For example, if a `Calendar Year` column is stored as a **Text** data type, the following DAX metric will fail due to the type incompatibility of the number 2016:

```
Sales in 2016 and Later = CALCULATE([Internet Sales], 'Date'[Calendar Year] >= 2016)
```

Figure 2.38: DAX measure expression

Revising `Calendar Year` to a whole number type avoids the need to use `VALUE` or `FORMAT` functions in each DAX measure. Power BI Desktop provides rich analysis capabilities for columns of the **Date** data type, including drill-down hierarchies, visual calendar pickers for filters, custom date filtering logic in slicers, and calculations such as for the first and last date. Given these capabilities, as well as DAX functionality with **Date** data types, converting **Text** and **Numeric** types to **Date** data types can provide significantly more options to develop Power BI content.

There's more...

While there are many topics that can be discussed regarding data types in Power Query, two are worth exploring in greater detail: **automatic data type detection** and **date with locale**. When enabled, automatic data type detection occurs when using unstructured data sources, such as flat files and Excel workbooks. When importing such data, a **Changed Type** step is added that uses a sampling or preview of each source column to determine the appropriate type.

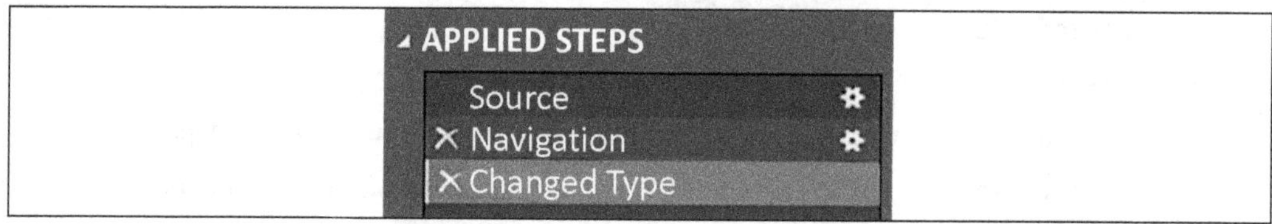

Figure 2.39: Automatic Data Type Selection Step

If the data sample does not reflect the full or future set of values for the column, the data type selected may be incorrect. Automatic type detection is not used with structured relational database systems such as SQL Server.

You can avoid automatic type detection via the **Data Load** options in the **File | Options and settings | Options** dialog.

As automatic detection is a **CURRENT FILE** option only, and since the setting is enabled by default, you currently need to disable this automatic type detection for each new file. It is recommended that you disable this for each file or manually remove the **Changed Type** step and make your own decisions regarding data type transformations.

Power Query also supports different locales or cultures. If there's any potential for **Date** data types to be sourced from a region with a different date standard than your local system, you should apply the **Locale** option to the `Table.TransformColumnTypes` function; for example, when a date column stores date values in the format `dd/mm/yyyy`, whereas the local system uses `mm/dd/yyyy`. Trying to convert this date directly on a desktop configured for US English causes an error as the first two digits are greater than 12. However, specifying the source locale in the transform expression allows for successful conversion. The Query Editor provides a simple interface for the source locale. Simply right-click on the column, expand **Change Type**, and then select **Using Locale...**.

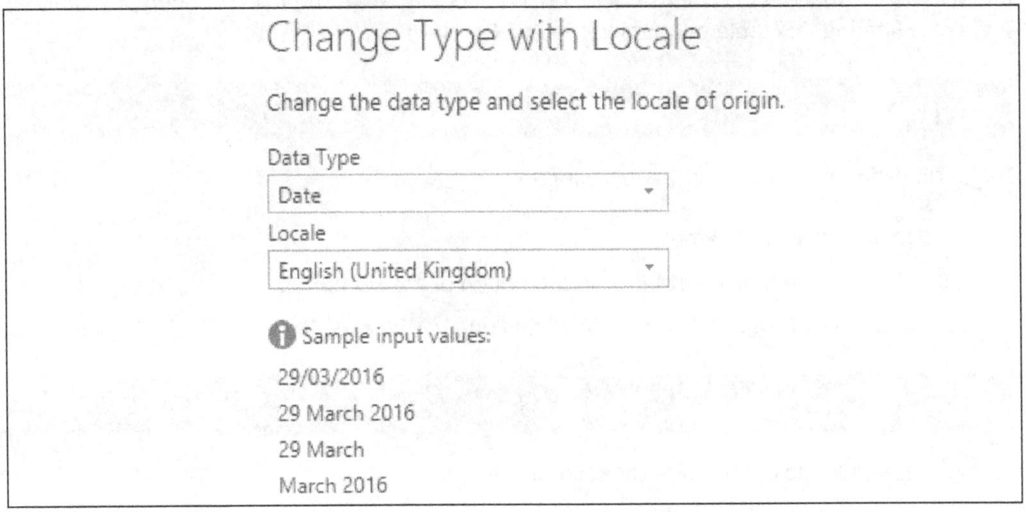

Figure 2.40: Change Type with Locale interface

Alternatively, you can add the locale to the expression itself directly:

```
DateLocale =
    Table.TransformColumnTypes(
        PreviousStep, {{ "Date", type date }}, "en-GB"
    )
```

See also

- `Table.AddColumn`: `http://bit.ly/3vGJZ6b`
- `Table.TransformColumnTypes`: `http://bit.ly/3s5AfjC`
- Data types in Power Query: `http://bit.ly/392iWIP`

- Language ID and tag reference: `http://bit.ly/3cXpPfw`
- 10 Common Mistakes You Do In #PowerBI #PowerQuery – Pitfall #2: `http://bit.ly/2otDbcU`
- Choosing Numeric Data Types in DAX: `http://bit.ly/2nOWYAm`

Visualizing the M library

To implement complex and less common data transformation requirements, it is often necessary to browse the M library to find a specific function or review the parameters of a specific function.

This short recipe provides a pre-built M query expression you can use to retrieve the M library into a table for analysis in Power BI Desktop. Additionally, an example is provided of visualizing and cross-filtering this table of functions on the Power BI report canvas.

Getting ready

To get ready for this recipe, do the following:

1. Open Power BI Desktop.
2. Click the **Transform data** icon in the ribbon of the **Home** tab.
3. Create a new **Blank Query** and call this query **MLibrary**.

How to Visualize M library

To implement this recipe, perform the following steps:

1. Enter the following M code in the **Advanced Editor**:

```
let
    Source = Record.ToTable(#shared),
    Rename = Table.RenameColumns(Source, {{"Name", "Function"}}),
    Sort = Table.Sort(Rename, {{"Function", Order.Ascending}}),
    Dupe = Table.DuplicateColumn(Sort, "Function", "Function2"),
    Split =
```

```
        Table.SplitColumn(
            Dupe, "Function2",
            Splitter.SplitTextByDelimiter(".", QuoteStyle.Csv),
            {"Group", "Detail"}
        ),
    MLibraryTable =
        Table.TransformColumnTypes(
            Split, {{"Group", Text.Type}, {"Detail", Text.Type}}
        )
in
    MLibraryTable
```

2. Click the **OK** button to close the **Advanced Editor**. The preview area should now look similar to that shown in *Figure 2.41*.

	Function	Value	Group	Detail
1	AI.ExecuteInProc	Function	AI	ExecuteInProc
2	AI.ExecuteInternal	Function	AI	ExecuteInternal
3	AI.ExternalSort	Function	AI	ExternalSort
4	AI.GetAutoMLEntity	Function	AI	GetAutoMLEntity
5	AI.SampleStratifiedWithHoldout	Function	AI	SampleStratifiedWithHoldout
6	AI.TestConnection	Function	AI	TestConnection
7	AIFunctions.Capacities	Function	AIFunctions	Capacities
8	AIFunctions.Contents	Function	AIFunctions	Contents
9	AIFunctions.ExecuteInternal	Function	AIFunctions	ExecuteInternal
10	AIFunctions.GetAutoMLEntity	Function	AIFunctions	GetAutoMLEntity
11	AIFunctions.PostProcess	Function	AIFunctions	PostProcess
12	AIInsights.Contents	Function	AIInsights	Contents
13	AIInsights.ContentsGenerator	Function	AIInsights	ContentsGenerator
14	AML.Execute	Function	AML	Execute
15	AML.ExecuteBatch	Function	AML	ExecuteBatch
16	Access.Database	Function	Access	Database

Figure 2.41: Query Editor view of library table function

3. Click on **Close and Apply** from the Query Editor.
4. The 1,000+ rows from the M library are now loaded to the **Data** mode.

5. Create a **visualization** that uses the `Function Groups` column for filtering.

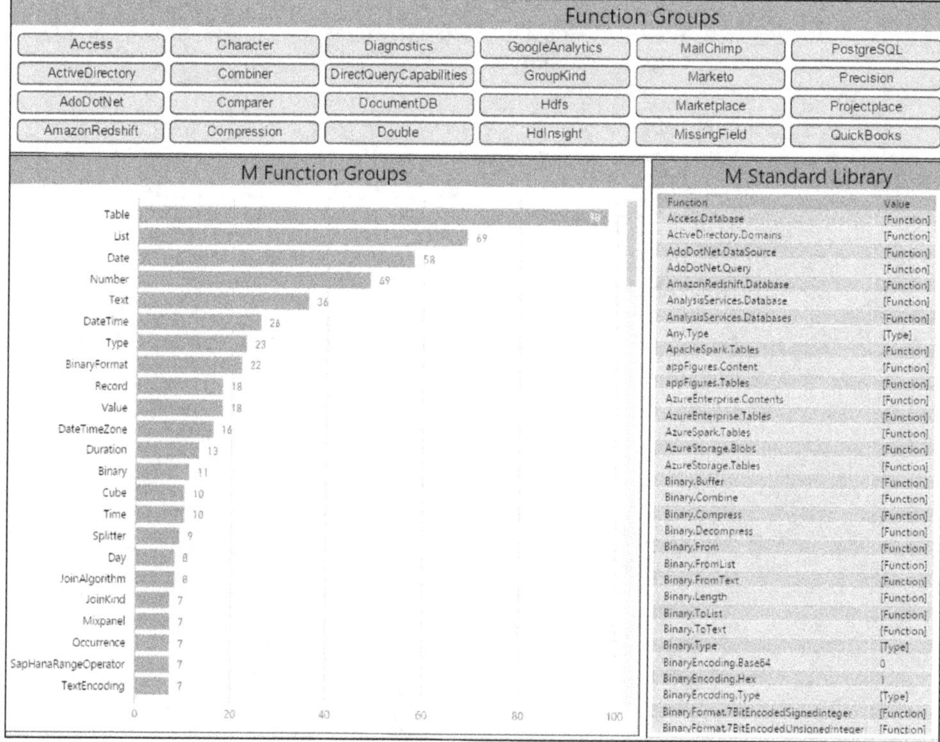

Figure 2.42: Report page of M standard library

How it works

The M expression leverages the `#shared` variable, which returns a record of the names and values currently in scope. The record is converted to a table value and then the `Function` column, originally `Name` in the context of the library, is split based on the period delimiter to allow for the `Group` column.

There's more...

M library details for every function are made available by entering the function without any parameters.

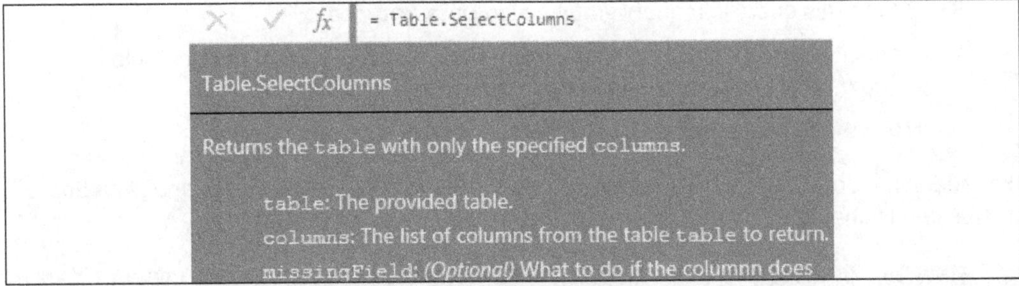

Figure 2.43: Library Function Details

See also

- Power Query function reference: `http://bit.ly/3bLKJ1M`

Profiling Source Data

The topic of data quality deals with the overall utility of datasets, and the ability to easily process and use the data for certain purposes, including analytics and reporting. Data quality is an essential component of data governance, ensuring that business data is accurate, complete, consistent, and valid. Good data quality is an essential element of any data analytics and reporting endeavor. Poor data quality can lead to incorrect analysis and decisions by the business—hence the phrase "garbage in, garbage out". Luckily, the Power Query Editor provides powerful data profiling tools to assist in quickly determining the quality of the data with which you are working. This recipe demonstrates how to unlock the powerful tools within the Power Query Editor for profiling columns and gaining a sense of the quality of the data being worked upon.

Getting ready

To get ready for this recipe, import the `FactCallCenter` table from the **AdventureWorksDW2019** database by doing the following:

1. Open Power BI Desktop and choose **Transform data** from the ribbon of the **Home** tab to open the **Power Query Editor**.
2. Create an **Import** mode data source query called `AdWorksDW`. This query should be similar to the following:

```
let
    Source = Sql.Database("localhost\MSSQLSERVERDEV",
"AdventureWorksDW2019")
in
    Source
```

3. Isolate this query in a query group called **Data Sources**.
4. Right-click `AdWorksDW` and choose **Reference**, select the **FactFinance** table in the data preview area, and rename this query **FactFinance**.
5. Move the **FactFinance** query to the **Other Queries** group.

For additional details on performing these steps, see the *Managing Queries and Data Sources* recipe in this chapter.

How to Profile Source Data

To implement this recipe, perform the following steps:

1. Select the **FactFinance** query.
2. In the **View** tab, check the box for **Column profile** in the **Data Preview** area of the ribbon.
3. Select a column to view the column statistics similar to those in *Figure 2.44*:

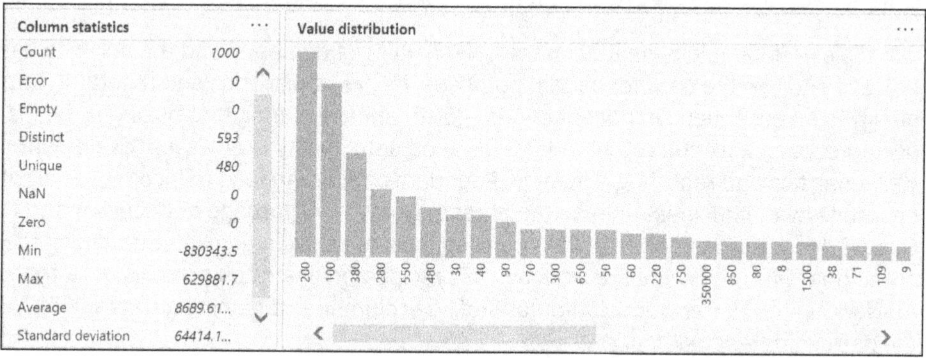

Figure 2.44: Column profile information

How it works

By default, the M query engine pulls the first 1,000 rows of data from the specified data source. This is the data used in the data preview area. The default of using only the first 1,000 rows of data can be changed by clicking on **Column profiling based on top 1000 rows** in the status bar in the bottom right and choosing **Column profiling based on the entire data set**. Statistics are collected on each column in the data source. When the **Column profile** feature is enabled, selecting a column causes column statistics and value distribution to display in the bottom half of the data preview area, including alongside this error counts, the number of distinct and unique values, minimum values, maximum values, and additional information that depends upon the data type of the column, as shown in *Figure 2.44*.

There's more...

Additional data quality dialogs are available in the Power Query Editor. From the **View** tab, check the box next to **Column quality** and **Column distribution**. Small visuals appear under the column headings. Hovering your mouse over this area provides a pop-up dialog that provides suggested actions as well as common data cleansing activities via the ellipsis menu (...).

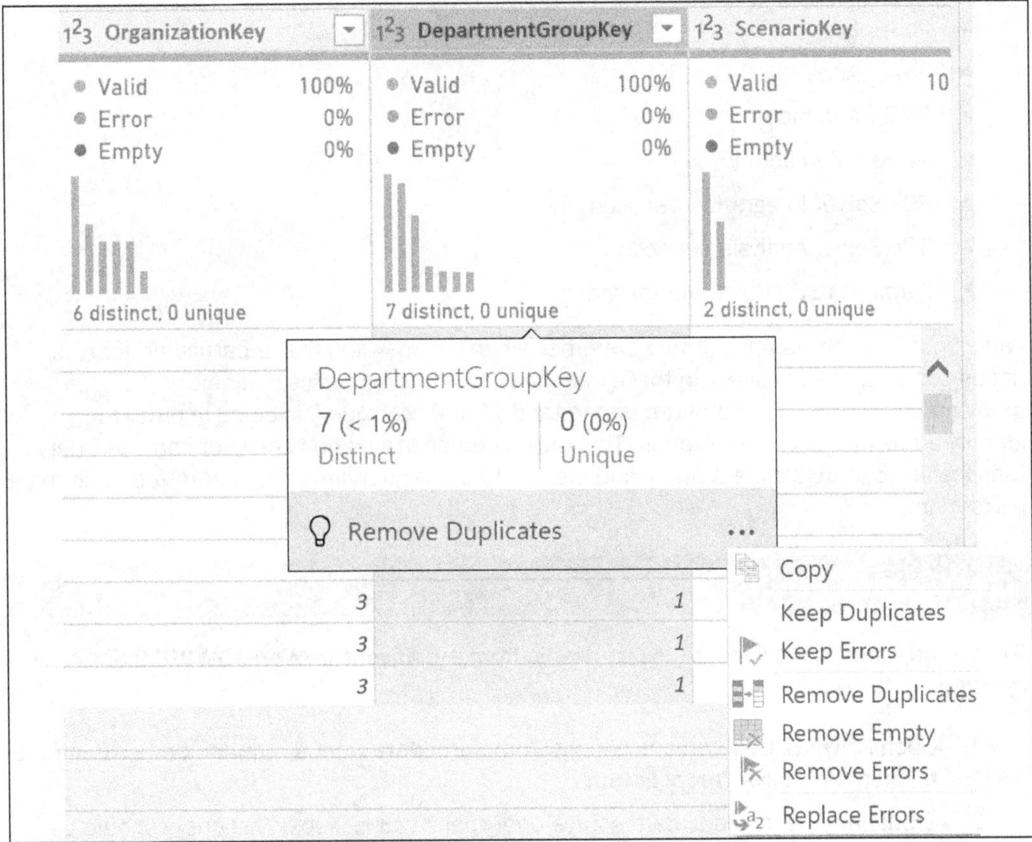

Figure 2.45: Column quality and Column distribution visuals

See Also

- *Using the data profiling tools*: `http://bit.ly/3c46s5g`

Diagnosing Queries

The Power Query M engine is an extremely powerful and fast data transformation and data preparation engine used across an array of products, including:

- Excel for Windows
- Excel for Mac
- Power BI
- Power Apps
- Power Automate
- Azure Data Factory
- SQL Server Integration Services
- SQL Server Analysis Services
- Dynamics 365 Customer Insights

While both fast and powerful, there are times when you may find that a particular query is not as performant as desired. In these instances, Query Diagnostics can help you pinpoint problematic expressions and better understand what Power Query is doing in order to identify areas for query optimization. This recipe demonstrates how the user can use Query Diagnostics to troubleshoot a query and identify how the query might be optimized to be more performant.

Getting ready

To get ready, import the `FactCallCenter` table from the **AdventureWorksDW2019** database by doing the following:

1. Open Power BI Desktop and choose **Transform data** from the ribbon of the **Home** tab to open the **Power Query Editor**.
2. Create an Import mode data source query called `AdWorksDW`. This query should be similar to the following:

   ```
   let
       Source = Sql.Database("localhost\MSSQLSERVERDEV",
   "AdventureWorksDW2019")
   in
       Source
   ```

3. Isolate this query in a query group called **Data Sources**.

4. Right-click `AdWorksDW` and choose **Reference**; select the **FactCurrencyRate** table in the data preview area, and rename the AdWorksDW query to **FactCurrencyRate**.
5. Move the **FactCurrencyRate** query to the **Other Queries** group.
6. In the **Power Query Editor**, select the **Tools** tab and then **Diagnostic Options**.
7. Ensure that the radio button for **Enable in Query Editor (does not require running as admin)** is selected and check all the boxes under the **Diagnostics Level** and **Additional Diagnostics** sub-headings.

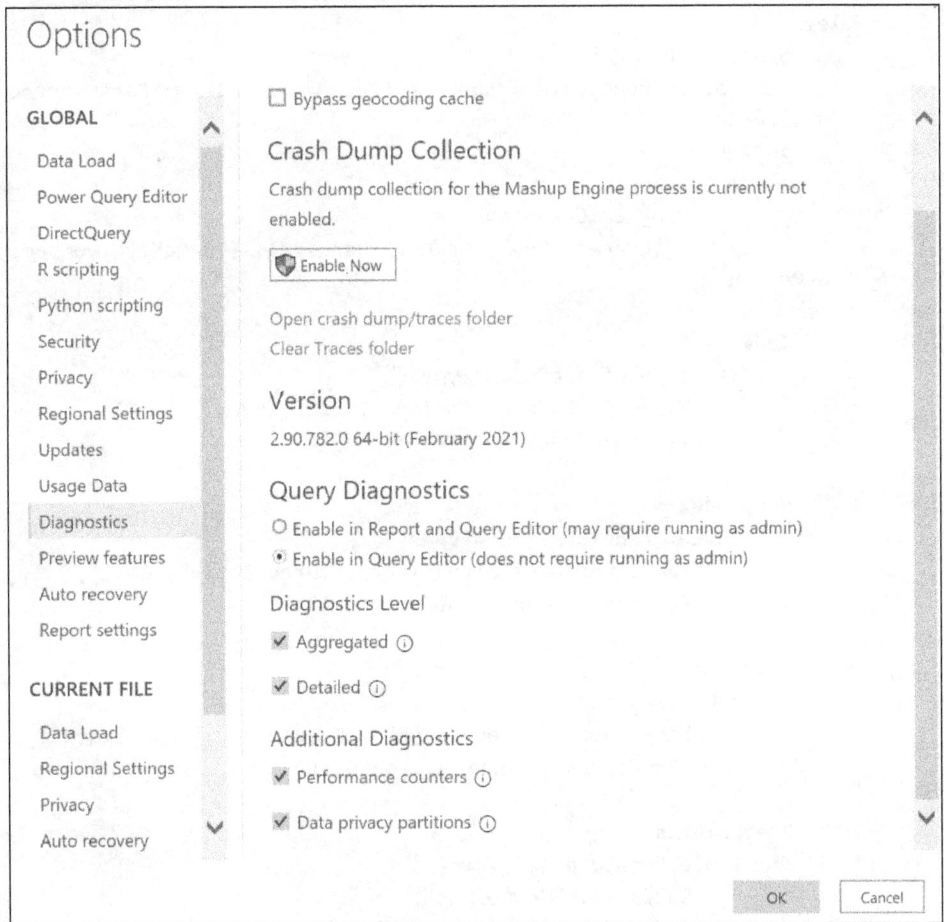

Figure 2.46: Query Diagnostic options

For additional details on performing these steps, see the *Managing Queries and Data Sources* recipe in this chapter.

How to Diagnose Queries

To implement this recipe, perform the following steps:

1. Select the **FactCurrencyRate** query, open **Advanced Editor,** and modify the query to calculate the daily change in currency rates.

```
let
    Source = AdWorksDW,
    dbo_FactCurrencyRate = Source{[Schema="dbo",Item="FactCurrencyRa
te"]}[Data],
    Sort =
        Table.Sort(
            dbo_FactCurrencyRate,
            {{"CurrencyKey", Order.Ascending}, {"DateKey", Order.
Ascending}}
        ),
    Index =
        Table.TransformColumnTypes(
            Table.AddIndexColumn(Sort, "Row Index", 1, 1),
            {{ "Row Index", Int64.Type }}
        ),
    PrevIndex =
        Table.TransformColumnTypes(
            Table.AddIndexColumn(Index, "Prev Index", 0, 1),
            {{ "Prev Index", Int64.Type }}
        ),
    SelfJoin =
        Table.NestedJoin(
            PrevIndex, {"Prev Index"}, PrevIndex, {"Row Index"},
            "NewColumn", JoinKind.LeftOuter
        ),
    PrevColumns =
        Table.ExpandTableColumn(
            SelfJoin, "NewColumn",
            {"EndOfDayRate", "CurrencyKey"}, {"PrevRate", "PrevKey"}
        ),
    AddChange =
        Table.AddColumn(
            PrevColumns, "Daily Change", each
            if [CurrencyKey] = [PrevKey] then [EndOfDayRate] -
[PrevRate]
```

```
            else null, type decimal
        ),
    SelectColumns =
        Table.SelectColumns(
            AddChange,
            {"CurrencyKey", "EndOfDayRate", "Date", "Daily Change"}
        )
in
    SelectColumns
```

2. You may have to wait several minutes for the preview data to display. To investigate what is going on, click on the **Tools** tab and then **Start Diagnostics**.
3. Click back on the **Home** tab and click **Refresh Preview**.
4. Wait for the preview data to refresh and then click back on the **Tools** tab and **Stop Diagnostics**.

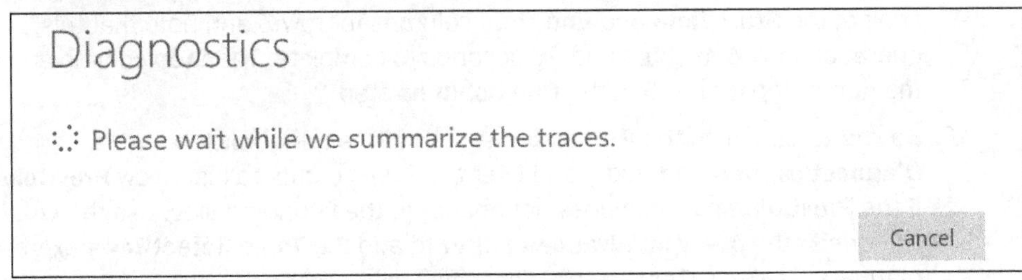

Figure 2.47: Diagnostics processing display

5. When the **Diagnostics** processing completes, you will have a new query group called **Diagnostics** containing four queries for **Diagnostics_Counters**, **Diagnostic_Detailed**, **Diagnostic_Aggregated**, and **Diagnostic_Partitions**. Each of these queries is suffixed with a date and time stamp of when the diagnostics were run, and each has loading disabled.

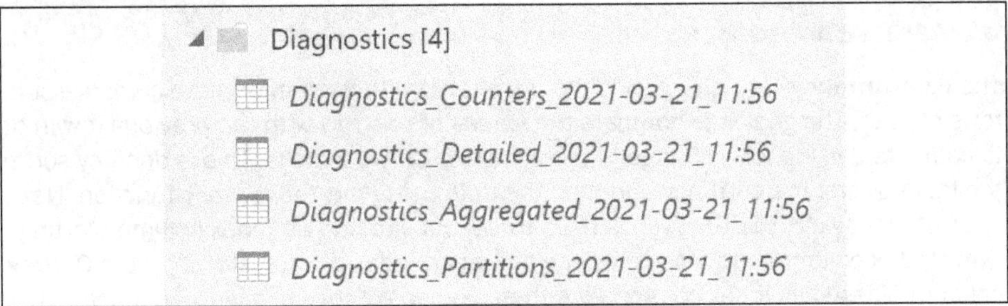

Figure 2.48: Diagnostics queries

6. Click on the **Diagnostics_Aggregated** query. Select the **Step**, **Category**, **Start Time**, **End Time**, **Exclusive Duration (%)**, and **Exclusive Duration** columns and remove the other columns.

7. Sort the **Exclusive Duration** column in descending order.

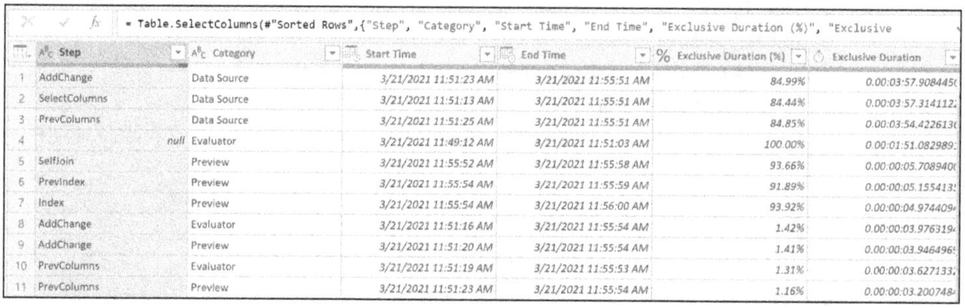

```
= Table.SelectColumns(#"Sorted Rows",{"Step", "Category", "Start Time", "End Time", "Exclusive Duration (%)", "Exclusive
```

	Step	Category	Start Time	End Time	Exclusive Duration (%)	Exclusive Duration
1	AddChange	Data Source	3/21/2021 11:51:23 AM	3/21/2021 11:55:51 AM	84.99%	0.00:03:57.908445
2	SelectColumns	Data Source	3/21/2021 11:51:13 AM	3/21/2021 11:55:51 AM	84.44%	0.00:03:57.314112
3	PrevColumns	Data Source	3/21/2021 11:51:25 AM	3/21/2021 11:55:51 AM	84.85%	0.00:03:54.422613
4	null	Evaluator	3/21/2021 11:49:12 AM	3/21/2021 11:51:03 AM	100.00%	0.00:01:51.082989
5	SelfJoin	Preview	3/21/2021 11:55:52 AM	3/21/2021 11:55:58 AM	93.66%	0.00:00:05.708940
6	PrevIndex	Preview	3/21/2021 11:55:54 AM	3/21/2021 11:55:59 AM	91.89%	0.00:00:05.155413
7	Index	Preview	3/21/2021 11:55:54 AM	3/21/2021 11:56:00 AM	93.92%	0.00:00:04.974409
8	AddChange	Evaluator	3/21/2021 11:51:16 AM	3/21/2021 11:55:54 AM	1.42%	0.00:00:03.976319
9	AddChange	Preview	3/21/2021 11:51:20 AM	3/21/2021 11:55:54 AM	1.41%	0.00:00:03.946496
10	PrevColumns	Evaluator	3/21/2021 11:51:19 AM	3/21/2021 11:55:53 AM	1.31%	0.00:00:03.627133
11	PrevColumns	Preview	3/21/2021 11:51:23 AM	3/21/2021 11:55:54 AM	1.16%	0.00:00:03.200748

Figure 49: Diagnostic results

8. Look for large jumps in the **Exclusive Duration** column; we see two such jumps between lines 3 and 4, and 4 and 5, with the larger jump being between lines 3 and 4. Also, note the high **Exclusive Duration (%)** value for row 3.
9. Look at the **Start Time** and **End Time** columns for row 3 and note that this operation took 4 minutes and 26 seconds to complete. The **Step** column shows that the query step for row 3 is the **PrevColumns** step.
10. Having zeroed in on the **PrevColumns** step of the query, click on the **Diagnostics_Detailed** query and filter the **Step** column to just show **PrevColumns.** If the **PrevColumns** value does not appear in the filtering dialog, use the **Load More** link or edit the query in **Advanced Editor** to add the **Table.SelectRows** expression manually: `Table.SelectRows(#"Changed Type", each [Step] = "PrevColumns")`.
11. Sort the query by the **Exclusive Duration (%)** column in **Descending** order.
12. Note that the **Operation** column for the top row is **DbDataReader**.

At this point, it should be evident that this query would likely be better done in the source database system as a view or stored procedure.

How it works

The **FactCurrencyRate** query joins the base table with itself in order to compare subsequent rows of data. The goal is to compare the values of one row with the previous row in order to compute a value for a change in currency rate between days. This is done by sorting the table by first the currency and then the date using the `Table.Sort` function. Next, the `Table.AddIndexColumn` function is used twice, once to add an index column starting from 1 (**Row Index** column) and a second time to add an index column starting from 0 (**Prev Index** column). These two index columns are then used in a `Table.NestedJoin` function to join the table to itself. The `Table.ExpandTableColumn` function is used to expose the previous row's **CurrencyKey** and **EndOfDayRate** columns of the previous row. This information can then be used to create the **Daily Change** column using the `Table.AddColumns` function, and finally, only the essential columns are selected using the `Table.SelectColumns` function.

When you start Query Diagnostics, query diagnostic information is logged to JSON and CSV files stored in the application's directory. These files can be located by looking at the **Source** step for aggregated, detailed, and partition diagnostic queries and the **CsvFiles** step of the **Counters** diagnostic query. For the Power BI Desktop Store App, the path should be similar to the following:

```
C:\Users\[user]\Microsoft\Power BI Desktop Store App\Traces\Diagnostics
```

These files record diagnostic information performed by the query engine during processes such as refreshing the preview data. Stopping Query Diagnostics ends logging of the diagnostic data and generates queries for each enabled Query Diagnostics feature: **Aggregated**, **Detailed**, **Performance counters**, and **Data privacy partitions**. As diagnostic logging is costly in terms of performance and system resources, it is recommended to only use Query Diagnostics when troubleshooting a query's performance. In addition, only enable the minimal amount of diagnostic logging required to identify the problem—for example, often just starting with the **Aggregated** diagnostic data is enough to identify the problematic step(s).

There's more...

There is also a **Diagnose Step** feature available for Query Diagnostics. To see how **Diagnose Step** can be used, follow these steps:

1. Open the **Diagnostic Options** from the ribbon of the Tools tab and uncheck the **Performance counters** and **Data privacy** partitions.
2. In the **Query Settings** pane, select the **SelfJoin** step. You can now either right-click the **SelfJoin** step and select **Diagnose** or select **Diagnose Step** in the ribbon of the **Tools** tab.
3. Once complete, two additional queries are added to the Diagnostics query group, **FactCurrencyRate_SelfJoin_Detailed** and **FactCurrencyRate_SelfJoin_Aggregated**, each suffixed with a date and time stamp.
4. Click on the **FactCurrencyRate_SelfJoin_Aggregated** query.
5. Add an **Index** column.
6. Sort the **Exclusive Duration** column in descending order.
7. Here we can see that the most expensive operation occurs early on in the process, at index 15 out of 3,000+ rows, and appears to be the initial selection of columns with the Data Source Query being the following:

```
select [_].[CurrencyKey],
    [_].[DateKey],
    [_].[AverageRate],
    [_].[EndOfDayRate],
    [_].[Date]
```

```
from [dbo].[FactCurrencyRate] as [_]
order by [_].[CurrencyKey],
        [_].[DateKey]
```

It should be evident that diagnosing a single step of a query is faster and consumes fewer system resources than analyzing the entire query. Thus, it is recommended that you run only **Aggregated** diagnostics over an entire query to identify problematic steps, and then run **Detailed** diagnostics on those steps individually. If you look at the **FactCurrencyRate_SelfJoin_Detailed**, the most expensive operation is on line **60**, and it is the **DbDataReader** operation. The SQL statement identified is actually on line **59** with the operation **Execute Query**. Thus, we can conclude that the most expensive operation performed was not in executing the query, but rather reading the data generated by the query.

See Also

- *Recording Query Diagnostics in Power BI*: `http://bit.ly/2ND2yqF`
- *Query Diagnostics*: `http://bit.ly/3lFz8ET`
- Reading query diagnostics: `http://bit.ly/3s8IFXA`

Conclusion

In this chapter, we dove into Power BI Desktop's Get Data experience and walked through the process of establishing and managing data source connections and queries. The ability to ingest and access data is crucial to every BI project. In Power BI, this data ingest and access is driven by a powerful functional language and query engine, M. The Power Query M language provides a robust, scalable, and flexible engine for data retrieval, cleansing, and transformation.

3

Building a Power BI Data Model

"The data model is what feeds and what powers Power BI."

- Kasper de Jonge, Senior Program Manager, Microsoft

The data models developed in Power BI Desktop are at the center of Power BI projects. These data models support data exploration and drive the analytical queries visualized in reports and dashboards. Properly designed data models leverage the data connectivity and transformation capabilities described in *Chapter 2, Accessing and Retrieving Data*, to provide an integrated view of distinct business processes and entities. Additionally, data models contain predefined calculations, hierarchies and groupings, and metadata to greatly enhance both the analytical power of the dataset and its ease of use. The combination of accessing and retrieving data coupled with the additional enhancements available in the data model serves as the foundation for the BI and analytical capabilities of Power BI.

In this chapter, we explore the primary processes of designing and developing robust data models. Common challenges in dimensional modeling are mapped to corresponding features and approaches in Power BI Desktop, including multiple grains and many-to-many relationships. Examples are also provided on how to embed business logic and definitions, develop analytical calculations with the DAX language, and configure metadata settings to increase the value and sustainability of models.

In this chapter, we will cover the following recipes:

- Designing a Data Model
- Implementing a Data Model
- Creating Relationships

- Configuring Model Metadata
- Hiding Columns and Tables
- Enriching a Model with DAX
- Supporting Virtual Table Relationships
- Creating Hierarchies and Groups
- Designing Column Level Security
- Leveraging Aggregation Tables

Technical Requirements

The following are required to complete the recipes in this chapter:

- Power BI Desktop
- Tabular Editor
- SQL Server with the **AdventureWorksDW2019** database installed. This database and instructions for installing it are available here: `http://bit.ly/2OVQfG7`
- Code samples and other materials can be downloaded from the following GitHub repository: `https://github.com/PacktPublishing/Microsoft-Power-BI-Cookbook-Second-Edition`

Designing a Data Model

Power BI Desktop lends itself to rapid, agile development in which significant data insights can be obtained quickly despite both imperfect data sources and an incomplete understanding of business requirements and use cases. However, rushing through the design phase can undermine the sustainability of the solution, as future needs cannot be met without structural revisions to the model or complex workarounds. A balanced design phase in which fundamental decisions, such as DirectQuery versus in-memory, are analyzed, while simultaneously using a limited prototype model to generate visualizations and business feedback can address both short- and long-term needs.

This recipe describes a process for designing a data model and identifies some of the primary questions and factors to consider while doing so.

Getting ready

Visually and analytically impressive examples of Power BI's reporting capabilities can often cause stakeholders to underestimate the effort and complexity associated with data integration and data modeling.

It is important to rein in any unrealistic expectations and confirm feasibility. Power BI is not the right tool for every job, so it is important to approach tasks through a methodical design approach. It is important to identify the top pain points and any unanswered business questions in the current state. Contrast this input with an assessment of feasibility and complexity (for example, data quality and analytical needs) along with targeting realistic and sustainable deliverables. A good design process will do just that.

Dimensional modeling best practices and star schema designs are directly applicable to Power BI data models. Short, collaborative modeling sessions can be scheduled with subject matter experts and the main stakeholders. With the design of the model in place, an informed decision about the model's data mode (Import or DirectQuery) can be made prior to development. The four-step dimensional design process is as follows:

1. **Choose the business process(es)**: The number and nature of processes to include depends on the scale of the sources and scope of the project. Business processes might include planning, sales, time reporting, general ledger, and many others.
2. **Declare the granularity**: For each business process (or fact) to be modeled, define the meaning of each row. These should be clear, concise business definitions, and each fact table should only contain one grain. Consider scalability limitations with Power BI Desktop and balance the needs between detail and history, such as choosing to have greater history but less granularity. Examples include:
    - One Row per Sales Order Line
    - One Row per General Ledger Account Balance per fiscal month

    In the first example, the granularity is at the sales order line versus, perhaps, the purchase order header; in the second, the granularity is at the fiscal month versus per day or fiscal quarter.

    Separate business processes, such as planning and sales, should never be integrated into the same table. Likewise, a single fact table should not contain distinct processes, such as shipping and receiving. Fact tables can be related to common dimensions but should generally never be related to each other in the data model (for example, **PO Header** and **Line level**).
3. **Identify the dimensions**: Dimensions should have a natural relationship with the business process or event at the given granularity. Compare the dimension with any existing dimensions and hierarchies in the organization (for example, **Store**). If so, determine whether there is a conflict, or whether additional columns may be required. Be aware of the query performance implications with large, high-cardinality dimensions, such as in customer tables with over two million rows. It may be necessary to optimize this relationship in the model or the measures and queries that use this relationship. See *Chapter 11, Enhancing and Optimizing Existing Power BI Solutions*, for more details.

4. **Identify the facts**: Facts should align with the business processes being modeled; for example, the sum of a quantity or a unique count of a dimension. Document the business and technical definition of the primary facts and compare this with any existing reports or metadata repository (for example, *Net Sales = Extended Amount - Discounts*). At this stage, you should be able to walk through top business questions and check whether the planned data model will support them. For example, the business might wish to answer the following question, "*What was the variance between Sales and Plan for last month for Bikes?*". Any clear gaps can be handled in one of three ways:

    - Revisit and modify the prior steps of this process
    - Remove the question from the scope of the data model
    - Plan to address the issue with additional logic in the model (M or DAX)

    Focus only on the primary facts at this stage, such as the individual source columns that comprise the cost facts. If the business definition or logic for a core fact has multiple steps and conditions, check whether the data model will naturally simplify it or whether the logic can be developed during data retrieval in order to avoid complex measures.

How to Design a Data Model

The Power BI model should preferably align with a corporate data architecture framework of standard facts and dimensions that can be shared across models. Though consumed by Power BI Desktop, existing data definitions and governance should be observed. Any new facts, dimensions, and measures developed with Power BI should supplement this architecture. To implement this recipe, follow these steps:

1. **Create a data warehouse bus matrix**: A matrix of business processes (facts) and standard dimensions is a primary tool for designing and managing data models, while also communicating the overall BI architecture. In this example, the business processes selected for the model are **Internet Sales**, **Reseller Sales**, and **General Ledger**.

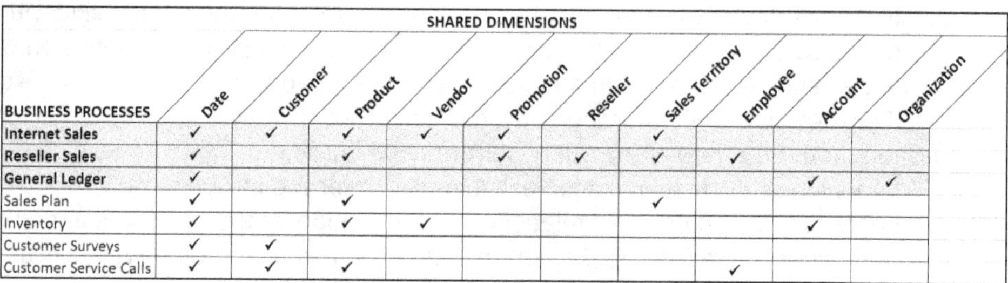

	SHARED DIMENSIONS									
BUSINESS PROCESSES	Date	Customer	Product	Vendor	Promotion	Reseller	Sales Territory	Employee	Account	Organization
Internet Sales	✓	✓	✓	✓	✓		✓			
Reseller Sales	✓		✓		✓	✓	✓	✓		
General Ledger	✓								✓	✓
Sales Plan	✓		✓				✓			
Inventory	✓		✓	✓					✓	
Customer Surveys	✓	✓								
Customer Service Calls	✓	✓	✓					✓		

Figure 3.1: Data Warehouse Bus Matrix

2. **Create an implementation bus matrix**: An outcome of the model design process should include a more detailed implementation bus matrix. Clarity and approval of the grain of the fact tables, the definitions of the primary measures, and all dimensions gives confidence when entering the development phase.

BUSINESS PROCESSES	Row Granularity	Measures	Date	Customer	Product	Promotion	Reseller	Sales Territory	Employee	Account	Organization	Department
Internet Sales	Sales Order Line (SKU)	Internet Sales Dollars and Units, Count of Customers and Products	✓	✓	✓	✓		✓				
Reseller Sales	Sales Order Line (SKU)	Gross and Net Sales, Discounts, Margin Amount and %	✓		✓	✓	✓	✓	✓			
General Ledger	GL Account Entity	Account Balance Amount	✓							✓	✓	✓

Figure 3.2: Implementation Bus Matrix: Internet Sales, Reseller Sales, and General Ledger

Power BI queries (M) and analysis logic (DAX) should not be considered as long-term substitutes for issues with data quality, master data management, and the data warehouse. If it is necessary to move forward, document the "technical debts" incurred and consider long-term solutions such as **Master Data Services** (**MDS**).

3. **Choose the dataset storage mode—Import, DirectQuery, or Composite**: With the logical design of a model in place, one of the top design questions is whether to implement this model with DirectQuery mode or with the default imported In-Memory mode.

   The default Import mode is highly optimized for query performance and supports additional modeling and development flexibility with DAX functions. With compression, columnar storage, parallel query plans, and other techniques an import mode model is able to support a large amount of data (for example, 50 million rows) and still perform well with complex analysis expressions. Multiple data sources can be accessed and integrated into a single data model and all DAX functions are supported for measures, columns, and role security. The chief disadvantages of import mode are dataset size limitations (1 GB for Pro, 10 GB for Premium) and the fact that data refreshes must be scheduled (eight times per day for Pro, 48 per day for Premium). An alternative to scheduled refreshes in the Power BI service is the use of REST APIs to trigger a data refresh of a published dataset. For example, an HTTP request to a Power BI REST API calling for the refresh of a dataset can be added to the end of a nightly update or ETL process script such that published Power BI content remains aligned with the source systems.

   A DirectQuery mode model provides the same semantic layer interface for users and contains the same metadata that drives model behaviors as Import mode models do. The performance of DirectQuery models, however, is dependent on the source system and how this data is presented to the model. By eliminating the import or refresh process, DirectQuery provides a means to expose reports and dashboards to source data as the data changes.

This also avoids the file size limit of import mode models. However, there are several limitations and restrictions to be aware of with DirectQuery:

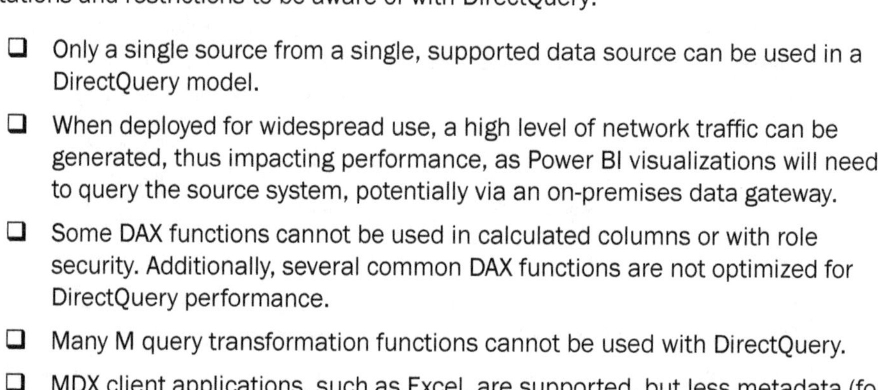

- Only a single source from a single, supported data source can be used in a DirectQuery model.
- When deployed for widespread use, a high level of network traffic can be generated, thus impacting performance, as Power BI visualizations will need to query the source system, potentially via an on-premises data gateway.
- Some DAX functions cannot be used in calculated columns or with role security. Additionally, several common DAX functions are not optimized for DirectQuery performance.
- Many M query transformation functions cannot be used with DirectQuery.
- MDX client applications, such as Excel, are supported, but less metadata (for example, hierarchies) are exposed.

Given these limitations and the importance of a "speed of thought" user experience with Power BI, DirectQuery should generally be used only on centralized and smaller projects in which visibility of updates of the source data is essential. If a supported DirectQuery system (for example, Teradata or Oracle) is available, the performance of core measures and queries should be tested. Also, confirm referential integrity in the source database and use the **Assume Referential Integrity** relationship setting in DirectQuery mode models. This will generate more efficient inner join SQL queries against the source database.

Composite models allow mixing DirectQuery and Import sources, or even multiple DirectQuery sources. While more complex, when configured correctly, composite models can combine the ability to retrieve near-real-time data from DirectQuery sources with the high query performance of Import models. When using composite models, the storage mode for each table can be specified within the model. It is best to designate dimension-type tables as **Import** or **Dual** storage mode, and fact-type tables as **DirectQuery** mode.

As an example, consider a model from this recipe with fact tables, Reseller Sales, Internet Sales, and General Ledger, along with dimensions such as Product and Sales Territory. Setting the dimension tables to Dual mode and the Internet Sales fact table to DirectQuery mode would allow the dimension tables to be quickly and efficiently retrieved from the in-memory (Import) model for rendering in a slicer, while simultaneously the Internet Sales table could use DirectQuery mode with the related dimension tables to enable real-time sales reporting via a single, efficient native SQL query.

How it works

Power BI can be fully delivered and managed by corporate BI professionals from data retrieval through visualization and content distribution.

Some BI and analytics organizations also adopt hybrid approaches in which different components of Power BI are developed and owned by different teams, such as the BI/IT teams providing an optimized data source, its supporting ETL process, and the analytical data model, including its measure definitions, relationships, and data refresh process.

Business teams can then leverage these assets in developing Power BI reports and dashboards, plus, optionally, Excel reports.

As Power BI projects can have widely varying and often overlapping needs (for example, security, data refresh, and scalability) it is important to adopt a process for allocating the appropriate resources and planning for the longer-term deployment, such as migrating important, relatively mature Power BI datasets to **Analysis Services** Tabular.

Power BI datasets and **SSAS** share the same database engine and architecture. Both tools support both Import and DirectQuery data models, and along with DAX and MDX client applications such as Power BI (DAX) and Excel (MDX). The DAX query engine comprises a formula and a storage engine for both Import and DirectQuery modes. The formula engine produces query plans, requests data from the storage engine, and performs any remaining complex logic not supported by the storage engine against this data.

In DirectQuery models, the source database is the storage engine—it receives SQL queries from the formula engine and returns the results to it. For In-Memory (Import) models, the imported and compressed columnar memory cache is the storage engine. See *Chapter 11, Enhancing and Optimizing Existing Power BI Solutions*, for more details.

There's more...

Several topics and specific questions are so common that a standard "project ingestion" form or document can be created to support design and planning meetings. These topics and questions include the following:

- **Data Sources**: Is all the data required in a given system? What other sources are required or currently used?
- **Security:** Will the data model contain PCII or sensitive data? Does any data need to be secured from certain users?
- **Version Control**: Are there existing reports or models with the same measures?
- **Complexity**: Can the source data be used directly or are transformations required?
- **Analytics**: Are any custom or advanced analytics required (for example, exception measures, statistical analyses)?
- **Data Refresh**: Is there a need for real-time access? If not, how frequently does the data need to be refreshed?

- **Model Scale**: How much historical data is required? How many rows per week/month/year are in the largest fact table?
- **Distribution**: Approximately how many users will need to access the reports and dashboards that this model will support?

The *Planning a Power BI Enterprise Deployment* whitepaper identifies the fundamental decisions and factors that guide Power BI deployments, including licensing, scalability and performance, data sources (cloud and on-premises), report visualization options, administration, and more.

See also

- Planning a Power BI Enterprise Deployment: `http://bit.ly/2NJ55Qg`
- The Ten Essential Rules of Dimensional Modeling: `http://bit.ly/1QijUwM`
- Using DirectQuery in Power BI Desktop: `http://bit.ly/2nUoLOG`
- DirectQuery in SSAS Tabular 2016 whitepaper: `http://bit.ly/2oe4Xcn`
- Announcing Data Refresh APIs: `http://bit.ly/2rOUd3a`
- Dataset modes in Power BI: `http://bit.ly/30P2HKF`
- Use composite models in Power BI: `http://bit.ly/3tKFTbr`
- Composite model guidance in Power BI: `http://bit.ly/3sd3aCz`

Implementing a Data Model

The implementation of a data model proceeds from the design phase described in the previous recipe. The design process and its supporting documentation clarify which entities to model, their granularity, the fact-to-dimension relationships, and the fact measures that must be developed. Additionally, the model mode (Import or DirectQuery) has already been determined, and any additional business logic to be implemented via M or DAX functions is also known. The different components of the model can now be developed, including data source connectivity, queries, relationships, measures, and metadata.

In this recipe, we walk through all the primary steps in the physical implementation of a model design. Three fact tables and their related dimensions are retrieved, relationships are created, and the core measures and metadata are added. When complete, the multi-fact data model can be exposed to business users for initial testing and feedback.

Getting ready

To prepare for this recipe, follow these steps:

1. Create a SQL view for each fact and dimension table to be represented in the data model. If you're unfamiliar with SQL views, see the *See also* section of this recipe.

   The views should only select the columns required of the model and apply the model's column names. Create views for the fact tables **FactResellerSales**, **FactInternetSales**, and **FactFinance**, as well as the dimensions **DimEmployee**, **DimReseller**, **DimPromotion**, **DimProduct**, **DimSalesTerritory**, **DimDepartmentGroup**, **DimOrganization**, **DimAccount**, **DimCustomer**, and **DimDate.**

   The layer of views protects the model from changes in the source system and provides visibility to administrators of the model's dependencies. Additionally, the views can de-normalize source tables via joins to conform to the structure of the model tables, and potentially include derived columns not available in the source. In the following SQL example, the product dimension view joins three tables, **DimProduct**, **DimProductCategory**, and **DimProductSubcategory**, and applies model column names.

```
select [$Outer].[ProductKey] as [ProductKey],
    [$Outer].[ProductSubcategoryKey2] as [ProductSubcategoryKey],
    [$Outer].[EnglishProductName] as [EnglishProductName],
    [$Outer].[Color] as [Color],
    [$Outer].[ListPrice] as [ListPrice],
    [$Outer].[Weight] as [Weight],
    [$Outer].[DaysToManufacture] as [DaysToManufacture],
    [$Outer].[EnglishDescription] as [EnglishDescription],
    [$Outer].[EnglishProductSubcategoryName] as
[EnglishProductSubcategoryName],
    [$Outer].[ProductCategoryKey2] as [ProductCategoryKey],
    [$Inner].[EnglishProductCategoryName] as [DimProductCategory.
EnglishProductCategoryName]
from
(
    select [$Outer].[ProductKey] as [ProductKey],
        [$Outer].[ProductSubcategoryKey2] as [ProductSubcategoryKey2],
        [$Outer].[EnglishProductName] as [EnglishProductName],
        [$Outer].[Color] as [Color],
        [$Outer].[ListPrice] as [ListPrice],
        [$Outer].[Weight] as [Weight],
        [$Outer].[DaysToManufacture] as [DaysToManufacture],
        [$Outer].[EnglishDescription] as [EnglishDescription],
        [$Inner].[EnglishProductSubcategoryName] as
[EnglishProductSubcategoryName],
        [$Inner].[ProductCategoryKey] as [ProductCategoryKey2]
    from
    (
```

```
        select [ProductKey] as [ProductKey],
            [ProductSubcategoryKey] as [ProductSubcategoryKey2],
            [EnglishProductName] as [EnglishProductName],
            [Color] as [Color],
            [ListPrice] as [ListPrice],
            [Weight] as [Weight],
            [DaysToManufacture] as [DaysToManufacture],
            [EnglishDescription] as [EnglishDescription]
        from [dbo].[DimProduct] as [$Table]
    ) as [$Outer]
    left outer join [dbo].[DimProductSubcategory] as [$Inner] on
([$Outer].[ProductSubcategoryKey2] = [$Inner].[ProductSubcategoryKey])
) as [$Outer]
left outer join [dbo].[DimProductCategory] as [$Inner] on
[$Outer].ProductCategoryKey2 = [$Inner].ProductCategoryKey
```

Defining the SQL views is especially important if a DirectQuery model is being supported. For DirectQuery model views, evaluate the efficiency of the query plans and the referential integrity between the views to support inner join DirectQuery queries.

2. Open Power BI Desktop.
3. Create an Import mode data source query called `AdWorksDW`. This query should be similar to the following:

```
let
    Source = Sql.Database("localhost\MSSQLSERVERDEV",
"AdventureWorksDW2019")
in
    Source
```

4. Isolate this query in a query group called **Data Sources** and disable loading.
5. Both of these can be done by right-clicking the query in the **Queries** pane.
6. Right-click `AdWorksDW` and choose **Reference**.
7. Build an M query for each dimension and fact table that accesses the SQL views defined in *step 1*. In this example, the `AdWorksDW` query contains the data source information, and a **vCH3R2_Products** view is accessed:

```
let
    Source = AdWorksDW,
    Data = Source{[Schema="dbo",Item="vCH3R2_Products"]}[Data]
in
    Data
```

8. Duplicate this query and replace the `Item` parameter with the source view for each remaining fact and dimension.

9. Separate the fact queries into a **Facts** query group.
10. Separate the dimension queries into a **Dimensions** query group.

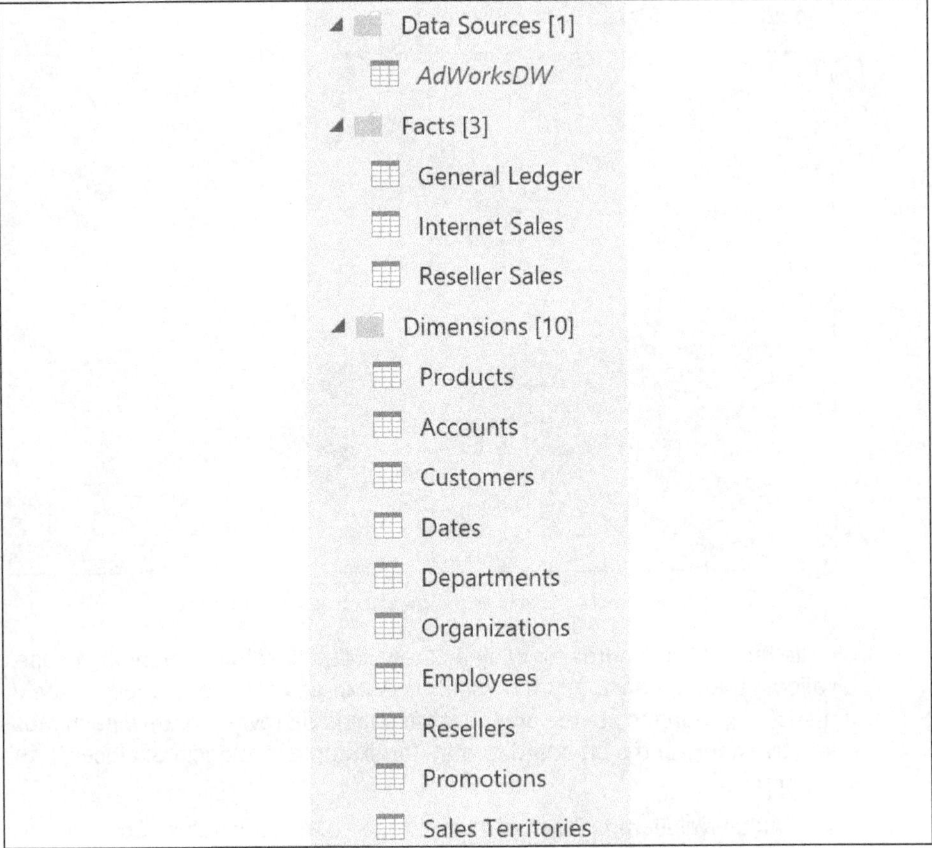

Figure 3.3: Dimensions, Facts, and Data Sources queries in Power Query Editor

11. Confirm that the column data types align with the design (for example, a fixed decimal number to avoid rounding issues).
12. Close the Power Query Editor and load the tables into the Power BI model by choosing **Close & Apply** from the ribbon of the **Home** tab.

How to Implement a Data Model

To implement this recipe, use the following steps:

1. In Power BI Desktop, select **Manage Relationships** from the **Modeling** tab of the **Report** view or the **Table tools** tab of the **Data** view and click the **New** button.

2. Create many-to-one, single-direction relationships from each fact table to its corresponding dimension table. Bidirectional relationships should only be implemented with clear guidance and evaluation. Date data type columns should be used for the `Date` table relationships.

Figure 3.4: Relationships view of a multi-fact data model

3. Write the core measures for each fact table identified in the planning phase and validate them for accuracy. If complex DAX expressions are needed for the core measures, then the source and retrieval should be reviewed. Give each measure an intuitive name and a standard format (for example, two decimal places, a thousands separator).
4. Add multi-level hierarchies in commonly used dimension tables such Product and Date. Hierarchies are essentially just groups of columns that allow for report authors to more easily navigate or drill between different levels of detail.
5. Set the **Default Summarization** and **Sorting of columns**, such as **Month Name**, sorted by **Month Number**.
6. Assign **Data Categories** to columns such as **Address** or **Postal Code** to support geographical visualization.
7. Hide columns from the fact tables such that only measure groups are visible.
8. Validation and user testing of the new model should follow implementation.
9. Model documentation can be developed via **Dynamic Management Views** (**DMVs**) to provide users with definitions and relationships. See the *Importing and visualizing dynamic management view (DMV) data* recipe of *Chapter 10, Administering and Monitoring Power BI*, for a detailed example of this pattern.

How it works

The steps in this recipe align with the logical flow of model development and can be implemented in discrete phases across teams or by an individual Power BI developer. Given the different lead times associated with the components of the model, it can be advantageous to move forward with a more mature or simple component such that business teams can engage and provide feedback as enhancements and other components are deployed.

Details on all primary metadata settings are included in this chapter in the following recipes:

- Configuring Model Metadata
- Hiding Columns and Tables
- Creating Hierarchies and Groups

All of these settings impact the usability and functionality of the data model and should not be neglected.

There's more...

If a model's source view is shared with other applications and may change or include columns not needed by the model, the `Table.SelectColumns()` M function can be used:

```
let
    Source = AdWorksDW,
    InternetSales = Source{[Schema="dbo",Item="vInternetSales"]}[Data],
    SalesColumns =
        Table.SelectColumns(
            InternetSales,{"ProductKey","OrderDateKey"},MissingField.UseNull
        )
in
    SalesColumns
```

Each column required by the table in the model is explicitly selected, and the `MissingField.UseNull` parameter allows the query to refresh successfully despite a specified column being missing—such as when a column's name has changed.

See also

- Create SQL Views: `https://bit.ly/2T3FzHF`
- Create and manage relationships in Power BI: `http://bit.ly/3tLwcJM`
- Model view in Power BI: `http://bit.ly/3vUXwag`
- Model data in Power BI: `http://bit.ly/3f8p7yT`
- Design a data model in Power BI: `http://bit.ly/3d28LVW`

Creating Relationships

One of the most important data modeling features of Power BI, as well as Analysis Services Tabular, is the control the modeler has over defining the filtering behavior between tables via relationships. In addition to one-to-many, single-direction relationships, Power BI models can contain bidirectional relationships, one-to-one relationships, many-to-many relationships, and even DAX measures that contain their own relationship filtering logic via functions such as `USERELATIONSHIP` and `CROSSFILTER`. These relationship tools, along with modifying the filter context of measures through DAX, can be used to support many-to-many modeling scenarios and provide alternative model behaviors for multiple business requirements.

In this recipe, we look at single-direction relationships, as well as the primary use cases for bidirectional relationships, and DAX-based cross-filtering.

Getting ready

To prepare for this recipe, follow these steps:

1. Open Power BI Desktop and choose **Transform data** from the ribbon of the **Home** tab to open the **Power Query Editor**.
2. Create an **Import** mode data source query called `AdWorksDW`. This query should be similar to the following:

```
let
    Source = Sql.Database("localhost\MSSQLSERVERDEV",
"AdventureWorksDW2019")
in
    Source
```

3. Isolate this query in a query group called **Data Sources** and disable loading.
4. Right-click `AdWorksDW` and choose **Reference**.
5. Select the **FactInternetSales** table and name this query **Internet Sales**.
6. Repeat *steps 4* and *5* to create a **Customers** query that imports **DimCustomer**, and a **Dates** query that imports **DimDate** tables.
7. Create a **Products** query based on the **DimProduct**, **DimProductCategory**, and **DimProductSubcategory** tables using the following code. Alternatively, use the SQL view for products from the previous recipe in this chapter, *Implementing a Data Model*.

```
let
    Source = AdWorksDW,
    Navigation = Source{[Schema="dbo",Item="DimProduct"]}[Data],
    Subcategory =
        Table.ExpandRecordColumn(
            Navigation, "DimProductSubcategory",
            {"EnglishProductSubcategoryName", "DimProductCategory"},
            {"Product Subcategory", "DimProductCategory"}
        ),
    Category =
        Table.ExpandRecordColumn(
            Subcategory, "DimProductCategory",
            {"EnglishProductCategoryName"}, {"Product Category"}
        )
in
   Category
```

8. Separate the fact query **Internet Sales** into a **Facts** query group by right-clicking the query in the Queries pane and choosing Move to Group and then New Group
9. Separate the dimension queries, **Customers**, **Dates**, and **Products** into a **Dimensions** query group.
10. Create a **Blank Query** called **Calculations** in the **Other Queries** group.
11. Choose **Close & Apply** in the ribbon of the **Home** tab to load the tables to the data model.

How to Create Relationships

To implement this recipe, use the following steps:

1. Create a relationship between the **Products** table and the **Internet Sales** table. This can be done in the **Model** view by dragging and dropping the **ProductKey** column in the **Products** table to the **ProductKey** column in the **Internet Sales** table. Alternatively, select **Manage relationships** in the ribbon of the **Modeling** tab while in the **Report** view or from the ribbon of the **Table tools** tab while in the **Data** view. This relationship should be one-to-many relationships between the **Products** table on the **One** side and the **Internet Sales** table on the **Many** side. The **Cross-filter direction** should be set to **Single**.

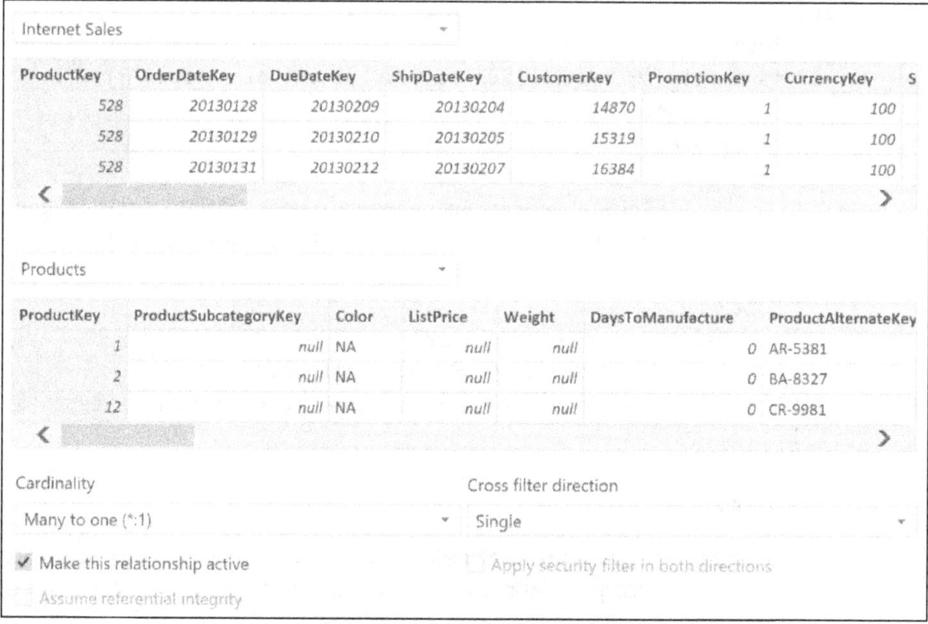

Figure 3.5: Creating a relationship between Products and Internet Sales

2. Create additional relationships between the other dimension tables and the **Internet Sales** table until your **Manage relationships** dialog box has the same relationships checked as shown in *Figure 3.6*.

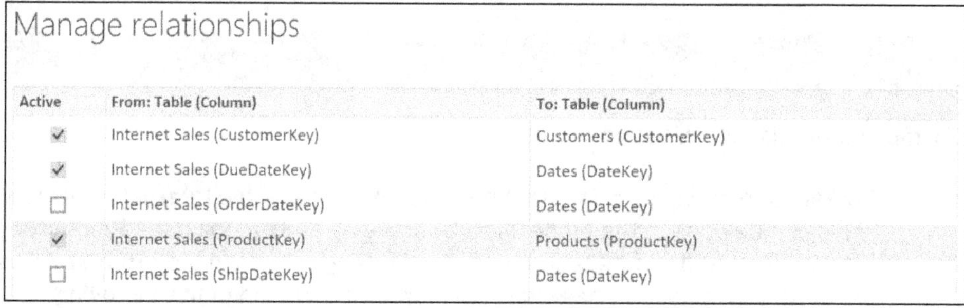

Figure 3.6: Table relationships in the Manage relationships dialog

3. The **Model** view of the dataset should now present, as shown in *Figure 3.7*:

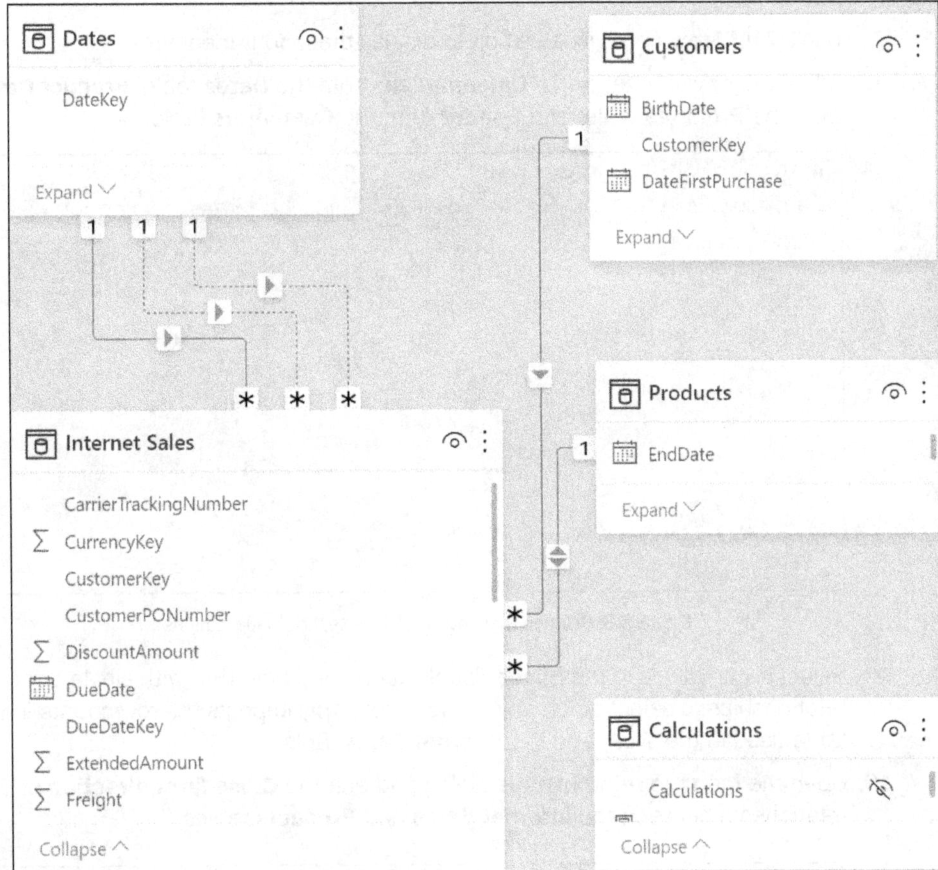

Figure 3.7: Model view of relationships

4. Right-click the **Dates** table and choose **Mark as date table** using **FullDateAlternateKey** as the **Date** column.
5. Create the following four DAX measures by right-clicking the **Calculations** table in the **Data** view and selecting **New measure**:

```
Sales Table Rows = COUNTROWS('Internet Sales')

Customers Table Rows = COUNTROWS('Customers')

Dates Table Rows = COUNTROWS('Dates')

Products Table Rows = COUNTROWS('Products')
```

6. Right-click the **Calculations** column in the **Calculations** table and choose **Hide in report view**.
7. Use a **Multi-row card** visualization to display these four measures.
8. Add a **Slicer** visualization for **CalendarYear** from the **Dates** table, **Product Category** from the **Products** table, and **Gender** from the **Customers** table.

60398
Sales Table Rows
18484
Customers Table R...
3652
Dates Table Rows
606
Products Table Rows

CalendarYear
2005
2006
2007
2008
2009
2010
2011
2012
2013
2014

Product Category
(Blank)
Accessories
Bikes
Clothing
Components

Gender
F
M

Figure 3.8: Relationship and cross-filter testing visualizations

9. Select slicer values in the **Slicer** visualizations and note that with single-direction relationships, a selection on any of the slicers only impacts the row counts in the table used in the slicer and the **Internet Sales** table.
10. Open the **Manage relationships** dialog and edit the **Cross-filter direction** of the relationship between the **Internet Sales and Products** tables.

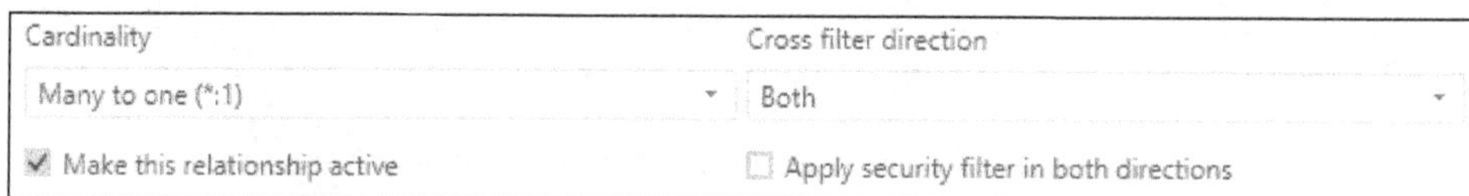

Figure 3.9: Bidirectional Relationship Configuration (Both) from the Edit Relationships Dialog

11. Slicer selections for **CalendarYear** and **Gender** now also filter the `Products` table.
12. Create a DAX measure that applies an alternative cross-filter behavior to the relationship in the model:

```
Products Table Rows (CF) =
    CALCULATE([Products Table Rows],
       CROSSFILTER('Internet Sales'[ProductKey],'Products'[ProductKey],O
neWay) )
```

13. Add this measure to the **Multi-row card** visualization and observe that this measure is unaffected by the **Gender** and **CalendarYear** slicers.
14. Write a DAX measure to propagate filter context. The following measure respects the filters applied to the `Internet Sales` table, such as `Customer Gender = "M"`:

```
Products Rows (Sales) = CALCULATE(COUNTROWS('Products'),'Internet
Sales')
```

15. Add this measure to the **Multi-row card** visualization and observe that this measure returns the same results as the bidirectional relationship when selecting values in the **Gender** and **CalendarYear** slicers, except when there are no slicer selections at all—then the measure returns **158**.
16. Write a DAX measure to use an inactive relationship between the **Dates** and **Internet Sales** tables:

```
Sales Table (Orders) =
    CALCULATE([Sales Table Rows],
        USERELATIONSHIP('Dates'[DateKey],'Internet Sales'[OrderDateKey])
)
```

17. Add this measure to the **Multi-row card** visualization and notice that different numbers are returned from the **Sales Table Rows** measure when selecting **CalendarYear** 2010 or higher.

How it works

Single-direction cross-filter relationships only propagate filters in the direction of the relationship. Thus, when **Products** is set to filter **Internet Sales** in a single-direction, other filters affecting **Internet Sales** are not propagated to the **Products** table. With bidirectional cross-filter relationships, filters affecting one side of the relationship are always propagated to the other side of the relationship unless DAX measures use functions such as CROSSFILTER() to override the default behavior defined by the model relationships.

Bidirectional relationships between fact and dimension tables should generally be avoided when the given dimension table is also related to other fact tables. This can cause over-filtering or unintended filter contexts. However, bidirectional relationships are an integral part of efficient solutions to common (and otherwise complex) modeling scenarios, such as actual versus budget and classic many-to-many scenarios.

Regarding the **Date** table relationships, the DAX time intelligence functions, such as `DATESYTD`, `DATEADD`, and `SAMEPERIODLASTYEAR`, all require either a relationship based on a date data type or a **Mark as date table** setting. Since the relationships for the **Date** table were formed on surrogate keys (20150101), the **Date** table needs to be marked as a **date table** in order for DAX time intelligence functions to operate properly.

The measure **Product Table Rows (CF)** overrides the bidirectional relationship to apply single-direction cross-filtering using the DAX function `CROSSFILTER`. Though limited to specific measures, the `CROSSFILTER` function can provide a simple and powerful supplement to the relationship cross-filtering defined in the model. The `CROSSFILTER` function requires an existing relationship (active or inactive) and always overrides the relationship settings of the model. The third parameter accepts the following values:

- `OneWay`
- `Both`
- `None`

Both bidirectional relationships and the `CROSSFILTER` function can be used with DirectQuery models. The **Global DirectQuery** setting **Allow unrestricted measures** needs to be enabled to use `CROSSFILTER`.

The **Products Rows (Sales)** measure implements bidirectional cross-filtering between the **Products** and **Internet Sales** tables by using the `CALCULATE` function to evaluate the **Products** table in the context of the **Internet Sales** table. Thus, filters affecting the **Internet Sales** table also impact the result of the `COUNTROWS` function on the **Products** table. This is true even when no slicers have selections, which is why the **Product Rows (Sales)** measure returns **158**, because only **158** products were sold over the internet. Keep in mind that relationships on their own only propagate active filters against a table. This is why the **Products Table Rows** measure returns all **606** products when no slicer selections are active.

The **Sales Table (Orders)** measure uses the `USERELATIONSHIP` function to utilize an inactive relationship in the model. Power BI data models reject ambiguous relationships, in which there are multiple possible cross-filtering paths between two tables. These duplicate relationships are set to an inactive status, but can still be used in DAX. As with the `CROSSFILTER` function, the `USERELATIONSHIP` function requires an existing relationship (active or inactive) and always overrides the relationship settings of the model.

There's more...

In the many-to-many model shown in *Figure 3.10*, multiple customers are associated with a given account, and some customers have multiple accounts.

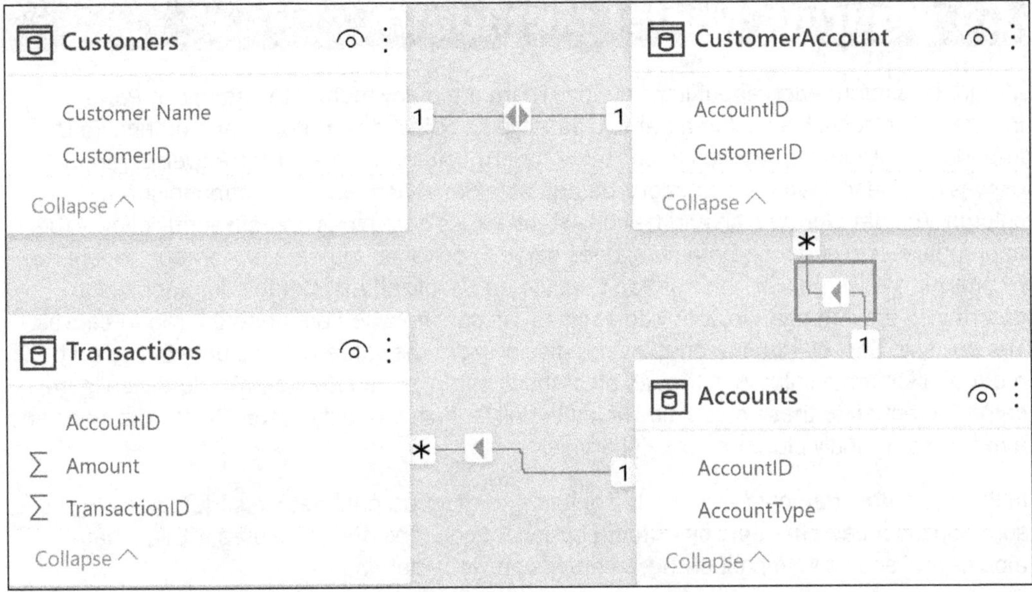

Figure 3.10: Many-to-many model with single-direction cross-filtering relationships

Given the highlighted single-direction relationship from the **Accounts** table to the **CustomerAccount** bridge table, a filter selection on the **Customer** table does not filter the **Transactions** table. By modifying the cross-filter direction of the relationship between `Accounts` and `CustomerAccount` to **Both**, a report visual by customer will now correctly display both the total amount from the fact table and the amounts associated with each customer.

A DAX alternative to the bidirectional relationship is the following:

```
M2M Tran Amount =
  CALCULATE([Tran Amount], SUMMARIZE(CustomerAccount,Accounts[Account ID]) )
```

The `SUMMARIZE` function leverages the one-to-many relationships of `Customers` and `Accounts` with the bridge table, via the `CALCULATE` function, and passes the filter context of `Customers` to the `Accounts` table, which filters transactions.

For similar many-to-many scenarios, bidirectional relationships are recommended over the DAX approach for manageability and performance reasons.

See also

- Create and manage relationships in Power BI Desktop: `http://bit.ly/3tLwcJM`
- Bidirectional cross-filtering whitepaper: `http://bit.ly/2oWdwbG`

Configuring Model Metadata

Metadata is information about information. There are many metadata settings in Power BI data models, such as column names, data types, object descriptions, and others. Four important metadata properties to configure for any column visible on the Power BI report canvas are the format, data category, default summarization, and the option to sort by column. The data formats should be consistent across data types and efficiently convey the appropriate level of detail. Data categories serve to enhance the data exploration experience by providing Power BI with information to guide its visualizations. Default summarization determines the aggregation, if any, to apply to the column when added to the report canvas. The ability to **Sort by Column** enables the displaying of the values in a column based on the order of a separate column. Although all of these settings are relatively simple to configure, careful attention to these properties helps to deliver higher-quality Power BI visualizations and a more user-friendly platform for self-service.

In this recipe, we demonstrate how to configure the format, data category, default summarization, and the **Sort by Column** option for columns and measures within a data model—and show the impact of these settings on visualizations.

Getting ready

To prepare for this recipe, follow these steps:

1. Open Power BI Desktop.
2. Create an Import mode data source query called `AdWorksDW`. This query should be similar to the following:

   ```
   let
       Source = Sql.Database("localhost\MSSQLSERVERDEV",
   "AdventureWorksDW2019")
   in
       Source
   ```

3. Isolate this query in a query group called **Data Sources** and disable loading.
4. Right-click `AdWorksDW` and choose **Reference**.
5. Select the **FactFinance** table and name this query **General Ledger**.
6. Repeat *steps 4* and *5* to create a **Dates** query that imports **DimDate** and a **Departments** query that imports **DimDepartmentGroup**.

7. Repeat *steps 4* and *5* to create a **Customers** query that imports **DimCustomer**.

```
let
    Source = AdWorksDW,
    Data = Source{[Schema="dbo",Item="DimCustomer"]}[Data],
    #"Expanded DimGeography" =
        Table.ExpandRecordColumn(
            Data, "DimGeography",
            {"City", "StateProvinceName",
             "EnglishCountryRegionName", "PostalCode"},
            {"City", "StateProvinceName",
             "CountryRegionName", "PostalCode"}
        )
in
    #"Expanded DimGeography"
```

8. Separate the dimension queries, **Customers**, and **Dates** into a **Dimensions** query group and the **General Ledger** query into a query group called **Facts**.
9. Create a **Blank Query** called **Calculations** in the **Other Queries** group.
10. Choose **Close & Apply** on the ribbon of the **Home** tab to load the tables to the data model.
11. Create the relationships shown in *Figure 3.11*, using the **Manage relationships** dialog box.

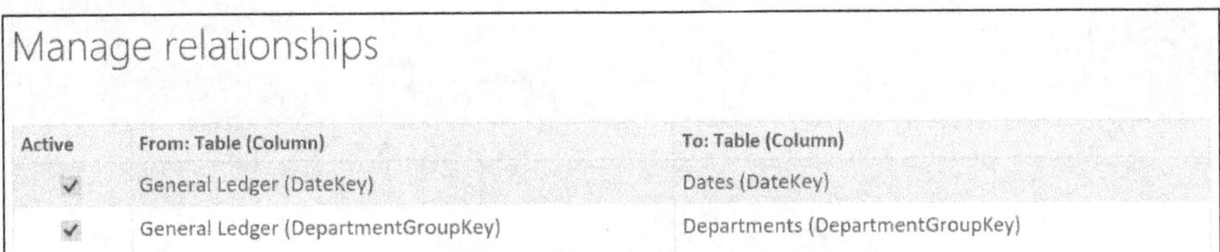

Figure 3.11: Relationships

How to Configure Model Metadata

To implement this recipe, use the following steps:

1. Select the **Data** view.
2. Use the **Fields** list on the right to navigate to the **Dates** table and select the **FullDateAlternateKey** column.

3. Use the **Format** drop-down in the ribbon of the **Column tools** tab to change the format to **3/14/2001 (m/d/yyyy)** or some other format.

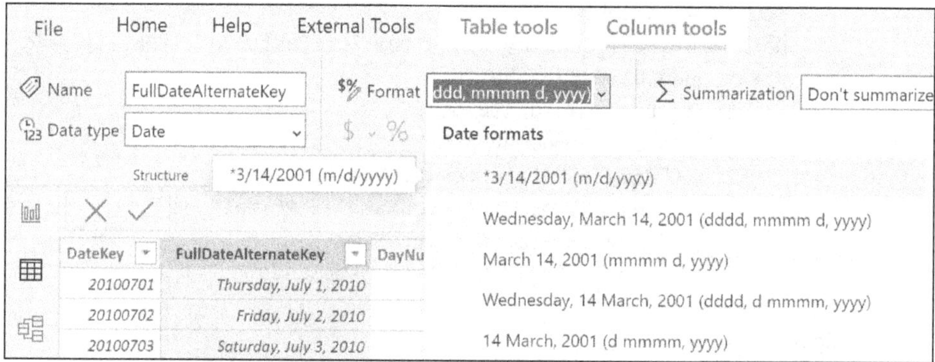

Figure 3.12: Column Formatting

4. Right-click the **Calculations** table and click **New measure** to create a measure with the code:

```
Finance = SUM('General Ledger'[Amount])
```

5. Select the **Finance** measure and change the format to **Currency** using the **Format** option in the **Measure tools** tab.

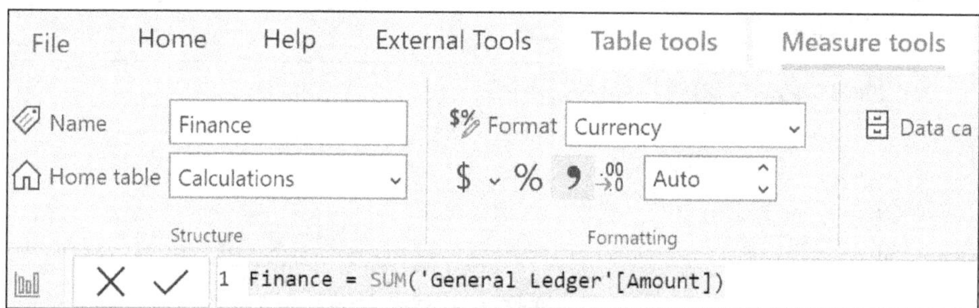

Figure 3.13: Measure Formatting

6. Right-click on the **Calculations** column in the **Calculations** table and choose **Hide in report view**.

7. While still in the **Data** view, select the **StateProvinceName** column in the **Customers** table, and from the **Column tools** tab change the **Data category** to **State or Province**.

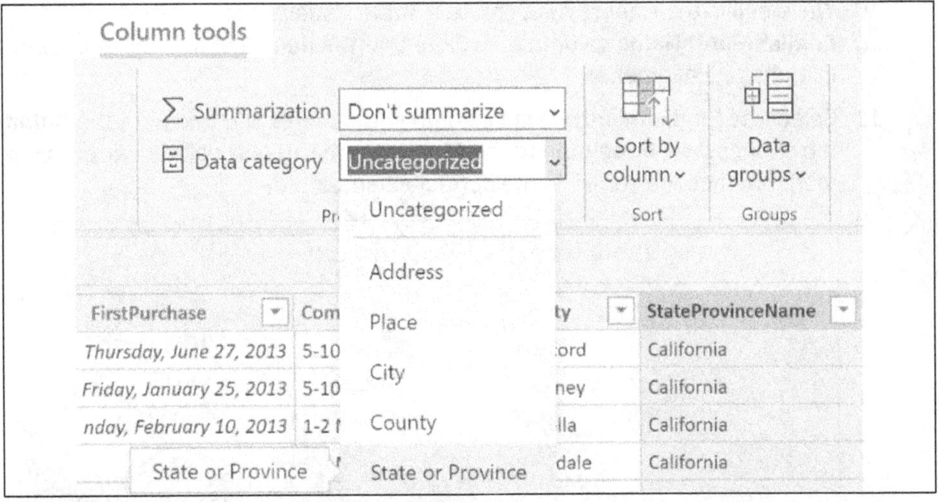

Figure 3.14: Data Category Selection

8. Repeat this procedure, setting the **City** column to **City**, the **CountryRegionName** column to **Country**, and the **PostalCode** column to **Postal code**. Note that a globe icon appears next to all of these columns in the field list.
9. Switch to **Report** view and create a **Map** visualization with **CountryRegionName** and **PostalCode** in the **Location** area and **CustomerKey** in the **Size** area. You can drill down to the postal code level and zoom in to investigate how many customers are in particular areas.

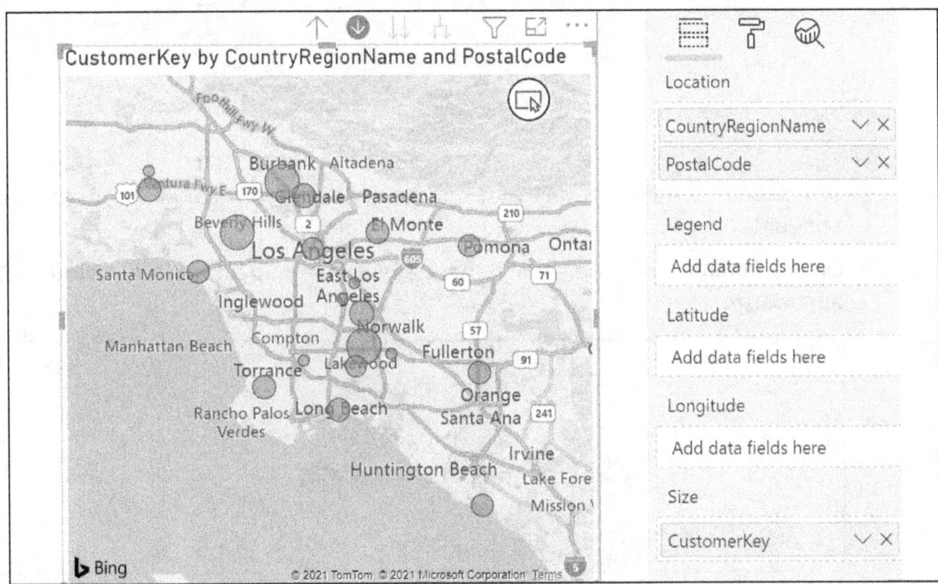

Figure 3.15: Default Visual of the Geographical Data Category

10. While still in the **Report** view, create a **Table** visualization with the **EnglishMonthName** column only. Note that the names of months appear in the table in alphabetical order.
11. Select the **EnglishMonthName** column in the **Fields** list, and from the **Column tools** tab change **Sort by column** to the **MonthNumberOfYear** column. After this action, the month names are sorted in the correct calendar order.

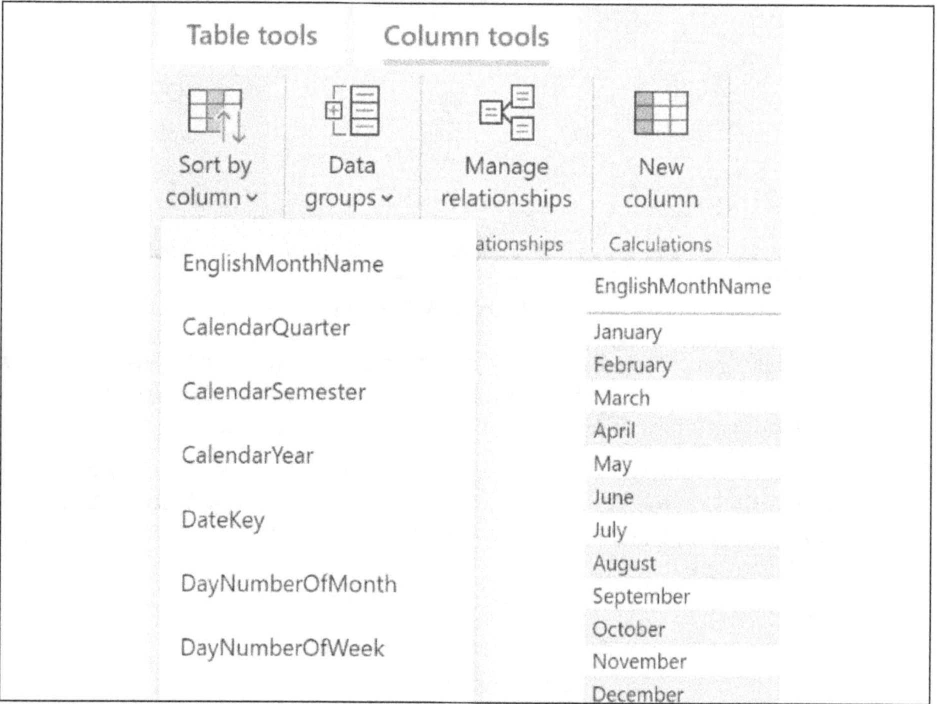

Figure 16: Sort by column

12. Switch back to the **Data** view and select the **AccountKey** column from the **General Ledger** table.
13. On the **Column tools** tab, change the default **Summarization** from **Count** to **Don't summarize**.

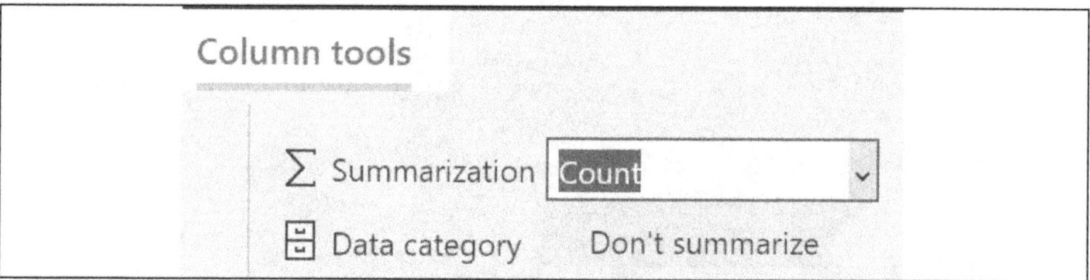

Figure 3.17: Default Summarization for Columns

How it works

The metadata settings for **Formatting**, **Data category**, **Summarization**, and **Sort by column** are all available from the **Column tools** or **Measure tools** tabs, whether you are in the **Data** view or **Report** view. Note that **Summarization** and **Sort by column** are not available for **Measures tools**. These metadata settings cannot be modified in the Power BI service once the model is published. Reports can be created and edited in the service, but data types, names, and other metadata are not available.

Formatting decisions should consider the impact of precision on visualizations. Fewer decimal places and more abbreviated date formats consume less space in reports and are easier to visually comprehend on dashboards. To understand how formatting works, consider a date data type. Date data types are actually stored as decimal numbers in the model engine. The integer portion of the number is the number of days since December 30, 1899. The decimal portion is the fraction of a day, with hours being 1/24 or .04166, minutes being 1/24/60 or .0006944, and seconds being 1/24/60/60 or .0000115740. Thus, the display formats for dates simply visually change how the base data is displayed to the user while keeping the underlying data unchanged. The user may see *1/1/1900 00:00:00* displayed on their screen, but internally in the data model, this is simply stored as 2.

Assigning a location **Data category** to columns assists Bing maps with geolocation and changes the default visualization for such columns to the **Map** visualization. The **Web URL** is important for such things as **mailto** email address links and any URL links exposed in reports. When the column is used in **Table** visualizations, email and link icons are displayed, respectively. Similarly, assigning an **Image URL** to a column displays the actual image when using **Table** visualizations. The **Barcode** data category can be useful for mobile applications.

When considering the use of **Sort by** columns, identify columns requiring custom sorting. Calendar text columns such as `Month` and `Weekday` are the most common candidates. Other columns may represent an organizational structure or entity hierarchy, such as general ledger accounts. The **Sort by column** sort must contain only one distinct value for each value in the column to be sorted. It is recommended to embed the sorting logic as deep into the BI architecture as possible. For example, the sorting column could be added to a dimension table in a data warehouse or the SQL view used to load the data model. If these options are not available, M query transformations are recommended over DAX calculated columns.

Text and date data type columns are set to **Don't summarize** by default when first loaded to Power BI models. These data types have default summarizations of **Count** and **Count (Distinct)**. In addition, the **Report** view provides the following aggregation options when using these data types in visualizations:

- **Text**: **First**, **Last**, **Count (Distinct)**, or **Count**
- **Date**: **Earliest**, **Latest**, **Count (Distinct)**, or **Count**

By default, **Whole number**, **Decimal number**, and **Fixed decimal number** are set to **Sum as the default summarization**. For numeric columns with default summarization applied, the Fields list applies a summation symbol and aggregates the column's values according to the default summarization setting when used in a report visualization. The same symbol is applied regardless of the default summarization configured (for example, **Average** and **Count**).

Simple DAX measures can deliver all **default summarization** options (**Sum**, **Min**, **Max**, **Average**, **Count**, and **Count Distinct**). Additionally, measure names such as **Count of Products** can help eliminate confusion regarding the default summarization icon. Many BI professionals prefer to replace fact columns with measures for this reason. Simple DAX expressions are used to perform the various aggregations or summarizations required in the data model; the fact columns are then hidden. When all fact columns are hidden, associated measures display at the top of the **Field** list. Additionally, using measures allows business logic to be applied, such as including or excluding certain values.

There's more...

While serving as an intern at Microsoft, Chelsie Eiden solved a long-standing issue with Power BI involving duration by implementing custom format strings in the September 2019 release of Power BI Desktop. Since the release of Power BI Desktop, there was always an issue aggregating durations and displaying them in the format of *HH:MM:SS*. This was the result of the model engine not including a true **Duration** data type, unlike the M query engine. You could convert durations to seconds to aggregate it, but you could not display aggregated durations that properly aggregated as numbers and displayed in the *hours, minutes, seconds* format in a visual. The reason was that there was no numeric formatting option for duration, and using the DAX `FORMAT` function turned a number into text. Custom format strings solved this issue by allowing the column to remain as a number, but also allowing the creation of a custom format for display purposes. Custom format strings can be applied to a column or measure using the **Properties** pane of the **Model** view, as shown in *Figure 3.18*.

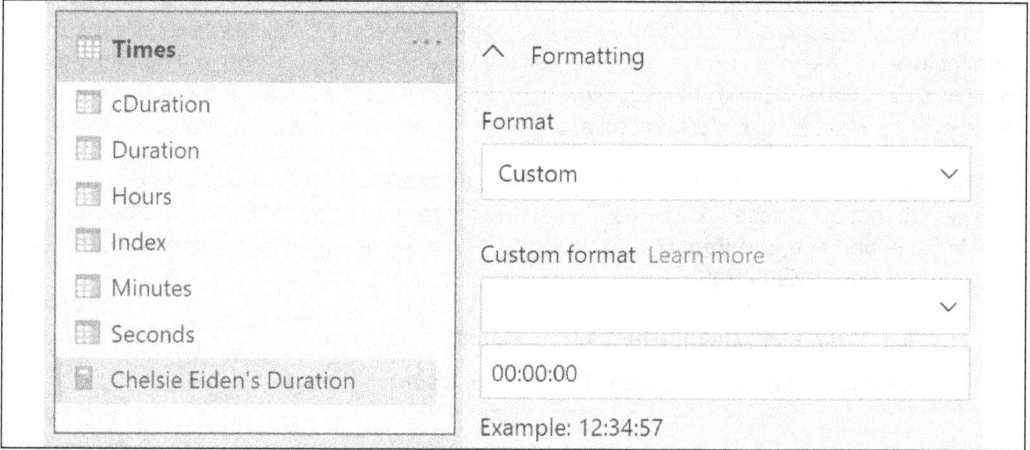

Figure 3.18: Custom format strings

DAX can be used to assist with sorting issues; for example, a DAX-calculated column can be created to support sorting of the **Calendar Yr-Mo** column with values such as *2016-Jan*. The DAX formula to create a **CalYr-Mo Sort** column is:

```
CalYr-Mo Sort = YEAR('Dates'[Date]) * 100 + MONTH('Dates'[Date])
```

This calculation results in values such as *201601*. The `YEAR` function is applied against the **Date** column and multiplied by 100 to add two digits. This product is then added to the results of the `MONTH` function applied against the **Date** column, which returns a value between 1 and 12. Although this approach is simple to implement and inexpensive in terms of resource usage, the values of the new column are not sequential, thus limiting the use of the column in Time Intelligence measures (for example, trailing 3 months). Sequential surrogate key columns for each grain of the date dimension, including fiscal calendars, is an essential component of robust date intelligence logic.

The DAX `RANKX` function can also be leveraged for sorting. For example, use the following DAX code to create a ranking column in the **Departments** table based upon the funding each **Department Group** receives in the **General Ledger**.

```
DeptGroupRank = RANKX('Departments',[Finance])
```

The ranking is based on the **Finance** measure created in this recipe. The **DeptGroupRank** column is re-evaluated during each refresh and thus the sort order could change to reflect the source data.

```
1 DeptGroupRank = RANKX('Departments',[Finance])
```

DepartmentGroupKey	ParentDepartmentGroupKey	DepartmentGroupName	DeptGroupRank
1		Corporate	5
2	1	Executive General and Administration	4
3	1	Inventory Management	3
4	1	Manufacturing	6
5	1	Quality Assurance	7
6	1	Research and Development	2
7	1	Sales and Marketing	1

Figure 3.19: RANKX Calculated Column

The **DepartmentGroupName** column can now have a **Sort by column** specified of **DeptGroupRank** to order departments by their funding, with **Sales and Marketing** being first (the most funding) and **Quality Assurance** being last (the least funding).

See also

- Specify data categories in Power BI Desktop: `http://bit.ly/2peNqPm`
- Tag barcode fields to enable barcode-scan filtering in mobile apps: `http://bit.ly/3re4dAV`
- Add hyperlinks (URLs) to a table or matrix: `http://bit.ly/39dxJ3r`
- Display images in a table or matrix in a report: `http://bit.ly/2Pkx1dE`
- Sort by column in Power BI Desktop: `http://bit.ly/2pFXhgh`
- Chelsie Eiden's Duration: `http://bit.ly/3lKFUtf`
- Custom format strings: `http://bit.ly/3sj648B`
- Use custom format strings in Power BI Desktop: `http://bit.ly/3cXAW8o`

Hiding Columns and Tables

Data models must balance the competing demands of functionality, scope, and usability. As additional tables, columns, measures, and other structures are added to meet various analytical needs, a model can quickly become confusing to end users. Therefore, it is important to minimize the visibility of columns and tables to provide an intuitive interface.

In this recipe, we demonstrate how to hide columns and even entire tables from report consumers.

Getting ready

To prepare for this recipe, follow these steps:

1. Open Power BI Desktop.
2. Create an Import mode data source query called `AdWorksDW`. This query should be similar to the following:

```
let
    Source = Sql.Database("localhost\MSSQLSERVERDEV",
"AdventureWorksDW2019")
in
    Source
```

3. Isolate this query in a query group called **Data Sources** and disable loading.
4. Right-click `AdWorksDW` and choose **Reference**.
5. Select the **FactInternetSales** table and name this query **Internet Sales**.
6. Repeat *steps 4* and *5* to create a **Departments** query that imports **DimDepartmentGroup** and an **Accounts** query that imports **DimAccount**.

7. Create a **Products** query based upon the **DimProduct**, **DimProductCategory**, and **DimProductSubcategory** tables using the following code. Alternatively, use the SQL view for products from a prior recipe in this chapter, *Implementing a Data Model*.

```
let
    Source = AdWorksDW,
    Navigation = Source{[Schema="dbo",Item="DimProduct"]}[Data],
    Subcategory =
        Table.ExpandRecordColumn(
            Navigation, "DimProductSubcategory",
            {"EnglishProductSubcategoryName", "DimProductCategory"},
            {"Product Subcategory", "DimProductCategory"}
        ),
    Category =
        Table.ExpandRecordColumn(
            Subcategory, "DimProductCategory",
            {"EnglishProductCategoryName"}, {"Product Category"}
        ),
    RemoveColumns =
        Table.SelectColumns(
            Category,
            {"ProductKey", "EnglishProductName", "DaysToManufacture",
             "Product Subcategory", "Product Category"}
        )
in
    RemoveColumns
```

8. Move the **Internet Sales** query to a query group called **Facts** and the **Departments**, **Accounts**, and **Products** queries to a query group called **Dimensions**.
9. Click **Close & Apply** in the ribbon of the **Home** tab to load the tables to the data model.
10. Create a relationship based on the **ProductKey** columns of both the **Products** table and the **Internet Sales** table.
11. Create the following four measures in the **Internet Sales** table:

```
Internet Sales = SUM('Internet Sales'[SalesAmount])

Internet Sales Freight = SUM('Internet Sales'[Freight])

Internet Sales Order Quantity = SUM('Internet Sales'[OrderQuantity])


Internet Sales Distinct Products =
    COUNTROWS(DISTINCT('Internet Sales'[ProductKey]) )
```

How to Hide Columns and Tables

To implement this recipe, use the following steps:

1. In the **Data** view's **Fields** pane, right-click a column in the **Internet Sales** table and select **Hide** in **Report** view. Notice that the "visible" icon with a strike-through is displayed to the right of the column in the **Fields** pane. Also, the columns are grayed out in the data viewing area.

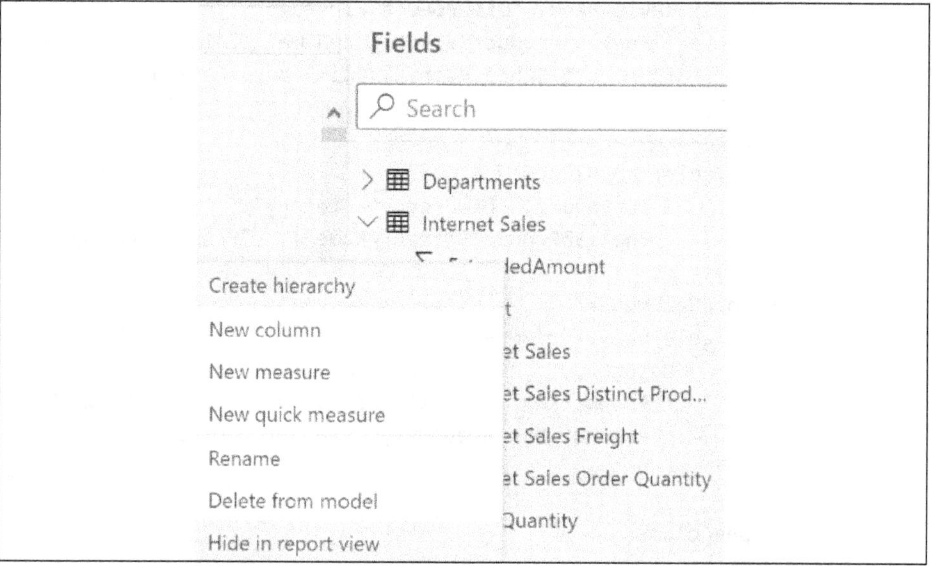

Figure 3.20: Hide in report view

2. Repeat this procedure for all columns (but not measures) in the **Internet Sales** table.
3. Once all the columns are hidden, switch to the **Report** view and observe that the **Internet Sales** table is now displayed above the other two tables, out of alphabetical order. In addition, the icon for this table is a calculator instead of a table.

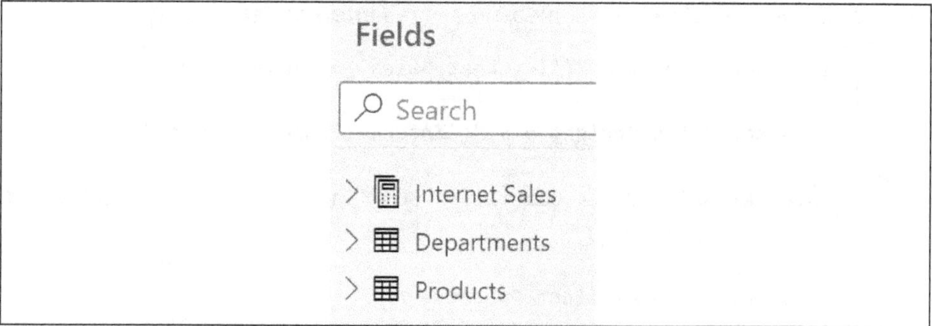

Figure 3.21: Measure table in the Report view Fields list

4. Switch back to the **Data** view, right-click the **EnglishProductName** column in the **Products** table, and choose **Create hierarchy**.
5. Right-click the **Product Category** column and choose **Add to hierarchy**, then the **EnglishProductName Hierarchy**.
6. Add **Product Subcategory** to the **EnglishProductName Hierarchy**.
7. Hide the **EnglishProductName**, **Product Category**, **Product Subcategory**, and **ProductKey** columns.
8. Switch to **Report** view and confirm that only the **DaysToManufacture** column and the **EnglishProductName Hierarchy** are visible under the **Products** table in the **Fields** pane.
9. Switch to the **Model** view, right-click the **Departments** table, and choose **Hide in report** view.
10. Switch to the **Report** view and confirm that the **Departments** table is no longer visible in the **Fields** pane.

How it works

Hiding columns and tables is an important step in developing professional data models that can be easily consumed by end users for self-service purposes; too many columns and tables can be confusing to end users. In general, hide any column which is not directly required in Power BI reports. Relationship key columns, fact table columns represented via measures, custom **Sort by** columns, and any degenerate dimensions should be hidden. Additionally, hide any measure which exclusively supports other measures and is not used directly in reports. Also hide entire tables if they exist solely for data modeling purposes, such as a bridge table in a many-to-many relationship. As this is only a visibility metadata setting, the hidden columns, measures, and tables can still be used in measures and accessed from other tools via DAX queries.

As demonstrated in this recipe, columns visible within hierarchies can be hidden as individual columns. Exposing both an individual column and a hierarchy that includes that same column can confuse users and lengthen the **Fields** list. Conversely, not hiding the individual column contained within a hierarchy provides greater flexibility, such as viewing the columns in the hierarchy on separate axes. The same is true when grouping columns. The grouping of column values described in the *Creating Hierarchies and Groups* recipe in this chapter is still possible with hidden columns. It should be noted that **Groups** and **Hierarchies** can both be hidden from the **Fields** list as well. In general, however, such structures would not have been created if those structures' visibility was not required.

Hiding columns and tables should also be considered in role-based security scenarios involving **row-level security** (**RLS**). Users mapped to security roles that forbid them from accessing all the rows of a table are still able to see related metadata, such as the table name, the table's column names, and any metric names not hidden. New object-level security features of SSAS 2017 and later can eliminate this visibility.

One option to simplify the **Fields** list is to consolidate measures into fewer home tables and hide unused tables. Dedicated measure group tables can be created to organize and group similar measures. Dedicated measure groups are empty tables created with queries that do not return rows or other sources, and that do not require a refresh. One method of creating dedicated measure group tables is to create a **Blank Query** called something along the lines of "*Calculations*", and then to load and apply this to the model. In the Desktop, create at least one measure in this table and hide the single column automatically created by the query that is named the same as the query/table. Measures can be created directly in this table, or existing measures can be associated with any table of the model via the **Home table** property available in the ribbon of the **Measure tools** tab.

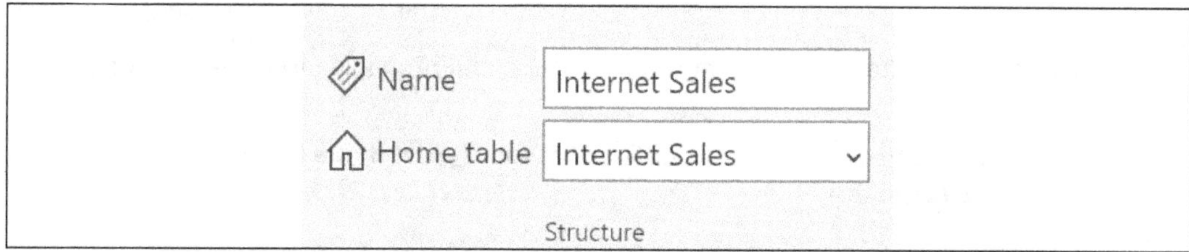

Figure 3.22: Measure Home table

There's more...

Pages can also be hidden from report readers in the case of reports that include multiple pages. To hide pages, right-click the **Page** tab and choose **Hide Page**. This can be useful to preserve pages used during development and troubleshooting, or when using tooltip pages.

Perspectives are essentially view definitions of models such that only a defined set of tables, columns, and metrics of a model are exposed to a given view. Power BI Desktop supports perspectives, although they must be created using an external tool such as Tabular Editor. To see how perspectives can be created and used, follow these steps:

1. From the **Report** view, select **Tabular Editor** in the ribbon of the **External Tools** tab.
2. In **Tabular Editor**, note that only the visible tables are displayed—the **Departments** table is missing. You can view hidden objects by choosing **Hidden Objects** from the **View** menu.
3. Right-click the **Perspectives** folder, choose **New Perspective**, and name the perspective **New Perspective**.
4. In the **Tables** folder, right-click the **Internet Sales** table and choose **Show in Perspectives**, then **All Perspectives**.
5. Repeat *step 4* for the **Products** table.

6. Expand the **Products** table, right-click the **DaysToManufacture** column, and choose **Hide in Perspectives** and then **New Perspective**.

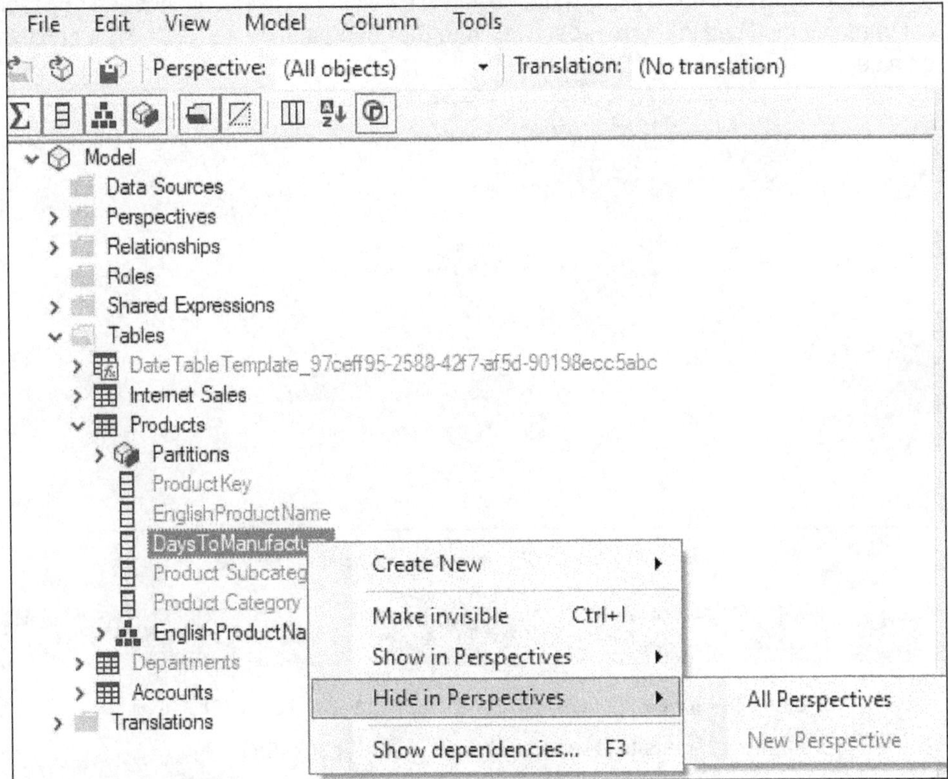

Figure 3.23: Tabular Editor

7. Right-click the **Accounts** table, choose **Hide in Perspectives**, and then **All Perspectives**.
8. Choose **Save** from the **File** menu.
9. Close the **Tabular Editor**.
10. Back in Power BI Desktop, create a second page, and then save the report.
11. Choose **Options and settings** and then **Options** from the **File** menu.
12. Under **CURRENT FILE** in **Report** settings, turn on the **Allow report readers to personalize visuals to suit their needs** option.
13. In the **Format** section of the **Visualizations** pane for your second page, notice the new **Personalize visual** section.
14. Set **Report-reader perspective** to **New Perspective**.

As the report editor, you will continue to see the entire model of all tables and columns not hidden in the model while in **Report** view in Power BI Desktop. However, when users are personalizing visuals on **Page 2** in the Power BI service, the users will not see any tables and columns not included in the perspective. Note that perspectives should not be considered to be a security mechanism in any regard.

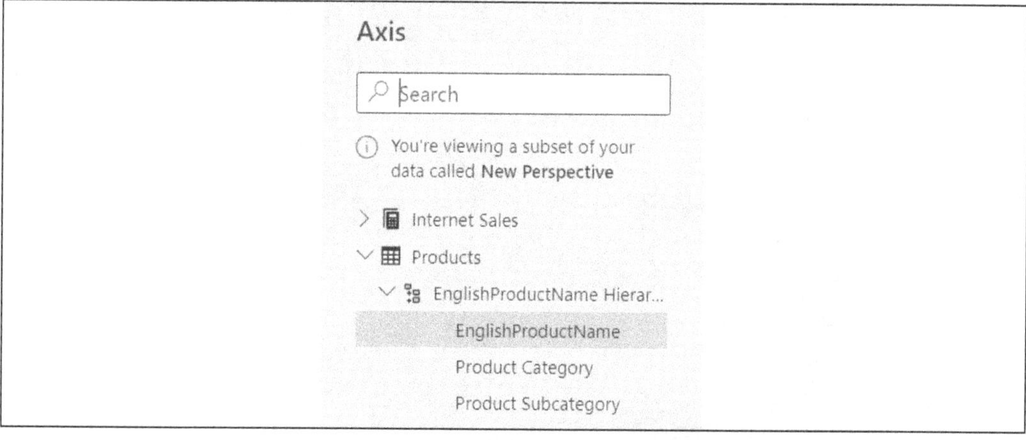

Figure 3.24: Personalize dialog visuals in Service

See also

- Let users personalize visuals in a report: `http://bit.ly/3cljuvm`
- Personalize visuals in a report: `http://bit.ly/2OZX8a8`

Enriching a Model with DAX

In order to drive user adoption and to provide a foundation to support more advanced analytics, it's essential that the logic embedded in core or 'base' DAX measures accurately reflect business definitions. These fundamental measures deliver version control across the many reports built from a data model and avoid the need for additional logic to be applied at the report layer. Clear definitions for required business metrics should be documented and the corresponding DAX measures should be validated for accuracy prior to deploying any reports using these new measures to a production environment.

Performance, usability, and version control are all fundamental characteristics of effective data models, but it is often the additional analytical context that sets models apart. Once fundamental measures have been implemented, additional DAX measures can be developed to support common and high-priority business analysis. These measures can often replace ad hoc and manual data analysis for business users as well as dedicated custom reports maintained by the BI organization. As measures are stored within the data model, the logic can be re-used in various combinations and in future projects.

When developing these metrics, it is important to identify the set of base measures to create, the data source to validate against, and the subject matter experts. Reconcile differences in definitions between source systems and any custom logic applied in reports. Request a project sponsor from a business organization to review and approve the definitions and validation. Finally, identify any conflicts with existing business definitions and advise of complexity in implementing the measures.

In this recipe, DAX measures are created to represent business definitions and support deeper analysis.

Getting ready

To prepare for this recipe, follow these steps:

1. Open Power BI Desktop.
2. Create an Import mode data source query called `AdWorksDW`. This query should be similar to the following:

```
let
    Source = Sql.Database("localhost\MSSQLSERVERDEV",
"AdventureWorksDW2019")
in
    Source
```

3. Isolate this query in a query group called **Data Sources** and disable loading.
4. Right-click `AdWorksDW` and choose **Reference**.
5. Select the **FactResellerSales** table and name this query **Reseller Sales**.
6. Repeat *steps 4* and 5 to create a **Currency Rates** query that imports **FactCurrencyRates**, an **Internet Sales** query that imports **FactInternetSales**, a **Dates** query that imports **DimDate**, and a **Customers** query that imports **DimCustomer**.
7. Add an **Index** column starting from 1 to the **Currency Rates** query, and filter the **CurrencyKey** column to **98**.
8. Create a **Products** query based on the **DimProduct**, **DimProductCategory**, and **DimProductSubcategory** tables using the following code. Alternatively, use the SQL view for products from a prior recipe in this chapter, *Implementing a Data Model*.

```
let
    Source = AdWorksDW,
    Navigation = Source{[Schema="dbo",Item="DimProduct"]}[Data],
    Subcategory =
        Table.ExpandRecordColumn(
            Navigation, "DimProductSubcategory",
```

```
                {"EnglishProductSubcategoryName", "DimProductCategory"},
                {"Product Subcategory", "DimProductCategory"}
            ),
        Category =
            Table.ExpandRecordColumn(
                Subcategory, "DimProductCategory",
                {"EnglishProductCategoryName"}, {"Product Category"}
            )
in
    Category
```

9. Move the **Reseller Sales**, **Internet Sales**, and **Currency Rates** queries to a query group called **Facts** and the **Dates**, **Products**, and **Customers** queries to a query group called **Dimensions**.
10. Create four blank queries called **Reseller Measures**, **Pricing Measures**, **Customer Measures**, and **Currency Measures** in the **Other Queries** group.
11. Click **Close & Apply** in the ribbon of the **Home** tab to load the tables to the data model.
12. Create the relationships shown in *Figure 3.25*.

Active	From: Table (Column)	To: Table (Column)
✓	Currency Rates (DateKey)	Dates (DateKey)
✓	Internet Sales (CustomerKey)	Customers (CustomerKey)
☐	Internet Sales (DueDateKey)	Dates (DateKey)
✓	Internet Sales (OrderDateKey)	Dates (DateKey)
✓	Internet Sales (ProductKey)	Products (ProductKey)
☐	Internet Sales (ShipDateKey)	Dates (DateKey)
☐	Reseller Sales (DueDateKey)	Dates (DateKey)
✓	Reseller Sales (OrderDateKey)	Dates (DateKey)
✓	Reseller Sales (ProductKey)	Products (ProductKey)
☐	Reseller Sales (ShipDateKey)	Dates (DateKey)

Figure 3.25: Model relationships

13. All of these relationships' cross-filtering directions should be **Single**, except for the **Internet Sales** to **Customers** relationship, which should be set to **Both**.
14. Switch to the **Data** view and hide the single columns in the **Reseller Measures**, **Pricing Measures**, **Customer Measures**, and **Currency Measures** tables.
15. Right-click on the **Date** table and choose **Mark as date table** using **FullDateAlternateKey** as the **Date column**.

How to Enrich a Model with DAX

To implement this recipe, use the following steps:

1. Switch to the **Data** view.
2. Create the following eight sales and cost DAX measures in the **Reseller Measures** table:

```
Reseller Discount Amount = SUM('Reseller Sales'[DiscountAmount])

Reseller Gross Sales =
    SUMX('Reseller Sales',
        'Reseller Sales'[UnitPrice] * 'Reseller Sales'[OrderQuantity])

Reseller Net Sales =
    CALCULATE( [Reseller Gross Sales] - [Reseller Discount Amount],
        'Reseller Sales'[ShipDate] <> DATEVALUE("12/31/2099") )

Reseller Product Cost =
    SUMX('Reseller Sales',
        'Reseller Sales'[OrderQuantity]*'Reseller
Sales'[ProductStandardCost])

Reseller Gross Margin % =
    DIVIDE([Reseller Gross Sales] - [Reseller Product Cost],
        [Reseller Gross Sales])

Reseller Margin % =
    DIVIDE([Reseller Net Sales] - [Reseller Product Cost],
        [Reseller Net Sales])


Reseller Count of Products Sold =
    CALCULATE(DISTINCTCOUNT('Products'[ProductAlternateKey]),
        'Reseller Sales')

Reseller Count of Sales Orders = DISTINCTCOUNT('Reseller
Sales'[SalesOrderNumber])
```

3. Create the following seven sales and cost DAX measures in the **Pricing Measures** table:

```
Effective Unit Price =
    DIVIDE(SUM('Reseller Sales'[ExtendedAmount]),
        SUM('Reseller Sales'[OrderQuantity]) )
```

```
25th Percentile Unit Price = PERCENTILE.INC('Reseller
Sales'[UnitPrice],.25)

75th Percentile Unit Price = PERCENTILE.INC('Reseller
Sales'[UnitPrice],.75)

Maximum Unit Price = MAX('Reseller Sales'[UnitPrice])

Median Unit Price = MEDIAN('Reseller Sales'[UnitPrice])

Minimum Unit Price = MIN('Reseller Sales'[UnitPrice])

Range of Unit Prices = [Maximum Unit Price] - [Minimum Unit Price]
```

4. Create the following three sales and cost DAX measures in the **Pricing Measures** table:

```
Count of Accessory But Not Bike Customers =
VAR BikeCustomers =
    SUMMARIZE(
        CALCULATETABLE('Internet Sales','Products'[Product Category] =
"Bikes"),
        'Customers'[CustomerAlternateKey])
VAR AccessoryCustomers =
    SUMMARIZE(
        CALCULATETABLE('Internet Sales',
            'Products'[Product Category] = "Accessories"),
        'Customers'[CustomerAlternateKey])
RETURN
    CALCULATE(
        DISTINCTCOUNT('Customers'[CustomerAlternateKey]),
        EXCEPT(AccessoryCustomers,BikeCustomers) )

Count of Bike Only Customers =
VAR BikeCustomers =
    SUMMARIZE(
        CALCULATETABLE('Internet Sales','Products'[Product Category] =
"Bikes"),
        'Customers'[CustomerAlternateKey]
    )
VAR ClothesAndAccessoryCustomers =
    SUMMARIZE(
        CALCULATETABLE('Internet Sales',
            'Products'[Product Category] IN {"Accessories","Clothing"}
        ), 'Customers'[CustomerAlternateKey])
```

```
RETURN
    CALCULATE(
        DISTINCTCOUNT('Customers'[CustomerAlternateKey]),
        EXCEPT(BikeCustomers,ClothesAndAccessoryCustomers) )

Count of Last Year Customers ex Current Year =
VAR CurrentYear = 2012
VAR LastYear = CurrentYear - 1
VAR LYCustomers =
    SUMMARIZE(
        CALCULATETABLE('Internet Sales',
            FILTER(ALL('Dates'),'Dates'[CalendarYear] = LastYear)
        ), 'Customers'[CustomerAlternateKey])
VAR CYCustomers =
    SUMMARIZE(
        CALCULATETABLE(
            'Internet Sales',
            FILTER(ALL('Dates'),'Dates'[CalendarYear] = CurrentYear)
        ), 'Customers'[CustomerAlternateKey])
RETURN
    CALCULATE(
        DISTINCTCOUNT('Customers'[CustomerAlternateKey]),
        EXCEPT(LYCustomers,CYCustomers) )
```

5. Create the following two DAX columns in the **Dates** table:

```
YearMonth = [CalendarYear]*100 + [MonthNumberOfYear]

YearMonthIndex =
    COUNTROWS(

SUMMARIZE(FILTER('Dates',[YearMonth]<EARLIER([YearMonth])),[YearMonth])
    ) + 1
```

6. Create the following eleven sales and cost DAX measures in the **Currency Measures** table:

```
Max Daily Rate = MAX('Currency Rates'[EndOfDayRate])

Last Rate =
    CALCULATE(DISTINCT('Currency Rates'[EndOfDayRate]),
        LASTNONBLANK('Dates'[FullDateAlternateKey],[Max Daily Rate]) )

Previous Daily Rate =
    CALCULATE([Last Rate],
        FILTER(ALL('Currency Rates'),
```

```
                'Currency Rates'[Index] = MAX('Currency Rates'[Index]) - 1)
)

Previous Monthly Rate =
    CALCULATE([Last Rate],
        FILTER(ALL('Dates'),
            'Dates'[YearMonthIndex] = MAX('Dates'[YearMonthIndex]) - 1)
)

Previous Year Rate =
    CALCULATE([Last Rate],
        FILTER(ALL('Dates'),
            'Dates'[CalendarYear] = MAX('Dates'[CalendarYear]) - 1) )

Daily Change % = DIVIDE([Last Rate],[Previous Daily Rate])
Monthly Change % = DIVIDE([Last Rate],[Previous Monthly Rate])
Yearly Change % = DIVIDE([Last Rate],[Previous Year Rate])
Daily Geometric Return = GEOMEANX('Currency Rates',[Daily Change %])-1
Daily Geometric Change = GEOMEANX('Currency Rates',[Daily Change %])-1
Yearly Geometric Change = GEOMEANX(DISTINCT('Dates'[CalendarYear]),[Year
ly Change %])-1
```

How it works

Measure definitions can be straightforward when the data is internally managed with processes and tools such as a data governance council, **Master Data Services** (**MDS**), **Data Quality Services**, and **Azure Data Catalog**. As per the *Power BI Governance and Deployment whitepaper*, Power BI projects and all BI projects greatly benefit from these data cleansing and information management tools. The data warehouse bus matrix and stakeholder matrix referenced in this chapter and *Chapter 4*, *Authoring Power BI Reports*, respectively, can help to focus the measure definition process on version control and transparency.

The names used for measures should be intuitive and specific to the business process. Preferably, a naming standard is followed to balance the detail of the name with the impact of text on visualizations. In a real project scenario, several additional measures would likely be created following validation. These might include Net Sales as a percentage of Gross Sales, Sales per Order, Quantity per Order, and Sales Not Shipped. These measures and more advanced measures would all leverage the validated measures.

For the **Reseller Measures**, the following business definitions are specified:

- Gross Sales is equal to Unit Price multiplied by Order Quantity with no discounts applied.

- Net Sales are Gross Sales reduced by Discounts and must have been shipped.
- Product Cost is equal to Product Standard Cost multiplied by Order Quantity.

Two columns exist in the source database reflecting **Reseller Gross Sales** and **Reseller Product Cost**. Performance and memory usage can be improved only by importing the price and quantity columns and multiplying them within the measure. For the **Reseller Gross Sales** measure, the `SUMX` function is used to iterate over the table specified in the first parameter. The calculation specified in the second parameter is performed for each row and then all rows are summed. The net sales measure deducts discounts from gross sales and only includes shipped products. Here it is assumed that the date value of `12/31/2099` is assigned for any sales orders that have not shipped.

Margin percentage measures reflecting both gross and net sales (with discounts) are required. These are the **Reseller Gross Margin %** and **Reseller Margin %** measures, respectively. **Margin Amount** measures might also be created and could replace the numerator of the **Margin %** measures. `DISTINCTCOUNT` can be used directly against foreign key relationship columns and any degenerate dimension columns on the fact table, such as **SalesOrderNumber**. Always use the `DIVIDE` function with the optional third parameter to avoid division by zero errors.

The distinct count of sales orders and products sold are also core measures used in many reports and are referenced by other measures. These are the **Reseller Count of Products Sold** and **Reseller Count of Sales Order** measures. The **Reseller Count of Products Sold** measure uses the natural key of the product in the filter context of the fact table to count unique products. Using the product key on the fact table would count multiple versions of a product, given slowly changing dimensions.

The **Pricing Measures** provide an example of supporting the deeper analysis of pricing trends. These measures are designed to accomplish the following:

- Describe the central tendency and distribution of prices.
- Account for the impact of product sales mix to support analysis of effective pricing versus product pricing.

The **Effective Unit Price** measure accounts for the impact of quantity sold and uses the existing sales and quantity metrics. The percentile and median measures **25th Percentile Unit Price**, **75th Percentile Unit Price**, and **Median Unit Price** help to better describe the distribution of prices. The `MEDIAN` function returns the 50th percentile of values in a column. The `PERCENTILE.INC` function is used for the 25th and 75th percentile.

The minimum, maximum, and range of unit prices provide additional context to the variability of the prices. Visuals can be created that use these measures to analyze pricing; see *Figure 3.26* as an example.

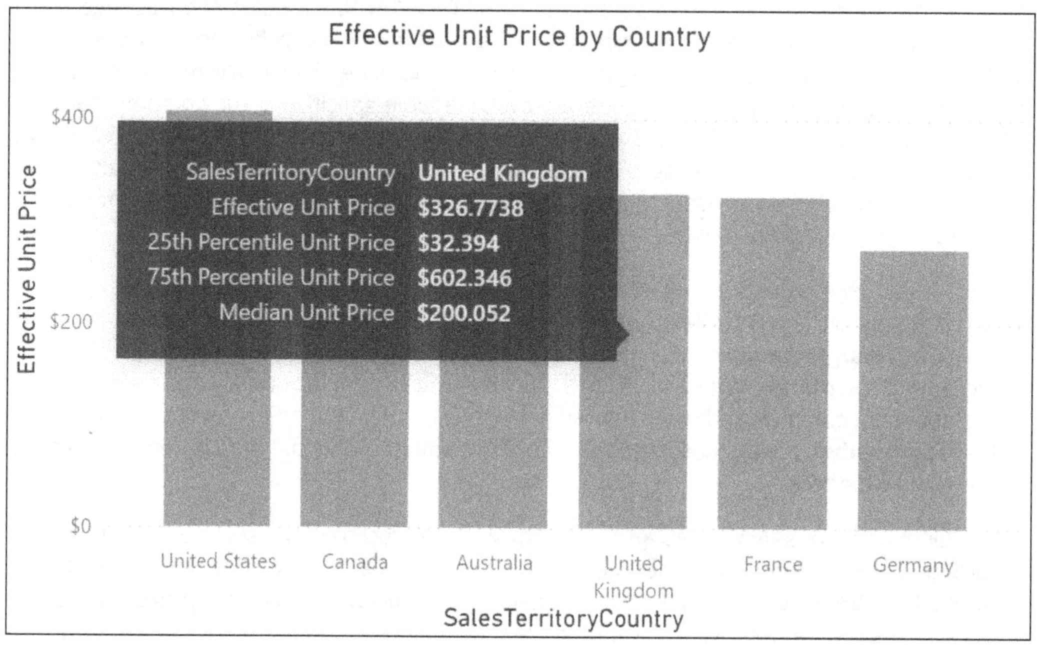

Figure 3.26: Example Power BI Pricing Reports

The visuals compare the average unit price metric to the new effective unit price metric. Pricing metrics are added to visual tooltips such that hovering over values in the charts provides additional context. Performance is not negatively impacted when adding measures to visuals from the same table due to measure fusion. The tooltip measures shown are from the same table and did not create additional DAX queries.

Embedding hierarchies in visuals with supporting measures can allow users to investigate interesting values by drilling up and down. Additionally, exception reports and notifications can be developed using the new measures as thresholds.

The **Customer Measures** serve as an example for finding cross-selling opportunities, as well as lapsed customers. The objective of these measures is to identify customer segments based on their purchase history across product categories. For example, the business wants to identify customers who have purchased a bike, but no bike accessories.

By creating a **Table** visualization that includes the **Product Category** column from the **Products** table and the distinct count of the **CustomerKey** from the **Customers** table, we can see that 18,484 distinct customers have made purchases across three product categories; this information can be seen in *Figure 3.27*.

Product Category	Count of CustomerKey
Accessories	15114
Bikes	9132
Clothing	6852
Total	**18484**

Figure 3.27: Unique Customers by Product Category

The **Count of Accessory But Not Bike Customers** and **Count of Bike Only Customers** measures help us to determine the number of customers that have bought clothing or accessories but not bikes, or bought bikes but not accessories, respectively. These measures can be used in **Card** visuals to show that there are far fewer bike-only customers than customers that only buy clothing or accessories, but not bikes. In addition, these measures can be used in **Table** visualizations that include the **CustomerAlternateKey** column to identify individual customers; when these measures are calculated at the individual customer level, the measures return either zero, or one and zero values are automatically filtered from the **Table** visualization by default. Note that you can click the drop-down arrow in the **Values** area for **CustomerAlternateKey** and choose **Show items with no data** to change this default behavior.

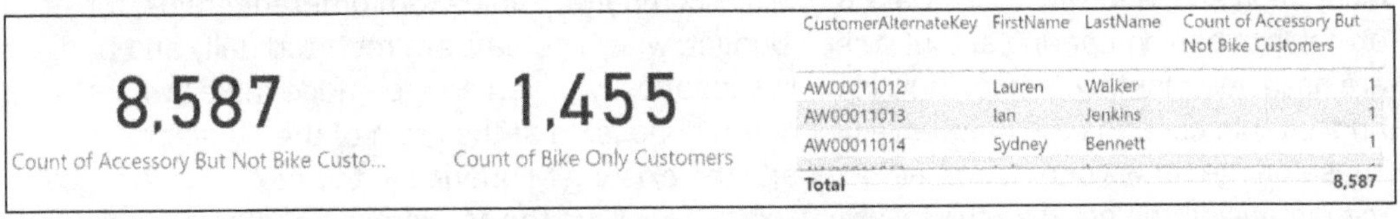

8,587
Count of Accessory But Not Bike Custo...

1,455
Count of Bike Only Customers

CustomerAlternateKey	FirstName	LastName	Count of Accessory But Not Bike Customers
AW00011012	Lauren	Walker	1
AW00011013	Ian	Jenkins	1
AW00011014	Sydney	Bennett	1
Total			8,587

Figure 3.28: Measures Count of Accessory But Not Bike Customers and Count of Bike Only Customers

The **Count of Accessory But Not Bike Customers** measure uses variables (VAR) to create the virtual tables `BikeCustomers` and `AccessoryCustomers` that store the distinct customer keys associated with the two product categories, Bikes and Accessories, respectively. The `SUMMARIZE` function groups the customer key values and `EXCEPT` performs the set-based operation. For the **Count of Bike Only Customers** measure, the syntax aligns with the structure of the first measure except for the use of the DAX IN operator to include accessories and clothing in the same group of customer keys. Given the power of these measures, they could be candidates for sales and marketing dashboards and exception reports; sales teams could focus on cross-selling bike-only customers and selling bikes to non-bike customers.

The **Count of Last Year Customers ex Current Year** measure demonstrates how to identify customers who made a purchase last year but have not yet made a purchase this year. The structure of this measure is similar to the two previous measures, except for the use of the `CALCULATETABLE` function to create a filtered table set. In the recipe, the `CurrentYear` variable is hardcoded to be `2012`. In a production dataset, this would likely be changed to something like `YEAR(TODAY())` in order to get the current year or `YEAR(MAX('Dates'[Date]))` to get the most current year in context. This measure can be used in **Card** or **Table** visualizations as well.

The **Currency Measures** provide an example of computing the geometric mean at the day, month, and year grains. In the **Last Rate** measure, the `LASTNONBLANK` function is needed for days where there might not be a rate logged in the data. This measure is used to compute the previous rate at the day, month, and year granularity (**Previous Daily Rate**, **Previous Monthly Rate**, and **Previous Year Rate**). The percentage change measures, **Daily Change** %, **Monthly Change** %, and **Yearly Change** % are the source values for the geometric mean calculations and thus are expressed as positive numbers. The `GEOMEANX` function iterates over tables at the different grains and computes the `Change %` measure for each row. The geometric mean (the product of values taken to the Nth root) is computed last against this list of values. The geometric change measures can be used in a multi-row card visualization, with 10 decimal points specified:

-0.0108542283	-0.0011481367	-0.0000349297
Yearly Geometric Change	Monthly Geometric Cha...	Daily Geometric Change

Figure 3.29: Geometric Mean Measures

There's more...

A common scenario with many data models is comparing tables with different grains, for example, when comparing actual versus budget, where actuals are reported daily and budgets are assigned monthly or quarterly. In such scenarios, you can create bridge tables where each bridge table contains the unique values of the dimension at the grain of the budget table. These bridge tables can potentially leverage the existing M queries in the model used to load the dimension tables. Take the following example, where the M expression references the **Dates** table query as its source and selects only the distinct values of the **Calendar Yr-Mo** column. If this is the grain of the budget table, this single-column table could be used as the bridge table.

```
let Source = Dates,
      YearMonthColumn = Table.SelectColumns(Source,{"Calendar Yr-Mo"}),
      RemoveDuplicates = Table.Distinct(YearMonthColumn)
in RemoveDuplicates
```

Alternatively, a simple SQL view could be created (`'Select Distinct [Calendar Yr-Mo] From dbo.DimDate'`) that selects the distinct values of the column; this view could be accessed from a new bridge table M query.

One-to-many relationships with single-direction cross-filtering from the bridge tables to the budget table can be created. Additional many-to-one relationships with bidirectional cross-filtering are then created between the bridge tables and their corresponding dimension tables. An example final model might look the same as that shown in *Figure 3.30*.

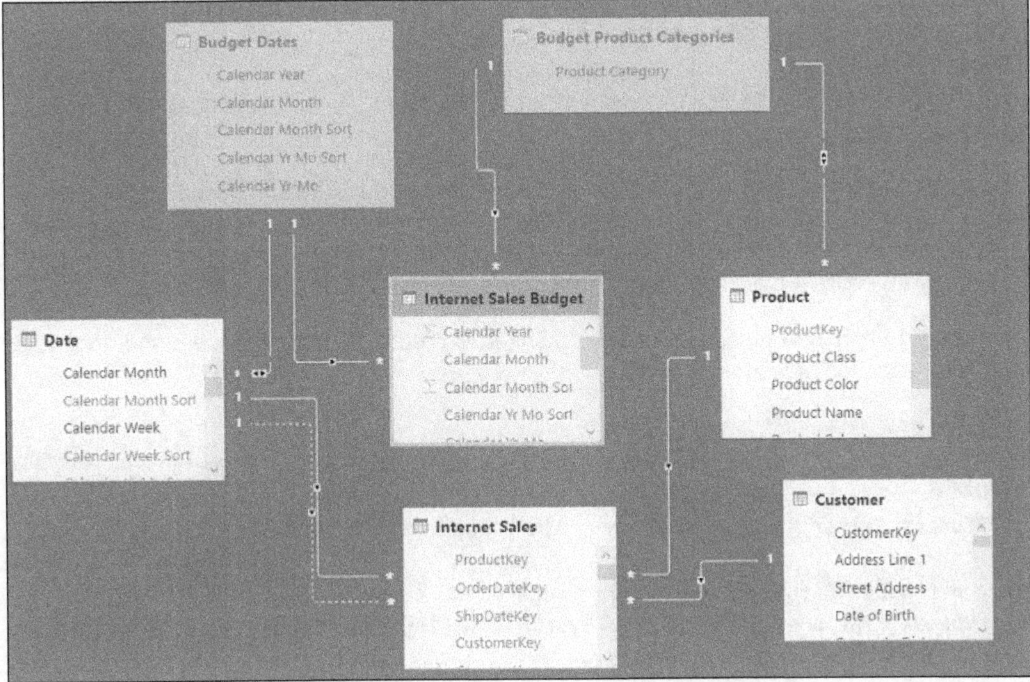

Figure 3.30: Internet Sales versus Budget Data Model

The two bidirectional relationships highlighted in the image allow filters on the **Date** and **Product** tables to propagate to the **Internet Sales Budget** table, in addition to the **Internet Sales** fact table.

The only remaining steps requiring some level of code are to avoid invalid filter contexts. For example, the **Internet Sales** fact table can of course be filtered by individual products and dates, but this granularity is not available for the **Internet Sales Budget** table and thus a blank value should be returned.

A filter test measure can be created to test for filter context. The filter test is used to protect against invalid sales to budget reports, with different filters applied to each fact table. The following measure checks whether filters have been applied at higher grains than the budget table:

```
Budget Filter Test =
 VAR CustomerFilter = ISCROSSFILTERED(Customer)
 VAR ProductGrain =
  ISFILTERED('Product'[Product Class]) || ISFILTERED('Product'[Product Color])
||
  ISFILTERED('Product'[Product Subcategory]) || ISFILTERED('Product'[Product
Name])
 VAR DateGrain =
```

```
  ISFILTERED('Date'[Calendar Yr-Wk]) || ISFILTERED('Date'[Date]) ||
ISFILTERED('Date'[Wk End Date])
RETURN
IF(CustomerFilter = TRUE() || ProductGrain = TRUE() || DateGrain =TRUE(),
 "Higher Grain", "Common Grain")
```

The ISFILTERED and ISCROSSFILTERED functions return Boolean values based on the filter context of the table or columns. The ISFILTERED function is limited to a single column in the model and is specific to the given column. The ISCROSSFILTERED function can check a single column or an entire table. Filters from other tables are included in the evaluation.

The **Budget Filter Test** measure can then be used to create a budget measure and an actual-to-budget variance measure:

```
Internet Sales Budget =
 VAR BudgetSales = sum('Internet Sales Budget'[Online Sales Budget])
RETURN
IF([Budget Filter Test] = "Common Grain", BudgetSales, BLANK())

Internet Sales Actual to Budget Variance =
IF(ISBLANK([Internet Sales Budget]),BLANK(), [Internet Sales] - [Internet Sales
Budget])
```

In this scenario, the requirement is to only test for a common grain, and return a blank otherwise. It is possible to build allocation logic into the DAX budget measure to account for higher grains. In general, these allocation rules are better implemented in the budget process itself or via ETL tools and query languages, such as SQL and M. These measures can be used to visualize variances between actuals and budget.

Product Category	2017-Jan	2017-Feb	2017-Mar	2017-Apr	2017-May	2017-Jun	2017-Jul
Accessories	($5,524)	($462)	$13,281	($3,103)	($16,784)	($1,876)	$8,120
Bikes	($66,393)	$98,532	($48,389)	$271,293	($336,043)	$465,368	$385,256
Clothing	($87)	$2,131	$2,679	$5,333	$266	($2,943)	($5,602)
Total	($72,005)	$100,200	($32,428)	$273,523	($352,562)	$460,549	$387,774

Figure 3.31: Internet Sales Actual versus Budget by Product Category and Year-Month

Matrix visuals provide functionality similar to Excel pivot tables and are therefore a good choice for budget versus actuals.

See also

- DAX function reference: http://bit.ly/3rrQFlt
- Governance and deployment approaches: http://bit.ly/1VLWdVg

Supporting Virtual Table Relationships

Virtual table relationships are DAX expressions implemented to filter one table from another when a relationship does not exist between the two. Report visualizations can then be constructed using both tables (and those related to it), and the DAX measures will update as though a normal relationship is defined. Virtual relationships are often used to address disparate grains of tables and to leverage performance segmentation tables.

Although physical relationships are the preferred long-term solution for both performance and manageability, virtual relationships provide an attractive alternative when physical relationships are not feasible. In this recipe, we provide virtual relationship examples that use both a custom performance segmentation table and an aggregated table.

Getting ready

To prepare for this recipe, follow these steps:

1. Open Power BI Desktop.
2. Create an Import mode data source query called `AdWorksDW`. This query should be similar to the following:

```
let
    Source = Sql.Database("localhost\MSSQLSERVERDEV",
"AdventureWorksDW2019")
in
    Source
```

3. Isolate this query in a query group called **Data Sources** and disable loading.
4. Right-click `AdWorksDW` and choose **Reference**.
5. Select the **FactInternetSales** table and name this query **Internet Sales**.
6. Repeat *steps 4* and *5* to create a **Dates** query that imports **DimDates**.
7. Create a **Customers** query using the following code:

```
let
    Source = AdWorksDW,
    dbo_DimCustomer = Source{[Schema="dbo",Item="DimCustomer"]}[Data],
    Country =
        Table.ExpandRecordColumn(
            dbo_DimCustomer, "DimGeography",
            {"EnglishCountryRegionName"}, {"Country"})
in
    Country
```

8. Create a **Products** query using the following code:

```
let
    Source = AdWorksDW,
    Navigation = Source{[Schema="dbo",Item="DimProduct"]}[Data],
    Subcategory =
        Table.ExpandRecordColumn(
            Navigation, "DimProductSubcategory",
            {"EnglishProductSubcategoryName", "DimProductCategory"},
            {"Product Subcategory", "DimProductCategory"}
        )
in
    Subcategory
```

9. Move the **Internet Sales** query to a query group called **Facts**, and the **Dates**, **Products**, and **Customers** queries to a query group called **Dimensions**.
10. Use an **Enter Data** query to create a **GrowthTiers** query in the **Other Queries** group.

Create Table

	GrowthTierKey	Growth Tier	Min	Max	*
1	1	Problem	-1	-.25	
2	2	Underperform	-.25	0	
3	3	Average	0	.25	
4	4	Overperform	.25	10	
*					

Name: GrowthTiers

Load Edit Cancel

Figure 3.32: Sales Growth Segmentation Table, GrowthTiers

11. Create a **SubCatPlan** query in the **Other Queries** group with the following code:

```
let
    Source = Products,
    Sales =
        Table.ExpandTableColumn(
            Source, "FactInternetSales",
            {"SalesAmount", "OrderDate"}, {"SalesAmount", "OrderDate"}
        ),
    RemoveNulls = Table.SelectRows(Sales, each [SalesAmount] <> null),
    Year =
        Table.AddColumn(
            RemoveNulls, "Calendar Year", each Date.Year([OrderDate])
        ),
```

```
    Month =
        Table.AddColumn(
            Year, "Calendar Month", each Date.MonthName([OrderDate])
        ),
    Group =
        Table.Group(
            Month,
            {"Calendar Year", "Calendar Month", "Product Subcategory"},
            {{"SalesAmount", each List.Sum([SalesAmount]),
                type nullable number}}
        ),
    Index = Table.AddIndexColumn(Group, "Index", 1, 1, Int64.Type),
    Plan =
        Table.AddColumn(
            Index, "Plan Amt",
            each if Number.IsEven([Index])
                then 1/Number.RandomBetween(5,10) * [SalesAmount] +
[SalesAmount]
                else (-1 * 1/Number.RandomBetween(5,10) * [SalesAmount])
+ [SalesAmount]
        ),
    Remove = Table.RemoveColumns(Plan,{"SalesAmount", "Index"}),
    Currency = Table.TransformColumnTypes(Remove,{{"Plan Amt", Currency.
Type}})
in
    Currency
```

12. Create a **Blank Query** called **Calculations** in the **Other Queries** group.
13. Click **Close & Apply** in the ribbon of the **Home** tab to load the tables to the data model.
14. Create the single cross-filtering relationships shown in *Figure 3.33*; note that there are no relationships for the **GrowthTiers** or **SubCatPlan** tables:

Active	From: Table (Column)	To: Table (Column)
✓	Internet Sales (CustomerKey)	Customers (CustomerKey)
☐	Internet Sales (DueDateKey)	Dates (DateKey)
✓	Internet Sales (OrderDateKey)	Dates (DateKey)
✓	Internet Sales (ProductKey)	Products (ProductKey)
☐	Internet Sales (ShipDateKey)	Dates (DateKey)

Figure 3.33: Model relationships

15. Switch to the **Data** view and hide the single column in the **Calculations** table.

16. Create the following measures in the **Calculations** table:

```
Sales Current Year =
    CALCULATE(SUM('Internet Sales'[SalesAmount]),
        FILTER(ALLEXCEPT('Internet Sales','Customers'),
            YEAR('Internet Sales'[OrderDate]) =
MAX('Dates'[CalendarYear]) ) )

Sales Previous Year =
    CALCULATE(
        SUM('Internet Sales'[SalesAmount]),
        FILTER(ALLEXCEPT('Internet Sales','Customers'),
            YEAR('Internet Sales'[OrderDate]) =
MAX('Dates'[CalendarYear])-1) )

Sales Growth =
    DIVIDE([Sales Current Year] - [Sales Previous Year],
        [Sales Previous Year], BLANK() )
```

17. Right-click the **Date** table and choose **Mark as date table** using **FullDateAlternateKey** as the **Date** column.

How to Support Virtual Table Relationships

To implement this recipe, use the following steps:

1. Create the `Sales Growth Tier` measure in the **Calculations** table:

```
Sales Growth Tier =
    VAR Growth = [Sales Growth]
    VAR Level1 =
        CALCULATE(MIN('GrowthTiers'[Max]), 'GrowthTiers'[GrowthTierKey]
= 1)
    VAR Level2 =
        CALCULATE(MIN('GrowthTiers'[Max]), 'GrowthTiers'[GrowthTierKey]
= 2)
    VAR Level3 =
        CALCULATE(MIN('GrowthTiers'[Max]), 'GrowthTiers'[GrowthTierKey]
= 3)
    VAR Level4 =
        CALCULATE(MIN('GrowthTiers'[Max]), 'GrowthTiers'[GrowthTierKey]
= 4)
RETURN
```

```
    SWITCH(TRUE(),
        ISBLANK(Growth), BLANK(),
        Growth <= Level1, CALCULATE(DISTINCT('GrowthTiers'[Growth
Tier]),
                'GrowthTiers'[GrowthTierKey] = 1),
        Growth <= Level2, CALCULATE(DISTINCT('GrowthTiers'[Growth
Tier]),
                'GrowthTiers'[GrowthTierKey] = 2),
        Growth <= Level3, CALCULATE(DISTINCT('GrowthTiers'[Growth
Tier]),
                'GrowthTiers'[GrowthTierKey] = 3),
        Growth <= Level4, CALCULATE(DISTINCT('GrowthTiers'[Growth
Tier]),
                'GrowthTiers'[GrowthTierKey] = 4
            ),"Unknown")
```

2. Create the virtual table relationship measure **Customer Countries** in the **Calculations** table:

```
Customer Countries =
    CALCULATE(DISTINCTCOUNT('Customers'[Country]),
        FILTER(ALL('Customers'[Country]),
            [Sales Growth] > MIN('GrowthTiers'[Min]) &&
            [Sales Growth] < MAX('GrowthTiers'[Max]) ) )
```

3. Create a **Slicer** visualization that uses the **CalendarYear** column from the **Dates** table.
4. Create a **Matrix** visualization with the **Country** column from the **Customers** table as **Rows** and the measures **Sales Growth**, **Sales Current Year**, **Sales Previous Year**, and **Sales Growth Tier** as **Values**.
5. Create a **Clustered column chart** visualization with the **Growth Tier** column from the **GrowthTiers** table as the **Axis**, and the **Customer Countries** measure as **Values**.

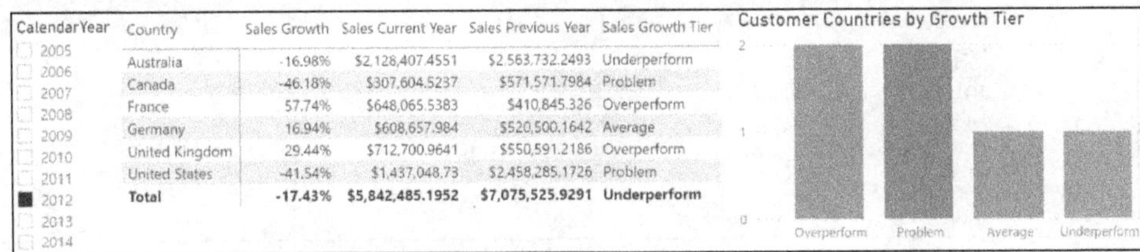

Country	Sales Growth	Sales Current Year	Sales Previous Year	Sales Growth Tier
Australia	-16.98%	$2,128,407.4551	$2,563,732.2493	Underperform
Canada	-46.18%	$307,604.5237	$571,571.7984	Problem
France	57.74%	$648,065.5383	$410,845.326	Overperform
Germany	16.94%	$608,657.984	$520,500.1642	Average
United Kingdom	29.44%	$712,700.9641	$550,591.2186	Overperform
United States	-41.54%	$1,437,048.73	$2,458,285.1726	Problem
Total	**-17.43%**	**$5,842,485.1952**	**$7,075,525.9291**	**Underperform**

Figure 3.34: Virtual relationship segmentation example

6. Save your work.

How it works

The goal of this recipe is to apply the **Growth Tier** segmentations from the disconnected **GrowthTiers** table to the measures of the data model. Two measures are used to form this virtual relationship, **Sales Growth Tier** and **Customer Countries.** The measures apply filters based on the segmentation table thresholds and the **Sales Growth** measure. In effect, these measures form the relationship between the tables in the data model through the calculations performed.

The **Sales Growth Tier** measure returns the text value of the **Growth Tier** column for the specified **Sales Growth** measure value in context. The existing `Sales Growth` measure and the four segment threshold values are stored in DAX variables (the `VAR` statements). The `SWITCH` function compares sales growth with the segment thresholds to assign the **Growth Tier** value. Providing `TRUE()` as the first parameter of the `SWITCH` function allows independent logical conditions to be evaluated in order (from top to bottom). This is similar to the `CASE` expression in SQL. The **Customer Countries** measure uses a simple `CALCULATE` statement to return a `DISTINTCOUNT` of countries filtered by the `MIN` and `MAX` limits of each **Growth Tier**.

The **Sales Growth Tier** measure could be used for analyzing other dimensions of the model, and at different grains; for example, if **StateProvinceName** was added to the **Customers** table and a hierarchy created, you could drill down with the matrix visual and see growth tiers by state/province.

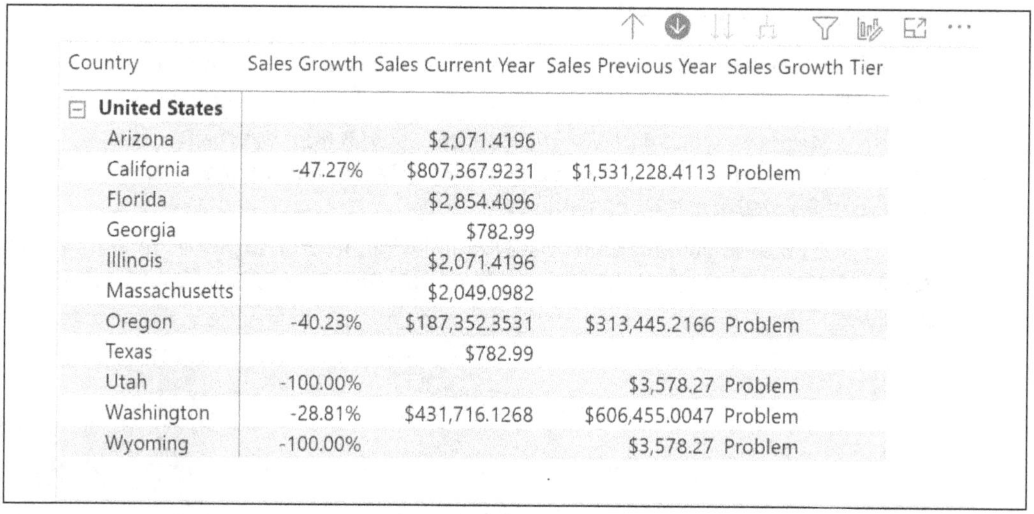

Country	Sales Growth	Sales Current Year	Sales Previous Year	Sales Growth Tier
⊟ **United States**				
Arizona		$2,071.4196		
California	-47.27%	$807,367.9231	$1,531,228.4113	Problem
Florida		$2,854.4096		
Georgia		$782.99		
Illinois		$2,071.4196		
Massachusetts		$2,049.0982		
Oregon	-40.23%	$187,352.3531	$313,445.2166	Problem
Texas		$782.99		
Utah	-100.00%		$3,578.27	Problem
Washington	-28.81%	$431,716.1268	$606,455.0047	Problem
Wyoming	-100.00%		$3,578.27	Problem

Figure 3.35: Drill Down into Problem Customer Country

There are options to modify data models to support physical relationships and thus avoid the limitations of virtual relationships. For example, a concatenated column such as Year-Month could be created for each table via SQL, M, or a DAX-calculated column.

Alternatively, bridge tables with bidirectional cross-filtering relationships provide simple solutions to many-to-many scenarios. Finally, for small fact tables, the `LOOKUPVALUE` function could be used in a calculated column supporting the relationship.

There's more......

The DAX `TREATAS` function was added in early 2017 and provides both simpler syntax and better performance than alternative virtual relationship methods involving `INTERSECT` or `FILTER` with a `CONTAINS` function parameter. We can use the `TREATAS` function to integrate a summary table, **SubCatPlan**, into our Power BI data model. This is useful when a business wants to filter plan data via the same **Products** and **Dates** tables they use regularly and to create actual versus plan reports. The grain of the `SubCatPlan` table is `Product Subcategory` by `Calendar Year` and `Calendar Month`; this is shown in *Figure 3.36*.

Product Subcategory	Calendar Year	Calendar Month	Plan Amt
Mountain Bikes	2013	January	*$313,596.6261*
Bottles and Cages	2013	January	*$2,284.3156*

Figure 3.36: Plan Summary Table for Virtual Relationships

Relationships from the **SubCatPlan** table to the **Date** and **Product** tables cannot be created directly given the many-to-many relationship. Each physical relationship in Power BI is based on a single column from each table, with one of the relationship columns uniquely identifying all the rows of its host table. This is consistent with SSAS Tabular and Power Pivot for Excel models.

To create a virtual table relationship with DAX, follow these steps:

1. Create the **Subcat Plan Amt** measure in the **Calculations** table. This measure filters the subcategory plan measure by the **Products** table and the **Dates** table:

```
Subcat Plan Amt =
    VAR ProductSubCats = VALUES('Products'[Product Subcategory])
    VAR DateTbl =
        SUMMARIZE('Dates','Dates'[CalendarYear],'Dates'[EnglishMonthNa
me])
RETURN
    CALCULATE(
        SUM('SubCatPlan'[Plan Amt]),
        TREATAS(ProductSubCats,'SubCatPlan'[Product Subcategory]),
        TREATAS(DateTbl,'SubCatPlan'[Calendar Year],'SubCatPlan'[Calendar
Month]))
```

2. Create a **Sales vs Plan** measure:

```
Sales vs Plan = SUM('Internet Sales'[SalesAmount]) - [Subcat Plan Amt]
```

3. Create a **Matrix** visualization with the **Product Subcategory** column from the **Products** table as **Rows**, the **EnglishMonthName** column from the **Dates** table as **Columns**, and the **Subcat Plan Amt** measure, **Sales vs Plan** measure, and the **SUM** of the **SalesAmount** column from the **Internet Sales** table as **Values**.

EnglishMonthName	January			February	
Product Subcategory	Subcat Plan Amt	SalesAmount	Sales vs Plan	Subcat Plan Amt	SalesAmount
Bike Racks	$1,362	$1,560	$198	$2,200	$2,520
Bike Stands	$1,111	$1,272	$161	$2,946	$2,544

Figure 3.37: Subcategory Plan versus Actual Matrix Visual

In the **Subcat Plan Amt** measure, variables are used to store tables representing the filtered values of the **Products** and **Dates** dimension tables. The `TREATAS` function transfers the variables to the corresponding plan column(s), thus filtering the **SubCatPlan** table. Any column with the same grain (or lower) than the **Product Subcategory**, **Calendar Year**, and **Calendar Month** columns can be used. Columns from other tables or columns without a virtual relationship will not filter the **SubCatPlan** table.

Bridge tables to support physical relationships to the **Products** and **Dates** tables could be created in this scenario. The two bridge tables would contain the unique product subcategory and month values, and one-to-many relationships would link the bridge tables to the **SubCatPlan**, **Product**, and **Date** tables. The **SubCatPlan** and bridge tables could be hidden from the **Report** view, and bidirectional relationships would be configured between the bridge tables and the **Products** and **Dates** tables. For better performance and manageability, physical relationships are recommended over virtual ones.

See also

- DAX function reference: `http://bit.ly/3rrQFlt`
- Physical and Virtual Relationships in DAX: `http://bit.ly/2oFpe8T`

Creating Hierarchies and Groups

Hierarchies and groups are data model structures that can be implemented to simplify the user and report authoring experience. Hierarchies provide single-click access to multiple columns of a table, enabling users to navigate through pre-defined levels, such as the weeks within a given month. Groups comprise individual values of a column that enable analysis and visualization of the combined total as though it is a single value. Hierarchies and groups have useful applications in almost all data models, and it is important to understand the relationship of these structures to the data model and visualizations.

This recipe provides an example of utilizing DAX parent- and child-hierarchy functions to create columns of a hierarchy. The hierarchy is then implemented into the data model, and a group is created to further benefit analysis.

Getting ready

To prepare for this recipe, follow these steps:

1. Open Power BI Desktop.
2. Create an Import mode data source query called `AdWorksDW`. This query should be similar to the following:

   ```
   let
       Source = Sql.Database("localhost\MSSQLSERVERDEV",
   "AdventureWorksDW2019")
   in
       Source
   ```

3. Isolate this query in a query group called **Data Sources** and disable loading.
4. Right-click `AdWorksDW` and choose **Reference**.
5. Select the **FactInternetSales** table and name this query **Internet Sales**.
6. Repeat *steps 4* and *5* to create a **General Ledger** query that imports **FactFinance**.
7. Create a **Products** query using the following code:

   ```
   let
       Source = AdWorksDW,
       Navigation = Source{[Schema="dbo",Item="DimProduct"]}[Data],
       Subcategory =
           Table.ExpandRecordColumn(
               Navigation, "DimProductSubcategory",
               {"EnglishProductSubcategoryName", "DimProductCategory"},
               {"Product Subcategory", "DimProductCategory"}
           ),
   in
       Subcategory
   ```

8. Create an **Accounts** query using the following code:

   ```
   let
       Source = AdWorksDW,
       dbo_DimCustomer = Source{[Schema="dbo",Item="DimAccount"]}[Data],
       Parent =
           Table.ExpandRecordColumn(
               dbo_DimCustomer, "DimAccount(ParentAccountKey)",
   ```

```
                {"AccountDescription"}, {"ParentAccountDescription"})
in
    Parent
```

9. Move the **Internet Sales** and **General Ledger** queries to a query group called **Facts**, and the **Products** and **Accounts** queries to a query group called **Dimensions**.
10. Click **Close & Apply** in the ribbon of the **Home** tab to load the tables to the data model.
11. Create the **Single** cross-filtering relationships shown in *Figure 3.38*.

Active	From: Table (Column)	To: Table (Column)
✓	General Ledger (AccountKey)	Accounts (AccountKey)
✓	Internet Sales (ProductKey)	Products (ProductKey)

Figure 3.38: Model relationships

How to Create Hierarchies and Groups

To implement this recipe, use the following steps:

1. In the **Data** view, create the following seven calculated columns in the **Accounts** table:

```
Path = PATH('Accounts'[AccountKey],'Accounts'[ParentAccountKey])

Account Level 1 =
    VAR __Key = PATHITEM('Accounts'[Path],1,1)
RETURN
    LOOKUPVALUE('Accounts'[AccountDescription],'Accounts'[AccountKey],
__Key)

Account Level 2 =
    VAR __Key = PATHITEM('Accounts'[Path],2,1)
RETURN
    LOOKUPVALUE('Accounts'[AccountDescription],'Accounts'[AccountKey],
__Key)

Account Level 3 =
    VAR __Key = PATHITEM('Accounts'[Path],3,1)
RETURN
    LOOKUPVALUE('Accounts'[AccountDescription],'Accounts'[AccountKey],
__Key)
```

```
Account Level 4 =
    VAR __Key = PATHITEM('Accounts'[Path],4,1)
RETURN
    LOOKUPVALUE('Accounts'[AccountDescription],'Accounts'[AccountKey],
__Key)

Account Level 5 =
    VAR __Key = PATHITEM('Accounts'[Path],5,1)
RETURN
    LOOKUPVALUE('Accounts'[AccountDescription],'Accounts'[AccountKey],
__Key)

Account Level 6 =
    VAR __Key = PATHITEM('Accounts'[Path],6,1)
RETURN
    LOOKUPVALUE('Accounts'[AccountDescription],'Accounts'[AccountKey],
__Key)
```

2. In the **Fields** list of the **Data** view, right-click the **Account Level 1** column and choose **Create hierarchy**.
3. Rename the **Account Level 1 Hierarchy** to **Account Hierarchy** by right-clicking the hierarchy and choosing **Rename**.
4. Right-click the **Account Level 2** column and choose **Add to hierarchy**, and then **Account Hierarchy**.
5. Repeat *step 4* for the **Account Level 3**, **Account Level 4**, **Account Level 5**, and **Account Level 6** columns in order.

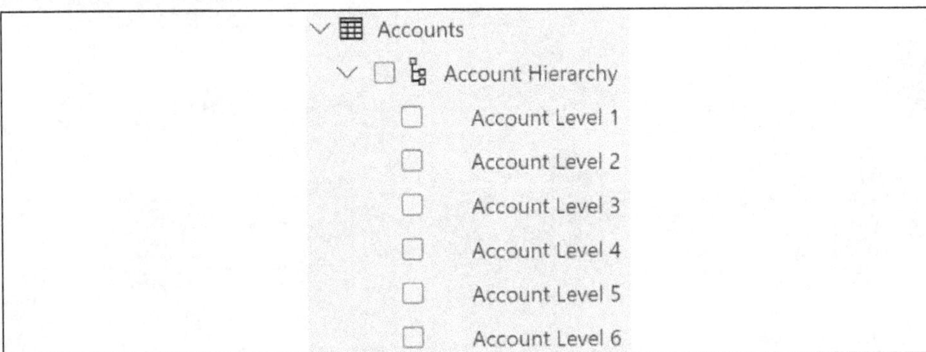

Figure 3.39: Hierarchy in the Fields list

6. Right-click the individual columns that comprise the hierarchy and choose **Hide in report view**.

7. Switch to the **Report** view and create a **Matrix** visualization with **Account Hierarchy** as **Rows** and the **Amount** column from the **General Ledger** table as **Values**.

Account Level 1	Amount
Balance Sheet	**1,107,010,918.52**
Assets	**553,505,459.26**
Current Assets	505,506,336.27
Other Assets	6,080,005.58
Property, Plant, Equipment	41,919,117.41
Liabilities and Owners Equity	**553,505,459.26**
Net Income	**239,257,169.18**
Statistical Accounts	**12,372,325.00**
Total	**1,358,640,412.70**

Figure 3.40: Matrix Visual of Account Hierarchy

8. In the **Fields** list, right-click the **Product Subcategory** column in the **Products** table and choose **New group**.
9. Rename the group **Product Subcategories** by editing the **Name** field.
10. Select **Caps** from the **Ungrouped values** area, press the **Group** button, and name the group **Bike Attire Accessories**.
11. Select **Gloves** from **Ungrouped values**, select **Bike Attire Accessories** from **Groups and members**, and then click the **Group** button to add **Gloves** to the **Bike Attire Accessories** group.
12. Check the box for **Include Other group** and click the **OK** button.

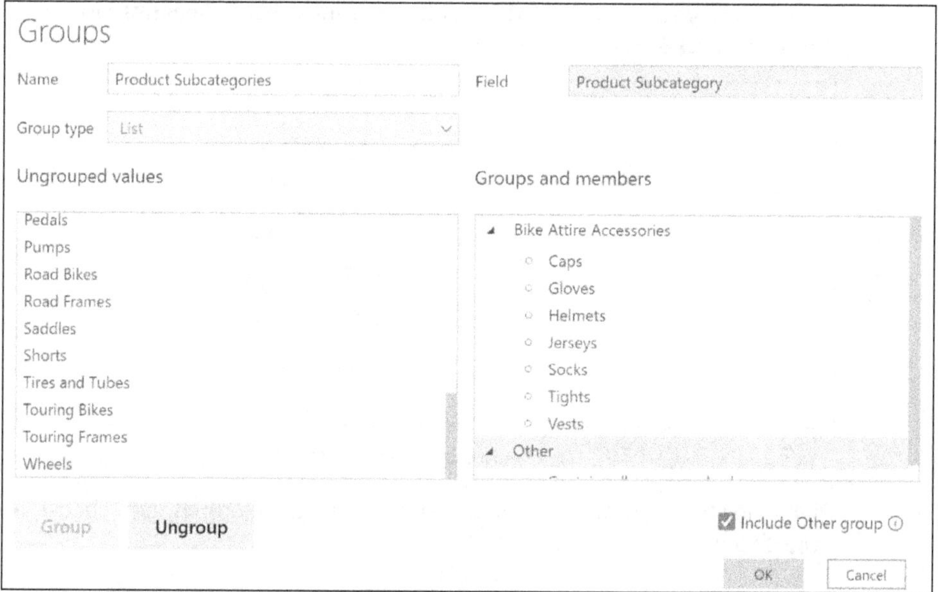

Figure 3.41: Groups Dialog

13. Create a **Clustered bar chart** visualization with the **Product Subcategories** group in the **Products** table as the **Axis**, and the **SalesAmount** column from the **Internet Sales** table as the **Values**.

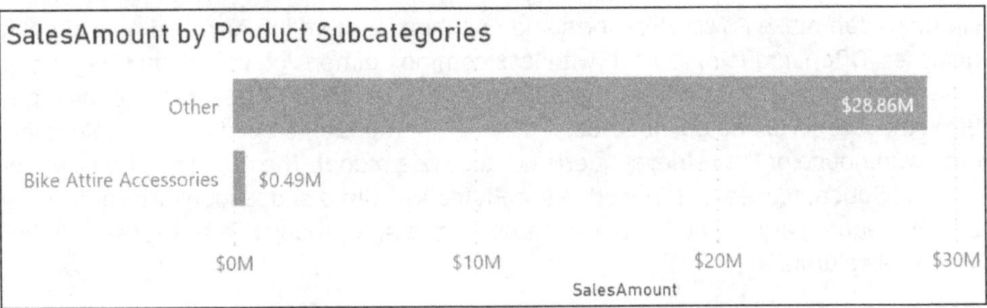

Figure 3.42: Product Subcategories Group with the Other group enabled

How it works

For the hierarchy created, the `PATH` function compares a child key column with the parent key column and returns a delimited text string containing all the parent members for the given row. The `PATHITEM` function returns the key value from a path from highest to lowest based on the position parameter. The third and final parameter of the `PATHITEM` function (1) specifies to return this value as an integer. The `LOOKUPVALUE` function compares the account key with the key returned by the `PATHITEM` function and returns the column specified by the first parameter, **AccountDescription**. Some rows have blank values for a given column because it is higher in the structure; for example, the **Balance Sheet** account does not have values for the columns of level 2 through 6. The calculated columns will appear in the **Fields** list with formula icons.

The hierarchy can now be added to visuals with a single click. Drilldown is available to navigate all six columns. Alternatively, in **Matrix** visualizations, the expand and collapse controls at the beginning of each row can be used to investigate the hierarchy. With the hierarchy in the **Fields** list, usability may be improved by hiding the individual columns. However, individual columns are needed to view a different order of the columns or to view the individual columns of the hierarchy on opposing axes.

Consider the hierarchy created in this recipe as a natural hierarchy versus an unnatural hierarchy. A natural hierarchy contains unique child values for each parent value and is the recommended structure of hierarchies. For example, each unique value in a **Fiscal Year** column would have 12 unique child values, such as "2017-Mar". An unnatural hierarchy would have the same child value repeated across multiple parent values.

In almost all scenarios, the SQL source views or M queries are preferable alternatives to DAX-calculated columns. The DAX parent-child functions used were developed for this scenario, and the **Accounts** table only has 100 rows.

Calculated columns and tables in DAX use the resources of the model during processing/refresh operations and are not compressed, thus increasing the memory footprint of the model. Thus, you should avoid calculated columns on large fact tables.

Grouping can make Power BI reports and dashboards more intuitive and help simplify analyses. Often, grouping is used with less common dimension values that might clutter data visualizations. If a particular grouping created in Power BI Desktop becomes pervasive throughout reports and dashboards, it may be appropriate to build the equivalent into the data warehouse or the retrieval queries of the data model. The name for the new groups, Product Subcategories, is exposed in the **Fields** list with a shape icon of a square segmented into four equal parts. In addition, the name for the new groups is also exposed in the **Data** view as a column.

By default, the **Include Other group** option in the **Groups** dialog box is not enabled. If enabled, all other distinct values or members of the column not included in a group are grouped into the **Other** group. In the **Data** view, members of the **Other** group are displayed as having the value **(Blank)**.

Creating and editing groups and hierarchies is only available in Power BI Desktop with the data model loaded. Users accessing the data model in the Power BI service are only able to use the existing groups and hierarchies. Groups and hierarchies can also be created in DirectQuery data models. Calculated columns can be created in DirectQuery models too, though performance can be negatively impacted.

There's more...

Grouping is also available for date and numerical data type columns and includes the concept of "binning," or grouping based upon values falling into particular ranges. For example, the **ListPrice** column from the **Products** table can be divided into equally sized bins for analysis across the ranges of prices. The specific size of a bin or a set number of bins can be selected. A similar dialog is available for date data types.

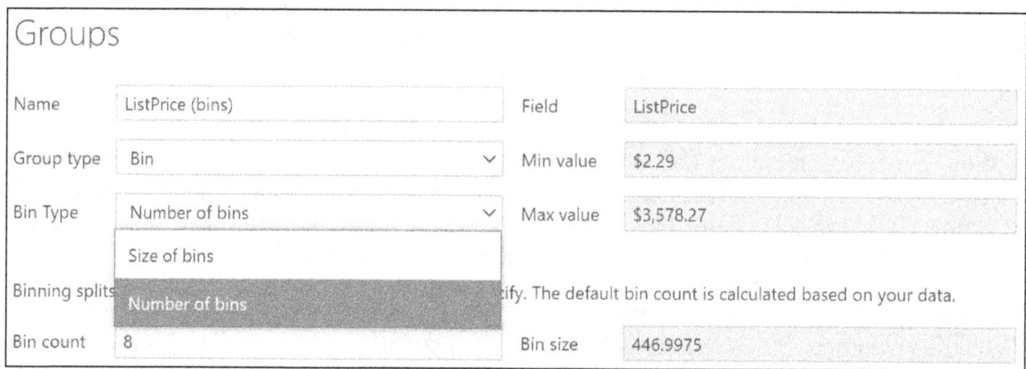

Figure 3.43: Grouping Bins for Numeric Data Type Column

See also

- DAX function reference: `http://bit.ly/3rrQFlt`
- Use grouping and binning in Power BI Desktop: `http://bit.ly/2pALaBc`

Designing Column Level Security

While not as common as **row-level security** (**RLS**), there are times when you may wish to hide particular columns in a data model from one group of report viewers, but not others. Power BI Desktop does not natively support column security. However, a carefully designed data model can achieve column level security using Power BI's native RLS functionality.

It should be noted that Microsoft has recently released **object-level security** (**OLS**) for securing tables and columns in Power BI Premium and Pro. This method of securing objects currently requires third-party tools, such as Tabular Editor. In addition, this method has the advantage of securing even the metadata about the objects such that report viewers without access will not even know that the tables and columns exist in the model. However, there are disadvantages to OLS as well; namely, by completely hiding the tables and columns in the model, it becomes difficult to create measures and report visualizations that work for a variety of users with and without access to certain tables and columns. This is such an issue that you may well conclude that it is not worth the time and trouble, and the reports should indeed be separate data models.

This recipe demonstrates a method of implementing column level security in Power BI Desktop that does not require OLS and works natively with Power BI Desktop at any licensing level. While the metadata about the secured column is viewable with report viewers without access to the secured column's values, this method has the advantage of being easier to author measures and report visualizations that work at any level of security within the model.

Getting ready

To prepare for this recipe, follow these steps:

1. Open Power BI Desktop.
2. Create an Import mode data source query called `AdWorksDW`. This query should be similar to the following:

```
let
    Source = Sql.Database("localhost\MSSQLSERVERDEV",
"AdventureWorksDW2019")
in
    Source
```

3. Isolate this query in a query group called **Data Sources** and disable loading.
4. Add a query called **Reseller Sales Intermediate** that references the **AdWorksDW** query, imports the **FactResellerSales** table, and adds an **Index** column starting at 1:

```
let
    Source = AdWorksDW,
    dbo_FactResellerSales = Source{[Schema="dbo",Item="FactResellerSal
es"]}[Data],
    Index =
        Table.AddIndexColumn(dbo_FactResellerSales, "Index", 1, 1,
Int64.Type)
in
    Index
```

5. Add a query called **Reseller Sales** that references the **Reseller Sales Intermediate** query and removes the **ProductStandardCost** and **TotalProductCost** columns:

```
let
    Source = #"Reseller Sales Intermediate",
    RemoveColumns =
        Table.RemoveColumns(Source,{"ProductStandardCost",
"TotalProductCost"})
in
    RemoveColumns
```

6. Add a query called **Reseller Costs** that references the **Reseller Sales Intermediate** query and selects the **ProductTotalCost**, **TotalProductCost**, and **Index** columns.

```
let
    Source = #"Reseller Sales Intermediate",
    SelectColumns =
        Table.SelectColumns(
            Source,{"ProductStandardCost", "TotalProductCost", "Index"})
in
   SelectColumns
```

7. Move the **Reseller Sales** and **Reseller Sales** queries to a query group called **Facts**, and the **Reseller Sales Intermediate** query to the **Other Queries** query group.
8. Click **Close & Apply** in the ribbon of the **Home** tab to load the tables to the data model.

How to Design Column Level Security

To implement this recipe, use the following steps:

1. Create a relationship between the **Reseller Costs** and **Reseller Sales** tables using the **Index** columns in both tables. Set this relationship to be one-to-many with the **Reseller Sales** table on the **One** side and the **Reseller Costs** table on the **Many** side.

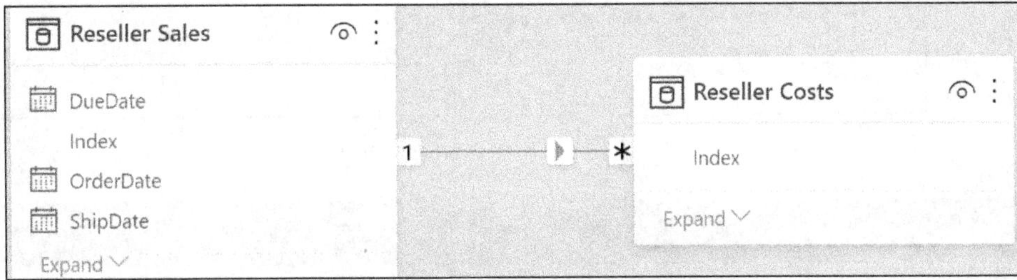

Figure 3.44: Many-to-one relationship required

2. Click **Manage roles** in the ribbon of the **Home** tab in the **Model** view or the **Modeling** tab in the **Report** view.
3. Use the **Create** button to create a **Sales Person** role with RLS on the **Reseller Cost** table with the DAX formula, `ISBLANK([Index])`, and **Save** the role.

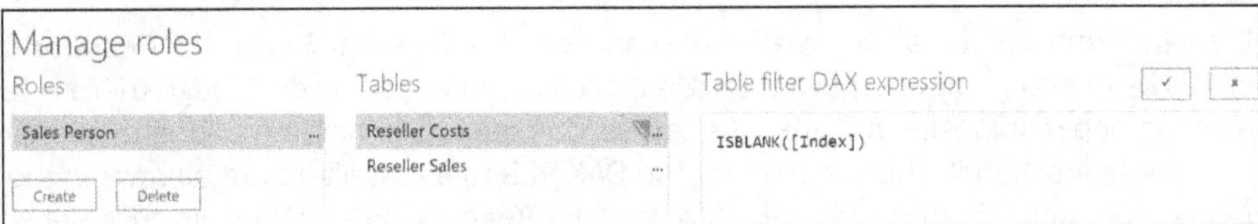

Figure 3.45: Manage roles dialog box

4. In the **Report** view, create a simple **Table** visualization using the **SalesOrderNumber** and **SalesAmount** columns from the **Reseller Sales** table, and the **ProductStandardCost** and **TotalProductCost** columns from the **Reseller Costs** table. Note that values are displayed for all columns.
5. Click on **View as** in the ribbon of the **Modeling** tab, select **Sales Person**, and then click the **OK** button.

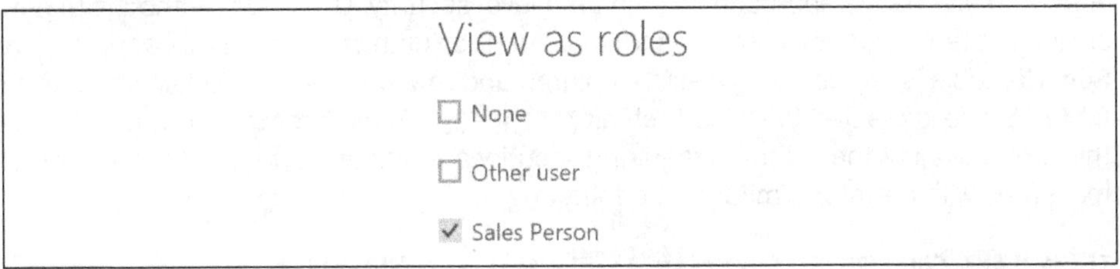

Figure 3.46: View as roles dialog

6. Wait for the visualization to refresh and notice that the **ProductStandardCost** and **TotalProductCost** columns are now blank.

Now viewing as: Sales Person

SalesOrderNumber	SalesAmount	ProductStandardCost	TotalProductCost
SO43659	$20,565.6206		
SO43660	$1,294.2529		
SO43661	$32,726.4786		

Figure 3.47: Viewing as a role

How it works

The keys to this recipe are the implementation of the **Index** column in an intermediate query, the characteristics of the relationship between the **Reseller Sales** and **Reseller Costs** tables, and the implementation of RLS via the **Sales Person** role.

Since the **Index** column is created in an intermediate table that both the **Reseller Sales** and **Reseller Costs** queries reference as their **Source**, we can be certain that there is a one-to-one match between the rows in the **Reseller Sales** and **Reseller Costs** tables.

It is vitally important that the relationship between the **Reseller Sales** and **Reseller Costs** tables be one-to-many and have a **Single** cross-filter direction, even though there is technically a one-to-one relationship between the tables. The reason is that one-to-one relationships must be bidirectional. This means that the DAX RLS rule that filters out all rows in the **Reseller Costs** table would in turn filter out all rows in the **Reseller Sales** table, which is not what is desired.

The DAX RLS rule, `ISBLANK([Index])`, filters out all rows in the **Reseller Costs** table for the **Sales Person** role since the **Index** column is never blank. Note that while the values are hidden, the metadata for the secured columns is still available in the model.

There's more...

There are alternative approaches to column level security. One such method is to have a single fact table and use measures to implement column security. In this approach, a dummy **Security** table is created with a single column and row, containing a single value. A similar DAX RLS rule is created for roles such as `ISBLANK([Column])` for this dummy table. Using this method, all of the columns requiring security are hidden in the model and replaced with measures with a syntax similar to the following:

```
IF(ISBLANK(COUNTROWS('Security')),BLANK(),SUM('Reseller
Sales'[TotalProductCost]))
```

This approach could be extended to handle multiple roles requiring different column security for each role by having a single row per role in the **Security** table with corresponding RLS rules such as `[Column] = "Sales Person"`, `[Column] = "Marketing"` and `[Column] = "Accounting"`. The DAX measures would be adjusted as appropriate. Note that while the values are hidden, the metadata for the secured columns is still available in the model. It is also possible to edit **Table Permissions** in **Tabular Editor**.

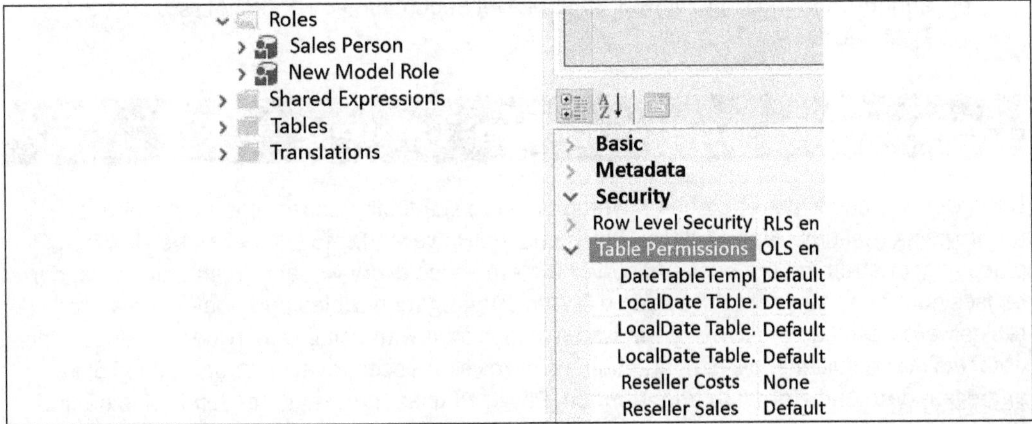

Figure 3.48: Table permissions for roles in Tabular Editor

Unfortunately, this is not fully supported by Power BI Desktop.

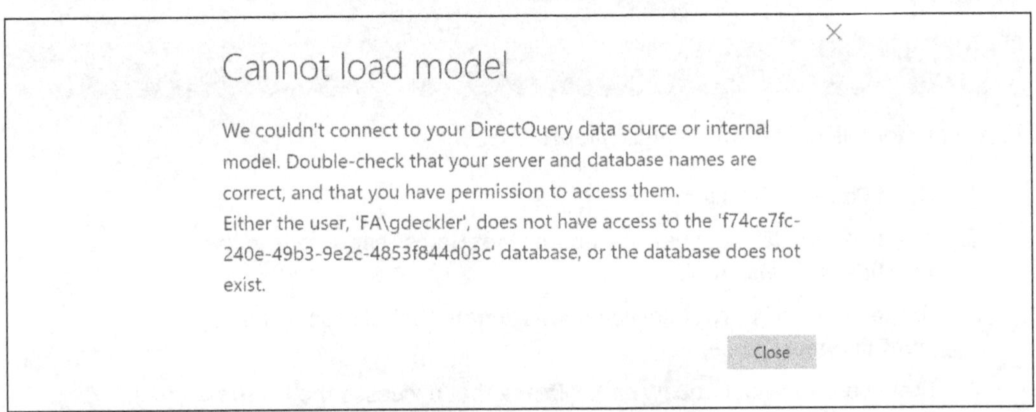

Figure 3.49: Error in Power BI Desktop

Finally, SSAS Tabular 2017 and newer versions implements true OLS that allows tables and columns to be completely shielded from **Roles**, including their metadata. Azure Analysis Services and Power BI Premium also support OLS.

See also

- Column Level Security: http://bit.ly/2P5Gc20
- Analysis Services tabular model object-level security: http://bit.ly/2PEbCMs
- Object Security in Analysis Services 2017: http://bit.ly/39m1P4S
- Announcing public preview of Object-Level Security in Power BI: https://bit.ly/3x182N0

Leveraging Aggregation Tables

DirectQuery mode is a great tool for overcoming the scalability issues of Import mode, or for providing real-time reporting to business users. However, DirectQuery can be slow and place a lot of strain on the backend server system, since every visual refresh and interaction causes queries to be sent to the source system. Aggregation tables and dual-mode storage tables were designed to fix the speed issues associated with using DirectQuery against large datasets in the millions, billions, and trillions of rows. In essence, aggregation tables pre-aggregate data and store it in Import mode. Power BI uses these aggregation tables behind the scenes when possible to limit the number of queries sent to the data source.

This recipe demonstrates how to create and configure an aggregation table for use in Power BI reports.

Getting ready

To prepare for this recipe, follow these steps:

1. Open Power BI Desktop.
2. Create a DirectQuery query called **Internet Sales** that accesses the **FactInternetSales** table.
3. Create a DirectQuery query called **Customers** that accesses the **DimCustomers** table.
4. Create a DirectQuery query called **Dates** that accesses the **DimDates** table.
5. Add a query called **Sales Agg** using the following code (edit the **Source** line):

```
let
    Source = Sql.Database("localhost\MSSQLSERVERDEV",
"AdventureWorksDW2019"),
    Navigation = Source{[Schema="dbo",Item="FactInternetSales"]}[Data],
    Group =
        Table.Group(Navigation, {"OrderDateKey", "CustomerKey"},
        {{"SalesAmount_Sum", each List.Sum([SalesAmount]), type number},
```

```
            {"UnitPrice_Sum", each List.Sum([UnitPrice]), type number}}),
        ChangeType =
            Table.TransformColumnTypes(Group,
                {{"SalesAmount_Sum", Currency.Type},
                 {"UnitPrice_Sum", Currency.Type}} )
    in
        ChangeType
```

6. Move the **Internet Sales** query to a query group called **Facts**, the **Customers** and **Dates** queries to a query group called **Dimensions**, and the **Sales Agg** query to the **Other Queries** query group.
7. Click **Close & Apply** on the ribbon of the **Home** tab to load the tables to the data model.
8. Create the following **Single-direction**, one-to-many relationships in the model, as shown in *Figure 3.50*.

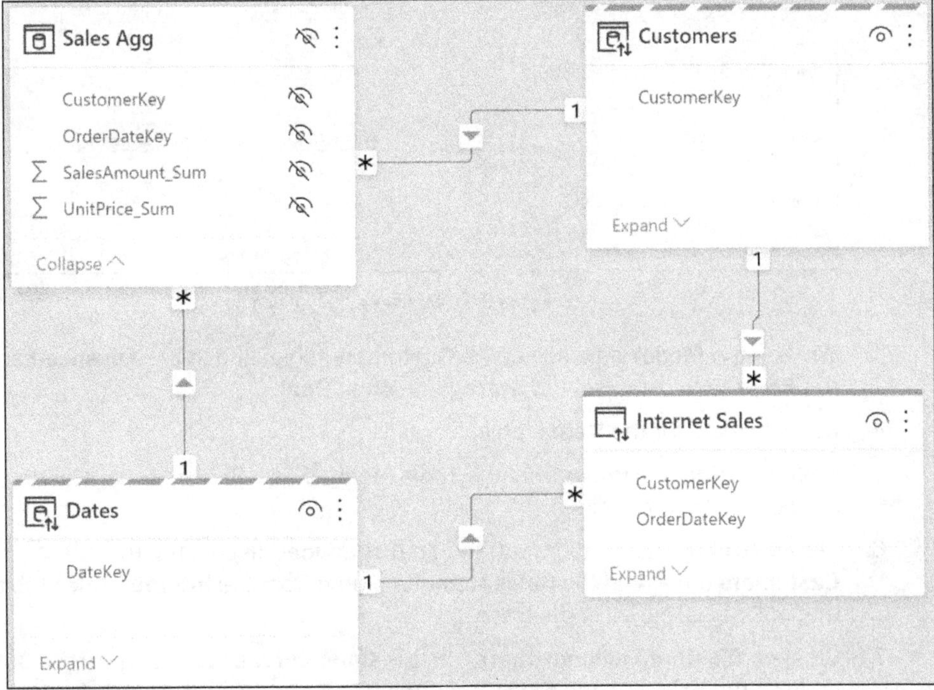

Figure 3.50: Model relationships

Note that you may have to use **Database credentials** for your data source instead of **Windows credentials**. In testing, we experienced problems using **Windows credentials** when attempting to create relationships with the **Sales Agg** table and the dimension tables.

How to do it

To implement this recipe, use the following steps:

1. In the **Model** view, right-click the **Sales Agg** table and choose **Manage aggregations**.
2. Create the aggregations shown below for the **Sales Agg** table and then click on the **Apply all** button.

Figure 3.51: Manage aggregations dialog

3. While in the **Model** view, select the **Customers** table, and in the **Advanced** area of the **Properties** pane, set the **Storage mode** to **Dual**.
4. Repeat *step 3* for the **Dates** table.
5. Open **SQL Server Profiler** from the **Tools** menu of SQL Server Management Studio and run a trace.
6. Create a **Table** visualization with the **EnglishEducation** column from the **Customers** table, and the **SalesAmount** column from the **Internet Sales** table. Note that nothing is logged in the trace.
7. Create a **Clustered column chart** with the **CalendarYear** column from the **Dates** table as the **Axis**, and the **SalesAmount** column from the **Internet Sales** table as **Values**. Again, nothing is logged.

How it works

It is imperative that the core fact table, **Internet Sales**, be set to **DirectQuery** storage mode, as aggregation tables only work with detail tables that are set to **DirectQuery** storage mode. The aggregation table itself, **Sales Agg**, must be set to **Import** storage mode. The two-dimensional tables, **Customers** and **Dates**, that have relationships to both the **Internet Sales** table and the **Sales Agg** table, should be set to **Dual** storage mode so that these tables can operate optimally in either mode. Configuring aggregation for a table automatically hides the table in the data model, as aggregation tables must be hidden.

Relationships must exist between the dimension tables and the aggregation table. This is because the aggregation table is used as a surrogate to the detailed, **DirectQuery** mode fact table when possible, and thus the aggregation table should have the same relationships to dimension tables as the fact table.

It is also important to keep column datatypes in mind when configuring aggregations. This is because the **Manage aggregations** dialog box enforces the rule that the **Detail Column** must have the same datatype as the **Aggregation Column**. The only exception to this rule is for **Summarizations** of **Count** and **Count table rows**. **Count** and **Count table rows** require integer aggregation columns but do not require matching datatypes for the **Detail Column**.

Additional restrictions include chained aggregations, the use of inactive relationships supported by the DAX `USERELATIONSHIP` function, and duplicate aggregations using the same **Summarization**, **Detail Table**, and **Detail Column**. None of those scenarios are supported.

There's more...

In order to operate properly, RLS expressions should filter the detail table as well as the aggregation table. In fact, once aggregations have been set on a table, RLS expressions that only filter the aggregation table and not the associated **Detail Table** are not allowed by the **Manage roles** dialog box.

The **Manage roles** dialog box includes the ability to set **Precedence**. This means that you can have multiple aggregation tables at different granularities, and set these aggregation tables' **Precedence** to allow them to be considered by a single subquery. For example, if the **Products** table was included in this model, you might create an aggregation table for **Product Category** and a separate aggregation table for **Product Subcategory**. You would set the granularity of the aggregation table for **Product Category** to 10, and the granularity of the aggregation table for **Product Subcategory** to 0. Subqueries will consider the aggregation table with the highest granularity first, and if that level of granularity is not sufficient, it will consider other aggregation tables of lower granularity.

See also

- Use aggregations in Power BI Desktop: `http://bit.ly/2Pgckjp`
- Power BI Fast and Furious with Aggregations: `https://bit.ly/3cpReI1`

Conclusion

In this chapter, we explored the primary processes of designing and developing robust data models in Power BI Desktop. Common data modeling challenges, including multiple grains and many-to-many relationships, were shown to be handled relatively easily with standard Power BI features. In addition, examples were provided for adding business logic and definitions developed using the DAX language. Finally, use cases for increasing the value and sustainability of models via metadata settings and advanced features were explored.

4

Authoring Power BI Reports

Power BI reports serve as the basic building blocks for dashboards, data exploration, and content collaboration and distribution in Power BI. Power BI Desktop provides abundant data visualization features and options, enabling the construction of highly targeted, user-friendly reports across devices. As each Power BI Desktop report can contain multiple pages with each page including multiple visuals, a single Power BI report can support multiple use cases, audiences, and business needs. For example, a KPI visual can be pinned to a dashboard in the Power BI Service, while a report page can support detailed, domain-specific analysis. These capabilities compete directly with visualization offerings from competitor analytics platforms and can be further extended with custom visuals and report themes.

The selection and configuration of Power BI visualization features in report design are essential to derive value from the data retrieval and modeling processes covered in *Chapter 2, Accessing and Retrieving Data*, and *Chapter 3, Building a Power BI Data Model*, respectively. In this chapter, we develop and describe the most fundamental report visualizations and design concepts. Additionally, guidance is provided to enhance and control the user experience when interacting with Power BI reports and consuming them on both Windows and mobile devices.

In this chapter, we will cover the following recipes:

- Building Rich and Intuitive Reports
- Filtering at Different Scopes
- Integrating Card Visualizations
- Using Slicers
- Controlling Visual Interactions

- Utilizing Graphical Visualizations
- Creating Table and Matrix visuals
- Enhancing Reports
- Formatting Reports for Publication
- Designing Mobile Layouts
- Creating Paginated Reports

Technical Requirements

The following are required to complete the recipes in this chapter:

- Power BI Desktop and a Power BI service account.
- Tabular Editor.
- SQL Server with the AdventureWorksDW2019 database installed. This database and instructions for installing are available here: `http://bit.ly/2OVQfG7`.
- `CH4_Start.pbix` contains the model used for this chapter and can be downloaded from the following GitHub repository: `https://github.com/PacktPublishing/Microsoft-Power-BI-Cookbook-Second-Edition`.

Building Rich and Intuitive Reports

Power BI Desktop provides the means to design reports that are both highly customized to specific use cases and requirements and aligned with a corporate BI standard. The design and development process for a report should naturally flow from the data modeling process as the measures, relationships, and dimensions from the model are utilized to visualize and analyze business questions. As the purpose and scope of Power BI reports can range widely, from dashboard visualizations to interactive analytical experiences to role-specific detail reporting, it is essential that report authoring features are aligned closely to these distinct use cases.

In this recipe, a report design planning process is shared to bring clarity to the primary design elements of Power BI reports, such as visualization types. Two finished report pages are described with supporting details included in the *How it works* section, and additional report design features and practices are discussed in *There's more...*.

Getting ready

A stakeholder matrix can help structure the report design planning process around the needs of the different parties accessing the model and reports. The stakeholders or business units, such as **Merchandising**, appear on the columns axis and replace the conformed dimensions (that is, **Product** or **Vendor**) that were used in the data warehouse bus matrix described in *Chapter 3, Building a Power BI Data Model*.

	Stakeholders							
BUSINESS PROCESSES	Executive	Sales	Finance	Marketing	Merchandising	eCommerce	Customer Service	Supply Chain
Internet Sales	✓	✓	✓	✓	✓	✓		
Internet Sales Plan	✓	✓	✓	✓	✓	✓	✓	✓
Reseller Sales	✓	✓	✓		✓			
General Ledger	✓		✓					
Inventory			✓	✓	✓	✓		
Customer Surveys	✓	✓	✓	✓		✓	✓	✓
Customer Service Calls			✓				✓	
Shipping			✓		✓			✓

Figure 4.1: Stakeholder matrix

In this example, the data model contains the four highlighted fact tables: **Internet Sales**, **Internet Sales Plan**, **Reseller Sales**, and **General Ledger**. When there can be multiple stakeholders within a given business function with their own unique needs and use cases, these stakeholders can be added as columns to the stakeholder matrix. In Power BI, there are many options for meeting the unique needs of different stakeholders with the same data model and underlying retrieval and data architecture.

How to Build Reports

While report development should be an agile process where feedback is regularly solicited from stakeholders as the report is designed and developed, having a solid planning and design process for a report upfront is extremely beneficial in understanding the scope and requirements of it. A single report should not attempt to address unrelated business questions or meet the needs of highly diverse users such as a corporate financial analyst or a store manager. Multi-scope reports can lead to convoluted user experiences and report-level customization that can be difficult to maintain and scale. The report planning and design process should answer the following five questions:

1. Who will be accessing this report?
2. What are the top priorities of this report in terms of business questions?
3. How will the report be accessed and utilized?

4. What is the velocity of data required, and does this impact the model?
5. Is Power BI the right tool for the report?

Regarding the first of these questions, just like a PowerPoint presentation, report pages should support a single theme and target a specific audience. As per the stakeholder matrix, there are often many disparate users and use cases for a given data model. Consider the following:

- If identified users have highly disparate needs, choose one user role and address the others separately.
- Page-level filtering and row-level security can provide a robust solution for a single team.
- Reports for various teams can be developed quickly if models include the required data and grain.
- Users deeply familiar with the data require less in the way of titles and descriptive text and labels.
- It is recommended to involve the business users or a representative early on in the report design process, and potentially before all elements of the data model are complete. Any initial iterations of the report and feedback can contribute to the design of the final report to be published.

The second question can be addressed as follows: The prioritized business questions directly drive visualization choices, such as line/bar charts and tables. If the trend or fluctuations of measures is the top priority, then line charts, with custom scales and supporting trend and reference lines, may be chosen. If precise individual data points are required, either as standalone numbers or in relation to one or two dimensions, then cards, KPIs, and tables or matrices should be used. The choice of visuals and the visuals' sizes, colors, and positioning on the canvas relative to other visuals should not be an arbitrary decision or guess. Consider the following:

- Establish the starting point for the analysis, including measures and grain such as weekly sales.
- Stakeholders often have many related questions and need to navigate the model quickly.
- Additional drilling and filtering features can be added to a report's starting point.
- Standard line, bar/column, and scatter chart visualizations have natural advantages in terms of visual perception and user comprehension. Other visuals should be utilized for their specific use cases and strengths, such as a Funnel visualization for stages of a process and a Waterfall visualization for the contributions of dimension values to an overall total.

How will the report be accessed and utilized? How a report will be accessed and how business users desire to interact with the report are key questions that should be answered before beginning report development. Report access and interactivity are key components that a report designer should understand in order to ensure that the report contains the proper elements, views, filters, and measures. Consider the following:

- Will users only view the report, or is the report a starting point for further analysis?
- If there is no interaction or limited interaction desired, plan to embed conditional logic and exceptions in the report.
- If there is high interaction, plan to use hierarchies, tooltips, and slicers to enable data exploration.
- How does the report relate to existing dashboards?
- Identify the components of the report that will contribute to an existing dashboard.
- If creating a new dashboard based on the report, identify the tiles and interaction.
- Will the report only be accessed via the web browser, or will mobile devices be used regularly?
- If mobile consumption is expected, reports can be designed to optimize this experience.
- Power BI dashboards can also be optimized for phone layout in the Power BI service.

What is the velocity of data required, and does this impact the model? The velocity of data required can impact the chosen storage mode, whether that is Import, DirectQuery, or Dual mode, or even streaming datasets. An Import mode model may work fine for business users that only need data to be refreshed once or twice a day, but business users with more immediate velocity may be better served by a DirectQuery model. Other factors can also influence the need to revise a data model, including:

- If a report requirement is systemic to all reports for a stakeholder group, consider revising the model.
- If complex report-level customization is required, or if the performance is poor, consider revising the model.
- These revisions often include new logical attributes or new DAX measures.

Finally, it's critical to understand that Power BI reports created in Power BI Desktop are not appropriate for every report type. Report requirements such as multi-page printing, email subscriptions with data attached in various file formats, and pixel-perfect formatting control are much more closely aligned with paginated reports created in Power BI Report Builder. Similarly, financial statement and accounting reports with custom layouts involving cell-level control and formatting are generally more suited for Excel. Thankfully these other two report types are fully supported in Power BI such that solutions can be developed that include all three distinct report types.

How it works

In this example, the stakeholder is the European Sales Territory Group, comprised of France, Germany, and the United Kingdom. The planning process revealed two primary types of users. The first type of user is the Europe Sales Group manager, who manages the entire sales territory. The second type of user is those managers that are responsible for the individual countries.

The top priorities identified are viewing and analyzing Internet Sales versus Plan, Reseller Sales, and sales margins at the monthly grain—by country and by product breakdowns in relation to category, subcategory, and model. The country managers desire a more granular geographic data at the state/province, city, and postal code levels. The overall organization operates on a fiscal calendar for accounting purposes, but the business stakeholders desire that the report uses calendar months when reporting data, instead of fiscal months. The business is also interested in comparing customers counts with internet sales over time.

With regard to how the reports will be accessed and utilized, the Europe Sales Group Manager needs key facts, figures, and trends for the entire European Sales Territory; the manager is not expected to interact heavily with the report, but should still have the opportunity to drill into the data if desired. The Europe Sales Group Manager desires a mobile report that they can view on their phones, since this individual is often traveling between countries and so is constantly mobile. The individual country managers desire the ability to analyze their own data in a highly interactive manner. Country-level managers are also accountable for the sales plan, but are interested in greater self-service flexibility and require some detailed reporting in tabular formats to expose specific values for several measures. Country managers are expected to access the report from their desktops in a web browser.

In terms of velocity, both Sales Group managers and country managers find it acceptable if the data is refreshed once or twice per day, given that the primary granularity of interest is monthly data. All parties also agree that using US English names, descriptions, and currency best meets the needs of the group. Given the requirements identified in the planning process, it is determined that the model must contain fact tables for Internet Sales, Reseller Sales, General Ledger, and Internet Sales Plan. In addition, the following dimensions are required: Products, Accounts, Customers with geographic data, Dates, Departments, Organizations, Employees, Resellers, Promotions, and Sales Territories. No single model currently contains all the information desired, and so it is determined that a new model will be developed.

With the gathering of requirements completed, it is determined that the report will consist of two to four primary report pages, one page per country (or a single drill-through country page), and one page for the Europe Sales Group Manager. All the report pages will include the same four priority measures of Monthly Internet Sales, Monthly Internet Margin %, Monthly Reseller Sales, and Monthly Reseller Margin % in the top left, as well as an **Internet Sales to Plan** chart displayed by calendar year and month. For the measures that do not have a target or goal (plan), a trailing 6-month average measure is used.

Considering performance and usability, it is determined to limit the number of visuals per page to four or five and to avoid dense "data extract or dump" visuals. This limit does not apply to Cards, Gauges, and KPI visualizations. DAX queries are generated for report visuals, and the queries associated with dense visuals such as tables or matrices with many rows and columns are much slower than Cards and KPI visuals. Additionally, report pages with many visuals can appear crowded and be complex to use. Additionally, opportunities will be investigated to apply simple filters (**Current Year** or **Prior Year**) at the report and page levels to further aid performance. The report will be filtered by Europe at the report level and by the individual countries at the page level for these particular pages.

A reliable predictor of a report's effectiveness is the ratio of business insights (measures, context, or analysis) to the user effort required to consume the information. Ideally, a report will offer out-of-the-box analytics that require nothing from the user beyond access and a basic knowledge of the terminology and domain. The more a user is required to scroll, click, and avoid unnecessary colors or data elements, the less effective the report will be.

After planning and design, mock-ups of the report pages are created, shown to users, and refined.

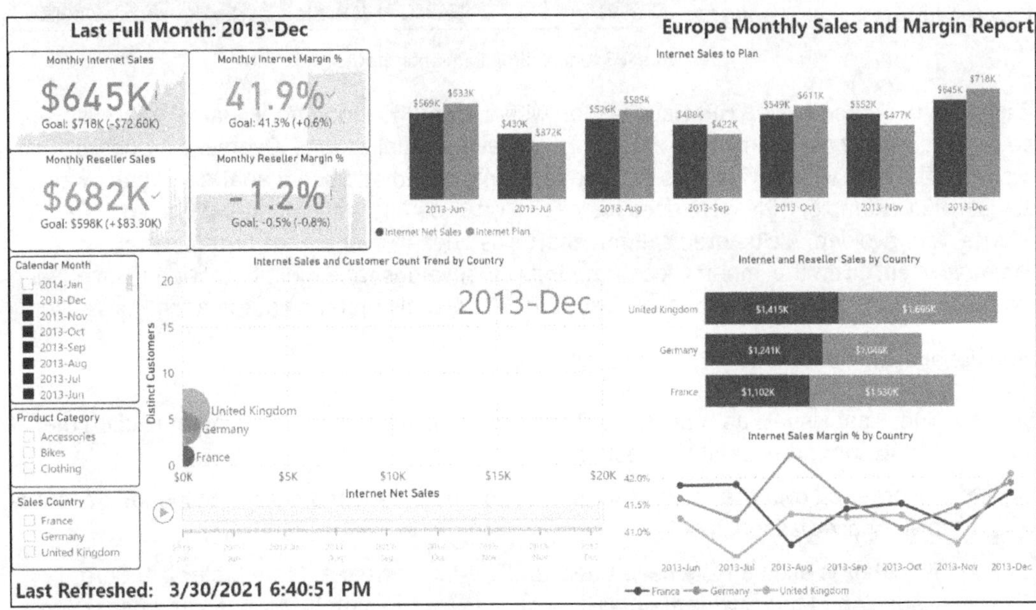

Figure 4.2: Europe Monthly Sales and Margin Report page

Figure 4.2 is a mock-up of a report at a regional level, while *Figure 4.3* displays similar information at the country level.

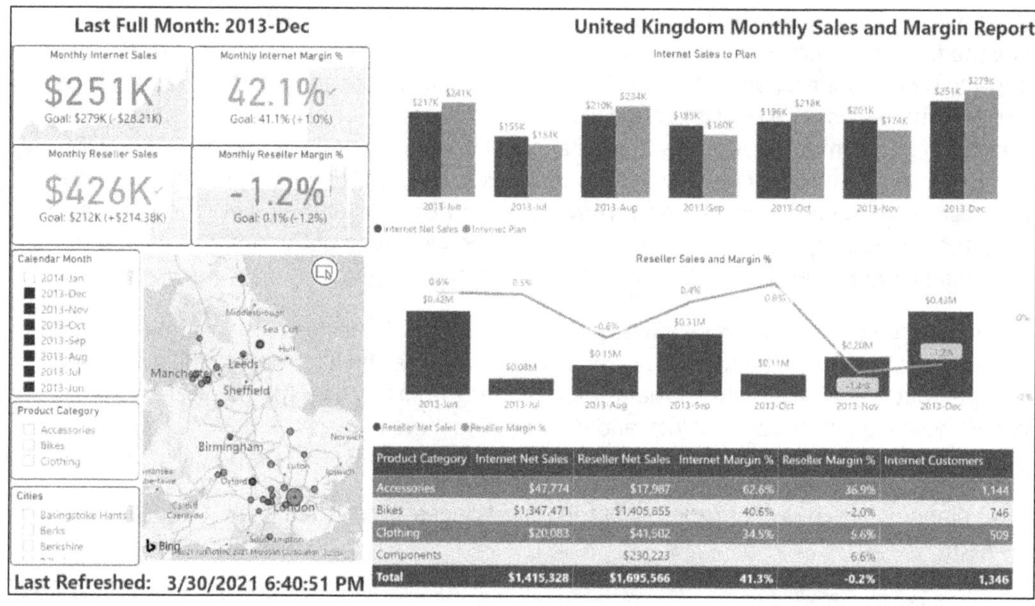

Figure 4.3: United Kingdom report page

Based on user feedback, a KPI visualization with a monthly trend and a goal measure is used to provide greater context compared to Card or Gauge visualizations. Overall, a standard visualization type with advantages in visual perception and additional analysis context was chosen. For example, KPIs were used instead of Card visuals; gauges, treemaps, and pie charts were avoided. A clustered column chart was chosen over a line chart for **Internet Sales to Plan**, given the importance of the individual values for each month. At a glance, each country report page also offers values with the KPIs visuals updating automatically.

Additional design decisions include the following:

- The slicer visuals as well as the **Play** axis on the scatter chart are organized on the left to support user filter selections.
- By hovering over the bubbles in the map or the bars in the chart, additional measures are exposed as tooltips.
- A textbox is used for the page titles, and the last refreshed date footer is a Card visual. An M query with the `DateTime.LocalNow` function is retrieved and passed to a DAX measure, returning text.
- The chart titles are customized, and the *y*-axis is removed when possible.

More details on the individual report components used in this example are contained within other recipes in this chapter.

There's more...

Similar to the simple—yet important—details with data modeling shared in *Chapter 3, Building a Power BI Data Model*, a number of design practices significantly improve the value and user adoption of Power BI reports:

- **Minimalism**: Any report element that is not strictly required for comprehension should be removed. Examples include images, redundant chart axes, verbose text, and unnecessary data legends.
- **Efficient visuals**: Leverage visuals and features that provide additional insights with the same amount of space; examples include KPI and combination chart visuals, tooltips, trend lines, and color saturation.
- **Meaningful colors**: Colors should be used to convey meaning, such as high or low variances to a target or measure. Use colors selectively and avoid overwhelming or distracting users with color variety or density.
- **Organized**: Report visuals should be aligned, distributed evenly, and situated near related visuals. The most important visuals should be near the top-left corner of the canvas, and white space should separate visuals.
- **Consistent**: Layout and formatting choices, such as visual placement, fonts, and text alignment should be consistent. For example, slicer visuals should always be placed on the left or top of the visual.

Regarding consistency, Power BI supports report themes that include a standard color palette, fonts, font sizes, and other metadata elements that control the defaults for reports and visualizations. Nearly every aspect of the default settings for a Power BI report can be controlled, including whether axis titles are shown, label orientation, legend markers, and essentially anything that appears in the **Format** pane for pages and visualizations.

Many organizations will have a standard report theme, or even standard report layouts. Often, these themes reflect the corporate brand and identity. In this example, a report theme is applied to a report such that users with color vision deficiency can comprehend it clearly:

- Download the **Color Blind Friendly** theme from the report theme gallery `https://aka.ms/pbithemes`. Use the `ColorblindSafe-Longer.json` file.
- Open `CH4_Start.pbix` in Power BI Desktop and save this file as `CH4_R1.pbix`.

In the ribbon of the **View** tab, click the drop-down arrow in the **Themes** area and choose **Browse for themes**:

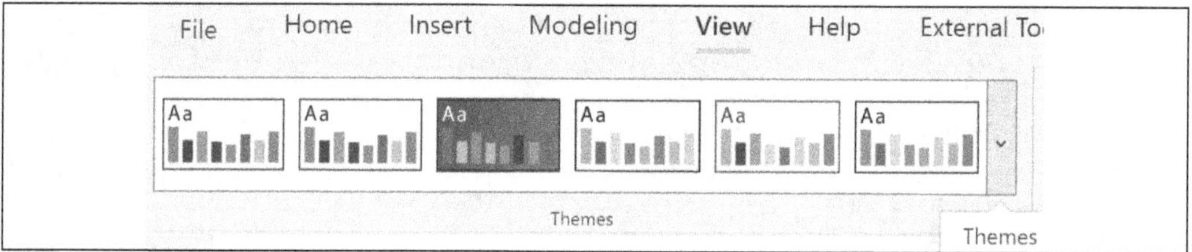

Figure 4.4: Report Themes

Browse to the downloaded JSON file, select it, and click **Open**. A message will appear, stating that the theme was imported successfully. Theme settings will be applied to the report. The colors available for formatting visuals now reflect the theme's colors. Save `CH4_R1.pbix`.

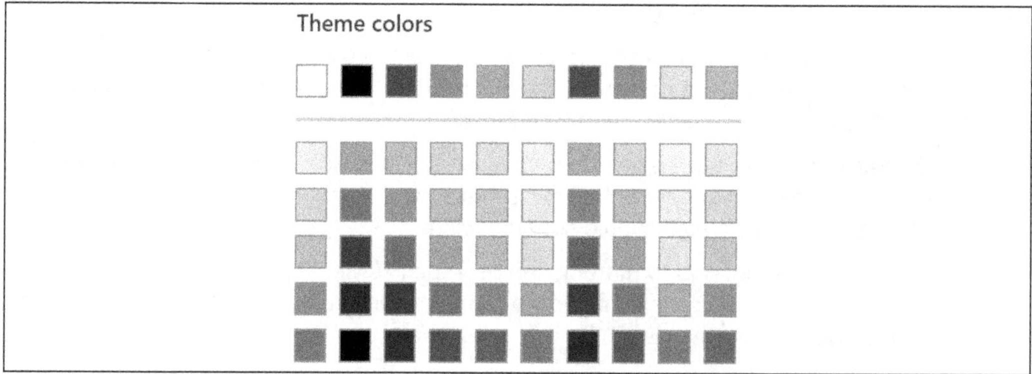

Figure 4.5: Report Theme colors applied to Formatting Pane of Power BI Report

Themes cannot be applied in the Power BI service, and some custom visuals do not apply report themes. Additionally, report themes do not impact the colors of images and do not override any custom color applied to a specific data point in a visual. It is important to apply themes early when developing reports to avoid situations where hours of formatting are suddenly undone after applying a theme!

Each report theme JSON file has a structure of elements of color code mapping consistent with that shown in *Figure 4.6*.

```
"name": "ColorblindSafe-Longer",
"dataColors": ["#074650", "#009292", "#fe6db6", "#feb5da", "#480091", "#b66dff", "#b5dafe", "#6db6ff", "#914800", "#23fd23"],
"background":"#FFFFFF",
"foreground": "#074650",
"tableAccent": "#fe6db6"
```

Figure 4.6: Color Blind Report Theme JSON file structure

Only the **Name** field is required in the JSON file. Any number of distinct codes can be entered in the `dataColors` field.

See also

- Visualizations in Power BI reports: `http://bit.ly/2poUeMv`
- Tips For Power BI Report Design – Best Practices: `http://bit.ly/3fmfXPf`
- Power BI Best Practices Guide: `http://bit.ly/3cxCs29`
- Power BI Community Themes Gallery: `https://aka.ms/pbithemes`
- Use report themes in Power BI Desktop: `http://bit.ly/31vBixz`
- Theme generator: `https://themes.powerbi.tips/`

Filtering at Different Scopes

Filters can be configured against Power BI reports at each level of the report architecture, including the entire report, the report page, and the individual visual. As report filters are configured at design time and not exposed on the canvas like slicers, filters provide a powerful, efficient method of customizing elements of reports to specific needs. Report- and page-level filters that align with the user or team accessing the report, or with specific entities to be analyzed, deliver immediate focus and a certain degree of organization. For example, a report page built for one product category can be duplicated for other product category pages, with each page containing a different page-level filter. Visual-level filters deliver greater flexibility, as complex filtering conditions, including measures, can be defined in addition to any report- and page-level filters.

In this recipe, examples are provided of implementing filters at the three different scopes. The **Top N** visual-level filter condition is demonstrated in this section, and an example of the DAX queries generated by the filter types is shared in *How it works.*

Getting ready

To prepare for this recipe, follow these steps:

1. Open the `CH4_R1.pbix` file and save it as `CH4_R2.pbix`.
2. Rename **Page 1** to `Europe` by right-clicking the page tab and choosing **Rename Page**:

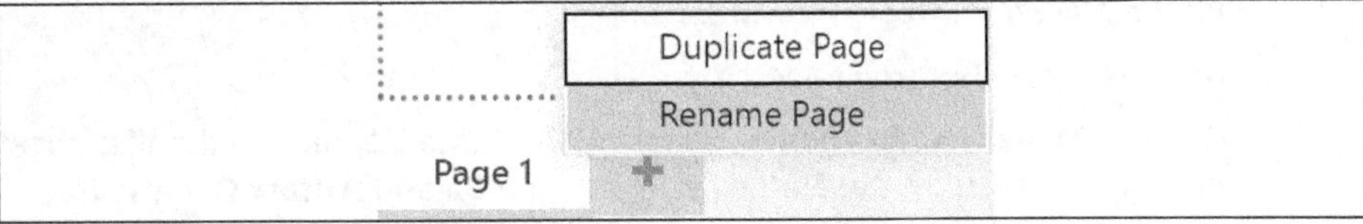

Figure 4.7: Page renaming and creation

3. Use the **+** icon to create four additional report pages named **France**, **Germany** and **United Kingdom**, and **Scratch**:

Figure 4.8: Report pages

4. Save your work.

How to Filter at Different Scopes

To implement this recipe, use the following steps:

1. Switch to the **Europe** page.
2. In the **Fields** pane, drag the **Sales Territory Group** column from the **Sales Territories** table to the **Filters on all pages** area in the **Filters** pane.
3. Select **Europe** using **Basic filtering**.

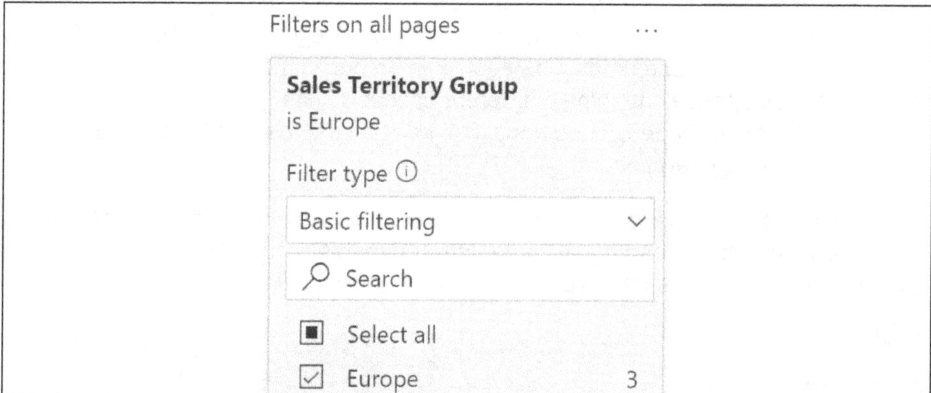

Figure 4.9: Report-level filter for European Sales and Margin Monthly Report

4. Similarly, on the country pages for **France**, **Germany**, and **United Kingdom**, drag the **Sales Territory Country** column from the **Sales Territories** table in the **Fields** pane to the **Filters on this page area** in the **Filters** pane, and select the respective country for the page from **Basic filtering**.
5. Now select the **Scratch** page.
6. Create a **Table visualization** by choosing the **Table visual** from the **Visualizations** pane, and then from the **Fields** pane, add the **Sales Territory Country** from the **Sales Territories** table and the **Internet Gross Sales** measure from the **Internet Sales** table.

7. Select the **Table visualization**, and in the **Filters** pane, expand the **Internet Gross Sales** area in the **Filters on this visual** section.
8. Select **is greater than** from the drop-down under **Show items when the value**, and in the field below the drop-down type `3000000`.
9. Click **Apply filter** to apply the filter to the visual.

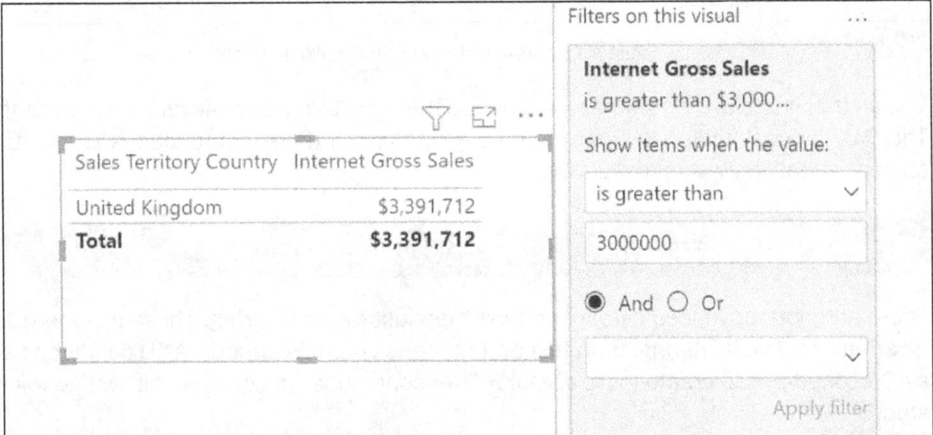

Figure 4.10: Visual-level filter

How it works

Report-level filters affect all pages in a report; thus, when filters are applied to the **Filters on all pages** area of the **Filters** pane, all visuals on all pages of the report respect this filter if a relationship to the dimension exists in the model and if DAX does not override the filter. For the report described in the previous recipe, it is determined that the European team does not need to view other sales groups or countries, and thus we filtered the entire report (all pages) for a **Sales Territory Group** of **Europe**. Similarly, page-level filters only affect the visuals on the page to which they are applied. Thus, we filtered each country page to the appropriate **Sales Territory Country**.

Report- and page-level filters are most commonly implemented at different levels of a dimension hierarchy that is relatively static and has few unique values, such as the example in this recipe. Date range filters should generally be applied either in the data retrieval queries or the report canvas, with visuals such as the date slicer. As these filters are applied to all visuals in the report or page, respectively, try to avoid filters against high-cardinality columns such as **ProductKey** or **Sales Order Number**. DAX measures cannot be used to define report- and page-level filters.

Visual-level filters can be based on both measures and columns from the data model. These measures and columns can be present in the visualization or not present.

The DAX queries created by Power BI reveal how the different layers of filters are implemented. Using DAX Studio, we can view the DAX variables used to store the report- and page-level filters (as well as slicer selections):

```
DEFINE
  VAR __DS0FilterTable =
    TREATAS({"Europe"}, 'Sales Territories'[Sales Territory Group])
```

Figure 4.11: DAX report-level filter variable in DAX Studio

Visual-level filters are also variables, but use the report- and page-level variables as inputs. The DAX queries created by Power BI take advantage of the latest functions and features, such as variables, `VAR`, and `TREATAS`.

There's more...

There are more advanced filtering options than just **Basic filtering**. These include **Advanced filtering** and **Top N** filtering. Both text and numeric columns support AND conditions as well as OR conditions to create more complex filter conditions. To see how this works, follow these steps:

1. Select the **Table visualization** created on the **Scratch** page.
2. In the **Filters** pane, clear the visual-level filter from **Internet Gross Sales**.
3. Expand the **Sales Territory Country** area in the **Filters on this visual** section and switch the **Filter type** to **Advanced filtering**.
4. Select **contains** from the **Show item when the value** drop-down, type the letter `a` in the field below, and then click **Apply filter**. The **United Kingdom** disappears from the **Table** visualization.
5. Clear this filter and change the **Filter type** to **Top N**.
6. Under **Show items**, choose **Top** and type the number `2`.
7. Drag the **Reseller Net Sales** measure from the **Reseller Sales** table to the **By value** area and click **Apply filter**. **Germany** now disappears from the table.

If complex filtering conditions are required, or if filters are needed against columns with many distinct values (for example, **Sales Order Number**), it may be beneficial to account for this logic in the data retrieval or model, thus simplifying the DAX queries generated.

Additionally, report-, page-, and visual-level filters can be overridden with DAX measures. To see how this works, create the following measure in the Sales Territories table:

```
Count Countries = COUNTROWS(ALL('Sales Territories'))
```

Use a **Card visualization** on the **Scratch** page to display this new measure and observe that the measure's value is **11**. Regardless of the report-, page-, and visual-level filters applied, this measure will always have a value of **11**. The DAX function `ALL` overrides the filters being applied to the **Sales Territories** table.

See also

- Filters and highlighting in Power BI reports: `http://bit.ly/39y0msh`
- Types of filters in Power BI reports: `http://bit.ly/3sBkMrQ`

Integrating Card visualizations

Card and Multi-row Card visualizations are often positioned at the top and left sections of report pages, given the importance of individual measures and small sets of measures. Although less graphically powerful and interactive than other visuals, cards are also the most common tiles pinned to Power BI dashboards and are also used frequently in phone layouts for mobile consumption. A common practice in report design is to start with a few high-level measures represented as card or KPI visuals and build additional chart and Table visuals around these.

This recipe demonstrates how to use card, Multi-row card, KPI, and Gauge visualizations—as well as text boxes.

Getting ready

To prepare for this recipe, follow these steps:

1. Open the **CH4_R2.pbix** file and save it as `CH4_R3.pbix`.
2. Switch to the **Scratch** page, and use *Ctrl-A* then *Delete* to remove any visuals.
3. Check the **Filters** pane and ensure that only the **Europe** filter is active.

How to Integrate Card visualizations

To implement this recipe, carry out the following steps:

1. Select the **Europe** page.
2. Create a **Card visualization** using the **Visualizations** pane and then in the **Fields** list select the **Last Full Month** measure from the **Calculations** table.

3. In the **Format** pane, switch the **Category** and **Background** sliders to **Off**.

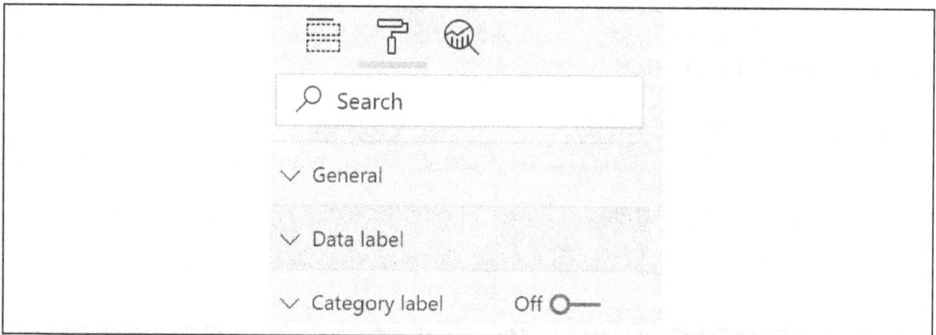

Figure 4.12: Format pane

4. Expand the **Data label** section, set the **Text size** to **18** and the **Font family** to **Segoe (Bold)**.
5. Expand the **General** section and set the **X Position** to **0**, **Y Position** to **0**, **Width** to **448**, and **Height** to **48**. It is generally considered better to set the **Width** and **Height** first, then the **X Position** and **Y Position**.
6. Click a blank area of the page canvas and repeat steps *2*, *3*, and *4* to create another **Card visualization** that displays the **Date Last Refreshed** measure; in the **General** section set the **X Position** to **168**, **Y Position** to **680**, **Width** to **305**, and **Height** to **36**.
7. Click a blank area of the page canvas, select **Text box** in the ribbon of the **Insert** tab, and type `Europe Monthly Sales and Margin Report`.
8. Use *Ctrl-A* to select all of the text and then change the font to **Segoe (Bold)**, set the text size to **18**, and right-justify the text.

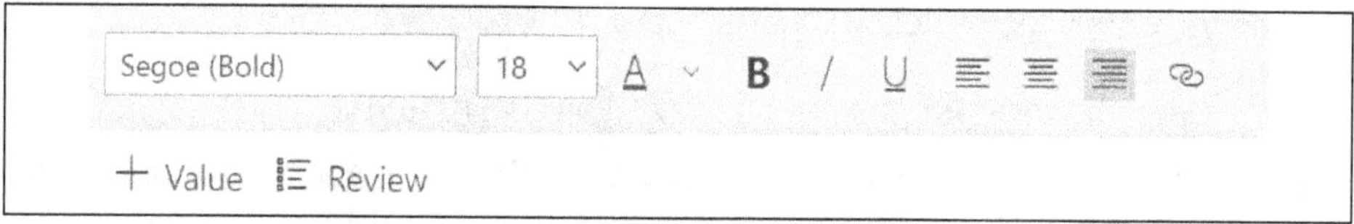

Figure 4.13: Settings to select when formatting

9. In the **Format text box** pane, switch the **Background** slider to **Off**, and in the **General** section set the **X Position** to **624**, **Y Position** to **0**, **Width** to **656**, and **Height** to **48**.
10. Select the **Text box** element just created and use *Ctrl-C* and then *Ctrl-V* to copy and paste the visual on the page.
11. Reposition the new **Text box** element, replace the text with **Last Refreshed:** and left-justify the text.
12. In the **General** section of the **Format text box** pane, set the **X Position** to **0**, **Y Position** to **675**, **Width** to **190**, and **Height** to **45**.

13. Click a blank area of the canvas, and from the **Visualizations** pane select the KPI visualization.
14. From the **Fields** list, expand the **Internet Sales** Table and select the **Internet Monthly Net Sales** measure as the **Indicator**, and the **Internet Monthly Sales Goal** measure as the **Target goals**. From the **Dates** table, use the **Year Month** column as the **Trend axis**.
15. Format the KPI visual just created by expanding the **Title** section, renaming the **Title** to **Monthly Internet Sales** and center-aligning the **Title**.
16. In the **Indicator** section, set the **Display units** to **Thousands**, the **Value decimal places** to **0**, and the **Text size** to **40**.
17. In the **General** section, set the **X Position** to **0**, **Y Position** to **48**, **Width** to **225**, and **Height** to **122**.
18. Turn the **Border** slider to **On**, expand the **Border** section, and set the **Radius** to **5**.
19. In the **Goals** section, change the **Label** from **Percent** to **Value**.

Figure 4.14: KPI visualization

20. Select the KPI visualization and use *Ctrl-C* and then *Ctrl-V* to copy and paste the visual.
21. Reposition the new KPI visual on the page and replace the **Indicator** and **Target goals** with the **Internet Monthly Margin %** and **Internet Monthly Margin % Goal** measures from the **Internet Sales** table, respectively.
22. Format this new KPI visualization by changing **Title** to **Monthly Internet Margin %**, the **Indicator Display units** to **Auto**, and in the **General** section set the **X Position** to **224** and the **Y Position** to **48**.
23. Hold down the *Ctrl* key and use your mouse to select both KPI visuals.
24. Use *Ctrl-C* and *Ctrl-V* to copy and paste both visuals and then reposition the visuals on the page.
25. For the **Monthly Internet Sales** visual, replace the **Indicator** and **Target goals** with the **Reseller Monthly Net Sales** and **Reseller Monthly Sales Goal** measures from the **Reseller Sales** table, respectively.
26. Format this new KPI visualization by changing **Title** to **Monthly Reseller Sales** and in the **General** section set the **X Position** to **0** and the **Y Position** to **168**.

27. For the **Monthly Internet Margin** % visual, replace the **Indicator** and **Target goals** with the **Reseller Monthly Margin** % and **Reseller Monthly Margin** % **Goal** measures from the **Reseller Sales** table, respectively.
28. Format this new KPI visualization by changing **Title** to **Monthly Reseller Margin** % and in the **General** section set the **X Position** to **224** and the **Y Position** to **168**.
29. Click a blank area of the page canvas, then use *Ctrl-A* and *Ctrl-C* to select and copy all visualizations on the **Europe** page.
30. Switch to the **France** page, use *Ctrl-V* to paste all of the visuals, and edit the **Text box** in the upper right to read **France** instead of **Europe**.
31. Repeat *step 30* for the **Germany** and **United Kingdom** pages.
32. Save your work.

How it works

To integrate Card visualizations most effectively, identify the following two items:

1. Which measures does the user need to have maximum visibility to (such as all devices, reports, and dashboards)?
2. Which measures are available or can be created to serve as a target or goal to compare these measures to?

Numbers without well-defined targets nor any trending indicators, such as standard Card visualizations, are simply less valuable than KPIs that provide this additional context. However, KPI visualizations require both an **Indicator** and a **Trend axis**. In addition, goal and target measures are one of the main benefits of integrating **Plan** and **Budget** fact tables into data models. If this integration is not an option, a historical average of the indicator measure such as the trailing three or six months can be used as the KPI's target goal.

The data model used in this recipe actually does both. The **Internet Sales Plan** table (hidden in **Report** view) has internet sales plan numbers broken down by region, country, year, month, and product subcategory. This fact table is used for the **Internet Monthly Sales Goal** measure. This measure looks at the **Today** measure in the **Dates** Table and determines the last fully completed month from **Today**. Because we are dealing with the **AdventureWorksDW2019** database where data is only posted until early 2014, we have set the **Today** measure to be **1/28/2014**. In a real-world scenario, the **Today** measure would be set to be equal to the DAX `TODAY` function. The other goal measures are calculated using an average of the previous six months, after the last fully completed month. The measure that calculates this date is the **6 Months Ago** measure in the **Dates** table.

Similarly, the target measures calculate their values for the most current, complete month, in this case December 2013. Alternatively, DAX measures could have been created that factored in the percentage of days completed in the month and applied that percentage to the target and goal measures.

While the KPI visualization should be preferred when displaying numeric values, the Card visualization can also be used quite effectively to display dynamic text data, such as the **Date Last Refreshed** column and **Last Refreshed** measure. The formula for the **Last Refreshed** measure is the following:

```
Last Full Month = "Last Full Month: " & FORMAT(EOMONTH([Today],-1),"yyyy-mmm")
```

The **Date Last Refreshed** column was created using the following Power Query query:

```
let Source = #table(type table[Date Last Refreshed=datetime], {{DateTime.
LocalNow()}}) in Source
```

Static text information can be displayed using a simple **Text box** element, such as the report/page title in the upper right and **Last Refreshed:** in the lower left. However, text boxes can also be made dynamic via Q&A functionality, accessed in the **Value** and **Review** dialogs of the **Text box** formatting dialog.

There's more...

Two additional card- and KPI-style visualizations are available in Power BI Desktop's default visualization library: the **Multi-row card** and **Gauge** visualizations. Multi-row cards are best organized around a common dimension and measure and are often placed to the right of **KPI** or **Gauge** visuals as supplemental details. To see **Multi-row Card** visualizations in action, follow these steps:

1. Switch to the **Scratch** page.
2. Select the **Multi-row Card visualization** from the **Visualizations** pane and place the **Internet Customer Count France**, **Internet Customer Count Germany**, and **Internet Customer Count United Kingdom** measures from the **Internet Sales** table in the **Fields** field of the visualization.

1,810	1,780	1,913
Internet Customer Count France	Internet Customer Count Germany	Internet Customer Count United Kingdom

Figure 4.15: Multi-row Card visualization

Power BI Desktop also includes a **Gauge** visualization that is a popular alternative to **Card** and **KPI** visualizations for dashboards. To see the **Gauge** visualization in action, follow these steps:

1. Copy the **Monthly Internet Sales** KPI visualization from the **Europe** page and paste it onto the **Scratch** page.
2. With the KPI visual selected, click the **Gauge** visualization in the **Visualizations** pane to convert the KPI visualization to a **Gauge** visualization.

3. Set the **Value** to the **Internet Monthly Net Sales** measure and the **Target value** to the **Internet Monthly Sales Goal** measure.

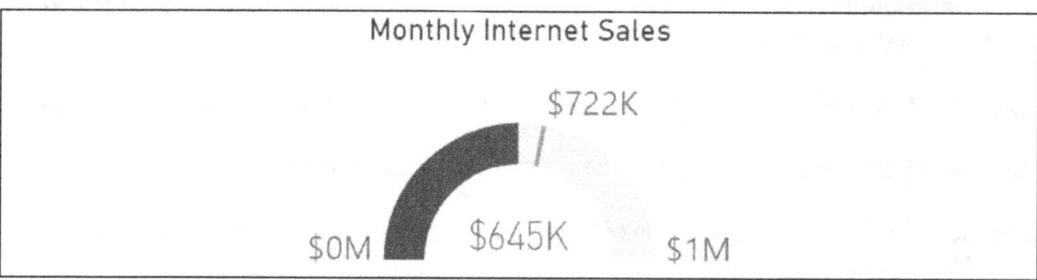

Figure 4.16: Gauge visualization comparing two measures (Value to Target value)

See also

- **Key Performance Indicator** (**KPI**) visuals: `http://bit.ly/3rFPxe7`
- Radial Gauge charts in Power BI: `http://bit.ly/2PgtTjv`
- Card visualizations (big number tiles): `http://bit.ly/3uaMPib`
- Copy and paste a visualization in Power BI: `http://bit.ly/39vECNL`
- Get started formatting Power BI visualizations: `http://bit.ly/3sGqzwm`

Using Slicers

Slicer visuals are the primary means for users to apply filter selections to other visuals of a report page, and thus their implementation greatly affects usability and analytical flexibility. Although user interaction with other visuals also applies cross-filtering to other visuals, slicers provide the fastest and most intuitive method to define specific filtering criteria, such as three specific months and two product categories. Slicer visuals also have unique formatting options for defining the selection behavior, including a **Select All** option.

An alternative to slicers is the use of the Filter pane. While perhaps not as obvious to end users and requiring specific training, the use of the Filter pane as opposed to slicers does provide the benefit of preserving space on the Canvas. However, while the Filter pane can provide some of the basic usage scenarios common to slicers, slicers provide much greater flexibility in terms of interactions with different visuals on a page, synchronization of slicers across specific pages, and the layout and position of filtering elements relative to other visuals.

In this recipe, we look at the primary use cases for slicers and the report design considerations, including selection properties and formatting options. The slicer filter configurations available for **Date** data types are also reviewed, and additional details on text search and alternative slicer visuals are provided.

Getting ready

To prepare for this recipe, follow these steps:

1. Open the `CH4_R3.pbix` file and save the file as `CH4_R4.pbix`.
2. Switch to the **Scratch** page and use *Ctrl-A* and then *Delete* to remove any visuals.
3. Check the **Filters** pane and ensure that only the **Europe** filter is active.

How to Use Slicers

To implement this recipe, use the following steps:

1. Select the **Europe** page.
2. Create a **Slicer** visualization using the **Visualizations** pane, and then in the **Fields** list select the **Year Month** column from the **Dates** table.
3. With the slicer selected, use the ellipses (**...**) to change the sorting to **Sort descending**.

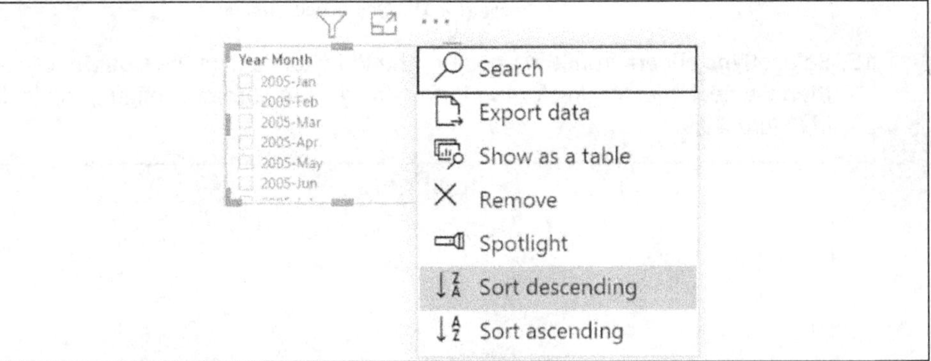

Figure 4.17: Slicer options

4. In the **Format** pane, switch the **Slicer header** to **Off**, the **Title** to **On**, and change the **Title** to **Calendar Month**.
5. In the **Format** pane, switch **Border** to **On** and set the **Radius** to **5**; in the **General** section, set the **X Position** to **0**, **Y Position** to **295**, **Width** to **160**, and **Height** to **178**.
6. Create a second slicer for the **Product Category** column in the **Products** table.
7. Right-click the **(Blank)** option in the **Slicer** and choose **Exclude**. Repeat this for **Components**.
8. In the **Format** pane, switch the **Slicer header** to **Off**, the **Title** to **On**, and change the **Title** to **Product Category**.

9. Also, in the **Format** pane, switch **Border** to **On** and set the **Radius** to **5**; in the **General** section, set the **X Position** to **0**, **Y Position** to **479**, **Width** to **160**, and **Height** to **95**.
10. Use *Ctrl-C* and then *Ctrl-V* to copy and paste the **Product Category** slicer.
11. Reposition the new slicer on the page, replace the slicer's **Field** with the **Sales Territory Country** column from the **Sales Territories** table, and edit the slicer's **Title** to **Country**.
12. Edit the **Country** slicer's **General** settings to set the **X Position** to **0**, **Y Position** to **580**, **Width** to **160**, and **Height** to **94**.
13. Select the three slicers and use *Ctrl-C* to copy.
14. Switch to the **France** page, use *Ctrl-V* to paste the slicers, and at the **Sync visuals** prompt select **Sync**.

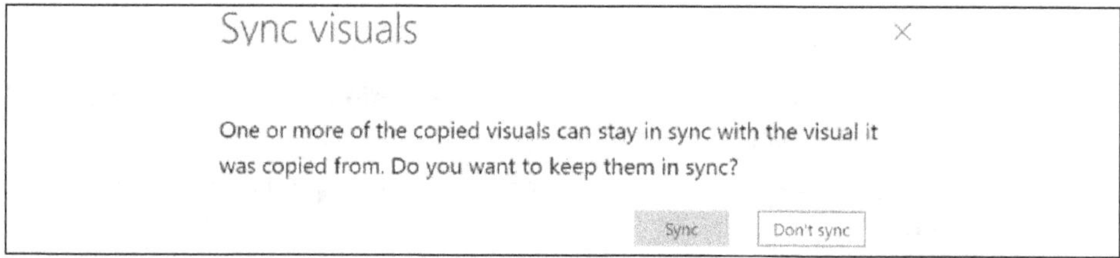

Figure 4.18: Sync visuals prompt

15. Select **Sync slicers** from the ribbon of the **View** tab, select the **Country** slicer, and then uncheck the syncing for the **France** page. The correct configuration is displayed in *Figure 4.19*.

Figure 4.19: Sync slicer controls

16. Close the **Sync slicers** pane, replace the **Country** slicer's **Field** with the **State/Province** column from the **Customers** table, and edit the **Title** to be **Regions**.
17. Copy the **Calendar Month** and **Product Category** slicers to the **Germany** and **United Kingdom** pages, choosing to **Sync** both times.
18. Copy the **Regions** slicer from the **France** page to the **Germany** and **United Kingdom** pages, but this time choose **Don't sync** in both instances.

19. On the **Germany** page, change the **Regions** slicer's **Title** to **States**.
20. On the **United Kingdom** page, replace the **Regions** slicer's **Field** with the **City** column from the **Customers** table, and change the **Title** to **Cities**.
21. On the **Europe** page, select the following values in the **Calendar Month** slicer: **2013-Dec**, **2013-Nov**, **2013-Oct**, **2013-Sept**, **2013-Aug**, and **2013-Jul**.
22. When switching to other pages, the **Calendar Month** slicer on those pages also has those selections.
23. Save your work.

How it works

Slicers are important Power BI visuals, and so careful thought should be given when identifying slicer column(s). Typically, slicer columns are parent-level dimensions such as year or region with few individual values. Choosing a column with few values allows these items to be exposed on the canvas as a list, instead of using a drop-down. Using too many slicers, or slicers with too many distinct values, detracts from the usability of report pages. Without significant DAX customization to interpret filter selections, users can be uncertain as to what filters have been applied. Measures cannot be used in slicers, but slicers support the use of hierarchies and ad hoc hierarchies in their **Field** area.

It is recommended to position slicers to the left of all other visuals on the page. Format the slicer visuals with borders and/or background colors to make the slicers stand out on the page. With regards to using the **Slicer header** or the **Title**, pick one of the two and be consistent for all slicers on the page. The **Slicer header** provides a **Clear selections** option (the eraser icon), as well as allowing you to switch a slicer from **List** to **Drop-down**, and vice versa.

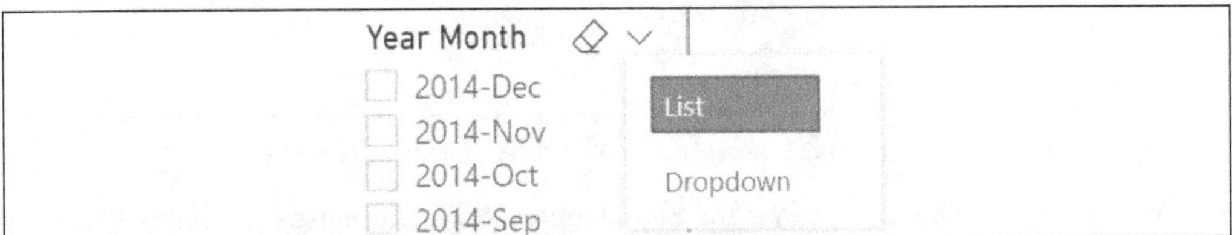

Figure 4.20: Slicer header options

Selecting items in the slicer cross-filters the other visuals on the page. Select the box next to an option once to select that value, and select the same box again to deselect the same value. Hold down the *Ctrl* key to select multiple values. This behavior can be controlled using the **Selection controls** area of the **Format** pane.

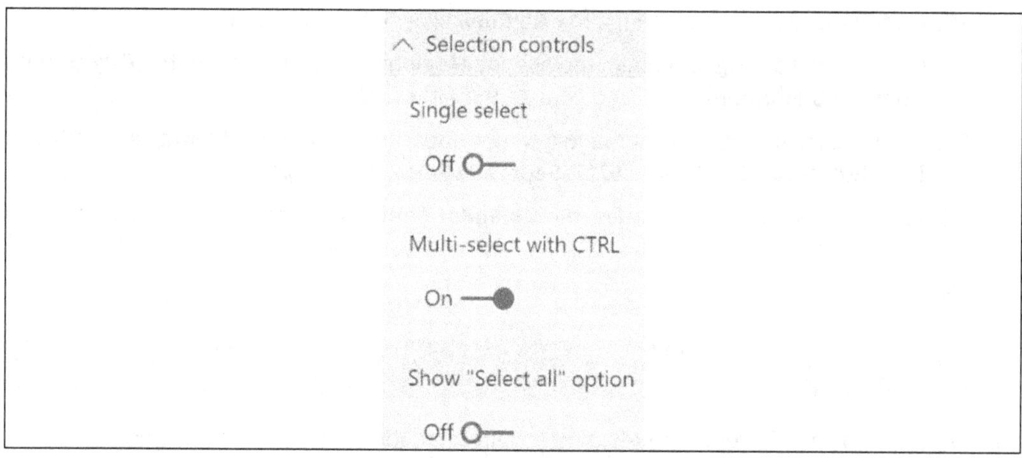

Figure 4.21: Slicer selection controls

You can also force only **Single select**. Turning off **Multi-select with CTRL** makes multiple selection possible without holding down the *Ctrl* key on the keyboard. Slicer item selection essentially becomes a set of checkboxes. The **Show "Select all"** option provides a quick method to select and deselect all values. The **Select all** option can be helpful if the slicer contains more than seven to 10 values. With **Select all**, the user can easily construct a filter to exclude only a few items from a long list.

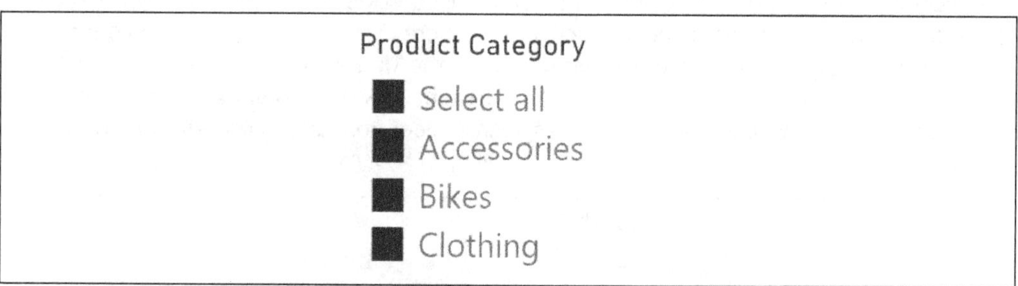

Figure 4.22: Select All Slicer Selection Control Turned On

Slicers can be searched by activating the **Search** option from the ellipses (**...**) menu of the slicer.

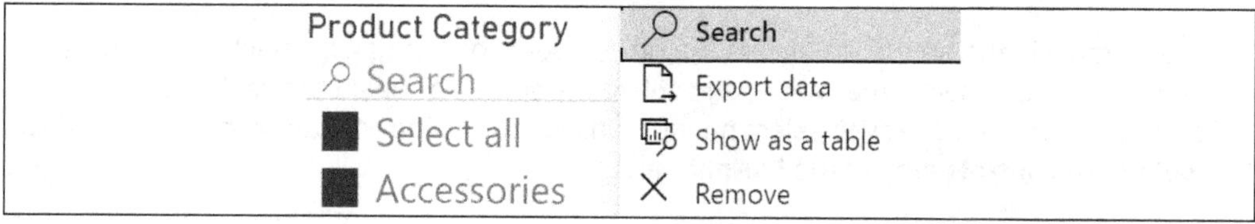

Figure 4.23: Slicer Search option

Activating this option presents a **Search** bar at the top of the items list. **Search** is useful for long lists of items.

Slicers can also be synchronized between report pages. Sync'd slicers means that items selected in a slicer on one page affect any other pages where there is a sync'd slicer. Copying and pasting a slicer between pages prompts the **Sync visuals** dialog box but can also be controlled via the **Sync slicers** pane. By default, slicers with the same **Field** on different pages are "grouped," but you can use the **Advanced options** to control these groupings. In addition to synchronization, the **Sync slicers** dialog box allows you to control whether a slicer is visible on a page. Coupling sync'd slicers with making slicers invisible on pages can be used to free up page canvas space.

There's more...

There are many options when it comes to slicers. In addition to the options discussed so far, there are also special types of slicers, such as horizontal slicers, range slicers, and relative date slicers.

Horizontal slicers are an alternative design that can be activated by changing the **Orientation** setting in the **General** format section of the **Format** pane. Horizontal orientation slicers are often placed along the top of report pages and can benefit mobile consumption.

Figure 4.24: Slicer visual with Horizontal Orientation

Slicer visuals contain powerful filtering options when used with **Date** data types, including graphical date selection, before/after criteria, relative dates, and relative times. The default slicer type for a **Date** data type is a date range slicer or **Between** slicer. The start and end points of the timeline can be selected and dragged to revise the filter condition. Alternatively, selecting the date input cells exposes a graphical calendar picker element for choosing a date. The **Before** and **After** filter options gray out the start and end date input cells of the **Between** dialog, respectively. The **Relative Date** option provides three input boxes. The first input box allows the selection of **Last**, **Next**, or **This**.

The middle input box allows the entry of a number and the last input box provides a drop-down for various date intervals; see *Figure 4.25*.

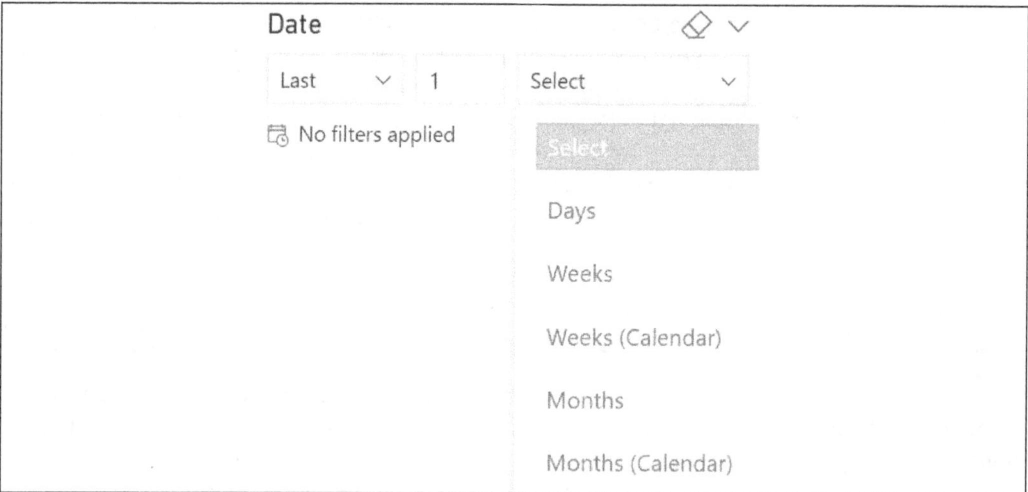

Figure 4.25: Standard slicer based on a Date column configured for a Relative Date Filter

In the **Format** pane, you can specify whether the current day is included in the relative date filter as well as an **Anchor Date**. The relative date filtering options of slicer visuals are also available as report-, page-, and visual-level filters. The **Relative Time** option function is similar to the **Relative Date** option, only the intervals are in **Minutes and Hours**.

The default slicers format for numeric data types is also the **Between** slicer. The **Less than or equal to** and **Greater than or equal to** options for numeric slicers are analogous to a Date slicer's **Before** and **After** options.

See also

- Slicers in Power BI: `http://bit.ly/3mkZcFX`
- Using slicers in the Power BI service: `http://bit.ly/3fsCdHr`

Controlling Visual Interactions

Power BI report pages are interactive by default, with all visuals, excluding slicers, cross-filtered via the selections applied to one visual. While this dynamic filter context is often helpful in exploring and analyzing across dimensions, there is often also a need to exclude certain visuals from this behavior. For example, a high-priority measure reflected in a card or KPI visual may be configured to ignore any filter selections from slicers and other visuals on the page. Additionally, rather than the default highlighting of cross-filtered visuals, it can be beneficial to exclusively display the related values in other visuals.

In this recipe, we provide examples of configuring interactivity between visuals.

Getting ready

To prepare for this recipe, follow these steps:

1. Open the `CH4_R4.pbix` file and save the file as `CH4_R5.pbix`.
2. Switch to the **Scratch** page and use *Ctrl-A* and then *Delete* to remove any visuals.
3. Check the **Filters** pane and ensure that only the **Europe** filter is active.

How to Control Visual Interactions

To implement this recipe, use the following steps:

1. Select the **Europe** page.
2. Select any visual and click **Edit interactions** in the ribbon of the **Format** tab.
3. Select the **Calendar Month** slicer.

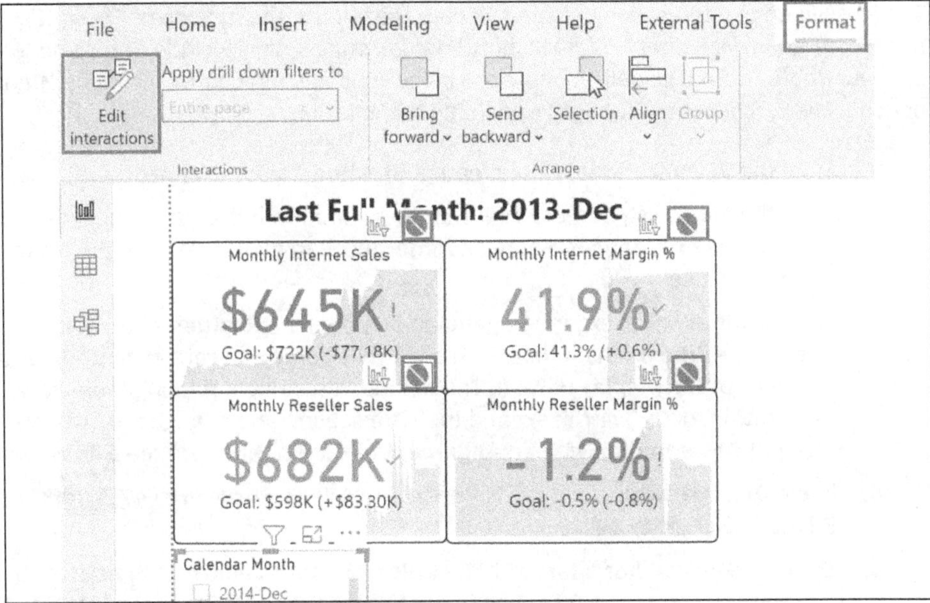

Figure 4.26: Edit interactions

4. Click on the **None** circle icon for the four KPI visualizations.
5. Repeat steps *3* and *4* with the **Product Category** and **Country** slicers.

6. Repeat steps *3*, *4*, and *5* for the **France**, **Germany**, and **United Kingdom** pages.
7. Select any visual and click **Edit interactions** in the ribbon of the **Format** tab to toggle off editing interactions.
8. Save your work.

How it works

In this example, it was determined that the KPI visualizations should always show the last full month's statistics for all products and all countries, states/provinces, and cities. To ensure this is the case, interactivity with all other visualizations on the pages is set to **None** instead of the default **Filter**, using the **Edit interactions** feature on Power BI Desktop.

It is important to realize that DAX measures can override cross-filtering behavior by using filter functions such as `ALL`, `ALLEXCEPT`, and `REMOVEFILTERS`. In fact, there actually was no need to set the interaction between the Calendar Month slicer and the KPI visuals to **None** because the DAX measures that drive the KPI visuals include the use of the `ALL` function for the **Dates** table as part of their calculations.

There's more...

The cross-filtering interactions between visualizations have the options of **Filter**, **Highlight**, and **None**—some visualizations, such as KPI visualizations, only include **Filter** and **None** options, whereas other visualizations, such as bar and column charts, include a **Highlight** option as well. To see the **Highlight** option, do the following:

1. From the **Visualizations** pane, create a **Clustered column chart**.
2. From the **Fields** list, add the **Year Month** column from the **Dates** table as the **Axis**, and add the **Internet Net Sales** and **Internet Plan** measures from the **Internet Sales** table as **Values**.
3. In the **Format** pane, expand **Legend** and change the **Position** to **Bottom**, turn off the **Title** on the **X axis**, turn the **Y axis** completely off, expand **Data labels**, and change the **Display units** to **Thousands**, the **Value decimal places** to **0**, and **Orientation** to **Horizontal**; expand the **Title** section and change the **Title text** to **Internet Sales to Plan** with an **Alignment** of **Center**, and turn the **Background** to **Off**.
4. In the **General** section, set the **X Position** to **449**, **Y Position** to **47**, **Width** to **831**, and **Height** to **241**.
5. Create a **Stacked bar chart** with the **Sales Territory Country** column from the **Sales Territories** table as the **Axis**, and in the **Values** field well, place the **Internet Net Sales** measure from the **Internet Sales** table, and the **Reseller Net Sales** measure from the **Reseller Sales** table.

6. In the **Format** pane, expand **Legend** and change the **Position** to **Bottom**, turn off the **Title** on the **Y axis**, turn off the **Title** on the **X axis**, and then turn the **X axis** completely off; expand **Data labels** and change the **Display units** to **Thousands**, expand the **Title** section and change the **Title text** to **Internet and Reseller Sales by Country** with an **Alignment** of **Center**, and turn the **Background** to **Off**.
7. In the **General** section, set the **X Position** to **753**, **Y Position** to **295**, **Width** to **527**, and **Height** to **212**.
8. Select the **Stacked bar chart** visual and click **Edit interactions** in the ribbon of the **Format** tab.
9. Change the cross-filtering on the **Clustered column chart** visual from **Highlight** to **Filter**.

Figure 4.27: Cross-filtering icons

10. Click on the **None** circle icon for the four KPI visualizations.
11. Select the **Clustered column chart** visual and click on the **None** circle icon for the four KPI visualizations.
12. Select any visual and click on **Edit interactions** in the ribbon of the **Format** tab to toggle editing interactions off.
13. Click on columns in the **Internet Sales Plan** visual and observe the highlighting on the **Internet and Reseller Sales by Country** visual.
14. Similarly, click on the bars in the **Internet and Reseller Sales by Country** visual and observe that the **Internet Sales Plan** visual is filtered.
15. Copy the **Internet Sales Plan** visual to the **France**, **Germany**, and **United Kingdom** pages.
16. Save your work.

See also

- Change how visuals interact in a report: `http://bit.ly/3cGQazB`
- Understand how visuals interact in a report: `http://bit.ly/3wgsQR3`

Utilizing Graphical Visualizations

Data visualization and exploration is central to Power BI, and the visualization types chosen in reports contribute greatly to user comprehension and adoption. Power BI Desktop includes an array of modern visuals, such as the Treemap and the Funnel, but also includes a set of rich formatting options for traditional line, bar/column, combination, and scatter charts. Additionally, five map visuals are available to analyze geographical data, and an entire library of custom visuals is available via the AppSource store, which is integrated into the Home ribbon and Visualizations pane of Power BI Desktop.

A common mistake of inexperienced report developers is the overuse of fancy or complex graphical visuals. Report developers should choose visuals based on their alignment to the business questions within the scope of the report and should always prioritize simplicity and ease-of-use.

This recipe provides examples of utilizing various graphical visualization types, such as the **Line chart**, **Line and Clustered column chart**, **Map**, and **Shape map**.

Getting ready

To prepare for this recipe, follow these steps:

1. Open the `CH4_R5.pbix` file and save the file as `CH4_R6.pbix`.
2. Switch to the **Scratch** page and use *Ctrl-A* then *Delete* to remove any visuals.
3. Check the **Filters** pane and ensure that only the **Europe** filter is active.

How to Utilize Graphical Visualizations

To implement this recipe, use the following steps:

1. Select the **Europe** page.
2. From the **Visualizations** pane, select the **Scatter chart** visualization and add the **Sales Territory Country** column from the **Sales Territories** table as the **Legend**.
3. From the **Internet Sales** table, add the **Internet Net Sales** measure as the **X Axis**, the **Internet Customer Count** measure as the **Y Axis**, and the **Internet Order Quantity Total** measure as the **Size**.
4. From the **Dates** table, add the **Date** column (*not* a **Date** hierarchy) to the **Play Axis**.

5. In the **General** section of the **Format** pane, set the **X Position** to **160**, **Y Position** to **295**, **Width** to **594**, and **Height** to **381**.
6. In the **Format** pane, set the **Legend** to **Off**, and expand the **Y Axis** section, and change the **Axis title** to **Distinct Customers**; then expand the **Title** section, change the **Title text** to **Internet Sales and Customer Count Trend by Country**, and set the **Alignment** to **Center**.

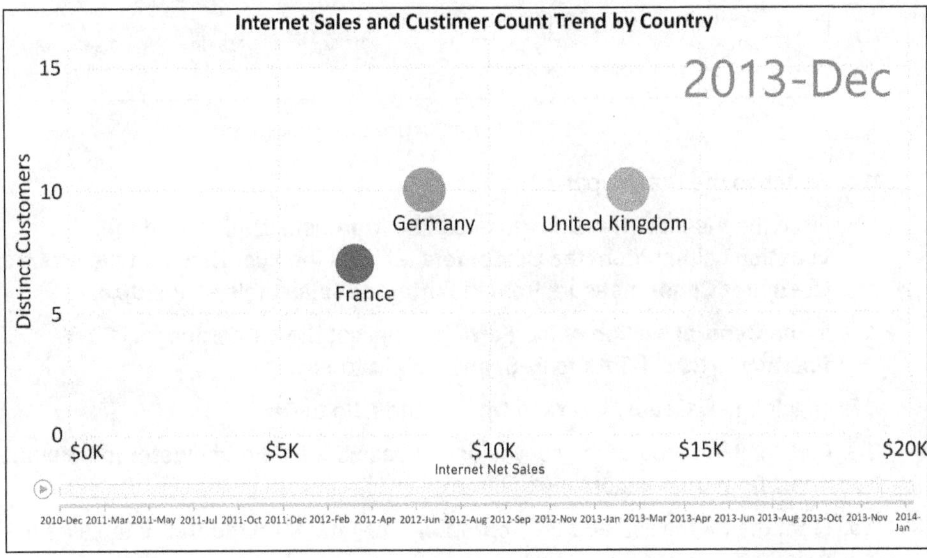

Figure 4.28: Scatter chart visualization

7. Click a blank spot on the page canvas, and from the **Visualizations** pane, select the **Line chart**.
8. Use the **Year Month** column from the **Dates** table as the **Axis**, the **Sales Territory Country** column from the **Sales Territories** table as the **Legend**, and the **Internet Margin %** measure from the **Internet Sales** table for **Values**.
9. In the **General** section of the **Format** pane, set the **X Position** to **754**, **Y Position** to **508**, **Width** to **526**, and **Height** to **212**.
10. Expand the **Legend** section, set the **Position** to **Bottom**, and delete the **Legend Name**.
11. Expand the **X Axis** and **Y Axis** sections and toggle the **Title** to **Off** for both.
12. Toggle **Data labels** to **Off**.
13. Expand the **Title** section, change the **Title text** to **Internet Sales Margin % by Country**, and set the **Alignment** to **Center**.

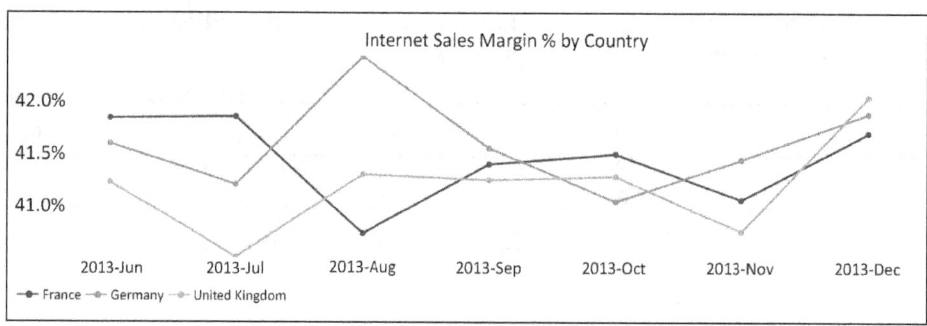

Figure 4.29: Line chart visualization

14. Switch to the **France** page.
15. From the **Visualizations** pane, select the **Map** visualization, add the **Location** column from the **Customers** table as the **Location**, and the **Internet Customer Count** measure from the **Internet Sales** table as the **Size**.
16. In the **General** section of the **Format** pane, set the **X Position** to **160**, **Y Position** to **295**, **Width** to **288**, and **Height** to **381**.
17. Toggle the **Category** labels to **Off** and the **Title** to **Off**.
18. Click a blank area of the canvas and choose the **Line and clustered column chart** from the **Visualizations** pane.
19. From the **Fields** list, add the **Year Month** column from the **Dates** table as the **Axis**.
20. From the **Reseller Sales** table, add the **Reseller Net Sales** measure as the **Column values** and the **Reseller Margin %** measure as the **Line values**.
21. In the **General** section of the **Format** pane, set the **X Position** to **448**, **Y Position** to **295**, **Width** to **832**, and **Height** to **232**.
22. Expand the **Legend** section and change the **Position** to **Bottom**.
23. Expand the **X Axis** and **Y Axis** sections and toggle the **Title** to **Off** for both, and then toggle the **Y Axis** to **Off**.
24. Expand the **Data labels** section and change the **Orientation** to **Horizontal**.
25. Expand the **Title** section and change the **Title text** to **Reseller Sales and Margin %**, with an **Alignment** of **Center**.
26. Turn the **Background** to **Off**.
27. Copy the **Map** and the **Line and clustered column chart** and paste onto the **Germany** and **United Kingdom** pages.
28. Switch to the **Germany** page and select the **Map** visual.
29. Change to using the **State/Province** column from the **Customers** table for **Location**.

30. With the **Map** visual selected, select **Shape map** from the **Visualizations** pane. If **Shape map** is not present, this visualization can be activated using **Preview features**, found by selecting **File** from the menu/ribbon, then **Options and settings**, and finally **Options**.
31. In the **Format** pane, expand the **Shape** section and change the **Map** to **Germany states**.
32. Save your work.

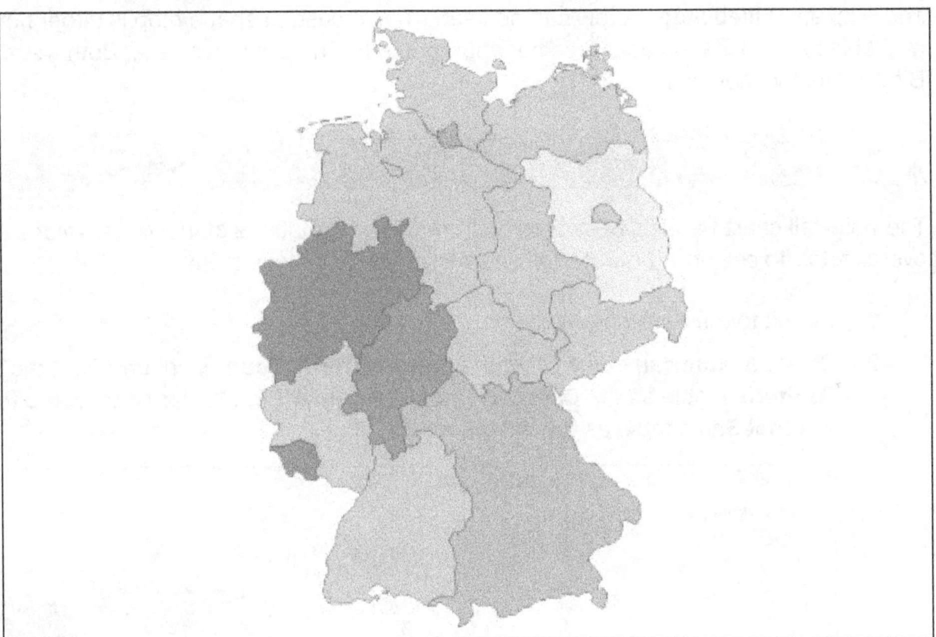

Figure 4.30: Shape map visualization

How it works

Choose column charts when individual values and their comparison is more important than the trend. Select bar charts when the axis category labels are long, as bar charts will display more of the label text than column charts. Use line charts when the trend or shape of data is more important than individual values and their comparison. Select scatter charts to demonstrate a correlation of a dimension between two measures. Choose special-purpose visuals such as Treemaps and Waterfall charts as supplements to standard visuals.

It is generally recommended to avoid pie charts, donut charts, gauges, and treemap visuals, given the advantages in visual perception and comprehension of other visuals. For example, the curved shapes of pie charts and gauges are more difficult to interpret than straight lines and the distance between points in column/bar and scatter charts, respectively.

On the **Scatter chart** visual, you can click the **Play** button to have the measures calculated for each date in the **Play** axis. The shapes will move and change sizes over time.

For the **Shape map** visuals, states with higher sales have greater color saturation by default, and the tooltips display when hovering over states. The available shape maps include a **Map keys** dialog that is used to plot your location column. Map keys can be viewed by clicking **View map keys** from the **Shape** option in the **Formatting** pane. Ensure that your location data matches the keys before using the given shape map.

The **Map** and **Filled map** visuals can be used when a custom shape map is either not available for the location data or is not appropriate for the given use case. Both visuals use Bing to plot location points.

There's more...

The waterfall chart visual is best used to show the contributions of individual values to an overall total. To see how the waterfall chart works, follow these steps:

1. Switch to the **Scratch** page.
2. Create a **Waterfall chart** using the **Sales Territory Country** column from the **Sales Territories** table as the **Category** and the **Internet Plan Variance** measure from the **Internet Sales** table as the **Values**.

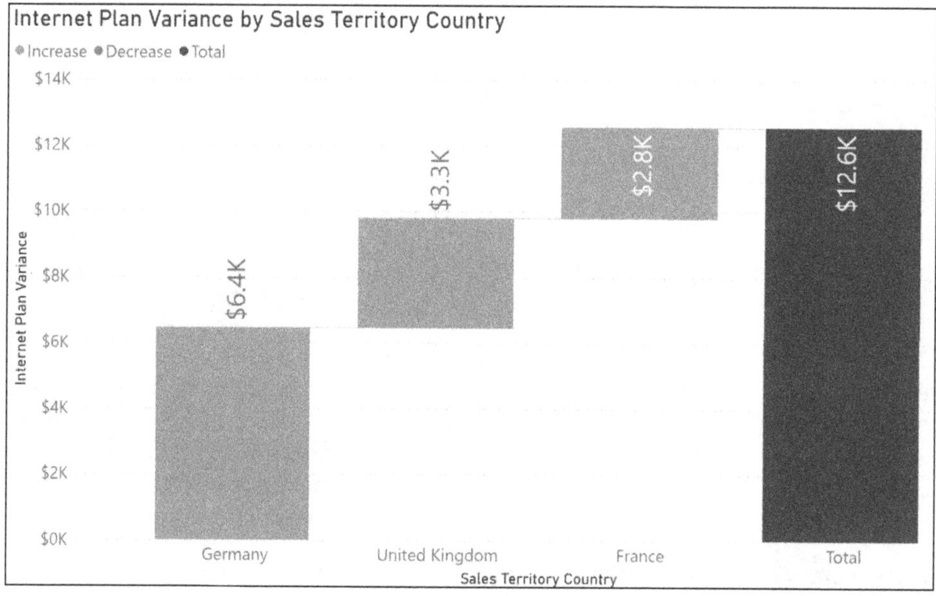

Figure 4.31: Waterfall chart

Waterfall charts should be sorted by the measure in order to support an intuitive "walk" from the components to the **Total** column. The default color formatting of red for negative and green for positive is usually appropriate. Additional columns can be added to the **Category** field in order to enable a drill-down dimension. The **Year Month** column from the **Dates** table or the **Product Category** from the **Products** table are good candidates. Additionally, a column can also be added to the **Breakdown** field. The **Breakdown** field calculates the variance and percentage variance of an individual dimension value between two category values. Adding the **Product Category** column to the **Breakdown** field displays the product categories with the most significant variances between the countries, with details available in tooltips.

Many chart types, such as line charts, have useful analytics options. To demonstrate these analytics capabilities, do the following:

1. On the **Scratch** page, create a **Line chart** with the **Year Month** column from the **Dates** table as the **Axis**, and the **Internet Net Sales** measure from the **Internet Sales** table as the **Values**.
2. Select the line chart and choose the **Analytics** tab.

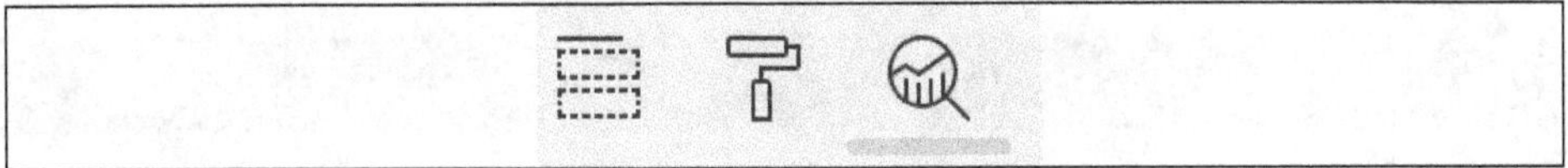

Figure 4.32: Analytics tab

3. Expand the **Average line** section and click **Add**.
4. Toggle the **Data label** to **On** and change the **Text** to **Name and value**.
5. A **Trend** line is available but only when the x-axis is set to **Continuous**. **Date** columns are a good choice to provide a **Continuous** axis. **Date** columns also make a **Forecast** analytic available.
6. A useful trick with line chart visuals is using a measure to add conditional formatting. Create the following measure in the **Internet Sales** table:

```
Variance Less Than 12% =
    IF(
        ABS([Internet Plan Variance]) < [Internet Net Sales]*.12,
        [Internet Net Sales],BLANK()
    )
```

7. Add this measure to the **Values** field well of the line chart. The conditional measure will be included in the line chart but will have a value (and not be blank) only when the condition is met. This approach follows general report design goals in providing more analytical value in the same space without impacting usability. Drill-down via the data hierarchy in the axis and additional measures in the tooltips provide further support in the same space on the report canvas.

See also

- Visualization types in Power BI: `http://bit.ly/3cHg2vh`

Creating Table and Matrix visuals

Table and Matrix visuals are appropriate when visibility of precise, individual values are needed, or when data is viewed at a detailed level, such as in individual transactions. Table visuals in Power BI conform to the classic "list" report format of columns and rows but support powerful cross-highlighting and formatting options, including conditional formatting. Matrix visuals include Table visual features and correspond to the layout and general functionality of pivot tables in Excel: two-dimensional representations of measures with the ability to drill up and down the row and column axes.

In this recipe, the various capabilities of Table and Matrix visualizations are demonstrated, including conditional formatting, drill-down, and cross-highlighting.

Getting ready

To prepare for this recipe, follow these steps:

1. Open the `CH4_R6.pbix` file and save the file as `CH4_R7.pbix`.
2. Switch to the **Scratch** page and use *Ctrl-A* and then *Delete* to remove any visuals.
3. Check the **Filters** pane and ensure that only the **Europe** filter is active.

How to Create Table and Matrix visuals

To implement this recipe, use the following steps:

1. Select the **France** page.
2. From the **Visualizations** pane, select the **Table visualization**.
3. Add the **Product Category** column from the **Products** table, the **Internet Net Sales**, **Internet Margin %**, and **Internet Customer Count** measures from the **Internet Sales** table, and the **Reseller Net Sales** and **Reseller Margin %** measures from the **Reseller Sales** table.
4. Rearrange the measures as necessary in the **Values** area for the visualization.
5. In the **Values** well for the visualization, double-click the **Internet Customer Count** measure and rename it to `Internet Customers`.

6. In the **General** section of the **Format** pane, set the **X Position** to **448**, **Y Position** to **526**, **Width** to **832**, and **Height** to **194**.
7. Expand the **Style** section and choose **Contrast alternating rows**.
8. Copy this visual to the **Germany**, **United Kingdom**, and **Scratch** pages.
9. On the **Scratch** page, use the drop-down for the **Reseller Margin %** measure in the **Values** well to apply **Conditional formatting** to the **Background color**.

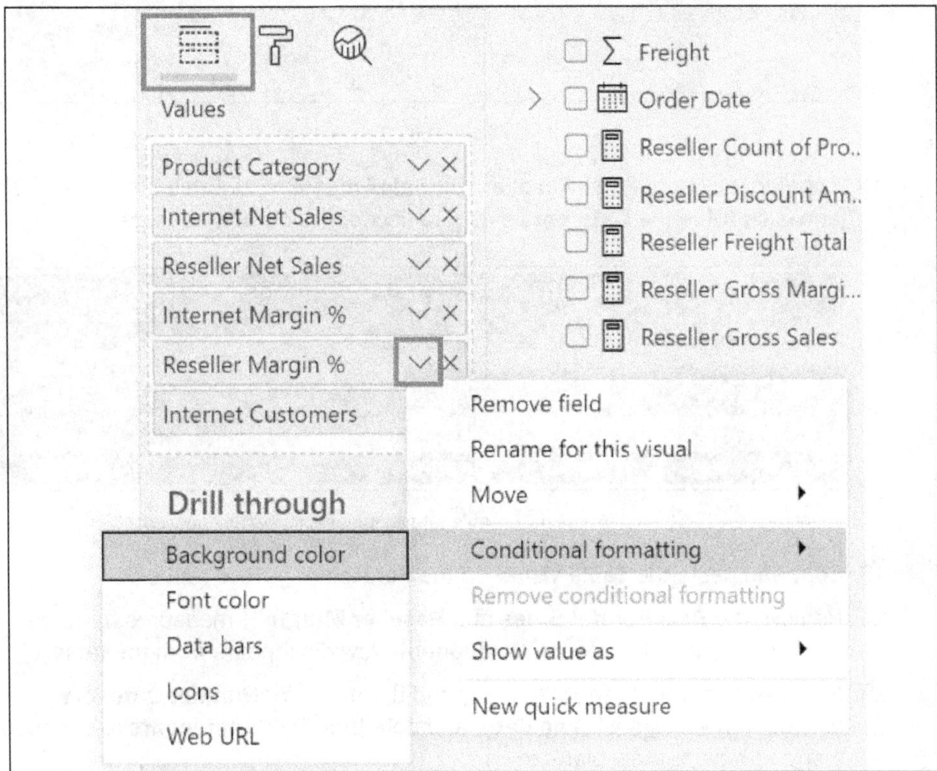

Figure 4.33: Conditional formatting

10. In the conditional formatting dialog, check the **Diverging** checkbox, and then click the **OK** button.

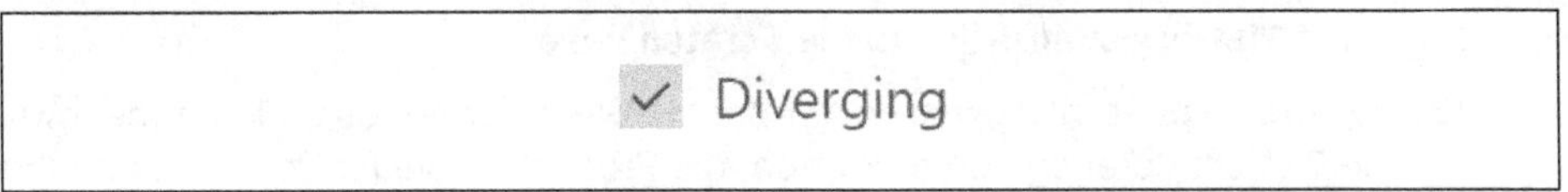

Figure 4.34: Diverging colors for conditional formatting

11. Conditionally format the background for **Internet Net Sales**, but this time change **Format by** to **Rules** and in the **Rules** change the drop-down to **is blank**.

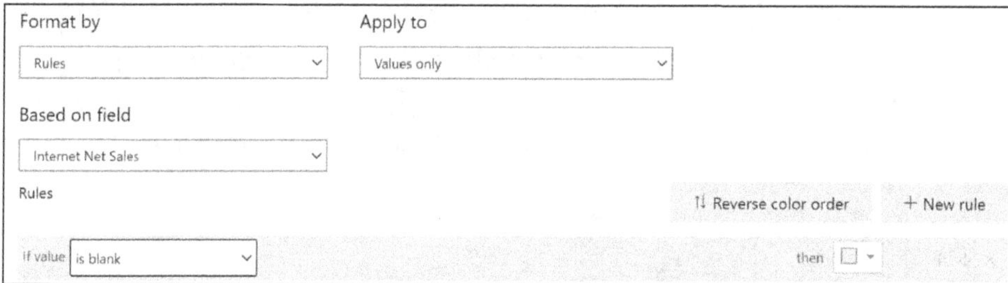

Figure 4.35: Format by rules

12. Conditionally format the **Reseller Net Sales** measure, but this time choose **Data bars** and click **OK** in the **Data bars** dialog to accept the default settings.

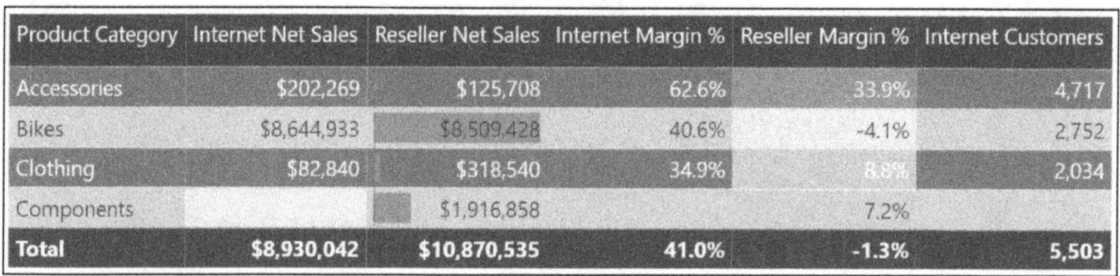

Product Category	Internet Net Sales	Reseller Net Sales	Internet Margin %	Reseller Margin %	Internet Customers
Accessories	$202,269	$125,708	62.6%	33.9%	4,717
Bikes	$8,644,933	$8,509,428	40.6%	-4.1%	2,752
Clothing	$82,840	$318,540	34.9%	8.8%	2,034
Components		$1,916,858		7.2%	
Total	**$8,930,042**	**$10,870,535**	**41.0%**	**-1.3%**	**5,503**

Figure 4.36: Table with conditional formatting applied

13. Copy and paste the **Table visual** on the **Scratch** page and reposition.
14. Remove the **Reseller Net Sales** and **Reseller Margin** % measures from this new visual and note that the **Components** row disappears from the table.
15. In the **Values** well for the visual, expand the menu for **Product Category**, choose **Show items with no data**, and note that the **Components** row reappears along with an entirely blank row.
16. In the **Values** well for the visual, expand the menu for **Internet Customers**, choose **Show value as** and then **Percent of grand total**, and note that percentages are now displayed in the **Internet Customers** column, and the blank row and the **Components** row disappear.
17. Add a **Matrix visualization** to the **Scratch** page.
18. Use the Sales Territory Hierarchy from the Sales Territories table for the rows, the Product Category Hierarchy from the Products table for Columns, and the Internet Net Sales measure from the Internet Sales table for Values.
19. Expand **Europe** using the **+** icon for the row.

20. Switch **Drill on** to **Columns**, choose the down arrow to turn on *drill* mode and click on the **Bikes** column.

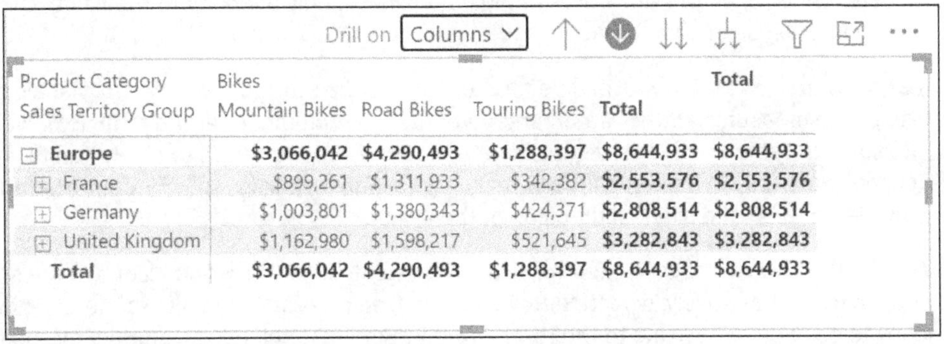

Product Category	Bikes				Total
Sales Territory Group	Mountain Bikes	Road Bikes	Touring Bikes	Total	
Europe	**$3,066,042**	**$4,290,493**	**$1,288,397**	**$8,644,933**	**$8,644,933**
France	$899,261	$1,311,933	$342,382	**$2,553,576**	**$2,553,576**
Germany	$1,003,801	$1,380,343	$424,371	**$2,808,514**	**$2,808,514**
United Kingdom	$1,162,980	$1,598,217	$521,645	**$3,282,843**	**$3,282,843**
Total	**$3,066,042**	**$4,290,493**	**$1,288,397**	**$8,644,933**	**$8,644,933**

Figure 4.37: Matrix visualization

21. Save your work.

How it works

Table and Matrix visualizations automatically filter out rows and columns for which there is no data. In effect, if the aggregations or measures in the **Values** area all evaluate to blank space, then the row is not displayed in the table. The **Show items with no data** feature overrides this default behavior but is not foolproof, as shown in the case of using the **Show value as** feature. An alternative approach is to construct measures in such a way that they return zero instead of a blank, as in the examples below:

```
Measure =
    VAR __Sum = SUM('Internet Sales'[Sales Amount])
RETURN
    IF(ISBLANK(__Sum),0,__Sum)
```

or

```
Measure = SUM('Internet Sales'[Sales Amount]) + 0
```

or

```
Measure =
    COALESCE(
        SUM('Internet Sales'[Sales Amount]),
        0
    )
```

Data bars can be displayed with the measure values, as per this example, or as standalone bars. Specific minimum and maximum threshold values can also be entered to drive the conditional formatting of the bars.

In addition to conditionally formatting background colors and data bars, conditional formatting is also available for fonts as well as icons. If the same formatting logic and colors are used for both font color scales and background color scales, only the color of the value will be displayed, such as in a heat map.

A **Show values as** option is available for measures added to Table and Matrix visuals to display the measure value as a percentage of the row, column, or grand total. However, measures in Table and Matrix visuals cannot currently be formatted to display units, nor decimal places, such as thousands or millions. For Table visuals, only **Percent of grand total** is available, given the single dimension of the visual.

With Matrix visuals, the rows hierarchy can be navigated via the **+** and **-** icons at the start of each row. Alternatively, selecting **Rows** for the **Drill on** drop-down allows the drill-down icons to be used to navigate to the row hierarchy. Similarly, selecting **Columns** for the **Drill on** dropdown allows the columns to be navigated to via the same drill-down icons. There are four drill-down icons: the up arrow icon drills up one layer in the hierarchy; the down arrow icon turns on *drill* mode. When drill mode is active (solid circle), then clicking on a row or column drills one layer deeper into the hierarchy for that particular column, or row, only. The double down arrow icon drills one layer deeper into the hierarchy for all rows or columns, but the parent hierarchy context is lost in this case. To drill one layer deeper into the hierarchy for all rows or columns and preserve the parent hierarchy context, use the forked down arrow icon.

There's more...

An additional conditional formatting option for Table and Matrix visualizations is **Web URL**. Using the **Web URL** conditional formatting makes the displayed value into a live link. To demonstrate how this works, do the following:

- On the **Scratch** page, create a **Table visualization** using the **Customer Name**, **Email**, and **Service URL** columns from the **Customers** table.
- In the **Values** well for the **Table visual**, access the **Conditional formatting** for the **Customer Name** measure and choose **Web URL**.
- In the **Web URL** dialog box, change **Based on field** to the **Email** column in the **Customers** table.

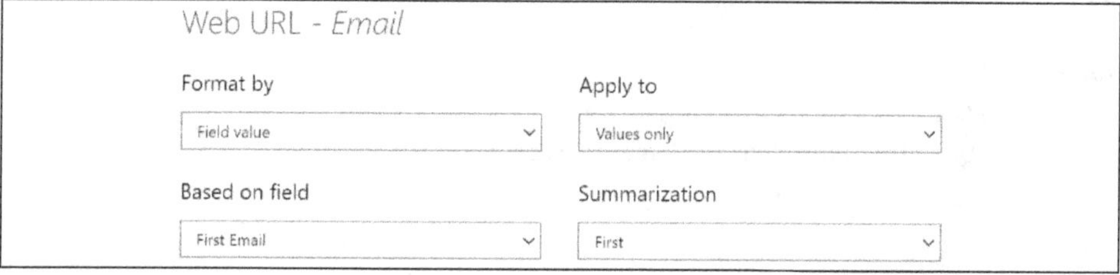

Figure 4.38: Web URL conditional formatting

- In the **Format** pane, expand the **Values** section and toggle the **URL icon** setting to **On**.

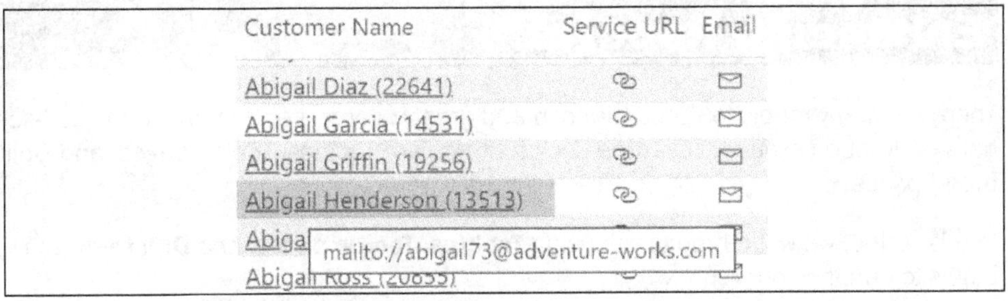

Customer Name	Service URL	Email
Abigail Diaz (22641)		
Abigail Garcia (14531)		
Abigail Griffin (19256)		
Abigail Henderson (13513)		
Abiga mailto://abigail73@adventure-works.com		
Abigail Ross (20855)		

Figure 4.39: Web URL conditional formatting and URL icons as live links

A unique option for Matrix visualizations is the ability to show multiple measures displayed on the rows of Matrix visuals. This is a very common use case in financial reporting. To see how this works, do the following:

- Create a Matrix visualization on the **Scratch** page with the **Product Category** from the **Products** table in the **Rows**, **Calendar Year** from the **Dates** table in the **Columns**, and the **Total Net Sales**, **Total Margin**, and **Total Margin %** measures from the **Calculations** table as **Values**.
- In the **Format** pane, expand the **Values** section and toggle the **Show on rows** option to **On**.

Product Category	2011	2012	2013	2014	Total
Accessories					
Total Net Sales		$15,356	$305,389	$7,233	**$327,977**
Total Margin		$4,835	$159,854	$4,528	**$169,217**
Total Margin %		31.5%	52.3%	62.6%	**51.6%**
Bikes					
Total Net Sales	$1,481,937	$4,189,725	$11,478,601		**$17,154,361**
Total Margin	$596,247	$843,180	$1,716,865		**$3,158,065**
Total Margin %	40.2%	20.1%	15.0%		**18.4%**
Total Net Sales	**$1,481,937**	**$4,803,937**	**$13,500,418**	**$10,187**	**$19,800,577**
Total Margin	**$596,247**	**$931,077**	**$1,987,117**	**$5,729**	**$3,521,945**
Total Margin %	**40.2%**	**19.4%**	**14.7%**	**56.2%**	**17.8%**

Figure 4.40: Matrix visual with three measures in the Values well displayed on rows

See also

- Table visualizations in Power BI reports and dashboards: `http://bit.ly/3fzJ6a4`
- Create a Matrix visual in Power BI: `http://bit.ly/2PN4Cxd`

- Conditional table formatting in Power BI Desktop: `http://bit.ly/3rMwvma`

Enhancing Reports

There are many report features that can add greater context and enhance the self-service data exploration experience. Three such features are Tooltips, Tooltip pages, and Drill through report pages.

In this recipe, we walk through the using **Tooltips**, **Tooltip** pages, and **Drill through report** pages to enhance our report.

Getting ready

To prepare for this recipe, follow these steps:

1. Open the `CH4_R7.pbix` file and save the file as `CH4_R8.pbix`.
2. Switch to the **Scratch** page and use *Ctrl-A* then *Delete* to remove any visuals.
3. Check the **Filters** pane and ensure that only the **Europe** filter is active.

How to Enhance Reports

To implement this recipe, use the following steps:

1. Select the **Germany** page.
2. Select the **Shape map** visualization.
3. In the **Fields** well, add the **Internet Net Sales**, **Internet Margin** %, and **Internet Sales Per Custome**r measures from the **Internet Sales** table to the **Tooltips** field.
4. Hover over a colored German state to see the new measures in the **Tooltip** pop-up:

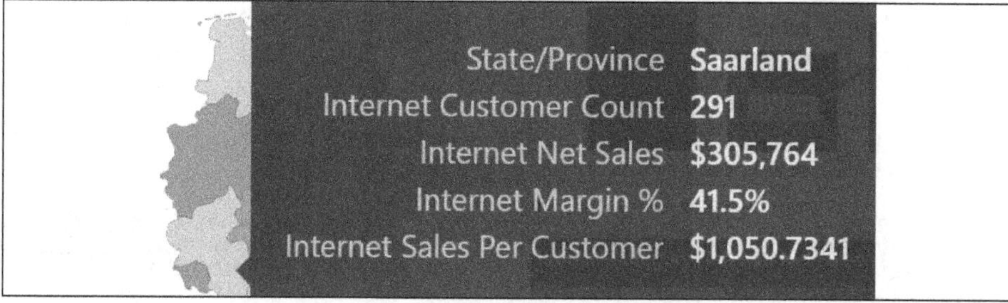

Figure 4.41: Additional measures displayed in Tooltip

5. Create a new **Page** called **Product Tooltip**.
6. In the **Format** pane, expand the **Page Information** section and toggle **Tooltip** to **On**.
7. Expand the **Page size** section and change the **Type** to **Tooltip**.
8. Create a **Clustered bar chart** visualization and resize to consume the entire page.
9. Add the **Product Subcategory** column from the **Products** table to the **Axis**.
10. Add the **Internet Net Sales** measure from the **Internet Sales** table to the **Values**.
11. In the **Filter** pane, apply a visual-level filter on **Product Subcategory**, choosing a **Top N** filter showing 5 items by **Internet Net Sales**.

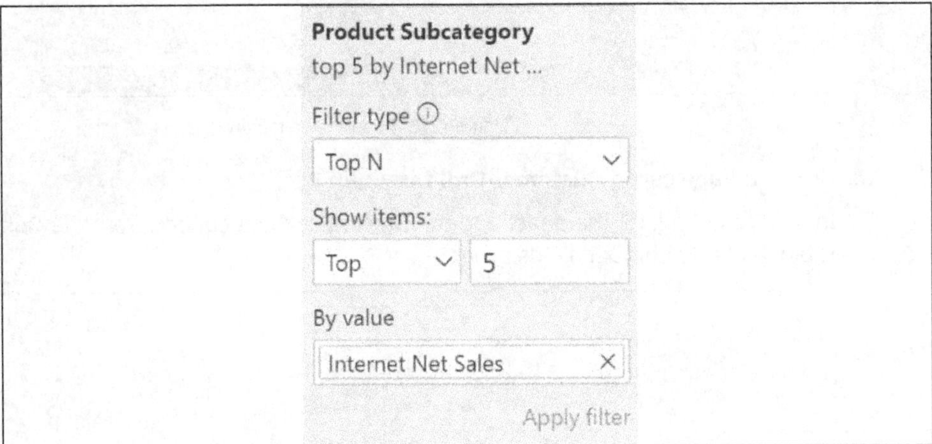

Figure 4.42: Tooltip visual filter

12. On the **Germany** page, select the **Table visual**.
13. In the **Format** pane, toggle the **Tooltip** to **On**.
14. Expand the **Tooltip** section, set **Type** to **Report** page, and **Page** to **Product Tooltip**.

15. Hovering over any cell in the table brings up the **Product Tooltip** page as a **Tooltip** for the subcategories within the **Product Category** for that row.

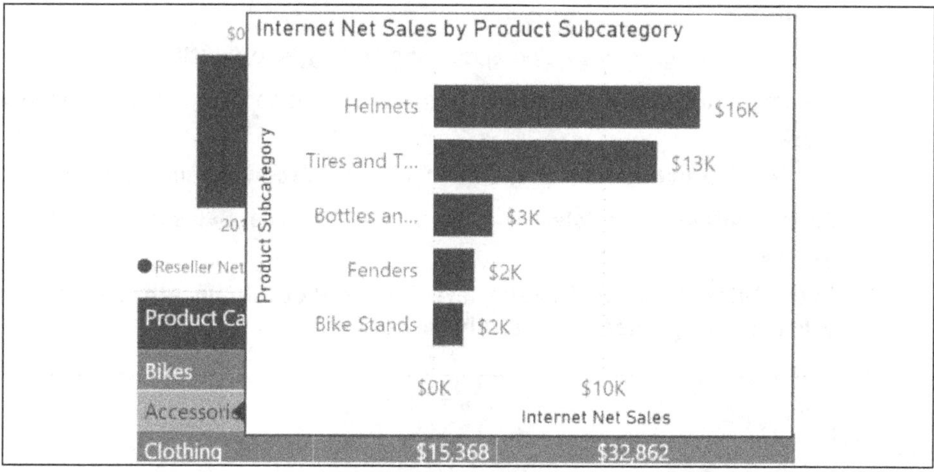

Figure 4.43: Report page tooltip

16. Create a **Page** called **Customer Drill through**.
17. In the **Fields** well for the page, add the **State/Province** column from the **Customers** table to the drillthrough fields area.

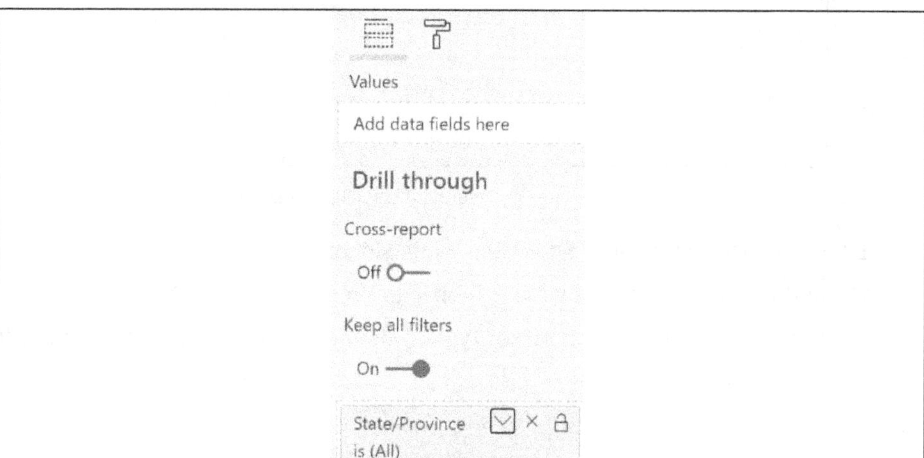

Figure 4.44: Page drillthrough fields

18. Note that a Back button is created automatically in the upper-left corner of the page.

Figure 4.45: Back button

19. Create customer-centric visuals, such as those shown in *Figure 4.46*.

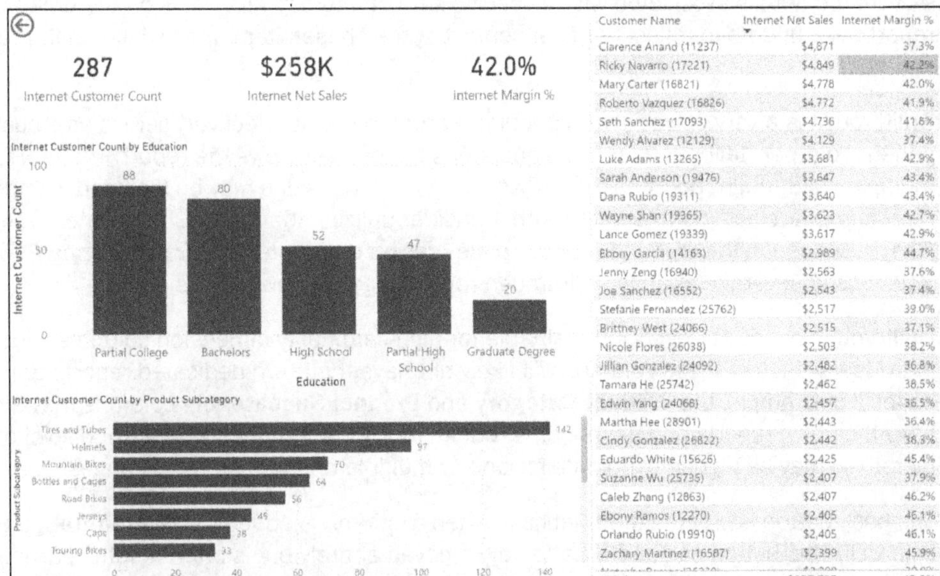

Figure 4.46: Customer Drill through page

20. On the **Germany** page, right-click one of the colored states, choose **Drill through** and then **Customer Drill through**.
21. Note that the drillthrough filters adopt the context passed in from the page and visual.

Figure 4.47: Drillthrough filters after drilling through

How it works

Tooltips and report page tooltips are excellent methods for increasing the information and analytical density of reports, providing additional insights within the same amount of report page real estate. Both tooltips and report page tooltips inherit the context of the visual at the granularity of the visual element being hovered over with the cursor. This means that any measures within tooltips and any visuals within a report page tooltip will reflect the current context of the user interacting with the report.

Report authors can also design drillthrough report pages to enable users to quickly and easily explore the details associated with a specific item of interest. All visuals on the drillthrough report page update to reflect the filter context of the chosen item upon which drillthrough was initiated.

Drillthrough is a very powerful and popular feature in that it effectively serves as a custom-generated report tailored to a user's questions as the user views the report. Therefore, multiple drillthrough report pages across common dimensions may be included with popular reports that are actively interacted with. Consider utilizing the Power BI templates (`.pbit` files) described in the *Working with templates* recipe of *Chapter 7, Parameterizing Power BI Solutions*, to leverage existing drillthrough report pages in new reports.

Drillthrough pages are especially valuable for high-cardinality dimension columns, since the individual values of these columns will likely not have their own dedicated reports or report pages. For example, the **Product Category** and **Product Subcategory** columns may already have their own reports and dashboards, but an individual **Product Model** (third level of this hierarchy) may be a good candidate for one or multiple drillthrough report pages.

The back button is created automatically when a column is added to the **drillthrough filters** field well. This button can be formatted or removed entirely but is often helpful, particularly with reports containing several pages. Alternatively, any **Shape** or **Image** that can be added via the **Insert** tab of the ribbon in Power BI Desktop can also be used as a back button for a drillthrough page.

There's more...

In the drillthrough area for a page, you may have noticed the **Cross-report** toggle. Power BI does indeed allow you to drill through between reports, and not just pages. The source report must be enabled to use drillthrough targets from other reports, either in the **Report settings** of the **CURRENT FILE** in **Options and settings**, or in the Power BI service. The target report would then be configured to toggle the **Cross-report** option to **On** and the drillthrough fields configured appropriately. It is important to note that **Cross-report** filtering requires that the dataset schema of the reports match.

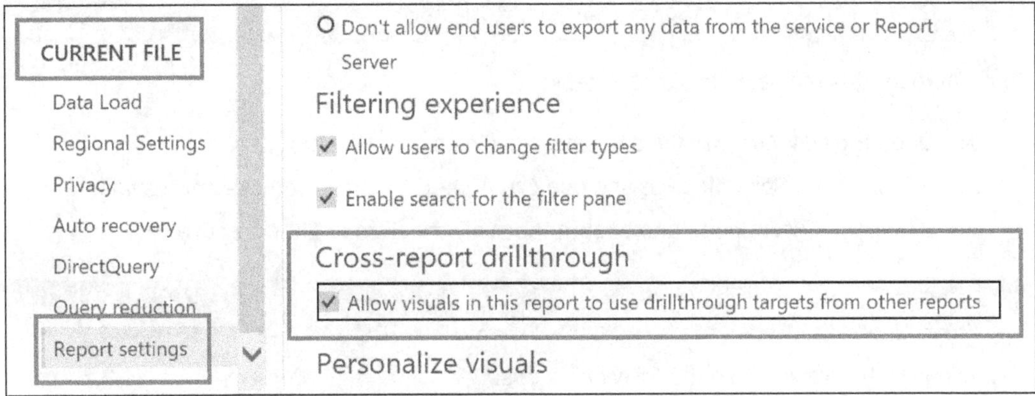

Figure 4.48: Cross-report drill through

See also

- Using report tooltip pages in Power BI: `http://bit.ly/2OdzeHA`
- Extend visuals with report page tooltips: `http://bit.ly/3cGwBHC`
- Set up drill through in Power BI reports: `http://bit.ly/31SH2lv`
- Use report page drillthrough: `http://bit.ly/3sKg5w0`
- Use cross-report drillthrough in Power BI Desktop: `http://bit.ly/3fzfQjJ`

Formatting Reports for Publication

Power BI Desktop includes features to control and enhance the formatting and layout of reports at a detailed level. Prior to publishing reports to the Power BI service, visuals can be aligned, sized, and evenly spaced to deliver an organized, symmetrical layout. Additionally, supplemental report elements, such as shapes, text boxes, and images, can be added to further organize and enrich report pages with textual and visual aids.

This recipe demonstrates how to control the positioning, alignment, and distribution of report visuals, as well as tips for presenting and working with visuals in groups. Additionally, helpful tips are presented for final clean-up items prior to publishing a report, as well as setting up Q&A after publishing.

Getting ready

To prepare for this recipe, follow these steps:

1. Open the `CH4_R8.pbix` file and save the file as `CH4_R9.pbix`.
2. Switch to the **Scratch** page and use *Ctrl-A*, then *Delete* to remove any visuals.
3. Check the **Filters** pane and ensure that only the **Europe** filter is active.

How to Format Reports

To implement this recipe, use the following steps:

1. Copy and paste the four KPI visuals from the **Europe** page to the **Scratch** page.
2. Move the KPI visuals around on the page, spacing them out vertically at different horizontal positions.
3. Notice the automatic alignment guides (the dashed red lines called *smart guides*) that appear when moving or resizing visuals.

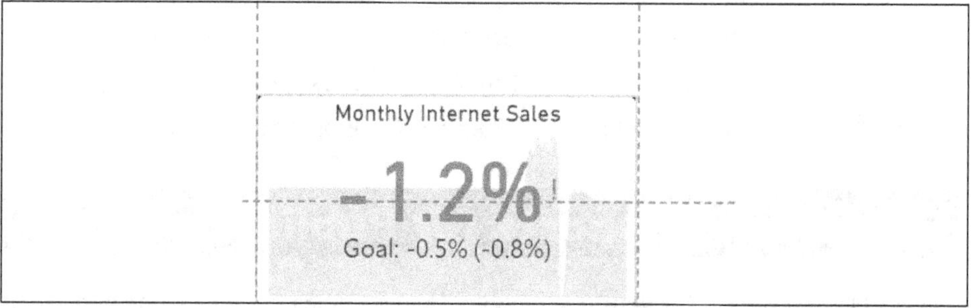

Figure 4.49: Automatic alignment guides

4. Use *Ctrl-A* to select all of the KPI visuals.
5. Select the **Format** tab in the ribbon, choose **Align**, and then **Align left**.

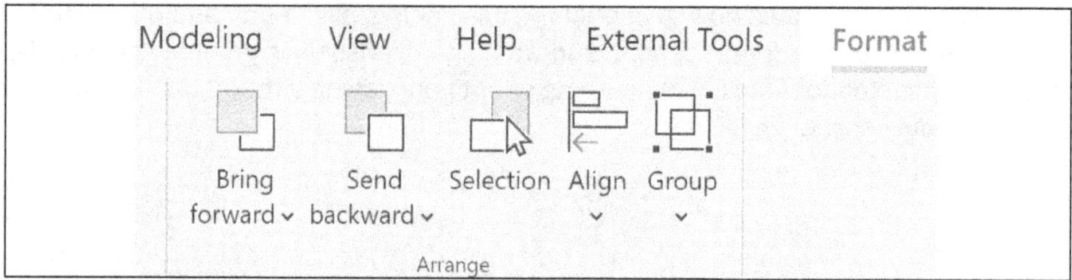

Figure 4.50: Arrange options in the Format ribbon

6. The visuals are all aligned to the leftmost visual.
7. Select **Align** again and choose **Distribute vertically**.
8. The visuals are distributed vertically on the page with equal spacing.
9. Select **Group** and then **Group** from the ribbon of the **Format** tab.
10. The visuals can now be moved around on the page as a single unit.
11. Select **Group** and then **Ungroup**.
12. Stack the visuals roughly on top of one another.
13. Click on a blank area of the page and then select the top visual.
14. From the **Format** tab, select **Send backward** and then **Send to back**.
15. Click on a blank area of the page canvas and note that the visual is now beneath all of the other visuals.
16. Select one of the visuals, and this time choose **Selection** from the ribbon of the **Format** tab to expose the **Selection** pane.

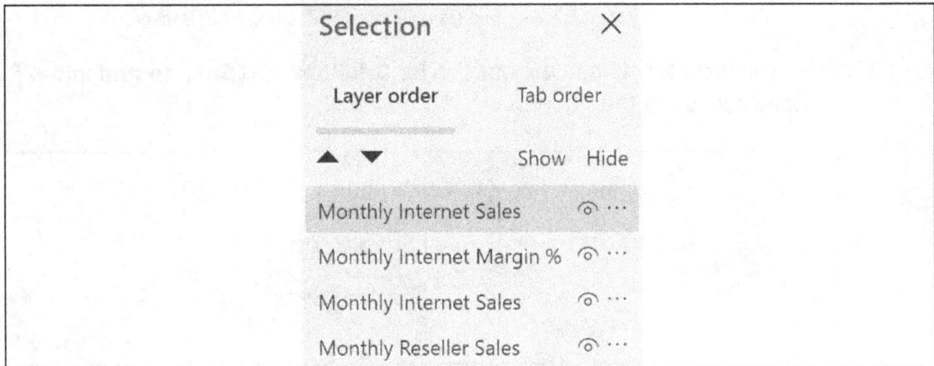

Figure 4.51: Selection pane

17. Use the up and down icons to change the **Layer order** of the visuals.
18. Switch to **Tab order** and again use the up and down icons to change the tab order of the visuals.
19. Close the **Selection** pane.
20. Space the KPI visualizations out horizontally on the page.
21. Select all of the visuals using *Ctrl-A*.
22. Select the **Format** tab, and in the ribbon choose **Align** | **Align top** and then **Align** | **Distribute horizontally**.
23. Convert each of the **KPI** visuals to **Card visual**s.
24. Toggle the **Border** and **Background** to **Off** for one of the KPI visuals.

25. With the **Card visual** selected, choose the **Format painter** from the ribbon of the **Home** tab.
26. Note that the cursor is now a paintbrush; select one of the other **Card visuals**.
27. Click the **Format painter** again and select the next **Card visual**; repeat for the last **Card visual** until all the **Card visuals** no longer have a **Border** or a **Background**.
28. Click on the **Insert** tab and choose **Shapes** in the ribbon and then **Rectangle**.
29. Enclose all of the **Card visuals** in the rectangle.
30. From the **Format** tab, use **Send backward** and then **Send to back** to put the rectangle behind the **Card visuals**.
31. Select *Ctrl-A* and then choose **Group** | **Group** from the ribbon of the **Format** tab.

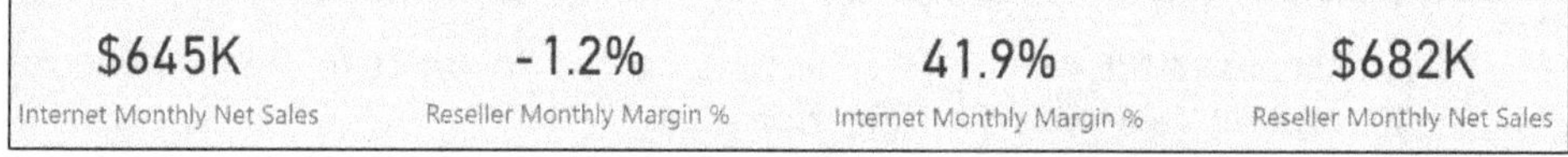

Figure 4.52: Grouped Card visuals with no Border or Background

32. From the **View** tab, check the options for **Gridlines** and **Snap to grid** in the **Page options** section of the ribbon.

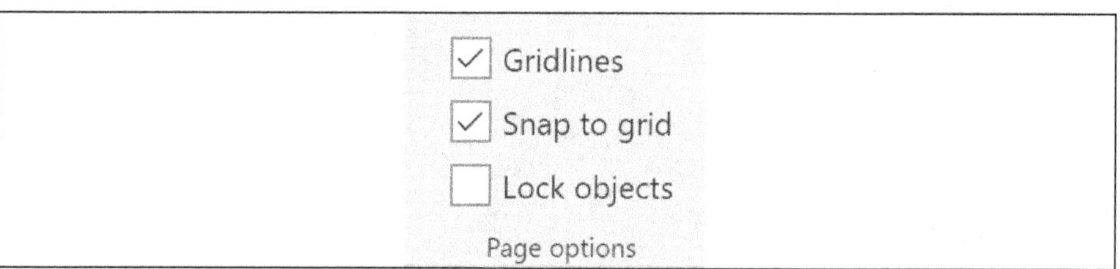

Figure 4.53: Page options in the View ribbon

33. Moving the group of visuals or resizing visuals now snaps to the grid points.
34. Deactivate **Gridlines** and **Snap to grid**.
35. Right-click the **Scratch** page tab and choose **Hide Page**.

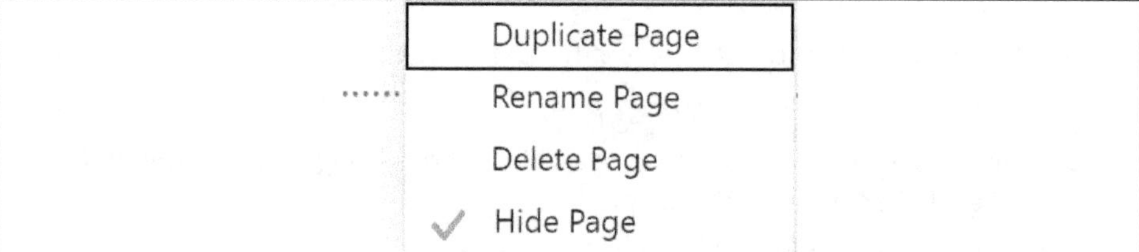

Figure 4.54: Hide Page

36. Repeat *step 32* for the **Product Tooltip** and **Customer Drill through** pages.
37. Use the **+** tab to add a page called **Information**.
38. On the **Information** page, use the **Insert** tab of the ribbon to create a **Text box** similar to the image in *Figure 4.55*.

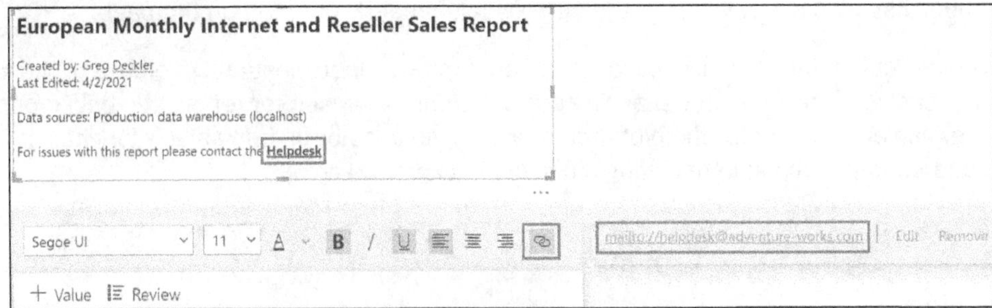

Figure 4.55: Information page of report with active mailto link

39. In this case, **Helpdesk** was selected and made into an active **mailto:** link.
40. From the **View** tab, choose **Lock objects** in the ribbon.
41. Select the **Europe** page and save your work.
42. From the **Home** tab, choose **Publish** in the ribbon to publish the report to the Power BI service.

How it works

Once a report is ready to be published, it is a good idea to use the **Lock objects** setting to prevent unintended movement or resizing of visual elements. It is important to note, however, that **Lock objects** only affects the movement or resizing of visuals by mouse and keyboard. The **X Position**, **Y Position**, **Width**, and **Height** settings in the **General** section of the **Format** pane can still reposition and resize visuals.

Before publishing a report, you should hide or remove pages used during development, such as the **Scratch** page. Pages used for report page tooltips should also be hidden. Drillthrough pages may or may not be hidden, depending on their utility in the report. Hidden pages will not be shown to the report reader when viewing the report in the Power BI service.

It is often a good idea to include an **Information** page. Information pages can be used to describe the data sources used in the report, helpful tips for navigating the report, and even support information.

Positioning and alignment are key qualities in a professional report. As demonstrated in this recipe, Power BI provides many options for ensuring that visuals are aligned and sized in symmetrical ways. The automatic alignment guides are present whenever moving or resizing a visual element on a page.

These alignment guides appear relative to the edges of other visual elements on the page, as well as "common" edges, such as the center of the page. Alternatively, the **Align** options present in the **Format** ribbon offer a way to mass-align many visuals simultaneously. In addition, the distribution options present in the **Align** options are a great way to ensure even spacing between similar visuals. The **Gridlines** and **Snap to grid** features available in the **View** ribbon can also assist you in getting the visuals properly oriented on the page.

Shapes can better organize visuals and can improve report aesthetics relative to the borders and backgrounds of each visual. Shapes are commonly used for report title backgrounds, and they can also customize the plot area of charts, such as by splitting a scatter chart into four squares, with each square having a distinct background color.

There's more...

With a report and dataset published to the Power BI service, we can now configure Q&A for the report. To see how this works, do the following:

1. View the **Germany** page in the Power BI service. Hover over one of the KPI visuals and use the pin icon to pin the visual to a dashboard.

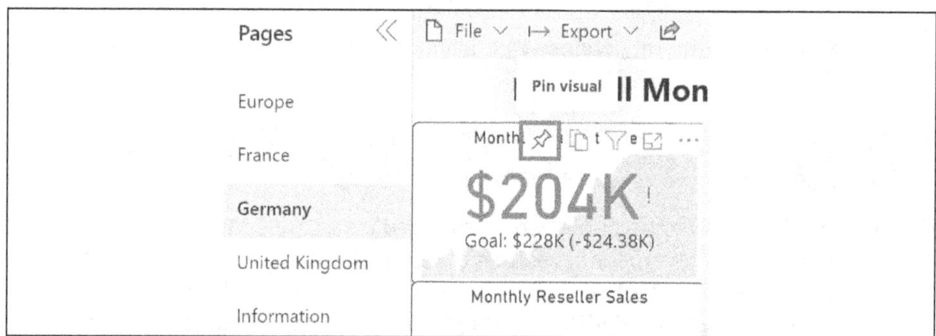

Figure 4.56: Pin visual

2. Select **New dashboard**, enter a name for the dashboard, and click the **Pin** button.

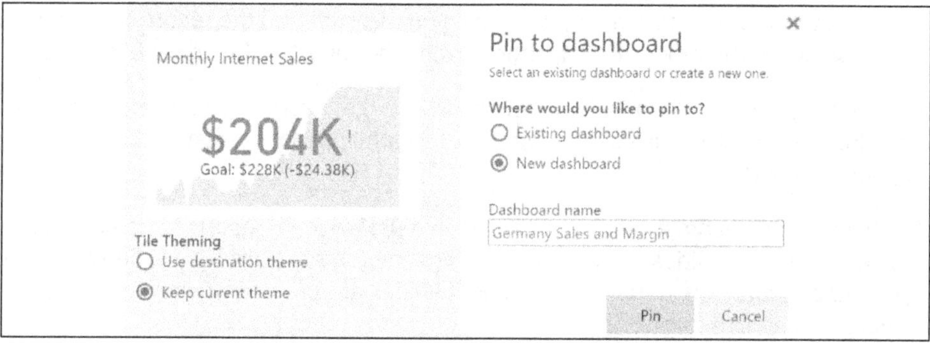

Figure 4.57: Pin to dashboard dialog

Q&A natural language queries are submitted from dashboards against the underlying datasets. In order for Q&A queries to access a dataset and its dependent reports, at least one tile of the given Q&A dashboard must be dependent on this dataset.

3. Navigate to the dashboard and note the **Ask a question about your data** prompt, then click the prompt.

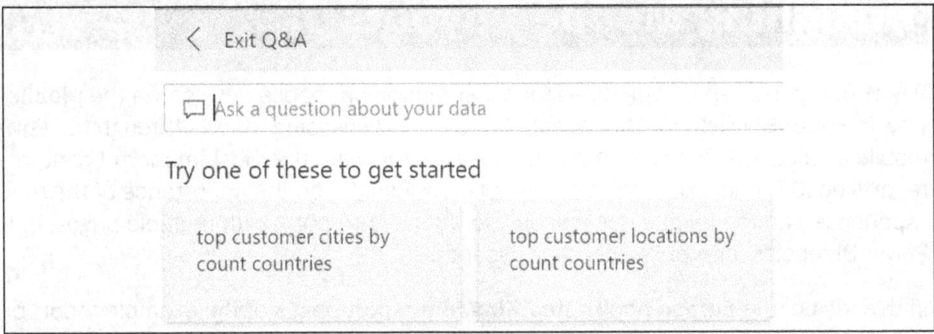

Figure 4.58: Dashboard Q&A

4. Test Q&A using your own questions, or one of the suggested questions; for example: *top Germany resellers by reseller net sales*.
5. Click on the gear icon in the top-right corner of the Power BI service and select **Settings**.
6. Select the **Datasets** tab and the specific dataset to be queried via Q&A.
7. Expand the **Featured Q&A questions** section and add questions; these questions will now appear as suggestions when using Q&A from the dashboard.

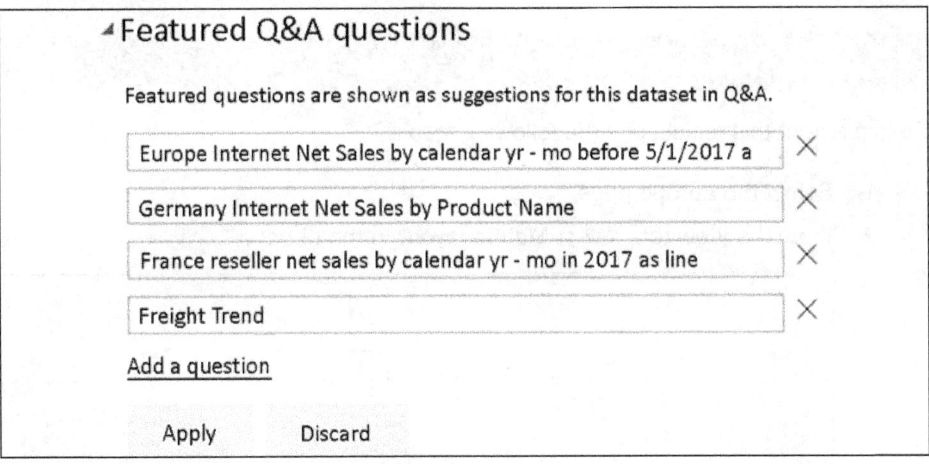

Figure 4.59: Featured Q&A questions option in Datasets Settings

See also

- Power BI best design practices for reports and visuals: `http://bit.ly/2poUeMv`
- Words and terminology that Q&A recognizes: `http://bit.ly/2pRIZdQ`

Designing Mobile Layouts

Power BI reports can be optimized for consumption on mobile devices via the **Mobile layout** view in Power BI Desktop. This layout allows users accessing reports through the Power BI mobile applications to more easily view and interact with the most important content of these reports on iOS, Android, or Windows mobile devices. Given the importance of the mobile experience and the unique design considerations for reports with multiple pages, optimizing Power BI reports for mobile access is essential.

In this recipe, the **Europe** and **United Kingdom** report pages of the example report provided in the first recipe of this chapter are configured with the **Mobile layout**. Additional details for optimizing Power BI dashboards are included in the *There's more...* section.

Getting ready

To prepare for this recipe, follow these steps:

1. Open the `CH4_R9.pbix` file and save the file as `CH4_R10.pbix`.
2. Switch to the **Scratch** page and use *Ctrl-A* and then *Delete* to remove any visuals.
3. Check the **Filters** pane and ensure that only the **Europe** filter is active.

How to Design Mobile Layouts

To implement this recipe, use the following steps:

1. Select the **Europe** page.
2. From the **View** tab, select **Mobile layout** in the ribbon.

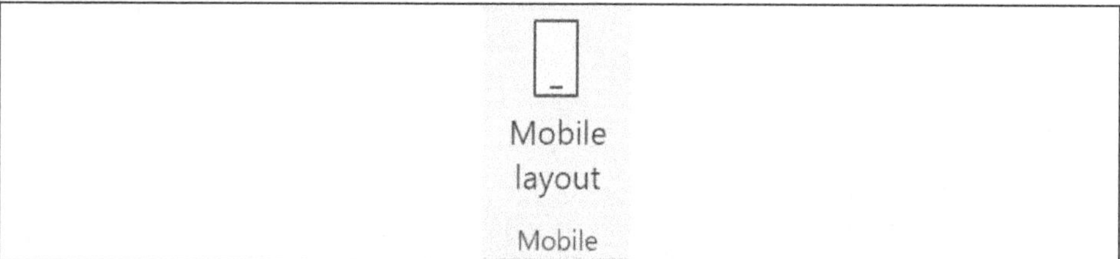

Figure 4.60: Mobile layout

3. Populate the Mobile layout view: click and drag the visualizations to the desired position in the device grid.

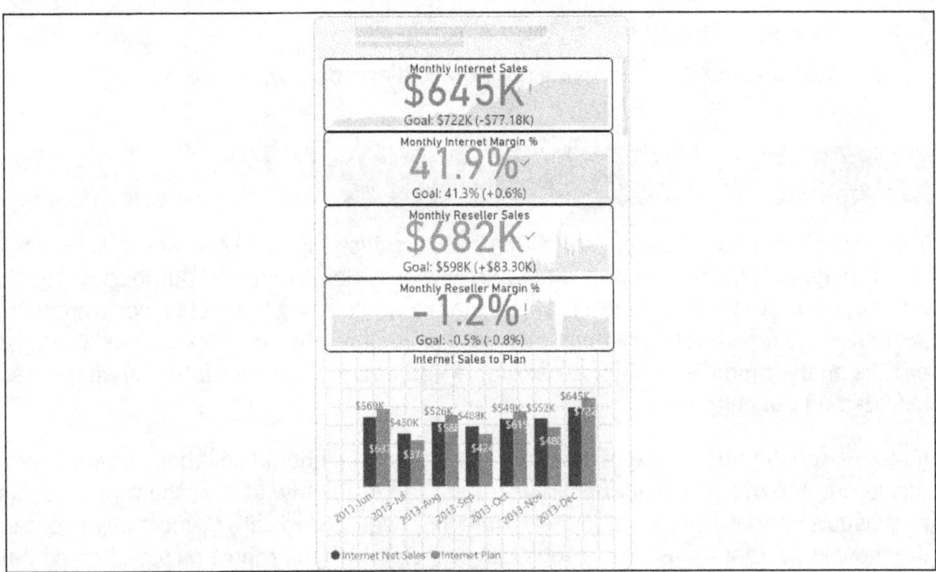

Figure 4.61: Populated Mobile layout

4. Switch to the **United Kingdom** page and also configure the **Mobile layout**.

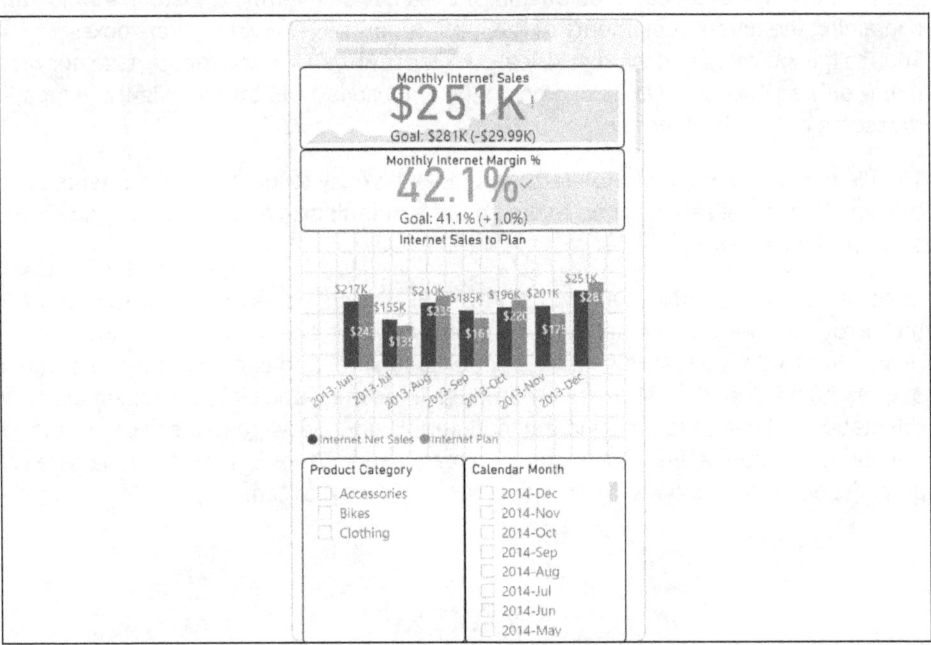

Figure 4.62: United Kingdom Sales and Margin Mobile layout

5. Exit **Mobile layout** by clicking on **Mobile layout** in the ribbon of the **View** tab.
6. Save your work.
7. Publish the report to the Power BI service.
8. Test the mobile views using the Power BI app on your phone.

How it works

The utilization of Power BI reports often varies significantly across devices. For example, a report page with multiple slicers and table or Matrix visuals may be appropriate for a detailed, interactive experience on a laptop but may not lend itself well to mobile consumption. In many scenarios, the user prefers simple, easy access to only a few high-level visuals, such as Cards or KPIs on their mobile device, rather than a sub-optimal representation of all the visuals included on the page.

If mobile consumption is expected, the report's authors should collaborate with users on this layout and overall experience. Given that the **Mobile layout** is at the report page scope and visuals cannot be combined from multiple pages, a dedicated report page containing the most important measures or KPIs can be helpful. These report pages often contain only numbers via Card, Gauge, or KPI visuals to provide a single, at-a-glance mobile view of the most important data points.

The phone layout presents a rectangular mobile device grid and a **Visualizations** pane containing the different elements of the given report page, including text boxes and shapes. Though it is possible to design mobile-optimized layouts for each report page, for most reports it may only be necessary to design one or two mobile layouts that highlight the most important measures or trends of the report.

The **Visualizations** pane of **Mobile layout** makes it easy to identify the elements to include or exclude. The visualizations snap to the grid at a default size and scale up or down on different sizes of mobile devices.

Once saved and published back to the Power BI service, users accessing the report from mobile devices will see the defined phone layout. In the absence of a mobile layout, mobile users will be advised that this has not been configured, and can adjust the orientation of their devices (to horizontal) to view the report page in a landscape view. Switching to a landscape orientation will open the report in the standard desktop view, regardless of whether or not the phone layout has been configured. The pages of a Power BI report can be accessed via swiping gestures from the side of the screen or the pages icon.

Figure 4.63: Switch to landscape view

There's more...

Many of the same interactive features of Power BI reports, such as drill mode and slicers, are also available through Power BI mobile applications. However, given the form factor limitations, it is important to evaluate the usability of these elements and consider whether mobile-friendly visuals, such as Cards or KPIs, can provide the necessary visibility.

As dashboards are created and modified in Power BI, the service allows a similar mobile optimization authoring experience for dashboards. From a dashboard in the Power BI service, click on the **Edit** drop-down, as demonstrated in *Figure 4.64*.

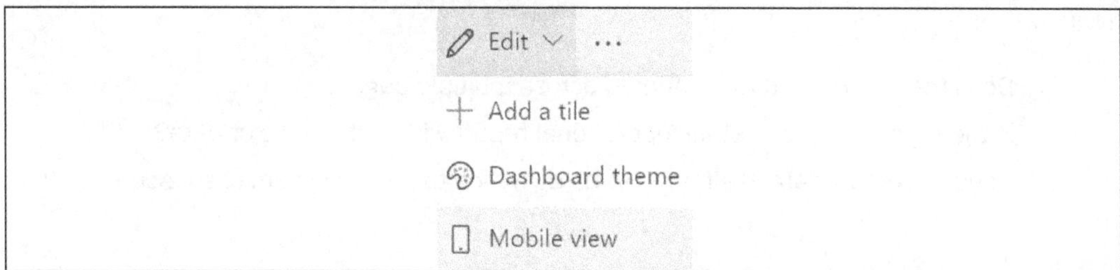

Figure 4.64: Mobile view for dashboard in the Power BI service

The mobile view and functionality are very similar to the mobile layout in Power BI Desktop. A pinned live page to a dashboard becomes one dashboard tile, and thus only one mobile visual. Therefore, pinning individual report visuals to tiles in dashboards is necessary to effectively configure mobile-optimized dashboards.

See also

- Power BI apps for mobile devices: `http://bit.ly/2q6SG8f`
- Tips for Mobile Friendly Report Development with Power BI: `https://bit.ly/3wpUJX8`

Creating Paginated Reports

Microsoft has made great strides to ensure that paginated reports (SSRS-style reports) are first-class citizens in the Power BI universe. Power BI Premium supports such reports, as does the **Power BI Report Server** (**PBIRS**). The most recent evidence that Microsoft still embraces paginated reports for Power BI is the announcement of a planned report-building experience within Power BI Desktop for the creation of paginated reports and the **Paginated report** visual released in May 2021.

At this time, however, paginated reports must still be created in a separate tool, Power BI Report Builder. This recipe demonstrates how to download and install Power BI Report Builder and use this tool to build a paginated report.

Getting ready

To prepare for this recipe, follow these steps:

1. Download Power BI Report Builder from this location: `https://bit.ly/2XOp1G1`.
2. Open the **PowerBIReportBuilder.msi** file.
3. Complete the installation using the wizard.

When considering paginated reports, it is useful to confirm whether a paginated report should indeed be developed. The following questions can help confirm that a paginated report is required:

1. Does the report need to be printed across multiple pages?
2. Is the report more of a static operational report with just a table of data?
3. Does the report data itself need to be delivered to people via email subscriptions?

Yes answers to one or more of these questions can help provide confirmation that a paginated report is required.

How to Create Paginated Reports

To implement this recipe, use the following steps:

1. Run the **Power BI Report Builder** app.
2. Upon opening **Power BI Report Builder**, choose **New Report** and **Table or Matrix Wizard**.

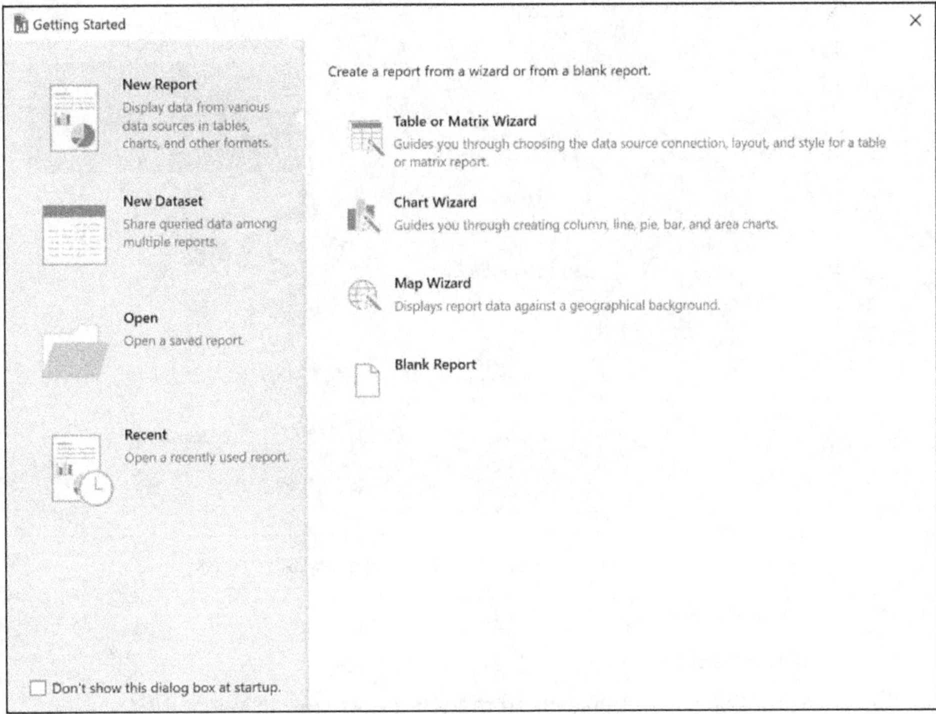

Figure 4.65: Report Builder Getting Started dialog

3. Choose **Create a dataset** and click **Next**.
4. Select **New** to create a new data source connection.
5. Choose the connection type **Microsoft SQL Server**.

6. Use the **Build** option to configure the data source; when finished, click the **OK** button.

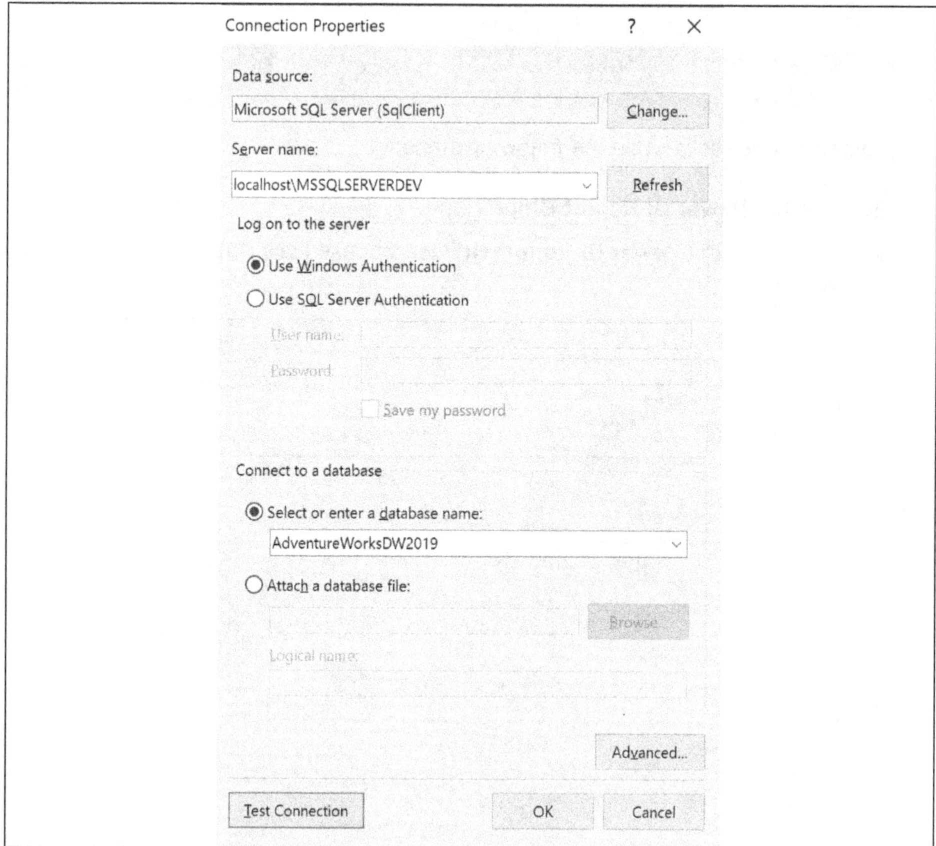

Figure 4.66: Creating a new data source

7. Click the **OK** button.
8. Click the **Next** button.
9. Expand **Views** and then expand the **vProducts** view to select the following fields:
    - **ProductKey**
    - **EnglishProductName**
    - **EnglishProductCategoryName**
    - **EnglishProductSubcategoryName**
    - **DaysToManufacture**
    - **Color**
10. Expand **Tables**, and then expand the **FactInternetSales** table to select the following fields:

- **ProductKey**
- **OrderQuantity**
- **UnitPrice**
- **DiscountAmount**
- **SalesAmount**
- **TaxAmt**
- **Freight**
- **OrderDate**

11. Expand the **Relationships** area, deselect **Auto Detect**, and press the **Add Relationship** icon.

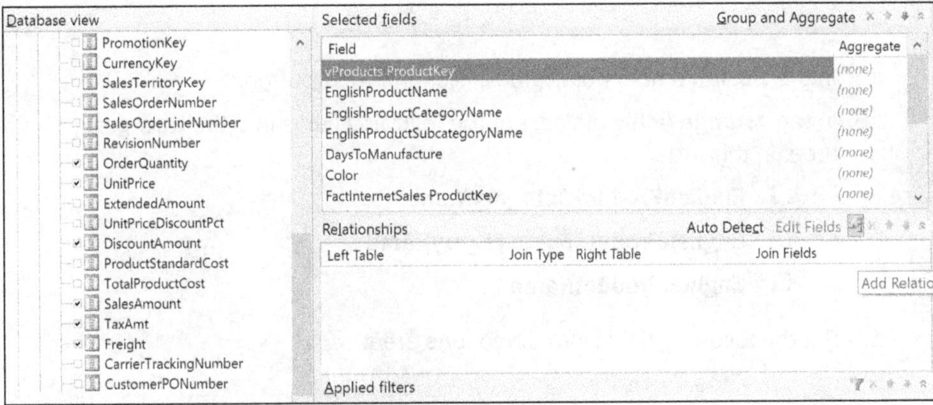

Figure 4.67: Add Relationship

12. Select **vProducts** for the **Left Table and FactInternetSales** as the **Right Table**.

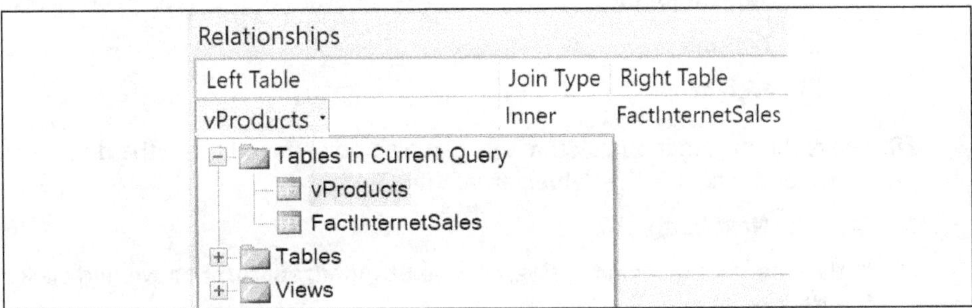

Figure 4.68: Join tables

13. Double-click the area under **Join Fields**.

14. In the **Edit Related Fields** dialog box, click the **Add Field** icon and then choose the **ProductKey** field from each table; click the **OK** button.

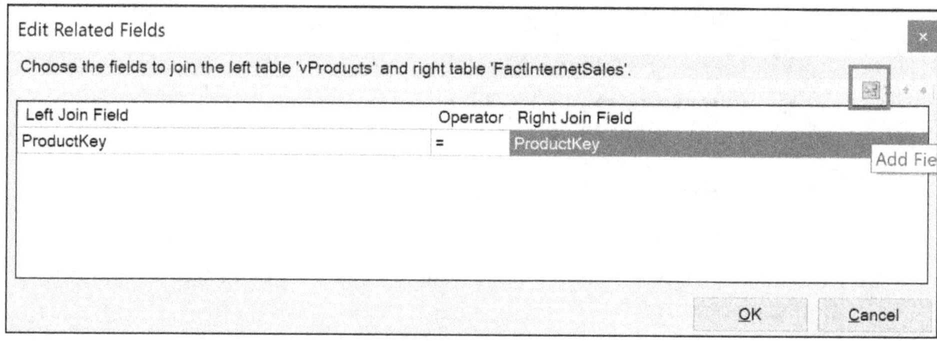

Figure 4.69: Edit related fields

15. In the **Design a query** dialog box, click the **Next** button.
16. In the **Arrange fields** dialog, put the following fields into the **Row groups** area, in this order:
    - **EnglishProductCategoryName**
    - **EnglishProductSubcategoryName**
    - **EnglishProductName**
17. Put the following fields into the **Values** area:
    - **OrderQuantity**
    - **UnitPrice**
    - **DiscountAmount**
    - **SalesAmount**
    - **TaxAmt**
    - **Freight**
18. Leave the aggregation as **Sum**; this can also be changed using the drop-down for the field in the **Values** area.
19. Click the **Next** button.
20. In the **Choose the layout** dialog, choose **Stepped, subtotal above** and click the **Next** button.
21. Click **Finish >>** on the **Preview** screen.

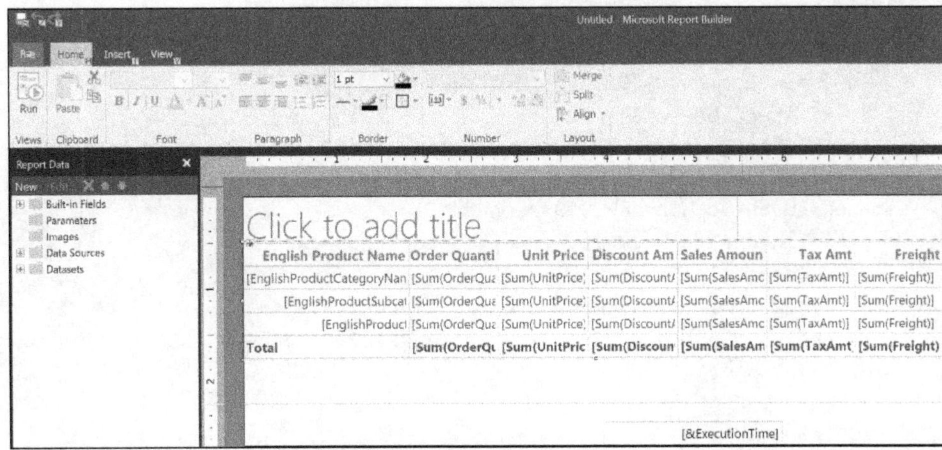

Figure 4.70: Report Builder design view

22. Click the **Run** button in the ribbon.

English Product Name	Order Quantity	Unit Price	Discount Amount	Sales Amount	Tax Amt	Freight
⊞ Accessories	36092	700759.9600	0	700759.9600	56060.7968	17520.5560
⊟ Bikes	15205	28318144.650	0	28318144.650	2265451.6245	707954.3109
⊞ Mountain Bikes	4970	9952759.5644	0	9952759.5644	796220.8062	248819.2140
⊞ Road Bikes	8068	14520584.036	0	14520584.036	1161646.7343	363014.9623
⊞ Touring Bikes	2167	3844801.0500	0	3844801.0500	307584.0840	96120.1346
⊞ Clothing	9101	339772.6100	0	339772.6100	27181.8088	8494.7422
Total	**60398**	**29358677.22**	**0**	**29358677.22**	**2348694.230**	**733969.6091**

4/2/2021 8:28:26 PM

Figure 4.71: Report matrix

23. Save the report as `CH4_R11.rdl`.

How it works

Report Builder is the newest report-building tool in a long line of such tools that use the **Report Definition Language** (**RDL**). RDL files are actually XML files. Here is the first part of the XML for the report just created:

```
<?xml version="1.0" encoding="utf-8"?>
<Report MustUnderstand="df" xmlns="http://schemas.microsoft.com/sqlserver/
reporting/2016/01/reportdefinition" xmlns:rd="http://schemas.microsoft.com/
SQLServer/reporting/reportdesigner" xmlns:df="http://schemas.microsoft.com/
sqlserver/reporting/2016/01/reportdefinition/defaultfontfamily">
  <df:DefaultFontFamily>Segoe UI</df:DefaultFontFamily>
```

```
    <AutoRefresh>0</AutoRefresh>
    <DataSources>
      <DataSource Name="DataSource1">
        <ConnectionProperties>
          <DataProvider>SQL</DataProvider>
          <ConnectString>Data Source=localhost\MSSQLSERVERDEV;Initial
  Catalog=AdventureWorksDW2019</ConnectString>
          <IntegratedSecurity>true</IntegratedSecurity>
        </ConnectionProperties>
        <rd:SecurityType>Integrated</rd:SecurityType>
        <rd:DataSourceID>a781f7ac-7bae-4de2-bf08-240a90e5e558</
  rd:DataSourceID>
      </DataSource>
    </DataSources>
    <DataSets>
      <DataSet Name="DataSet1">
        <Query>
          <DataSourceName>DataSource1</DataSourceName>
```

RDL files have been used in conjunction with SSRS since SSRS was first released. Power BI Report Server and Power BI Premium both support RDL files. If you have either Power BI Report Server or Power BI Premium, you can use the **Publish** button in the ribbon of the **Home** tab to publish the report.

Unlike Power BI Desktop, you do not import data into an RDL file. Datasets comprise the data source, queries, and field definitions stored within the RDL file. Thus, running a report always makes one or more queries back to the data source(s).

There's more...

There is a tremendous amount of functionality and capability present in Power BI Report Builder—functionality that is far beyond the scope of a single recipe. However, some of the highlights include the ability to use Power BI datasets in the service as data sources, numerous available visual elements, calculated fields, and formatting.

When adding a **Data Source**, the option exists to **Add Power BI Dataset Connection**. After signing into the Power BI service, you can select any dataset in any workspace to which you have access. Once you have added the Power BI dataset data source, you can create a dataset with that data source. A **Query Designer** window is available for constructing queries against the dataset.

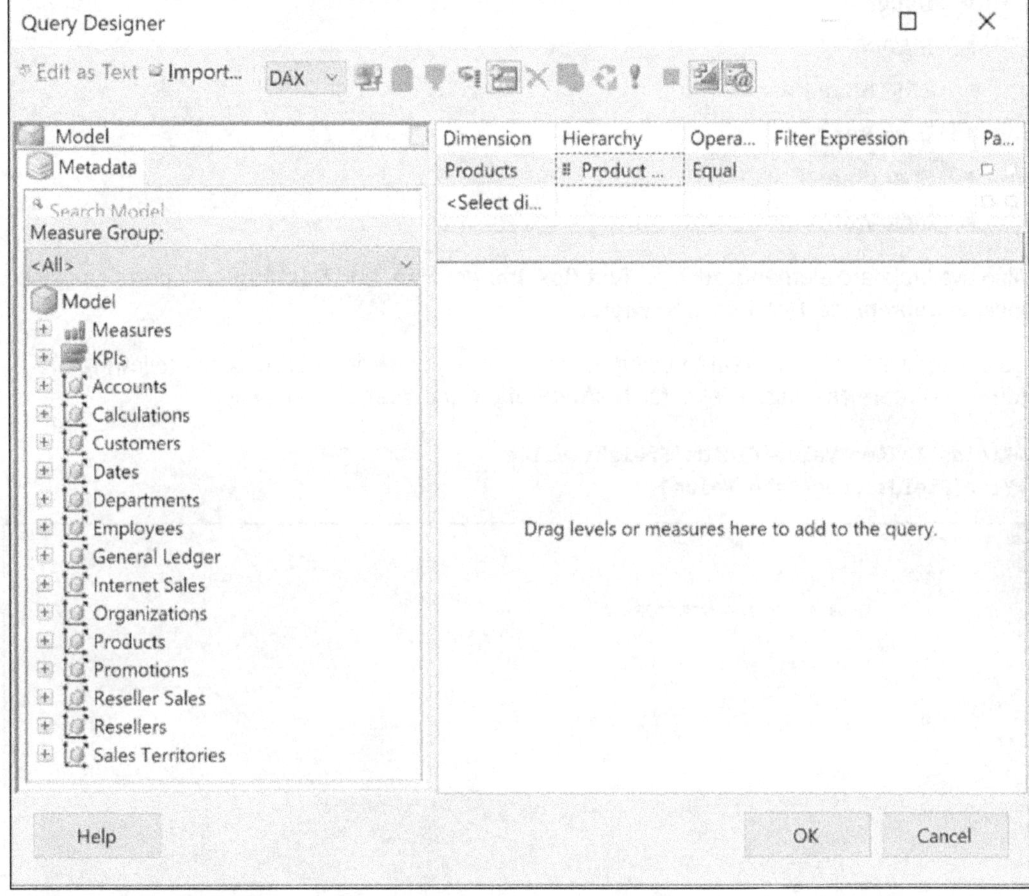

Figure 4.72: Query Designer

Power BI Report Builder includes a number of visual elements available in the **Insert** menu, including:

- **Table**
- **Matrix**
- **List**
- **Column Chart**
- **Line Chart**
- **Pie Chart**
- **Bar Chart**
- **Area Chart**

- **Gauge**
- **MAP**
- **ESRI Shapefile**
- **Data Bar**
- **Sparkline**
- **Indicator**

Also available are elements such as **Text Box**, **Image**, **Line**, and **Rectangle**. Reports can also include **Subreports**, **Headers**, and **Footers**.

Calculated fields can be created using numerous functions and operators; the following two formulas create calculated fields for **TaxAndFreight** and **Year**, respectively:

```
=Fields!TaxAmt.Value+Fields!Freight.Value
=Year(Fields!OrderDate.Value)
```

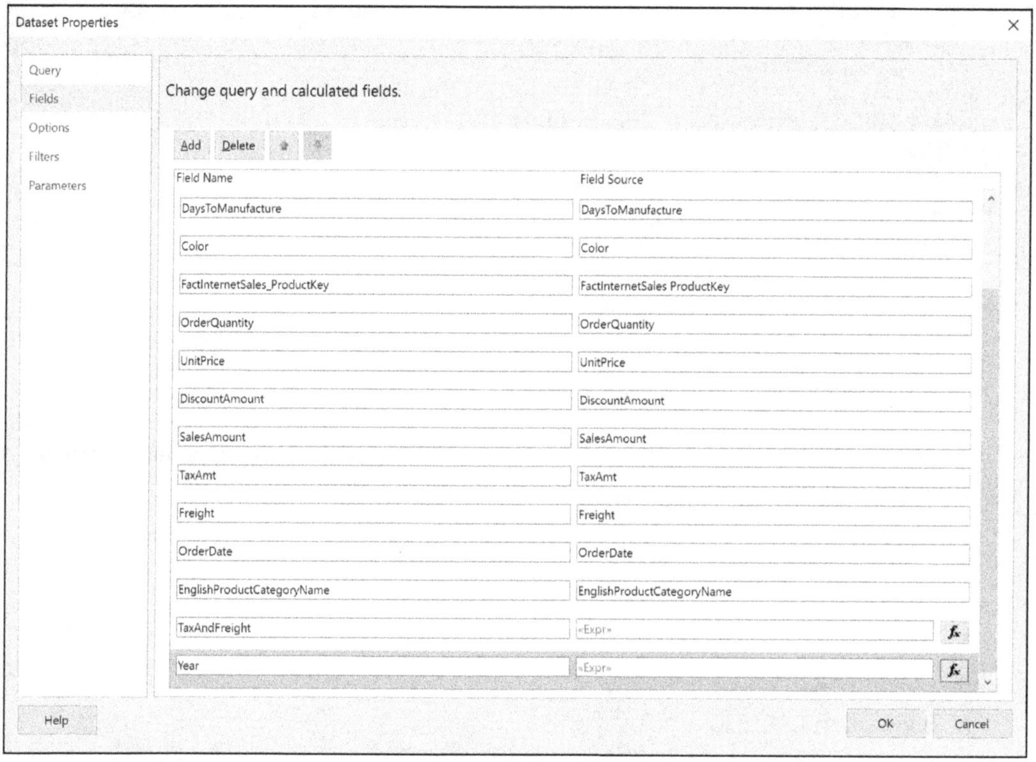

Figure 4.73: Dataset Properties

You can format cells by clicking on the cell in the grid and then using the ribbon of the **Home** tab to format information that appears in the column and row. For example, row headers can be put in bold and monetary fields set to **Currency**.

Year	Product	Order Quantity	Unit Price	Discount Amount	Sales Amount	Tax & Freight
2010	⊞ Bikes	14.00	$43,421.04	0.00%	$43,421.04	$4,559.21
2011	⊞ Bikes	2,216.00	$7,075,525.93	0.00%	$7,075,525.93	$742,930.34
2012	⊞ Accessories	106.00	$2,147.08	0.00%	$2,147.08	$225.45
	⊞ Bikes	3,269.00	$5,839,695.33	0.00%	$5,839,695.33	$613,168.15
	⊞ Clothing	22.00	$642.79	0.00%	$642.79	$67.49
2013	⊞ Accessories	34,409.00	$668,241.53	0.00%	$668,241.53	$70,166.85
	⊞ Bikes	9,706.00	$15,359,502.3	0.00%	$15,359,502.3	$1,612,748.23
	⊞ Clothing	8,686.00	$323,806.45	0.00%	$323,806.45	$34,000.09
2014	⊞ Accessories	1,577.00	$30,371.35	0.00%	$30,371.35	$3,189.06
	⊞ Clothing	393.00	$15,323.37	0.00%	$15,323.37	$1,608.97
	Total	**60,398.00**	**$29,358,677.2**	**0.00%**	**$29,358,677.2**	**$3,082,663.84**

Internet Sales

Figure 74: Paginated report

See also

- Power BI Report Builder: `http://bit.ly/3rLCg3I`
- Sample Power BI paginated reports: `http://bit.ly/2PonXVE`
- What are paginated reports in Power BI Premium?: `http://bit.ly/31F4tOS`

Conclusion

Power BI reports serve as the foundation for dashboards, data exploration, and content collaboration and distribution in Power BI. Power BI Desktop provides data visualization features and options in abundance, enabling the construction of highly targeted and user-friendly reports across devices. In this chapter, we developed and described the most fundamental report visualizations and design concepts. Additionally, guidance was provided to enhance and control the user experience when interacting with Power BI reports and consuming them on Windows and mobile devices.

5

Working in the Service

"A dashboard is really a content aggregator. It lets you bring together lots of different data sources in one place so you can have a 360 degree view of your business on one dashboard."

- Adam Wilson, group program manager for the Power BI service

Power BI dashboards are collections of tiles created in the Power BI service, representing the visuals from one or many Power BI reports and, optionally, other sources, such as Excel and SQL Server Reporting Services (SSRS). Dashboards are best utilized to centralize essential key performance indicators (KPIs), measures, and trends in a visual- and mobile-optimized layout. Additionally, dashboards can provide an entryway to other dashboards or reports and are further enhanced with URL links, streaming data, images, web content, and interactivity.

In this chapter, Power BI dashboards are constructed to provide intuitive, at-a-glance monitoring of critical measures and high-impact business activities. The unique features of dashboards, such as Q&A natural language queries, data alerts, and the integration of other report types—such as Excel and SSRS—are also included. Finally, the creation of additional content objects, such as streaming datasets and dataflows, is also included.

In this chapter, we will cover the following recipes:

- Building a Dashboard
- Preparing for Q&A
- Adding Alerts and Subscriptions
- Deploying Content from Excel and SSRS
- Streaming Datasets
- Authoring Dataflows

Technical Requirements

The following are required to complete the recipes in this chapter:

- Power BI Desktop and a Power BI service account.
- SQL Server with the `AdventureWorksDW2019` database installed. This database and instructions for installing it are available here: `http://bit.ly/2OVQfG7`.
- Files for this chapter and can be downloaded from the following GitHub repository: `https://github.com/PacktPublishing/Microsoft-Power-BI-Cookbook-Second-Edition`.

Building a Dashboard

With a robust dataset and multiple reports created in Power BI Desktop, dashboards can be developed in the Power BI service to consolidate the most valuable KPIs, measures, and visualizations onto a single pane of glass. Additionally, dashboards provide an access point to the detailed reports supporting the tiles and are optimized for mobile access through the Power BI mobile application.

Power BI dashboards are commonly used by executives and senior managers who desire an intuitive, consolidated view of relevant KPIs and visualizations. In many cases, these stakeholders will almost exclusively rely on dashboards rather than the more detailed and interactive reports underlying the dashboards. Such dashboards are often sourced from reports built against multiple datasets reflecting different business processes and functional areas such as Accounting and Supply Chain. Enterprise dashboards typically utilize card and KPI visuals to focus on strategic objectives and maximize canvas space. Given the scale and breadth of data sources for a modern enterprise, a significant level of coordination is required to ensure that all datasets supporting the dashboard represent an appropriate level of data quality and governance.

The report design planning process described in *Chapter 4, Authoring Power BI Reports*, is directly applicable to dashboards as well. It is important to confirm that the existing data model (or models) support the required business questions and metrics exposed in a dashboard.

In this recipe, a sales dashboard is created for the North American sales management team. Four reports have been built against the same Power BI dataset (data model) and the visuals from these reports are pinned as tiles to the sales dashboard.

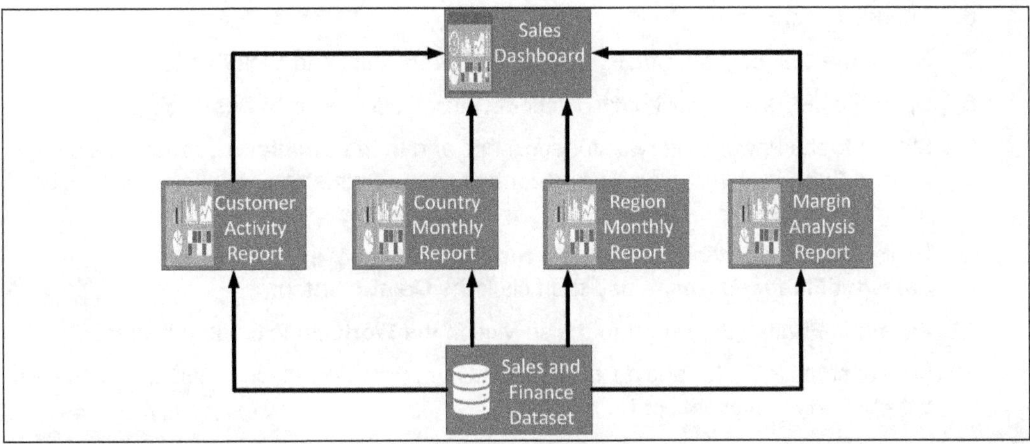

Figure 5.1: North America sales dashboard structure: 4 reports and 1 dataset

Getting Ready

To prepare for this recipe, follow these steps:

1. Log in to the Power BI service.
2. Click on **Workspaces** in the left navigation pane and select **Create a workspace** at the bottom of the fly-out. If you cannot create a workspace, check with your Power BI administrator, as they may have disabled this option.

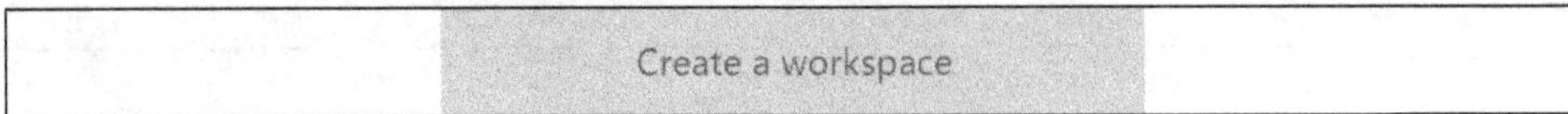

Figure 5.2: Create a workspace

3. In the **Create a workspace** dialog, enter a **Workspace name** and click **Save**.
4. In the center area, click **Add content**.
5. In the **Get Data** dialog, click the **Get** button for **Files**.

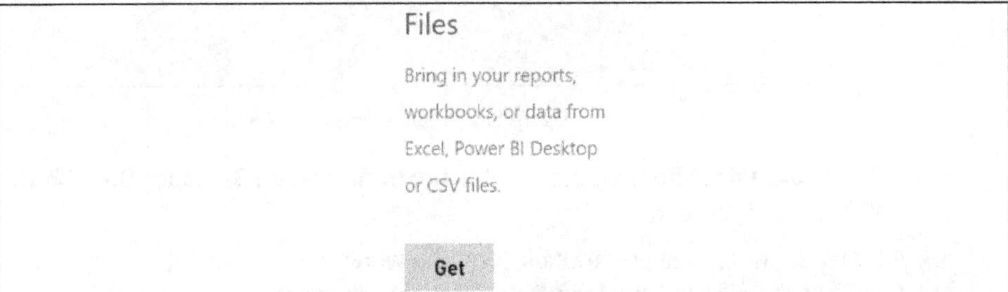

Figure 5.3: Get Data, Files

6. Choose **Local File**.
7. Select the `CH5_R1_SalesAndFinanceDataset.pbix` file and click **Open**.
8. Open the `CH5_R1_RegionMonthlyReport.pbix` file in Power BI Desktop.
9. Sign in to the Power BI service if necessary, and in the **Unable to connect** dialog, choose **Edit**. If you receive an error, contact your administrator to allow a connection to live datasets.
10. On the **Select a dataset to create a report** page, choose the **CH5_R1_SalesAndFinanceDataset**, and then click the **Create** button.
11. **Save** and **Publish** the report to the service in the **Workspace** created in *step 3*.
12. Repeat *steps 8*, *9*, *10*, and *11* for `CH5_R1_CountryMonthlyReport.pbix`, and `CH5_R1_MarginAnalysisReport.pbix`.

If you are unable to create a **Workspace** in the Power BI service, you can use **My workspace** instead. After completing these steps, the reports all have a live connection back to the dataset, `CH5_R1_SalesAndFinanceDataset`.

How to Build a Dashboard

To implement this recipe, use the following steps:

1. In the Power BI service, select the workspace created in the *Getting started* section of this recipe.
2. In the central area, click **New** and then choose **Dashboard**.

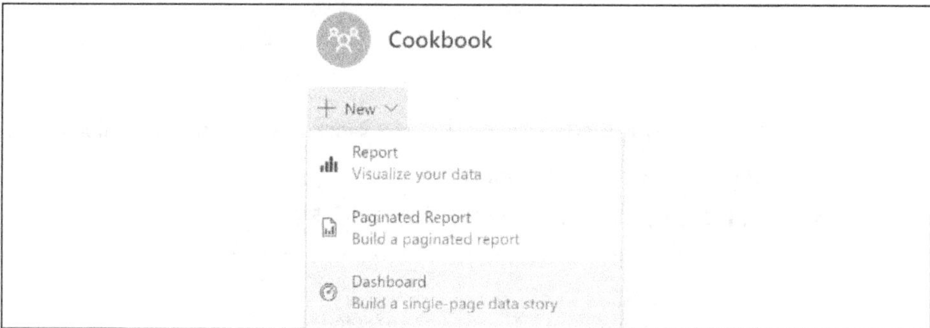

Figure 5.4: Create a new dashboard

3. In the **Create dashboard** dialog, enter **North American Sales** for **Dashboard name** and then click **Create**.
4. A blank dashboard is created; click on the workspace in the left navigation pane and note that the **North American Sales** dashboard is shown in the list.
5. In the service, open the **CH5_R1_RegionMonthlyReport** report and navigate to the **North America** page.

6. Hover your mouse over the **Monthly Internet Sales** KPI visualization and click the pin visual icon.

Figure 5.5: Pin visual

7. In the **Pin to dashboard** dialog, choose **Existing dashboard**, select **North American Sales**, and then click the **Pin** button.

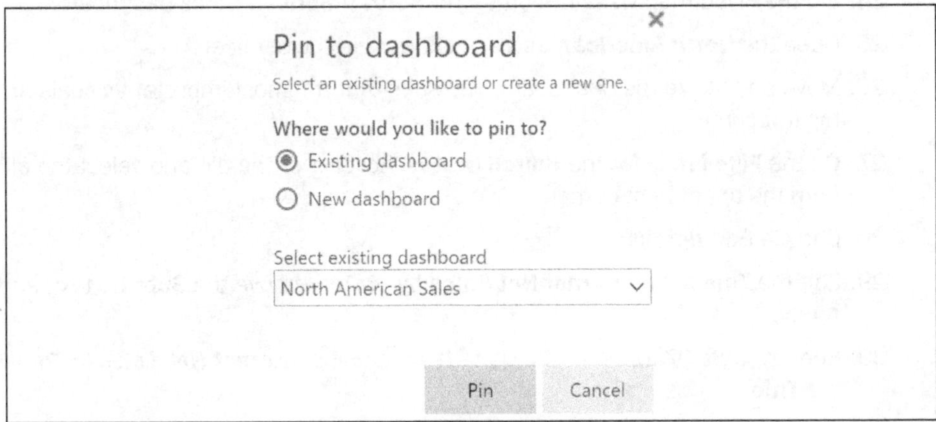

Figure 5.6: Pin to dashboard

8. Pin the **Monthly Internet Margin %** KPI visualization to the **North American Sales** dashboard.
9. Open the **CH5_R1_MarginAnalysisReport** report in the service.
10. In the **Sales Group** slicer, choose **North America.**
11. In the **Calendar Month** slicer, choose **2013-Dec, 2013-Nov, 2013-Oct, 2013-Sep, 2013-Aug**, and **2013-Jul.**
12. Pin the **Net Sales vs. Last Year** clustered column chart visualization to the **North American Sales** dashboard.
13. Open the **CH5_R1_CustomerActivityReport** report in the service.
14. In the **Sales Group** slicer, choose **North America.**
15. In the **Calendar Month** slicer, choose **2013-Dec, 2013-Nov, 2013-Oct, 2013-Sep, 2013-Aug**, and **2013-Jul.**
16. Pin the **Monthly Customers** KPI visualization to the **North American Sales** dashboard.

17. Pin the **YTD Net Sales vs. Last Year** gauge visualization to the **North American Sales** dashboard.
18. Pin the **Customer Count by Region** stacked column chart visualization to the **North American Sales** dashboard.
19. Pin the **YTD Net Sales by Region** clustered bar chart visualization to the **North American Sales** dashboard.
20. Open the **CH5_R1_CountryMonthlyReport** report in the service.
21. Navigate to the **United States** report page.
22. Pin the filled map visualization to the **North American Sales** dashboard.
23. Navigate to the **Canada** report page.
24. Pin the Filled map visualization to the **North American Sales** dashboard.
25. Open the **North American Sales** dashboard in the service.
26. Move and resize the dashboard tiles such that the most important visuals are in the top-left corner.
27. On the **Filled** map for the **United States**, hover over the tile and select the ellipsis (**...**) from the upper-right corner.
28. Choose **Edit details**.
29. Edit the **Title** to be **Internet Net Sales by State**, remove the **Subtitle** text, and click **Apply**.
30. Repeat *steps 27* to *29* for the Canada map using **Internet Net Sales by Province** as the **Title**.

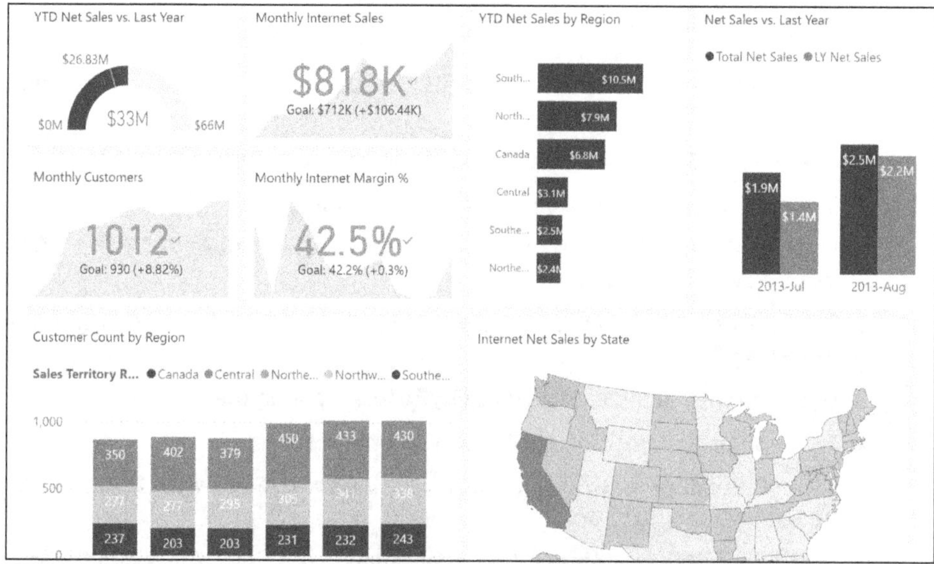

Figure 5.7: North American Sales dashboard

The dashboard provides an overview of the measures most important to the North America sales team. You can access any of the four underlying reports by clicking on a dashboard tile.

Note that resizing and moving dashboard tiles can be tricky at first. Hovering over a dashboard tile with your cursor displays a single resizing handle in the bottom-right corner of the tile. Click on this resizing handle to resize the tile. Tiles resize to preconfigured tile sizes displayed by the gray box displayed around the tile while resizing. When moving a tile, click and hold on the tile to move the tile around on the dashboard. Other tiles will automatically move depending upon where you place the tile. Release the mouse button to place the tile.

31. Just above the main dashboard area, select **Edit** and then **Add a tile**.

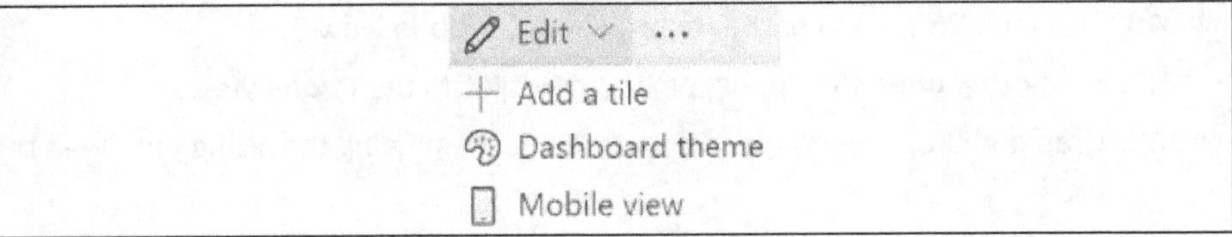

Figure 5.8: Dashboard Edit menu

32. In the **Add a tile** panel, choose **Image**, then click **Next**.
33. In **URL**, place the following link: `https://bit.ly/3mhzBxv`.
34. Check the **Set custom link** checkbox.
35. Set **Link type** to **External link** and **URL** to `http://www.adventure-works.com`.

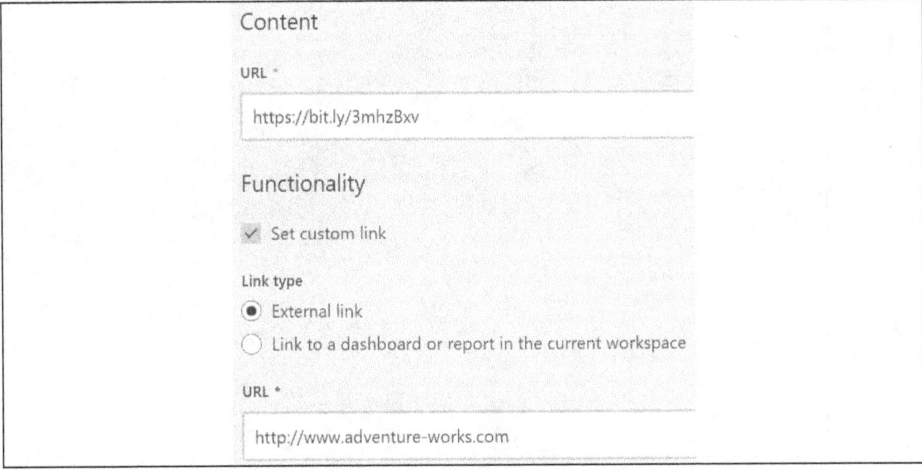

Figure 5.9: Image tile settings

36. Click the **Apply** button.
37. Add another tile, this time a **Text** box.
38. Add text to the **Content** area; notice that you can use the **Insert link** icon to add active links.

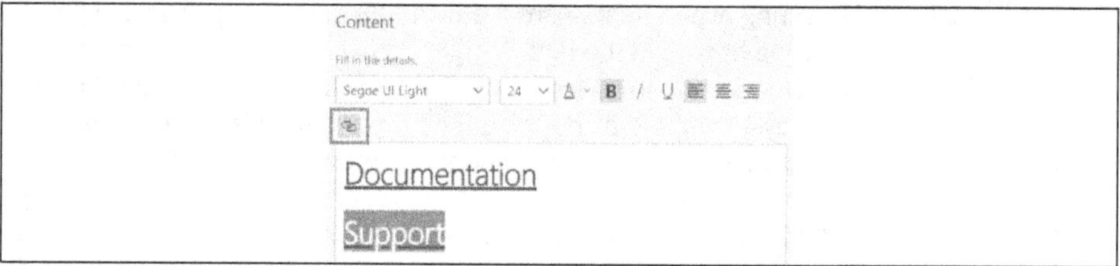

Figure 5.10: Text box tile settings

39. Click the **Apply** button.
40. From the **Edit** menu of the report, choose **Mobile view**.
41. In the **Unpinned tiles** pane, pin the new tiles to the **Phone view**.
42. Drag and drop tiles to reposition or resize them using the sizing handle at the lower right.

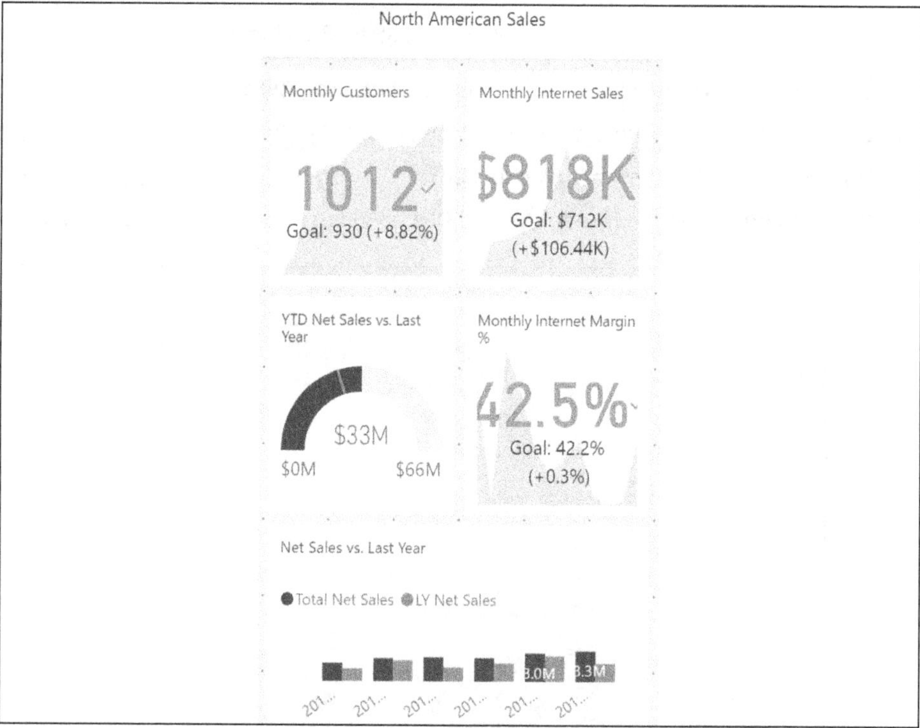

Figure 5.11: Dashboard Mobile view

43. When finished, at the upper right, select the dropdown for **Phone view** and switch to **Web view**.

How it works

It is important to understand that dashboard tiles maintain the filter context at the time the report visual is pinned. This is often a source of confusion for users and designers alike, as depending upon the design, a tile may appear to not update. For example, in the recipe, the last six months of 2013 were selected in the slicer before pinning the **Net Sales vs. Last Year** tile. Assuming that December 2013 is "today," when the data comes in for January 2014, this **Net Sales vs. Last Year** tile would not reflect data for January 2014. The tile would have to be unpinned and re-pinned with the new month included. To avoid situations like this, use **Relative Date** slicers/filters or base filtering on a flag field column that returns 1 if data is within a chosen range and 0 otherwise. This can be done in DAX or M; a DAX example is as follows:

```
6MonthFlag Column =
    VAR __Today = TODAY()
    VAR __EOM6Months = EOMONTH(__Today,-6)
    VAR __MinDate = DATE(YEAR(__EOM6Months),MONTH(__EOM6Months),1)
RETURN
    IF('Dates'[Date] >= __MinDate && 'Dates'[Date] <= __Today,1,0)
```

As demonstrated, dashboard tiles do not have to come from reports and can be added manually to include Image, Video, Text box, Web content, and Streaming data. In addition, a single dashboard can have tiles that come from reports that do not share the same dataset. Thus, if each of the four recipes in this model used different datasets, the exact same dashboard could still be created, as long as the reports all existed within the same workspace. In large enterprise organizations with many dashboards and reports, dashboards are sometimes used purely as a navigation device. By adding tiles of images or text, and using the ability to set custom links, a dashboard could be configured simply to link to other organizational dashboards.

There's more

By default, the tiles of a dashboard are independent of each other, and cannot be filtered or interacted with, such as when cross-filtering between visualizations. Additionally, modifications to reports after visuals have been pinned to dashboards, such as filter and layout changes, are not automatically reflected in the dashboards. In many scenarios, the users consuming a dashboard want to retain the interactive filtering experience of Power BI reports from within their dashboard, and so it can be helpful to automatically synchronize reports with dashboards. Luckily, Power BI supports the pinning of entire report pages to a dashboard. To see how this works, do the following:

1. Open the report **CH5_R1_RegionMonthlyReport** in the service.

2. From the menu bar of the report, click the ellipsis (**...**) and choose **Pin to a dashboard**.

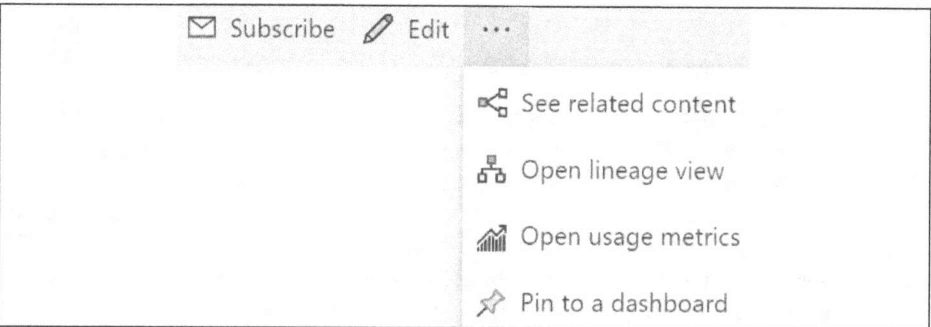

Figure 5.12: Pin to a dashboard

3. After selecting **Pin to a dashboard**, choose **Existing dashboard**, select the **North American Sales** dashboard, and click the **Pin live** button.
4. Navigate to the **North American Sales** dashboard, scroll down, and note that the report is now pinned as a tile.

The user of the dashboard can interact with the region and date slicers and other visuals on the live page. Given the size of the report page, it is generally not a good idea to pin a live report page to the **Mobile view**. The ellipsis at the top right of the live page tile includes the option **Go to report** link to access all pages of the live page report. Modifications to the underlying report will be reflected on the pinned live page. The other visuals link to their report pages.

See also

- Intro to dashboards for Power BI designers: `http://bit.ly/31KvIrv`
- Tips for designing a great Power BI dashboard: `http://bit.ly/2PspxG3`
- Add images, videos, and more to your dashboard: `https://bit.ly/31QypHP`

Preparing for Q&A

Q&A can be a powerful method of enabling users to explore datasets, enabling them to directly submit their own questions in both the Power BI service and through the Power BI mobile application. The tables and measures of each dataset, represented by a tile on the dashboard, are available to answer Q&A questions.

This recipe provides data model design and metadata tips to prepare a dataset for Q&A. Additionally, synonyms are added to a Power BI Desktop data model to improve the accuracy of natural language queries.

Getting ready

To prepare for this recipe:

- Complete the first recipe in this chapter, *Building a Dashboard*.

How to Prepare for Q&A

To implement this recipe, use the following steps:

1. Open the **North American Sales** dashboard.
2. At the upper left of the dashboard, click **Ask a question about your data**.

Figure 5.13: Power BI Q&A

3. Type the following: `wholesaler net sales by country`.
4. Notice that the word **wholesaler** is double-underlined in red, **net sales** is underlined in blue, and **country** is underlined with a dashed red line.

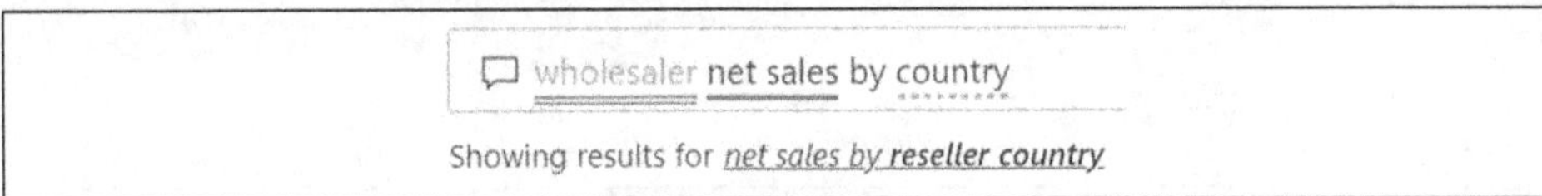

Figure 5.14: Showing results for net sales by reseller country

5. Hover over one of the map bubbles displayed and notice that the tooltip reads **Total Net Sales**, and *not* **Reseller Net Sales.**
6. Click the thumbs-down icon in the lower-right corner of the screen.
7. Open the file `CH5_R1_SalesAndFinanceDataset.pbix`.
8. Change to the **Model** view.
9. Click **Q&A setup** in the ribbon of the **Home** tab.

10. In the **Q&A setup** dialog, click the **Review questions** tab and notice that the question asked is present in the list. Note that you may have to wait a few minutes, using the refresh icon for the question to display.

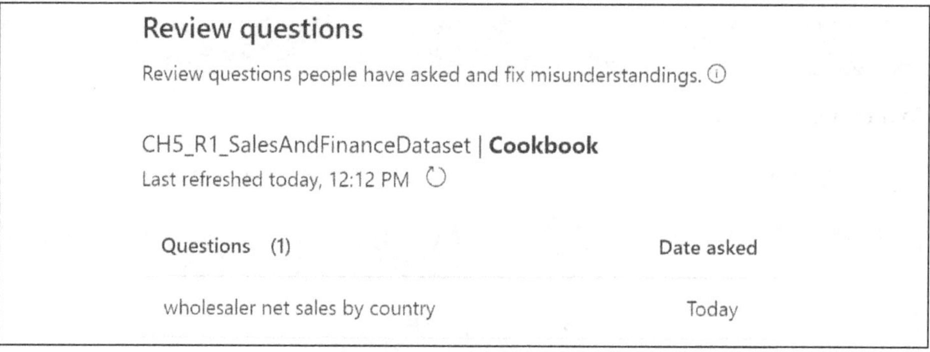

Figure 5.15: Review questions

11. Click the pencil icon under the **Fix needed** column. Note that if the question does not appear after a few minutes, simply proceed to the **Teach Q&A** tab, enter the question **wholesaler net sales by country**, click the **Submit** button, and proceed to *Step 13*.
12. The **Teach Q&A** tab is opened with the question displayed.
13. The word "wholesaler" is flagged between two handles; in **Define the terms Q&A didn't understand**, type **reseller** in the input field (see *Figure 5.16*).

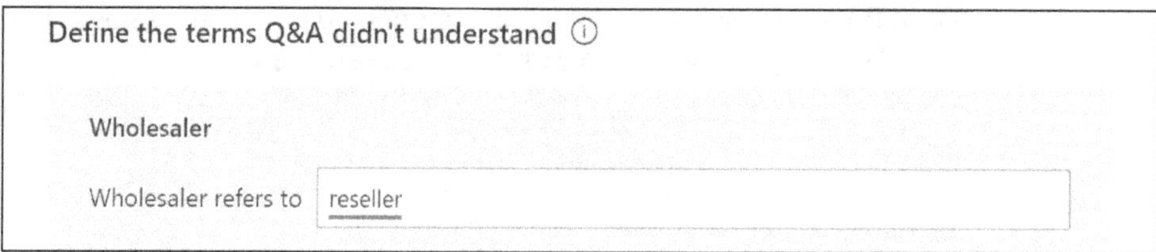

Figure 5.16: Adding synonym for reseller

14. Click **Save**, but notice that the map visual is still not correct.
15. Drag the right handle (the red stick and circle) to include the entire phrase **wholesaler net sales** and click **Submit.**

Figure 5.17: Adding term for wholesaler net sales

16. In the **Define the terms Q&A didn't understand** dialog box, type **reseller net sales** in the input field and notice that the map updates; the correct information is now displayed in the tooltip.

17. Click the **Save** button.
18. Click the **Manage terms** tab and notice that **wholesaler** and **wholesaler net sale** are now defined as terms with the correct definitions.
19. Click on the **Field synonyms** tab, expand the **Resellers** table and note that the **wholesaler** synonym has been added for the **Resellers** table.

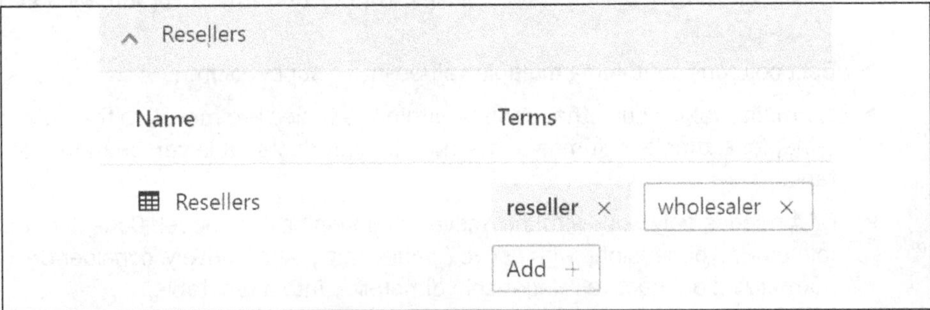

Figure 5.18: Table synonym

20. Expand the **Reseller Sales** table, scroll down, and see that the **wholesaler net sale** synonym has been added to the **Reseller Net Sales** measure.

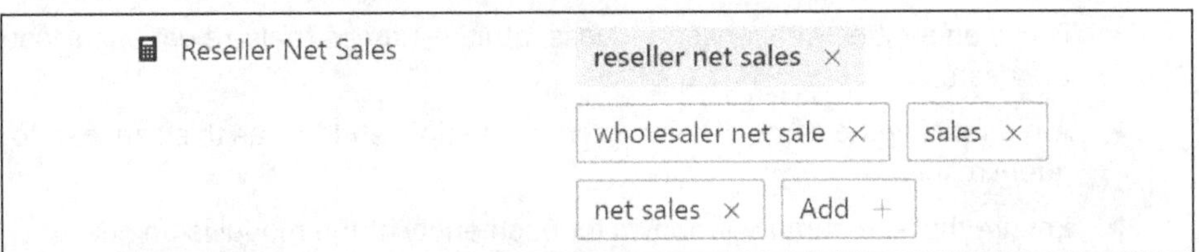

Figure 5.19: Measure synonym

21. Close the **Q&A setup** dialog using the close button in the upper-right corner.

How it works

Power BI Q&A supports Import mode and live connections to Azure Analysis Services, SQL Server Analysis Services (with a gateway), and Power BI datasets. RLS is supported for those data sources. Additionally, Q&A supports DirectQuery to SQL DirectQuery sources, such as Azure SQL Database, Azure Synapse Analytics, and SQL Server 2019. Q&A is not supported for composite data models or Reporting Services.

Synonyms are a crucial part of making sure that business users find the Q&A experience easy and intuitive—as well as getting the right answers to their questions. Synonyms allow a semantic layer to be added to the data model that uses business terminology instead of purely just the names of tables, columns, and measures within the model. Tables, columns, and measures can be included or excluded from Q&A and can have synonyms defined.

Some general tips for setting up a Q&A include the following:

- Revise any columns with incorrect data types, such as dates or numbers that are stored as text data types.
- Set the default summarization for dimension columns to **Do not summarize**.
- Associate geographical columns, such as states and zip codes, with a related data category.
- Split columns containing multiple values into distinct columns.
- Normalize tables such that entities within the tables are moved to their own distinct table; for example, columns of a vendor in a products table can be moved to a vendor table.
- Q&A queries only work with the active relationships of a model. Consider dedicated role-playing dimensions with active relationships. Alternatively, consider de-normalizing an inactive relationship dimension into a fact table.
- Define the top or most common natural language questions and test for accuracy in Power BI.
- Identify the gaps between the names of data model entities and the names used in natural language queries.
- Focus on entities with longer and less intuitive names that are not used casually by the users.
- Avoid reusing the same synonym across multiple entities, as this can lead to incorrect query results.
- Ensure that the primary synonym for each entity of the model is unique.

There's more

Q&A may not be appropriate for certain dashboards and datasets. For example, the Q&A search bar **Ask a question about your data** may be a distraction to users who only want to view the KPIs and other information as presented. Additionally, if the dataset requires a gateway, such as an on-premises SSAS server or a DirectQuery Power BI Desktop model to an on-premises source, Q&A may be avoided, given the additional (and potentially inefficient) queries and performance considerations.

To enable or disable Q&A, follow these steps:

1. In the Power BI service, access the app workspace containing the dashboard.
2. Use the three vertical dots and click **Settings**.

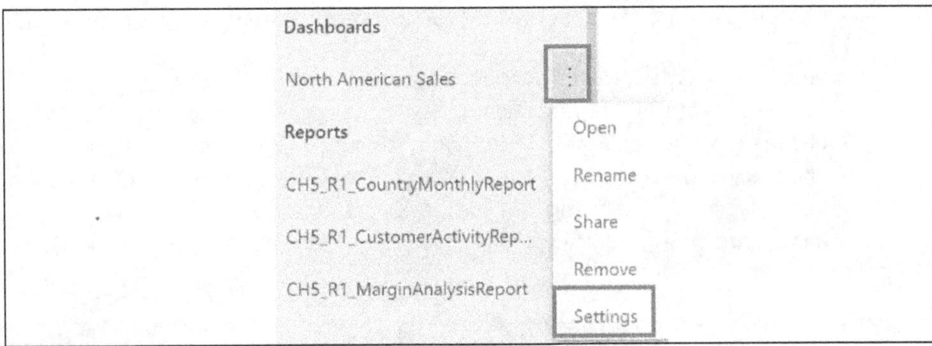

Figure 5.20: Dashboard settings

3. Check or uncheck the box for **Show the Q&A** search box on this dashboard.

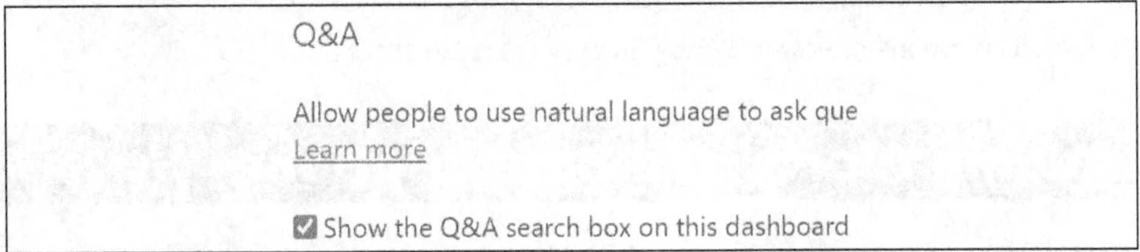

Figure 5.21: Show the Q&A search box on this dashboard

The entire semantic layer definition that drives Q&A can be exported, modified, and imported via Power BI Desktop using the **Linguistic schema** option in the ribbon of the **Home** tab while in **Model view**. The exported file is a YAML file. YAML (YAML Ain't Markup Language) is a human-readable text file used for data serialization. The portion of the YAML file after adding the wholesaler net margin synonym looks like the following:

```
reseller_sale.reseller_net_sales:
  Definition:
    Binding: {Table: Reseller Sales, Measure: Reseller Net Sales}
  State: Generated
  Terms:
  - reseller net sales: {State: Generated}
  - wholesaler net sale: {LastModified: '2021-04-05T16:58:30.2996117Z'}
  - sales: {State: Generated, Weight: 0.97}
  - net sales: {State: Generated, Weight: 0.97}
  - sale: {State: Suggested, Weight: 0.97}
  - net sale: {State: Suggested, Weight: 0.97}
  - reseller net sale: {Type: Noun, State: Suggested, Weight: 0.739}
  - wholesaler net auction: {Type: Noun, State: Suggested, Weight: 0.492}
  - net auction: {Type: Noun, State: Suggested, Weight: 0.485}
```

```
    - wholesaler net transaction: {Type: Noun, State: Suggested, Weight: 0.482}
    - auction: {Type: Noun, State: Suggested, Weight: 0.476}
    - net transaction: {Type: Noun, State: Suggested, Weight: 0.475}
    - wholesaler net deal: {Type: Noun, State: Suggested, Weight: 0.468}
    - wholesaler net trade: {Type: Noun, State: Suggested, Weight: 0.468}
    - wholesaler net vending: {Type: Noun, State: Suggested, Weight: 0.468}
    - wholesaler net retailing: {Type: Noun, State: Suggested, Weight: 0.468}
```

See also

- Use Power BI Q&A to explore and create visuals: `http://bit.ly/2QYa7JN`
- Best practices to optimize Q&A: `http://bit.ly/3cSddYp`
- Limitations of Power BI Q&A: `http://bit.ly/2PtCrDL`

Adding Alerts and Subscriptions

Alerts can be configured on the tiles of dashboards to provide a notification that a specific condition has been met. Alert rules and options can be managed in the Power BI service, and notifications can be limited to the notification center in Power BI or shared via email. Data-driven alerts enhance the value of Power BI dashboards, as they immediately bring attention to significant events or outcomes as the dataset supporting the dashboard tile is refreshed. Power BI dashboards and reports also support subscriptions. Subscriptions send images and links of refreshed reports and dashboards directly to user inboxes according to the defined schedule. Additionally, paginated report subscriptions can be configured to attach report data to subscription emails in common file formats such as Excel and PDF.

This recipe demonstrates how to create and configure alerts and subscriptions, as well as how to use this functionality to unlock even more powerful functionality through the use of Power Automate.

Getting ready

To prepare for this recipe:

- Complete the first recipe in this chapter, *Building a Dashboard*.

How to Add Alerts and Subscriptions

To implement this recipe, use the following steps:

1. Open the **North American Sales** dashboard in the Power BI service.
2. Hover over the **Monthly Customers** KPI tile, click the ellipsis (...) in the upper-right corner, and select **Manage alerts**.
3. In the **Manage alerts** pane, click **Add alert rule**.
4. Edit **Alert title**, **Condition**, and **Threshold** and ensure that the **Send me email, too** checkbox is selected.

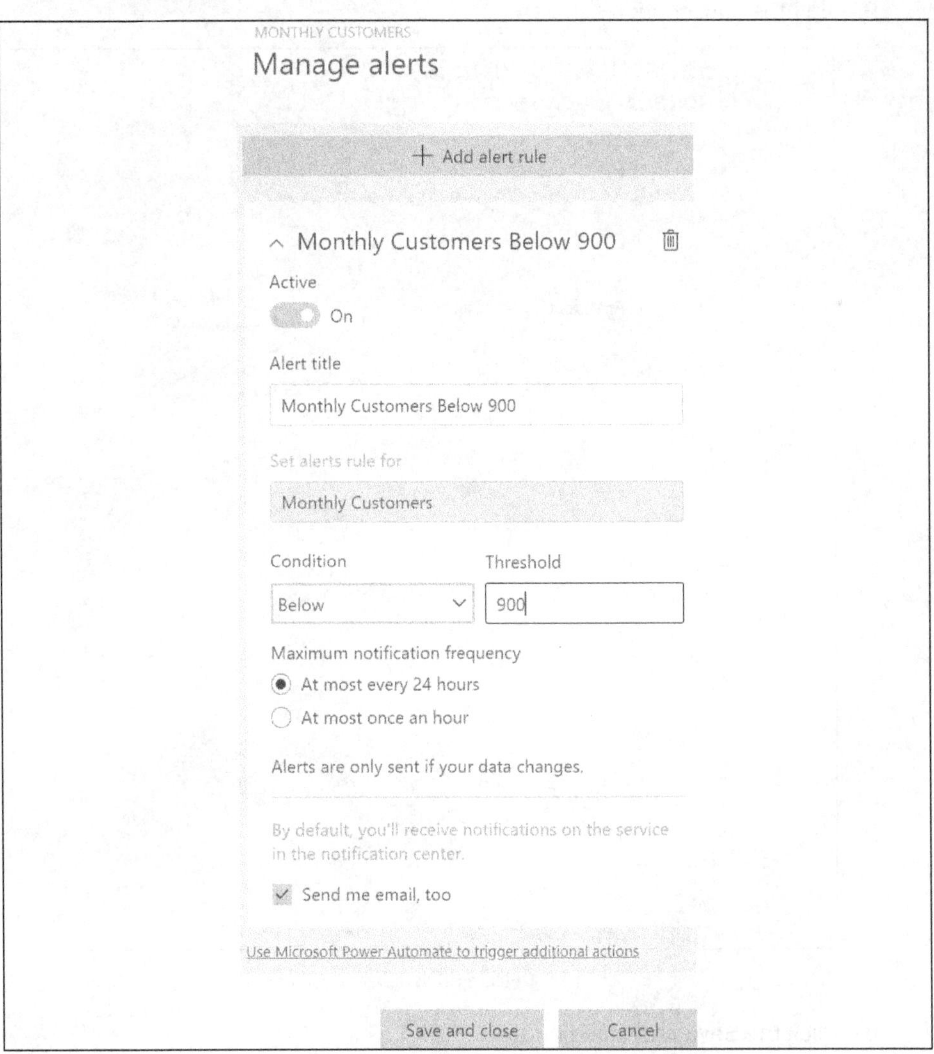

Figure 5.22: Alert creation

5. Click the **Save and close** button to save the alert.
6. Create another alert on the same KPI visual named **Monthly Customers Above 1100**, with the appropriate **Condition** and **Threshold** set.
7. In the ribbon for the dashboard, choose **Subscribe**.

File
Share
Chat in Teams
Comment
Subscribe
Edit

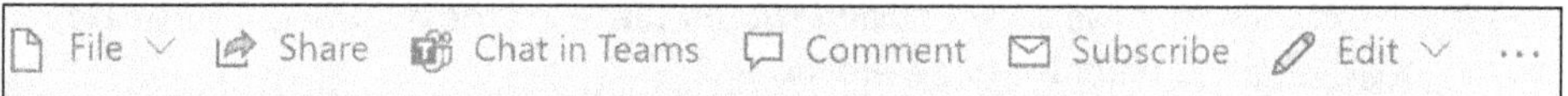

Figure 5.23: Dashboard ribbon

8. Click the **Add new subscription** button.
9. Edit the subscription settings.

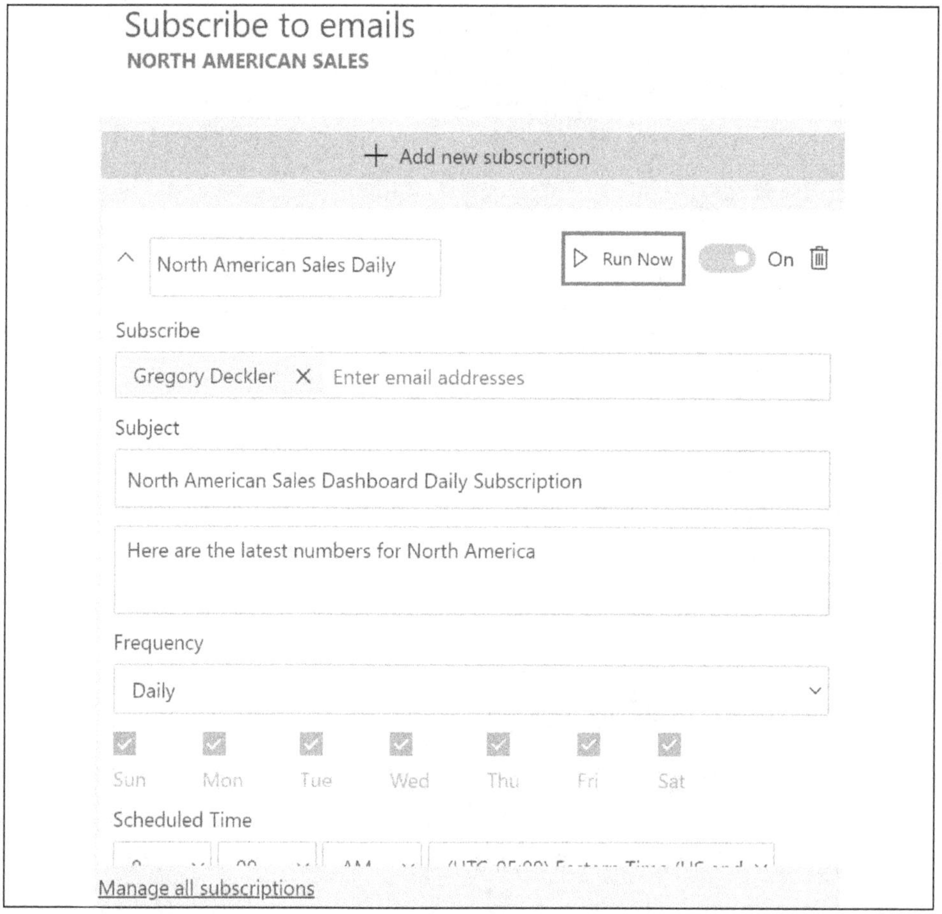

Subscribe to emails
NORTH AMERICAN SALES
Add new subscription
North American Sales Daily
Run Now
On
Subscribe
Gregory Deckler
Enter email addresses
Subject
North American Sales Dashboard Daily Subscription
Here are the latest numbers for North America
Frequency
Daily
Sun
Mon
Tue
Wed
Thu
Fri
Sat
Scheduled Time
Manage all subscriptions

Figure 5.24: Subscription creation

10. Click the **Save and close** button.

11. Click **Subscribe** in the ribbon again.
12. This time, expand the subscription just created.
13. Click **Run Now** to test the subscription (see *Figure 5.24*).
14. Within minutes, you should receive an email from Microsoft Power BI, with a subject line of the name of your subscription, and an email body similar to that shown in *Figure 5.25*.

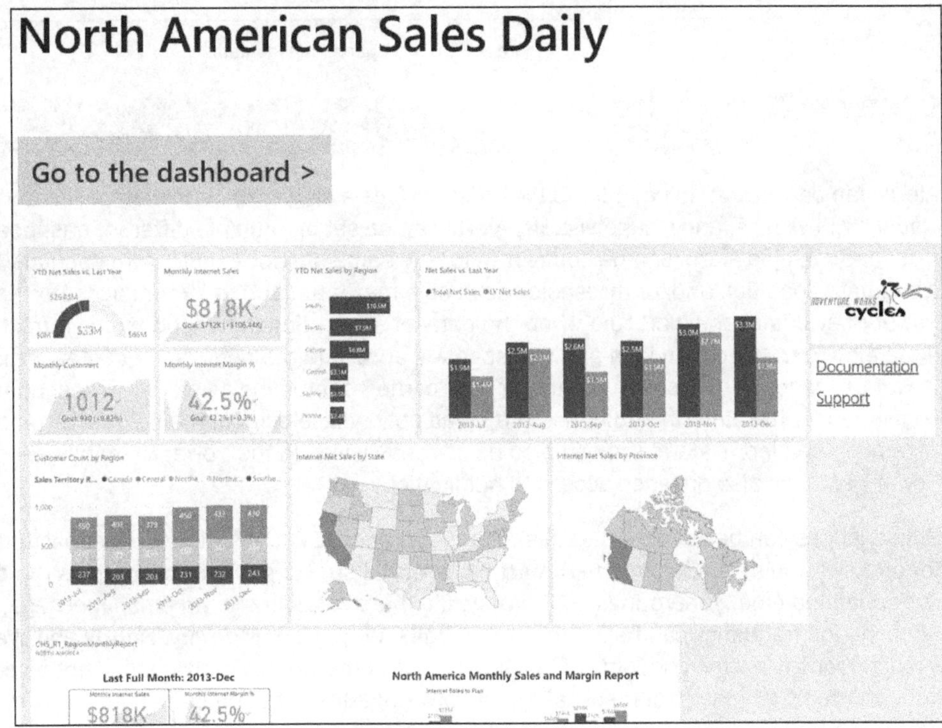

Figure 5.25: Subscription message body

15. In the Power BI service, click the gear icon in the upper-right corner and choose **Settings**.
16. Click the **Alerts** tab and note that you will have alerts appear.

Cookbook

ALERT	DASHBOARD	DATE CREATED	
Monthly Customers Below 900	North American Sales	Apr 5, 2021, 8:46:05 PM	On
Monthly Customers Above 1100	North American Sales	Apr 5, 2021, 8:47:37 PM	On

Figure 5.26: Alert management

17. Click the **Subscriptions** tab and note that your subscription has also appeared.

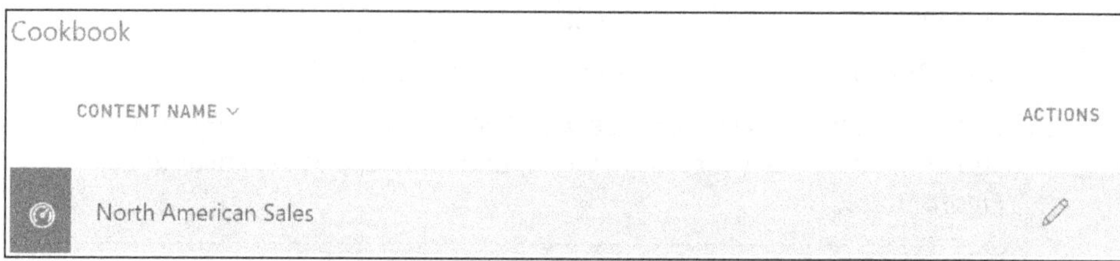

Figure 5.27: Subscription management

How it works

Alerts can only be set on dashboard tiles that surface a single numeric metric, like Card visuals, KPI visuals, and Gauge visuals. Alerts can be set on multiple different dashboard tiles, and multiple alerts can be configured for the same dashboard tile, with each alert having a separate condition and/or threshold—such as a maximum and minimum accepted value. Power BI evaluates the alert rule when the dataset supporting the dashboard is refreshed. If the alert is triggered, an icon and message will appear in the notification center in the Power BI service (a bell icon in the upper-right corner) containing a link to the dashboard tile configured for the alert. In addition, if the email option is selected, an email will also be sent regarding the alert. Data alerts can also be set and viewed in the Power BI mobile apps—Power BI mobile also provides access to notifications.

Subscriptions can be set on either dashboards or reports. When setting up a subscription for a report, you must choose the **Report** page for the subscription. Subscriptions run at the appointed time, generating a PNG image file that is attached to an email message. Subscription frequency can be set to **Hourly**, **Daily**, **Weekly**, or **Monthly**. **Hourly** and **Weekly** subscriptions allow the choosing of individual days of the week. A single subscription can support multiple email addresses, allowing Power BI admins to configure subscriptions for other users.

There's more

Alerts in the Power BI service are limited to the sending of emails only to the creator of that alert. However, Power Automate can be used to notify others via email, or even trigger complex workflows. To see how this works, carry out the following:

1. In the Power BI service, click the gear icon in the upper-right corner and choose **Settings**.
2. Choose the **Alerts** tab and click **Edit** for the **Monthly Customers Above 1100** alert.
3. In the **Manage alerts** pane at the bottom, click **Use Microsoft Power Automate to trigger additional actions**.

4. A new tab is opened for Power Automate for a template called **Trigger a flow with a Power BI data-driven alert**.
5. Click the **Try it now** button.
6. If necessary, sign in to your work account.

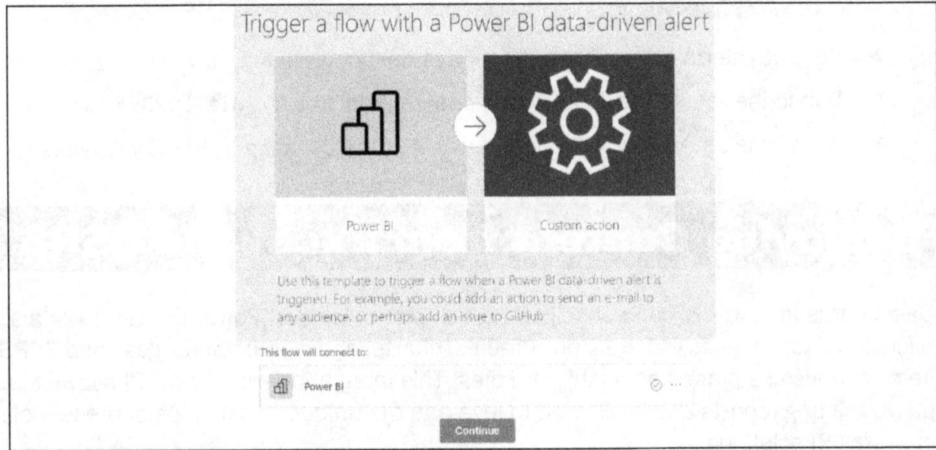

Figure 5.28: Trigger a flow with a Power BI data-driven alert

7. Click the **Continue** button.
8. From the **Alert Id** dropdown, choose the specific Power BI data alert to trigger the flow, and then click the **New Step** button.
9. Find the **Mail** action and select it.
10. Configure the email notification using **Dynamic content** and click the **Save** button.

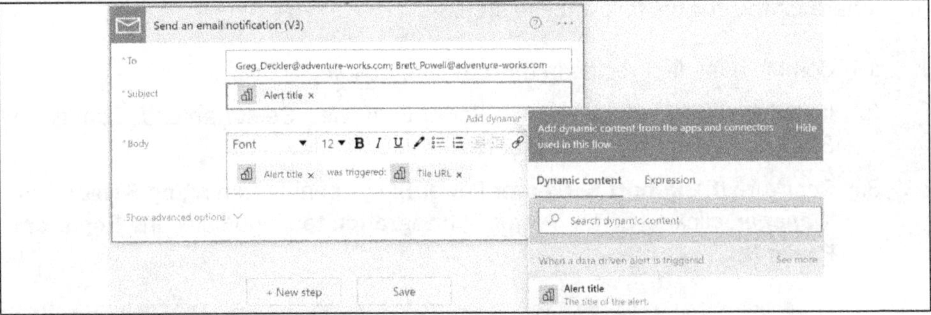

Figure 5.29: Configure custom email notification for alert

11. Select **Save** to save, and **Test** to test the flow. Select the **Manually** option.
12. Verify that the flow appears when selecting the **My flows** tab in the left navigation pane.

Given the value of alerts to stakeholders and the low effort required in creating and managing alerts and notifications in Power BI and Power Automate, dedicated alert dashboards can be developed to reduce the amount of analysis and monitoring required.

See also

- Set data alerts on the Power BI service dashboards: `http://bit.ly/2R40ebL`
- Subscribe yourself to reports and dashboards: `http://bit.ly/3fJphwU`
- Subscribe others to your reports and dashboards: `http://bit.ly/3wynW2a`

Deploying Content from Excel and SSRS

Dashboards in Power BI can consolidate much more than just Power BI report visuals. Microsoft Excel objects—such as pivot tables, charts, and workbook ranges—and SSRS report items can also be pinned as dashboard tiles. This integration with Power BI allows teams to utilize existing reports and skills, and to leverage the unique capabilities of these tools as part of overall BI solutions.

In this recipe, a pivot table and pivot chart from an Excel workbook are integrated into an existing Power BI dashboard. Additionally, an SSRS report item is also pinned to this dashboard. For more advanced integration examples, see *Chapter 13, Integrating Power BI with Other Applications*.

Getting ready

To prepare for this recipe, follow these steps:

1. Complete the first recipe in this chapter, *Building a Dashboard*.
2. Install Analyze in Excel from the Power BI service. See *Chapter 1, Configuring Power BI Tools*, for details on this process.
3. Configure the **Report Server** for Power BI by opening **Reporting Server Configuration Manager**, clicking on the Power BI **Integration** tab, and selecting **Register with Power BI**.

How to Deploy Excel and SSRS Content

To implement this recipe, use the following steps:

1. Open the report **CH5_R1_CountryMonthlyReport** in the service.
2. In the **Report** ribbon, select **Export** and then **Analyze in Excel**.

3. Open the `CH5_R1_SalesAndFinanceDataset.xlsx` file from your **Downloads** folder.
4. In the **Protected View** warning box, click **Enable Editing**.
5. In the **Security Warning** box, click **Enable Content**.
6. Select a cell in the **PivotTable1** area.
7. In the **PivotTable Fields** pane, find the **Internet Sales** group with a summation icon in front of it and place **Internet Net Sales** in the **Values** area.
8. Scroll down to find the **Dates** group with the table icon in front of it and drag and drop the **Year Month** field into the **Rows** area.

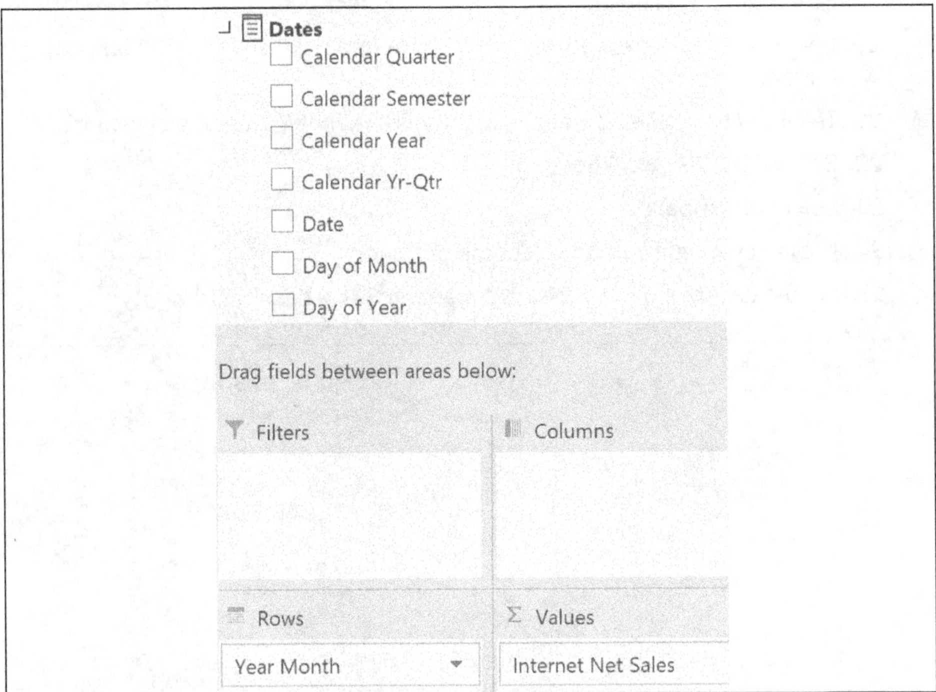

Figure 5.30: Pivot table configuration

9. Select **Insert Slicer** from the ribbon of the **Analyze** tab.
10. In the **Insert Slicers** dialog, select **Country** from the **Customers** table and then click **OK**.
11. Select a cell in the pivot table and then choose **PivotChart** from the ribbon of the **Analyze** tab.
12. In the **Insert Chart** dialog, choose **Column**, then **Clustered Column**, and click **OK**.
13. Select **United States** in the slicer.

14. Save the Excel file to your OneDrive for Business directory as `CH5_R4_Workbook` and close Excel.
15. In the Power BI service, open the workspace with the **North American Sales** dashboard.
16. In the lower-left corner, choose **Get data**.
17. In the **Get Data** dialog, select the **Get** button in the **Files** section under **Create new content**.
18. Choose **OneDrive - Business**.
19. Select the Excel file and then click the **Connect** button.
20. Under **Connect, manage, and view Excel in Power BI**, click the **Connect** button.
21. The Excel file name now appears in the **Workbooks** area of the workspace.
22. Select **CH5_R4_Workbook**.
23. Select **PivotChart**.
24. In the upper-right corner, select the pin icon.
25. Pin the dashboard to the **North American Sales** dashboard.

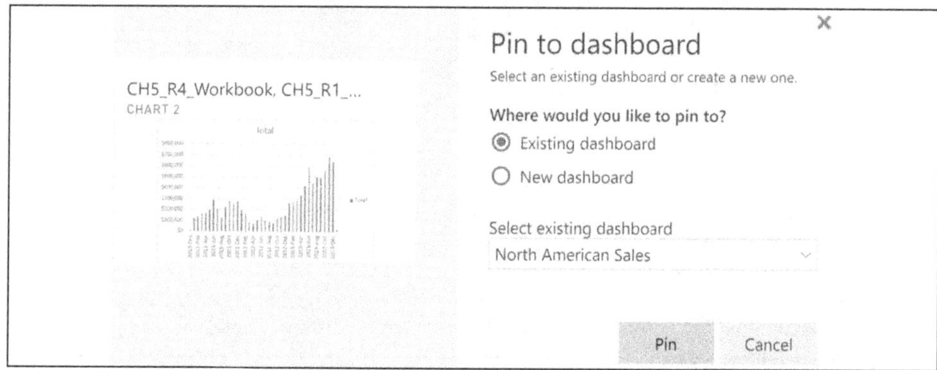

Figure 5.31: Pin Excel PivotChart to dashboard

26. Navigate to the **North American Sales** dashboard to view the pinned **PivotChart** tile at the bottom of the dashboard.

How it works

This recipe demonstrates how to publish the workbook from Excel to Power BI and then pin items from the workbook report in the Power BI service. Using this method, once published, the workbook cannot not be refreshed. This means that after pinning items directly from the Excel workbook to the dashboard, the connection to the dataset hosted in the Power BI service must be periodically refreshed, with the tile being removed and re-pinned.

To avoid this manual and local refresh process, Excel report visuals can be built on top of an Excel data model; this Excel workbook can be published to the Power BI service. Published workbooks, containing data models, can be configured for a scheduled refresh in the Power BI service, and their dependent reports will be updated to reflect these refreshes.

Recently, Microsoft added the ability for connected PivotTable refresh in Excel for the web. This means that PivotTables connected to Power BI inside Excel for the web can now be refreshed. A connected PivotTable can be created either via the service by choosing the **Analyze in Excel** option for a report or in Excel by choosing the **From Power BI** option when inserting a PivotTable.

There's more

It is also possible to pin SSRS report elements to Power BI dashboards. To see how this works, do the following:

1. Create or identify the SSRS report to support the dashboard.
2. Publish this report to the SSRS report server, or open this report on the report server.
3. From the report server browser window, click the Power BI icon and sign in with the appropriate Power BI account.
4. Click on the SSRS report item to pin:

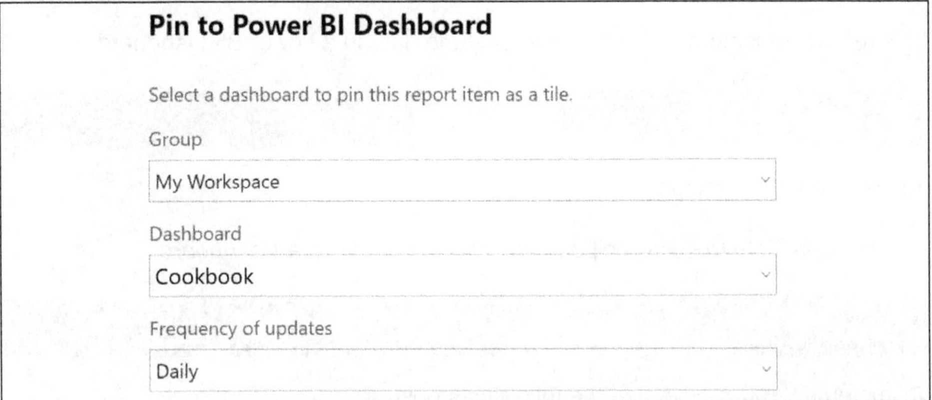

Figure 5.32: Pin to Power BI from SSRS 2016

5. From the **Pin to Power BI Dashboard** dialog, choose the workspace and dashboard to pin the item to.

The update frequency creates an SSRS subscription to keep the tile updated in Power BI. You can also pin charts, gauge panels, maps, and images from SSRS reports to Power BI dashboards, provided these items are within the report body (and not the page header or footer). You cannot currently pin tables, matrices, or list report items from SSRS reports.

SSRS and Excel are now much more deeply integrated in Power BI than the first edition of this book. In the case of SSRS, almost all of the same granular, 'pixel perfect' report design features are supported with paginated reports for Power BI premium customers. Likewise, Excel reports built with external data connections to Power BI datasets can also be published to Power BI and included in the same Power BI apps alongside paginated and Power BI reports.

See also

- Pin a tile to a Power BI dashboard from Excel: `http://bit.ly/2PI6RC1`
- Power BI Report Server Integration (Configuration Manager): `http://bit.ly/3sTGGqA`
- Pin paginated report items to Power BI dashboards: `http://bit.ly/3rVQfE7`
- Connected PivotTable refresh in Excel for the web is now 100% available to Office tenants: `https://bit.ly/3yM3kmS`

Streaming Datasets

Streaming datasets allow Power BI dashboards to display real-time data. Real-time data sources are generally Internet of Things (IoT) devices, but can also include such things as social media applications and stock prices.

This recipe demonstrates how to use real-time data in a Power BI dashboard.

Getting ready

To prepare for this recipe:

- Complete the first recipe in this chapter, *Building a Dashboard*.

How to Stream Datasets

To implement this recipe, use the following steps:

1. Navigate to the workspace where **North American Sales** is located in the service.
2. Under the workspace name, select **New**, and then **Streaming dataset**.

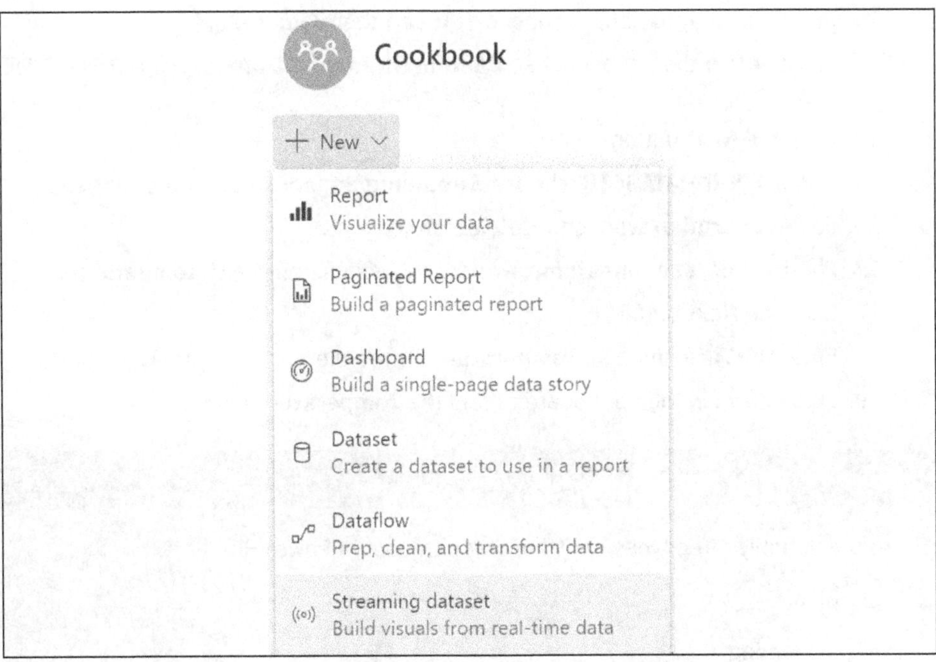

Figure 5.33: Create a new Streaming dataset

3. In the **New streaming dataset** pane, choose **PUBNUB** and click **Next**.
4. Name the dataset **Streaming Sensor Data**.
5. Use the following `Sub-key: sub-c-5f1b7c8e-fbee-11e3-aa40-02ee2ddab7fe`.
6. Use the following **Channel: pubnub-sensor-network**.
7. Click the **Next** button.
8. The next page shows the schema of the dataset; click the **Create** button.
9. The **Streaming Sensor Data** dataset appears in the workspace.
10. Navigate to the **North American Sales** dashboard.

11. In the dashboard ribbon, choose **Edit** and then **Add a tile**.
12. In the **Add a tile** pane, choose **Custom Streaming Data** from the **REAL-TIME DATA** area.
13. Click the **Next** button.
14. Under **YOUR DATASETS**, choose **Streaming Sensor Data**, and click **Next**.
15. For **Visualization type**, choose **Line chart**.
16. For the **Axis**, use **timestamp**, and for **Values** use **ambient_temperature**.
17. Click the **Next** button.
18. Enter the **Title** name as **Temperature** for the tile and click the **Apply** button.
19. Scroll down in the dashboard to find the **Temperature** tile.

How it works

There are actually three types of streaming datasets in Power BI:

- Push
- Streaming
- PubNub

Push datasets have an external program that pushes data into Power BI; the data is stored within Power BI as a dataset. Push datasets store the information permanently in Power BI, which can then be used to create reports. With push datasets, visuals are built via reports and then pinned to dashboards. Push datasets are limited to 1 request per second, 16 MB per request, and 1 million rows per hour.

Streaming datasets push data to Power BI, but do not store data within a Power BI dataset. Therefore, streaming datasets cannot be used in reports—only dashboards. Streaming datasets are limited to 5 requests per second and 15 KB per request but have no limits on the number of rows processed per hour.

PubNub datasets also do not store data in Power BI, and therefore can only be used on dashboards. There are no limits regarding the requests sent per second, or the amount of data sent per request, because the Power BI web client uses the PubNub SDK to read existing PubNub data streams, instead of the information being pushed to Power BI.

Push and streaming datasets can be created using the Power BI REST API, the **API** option in the service when creating a new streaming dataset via Azure Stream Analytics.

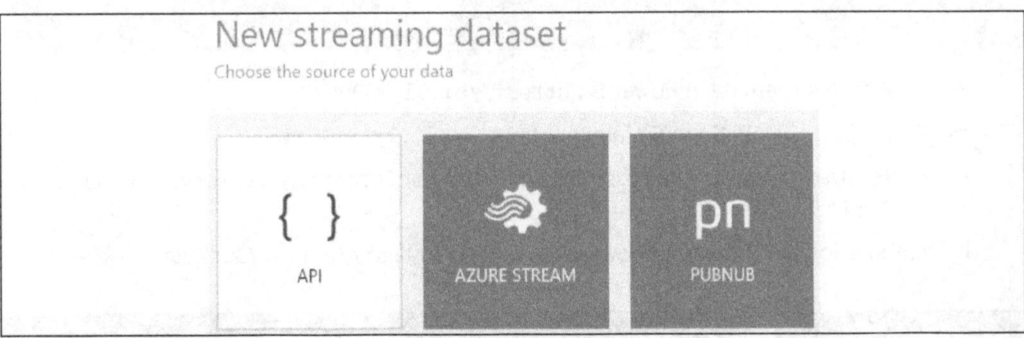

Figure 5.34: New streaming dataset options

When creating a streaming dataset using the **API** option in the service, the configuration screen includes a toggle for **Historic data analysis**. This toggle is **Off** by default, and will create a streaming dataset—toggling **Historic data analysis** to **On** creates a push dataset. Once the PUSH/STREAMING dataset is created, the Push Datasets functions of the Power BI REST API can be used to push data into the dataset.

The Azure Stream option in the Power BI service is not fully implemented at the time of writing, but when implemented will provide an interface for integrating Azure Stream Analytics data into Power BI. Currently, you must activate the Power BI integration from Azure Stream Analytics. Power BI is an output option for Azure Stream Analytics data. Setting Power BI as an output from Azure Stream Analytics creates a Power BI dataset that can take advantage of both push and streaming. By default, this dataset stores 200,000 rows of data, and data is expired via first-in-first-out (FIFO).

There's more

Another option when it comes to real-time or near-real-time data is to use **Automatic page refresh**. Automatic page refresh is used on report pages to set a refresh interval for visuals that is only active when the report is being viewed—the option is not available for Import data sources. Automatic page refresh is configured in Power BI Desktop or the Power BI service in the **Format** options for the page. The **Refresh** type can be configured to either a fixed interval or based upon a change detection configuration. Change detection support varies by storage mode, source, and whether you are using dedicated (Premium) or shared capacity. Shared capacities do not support change detection for any storage mode or source. The minimum refresh fixed interval also varies by storage mode, source, and type of capacity. For dedicated capacity, the minimum refresh fixed interval is one second, except for Azure Analysis Services, where it is 30 minutes. For shared capacity, the minimum refresh fixed interval is 30 minutes for all storage modes and sources.

See also

- Real-time streaming in Power BI: `https://bit.ly/39NhYRg`
- Power BI REST API Push Datasets: `https://bit.ly/3dDVW4u`
- Azure Stream Analytics: `https://azure.microsoft.com/en-us/services/stream-analytics/`
- Automatic page refresh in Power BI Desktop: `https://bit.ly/3utXO6q`

Authoring Dataflows

Dataflows are reusable, scalable self-service ETL (extract-transform-load) artifacts created exclusively in the Power BI cloud service. Dataflows utilize the same Power Query (M) language for data access and transformation that has existed within Power BI Desktop but can be shared across datasets and, with Power BI premium capacity, can support large, resource-intensive workloads.

This recipe demonstrates how to create a dataflow within the Power BI service, and how that dataflow can then be leveraged within Power BI Desktop.

Getting ready

To prepare for this recipe, follow these steps:

1. Download the `CH5_R7_AuthoringDataflows.xlsx` file from the following GitHub repository: `https://github.com/PacktPublishing/Microsoft-Power-BI-Cookbook-Second-Edition`.
2. Save the `CH5_R7_AuthoringDataflows.xlsx` file to your OneDrive for Business directory.

How to Author Dataflows

To implement this recipe, perform the following steps:

1. Open a workspace in the Power BI service.
2. Under the workspace name, select **New** and then **Dataflow**.
3. Choose **Add new tables** under the **Define new tables** area.

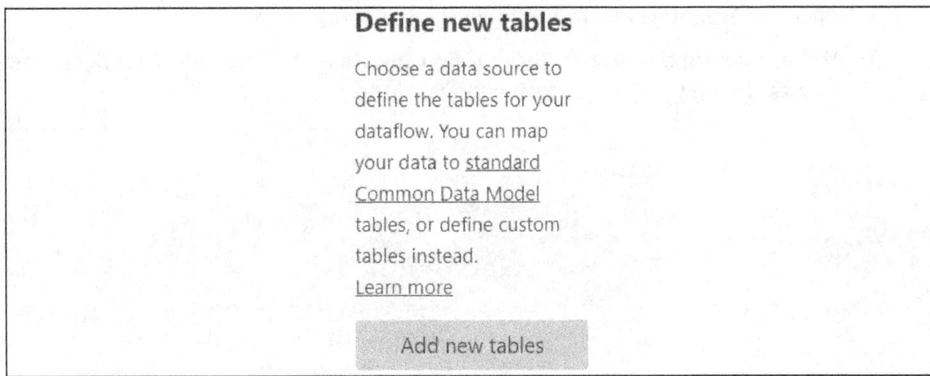

Figure 5.35: Define new tables

4. From the All categories tab, choose Excel under Data sources.

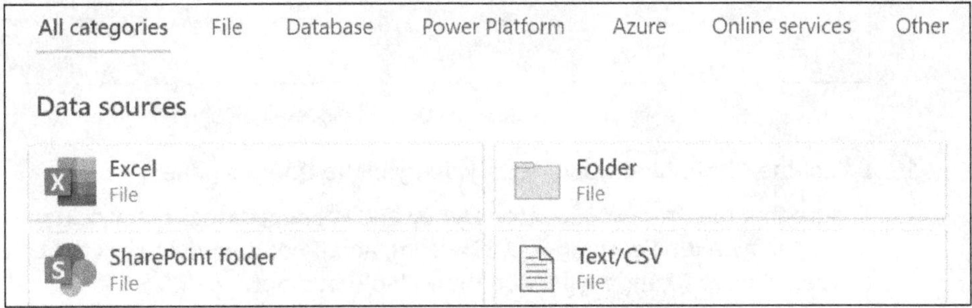

Figure 5.36: Data sources

5. For **Connection settings**, click the **Browse OneDrive** button, select the `CH5_R7_AuthoringDataflows.xlsx` file, and click **Open**.
6. Click the **Next** button in the lower-right corner.
7. Select **DimProduct**, **DimProductCategory**, and **DimProductSubcategory**.

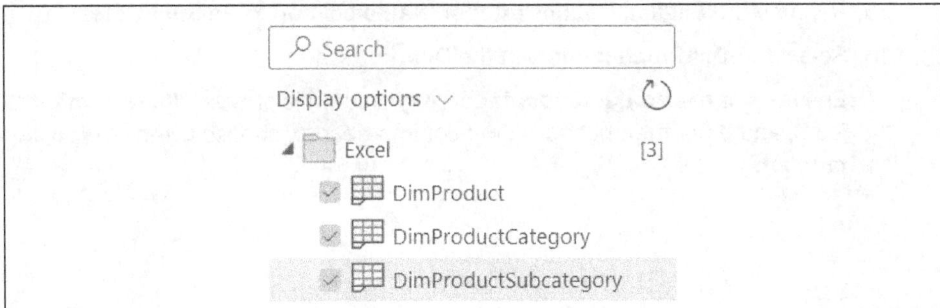

Figure 5.37: Choose data

8. Click the **Transform Data** button in the lower-right corner.
9. You are now in the **Power Query – Edit queries** interface, which works in the same way as the Power Query interface in Desktop.

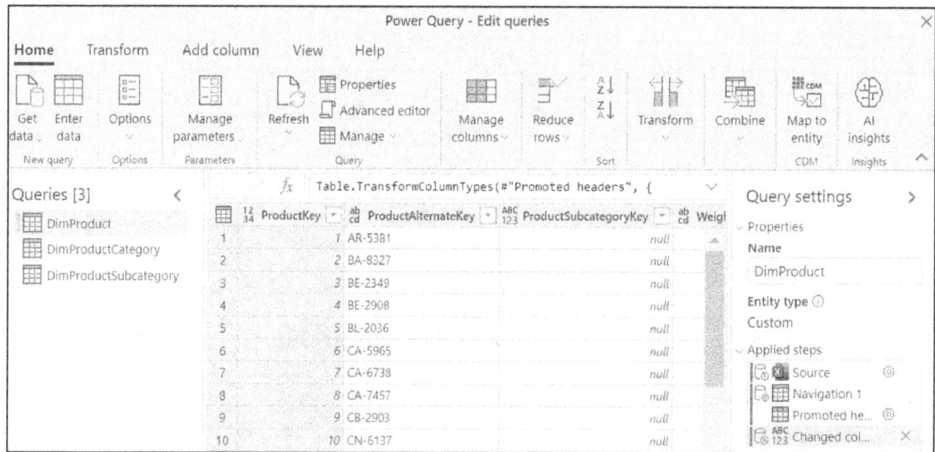

Figure 5.38: Power Query in the Power BI service

10. Select the **DimProductSubcategory** query in the **Queries** pane.
11. Ensure that the **ProductSubcategoryKey** and **ProductCategoryKey** columns are of the type **Whole number** (**1234** icon), and if not then right-click the column header, choose **Change type**, and then **Whole number**.
12. Right-click the **EnglishProductSubcategoryName** column header, choose **Rename**, and rename the column to **Product Subcatgory**.
13. Select the **DimProductCategory** query in the **Queries** pane.
14. Ensure that the **ProductCategoryKey** column is of type **Whole number** (**1234** icon), and if not then right-click the column header and choose **Change type**, then **Whole number**.
15. Rename the **EnglishProductCategoryName** column to **Product Category**.
16. Select the **DimProduct** query in the **Queries** pane.
17. Ensure that the **ProductSubcategoryKey** column is of type **Whole number** (**1234** icon), and if not then right-click the column header, choose **Change type**, then **Whole number**.

18. Rename the **EnglishProductName** column to **Product Name**.
19. Click **Merge queries** in the ribbon of the **Home** tab.

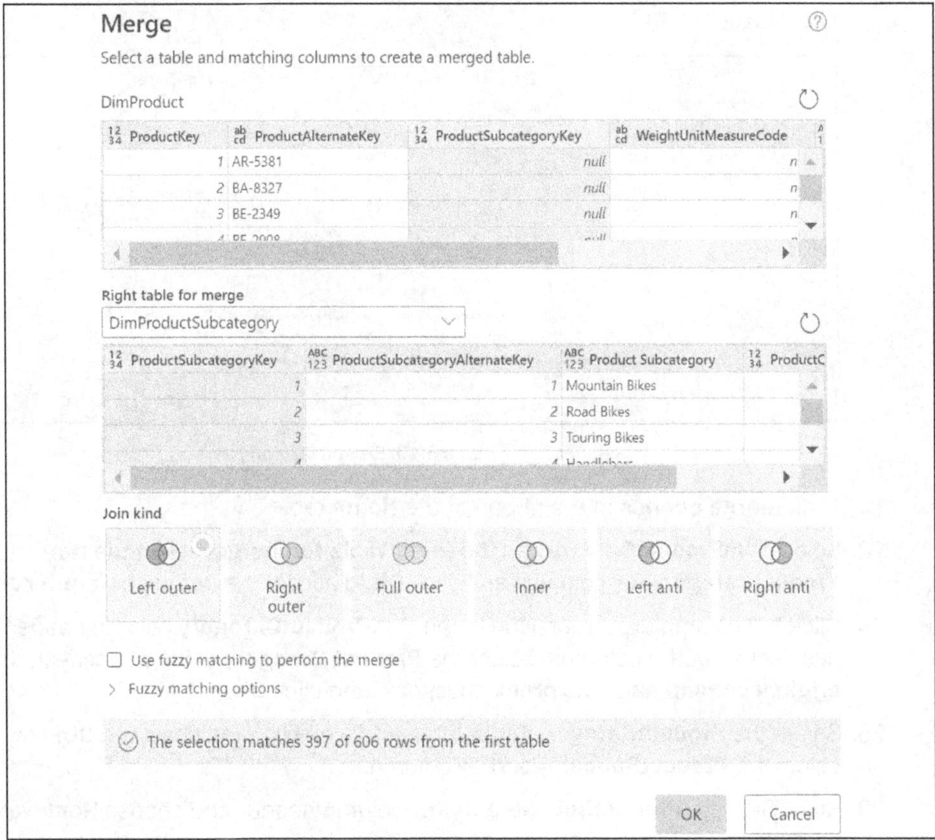

Figure 5.39: Merge dialog

20. Select **DimProductSubcategory** as the **Right table for merge**, select the two **ProductSubcategoryKey** columns, and click **OK** to accept the default **Left outer Join kind**.

21. Click the column expansion icon in the **DimProductSubcategory** column header, deselect all of the columns, select the **Product Subcategory** and **ProductCategoryKey** columns, and uncheck the **Use original column name as prefix** checkbox; click **OK**.

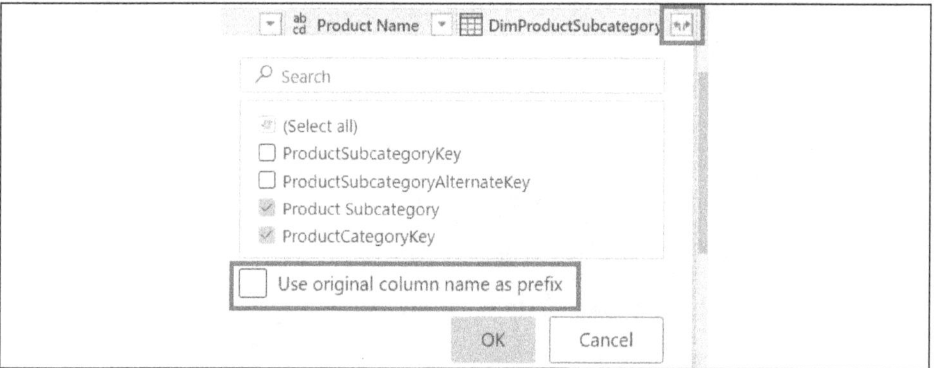

Figure 5.40: Expand column

22. Click **Merge queries** in the ribbon of the **Home** tab.
23. Select **DimProductCategory** as the **Right table for merge**, select the two **ProductCategoryKey** columns and click **OK** to accept the default **Left outer Join kind**.
24. Click the column expansion icon in the **DimProductCategory** column header, deselect all of the columns, select the **Product Category** column, uncheck the **Use original column name as prefix** checkbox, and click **OK**.
25. Select the **ProductCategoryKey** column and while holding down the **Ctrl** key, select the **ProductSubcategoryKey** column.
26. Right-click the **ProductSubcategoryKey** column header and choose **Remove columns**.
27. Right-click the **DimProductCategory** query in the **Queries** pane and deselect **Enable load**.
28. Disable load on the **DimProductSubcategory** query as well.
29. In the lower-right corner, click the **Save & Close** button.
30. **Name** the dataflow **Products** and click the **Save** button.

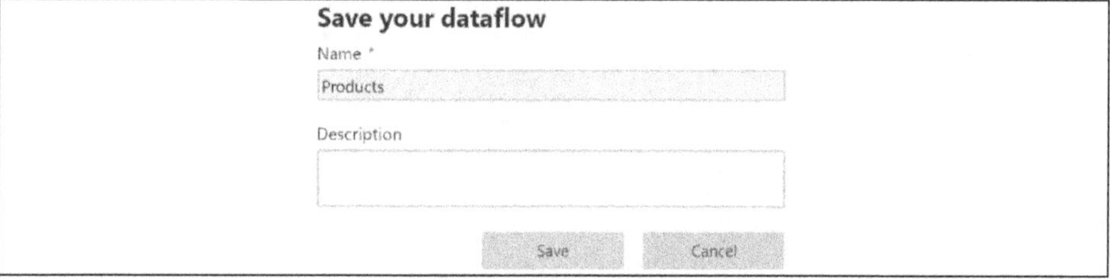

Figure 5.41: Save your dataflow

31. Click back on the workspace and note that the **Products** dataflow has appeared.

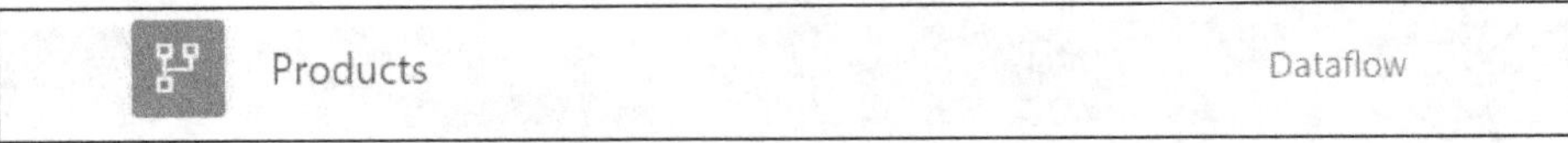

Figure 5.42: Products dataflow

32. Hover over the **Products** dataflow and click the **Refresh now** icon.

How it works

Dataflows allow Power Query queries to be built in the Power BI service. Furthermore, unlike Power Query queries built in the Power BI Desktop, dataflows are reusable across multiple datasets (models). Since dataflows and Power Query queries built in the Power BI Desktop use the same underlying M code technology, it is actually possible to take queries built in the Power BI Desktop and easily migrate them to dataflows using the **Advanced Editor** capability to copy and paste the code between the desktop and a dataflow, or using the **Import Model** feature when creating a dataflow.

Dataflows ingest data from sources into Common Data Model-compliant (Dataverse) folders stored in Azure Data Lake Storage Gen2. Dataflows also allow you to expose data in your own Azure Data Lake Gen2 storage to other Azure services. Once created, a dataflow must be refreshed at least once to initialize the data within the Azure Data Lake Gen2 storage. Dataflows support similar settings to datasets, in that you can configure scheduled refreshes and utilize gateways when refreshing data.

Dedicated capacities, such as Premium, support additional dataflow functionality, such as the following:

- Enhanced compute engine, enabling dataflows to leverage `DirectQuery`
- Refresh linked tables from other dataflows
- **Automated Machine Learning** (**AutoML**) and Cognitive Services

There's more

Once created, dataflows can be used in Power BI Desktop as data sources. To see how this works, do the following:

1. Open a new Power BI Desktop file.
2. Select **Get data** from the ribbon of the **Home** tab and choose **Power BI dataflows**.
3. Expand the workspace where the **Products** dataflow was created.
4. Expand the **Products** dataflow.
5. Choose the `DimProduct` table and then click the **Load** button.

The `DimProduct` table has now been added to the dataset.

See also

- Introduction to dataflows and self-service data prep: `https://bit.ly/3uCjNZf`
- Creating a dataflow: `https://bit.ly/2RiiGPV`
- Configure and consume a dataflow: `https://bit.ly/2RhlVHm`
- Dataflows best practices: `https://bit.ly/3cZIIQr`
- Dataflows limitations and considerations: `https://bit.ly/3t2UChM`
- Premium features of dataflows: `https://bit.ly/3fZXLLA`
- Build a Machine Learning model in Power BI: `https://bit.ly/3d1XGp7`
- Use Machine Learning—Cognitive Services with dataflows: `https://bit.ly/3fT3nYk`

Conclusion

The Power BI service provides the capability to create and share additional BI objects, such as dashboards, apps, streaming datasets, and dataflows; these components can be enriched and enhanced with alerts, subscriptions, images, and web content. In this chapter, Power BI dashboards were constructed to provide simple, at-a-glance monitoring of critical measures and high-impact business activities. The unique features of dashboards, such as Q&A natural language queries, data alerts, and the integration of other report types—such as Excel and SSRS—was also included. Finally, the creation and use of streaming datasets and dataflows was also covered.

6

Getting Serious with Date Intelligence

Date intelligence refers to a broad set of data modeling patterns and functions that enable analysis across time periods. In this chapter and throughout this book, we use date intelligence to refer to this broad set of data modeling patterns and to distinguish the concept from DAX time intelligence functions. This is done for two reasons. First, to be more technically precise, date intelligence deals with dates (days, months, years), not time (hours, minutes, seconds). Second, DAX time intelligence functions are only useful if dealing with a standard (Gregorian) calendar, but many businesses use a financial calendar that is different than a standard calendar year. Date intelligence, the broad concept, is applicable to both the standard (Gregorian) calendar as well as custom financial calendars.

Fundamental measures, such as reseller net sales, as created in *Chapter 3, Building a Power BI Data Model*, are supplemented with date intelligence measures to calculate year-to-date, prior period, and many other custom time period calculations. These measures are then used in combination to support growth and variance measures and are often utilized as **Key Performance Indicators** (**KPIs**) in Power BI dashboards, given their ability to convey additional context and insight. When implemented properly, date intelligence dramatically expands the analytical power of a data model and simplifies report and dashboard development.

This chapter contains recipes for preparing a data model to support robust date intelligence and authoring custom date intelligence measures. We will cover the following recipes:

- Building a Date Dimension Table
- Prepping the Date Dimension via the Query Editor
- Authoring Date Intelligence Measures
- Developing Advanced Date Intelligence Measures

- Simplifying Date Intelligence with DAX and Calculated Tables
- Leveraging Calculation Groups

Technical Requirements

The following are required to complete the recipes in this chapter:

- Power BI Desktop
- Tabular Editor
- SQL Server with the AdventureWorksDW2019 database installed. This database and instructions for installing it are available here: `http://bit.ly/2OVQfG7`
- Files for this chapter can be downloaded from the following GitHub repository: `https://github.com/PacktPublishing/Microsoft-Power-BI-Cookbook-Second-Edition`

Building a Date Dimension Table

A date dimension is needed by almost all data models and particularly those that require date intelligence calculations (e.g. Year-to-Date, Year-over-Year) and company-specific calendars. Building a robust date table in the source system provides significant long-term value across BI projects and tools. A complete date table accounts for all the required grains or hierarchy levels of both the standard (Gregorian) calendar and any fiscal calendar specific to the organization. Additionally, surrogate key columns aligned to each grain are included to drive the sort order of report attributes and to enable date intelligence expressions.

This recipe includes a design phase to identify the required date dimension columns and a process for adding a date intelligence surrogate key column to a dimension.

Getting ready

Full date tables are available from various sources:

- **The Kimball Group downloadable Excel file**: `http://bit.ly/2rOchxt`
- **A T-SQL approach**: `http://bit.ly/2s6tuPT`
- **A Power Query calendar**: `https://bit.ly/3uxcf9Z`
- **A DAX 445 Custom Financial Calendar**: `https://bit.ly/39SOVeZ`

A date table containing only the `DateKey`, `Date`, `Calendar Year`, and `Calendar Month Number` columns for the years 2010 to 2030 can be downloaded from the GitHub repository for this book. Download CH6_DateTable.xlsx from the following GitHub repository: `https://github.com/PacktPublishing/Microsoft-Power-BI-Cookbook-Second-Edition`

Date tables should contain a single row for every calendar date (no gaps). Given the small size (a 20-year span is approximately 7,600 rows inclusive of the last year), include all necessary history and three or more future years.

How to Build a Dimension Table

To implement this recipe, carry out the following steps:

1. Identify and document the required columns of the date dimension and identify any gaps with the existing table.

   Like other dimension tables, teams can often incrementally improve their date dimension table over time with additional logic. For example, if the great majority of analysis revolves around a fiscal calendar and at a certain granularity, then these columns can be targeted first. Mature date tables inclusive of standard and financial calendars, sequential surrogate columns, and logical or dynamic columns—such as `Fiscal Period Status`—are often quite wide, with over 40 columns. Required date dimension columns include the following:

   - The `Prior Year Date` and `Prior Period Date` columns for both standard and financial calendars
   - Natural hierarchy attributes for all levels, such as `2013`, `2013-Q3`, `2013-Sep`, `2013-Wk39`, and `9/25/2013`

   The natural hierarchy (one parent for each child value) allows users to easily navigate Power BI report visuals via drill-down and next-level commands. Without natural hierarchies, the context of the parent value is lost when drilling into the given parent. For example, drilling into the year 2017 would display each month's name, but the year associated with this month would only be visible in the tooltips by hovering over the chart. With natural hierarchies, this context is not lost as a `Calendar Yr-Mo` column might contain values such as `2017-Aug`.

   Power BI provides a method of working around unnatural hierarchies in report visuals via the **Expand all down one level in the hierarchy** drilling feature. However, this can lead to dense axis labels when multiple levels of a hierarchy are used. Given date intelligence requirements as well as the needs of other visualizations, it is recommended to build your date table to support natural hierarchies. When building natural hierarchies, consider building the following support columns:

   - An integer column that corresponds to the chronological order of each string column, such as `Weekday`. For example, a `Weekday Number` column, with values of 1 through 7, will set the `Sort By` property of `Weekday`.
   - Multiple "X in Y" columns, such as `Day in Year`, `Day in Month`, `Week in Month`, and `Week in Year`, stored as integers.
   - Indicator columns, such as `Weekday Indicator`, `Holiday Indicator`, and `Working Day Indicator`. The values for these columns should be report-friendly, such as `Holiday` and `Non-Holiday`.

- ❑ Starting and ending date columns for the different grains supported, such as `Week Ending Date` and `Period Ending Date`.

2. Look to integrate other calendars, such as a periods or fiscal calendar, into the same date table in the source database. Distinct views can be created to support role-playing dimensions. See the *There's more...* section.
3. Identify common date manipulations taking place in the existing reports, or by business users in Excel or Power BI, and consider adding a date dimension column to eliminate or simplify this work.
4. Ensure that date columns (for example, `Prior Year Date`) and number columns (such as `Calendar Year`) are stored as date and integer data types, respectively, as this allows arithmetic and DAX functions, such as `MAX` and `MIN`, to operate without any type conversion.

   If the date dimension table is updated daily as part of a data warehouse **Extract-Transform-Load** (**ETL**) process, columns identifying the current and prior periods such as `IsCurrentFiscalPeriod` and `IsPrior60Days` are also common.
5. Consider adding two columns to the date table stored in the relational database, a natural hierarchy string (`2009-Jan`), and an integer column, such as `Calendar Year Month Number` (`200901`).
6. Create a table with three columns, `Calendar Year`, `Calendar Month Number`, and an `identity` column with an increment value of 1, `Calendar Yr Mo Index`:

```
Create Table dbo.TempTblYearMo
( [Calendar Year] int not null
, [Calendar Month Number] tinyint not null
, [Calendar Yr Mo Index] smallint identity(1,1) not null)
```

7. Execute an `INSERT INTO` SQL statement to load this table.
8. `SELECT`, `GROUP`, and `ORDER BY` the `Calendar Year` and `Calendar Month Number` columns from the existing date table.

   The `ORDER BY` clause of the `SELECT` statement should order by `Calendar Year` and then by `Calendar Month Number`. The temporary table's index column (`Calendar Yr Mo Index`) is now populated in sequential order by month across years, as per *Figure 6.1*.

Calendar Year	Calendar Month Number	Calendar Yr Mo Index
2016	11	95
2016	12	96
2017	1	97
2017	2	98

Figure 6.1: TempTblYearMo table loaded from the INSERT INTO statement

9. Execute an UPDATE statement that populates the Calendar Year Month Number column with the identity value:

```
UPDATE DBO.DimFinDateTestTbl
SET [Calendar Year Month Number] = T.[Calendar Yr Mo Index]
FROM
DBO.DimFinDateTestTbl as D INNER JOIN dbo.TempTblYearMo as T
ON D.[Calendar Year] = T.[Calendar Year] AND D.[Calendar Month Number] =
T.[Calendar Month Number]
```

The following query in *Figure 6.2* displays the sequentially increasing Calendar Year Month Number column on the date table.

Date	Calendar Yr-No	Calendar Year Month Number
2017-12-30	2017-Dec	108
2017-12-31	2017-Dec	108
2018-01-01	2018-Jan	109
2017-01-02	2018-Jan	109

Figure 6.2: Date table with the Calendar Year Month Number column updated

10. Repeat this process for other natural hierarchy columns, such as Year-Qtr and Year-Wk, and drop the temporary tables.
11. When loaded to the model, the surrogate columns should be hidden from Report View and used as the Sort By column.
12. Implement hierarchies in the Fields list as per the *Creating Hierarchies and Groups* recipe, shared in *Chapter 3, Building a Power BI Data Model*.

SQL window functions can be helpful in creating certain "X in Y" date dimension columns. For example, the following DENSE_RANK function returns the calendar week number of the given calendar month:

```
OVER(PARTITION BY D.[CALENDAR YEAR MONTH NUMBER] ORDER BY D.[Calendar Week
Number in Year])
```

For DirectQuery data models in which the SQL queries defining the tables of the model are executed at runtime, it is best to move as much data transformation logic back to the source system. Complex SQL queries, DAX calculated columns, and M query expression logic can all lead to inefficient query plans, and so negatively impact the performance of DirectQuery solutions.

How it works...

Date intelligence measures reference the surrogate key columns to easily define specific time period filter conditions, such as in `Internet Net Sales (Trailing 3 Periods)`:

```
Internet Net Sales (Trailing 3 Periods) =
    CALCULATE(
        [Internet Net Sales],
        FILTER(
            ALL('Date'),
            'Date'[Calendar Year Month Number] >=
                MAX('Date'[Calendar Year Month Number])-2
            &&
            'Date'[Calendar Year Month Number] <=
                MAX('Date'[Calendar Year Month Number])
        )
    )
```

The `Internet Net Sales (Trailing 3 Periods)` can be used in visuals as shown in *Figure 6.3*.

Calenar Yr-Mo	Calendar Year Month Number	Internet Net Sales	Internet Net Sales (Trailing 3 Periods)
2017-May	101	$1,169,589	$3,265,519
2017-Apr	100	$1,046,023	$2867,279
2017-Mar	99	$1,049,907	$2,678,946

Figure 6.3: Trailing 3 Periods measure includes Calendar Year Month Number values 99 through 101 for 2017-May

If the `Calendar Year Month Number` column was not sequential, it would not be possible to refer to months across years without complex logic, such as the trailing three-month average of `2017-Jan`. Note that in this example, May 2017 is the current month and so was included, but often only the completed (or previous) months are included in these calculations

The SQL view used by the data model should dynamically filter the required dates, such as the trailing three years:

```
FROM DBO.DimFinDate as D
WHERE
D.[Date] BETWEEN DATEADD(YEAR,-3,CAST(CURRENT_TIMESTAMP AS date)) AND
CAST(CURRENT_TIMESTAMP as date)
```

In this example, only the current system date and three prior calendar years are loaded to the data model.

There's more...

An alternative to "secondary relationships" (inactive relationships) via the `USERELATIONSHIP` function described in *Chapter 3, Building a Power BI Data Model,* is to have multiple date dimension tables in the data model, each with a single, active relationship based on a different date column of the fact table. For example, a model would have `Order Date`, `Ship Date`, and `Delivery Date` dimension tables. This approach, called **role-playing tables**, reduces the volume of custom measures that must be developed and maintained in the model. If choosing this approach, create separate views against the source date dimension table, corresponding to each role-playing table. Apply column aliases in each view associating the attribute to the date (for example, `Ship Date Year` or `Ship Date Month`).

If the source fact table only contains a surrogate key, commonly in the `YYYYMMDD` format, the source views utilized by the data model can include the following conversion logic:

```
CONVERT(date,(CAST(F.OrderDateKey AS nvarchar(8)))) as [Order Date-Convert]
```

The `DATEFROMPARTS` function in SQL Server can be used for many other date conversion or logical needs.

As a general practice we recommend developing a single date dimension table in a corporate data warehouse system such as Azure Synapse Analytics and leveraging this dimension across multiple datasets. In many cases, a Power BI dataset targeting a particular business process and team will require custom date filtering or grouping not supported by the existing date dimension table in the data warehouse. In these scenarios, the additional logic can be incorporated into a SQL view object specific to the dataset or, if the requirement is expected to be common across many datasets, the new logic or columns could be built into the data warehouse dimension table.

Preparing the Date Dimension via the Query Editor

In some BI environments, it is not feasible to alter the source date table as per the previous recipe or even modify the SQL view used to load the date dimension table. In these situations, Power BI Desktop's Query Editor and M expressions can serve as an effective alternative to deliver the same columns necessary to drive robust date intelligence analysis.

In this recipe, an example date dimension M query is shared that builds common date attributes as well as dynamic logical columns. Additionally, a process for adding sequential date intelligence columns via M expressions is also included.

Getting ready

To prepare for this recipe:

- Download CH6_DateTable.xlsx from the following GitHub repository: https://github.com/PacktPublishing/Microsoft-Power-BI-Cookbook-Second-Edition

How to Prepare the Date Dimension

To implement this recipe, perform the following steps:

1. Create a new Power BI Desktop file.
2. Open the Power Query Editor by clicking Transform Data from the ribbon of the Home tab.
3. Create a query that imports the Dates sheet from CH6_DateTable.xlsx, and call this query BaseDateTable.
4. Create an M query that references the BaseDateTable query, retrieves the last three years of dates, and computes 11 additional columns via M functions:

```
let
    Dates = BaseDateTable,
    CurrentDate = DateTime.Date(DateTime.LocalNow()),
    CurrentYear = Date.Year(DateTime.Date(DateTime.LocalNow())),
    CurrentMonth = Date.Month(DateTime.Date(DateTime.LocalNow())),
    FilteredDates =
        Table.SelectRows(
            Dates,
            each [Date] >=
            Date.AddYears(CurrentDate,-3) and [Date] <= CurrentDate
        ),
    DateCol = Table.SelectColumns(FilteredDates,"Date"),
    YearCol =
        Table.AddColumn(
            DateCol, "Year", each Date.Year([Date]), Int64.Type
        ),
    MonthNameCol =
        Table.AddColumn(
            YearCol, "Month Name", each Date.MonthName([Date]), type
text
        ),
    YearMonthCol =
        Table.AddColumn(
            MonthNameCol, "Year-Mo",
            each Text.From([Year]) & "-" & [Month Name], type text
```

```
        ),
    MonthNumberCol =
        Table.AddColumn(
            YearMonthCol, "Month Number", each Date.Month([Date]),
Int64.Type
        ),
    WeekdayNameCol =
        Table.AddColumn(
            MonthNumberCol, "Weekday", each Date.DayOfWeekName([Date]),
            type text
        ),
    DayNumberOfWeekCol =
        Table.AddColumn(
            WeekdayNameCol, "Weekday Number",
            each Date.DayOfWeek([Date]), Int64.Type
        ),
    YearStatusCol =
        Table.AddColumn(DayNumberOfWeekCol, "Year Status", each
            if Date.IsInCurrentYear([Date]) = true then "Current Year"
            else if [Year] = CurrentYear - 1 then "Prior Year"
            else "Other Year", type text
        ),
    MonthStatusCol =
        Table.AddColumn(YearStatusCol, "Month Status", each
            if [Year Status] = "Current Year" and [Month Number] =
CurrentMonth
            then "Current Month" else
            if [Year] =
                    Date.Year(
                        Date.AddMonths(DateTime.Date(DateTime.
LocalNow()),-1)
                    )
                and [Month Number] =
                    Date.Month(
                        Date.AddMonths(DateTime.Date(DateTime.
LocalNow()),-1)
                    )
            then "Prior Month" else "Other Month", type text
        ),
    DayInMonthCol =
        Table.AddColumn(
            MonthStatusCol, "Day in Month", each Date.Day([Date]),
Int64.Type
        ),
    WeekOfYearCol =
```

```
            Table.AddColumn(
                DayInMonthCol, "Week of Year", each Date.WeekOfYear([Date]),
                Int64.Type
            ),
        WeekOfMonthCol =
            Table.AddColumn(
                WeekOfYearCol, "Week of Month",
                each Date.WeekOfMonth([Date]), Int64.Type
            )
    in
        WeekOfMonthCol
```

5. Name this query `DatesInterim`.
6. Create a new query called `Dates` that adds a surrogate sequential column to be used in date intelligence measures:

```
let
    Source = BaseDateTable,
    YearMonthCols =
        Table.Distinct(
            Table.SelectColumns(
                Source, {"Calendar Year","Calendar Month Number"}
            )
        ),
    YearMonthColSort =
        Table.Sort(
            YearMonthCols,
            {
                {"Calendar Year", Order.Ascending},
                {"Calendar Month Number", Order.Ascending}
            }
        ),
    YearMonthColIndex =
        Table.AddIndexColumn(YearMonthColSort, "YearMonthIndex",1,1),
    JoinedDateTable =
        Table.NestedJoin(
            DatesInterim, {"Year", "Month Number"},
            YearMonthColIndex, {"Calendar Year","Calendar Month
Number"},
            "Year-Mo Index", JoinKind.Inner
        ),
    IndexColumnAdded =
        Table.ExpandTableColumn(
            JoinedDateTable,
            "Year-Mo Index",{"YearMonthIndex"},{"Year Month Number"}
```

```
        )
in
    IndexColumnAdded
```

7. Disable loading on `BaseDateTable` and `DatesInterim` by right-clicking the queries and deselecting `Enable load`. Only the `Dates` query needs to be loaded into the data model.

How it works...

For the `DatesInterim` query, the `CurrentDate`, `CurrentMonth`, and `CurrentYear` expressions can be stored as separate queries. The `DateTime.LocalNow` function is used in dynamic M date logic, similar to the `CURRENT_TIMESTAMP` function used in SQL statements. A filter is applied via the `Table.SelectRows` function to only retrieve the last three years of dates, and conditional logic is used to populate dynamic `Year Status` and `Month Status` columns (for example, `Current Year`). The rest of the expressions use functions of the `Date` object class or concatenate columns.

Despite a minimal date table available in the source system (all that is required is a column containing dates), the M query generates a useful date dimension table for a model with many of the most common and important columns.

For the final `Dates` query, two additional columns (`Calendar Year` and `Calendar Month Number`) are used, although we could have performed a self-joining query with the `Year` and `Month Number` columns in the `DatesInterim` query. For example, if we rename the `Dates` query to `DatesInterim2`, we can create the final `Dates` table that adds a sequential index for `Year Week Number` as well:

```
let
    Source = DatesInterim2,
    YearMonthWeekCols =
        Table.Distinct(
            Table.SelectColumns(
                Source, {"Year", "Month Number", "Week of Year"}
            )
        ),
    YearMonthWeekColSort =
        Table.Sort(
            YearMonthWeekCols,
            {
                {"Year", Order.Ascending},
                {"Month Number", Order.Ascending},
                {"Week of Year", Order.Ascending}
            }
```

```
        ),
    YearMonthWeekColIndex =
        Table.AddIndexColumn(YearMonthWeekColSort, "YearMonthWeekIndex",1,1),
    JoinedDateTable =
        Table.NestedJoin(
            DatesInterim2,{"Year", "Month Number", "Week of Year"},
            YearMonthWeekColIndex, {"Year", "Month Number", "Week of Year"},
            "Year-Mo-Wk Index", JoinKind.Inner
        ),
    IndexColumnAdded =
        Table.ExpandTableColumn(
            JoinedDateTable,
            "Year-Mo-Wk Index", {"YearMonthWeekIndex"},{"Year Month Week
Number"}
        )
in
    IndexColumnAdded
```

The `Table.AddIndexColumn` function is applied to the sorted `DatesInterim2` table to create the sequential column, `YearMonthWeekColIndex`. The `DatesInterim2` query is then joined to the table containing this new column. Finally, the joined table is expanded using the `Table.ExpandTablecolumn` function.

The `Year-Mo` column (that is, `2016-Dec`) can now be sorted by the `Year Month Number` column in the data model and DAX measures can reference the `Year Month Number` column to apply date intelligence filter conditions, such as the trailing six months.

There's more...

The `Table.AddIndexColumn` function used in this recipe is not currently supported in DirectQuery mode for SQL Server, and thus the full M query from the date dimension M query section of this recipe cannot be used in DirectQuery data models.

Since the data access queries defining the dimension and fact tables in DirectQuery models are executed at runtime, these queries should be as simple as possible. For example, these queries should avoid joins, derived tables, subqueries, data type conversions, case statements, and so on. Simple, performant, or optimized queries are especially important for the queries used to access the largest tables of the model. To ensure sufficient performance in Power BI with DirectQuery models, large source tables of DirectQuery models should be optimized for read performance with features such as the columnstore index of SQL Server and table partitions.

See also

- **Power Query Date functions**: `https://bit.ly/3wSCMAz`
- **Power Query Table functions**: `https://bit.ly/3wMxlmC`

Authoring Date Intelligence Measures

With a complete date dimension table in place, date intelligence measures can be developed to support common requirements, such as `year-to-date`, `year-over-year`, and rolling history, as well as more complex, context-specific behaviors.

The date intelligence patterns described in this recipe are applicable to both standard and non-standard financial calendars, as they leverage fundamental DAX functions and the sequential date intelligence columns created earlier in this chapter.

This recipe includes examples of core `year-to-date` and prior year measures, as well as a more advanced dynamic prior period measure that adjusts to all grains of the date dimension.

Getting ready

To prepare for this recipe, follow these steps:

1. Complete the *Preparing the Date Dimension via the Query Editor* recipe in this chapter, or have a date table with the same columns as in that recipe.
2. Edit the initial part of the `DatesInterim` query to load all rows, and not just the first three years. The code snippet below represents the initial part of the query with the `FilteredDates` expression removed. The rest of the query is the same as the recipe. Note that the `DateCol` expression now refers to the `Dates` expression instead of the `FilteredDates` expression:

    ```
    Dates = BaseDateTable,
    CurrentDate = DateTime.Date(DateTime.LocalNow()),
    CurrentYear = Date.Year(DateTime.Date(DateTime.LocalNow())),
    CurrentMonth = Date.Month(DateTime.Date(DateTime.LocalNow())),
    DateCol = Table.SelectColumns(Dates,"Date"),
    ```

3. Add two additional columns to the end of the DatesInterim query for Prior Year Date and Prior Month Date using the following code:

    ```
    PriorYearDate =
            Table.AddColumn(
                WeekOfMonthCol, "Prior Year Date", each Date.
    AddYears([Date],-1)
            ),
        PriorMonthDate =
    ```

```
        Table.AddColumn(
            PriorYearDate, "Prior Month Date", each Date.
AddMonths([Date],-1)
        )
in
    PriorMonthDate
```

4. Import the `FactInternetSales` table from the `AdventureWorksDW2019` database.
5. Create a relationship between the `Date` column in the `Dates` table and the `OrderDate` column in the `FactInternetSales` table.
6. Mark the `Dates` table as a date table using the `Date` column.

Plan for a standard measure naming convention to identify the date intelligence logic, such as `Sales (PYTD)`. Symbol characters, such as currency (`$`) or percentage (`%`), can also help users browse the measures. Document the types of date intelligence measures to be implemented and for which measures of the model. Create a date intelligence measure matrix for documentation and to support communication with stakeholders.

Date Intelligence Measures	YTD	MTD	WTD	PY	PM	PMTD	YOY	YOY %	YOY YTD %	Rolling 12
Internet Sales	✓	✓	✓	✓	✓	✓	✓	✓	✓	✓
Internet Orders	✓	✓	✓	✓	✓	✓	✓	✓	✓	✓
Reseller Sales	✓	✓	✓	✓	✓	✓	✓	✓	✓	✓

Figure 6.4: Date intelligence measure matrix

Conduct reviews and/or quality assurance testing with business users to validate the logic and walk through use cases when designing reports. Given the volume of new measures to be developed, it is best to receive business approval for one or two measures prior to applying the date intelligence logic to other measures.

How to Author Date Intelligence Measures

To implement this recipe, perform the following steps:

1. Create a simple Internet Sales measure:

```
Internet Sales = SUM('FactInternetSales'[SalesAmount])
```

2. Create `Year-to-Date (YTD)`, `Month-to-Date (MTD)`, and `Week-to-Date (WTD)` measures:

```
Internet Sales (YTD) =
    CALCULATE([Internet Sales],
```

```
        FILTER(ALL('Dates'),
            'Dates'[Year] = MAX('Dates'[Year]) &&
            'Dates'[Date] <= MAX('Dates'[Date])))

Internet Sales (MTD) =
    CALCULATE([Internet Sales],
        FILTER(ALL('Dates'),
            'Dates'[Year Month Number] = MAX('Dates'[Year Month Number])
&&
            'Dates'[Date] <= MAX('Dates'[Date])))

Internet Sales (WTD) =
    CALCULATE([Internet Sales],
        FILTER(ALL('Dates'),
            'Dates'[Year Week Number] = MAX('Dates'[Year Week Number])
&&
            'Dates'[Date] <= MAX('Dates'[Date])))
```

3. Create `Prior Year (PY)`, `Prior Year to Date (PYTD)`, and `Prior Month to Date (PMTD)` measures:

```
Internet Sales (PY) =
    CALCULATE([Internet Sales],
        FILTER(ALL('Dates'),
            'Dates'[Date] >= MIN('Dates'[Prior Year Date]) &&
            'Dates'[Date] <= MAX('Dates'[Prior Year Date])))
Internet Sales (PYTD) =
    CALCULATE([Internet Sales],
        FILTER(ALL('Dates'),
            'Dates'[Year] = MAX('Dates'[Year]) - 1 &&
            'Dates'[Date] <= MAX('Dates'[Prior Year Date])))

Internet Sales (PMTD) =
    CALCULATE([Internet Sales],
        FILTER(ALL('Dates'),
            'Dates'[Year Month Number] = MAX('Dates'[Year Month Number])
- 1 &&
            'Dates'[Date] <= MAX('Dates'[Prior Month Date])))
```

4. Use the current year and prior year measures to create `Year-over-Year (YOY)` measures:

```
Internet Sales (YOY YTD) = [Internet Sales (YTD)] - [Internet Sales
(PYTD)]
Internet Sales (YOY YTD %) = DIVIDE([Internet Sales (YOY YTD)],[Internet
Sales (PYTD)])
```

5. Build logic into date intelligence measures to account for alternative subtotal filter contexts, such as when a prior period measure is calculated in a yearly, quarterly, or weekly subtotal context:

```
Internet Sales (Prior Period) =
    VAR Periods = DISTINCTCOUNT('Dates'[Year Month Number])
RETURN SWITCH(TRUE,
    HASONEVALUE('Dates'[Date]),
        CALCULATE([Internet Sales],
            FILTER(ALL('Dates'),'Dates'[Date] = MAX('Dates'[Date])-1)),
    HASONEVALUE('Dates'[Year Week Number]),
        CALCULATE([Internet Sales],
            FILTER(ALL('Dates'),
                'Dates'[Year Week Number] = MAX('Dates'[Year Week
Number])-1)),
    CALCULATE([Internet Sales],
        FILTER(ALL('Dates'),
            'Dates'[Year Month Number] >=
                MIN('Dates'[Year Month Number]) - Periods &&
            'Dates'[Year Month Number] <=
                MAX('Dates'[Year Month Number]) - Periods )))
```

6. Create a `Matrix` visualization that uses the `Year` column from the `Dates` table for columns and the `Internet Sales (YTD)` and `Internet Sales (PYTD)` as values

How it works...

When designing date intelligence measures, it is important to understand that the definition of "current" and "prior" are defined by the context of the visualization in which the measures operate. The `FILTER` function iterates each row (a date) to determine which rows are passed to the `CALCULATE` function. The `ALL` function removes all existing date table filters, thereby allowing filter conditions in the measure to access all rows of the date table.

For the "current" date period measures, each measure expression sets an "equal to" condition on the column representing the intended granularity; this column respects the filter context of the report query via `MAX`. If the source query to the date table is filtered to only retrieve dates equal to or less than the current date, these measures will default to the current year, month (or period), and week when added to reports.

Note that the `Year Month Number` and `Year Week Number` columns should be sequentially increasing integers.

For the "prior" date period measures, applying both the `MIN` and `MAX` filter conditions against the prior date columns selects the corresponding date ranges. Subtracting a value (1 in this example) from the `MAX` of the column shifts the selected time period backward.

Growth or variance measures that calculate the difference between the current time period value of a measure and a prior time period such as Year-over-Year (YOY) growth can be created with new measures that subtract the previous time period measure from the current period measure. Additional growth or variance measures expressed in percentages can use the DIVIDE function for computing this difference as a percentage of the previous time period value.

Prior period date columns allow the prior time period measures to apply simple filter expressions relative to the active date filter context down to the individual date granularity. In the absence of these columns and for period- or month-level date tables, measure filter conditions can be written as follows:

```
Prior Year (PY) = 'Dates'[Year Month Number] = MAX('Dates'[Year Month Number]) -
12)
Prior Month (PM) = 'Dates'[Year Month Number] = MAX('Dates'[Year Month Number])
- 1)
```

For the dynamic prior period measure, Internet Sales (Prior Period), the DAX variable (Periods) computes the number of periods in the current filter context, such as 12 if a year is the subtotal, 3 if it is a quarter, or 1 for an individual period. Test conditions with HASONEVALUE check whether a single date or week is selected, and return the corresponding previous day or week, respectively. The remaining date grains (Year, Quarter, Period) are accounted for by the Periods variable; this value is subtracted from both the MIN and the MAX of the period number of the given context. This example underscores the importance of sequential date intelligence columns for accessing specific time frames across grains to apply custom filter conditions.

There's more...

DAX includes a full set of time intelligence functions, such as DATESYTD and SAMEPERIODLASTYEAR, which, given a standard (Gregorian) calendar, can compute the same values as the expressions in this recipe. Although these functions generally improve readability relative to the examples in this recipe, the use (and knowledge) of core DAX functions, such as FILTER, MAX, and MIN, is necessary when working with non-standard calendars—such as fiscal calendars and more complex scenarios. Considering that the vast majority of DAX time intelligence functions are simply syntax sugar for the FILTER function and the simplifying assumptions regarding calendar dates, it is unwise to rely on DAX time intelligence functions to be of any meaningful use in many real-world scenarios.

It is often surprising for many individuals new to business intelligence how differently organizations measure and conceptualize time; this can be particularly true regarding weeks. Here again, the DAX time intelligence functions are useless, as there are no included week functions. When dealing with weeks, different organizations start weeks on different days within a week. Thus, when assigning week numbers at either a yearly or monthly grain, it is important to bear this in mind.

Furthermore, organizations will also treat partial weeks differently as well. For example, in the final `Dates` table, there is a single entry for `Year Week Number` of `54`. This is because the year 2010 ends with a partial 53rd week. A single day of this week, Saturday, January 1st, 2011, falls outside of 2010. Organizations will treat these partial weeks differently, either including that single day as part of the week starting in 2010, as its own week, or as part of the first full week of 2011.

See also

- **DAX FILTER function**: `https://bit.ly/2Q1S45q`
- **DAX HASONEVALUE function**: `https://bit.ly/3wXSEBE`
- **DAX time intelligence functions**: `https://bit.ly/3mKWtWp`
- **To **bleep** with Time Intelligence**: `https://bit.ly/3gaUHN6`

Developing Advanced Date Intelligence Measures

Date intelligence measures are often at the center of the most visible Power BI reports and dashboards, as well as more complex business analyses. Therefore, given the unique requirements of each organization and BI project, it is important to understand how to go beyond the standard patterns described in the previous recipe to efficiently embed custom logic. Additionally, the ability to answer the business question "When did X occur (or not occur)?" is a powerful supplement to data models that can be supported via DAX measure logic.

In this recipe, an example is provided of a measure that identifies the dates in which sales were not recorded for a specific region and product category. In addition, a custom prior year-to-date measure is described with default (no filter) behavior and the exclusion of incomplete periods from the current year.

Getting ready

To prepare for this recipe, follow these steps:

1. Open Power BI Desktop.
2. Complete the *Preparing the Date Dimension via the Query Editor* recipe from this chapter.
3. Create an Import mode data source query called `AdWorksDW`. This query should be similar to the following:

```
let
    Source = Sql.Database("localhost\MSSQLSERVERDEV",
```

```
"AdventureWorksDW2019")
in
    Source
```

4. Isolate this query in a query group called `Data Sources` and `disable loading`.
5. Right-click the `AdWorksDW` and choose `Reference`.
6. Select the `FactInternetSales` table and name this query `Internet Sales`.
7. Repeat *steps 5* and *6* for the `DimSalesTerritory` table and name this query `Sales Territories`.
8. Create a `Products` query based upon the `DimProduct`, `DimProductCategory`, and `DimProductSubcategory` tables using the following code.

```
let
    Source = AdWorksDW,
    Navigation = Source{[Schema="dbo",Item="DimProduct"]}[Data],
    Subcategory =
        Table.ExpandRecordColumn(
            Navigation, "DimProductSubcategory",
            {"EnglishProductSubcategoryName", "DimProductCategory"},
            {"Product Subcategory", "DimProductCategory"}
        ),
    Category =
        Table.ExpandRecordColumn(
            Subcategory, "DimProductCategory",
            {"EnglishProductCategoryName"}, {"Product Category"}
        )
in
   Category
```

9. Separate the fact query, `Internet Sales`, into a `Facts` query group.
10. Separate the dimension queries, `Dates`, `Sales Territories`, and `Products`, into a `Dimensions` query group.
11. Create a `Blank Query` called `Calculations` in the `Other Queries` group.
12. Select `Close & Apply` in the ribbon of the `Home` tab to load the tables to the data model.
13. Create a relationship using the `Date` column from the `Dates` table and the `OrderDate` column of the `Internet Sales` table.
14. Create a relationship between the `Internet Sales` table and the `Products` and `Sales Territories` tables using the `ProductKey` column and `SalesTerritoryKey` column, respectively.
15. Set the `Sort By` column for the `Year-Mo` column in `Dates` to be the `Year Month Number` column.

How to Develop Advanced Date Intelligence Measures

To implement this recipe, carry out the following steps:

1. Create a measure that counts the rows (days) that do not have corresponding fact table rows, given the following conditions:

```
Days Without Northwest Bike Sales =
    COUNTROWS(
        FILTER('Dates',
            ISEMPTY(CALCULATETABLE('Internet Sales',
                FILTER(CROSSJOIN(ALL('Sales
Territories'),ALL('Products')),
                    'Sales Territories'[SalesTerritoryRegion] =
"Northwest" &&
                        'Products'[Product Category] = "Bikes")))))
```

2. Create Power BI report visualization to analyze the measure. The result of doing this is shown in *Figure 6.5*.

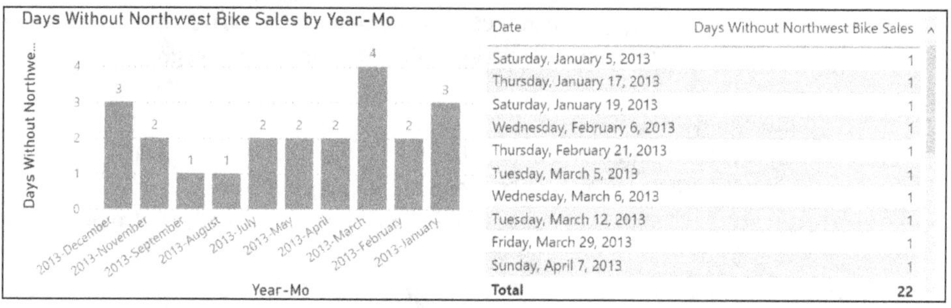

Figure 6.5: 22 days in 2013 in which the Northwest region did not generate any bike sales

How it works...

In this example, a new measure must count the days in which the Northwest sales region did not have any online sales for the `Bikes` product category. Any existing filters on the `Product` and `Sales Territory` tables are removed via `CROSSJOIN` of the `ALL` clauses. The `Internet Sales` fact table is then filtered for the `Northwest` region and the `Bikes` category, and `ISEMPTY` is applied for each date in the filter context. Only the dates with no rows are returned by `FILTER` to be counted.

The use of `CROSSJOIN` is necessary to remove filters on columns from separate tables of the model. A single `ALL` function can be used to remove one or more columns from the filter context of a single table, such as `ALL('Product'[Product Color],'Product'[Product Class])`.

There's more...

Prior period date intelligence measures can become quite complex. For example, consider the scenario where for a Prior Year-to-Date measure at the monthly grain, the business requirements are to filter the prior year by only the completed periods of the current year (only compare completed against completed). The goal is to calculate the Prior Year-to-Date value (completed periods only) automatically without any date columns in the report, and return a blank if the current period, which is incomplete, is selected in report visuals. To implement this measure, perform the following steps:

1. In the `Calculations` table, create the following measures:

```
Today = DATE(2013,6,28)

Current Year = LOOKUPVALUE('Dates'[Year],'Dates'[Date],[Today])

Current Period = LOOKUPVALUE('Dates'[Year Month Number],'Dates'[Date],
[Today])

Last Complete Period = [Current Period] - 1

Last Complete Month = LOOKUPVALUE('Dates'[Month Number],'Dates'[Year
Month Number],[Last Complete Period])

Internet Sales = SUM('FactInternetSales'[SalesAmount])
```

2. Hide the `Calculations` column in the `Calculations` table from the `Report View`
3. Create a measure in the `Calculations` table with multiple pairs of conditions and results to account for the filter contexts and requirements:

```
Sales (PYTD-Custom) =
SWITCH(TRUE(),
    NOT(ISCROSSFILTERED('Dates')),
        CALCULATE([Internet Sales],
            FILTER(ALL('Dates'),
                'Dates'[Year] = [Current Year]-1 &&
                'Dates'[Month Number] <= [Last Complete Month])),
    HASONEVALUE('Dates'[Year Month Number]) &&
        MAX('Dates'[Year Month Number]) > [Last Complete
Period],BLANK(),
    HASONEVALUE('Dates'[Year Month Number]) &&
        MAX('Dates'[Year Month Number]) <= [Last Complete Period],
        CALCULATE([Internet Sales],
            FILTER(ALL('Dates'),'Dates'[Year] = MAX('Dates'[Year])-1 &&
            'Dates'[Year Month Number] <= MAX('Dates'[Year Month
Number])-12)),
```

```
        MAX('Dates'[Year]) = [Current Year],
            CALCULATE([Internet Sales],
            FILTER(ALL('Dates'),'Dates'[Year] = [Current Year]-1 &&
            'Dates'[Month Number] <= [Last Complete Month])),
        CALCULATE([Internet Sales],
            FILTER(ALL('Dates'),
            'Dates'[Year] = MAX('Dates'[Year])-1 &&
            'Dates'[Year Month Number] <= MAX('Dates'[Year Month
    Number])-12)))
```

Since we are dealing with historical information in the Adventure Works database, the `Today` measure is set to a specific date. In a production scenario, the `Today` measure would be something like `Today = TODAY()` or, if you are filtering your date table in your query to only be through the current day, `Today = MAX('Dates'[Date])`. The rest of the measures are derived from the `Today` measure and use simple `LOOKUPVALUE` expressions.

By passing `TRUE` as the expression parameter to `SWITCH`, the first `<value>` condition (such as no filters applied) that evaluates to `True` will result in the corresponding result expression.

The first condition `NOT(ISCROSSFILTERED)` handles whether any date filter has been applied from any date column. The second condition tests for individual periods that are not yet complete, and returns a `BLANK`. The third condition accounts for individual periods prior to or equal to the last complete period. The fourth condition is specific to the subtotal of the current year (= `[Current Year]`); this rule excludes the incomplete period. All other filter contexts are accounted for in the final expression—a standard Prior Year-to-Date calculation at the period grain.

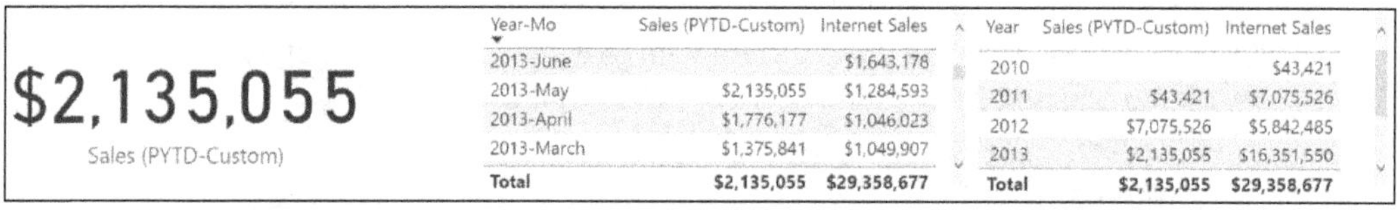

$2,135,055

Sales (PYTD-Custom)

Year-Mo	Sales (PYTD-Custom)	Internet Sales
2013-June		$1,643,178
2013-May	$2,135,055	$1,284,593
2013-April	$1,776,177	$1,046,023
2013-March	$1,375,841	$1,049,907
Total	**$2,135,055**	**$29,358,677**

Year	Sales (PYTD-Custom)	Internet Sales
2010		$43,421
2011	$43,421	$7,075,526
2012	$7,075,526	$5,842,485
2013	$2,135,055	$16,351,550
Total	**$2,135,055**	**$29,358,677**

Figure 6.6: Custom PYTD measure computes the correct value without any filter (card visual) and across date hierarchy levels

Note that a blank (no value) is returned for the current period (`2013-Jun`) as per the requirements.

Remember that the data models created in Power BI can be consumed in self-service scenarios, such as with Excel pivot tables, and business users will want or expect the new measures to "just work" across filter conditions. However, in the rapid, agile delivery of Power BI, only the most important or core filter contexts can be implemented in the first iterations.

See also

- DAX `LOOKUPVALUE` function: `https://bit.ly/3gdjZKl`

- DAX `CROSSJOIN` function: `https://bit.ly/2Ryr3qx`
- DAX `HASONEVALUE` function: `https://bit.ly/3wXSEBE`

Simplifying Date Intelligence with DAX and Calculated Tables

In addition to the M query transformations described earlier in this chapter, DAX table functions can also be used in Power BI Import mode models to enhance and simplify date intelligence. DAX queries can access existing tables in the data model, and the tables evaluated during refresh can be used in relationships and measure calculations like all other tables. Similar to calculated columns, calculated tables should be rarely used–given the transformation capabilities of M, SQL, and ETL tools–but can be valuable supplements to models for small tables, such as role-playing date dimensions and bridge tables.

This recipe provides an example of using DAX calculated tables to support role-playing date dimensions. Additionally, a single row table is created via DAX to simplify common date intelligence measures.

Getting ready

To prepare for this recipe, follow these steps:

1. Open Power BI Desktop.
2. Create an Import mode data source query called `AdWorksDW`. This query should be similar to the following:

   ```
   let
       Source = Sql.Database("localhost\MSSQLSERVERDEV",
   "AdventureWorksDW2019")
   in
       Source
   ```

3. Isolate this query in a query group called `Data Sources` and disable loading.
4. Right-click `AdWorksDW` and choose `Reference`.
5. Select the `FactInternetSales` table and name this query `Internet Sales`.
6. Repeat *steps 5* and *6* for the `DimDate` table and name this query `Order Dates`.
7. Separate the fact query, `Internet Sales`, into a `Facts` query group.
8. Separate the dimension query, `Order Dates`, into a `Dimensions` query group.
9. Create a `Blank Query` called `Calculations` in the `Other Queries` group.
10. Choose `Close & Apply` in the ribbon of the `Home` tab to load the tables to the data model.

11. Create a relationship using the `FullDateAlternateKey` column from the `Order Dates` table and the `OrderDate` column of the Internet Sales table.

How to Simplify Date Intelligence

To implement this recipe, perform the following steps:

1. From `Report View`, click on `New Table` in the ribbon of the `Modeling` tab
2. In the formula bar, assign a name to the date dimension table, such as `Shipment Dates`, and use the `SELECTCOLUMNS` function to retrieve date columns from the existing date dimension table:

```
Shipment Dates =
    SELECTCOLUMNS('OrderDates',
        "Shipment Date", 'OrderDates'[FullDateAlternateKey],
        "Shipment Year", 'OrderDates'[CalendarYear],
        "Shipment Month", 'OrderDates'[EnglishMonthName],
        "Last Refreshed", NOW()
    )
```

3. As per the example, apply column aliases (`Shipment...`) to avoid confusion with other date tables in the model
4. Create a relationship between the `Shipment Date` column in the `Shipment Dates` table and the `ShipDate` table in the `Internet Sales` table
5. Rename the `FullDateAlternateKey` column in the `Order Dates` table to `Order Date`

How it works...

The model now has two date dimension tables with active relationships to the fact table, order date, and shipment date in this example. Generally, when role-playing date dimensions are used, aliases are applied to all tables and columns, thus requiring the date table and its columns to be renamed as `Order Dates`. However, if the new role-playing date tables will be rarely used, then aliases may only be necessary for these new role-playing date tables.

There's more...

One option to further simplify date intelligence measures is to embed a calculated table in a model that generates values frequently used as filter conditions:

1. Create a `Today` measure in the `Calculations` table:

```
Today = DATE(2013,6,28)
```

2. Hide the `Calculations` column in `Report View` and note that the `Calculations` table's icon changes from a table to a calculator. This measure table will remain above other non-measure-only tables in the `Fields` list.
3. While in `Report View`, select `New Table` from the ribbon of the `Modeling` tab and enter the following DAX query:

```
Date Parameters =
    VAR __Today = [Today]
    VAR __CurrentFiscalYear =
        LOOKUPVALUE('OrderDates'[FiscalYear], 'OrderDates'[Order
Date],__Today)
    VAR __CurrentFiscalQuarter =
        LOOKUPVALUE('OrderDates'[FiscalQuarter],
            'OrderDates'[Order Date],__Today)
RETURN
    ROW(
        "Last Refreshed", NOW(),
        "Today", __Today,
        "30 Days Prior", __Today - 30,
        "90 Days Prior",__Today - 90,
        "Current Fiscal Year", __CurrentFiscalYear,
        "Prior Fiscal Year", __CurrentFiscalYear-1,
        "Current Fiscal Quarter", __CurrentFiscalQuarter
    )
```

4. Hide the parameters table from the `Report` view.

Last Refreshed	Today	30 Days Prior	90 Days Prior	Current Fiscal Year	Prior Fiscal Year	Current Fiscal Quarter
9/2/2021 12:41:21 PM	6/28/2013	5/29/2013	3/30/2013	2012	2011	4

Figure 6.7: Sample of the single row table (Date Parameters) created via the DAX calculated table query

5. Create date intelligence measures that leverage the values stored in the calculated table:

```
Internet Sales = SUM('Internet Sales'[SalesAmount])

Last 90 Days Sales =
    CALCULATE([Internet Sales],
        'OrderDates'[Order Date] >= DISTINCT('Date Parameters'[90 Days
Prior])
        &&
        'OrderDates'[Order Date] <= DISTINCT('Date Parameters'[Today]))
```

Since we are dealing with historical information in the Adventure Works database, the `Today` measure is set to a specific date. In a production scenario, the `Today` measure would be something like `Today = TODAY()` or, if you are filtering your date table in your query to only be through the current day, `Today = MAX('Dates'[Date])`.

An underscore or other leading character can be used in front of variable names to ensure that a variable's name does not conflict with reserved words, and also to distinguish variables and DAX added columns from actual columns and tables in the data model.

The `DISTINCT` function retrieves the single value from the table for comparison with the corresponding date dimension column in the filter condition of `CALCULATE`. One may be tempted to use the `MAX` or `MIN` functions here in place of `DISTINCT`, but this will generate an error that the `MAX` or `MIN` function has been used in a True/False expression that is used as a table filter expression.

See also

- DAX `SELECTCOLUMNS` function: `https://bit.ly/2OSw4JA`
- DAX `LOOKUPVALUE` function: `https://bit.ly/3gdjZKl`
- DAX `ROW` function: `https://bit.ly/3dobQ3R`

Leveraging Calculation Groups

When working with date intelligence, it is common to have many quasi-redundant measures that calculate various different metrics for YTD, MTD, PY, PYTD, PMTD, and other common date intelligence intervals. For example, business users may be interested in a year-to-date, year-over-year, and year-over-year percentage calculation for the gross sales, net sales, and other measures. Normally, this would require nine DAX measures to calculate these measures at each of those date intelligence intervals.

Calculation groups can greatly assist in reducing the number of measures required by allowing a DAX expression to be reused for any measure. In the example given, this means that three DAX expressions could serve the needs of the nine DAX expressions required without the use of calculation groups.

This recipe demonstrates the use of calculation groups in the context of date intelligence in order to eliminate redundant DAX expressions.

Getting ready

To prepare for this recipe, follow these steps:

1. Open Power BI Desktop.
2. Create an Import mode data source query called `AdWorksDW`. This query should be similar to the following:

```
let
    Source = Sql.Database("localhost\MSSQLSERVERDEV",
```

```
"AdventureWorksDW2019")
in
    Source
```

3. Isolate this query in a query group called `Data Sources` and disable loading.
4. Right-click `AdWorksDW` and choose `Reference`.
5. Select the `FactInternetSales` table and name this query `Internet Sales`.
6. Repeat *steps 4* and *5* for the `DimDate` table and name this query `Order Dates`.
7. Separate the fact query, `Internet Sales`, into a `Facts` query group.
8. Separate the dimension query, `Order Dates`, into a `Dimensions` query group.
9. Create a `Blank Query` called `Calculations` in the `Other Queries` group.
10. Select `Close & Apply` in the ribbon of the `Home` tab to load the tables to the data model.
11. Create a relationship using the `FullDateAlternateKey` column from the `Order Dates` table and the `OrderDate` column of the Internet Sales table.
12. Rename the `FullDateAlternateKey` column to `Date`.
13. Mark the `Order Dates` table as a date table using `Date` as the `Date` column.
14. In the `Calculations` table, create some simple measures:

```
Internet Sales = SUM('Internet Sales'[SalesAmount])

Orders = COUNTROWS('Internet Sales')
```

15. Hide the `Calculations` column in the `Calculations` table.
16. Set the `Sort by` column for the `EnglishMonthName` column to the `MonthNumberOfYear` column.

How to Leverage Calculation Groups

To implement this recipe, carry out the following steps:

1. Select `Tabular Editor` from the ribbon of the `External Tools` tab
2. In `Tabular Editor`, select `Model` and then `New Calculation Group`
3. Name the new calculation group `Date Intelligence Group`
4. Expand `Date Intelligence Group`, right-click `Calculation Items`, and choose `New Calculation Item`

5. Create a `Current` calculation item with the formula `SELECTEDMEASURE()`

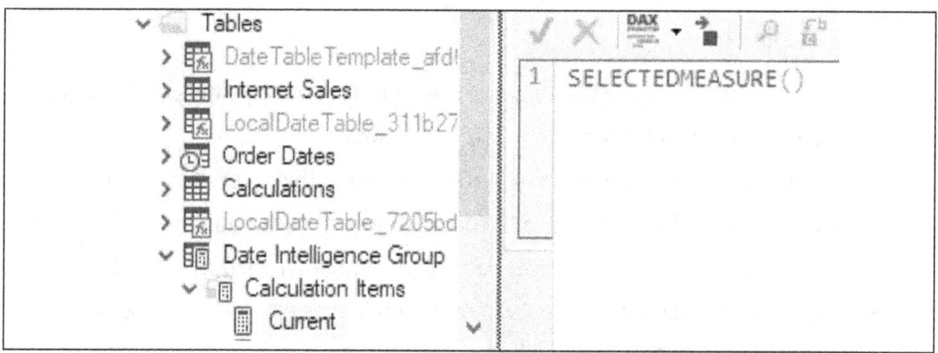

Figure 6.8: Creation of the Current calculation item

6. Repeat *steps 4* and *5* to create the following calculation items:

   For YTD:

```
CALCULATE(SELECTEDMEASURE(),
    FILTER(ALL('Order Dates'),
         'Order Dates'[CalendarYear] = MAX('Order Dates'[CalendarYear])
&&
        'Order Dates'[Date] <= MAX('Order Dates'[Date])))
For MTD:
CALCULATE(SELECTEDMEASURE(),
    FILTER(ALL('Order Dates'),
        'Order Dates'[CalendarYear] = MAX('Order Dates'[CalendarYear])
&&
        'Order Dates'[MonthNumberOfYear] = MAX('Order
Dates'[MonthNumberOfYear])
 && 'Order Dates'[Date] <= MAX('Order Dates'[Date])))
For QTD:
CALCULATE(SELECTEDMEASURE(),
    FILTER(ALL('Order Dates'),
        'Order Dates'[CalendarYear] = MAX('Order Dates'[CalendarYear])
&&
        'Order Dates'[CalendarQuarter] = MAX('Order
Dates'[CalendarQuarter]) &&
        'Order Dates'[Date] <= MAX('Order Dates'[Date])))
For PY:
VAR __MaxDate = MAX('Order Dates'[Date])
VAR __MinDate = MIN('Order Dates'[Date])
RETURN
    CALCULATE(SELECTEDMEASURE(),
```

```
        FILTER(ALL('Order Dates'),
            'Order Dates'[Date] >=
                DATE(YEAR(__MinDate)-1,MONTH(__MinDate),DAY(__MinDate))
&&
            'Order Dates'[Date] <=
                DATE(YEAR(__MaxDate)-1,MONTH(__MaxDate),DAY(__
MaxDate))))
For PY YTD:
VAR __MaxDate = MAX('Order Dates'[Date])
RETURN
    CALCULATE(SELECTEDMEASURE(),
        FILTER(ALL('Order Dates'),
            'Order Dates'[CalendarYear] =
                MAX('Order Dates'[CalendarYear])-1 &&
            'Order Dates'[Date] <=
                DATE(
                    YEAR(__MaxDate)-1,
                    MONTH(__MaxDate),
                    DAY(__MaxDate))))
For YOY:
SELECTEDMEASURE()
    - CALCULATE(SELECTEDMEASURE(),'Date Intelligence Group'[Name] =
"PY")
For YOY %:
DIVIDE(
    CALCULATE(SELECTEDMEASURE(),'Date Intelligence Group'[Name] ="YOY"),
    CALCULATE(SELECTEDMEASURE(),'Date Intelligence Group'[Name] ="PY"))
```

7. For the `YOY %` calculation item, set the `Format String Expression` to `0.00%;-0.00%;0.00%`
8. In `Tabular Editor`, select `File` and then `Save`
9. In Power BI Desktop, click `Refresh now` in the warning box regarding refreshing calculation groups

One or more calculation groups need to be manually refreshed. Refresh now

Figure 6.9: Manually refreshing calculation groups

10. Create a `Matrix` visualization with the `CalendarYear` and `EnglishMonthName` columns from the `Order Dates` table as `Rows`, the `Internet Sales` measure as `Values`, and the `Name` column from the `Date Intelligence Group` as `Columns`
11. Add the `Orders` measure to the `Matrix` visualization as `Values`

How it works...

Currently, Power BI Desktop does not provide a method for creating and editing calculation groups, so this must be done in Visual Studio or Tabular Editor.

The `SELECTEDMEASURE` function takes the current measure in context and replaces the values returned by the measure with the calculations from the calculation group. The format of the value returned (Currency, Whole Number, Decimal) corresponds with the format of the selected measure, unless overridden by a specified `Format String Expression`. For numeric values, the `Format String Expression` should always include three format specifications separated by semi-colons for positive, negative, and zero values.

The order of the calculation items returned will be alphabetical when the `Ordinal` property is set to `-1` for all calculation items. This order can be overridden by specifying `Ordinal` numbers from `0` and higher. Lower `Ordinal` numbers display first.

There's more...

The same results can be achieved using DAX time intelligence functions with the caveat that DAX time intelligence functions assume a standard (Gregorian) calendar, and thus should be avoided when dealing with fiscal calendars and more complex scenarios. To see how this works, do the following:

1. In `Tabular Editor`, select `Model` and then `New Calculation Group`
2. Name the new calculation group `Time Intelligence Group`
3. Create the following calculation items:
    - **Current**: `SELECTEDMEASURE()`
    - **YTD**: `CALCULATE(SELECTEDMEASURE(), DATESYTD('Order Dates'[Date]))`
    - **MTD**: `CALCULATE(SELECTEDMEASURE(), DATESMTD('Order Dates'[Date]))`
    - **QTD**: `CALCULATE(SELECTEDMEASURE(), DATESQTD('Order Dates'[Date]))`
    - **PY**: `CALCULATE(SELECTEDMEASURE(), SAMEPERIODLASTYEAR('Order Dates'[Date]))`
    - **PY YTD**: `CALCULATE(SELECTEDMEASURE(),SAMEPERIODLASTYEAR('Order Dates'[Date]),'Time Intelligence Group'[Name]= "YTD")`
    - **YOY**: `SELECTEDMEASURE()-CALCULATE(SELECTEDMEASURE(),'Time Intelligence Group'[Name] = "PY")`
    - **YOY %**: `DIVIDE(CALCULATE(SELECTEDMEASURE(),'Time Intelligence Group'[Name] ="YOY"),CALCULATE(SELECTEDMEASURE(),'Time Intelligence Group'[Name] ="PY"))`

4. Duplicate `Page 1`
5. Select the matrix visualization on `Duplicate of Page 1` and replace the columns with the `Name` column from the `Time Intelligence Group`

The numbers in both matrices are identical.

See also

- Calculation groups in Analysis Services tabular models: `https://bit.ly/3tlJRYd`
- `DAX SELECTEDMEASURE` function: `https://bit.ly/3sv5XWN`

Conclusion

This chapter provided recipes for preparing a data model to support robust date intelligence and for authoring custom date intelligence measures. Date intelligence provides a broad set of data modeling patterns and functions that enable analysis across time periods. The measures created for date intelligence can be used in combination with one another to support growth and variance measures and are often utilized as KPIs in Power BI dashboards. When properly implemented, date intelligence dramatically expands the analytical power of a data model and simplifies report and dashboard development.

7

Parameterizing Power BI Solutions

With the foundation of a Power BI deployment in place, components of the data retrieval and report design processes—as well as the user experience—can be parameterized to deliver greater flexibility for both technology services and users. For example, query parameters can isolate and restrict data sources to support changing source systems, templates can enable parameterized report development against pre-defined metadata, and M and DAX functions can deliver custom integration and analytical capabilities.

The recipes in this chapter cover both standard parameterization features and techniques in Power BI, as well as more advanced custom implementations. Examples of parameterizing data sources, queries, user-defined functions, and reports further express the power of the M language and its integration with other Power BI Desktop features. Additional examples, such as URL-based parameter filters, a dedicated forecasting or what-if? tool, and user selection parameter tables, utilize both the transformation and analytical features of Power BI to empower users with greater control over the analysis and visualization of Power BI data models.

In this chapter, we will cover the following recipes:

- Filtering reports dynamically
- Leveraging query parameters
- Working with templates
- Converting static queries to dynamic functions
- Capturing user selections with parameter tables
- Forecasting with what-if analysis

Technical requirements

The following are required to complete the recipes in this chapter:

- Power BI Desktop
- SQL Server with the `AdventureWorksDW2019` database installed. This database and the instructions for installing it are available here: `http://bit.ly/2OVQfG7`
- Files for this chapter can be downloaded from the following GitHub repository: `https://github.com/gdeckler/PowerBICookbook2ndEdition`

Filtering reports dynamically

In addition to the report filter options in Power BI Desktop covered in *Chapter 4, Authoring Power BI Reports*, filters can also be applied to published Power BI reports via the URL string. Rather than multiple, dedicated reports and report pages with distinct filter conditions, URL links with unique query strings can leverage a single published report in the Power BI service. Additionally, URL links can be embedded within a dataset such that a published report can expose links to other reports with a pre-defined filter condition.

In this recipe, two URL strings are created to demonstrate single and multiple filter parameter syntax. The second example creates a URL string for each row of the `Product` dimension table via an M query and exposes this dynamic link in a report visual.

Getting ready

To prepare for this recipe, follow these steps:

1. Download `CH7_R1.pbix` from the following GitHub repository: `https://github.com/PacktPublishing/Microsoft-Power-BI-Cookbook-Second-Edition`
2. Open `CH7_R1.pbix` in Power BI Desktop.
3. Edit the `AdWorksDW` query and change the `Source` line to point to your SQL server with the `AdventureWorksDW2019` database installed.
4. Publish the report to the Power BI service.

How to filter reports dynamically

To implement this recipe, perform the following steps:

1. Open the report in the Power BI service.

2. Replace the query string in the URL with the following and press *Enter*:

```
?filter=Products/ProductCategory eq 'Bikes'
```

3. To apply multiple URL filter parameters, separate the column filters with an `and` operator, as in the following example:

```
?filter=Products/ProductCategory eq 'Bikes' and Dates/CalendarYear eq
2013
```

4. Copy the report URL, without including the query string (the portion after and including the `?`).
5. Open `CH7_R1.pbix` in Power BI Desktop
6. Edit the **Products** query in Power Query Editor.
7. Add a column called **Product URL** to the **Products** table by using **Custom Column** in the ribbon of the **Add Column** tab, with a format similar to the following:

```
"https://app.powerbi.com/groups/[...]/reports/[...]/
[...]?filter=Products/ProductName eq '" & [ProductName] & "'"
```

Note that **[...]** will be replaced with your unique IDs.

8. Close and apply the query changes to apply them to the model.
9. Change the **Data category** for the **Product URL** column in the **Products** table to **Web URL**.
10. Add a second page to the report.
11. Create a **Table** visualization with the **ProductName** column from the **Products** table, the **Total Net Sales** measure from the **Calculations** table, and the **Product URL** column from the **Products** table.
12. With the **Table** visualization selected, use the **Format** pane, expand the **Values** section, and toggle the **URL icon** to **On**.
13. Save and publish the report.
14. Open the report in the Power BI service, navigate to **Page 2**, and click on one of the URL icons for a product.

How it works...

URL filters can be applied to any column in the data model that is of a text or numeric data type. The column does not have to be visible in the `Fields` list or used in one of the `Filtering` field wells in the `Report` view to be used in a URL filter.

The syntax is <Report URL>?filter=Table/Column eq 'value'. The table and field names (without spaces) are case sensitive, and the `'value'` must be enclosed in single quotes for text values. Do not use single quotes for numeric values, however.

Table and column names used in URL filters must not contain spaces. In the event that you want to have a friendly name for report users for columns, you can duplicate a friendly name column, remove the spaces from the duplicate column name, and then hide the duplicate column name from the report view. In this way, you can have a column for use in reports and a duplicate column that can be used as URL filters. When using duplicate columns, given the additional resources required of the new column(s), try to limit the columns to those with few distinct values. Additionally, a single hidden column with no spaces can be created based on the concatenation of multiple columns to simplify the URL strings.

There's more...

A report visual from a custom URL with a query string can be pinned to a dashboard, and the dashboard tile will reflect the filter condition following refreshes. However, by default, selecting the pinned dashboard tile will navigate to the unfiltered source report. The custom URL can be associated with a dashboard tile to control the dashboard navigation, as demonstrated in *Figure 7.1*:

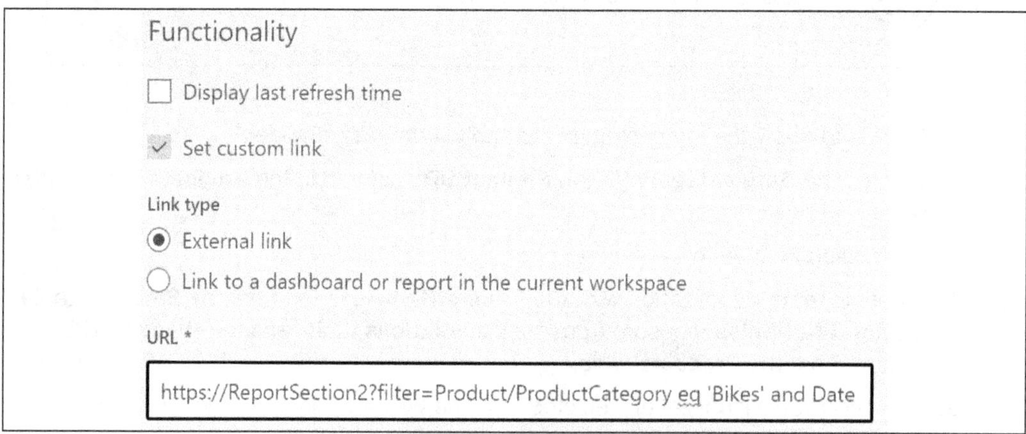

Figure 7.1: Custom URL link for a Power BI dashboard tile

See also

- Filter a report using query string parameters in the URL: `https://bit.ly/3swEJPF`

- Guy in a Cube – Filter a report with a URL query string parameter: `http://bit.ly/2s5hXSW`

Leveraging query parameters

Parameters are a primary component in building flexible, manageable query retrieval processes, as well as enabling simple filter selections. Hardcoded values in queries can be replaced with parameters, and a single parameter can be leveraged by multiple queries, thereby reducing development time and maintenance. Parameters are required to configure incremental data refresh policies on datasets and are commonly used to limit the volume of data loaded to a local instance of Power BI Desktop relative to the published Power BI dataset.

Parameters can also be useful during development in order to filter fact tables or large dimension tables to only a subset of data. Very large Power BI files can become slow and difficult to work with and thus the dataset author can add a filter via a parameter so that only a subset of rows are loaded locally. The dataset author can then simply revise the parameter such that all rows are loaded. This can be done just prior to publishing or after publishing via APIs and scripts that revise the parameter values in the Power BI service.

In this recipe, a parameter is used to filter a fact table query for a specified number of days relative to the current date. An additional, more advanced example is shared to apply parameters to a fact table query on both a dimension column as well as a date range.

Getting ready

To prepare for this recipe, follow these steps:

1. Open a Power BI Desktop file locally and access the **Power Query Editor** by clicking on **Transform Data** in the ribbon of the **Home** tab.
2. Create a query named `AdWorksDW` similar to the following:

   ```
   let
       Source = Sql.Database("localhost\MSSQLSERVERDEV",
   "AdventureWorksDW2019")
   in
       Source
   ```

3. Disable the load on the `AdWorksDW` query and place it in a `Data Sources` query group.

How to leverage query parameters

To implement this recipe, perform the following steps:

1. Create a blank query called `CurrentDate` and disable the loading of the query by right-clicking the query and then deselecting **Enable load**:

```
let
    Source = #date(2014,1,28)
in
    Source
```

2. From the **Home** tab of **Power Query Editor**, click on the **Manage Parameters** dropdown and select **New Parameter**:

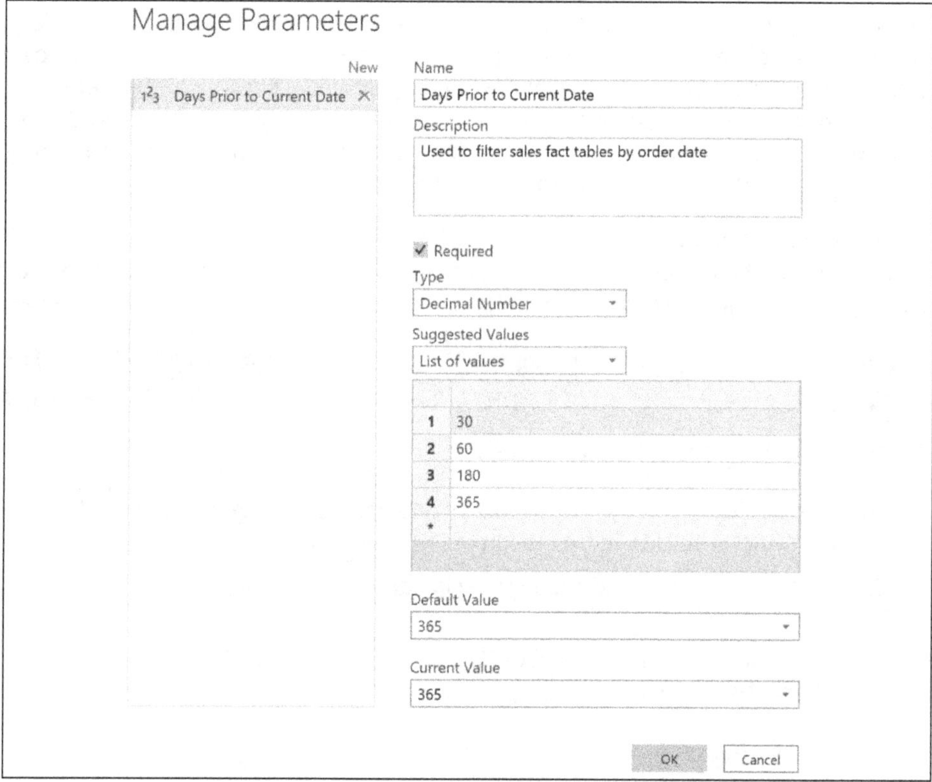

Figure 7.2: New parameter created for filtering fact table queries

3. Give the query the name **Days Prior to Current Date**, a data type of **Decimal Number**, and, for this example, enter a list of suggested values. Values outside this suggested list can also be applied to the parameter when necessary.
4. Based on the **List of values**, enter a **Default Value** and **Current Value**.

5. Create a new blank query called `StartDate` that computes a date value based on the **CurrentDate** query and the new parameter, and then disable the load:

```
let
    Source = Date.AddDays(CurrentDate,- #"Days Prior to Current Date")
in
    Source
```

   In this example, a date 365 days prior to the current date is returned based on the default parameter value.

6. Create an **Internet Sales** query based on the following M code:

```
let
    Source = AdWorksDW,
    dbo_FactInternetSales =
        Source{[Schema="dbo",Item="FactInternetSales"]}[Data],
    ChangeType = Table.TransformColumnTypes(
        dbo_FactInternetSales,{{"OrderDate", type date}}),
    RowFilter = Table.SelectRows(
        ChangeType,
        each [OrderDate] >= StartDate and [OrderDate] <= CurrentDate)
in
    SalesTerritoryJoin
```

7. Click on **Close & Apply** from the **Home** tab of Query Editor.
8. Optionally, build a report or query against the refreshed fact table to validate the filter.
9. From the **Home** tab of the **Report** view, click on the **Transform data** dropdown in the ribbon and select **Edit Parameters**:

Figure 7.3: Editing parameters from the Report view

10. Either select a suggested value from the drop-down menu or enter a number in the input box and click on **OK**.

11. Click on **Apply Changes** from the warning dialog. `StartDate` and the fact table queries impacted by the parameter change will both be refreshed.

How it works...

In a production scenario, the `CurrentDate` query would not be hardcoded to a date and would be something similar to the following:

```
let
    Source = DateTime.Date(DateTime.LocalNow())
in
    Source
```

The `StartDate` query uses the parameter to calculate a date prior to the `CurrentDate` by a number of days selected from the list of values. Parameters can be referenced within queries, just like referencing other queries or steps in a query, in which the same rules also apply. When parameters include spaces in their names, referencing the parameter must be preceded by a hashtag, #, and double quotes, and suffixed by double quotes (`#"Days Prior to Current Date"`). Parameters that do not include spaces in their names can be referenced directly without the prefix or suffix.

The `Internet Sales` query uses the `Table.SelectRows` function in the `RowFilter` step to filter the `FactInternetSales` table using the `OrderDate` column to be greater than or equal to `StartDate` (a date value). It is important that the data type of the `OrderDate` column and the data type of the `StartDate` query match one another. For example, `Date` data types cannot be compared to `DateTime` data types.

Currently, parameters cannot be created or edited in the Power BI service. The parameter values configured when published will be used for each refresh.

When considering your own scenarios, identify candidates for query parameters, such as hardcoded date filters and dimension attributes with few distinct values (for example, department groups). Identify scenarios in which certain business users or teams require edit rights to a dataset (that is, source queries, model relationships, and measures), but only need a small, highly filtered model for self-service development.

There's more...

Queries can be affected by multiple parameters. In addition, parameters can also use queries for their `Suggested Values`. To see how to use multiple parameters in a query, as well as how to use a query to provide `Suggested Values` for a parameter, do the following:

1. In **Power Query Editor**, create a query called **SalesTerritoryGroupsList** that returns the distinct **Sales Territory Groups** from the **DimSalesTerritory** table and disable loading of the query:

```
let
    Source = AdWorksDW,
    Navigation = Source{[Schema="dbo",Item="DimSalesTerritory"]}[Data],
    RemoveColumns = Table.SelectColumns(Navigation,{"SalesTerritoryGro
up"}),
    FilterNA = Table.SelectRows(RemoveColumns, each
([SalesTerritoryGroup] <> "NA")),
    RemoveDups = Table.Distinct(FilterNA),
    List = Table.ToList(RemoveDups)
in
    List
```

2. Click on **New Parameter** from the **Manage Parameters** dropdown in the ribbon of the **Home** tab.
3. Create a parameter called **Territory Group** with a **Text** data type that uses the **SalesTerritoryGroupsList** query for **Suggested Values**:

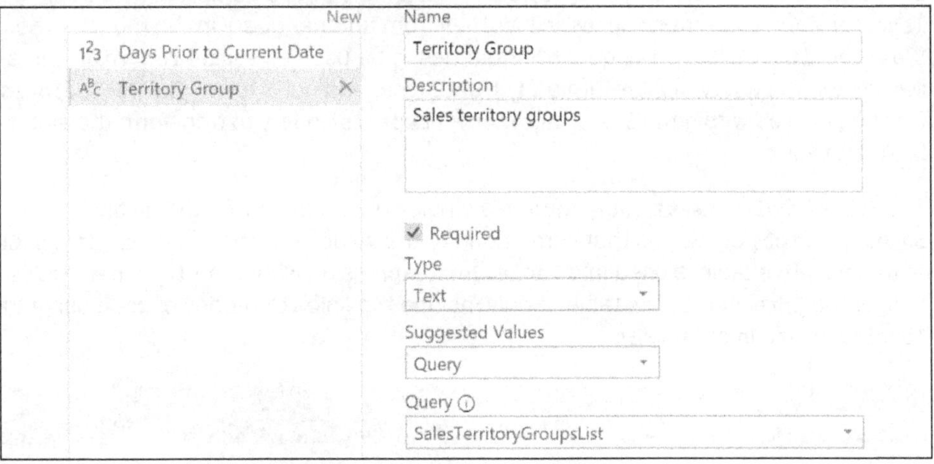

Figure 7.4: Territory Group parameter

4. Create a **SalesTerritoryKeys** query that selects the unique key values associated with this dimension using the value set by the **Territory Group** parameter and disable the load:

```
let
    Source = AdWorksDW,
    Navigation = Source{[Schema="dbo",Item="DimSalesTerritory"]}[Data],
    ParamFilter = Table.SelectRows(Navigation, each
[SalesTerritoryGroup] = #"Territory Group"),
    KeyColumn = Table.Distinct(Table.SelectColumns(ParamFilter,{"SalesTe
rritoryKey"}))
in
    KeyColumn
```

5. Within the **Internet Sales** table query, create an inner join expression step against the new **SalesTerritoryKeys** query:

```
let
    Source = AdWorksDW,
    dbo_FactInternetSalesReason = Source{[Schema="dbo",Item="FactInterne
tSales"]}[Data],
    ChangeType = Table.TransformColumnTypes(dbo_FactInternetSalesReason,
{{"OrderDate", type date}}),
    RowFilter = Table.SelectRows(ChangeType, each [OrderDate] >=
StartDate and [OrderDate] <= CurrentDate),
    SalesTerritoryJoin = Table.Join(RowFilter,"SalesTerritoryKey",SalesT
erritoryKeys,"SalesTerritoryKey",JoinKind.Inner)
in
    SalesTerritoryJoin
```

The `Internet Sales` table is now filtered by both the `Days Prior to Current Date` parameter and the `Territory Group` parameter. Instead of a static list of values, `Territory Group` derives `Suggested Values` from another query in the model – the `SalesTerritoryGroupsList` query. For queries to be used as `Suggested Values` in a parameter, the query must return a `List` data type, and not a table. The `Table.ToList` function is used within the `SalesTerritoryGroupsList` query to transform the single-column table into a list.

The `SalesTerritoryKeys` query returns a single column table with the distinct `SalesTerritoryKey` values that correspond to the value chosen for the `Territory Group` parameter. This table is used in a `Table.Join` expression within the `Internet Sales` query to filter the `Internet Sales` table to only include the sales territories chosen using the `Territory Group` parameter.

See also

- Using parameters: `https://bit.ly/37rXLP6`
- Edit parameter settings in the Power BI service: `https://bit.ly/3iuC1sn`

Working with templates

Power BI templates can be created from Power BI Desktop files as a means of providing users and other report authors with access to pre-defined metadata, such as M queries, DAX measures, model relationships, and report visualizations. As the template files do not contain actual data, they are very lightweight and, for import mode models, data is only retrieved when the template is opened. Additionally, if query parameters have been configured, a user interface is provided for entering parameter values, and these parameters can be integrated with the source queries and other components of the dataset.

In this recipe, a parameter and supporting query are added to a Power BI Desktop file to support the distribution of a Power BI template.

Getting ready

To prepare for this recipe, follow these steps:

1. Download `CH7_R3_Start.pbix` from the following GitHub repository: `https://github.com/PacktPublishing/Microsoft-Power-BI-Cookbook-Second-Edition`.
2. Edit the `AdWorksDW` query to point to your copy of the `AdventureWorksDW2019` database.

How to work with templates

In this example, the goal is to provide a Power BI template that only retrieves data for a single customer country. To implement this recipe, perform the following steps:

1. Open `CH7_R3_Start.pbix` in Power BI Desktop.
2. Choose **Transform data** from the ribbon of the **Home** tab to open **Power Query Editor**.
3. In the **Queries** pane, right-click an empty area and choose **New Group** to create a new query group called **Parameters**.
4. Right-click **Other Queries** and create a `List` query called **CustomerCountries** to retrieve the **Country** names from the **Customers** query:

```
let
    Source = Customers,
    SelectColumn = Table.SelectColumns(Source,{"Country"}),
    Distinct = Table.Distinct(SelectColumn),
    List = Table.ToList(Distinct)
in
    List
```

5. Disable the load for the **CustomerCountries** query.
6. Right-click the **Parameters** query group and choose **New Parameter**.
7. Create a parameter called **Customer Country** with **Text** as the type, **Suggested Values** for the **CustomerCountries** query, and **United States** as the current value.
8. In the **Other Queries** group, create a query called **CustomerKeys** that references the **Customer Country** parameter, and disable the load on this query:

```
let
    CountryParamFilter = Table.SelectRows(Customers, each [Country] =
#"Customer Country"),
    CustomerKeys = Table.SelectColumns(CountryParamFilter,
```

```
{"CustomerKey"})
in
    CustomerKeys
```

9. Modify the **Internet Sales** fact table query to respect the parameter selection:

```
let
    Source = AdWorksDW,
    dbo_FactInternetSales = Source{[Schema="dbo",Item="FactInternetSal
es"]}[Data],
    ChangeType =
        Table.TransformColumnTypes(dbo_FactInternetSales,
            {
                {"OrderDate", type date},
                {"DueDate", type date},
                {"ShipDate", type date}
            }
        ),
    CustomerJoin =
        Table.Join(ChangeType,
        "CustomerKey",CustomerKeys,"CustomerKey",JoinKind.Inner
    )
in
    CustomerJoin
```

10. Click **Close & Apply** from the ribbon of the **Home** tab and then save the PBIX file.
11. From the **File** menu of the **Report** view, select **Export** and then **Power BI template**.
12. Optionally, give the template a description describing the parameter logic.
13. Choose a folder path for the template (`.pbit`).
14. Open the template file; the parameters dialog is opened, as shown in *Figure 7.5*:

Figure 7.5: Parameter dialog when opening the Power BI template (.PBIT)

15. Choose **Australia** from the list and then select the **Load** button.
16. Save the file as a new **Power BI Desktop** (**PBIX**) file.

How it works...

When opening a Power BI template, if there are any parameters defined, the parameters dialog will open, allowing the user to specify the parameter values. In the recipe, the `Customer Country` parameter is defined. This parameter uses `Suggested Values`, which come from the `CustomerCountries` query; this is a `List` query in that it returns a `List` object instead of a `Table` object. Only queries that return lists can be used as `Suggested Values` for parameters.

The `CustomerKeys` query uses the chosen `Customer Country` parameter value to return a single-column table of `CustomerKey` values from the `Customers` query. Since the `CustomerKey` column is the surrogate key used in the customer-to-sales relationship, it is not necessary to apply any transformations to remove duplicates, as each value is already unique. The `CustomerKeys` query is then used within the `CustomerJoin` expression in the `Internet Sales` query to return only the sales for the specified `CustomerKeys`, which belong to the chosen `Customer Country`.

Distributing templates can introduce version control and manageability issues. Therefore, prior to designing parameters and creating templates, confirm whether the report authoring capabilities of Power BI Desktop against a published dataset in Power BI are insufficient. If insufficient, identify the modifications that users need to implement, such as additional data sources or query transformations, and consider whether these changes can be implemented in the existing dataset. Identify the scope and goals of the templates, such as the years of data and specific dimensions required. Parameters will be designed based on these requirements to retrieve the minimum amount of data needed.

There's more...

In some cases, such as, perhaps, an **Independent Software Vendor** (**ISV**), report templates can be created that utilize a standard data schema, such as the vendor's database that supports their third-party application. In these cases, the ISV can create a standard Power BI report template, complete with visuals, and distribute this template to its customers. In such circumstances, the database connection information can be parameterized, since each customer has their own local copy of the database. To see how this can work, follow these steps:

1. Open `CH7_R3_Start.pbix` in Power BI Desktop.
2. Choose **Transform data** from the ribbon of the **Home** tab to open **Power Query Editor**.
3. Right-click the **Parameters** query group and choose **New Parameter**.
4. In the **Manage Parameters** dialog, create a parameter called **SQL Server Instance** with **Text** as the type and a **Current Value** of the SQL Server instance that hosts your `AdventureWorksDW2019` database (in other words, `localhost\MSSQLSERVERDEV`).
5. While still in the **Manage Parameters** dialog, select **New** and create a parameter called **SQL Database** with **Text** as the type, and a **Current Value** of the database name of the `AdventureWorksDW2019` database.

6. Click the **OK** button to exit the **Manage Parameters** dialog.
7. Edit the `AdWorksDW` query to use the new parameters:

```
let
    SQLInstance =
        if #"SQL Server Instance" = null
            then "localhost\MSSQLSERVERDEV" else #"SQL Server Instance",
    SQLDatabase =
        if #"SQL Database" = null
            then "AdventureWorksDW2019" else #"SQL Database",
    Source = Sql.Database(SQLInstance, SQLDatabase)
in
    Source
```

In this case, the modified `AdWorksDW` query demonstrates how to account for parameters that may not be required. The query uses `if` statements to determine whether the parameter value is `null` and, if so, uses a default value for the `SQLInstance` and `SQLDatabase` expressions. If saved as a template, these parameters for the `SQL Server Instance` and `SQL Database` would be presented to the user upon opening the PBIT file. This would allow the user to connect to their own local copy of the database to retrieve the data used in the report. The user can then save the file as a PBIX.

See also

- Using templates in Power BI Desktop: `https://bit.ly/3gpXtxX`

Converting static queries to dynamic functions

In addition to the standard library of functions available to M queries, user-defined functions can be created to encapsulate the logic of queries for dynamic application against parameter inputs. Like SQL-stored procedures, M functions can be created with or without input parameters, which can be required or optional. Additionally, as functions are values in the M language, just like table and list values, they can be invoked on demand and in multiple areas within a given Power BI data model.

In this recipe, a function is created to support the integration of a list of employee IDs maintained outside the data warehouse environment. The function accepts the employee ID values as parameter inputs and retrieves related column values.

Getting ready

To prepare for this recipe, follow these steps:

1. Download `Employees.xlsx` from the following GitHub repository: `https://github.com/PacktPublishing/Microsoft-Power-BI-Cookbook-Second-Edition`.
2. Open a **Power BI Desktop** file locally and access **Power Query Editor** by clicking on **Transform Data** in the ribbon of the **Home** tab.
3. Create a query named `AdWorksDW` similar to the following:

```
let
    Source = Sql.Database("localhost\MSSQLSERVERDEV",
"AdventureWorksDW2019")
in
    Source
```

4. Disable the load on the `AdWorksDW` query and place it in a `Data Sources` query group.
5. Create an `Employees` query that references the `AdWorksDW` query and imports the `DimEmployee` table:

```
let
    Source = AdWorksDW,
    dbo_DimEmployee = Source{[Schema="dbo",Item="DimEmployee"]}[Data],
    FullName =
        Table.CombineColumns(
            dbo_DimEmployee,
            {"FirstName", "LastName"},
            Combiner.CombineTextByDelimiter(" ", QuoteStyle.None),
            "EmployeeName"
        )
in
    FullName
```

6. Place the `Employees` query into a query group called `Dimensions` and disable the load.

How to convert static queries

To implement this recipe, perform the following steps:

1. Create an M query called `EmployeeKeysAdHoc` in the **Other Queries** group that retrieves the employee IDs from the Excel workbook:

```
let
    Source = Excel.Workbook(File.Contents("C:\Employees.xlsx"), null,
true),
    Employees_Sheet = Source{[Item="Employees",Kind="Sheet"]}[Data],
```

```
    Headers = Table.PromoteHeaders(Employees_Sheet,
[PromoteAllScalars=true]),
    TypeConversion =
        Table.TransformColumnTypes(
            Headers,{{"EmployeeAlternateKey", type text}}
        ),
    RemoveNullsAndDups =
        Table.Distinct(
            Table.SelectRows(TypeConversion, each
[EmployeeAlternateKey]<>null)
        )
in
    RemoveNullsAndDups
```

2. Disable the load on the **EmployeeKeysAdHoc** query.
3. Create a function that retrieves the required employee column values for a given `Employee ID` input parameter from the **Employees** query by creating a **Blank Query**, using the following code:

```
(EmployeeID as text) =>
    let
        EmployeeDimFilter =
            Table.SelectRows(
                Employees,
                each [EmployeeNationalIDAlternateKey] = EmployeeID and
                [EndDate] = null),
        EmployeeColumnSelection = Table.SelectColumns(
             EmployeeDimFilter,
             {"EmployeeName", "DepartmentName", "EmailAddress"})
in
    EmployeeColumnSelection
```

4. Name this function **EmployeeDetailFunction** and place it in a **Functions** query group. A formula (`fx`) icon in the Query Editor will identify the value as a function.
5. Create a new blank query in the **Other Queries** group that references the **EmployeeKeysAdHoc** query; name this new query **EmployeeIDLookup**.
6. Add an expression that invokes the **EmployeeDetailFunction** function in a `Table.AddColumn` function, and then expand the column to expose the three columns returned from the **EmployeeDetailFunction** function using the `Table.ExpandTableColumn` function:

```
let
    Source = EmployeeKeysAdHoc,
    CallFunction =
        Table.AddColumn(
            Source,
```

```
                "FunctionTbl", each EmployeeDetailFunction([EmployeeAlternat
eKey])
            ),
        Expand =
            Table.ExpandTableColumn(
                CallFunction,
                "FunctionTbl",
                {"EmployeeName", "DepartmentName", "EmailAddress"},
                {"EmployeeName", "DepartmentName", "EmailAddress"}
            )
in
    Expand
```

7. Click on **Close & Apply** in the ribbon of the **Home** tab and save your work.

How it works...

In this example, a business team maintains a list of employee IDs in an Excel workbook and wants the ability to access several columns from the employee dimension table in the data model related to these IDs. In the `EmployeeKeysAdHoc` query, three M transformation functions are applied to protect the integration process: a data type conversion to text, the removal of any null values, and the removal of any duplicates. Data cleansing operations are always recommended when importing from files and unstructured data sources.

In the `EmployeeDetailFunction` function, the `EmployeeID` parameter is first defined as a required text-type input parameter. The parameter is then used in the `EmployeeDimFilter` expression as part of a `Table.SelectRows` filtering function. Given that the `Employees` table has type 2 slowly changing dimension logic applied, with multiple rows possible per employee, it is necessary to filter for the current employee row according to the `EmployeeDimFilter` variable expression (`[End Date = null]`). Setting this filter condition ensures that only the current or "active" row (no end date) for the employee is returned.

Slowly changing dimension logic that inserts and/or updates rows for core dimensions as the entities in these dimensions change is an essential feature of data warehouses. The entities represented by such dimensions can be things like products or employees. Power BI dataset designers must be aware of this logic as represented in dimension columns, such as surrogate keys and alternate or business keys, and develop M and DAX expressions accordingly.

With the filters applied, a simple `Table.SelectColumns` expression is used to retrieve the three required columns. A `Table` value is returned for each row, and each table contains columns for the given employee ID from the Excel workbook. As per the M expression code, the `EmployeeDetailFunction` function accepts the values from the `EmployeeNationalIDAlternateKey` column as its parameter inputs.

Changes to the list of employee keys in the Excel workbook will be reflected in the Power BI report with each refresh. Additional columns and logic can be added to the function and, as the function is only metadata, it can be used in other data transformation scenarios—in this model or in other models—with access to the `Employees` table.

The function in this recipe (Excel-based list), as well as functions applied against relational database sources that support query folding, still requires local resources of the M engine. This is demonstrated in *Figure 7.6*:

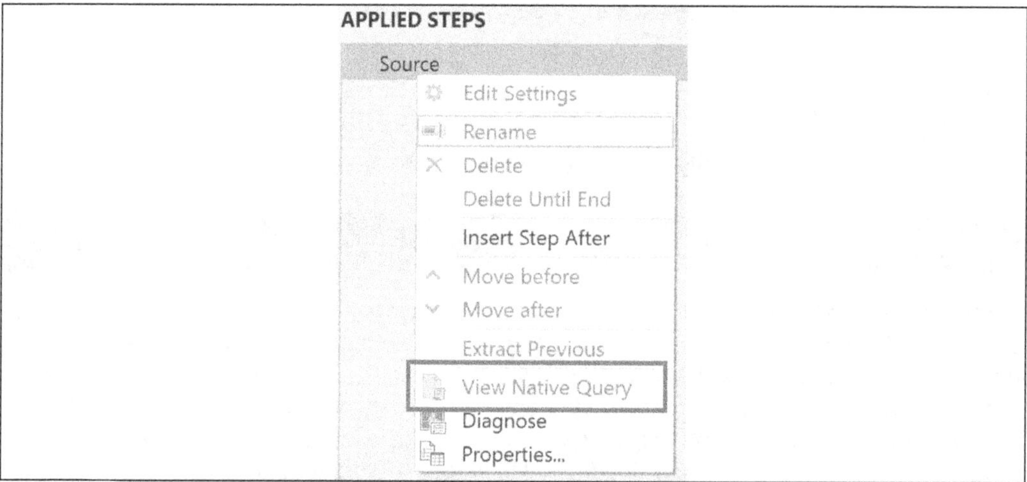

Figure 7.6: No query folding for an invoked M function

Given local resource usage and the iterative nature of functions, try to limit or avoid the use of functions against many rows, as well as functions with complex, multi-step logic. In this recipe, for example, the list of employees was very small and the function only selected a few columns from a small dimension table. Since join functions (`Table.Join, Table.NestedJoin`) and filter expressions are folded back to relational database sources, query authors should design query processes to achieve the same results as functions, but without row-by-row iterations and, hence, the local or gateway resource usage.

There's more...

The Excel file connection information can be parameterized. To see how this works, perform the following steps:

1. In Power Query Editor, choose **Manage Parameters** and then **New Parameter** in the ribbon of the **Home** tab.
2. Create a parameter called **ExcelFolder** as **Text** and set **Current Value** to the folder path where the `Employees.xlsx` file is located, with no trailing backslash, \, in the path.

3. Create a second parameter called **ExcelFile** as **Text** and set **Current Value** to `Employees.xlsx`.
4. Move the **ExcelFolder** and **ExcelFile** parameters to a **Parameters** query group.
5. Create a new **Blank Query** in the **Other Queries** group called **ExcelFilePath** and disable the load:

```
let
    ExcelPath = ExcelFolder & "\" & ExcelFile
in
    ExcelPath
```

6. Edit the `Source` line of the `EmployeeKeysAdHoc` query to use the `ExcelFilePath` query:

```
Source = Excel.Workbook(File.Contents(ExcelFilePath), null, true),
```

The path and filename of the Excel file are now controlled by the `ExcelFolder` and `ExcelFile` parameters.

See also

- Writing Custom Functions in Power Query M: `https://bit.ly/3xnPuYc`

Capturing user selections with parameter tables

An alternative method for providing parameter functionality to users of Power BI reports is via dedicated parameter tables. In this approach, the parameter values of a table are either computed during the dataset refresh process or are loaded as a one-time manual operation. DAX measures reference this parameter table and other tables and expressions of the model to enrich the self-service analysis experience and support Power BI report development. This approach is best suited for parameters that change infrequently since hard-coded parameter tables within Power BI means that the dataset owner must make such changes. If parameters need to change frequently, it may be better to have a database table or external file for the parameter table that is easier to edit and change.

The example in this recipe involves providing simple visibility to four alternative scenarios to the baseline annual sales plan—10 and 20 percent above and below the baseline plan. An inline set of scenario values are embedded in the data model, and DAX measures are used to capture filter context—such as business user selections—and compute the corresponding scenario logic.

Getting ready

To prepare for this recipe, follow these steps:

1. Open a Power BI Desktop file locally and access **Power Query Editor** by clicking on **Transform Data** in the ribbon of the **Home** tab.
2. Create a query named `AdWorksDW` similar to the following:

```
let
    Source = Sql.Database("localhost\MSSQLSERVERDEV",
"AdventureWorksDW2019")
in
    Source
```

3. Disable the load on the `AdWorksDW` query and place it in a `Data Sources` query group
4. Right-click the `AdWorksDW` query and choose **Reference**.
5. Create a `Products` query using the following code:

```
let
    Source = AdWorksDW,
    Navigation = Source{[Schema="dbo",Item="DimProduct"]}[Data],
    Subcategory =
        Table.ExpandRecordColumn(
            Navigation, "DimProductSubcategory",
            {"EnglishProductSubcategoryName", "DimProductCategory"},
            {"Product Subcategory", "DimProductCategory"}
        ),
    Category =
        Table.ExpandRecordColumn(
            Subcategory, "DimProductCategory",
            {"EnglishProductCategoryName"}, {"Product Category"}
        )
in
   Category
```

6. Create a `CategoryPlan` query with the following code:

```
let
    Source = Products,
    Sales =
        Table.ExpandTableColumn(
            Source, "FactInternetSales",
            {"SalesAmount", "OrderDate"}, {"SalesAmount", "OrderDate"}
        ),
    RemoveNulls = Table.SelectRows(Sales, each [SalesAmount] <> null),
    Year =
```

```
            Table.AddColumn(
                RemoveNulls, "Calendar Year", each Date.Year([OrderDate])
            ),
        Month =
            Table.AddColumn(
                Year, "Calendar Month", each Date.MonthName([OrderDate])
            ),
        MonthNum =
            Table.AddColumn(
                Month, "Month Number", each Date.Month([OrderDate])
            ),
        Group =
            Table.Group(MonthNum, {"Calendar Year", "Calendar Month",
    "Product Category", "Month Number"}, {{"SalesAmount", each List.
    Sum([SalesAmount]), type nullable number}}),
        Index = Table.AddIndexColumn(Group, "Index", 1, 1, Int64.Type),
        Plan =
            Table.AddColumn(
                Index, "Plan Amt",
                each if Number.IsEven([Index])
                    then 1/Number.RandomBetween(5,10) * [SalesAmount] +
    [SalesAmount]
                    else (-1 * 1/Number.RandomBetween(5,10) * [SalesAmount])
    + [SalesAmount]
            ),
        YearMonthSort =
            Table.AddColumn(
                Plan, "YearMonthSort", each [Calendar Year] * 100 + [Month
    Number]
            ),
        YearMonth =
            Table.CombineColumns(
                Table.TransformColumnTypes(
                    YearMonthSort, {{"Calendar Year", type text}}, "en-US"
                ),
                {"Calendar Year", "Calendar Month"},
                Combiner.CombineTextByDelimiter("-", QuoteStyle.None),"Year-
    Month"),
        Currency = Table.TransformColumnTypes(YearMonth,{{"Plan Amt",
    Currency.Type}})
    in
        Currency
```

7. Move the **CategoryPlan** query to a query group called **Facts**, and the **Products** query to a query group called **Dimensions**.

8. Disable the load for the **Products** query.
9. Select **Close & Apply** from the ribbon of the **Home** tab.
10. Set the **Sort By** column for the **Year-Month** column in the `CategoryPlan` table to the `YearMonthSort` column.
11. Save your work.

How to capture user selections

To implement this recipe, perform the following steps:

1. In Power BI Desktop, while in the **Report** view, click on **New Table** in the ribbon of the **Modeling** tab.
2. Use the DAX `DATATABLE` function to create a calculated table with the scenario name, scenario value, and a sort key:

```
Plan Scenarios =
    DATATABLE(
        "Plan Scenario", STRING,
        "Var to Plan", DOUBLE,
        "Scenario Sort", INTEGER,
        {
            {"Plan",1,3},{"10% Above Plan",1.1,2},
            {"20% Above Plan",1.2,1},
            {"10% Below Plan",.9,4},
            {"20% Below Plan",.8,5}
        }
    )
```

3. Select the new table (**Plan Scenarios**) in the **Data** view, and set the **Plan Scenario** column to sort by the **Scenario Sort** column using the **Sort by column** feature in the **Column tools** tab of the ribbon.
4. Right-click on the **Scenario Sort** and **Var to Plan** columns and select **Hide in Report View**.

5. Return to the **Report** view and create a measure that retrieves the filter context of the **Plan Scenario** column:

```
Sales Plan Scenario Filter Branch =
    SWITCH(TRUE(),
        NOT(ISFILTERED('Plan Scenarios'[Plan Scenario])),
            "No Selection",
        NOT(HASONEFILTER('Plan Scenarios'[Plan Scenario])),
            "Multiple Selections",
        "Single Selection"
    )
```

6. Create a **Plan Amount** measure:

```
Plan Amount = SUM('SubCatPlan'[Plan Amt])
```

7. Create an **Internet Sales Plan Scenario** measure that dynamically calculates a budget/plan amount based on the filter context (slicers, visuals):

```
Internet Sales Plan Scenario =
    VAR FilterContext = [Sales Plan Scenario Filter Branch]
RETURN
    SWITCH(TRUE(),
        FilterContext = "Single Selection",
            MIN('Plan Scenarios'[Var to Plan]) * [Plan Amount],
        FilterContext = "No Selection",
            [Plan Amount],
        FilterContext = "Multiple Selections",BLANK()
    )
```

8. Apply a currency format to the **Plan Amount** and **Internet Sales Plan Scenario** measures.

9. Create visualizations to display the different plan scenarios; an example is shown in *Figure 7.7*:

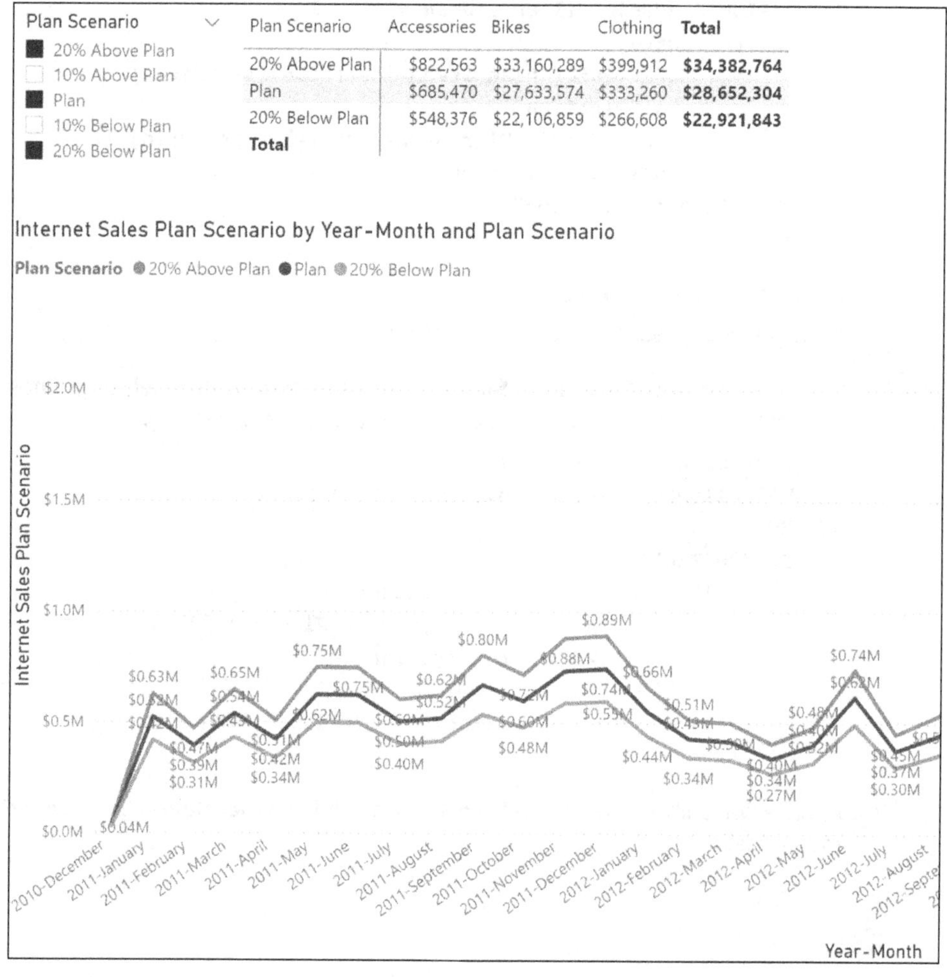

Plan Scenario	Accessories	Bikes	Clothing	**Total**
20% Above Plan	$822,563	$33,160,289	$399,912	**$34,382,764**
Plan	$685,470	$27,633,574	$333,260	**$28,652,304**
20% Below Plan	$548,376	$22,106,859	$266,608	**$22,921,843**
Total				

Figure 7.7: Visualizations of plan scenarios

How it works...

When using the DAX `DATATABLE` function in the `Plan Scenarios` table, the column names and types are declared, and each row is enclosed in curly braces—`List` values in M queries. Ideally, the new scenario table can be persisted within a data warehouse and the Power BI solution can be resilient to changes in scenario names and values.

As per other recipes, using DAX to create tables or columns should generally be thought of as a secondary and temporary option, such as in proof-of-concept scenarios, or in narrow, static use cases, such as a Power BI model owned and maintained by a business team.

The intermediate measure, `Sales Plan Scenario Filter Branch`, simplifies the parameter selection measure by computing one of the three possible filter contexts: `No Selection`, `Single Selection`, or `Multiple Selections`. This measure can be hidden from the report view's `Fields` list.

The scenario measure, `Internet Sales Plan Scenario`, passes the intermediate measure into the `FilterContext` variable and leverages the existing `Plan Amount` measure. If a single scenario selection has been made, such as on a slicer visual, then only a single value will be active in the `Plan Scenarios` table, and this will be retrieved via the `MIN` function. Generally, defaulting to a standard or base value if no selections have been made, and returning a blank if multiple selections are made, is appropriate for minimizing complexity and user confusion.

A standard slicer is the most straightforward method of exposing the parameter values in reports, and the descending order of scenario values (based on the `Sort By` column) makes the slicer intuitive for users. As per the matrix visual, the `Plan Scenario` column can also be used within report visuals. Additionally, any dimension table with a relationship to the plan/budget fact table, such as a `Products` table, can be used in report visualizations with the new scenario measure as well. The slicer can be used to control chosen plan scenarios, or visual-level filters can be applied to only display one or a few of the five scenario values.

Disconnected parameter tables are one of the more powerful and easily implemented patterns in Power BI, with many published examples available, such as enabling the user to filter reports for their own TOP criteria (in other words, Top 5, 10, 15, 20) through slicers. A more dynamic and analytical approach involves computing parameter values via M queries with each refresh, such as the standard deviation, median, and average of prices, and then using these query results in DAX measures.

There's more...

Parameter tables can also be used to dynamically filter Power Query queries when using DirectQuery sources. This means that users can dynamically filter the information coming back from a DirectQuery query using report slicers. This functionality may still be in preview at the time this book is published, but more information regarding this functionality is provided in the *See also* section of this recipe.

See also

- Dynamic M query parameters in Power BI Desktop (preview): `https://bit.ly/2QYrvhq`

Forecasting with what-if analysis

Power BI can be used to directly support the creation of forecasts, budgets, and other planned values of future business measures and events. The relationships and logic of these datasets, which are commonly implemented in Excel formulas and maintained by business teams, can be efficiently replicated within a dedicated Power BI Desktop file. Isolating the what-if input variables from the forecast creation, storage, and visualization in Power BI enables users to more easily create, analyze, and collaborate on business forecasts.

In this recipe, a Power Desktop model is used to ingest forecast-variable inputs from Excel, and process these variables with a dynamic transformation process to generate a forecast table available for visualization. This design enables business teams to rapidly iterate on forecasts, and ultimately supports an official or approved forecast or plan that could be integrated with other data models.

Getting ready

To prepare for this recipe, follow these steps:

1. Download `Forecast.xlsx` from the following GitHub repository: `https://github.com/PacktPublishing/Microsoft-Power-BI-Cookbook-Second-Edition`.
2. Open a **Power BI Desktop** file locally and access **Power Query Editor** by clicking on **Transform Data** in the ribbon of the **Home** tab.
3. Create a query named `AdWorksDW`, similar to the following:

```
let
    Source = Sql.Database("localhost\MSSQLSERVERDEV",
"AdventureWorksDW2019")
in
    Source
```

4. Disable the load on the `AdWorksDW` query and place it in a `Data Sources` query group.
5. Right-click the `AdWorksDW` query and choose **Reference**.
6. Rename the query `Internet Sales`, choose the `FactInternetSales` table, and change the `OrderDate` column to be of the `Date` data type:

```
let
    Source = AdWorksDW,
    dbo_FactInternetSales = Source{[Schema="dbo",Item="FactInternetSal
es"]}[Data],
    DateType = Table.TransformColumnTypes(
        dbo_FactInternetSales,{{"OrderDate", type date}})
```

```
in
    DateType
```

7. Repeat *steps 5* and *6*, creating a `Sales Territories` query that points to the `DimSalesTerritory` table, and a `Dates` query that points to the `DimDates` table.
8. Add `YearMonth` and `YearMonthSort` columns to the `Dates` table:

```
let
    Source = AdWorksDW,
    dbo_DimDate = Source{[Schema="dbo",Item="DimDate"]}[Data],
    YearMonth = Table.AddColumn(
        dbo_DimDate, "YearMonth",
        each Text.From([CalendarYear]) & "-" & Text.
Start([EnglishMonthName],3)
    ),
    YearMonthSort = Table.AddColumn(
        YearMonth, "YearMonthSort", each [CalendarYear]*100+[MonthNumber
OfYear])
in
    YearMonthSort
```

9. Select **Close & Apply** from the ribbon of the **Home** tab.
10. Switch to the **Model** view and create a relationship between the `SalesTerritoryKey` columns in the `Internet Sales` and `Sales Territories` tables.
11. Create a relationship between the `DateKey` column in the `Dates` table and the `OrderDateKey` column in the `Internet Sales` table.
12. Set `Sort by column` for the `YearMonth` column in the `Dates` table to the `YearMonthSort` column.

How to forecast with what-if analysis

To implement this recipe, perform the following steps:

1. In **Report** View, choose **Transform data** from the ribbon of the **Home** tab.
2. Create a query in the `Data Sources` query group called **ForecastFile** that points to the `Forecast.xlsx` file and disable the load:

```
let
    Source = Excel.Workbook(File.Contents("C:\Forecast.xlsx"), null,
true)
in
    Source
```

3. Right-click the **ForecastFile** query and choose **Reference**.

4. Rename the query `ForecastYear` and use the following code:

```
() =>
    let
        Source = ForecastFile,
        FY = Source{[Item="ForecastYear",Kind="DefinedName"]}[Data],
        Rename = Table.RenameColumns(FY,{{"Column2", "ForecastYear"}}),
        SelectColumn = Table.SelectColumns(Rename,{"ForecastYear"}),
        Record = Table.Max(SelectColumn,{"ForecastYear"}),
        Year = Record.Field(Record,"ForecastYear")
    in
        Year
```

5. Move the `ForecastYear` function to a query group called `Forecast`.
6. In the `Forecast` query group, create a query called `ForecastTotalGrowth` and disable the load:

```
let
    Source = ForecastFile,
    Forecast = Source{
        [Item="TotalSalesGrowthBaseForecast",Kind="DefinedName"]}[Data],
    Promote = Table.PromoteHeaders(Forecast, [PromoteAllScalars=true]),
    Unpivot = Table.UnpivotOtherColumns(
        Promote, {"Value"}, "Attribute", "Value.1"),
    RemoveColumn = Table.RemoveColumns(Unpivot,{"Value"}),
    Rename = Table.RenameColumns(
        RemoveColumn,{{"Attribute", "Month"}, {"Value.1", "Sales 
Growth"}}),
    ChangeToPercent = Table.TransformColumnTypes(
        Rename,{{"Sales Growth", Percentage.Type}})
in
    ChangeToPercent
```

7. In the `Forecast` query group, create a query called `ForecastAllocation` and disable the load:

```
let
    Source = ForecastFile,
    Allocation = Source{[Item="SalesGroupAllocation",Kind="DefinedNa
me"]}[Data],
    Promote = Table.PromoteHeaders(Allocation, [PromoteAllScalars=true]),
    Unpivot = Table.UnpivotOtherColumns(
        Promote, {"Group"}, "Attribute", "Value"),
    Rename = Table.RenameColumns(Unpivot,
        {
            {"Group", "Sales Territory"}, {"Attribute", "Month"},
            {"Value", "Allocation"}
```

```
        }),
    ChangeToPercent = Table.TransformColumnTypes(
        Rename,{{"Allocation", Percentage.Type}})
in
    ChangeToPercent
```

8. In the `Forecast` query group, create a function called `CurrentDate`:

```
() as date =>
    let
        Current = Date.FromText("6/28/2013")
    in
        Current
```

9. In the `Forecast` query group, create a query called `PriorYearMonthlySales` and disable the load:

```
let
    CurrentYear = Date.Year(CurrentDate()),
    CurrentMonth = Date.Month(CurrentDate()),
    WorkingMonth =
        if Date.DaysInMonth = Date.Day(CurrentDate())
            then CurrentMonth - 1 else CurrentMonth,
    PYJoin = Table.Join(
        #"Internet Sales","OrderDate",
        Dates,"FullDateAlternateKey",JoinKind.Inner),
    PYFilter = Table.SelectRows(PYJoin, each [CalendarYear] =
CurrentYear-1 and
        [MonthNumberOfYear] >= WorkingMonth),
    PYGroup = Table.Group(
        PYFilter,{"CalendarYear", "MonthNumberOfYear",
"EnglishMonthName"},
        {"Sales", each List.Sum([SalesAmount]), Currency.Type}),
    RemoveColumns = Table.RemoveColumns(PYGroup,{"MonthNumberOfYear"}),
    Month = Table.TransformColumns(
        RemoveColumns,
        {{"EnglishMonthName", each Text.Start(_, 3), type text}}),
    Rename = Table.RenameColumns(Month,{{"EnglishMonthName", "Month"}})
in
    Rename
```

10. In the `Forecast` query group, create a query called `CurrentYearMonthlySales` and disable the load:

```
let
    CurrentYear = Date.Year(CurrentDate()),
    CurrentMonth = Date.Month(CurrentDate()),
    WorkingMonth =
```

```
        if Date.DaysInMonth = Date.Day(CurrentDate())
            then CurrentMonth else CurrentMonth - 1,
    PYJoin = Table.Join(
        #"Internet Sales","OrderDate",
        Dates,"FullDateAlternateKey",JoinKind.Inner),
    PYFilter = Table.SelectRows(PYJoin, each [CalendarYear] =
CurrentYear and
        [MonthNumberOfYear] <= WorkingMonth),
    PYGroup = Table.Group(
        PYFilter,{"CalendarYear", "MonthNumberOfYear",
"EnglishMonthName"},
        {"Sales", each List.Sum([SalesAmount]), Currency.Type}),
    RemoveColumns = Table.RemoveColumns(PYGroup,{"MonthNumberOfYear"}),
    Month = Table.TransformColumns(
        RemoveColumns,
        {{"EnglishMonthName", each Text.Start(_, 3), type text}}),
    Rename = Table.RenameColumns(Month,{{"EnglishMonthName", "Month"}})
in
    Rename
```

11. In the Forecast query group, create a query called SalesForecastBase and disable the load:

```
let
    History = Table.Combine({CurrentYearMonthlySales,PriorYearMonthlySal
es}),
    JoinForecast = Table.NestedJoin(
        History, "Month", ForecastTotalGrowth,"Month",
        "Fcst Column", JoinKind.Inner),
    ForecastColumns = Table.ExpandTableColumn(
        JoinForecast, "Fcst Column", {"Sales Growth"}, {"Sales
Growth"}),
    MonthlyForecast = Table.AddColumn(
        ForecastColumns,
        "Forecast Sales", each ([Sales Growth]+1) * [Sales], Currency.
Type),
    AddForecastYear = Table.AddColumn(
        MonthlyForecast,"Forecast Year",each ForecastYear()),
    RemoveColumns = Table.RemoveColumns(
        AddForecastYear,{"CalendarYear", "Sales", "Sales Growth"})
in
    RemoveColumns
```

12. In the `Forecast` query group, create a query called `Sales Forecast`:

```
let
    Source = Table.NestedJoin(
        ForecastAllocation, "Month",
        SalesForecastBase, "Month", "AllocationTable", JoinKind.
LeftOuter),
    ExpandAllocation = Table.ExpandTableColumn(
        Source, "AllocationTable", {"Forecast Sales", "Forecast Year"},
        {"Forecast Sales Total", "Forecast Year"}),
    AddAllocationForecast = Table.AddColumn(
        ExpandAllocation, "Forecast Sales",
        each [Allocation] * [Forecast Sales Total], Currency.Type),
    RemoveColumns = Table.RemoveColumns(
        AddAllocationForecast,{"Allocation", "Forecast Sales Total"}),
    YearMonth = Table.CombineColumns(
        Table.TransformColumnTypes(RemoveColumns,
        {{"Forecast Year", type text}}, "en-US"),
        {"Forecast Year", "Month"},
        Combiner.CombineTextByDelimiter("-", QuoteStyle.
None),"YearMonth")
in
    YearMonth
```

13. In the `Other Queries` query group, create a query called `ForecastDateBridge`:

```
let
    Dates = Table.Distinct(
        Table.SelectColumns(
            Table.SelectRows(Dates,
                each [FullDateAlternateKey] <= CurrentDate()),
            {"YearMonth"})),
    Forecast = Table.Distinct(
        Table.SelectColumns(#"Sales Forecast", {"YearMonth"})),
    YearMonths = Table.Combine({Dates, Forecast})
in
    YearMonths
```

14. In the `Other Queries` query group, create a query called `ForecastTerritoryBridge`:

```
let
    Territories = Table.Distinct(
        Table.SelectColumns(#"Sales Territories","SalesTerritoryGroup"))
in
    Territories
```

15. Click **Close & Apply** from the ribbon of the **Home** tab and save your work.
16. Create a relationship between the `YearMonth` columns of the `Dates` table and the `ForecastDateBridge` table, and set **Cross filter direction** to **Both**.
17. Create a relationship between the `YearMonth` columns of the `ForecastDateBridge` table and the `Sales Forecast` table.
18. Hide the `ForecastDateBridge` table from the **Report** view.
19. Create a relationship between the `SalesTerritoryGroup` columns of the `Sales Territory` table and the `ForecastTerritoryBridge` table, and set **Cross filter direction** to **Both**.
20. Create a relationship between the `SalesTerritoryGroup` column in the `ForecastTerritoryBridge` table and the `Sales Territory` column in the `Sales Forecast` table.
21. Hide the `ForecastTerritoryBridge` table from the **Report** view. The final data model is displayed in *Figure 7.8*:

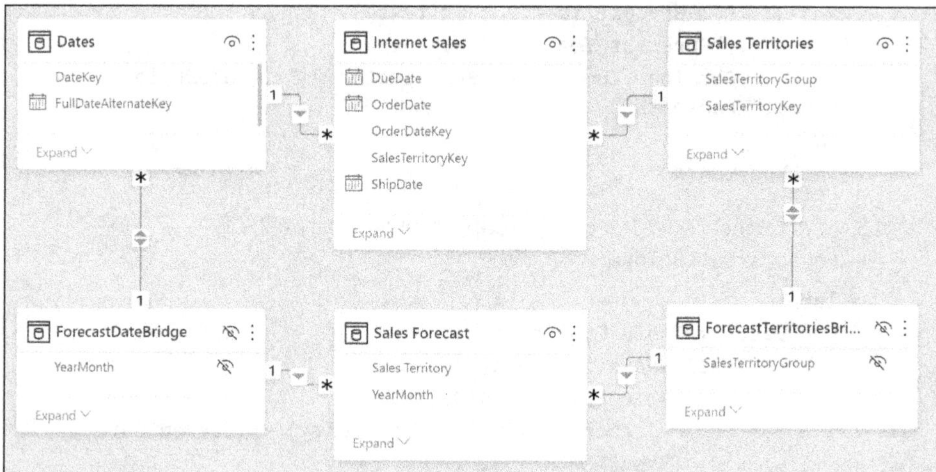

Figure 7.8: Final model for forecasting

22. Create a `Today` measure:

```
Today = DATE(2013,6,28)
```

23. Create a `Total Sales Amount` measure:

```
Total Sales Amount =
    SWITCH(TRUE(),
        ISBLANK(COUNTROWS('Sales Forecast')),
```

```
            IF(
                MAX('Dates'[FullDateAlternateKey])<[Today],
                SUM('Internet Sales'[SalesAmount]),
                BLANK()
            ),
        SUM('Sales Forecast'[Forecast Sales])
    )
```

24. Create a Line chart visualization using the `YearMonth` column from the `Dates` table as `Axis`, and the `Total Sales Amount` measure as `Values`.
25. Add a Slicer visualization using the `SalesTerritoryGroup` column from the `Sales Territories` table, as shown in *Figure 7.9*:

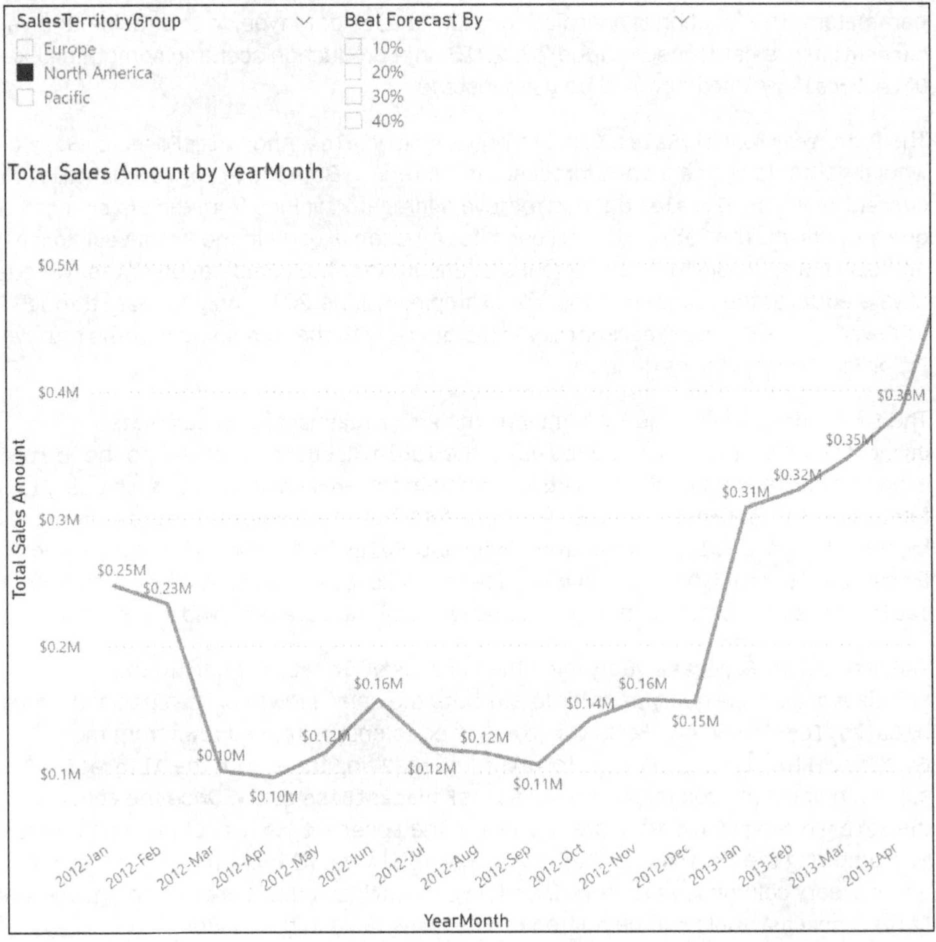

Figure 7.9: Historical and forecasted sales

How it works...

The `ForecastYear`, `ForecastTotalGrowth`, and `ForecastAllocation` queries use the named ranges in the `Forecast.xlsx` file to import the required forecast information. The `ForecastYear` query is a function with no input parameters that returns the single numeric value for the forecast year. The `ForecastTotalGrowth` and `ForecastAllocation` queries use the `Table.UnpivotOtherColumns` function to unpivot the month columns in the data to return 12 rows and 36 rows, respectively. In the `ForecastTotalGrowth` query, each row represents a month in the forecast year and the forecasted growth percentage year-on-year. In the `ForecastAllocation` query, each row represents the expected allocation of the forecasted growth by `Sales Territory` and `Month`.

The `CurrentDate` query specifies a date for the current date by using a function with no input parameters. The function is specified to return a `Date` data type. In this recipe, the value for `CurrentDate` is hardcoded to June 28, 2013. In a production scenario something like the `Date.LocalNow` function would be used instead.

The `PriorYearMonthlySales`, `CurrentYearMonthlySales`, and `SalesForecastBase` queries work together to create a base forecast for the report. Both the `PriorYearMonthlySales` and `CurrentYearMonthlySales` queries retrieve aggregated values from the `Internet Sales` query by `Month`. The `Table.SelectRows` filter function is used in the `PriorYearMonthlySales` and `CurrentYearMonthlySales` queries to ensure that the combination of the two queries is always equal to the full 12 months. For example, in June 2013, only January through May are retrieved by the `CurrentYearMonthlySales` query, with the remaining months retrieved by the `PriorYearMonthlySales` query.

The `SalesForecastBase` query combines the `PriorYearMonthlySales` and `CurrentYearMonthlySales` queries using the `Table.Combine` function into the `History` expression. The combined table is then joined to the `ForecastTotalGrowth` query to add the forecasted `Sales Growth` column. The base forecast, the `Forecast Sales` column, is created by multiplying the `Sales` column from `Internet Sales` by 1 + the `Sales Growth` percentage. Finally, the `Forecast Year` column is added by calling the `ForecastYear` function from a `Table.AddColumn` expression and unnecessary columns are removed.

The final `Sales Forecast` query joins the `ForecastAllocation` query to the `SalesForecastBase` query in order to attribute the sales growth of the specified allocation by `Sales Territory`. A `Left.Outer` join is used to ensure that all rows from the `ForecastAllocation` query are present in the resulting table, with the `AllocationTable` column holding the columns from the `SalesForecastBase` query. Once the columns from the `SalesForecastBase` table are expanded, the `Forecast Sales` column can be created by multiplying the `Forecast Sales Total` column by the `Allocation` column. Finally, unnecessary columns are removed, and a `YearMonth` column is created to ensure that the `Sales Forecast` table can be related to the `Dates` table in the model.

The `ForecastDateBridge` and `ForecastTerritoriesBridge` tables each contain unique values for `YearMonth` and `SalesTerritoryGroup`, respectively. These tables are used in the model to bridge the different granularities between the `Dates` table, the `Sales Territories` table, and the `Sales Forecast` table.

The `Total Sales Amount` measure determines whether the measure is executing in a current or future `YearMonth`, and calculates the value by either summing the `SalesAmount` column from the `Internet Sales` table for current `YearMonth` values, or by summing the `Forecast Sales` column from the `Sales Forecast` table for future `YearMonth` values.

There's more...

The forecasting can be modified to include a what-if parameter that can be chosen by the user to visualize beating the forecast by specified percentages. To demonstrate how this works, perform the following steps:

1. In the **Report** view, choose **New parameter** from the ribbon of the **Modeling** tab.
2. Name the parameter `Beat Forecast By`, choose `Decimal number` for the data type, set **Minimum** to `0.1`, **Maximum** to `0.4`, and **Increment** to `0.1`:

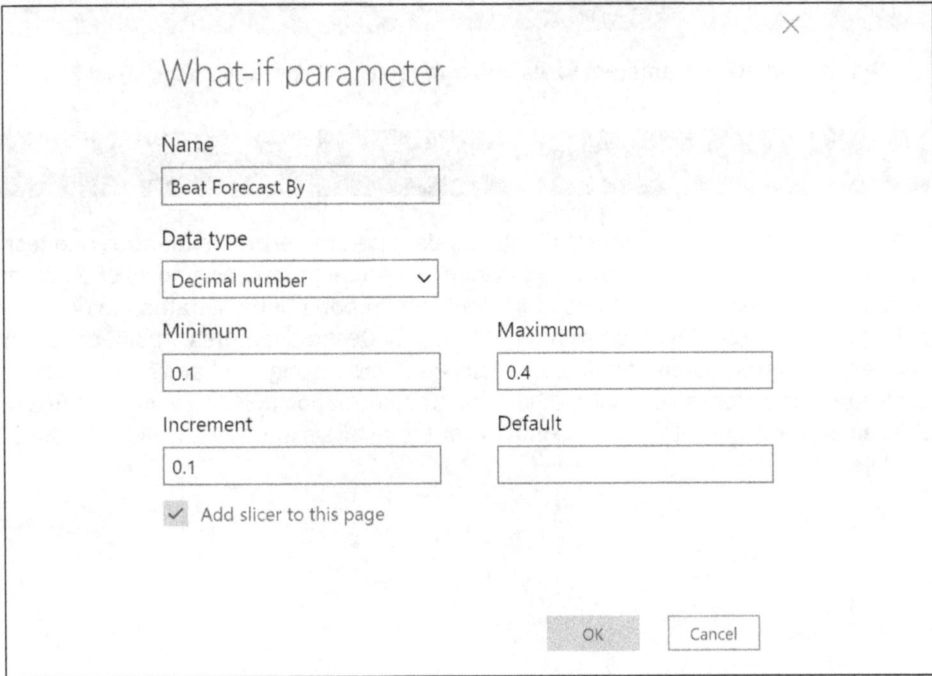

Figure 7.10: What-if parameter

3. Modify the `Total Sales Amount` measure as follows:

```
Total Sales Amount =
    VAR __BeatForecastValue = [Beat Forecast By Value]
    VAR __ForecastIncrease =
        IF(ISBLANK(__BeatForecastValue),1,1+__BeatForecastValue)
RETURN
    SWITCH(TRUE(),
        ISBLANK(COUNTROWS('Sales Forecast')),
            IF(
                MAX('Dates'[FullDateAlternateKey])<[Today],
                SUM('Internet Sales'[SalesAmount]),
                BLANK()
            ),
        SUM('Sales Forecast'[Forecast Sales]) * __ForecastIncrease
    )
```

Users can now use the `Beat Forecast By` slicer to control what-if scenarios, regarding exceeding the sales forecast by the specified percentages.

See also

- Use what-if parameters to visualize variables: `https://bit.ly/2QsmNZu`

Conclusion

The recipes in this chapter covered both standard parameterization features and techniques in Power BI as well as more advanced custom implementations. Examples of parameterizing data sources, queries, user-defined functions, and reports demonstrated the power of the M language and its integration with other Power BI Desktop features. Additional examples, such as URL-based parameter filters, a dedicated forecasting or what-if? tool, and user selection parameter tables, utilized both the transformation and analytical features of Power BI to empower users with greater control over the analysis and visualization of Power BI data models.

8

Implementing Dynamic User-Based Visibility in Power BI

Data security, wherein users or groups of users are prevented from viewing a portion of a dataset, is often a top requirement in Power BI deployments. Security implementations can range in complexity from mapping a few security groups to their associated row-level security roles based on a single dimension value such as department or region to dynamic, user-based security involving dedicated user permissions tables and dynamic DAX functions. Given the variety of use cases and the importance of this feature to securely share a dataset across stakeholders, it is important to understand the process and techniques available for developing, testing, and operationalizing data security roles.

In addition to **row-level security** (**RLS**) roles, dynamic, user-based filter context techniques can also be used to simplify and personalize the user experience. For example, the filter conditions built into reports, as well as the interactive filter selections from end users, can be dynamically updated and displayed in intuitive visuals to aid comprehension. In more advanced scenarios, DAX measures themselves can be filtered based on information about the user interacting with the content to deliver a personalized experience. This chapter contains detailed examples of building and deploying dynamic, user-based security for both Import and DirectQuery datasets, as well as examples of dynamic filter context functionality to enhance the user experience.

In this chapter, we will cover the following recipes:

- Capturing Current User Context
- Defining RLS Roles and Filter Expressions
- Designing Dynamic Security Models

- Building Dynamic Security for DirectQuery
- Displaying the Current Filter Context
- Avoiding Manual User Clicks

Technical Requirements

The following are required to complete the recipes in this chapter:

- Power BI Desktop.
- SQL Server with the `AdventureWorksDW2019` database installed. This database and the instructions for installing it are available here: `http://bit.ly/2OVQfG7`.
- Files for this chapter and can be downloaded from the following GitHub repository: `https://github.com/PacktPublishing/Microsoft-Power-BI-Cookbook-Second-Edition`.

Capturing Current User Context

The foundation of dynamic user security and visibility in Power BI is the ability to extract the **user principal name** (**UPN**) or login credential of the business user connected to content in the Power BI service. The `USERPRINCIPALNAME` DAX function retrieves this text value and thus enables filter expressions to be applied to the tables of a model in security roles. In addition to RLS roles, which override and impact all DAX measures of a dataset, the UPN or "current user" text value can be used by DAX measures to retrieve the UPN prefix and suffix, or filter other measures.

In this recipe, DAX measures are added to a data model to dynamically retrieve the UPN as well as the UPN's prefix and suffix. Additional detail on authentication in Power BI and the `USERNAME` function, an alternative dynamic DAX function that also retrieves the UPN in the Power BI service, is also covered.

Getting ready

To prepare for this recipe, follow these steps:

1. Open a new file in Power BI Desktop and sign in
2. Click **Transform data** from the ribbon of the **Home** tab
3. In the Power Query Editor, create a new **Blank** query called **Dynamic User Measures**
4. Click **Close & Apply** from the ribbon of the **Home** tab
5. Switch to **Data** view and hide the **Dynamic User Measures** column in the **Dynamic User Measures** table

How to Capture User Context

To implement this recipe, use the following steps:

1. In the **Data** view, create three DAX measures in the **Dynamic User Measures** table:

```
User Principal Name = USERPRINCIPALNAME()

UPN Prefix = LEFT([User Principal Name], SEARCH("@",[User Principal
Name]) - 1)

UPN Suffix =
    RIGHT(
        [User Principal Name],
        LEN([User Principal Name]) - LEN([UPN Prefix]) - 1)
```

2. Create a **Table** visualization and add the three measures to the table as **Values**

User Principal Name	UPN Prefix	UPN Suffix
BrettP@FrontlineAnalytics.onmicrosoft.com	BrettP	FrontlineAnalytics.onmicrosoft.com

Figure 8.1: UPN measures

3. Publish the report to the Power BI service
4. Add a separate user to the workspace or share the report with another user
5. Request this user to log in to the workspace to view the report or log on with the alternate user's credentials

User Principal Name	UPN Prefix	UPN Suffix
JenLawrence@FrontlineAnalytics.onmicrosoft.com	JenLawrence	FrontlineAnalytics.onmicrosoft.com

Figure 8.2: The function returns the UPN of the different logged-in user

How it works ...

It is not technically necessary to create these measures in a data model in order to implement dynamic security or visibility, but this approach simplifies development since measure expressions can be reused and hidden from users.

Power BI uses **Azure Active Directory** (**AAD**) to authenticate users who log in to the Power BI service, and the Power BI login credentials (such as `BrettP@FrontlineAnalytics.onmicrosoft.com`) are used as the effective username whenever a user attempts to access resources that require authentication. The `USERPRINCIPALNAME` DAX function returns the email address used to log in to Power BI. For organizations that use work email addresses for Power BI logins, this effective username maps to a UPN in the local active directory.

In Power BI service-to-on-premises scenarios, such as with SSAS cubes on-premises, the effective username (login credentials) from the Power BI service is mapped to a UPN in the local active directory and resolved to the associated Windows domain account.

If security roles have not been configured on the dataset, the member of the workspace, (JenLawrence for example) will see her UPN via either read or edit rights in the workspace. If security roles have been configured for the dataset, the member will either require edit rights in the workspace or can be added to one of the security roles defined for the dataset, and granted read access to the workspace. Security roles are applied to read-only members of app workspaces. Alternatively, the app workspace admin or workspace members with edit rights can test the security of users who are mapped to a security role but are not members of the workspace.

There's more ...

The `USERNAME` DAX function returns the user's domain login in the format `domain\user` locally, but returns the user principal name (the user's login credential) in the Power BI service. Therefore, security role filter expressions, user permissions tables, and any other dynamic user functionality added to Power BI datasets should align with the UPN email address format provided by `USERPRINCIPALNAME`.

In locally shared data models, DAX text functions can be used to extract the domain and username from `USERNAME`, like with `USERPRINCIPALNAME` in this recipe's example:

```
User Name = USERNAME()

User Name Domain = LEFT([User Name], SEARCH("\", [User Name]) - 1)

User Name Login =
    RIGHT([User Name], LEN([User Name]) - LEN([User Name Domain]) - 1)
```

User Name	User Name Domain	User Name Login
ATLAS\Brett Powell	ATLAS	Brett Powell

Figure 8.3: The USERNAME function used locally and outside of the Power BI service

The `USERNAME` function is commonly used in dynamic security implementations with SSAS tabular models. `USERPRINCIPALNAME` was introduced to simplify user identity, as it returns the UPN (email address format) locally and in the Power BI service. A rare exception to this is when a PC is not joined to a domain. In this unlikely scenario, `USERPRINCIPALNAME` returns the domain and username in (`domain\user`) format, just like `USERNAME`.

There is also a `USEROBJECTID` DAX function that returns the current user's object ID from AAD when used in the context of the Power BI service or Azure Analysis Services. When used with SQL Server Analysis Services on-premises, the user's **Security Identifier** (**SID**) is returned.

See also

- Power BI security documentation and whitepaper: `http://bit.ly/22NHzRS`
- DAX `USERPRINCIPALNAME` function: `https://bit.ly/3dMDhVc`
- DAX `USERNAME` function: `https://bit.ly/2RRFuWT`
- DAX `USEROBJECTID` function: `https://bit.ly/3aCEXPo`

Defining RLS Roles and Filter Expressions

Data security should always be top of mind and BI teams and developers should strive to ensure that users are never granted greater access or permission than is necessary to perform a legitimate business function.

In the context of Power BI projects, the question "Who should be able to see what?" should be well defined and documented before any reports are published or read access to the dataset is granted. Additionally, there should be a well-defined process for creating and managing the security groups used in security implementations.

The data security of Power BI models comprises security roles defined within the model, with each role containing a unique set of one or more DAX filter expressions. Roles and their associated filter expressions are created in Power BI Desktop, and users or groups are mapped to security roles in the Power BI service. A single DAX filter expression can be applied to each table of a model within a given security role, with users having the option of being mapped to multiple security roles. The filter expressions applied to tables within a security role also filter other tables in the model via relationships defined in the model, like the filters applied to Power BI reports, and are applied to all queries submitted by the security role member.

This recipe contains an end-to-end example of configuring, deploying, and validating RLS roles, applicable to both Import and DirectQuery data models. Additional guidance on a consolidated security role table that improves the manageability of changing security requirements is also included.

Getting ready

To prepare for this recipe, follow these steps:

1. Open a Power BI Desktop file locally and access the **Power Query Editor** by clicking on **Transform Data** in the ribbon of the **Home** tab
2. Create a query named **AdWorksDW** similar to the following:

```
let
    Source = Sql.Database("localhost\MSSQLSERVERDEV",
"AdventureWorksDW2019")
in
    Source
```

3. Disable load on the **AdWorksDW** query and place it into a **Data Sources** query group
4. Right-click the **AdWorksDW** query and choose **Reference**
5. Rename the query **Internet Sales** and choose the **FactInternetSales** table
6. Repeat steps *4* and *5*, creating a **Resellers** query that points to the **DimResellers** table, a **Reseller Sales** query that points to the **FactResellerSales** query, a **Sales Territories** query that points to the **DimSalesTerritory** table, and a **Dates** query that points to the **DimDate** table
7. Create a **Customers** query using the following code:

```
let
    Source = AdWorksDW,
    dbo_DimCustomer = Source{[Schema="dbo",Item="DimCustomer"]}[Data],
    DimGeography = Table.ExpandRecordColumn(
        dbo_DimCustomer, "DimGeography",
        {"DimSalesTerritory"}, {"DimSalesTerritory"}),
    SalesTerritory = Table.ExpandRecordColumn(
        DimGeography, "DimSalesTerritory",
        {"SalesTerritoryGroup"}, {"SalesTerritoryGroup"})
in
    SalesTerritory
```

8. Create a **Products** query using the following code:

```
let
    Source = AdWorksDW,
    Navigation = Source{[Schema="dbo",Item="DimProduct"]}[Data],
    Subcategory =
        Table.ExpandRecordColumn(
            Navigation, "DimProductSubcategory",
```

```
                {"EnglishProductSubcategoryName", "DimProductCategory"},
                {"Product Subcategory", "DimProductCategory"}
            ),
        Category =
            Table.ExpandRecordColumn(
                Subcategory, "DimProductCategory",
                {"EnglishProductCategoryName"}, {"Product Category"}
            )
    in
       Category
```

9. Move the **Internet Sales** and **Reseller Sales** queries to a **Facts** query group and the **Sales Territories**, **Dates**, **Customers**, **Resellers**, and **Products** queries to a **Dimensions** query group
10. In the **Other Queries** group, create a **Blank** query called **Calculations**
11. Select **Close & Apply** from the ribbon of the **Home** tab
12. Switch to the **Model** view and create a relationship between the **SalesTerritoryKey** columns in the **Internet Sales** and **Sales Territories** tables
13. Create a relationship between the **SalesTerritoryKey** columns in the **Reseller Sales** and **Sales Territories** tables
14. Create a relationship between the **ProductKey** columns in the **Reseller Sales** and **Products** tables
15. Create a relationship between the **ProductKey** columns in the **Internet Sales** and **Products** tables
16. Create a relationship between the **DateKey** column in the **Dates** table and the **OrderDateKey** column in the **Internet Sales** table
17. Create a relationship between the **DateKey** column in the **Dates** table and the **OrderDateKey** column in the **Reseller Sales** table
18. Create a relationship between the **CustomerKey** columns in the **Internet Sales** and **Customers** tables
19. Create a relationship between the **ResellerKey** columns in the **Reseller Sales** and **Resellers** tables
20. Save your work

Define and document the security role requirements to be implemented, and the members or groups of these roles. Use the bus matrix diagrams (*Figure 3.1* and *Figure 3.2*) described in *Chapter 3, Building a Power BI Data Model*, to help communicate what data is currently stored in the model. Validate that role security is indeed required (not report or model filters), given the risk or sensitivity of the data.

Do not confuse security role filters with the various other forms of filters in Power BI, such as report-, page-, and visual-level filters, as well as filter logic in DAX measures. RLS role filters are applied to all queries of security role members, effectively producing a virtual subset of the data model for the given role at query time. Given the performance implications of compounding security role filters with report query filters, all user experience and analytical filters should be implemented outside of the security role filters. Security filters should be exclusively used for securing sensitive data.

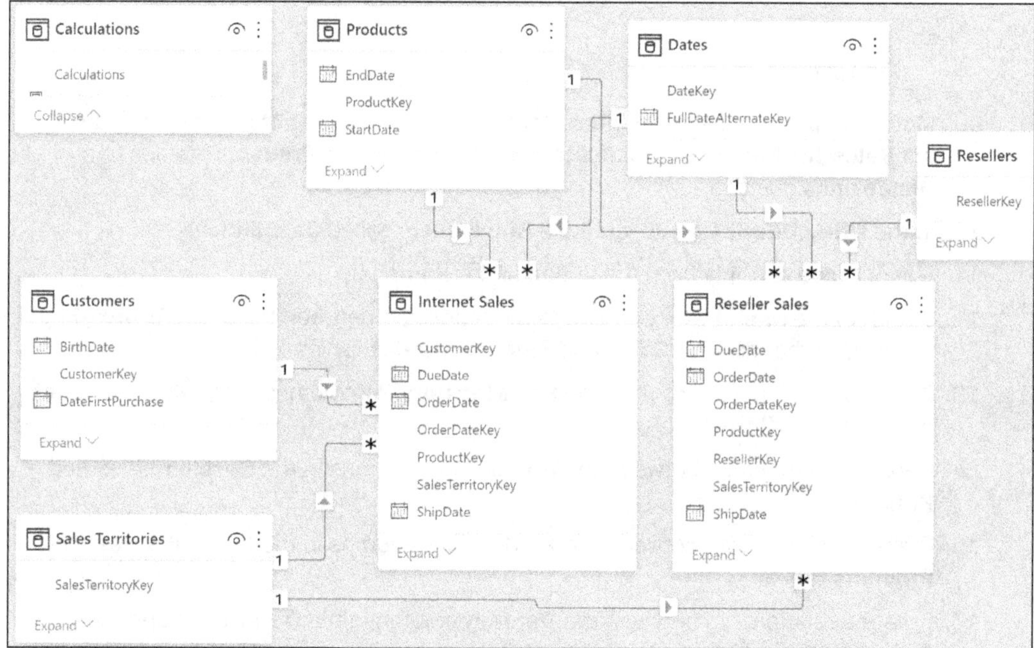

Figure 8.4: Model for RLS roles and filter expressions

How to Define RLS Roles and Filter Expressions

To implement this recipe, use the following steps:

1. In the **Report** view, create the following measures in the **Calculations** table:

```
Customers Row Count = COUNTROWS('Customers')

Internet Sales Row Count = COUNTROWS('Internet Sales')

Products Row Count = COUNTROWS('Products')

Reseller Sales Row Count = COUNTROWS('Reseller Sales')
```

```
Resellers Row Count = COUNTROWS('Resellers')

Sales Territories Row Count = COUNTROWS('Sales Territories')
Dates Row Count = COUNTROWS('Dates')
```

2. Create a simple Table visualization using the measures created in the previous step. An example is shown in *Figure 8.5*.

Customers Row Count	Internet Sales Row Count	Products Row Count	Reseller Sales Row Count	Resellers Row Count	Sales Territories Row Count	Dates Row Count
18,484	60,398	606	60,855	701	11	3652

Figure 8.5: Row count measures in a table visual of the Power BI data model

3. Hide the **Calculations** column in the **Calculations** table.
4. Click **Manage roles** in the ribbon of the **Modeling** tab.
5. Click the **Create** button and name the new role **United States Online Bike Sales**.
6. Create the following four table filter DAX expressions on the **Customers**, **Products**, **Resellers**, and **Sales Territories** tables, respectively:

```
[SalesTerritoryGroup] = "North America"
[Product Category] = "Bikes"
FALSE()
[SalesTerritoryCountry] = "United States"
```

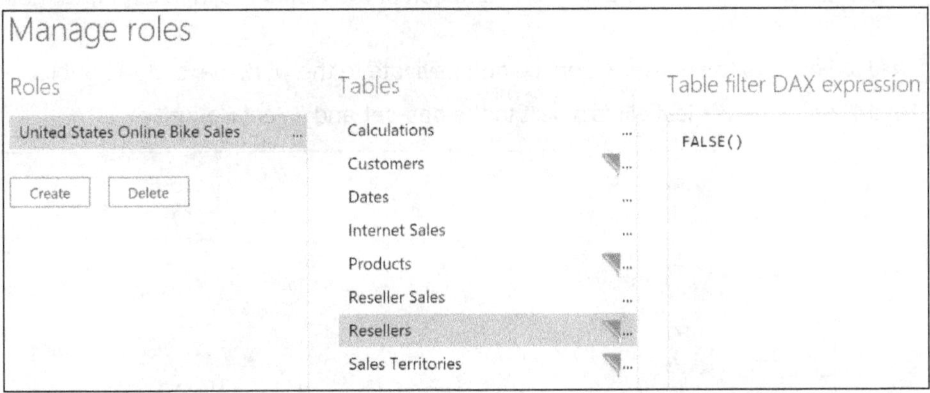

Figure 8.6: Role security definitions for United States Online Bike Sales

7. Click **Create** and name the new role **Europe Reseller Mountain and Touring**.
8. Create the following three table filter DAX expressions on the **Customers**, **Resellers**, and **Sales Territories** tables, respectively:

```
FALSE()
[ProductLine] IN {"Mountain","Touring"}
[SalesTerritoryGroup] = "Europe"
```

9. Click the **Save** button.

10. Click **View as** in the ribbon of the **Modeling** tab, choose the **United States Online Bike Sales** role, click the **OK** button, and note that the row counts in the Table visualization change, with the **Reseller Sales Row Count** and **Reseller Row Count** measures being blank.

Now viewing as: United States Online Bike Sales

Customers Row Count	Internet Sales Row Count	Products Row Count	Reseller Sales Row Count	Resellers Row Count	Sales Territories Row Count	Dates Row Count
9,390	4,907	125			5	3652

Figure 8.7: Viewing the row count measures as a member of the United States Online Bike Sales role

11. Click **View as** in the ribbon of the **Modeling** tab, choose the **Europe Reseller Mountain and Touring** role and uncheck the **United States Online Bike Sales** role, click the **OK** button, and note that the row counts in the Table visualization change with the **Internet Sales Row Count** and **Customers Row Count** measures being blank.

Now viewing as: Europe Reseller Mountain and Touring

Customers Row Count	Internet Sales Row Count	Products Row Count	Reseller Sales Row Count	Resellers Row Count	Sales Territories Row Count	Dates Row Count
		606	5,941	401	3	3652

Figure 8.8: Viewing the row count measures as a member of the Europe Reseller Mountain and Touring role

12. Save the file, click **Publish** in the ribbon of the **Home** tab, and deploy to the Power BI service.
13. Log in to the Power BI service and navigate to the workspace of the published report.
14. Click the vertical ellipsis next to the dataset and select **Security**.

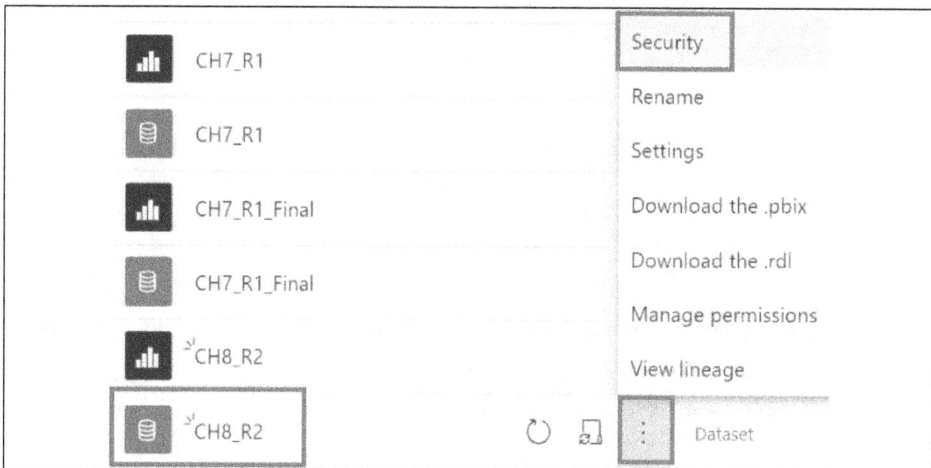

Figure 8.9: Opening the security settings for a published Power BI dataset in an app workspace

15. Members for each role can be added by entering the email addresses of the users and clicking the **Add** button.

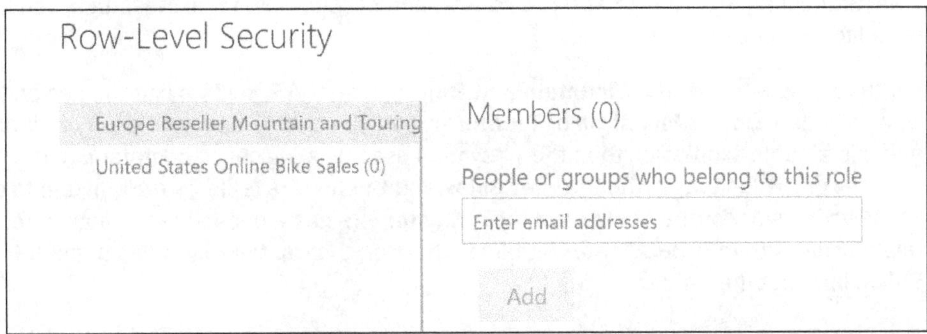

Figure 8.10: Row-Level Security dialog

How it works

The filter expressions in **RLS** roles are always enforced and override any filtering logic in connected reports or DAX measures. BI developers responsible for a model with RLS roles defined should be able to communicate how the RLS logic impacts common reports and measures to report authors and other stakeholders.

Filters applied in security roles traverse relationships just like filters in Power BI reports and filters applied in DAX measures. For example, a security filter on a product dimension table will flow from the **Products** table (the one side of a relationship) to the many side (**Internet Sales**), but will stop there, and neither will they flow to other tables related to **Internet Sales** unless bidirectional relationships have been enabled between **Internet Sales** and these other dimension tables. Note that when viewing by either role or no roles, the **Dates Row Count** measure remains the same, because there is no direct filter applied—nor are any of the DAX filter expressions propagated to the **Dates** table through relationships.

The data model contains both internet sales and reseller sales, but each role should be restricted to their specific business process (fact table). Additionally, the **United States Online Bike Sales** role should be able to view North America customer details (Canada and United States), but only sales for United States customers purchasing products in the bike category. The **Sales Territories** filter ensures that members will only see sales data associated with United States customers. The **Customers** table filter allows the security members the option to view Canada and United States customers. The `FALSE` function is used to filter every row of the **Resellers** table, which also filters the related **Reseller Sales** table.

The two reseller table measures return a blank value, given the `FALSE` security filter. The **Internet Sales** table is filtered by the **Products** filter (Bikes) and the **Sales Territories** filter (United States). The **Internet Sales** table is also filtered by the **Customers** filter, but the **Sales Territories** filter is more restrictive.

Even for experienced Power BI developers and for relatively simple requirements, it can be helpful to apply a single security filter at a time and to observe the impact on row counts. A standard testing report page with row counts, and possibly fact table measures, can help expedite the process.

For the **European Reseller Mountain and Touring** role, the **Resellers** filter makes only rows with a **ProductLine** of **Mountain** or **Touring** visible. The `IN` DAX operator is a more intuitive and sustainable expression than the || symbol used as a logical `OR` operator in older versions of the language. The **Internet Sales** and **Customers** tables are blank due to the `FALSE` expression for the **Customers** table. **Customers** has a one-to-many, single-direction relationship with **Internet Sales**. Therefore, filters on the **Customers** table impact **Internet Sales**, but not other tables.

The **Sales Territories** table has three rows remaining (France, Germany, and United Kingdom) due to the Europe filter. The **Reseller Sales** fact table is impacted by both the **Sales Territories** filter and the **Reseller ProductLine** filter (**Mountain** or **Touring**). The filters from the **Resellers** and **Sales Territories** tables flow to the **Reseller Sales** table, but stop there and do not impact other tables.

In gathering security requirements, and again in a testing or **quality assurance** (**QA**) phase, communicate which tables are not impacted by the security filters to stakeholders. Users may falsely believe that a **Products** table security filter will also filter another dimension table, such as a **Stores** dimension, since only certain products are sold in certain stores. However, if the **Stores** table is queried directly and there is not a bidirectional relationship between **Stores** and a **Sales** fact table, all the stores would be accessible. Only when a sales measure is used in a visual would stores with blank values (given the **Products** filter) be discarded by default, and even then, a user could access these stores via **Show items with no data setting**. To secure these tables and avoid bidirectional cross-filtering for these relationships, additional table-specific security filters may be needed.

There's more

Security role definitions are specific to a given Power BI model (dataset). The management overhead and risk of maintaining common security roles and business definitions across multiple Power BI models, in addition to excess resource usage, should motivate IT/BI teams to consider consolidating these models to a single Power BI premium dataset or optionally an Analysis Services model. The management overhead and risk of maintaining common security roles and business definitions across multiple Power BI models can motivate IT/BI teams to consolidate data models when feasible, and to consider a **SQL Server Analysis Services** (**SSAS**) or **Azure Analysis Services** model as a more efficient and secure long-term solution.

As more roles and role filter requirements are required of a data model, a central security role table can be built into a data warehouse with the names of distinct roles associated with the values of the columns to be secured. Queries against this table can be used by Import or DirectQuery data models to implement these roles via relationships.

See also

- Row-level security (RLS) with Power BI: `https://bit.ly/3nhx3zW`
- Row-level security (RLS) guidance in Power BI Desktop: `https://bit.ly/3tUH3kY`

Designing Dynamic Security Models

Dynamic security models in Power BI filter tables are based on the relationship of the logged-in user to a column or columns stored in the data model. The `USERPRINCIPALNAME` DAX function returns the user's UPN, as per the first recipe of this chapter, and a filter expression of a security role accepts this value as a parameter. Like all filters in Power BI data models, the filters applied in security roles also filter other tables via one-to-many and bidirectional relationships. Security roles can also blend dynamic, user-based filters with standard security filters to further restrict the visibility of members mapped to these roles.

This recipe implements dynamic security on an **Employees** dimension table. The result is that logged-in users (employees) can only view their own data and the data of those who report to them directly or indirectly via other managers.

Getting ready

To prepare for this recipe, follow these steps:

1. Open a Power BI Desktop file locally and access the **Power Query Editor** by clicking on **Transform Data** in the ribbon of the **Home** tab
2. Create a query named **AdWorksDW** similar to the following:

   ```
   let
       Source = Sql.Database("localhost\MSSQLSERVERDEV",
   "AdventureWorksDW2019")
   in
       Source
   ```

3. Disable load on the **AdWorksDW** query, and place it into a **Data Sources** query group
4. Right-click the **AdWorksDW** query and choose **Reference**
5. Rename the query **Employees**, choose the **DimEmployee** table, and move it to the **Other Queries** query group
6. Select **Close & Apply** from the ribbon of the **Home** tab
7. Switch to the **Data** view and create the following calculated columns:

   ```
   Employee Name = SWITCH(TRUE(),
       ISBLANK([MiddleName]),[FirstName] & " " & [LastName],
       [FirstName] & " " & LEFT([MiddleName],1) & ". " & [LastName])
   ```

```
Manager Name = LOOKUPVALUE(
    Employees[Employee Name],[EmployeeKey],[ParentEmployeeKey])

ManagementPath = PATH(Employees[EmployeeKey],Employees[ParentEmployeeK
ey])

ManagementPathLength = PATHLENGTH([ManagementPath])
```

8. Set the **EmployeeKey** and **ParentEmployeeKey** columns default **Summarization setting** to **Don't summarize**
9. Save your work

Establish the technical feasibility of dynamic security early in a Power BI deployment, such as through the existence and quality of employee-manager hierarchy sources, and the role security implications/options of Import versus DirectQuery models. As per the other recipes in this chapter, simple tables and relationships can be used as an alternative to relatively complex DAX expressions such as `PATHCONTAINS`. Additionally, for DirectQuery models, consider the option to leverage the existing security model of the source database rather than defining new RLS roles.

How to Build Dynamic Security Models

To implement this recipe, use the following steps:

1. In the **Report** view, create a simple Table visualization using the **Employee Name**, **Manager Name**, **EmployeeKey**, **ParentEmployeeKey**, **EmailAddress**, **ManagementPath**, and **ManagementPathLength** columns, as shown in *Figure 8.11*

Employee Name	Manager Name	EmployeeKey	ParentEmployeeKey	EmailAddress	ManagementPath	ManagementPathLength
A. Scott Wright	Peter J. Krebs	46	23	ascott0@adventure-works.com	112|23|46	3
Alan J. Brewer	A. Scott Wright	174	46	alan0@adventure-works.com	112|23|46|174	4
Alejandro E. McGuel	Brenda M. Diaz	33	214	alejandro0@adventure-works.com	112|23|214|33	4
Alex M. Nayberg	Jeff V. Hay	159	126	alex0@adventure-works.com	112|23|126|159	4

Figure 8.11: Table visual of the Employees table columns

2. Create the following DAX measures:

```
Current User Principal Name = "ascott0@adventure-works.com"

Current User EmployeeKey = LOOKUPVALUE(Employees[EmployeeKey],
    Employees[EmailAddress],[Current User Principal Name])

Current User Name = LOOKUPVALUE(Employees[Employee Name],
    Employees[EmailAddress],[Current User Principal Name])

Current User Manager = LOOKUPVALUE(Employees[Manager Name],
    Employees[EmployeeKey],[Current User EmployeeKey])
```

```
Current User Org Level = CALCULATE(MAX(Employees[ManagementPathLength]),
    FILTER(ALL(Employees),Employees[EmployeeKey] = [Current User
EmployeeKey]))

Employee Row Count = COUNTROWS('Employees')
```

3. Select **Manage roles** in the ribbon of the **Modeling** tab
4. Click **Create** and name the role **Current User**, with a table filter DAX expression on the **Employees** table of the following:

```
PATHCONTAINS(Employees[ManagementPath],[Current User EmployeeKey])
```

Figure 8.12: Dynamic filter expression applied to Employees table for security role Current User

5. Click the **Save** button
6. Create a **Multi-card** visualization using the **Current User Name**, **Current User Manager**, **Current User Org Level**, and **Employee Row Count** measures as **Fields**
7. Select **View as** in the ribbon of the **Modeling** tab and choose the **Current User** role

Now viewing as: Current User

A. Scott Wright — Current User Name
Peter J. Krebs — Current User Manager
3 — Current User Org L...
6 — Employee Row Count

Employee Name	Manager Name	EmployeeKey	ParentEmployeeKey	EmailAddress	ManagementPath	ManagementPathLength
A. Scott Wright	Peter J. Krebs	46	23	ascott0@adventure-works.com	112|23|46	3
Alan J. Brewer	A. Scott Wright	174	46	alan0@adventure-works.com	112|23|46|174	4
Brian P. LaMee	A. Scott Wright	210	46	brian1@adventure-works.com	112|23|46|210	4
Sairaj L. Uddin	A. Scott Wright	135	46	sairaj0@adventure-works.com	112|23|46|135	4
William S. Vong	A. Scott Wright	98	46	william0@adventure-works.com	112|23|46|98	4
William S. Vong	A. Scott Wright	99	46	william0@adventure-works.com	112|23|46|99	4

Figure 8.13: Viewing the report as A. Scott Wright

8. Edit the **Current User Principal** Name measure to be *peter0@adventure-works.com*

Now viewing as: Current User

Peter J. Krebs — Current User Name
Ken J. Sánchez — Current User Manager
2 — Current User Org L...
202 — Employee Row Count

Employee Name	Manager Name	EmployeeKey	ParentEmployeeKey	EmailAddress	ManagementPath	ManagementPathLength
A. Scott Wright	Peter J. Krebs	46	23	ascott0@adventure-works.com	112|23|46	3
Alan J. Brewer	A. Scott Wright	174	46	alan0@adventure-works.com	112|23|46|174	4
Alejandro E. McGuel	Brenda M. Diaz	33	214	alejandro0@adventure-works.com	112|23|214|33	4
Alex M. Nayberg	Jeff V. Hay	159	126	alex0@adventure-works.com	112|23|126|159	4
Alice O. Ciccu	Jinghao K. Liu	38	40	alice0@adventure-works.com	112|23|40|38	4
Andreas T. Berglund	Peng J. Wu	149	43	andreas0@adventure-works.com	112|23|204|43|149	5

Figure 8.14: Viewing the report as Peter J. Krebs

How it works

In a production environment, the **Current User Principal Name** measure would not be hardcoded to an email address, but would rather take the form of the following formula:

```
Current User Principal Name = USERPRINCIPALNAME()
```

The DAX functions used in this recipe are specific to a parent-child hierarchy that exists in the **DimEmployee** source table. The **DimEmployee** table contains an email address column that would correspond to the value returned by the DAX `USERPRINCIPALNAME` function when logged into the Power BI service. Additionally, this recipe is exclusive to Import mode datasets, as parent-child DAX functions are not currently supported in DirectQuery mode models for either calculated columns or security filter expressions.

The **Employees** table has 296 rows, but a logged-in user should only see her data and the data of those that report to her directly or indirectly. For example, a vice president should still have visibility to a manager even if the manager reports to a senior manager who reports to the vice president. The senior manager, however, should not be able to view the vice president's data or the data of a different senior manager. Visibility is limited to the current user's data and the data of those employees who report to them directly or indirectly via other managers.

The **EmployeeKey** value is the last item in the **ManagementPath** column via the `PATH` function. The **Current User EmployeeKey** measure, which uses the **Current User Principal** Name to retrieve the **EmployeeKey** value, is passed as the item parameter to the `PATHCONTAINS` function in the RLS filter expression. The calculated column created in *step 1*, **ManagementPath**, provides the string of values for each **Employees** row to be evaluated against.

There's more

RLS expressions can significantly degrade query performance, as these filters will be applied in addition to other filters and expressions from Power BI reports when members of security roles access this content. As a general rule, try to use relationships between tables with low cardinality to implement dynamic security, as per the following recipe in this chapter. Utility or information functions, such as `LOOKUPVALUE`, `CONTAINS`, and `PATHCONTAINS`, can meet complex security rules in Import mode models but can be very expensive from a performance standpoint when applied against larger-dimension tables—such as customer or product tables containing more than one million rows.

See also

- Row-level security (RLS) with Power BI: `https://bit.ly/3nhx3zW`
- Row-level security (RLS) guidance in Power BI Desktop: `https://bit.ly/3tUH3kY`

Building Dynamic Security for DirectQuery

Dynamic row-level security roles can be implemented in DirectQuery models via relationships, and with specifically bidirectional cross-filtering between user security tables and the dimension tables to be secured. DAX information functions, commonly used in the role security expressions of Import mode models, such as `CONTAINS` and `LOOKUPVALUE`, are not supported in DirectQuery mode models, thus requiring a relationship-based security design. Although limited to this single approach, dynamic security can be quickly developed for DirectQuery models and maintained easily, without the need for complex DAX security expressions.

This recipe walks through the steps and settings necessary to support dynamic security in a DirectQuery model.

Getting ready

To prepare for this recipe, follow these steps:

1. Open a Power BI Desktop file locally and access the **Power Query Editor** by clicking on **Transform Data** in the ribbon of the **Home** tab
2. Create a new query that accesses your copy of the **AdventureWorksDW2019** database on your SQL Server, ensuring that the **Data Connectivity** mode is set to **DirectQuery**
3. Choose the **FactInternetSales** table in the **Navigation** dialog
4. Rename the query **Internet Sales**
5. Right-click the **Internet Sales** query and choose **Duplicate**
6. Change the **Navigation** step to point to the **DimSalesTerritory** table
7. Rename the query **Sales Territories**
8. Right-click the **Internet Sales** query and choose **Duplicate**
9. Change the **Navigation** step to point to the **DimEmployee** table
10. Rename the query **Employees**
11. Edit the **Employees** query to be the following (replacing the **Source** line with the instance of your SQL Server):

```
let
    Source = Sql.Database("localhost\MSSQLSERVERDEV",
"AdventureWorksDW2019"),
    dbo_DimEmployee = Source{[Schema="dbo",Item="DimEmployee"]}[Data],
    ExpandSalesTerritory = Table.ExpandRecordColumn(
        dbo_DimEmployee, "DimSalesTerritory",
        {"SalesTerritoryCountry"}, {"SalesTerritoryCountry"}),
```

```
        RemoveColumns = Table.SelectColumns(
            ExpandSalesTerritory,
            {"SalesTerritoryCountry", "EmployeeKey",
            "EmployeeNationalIDAlternateKey", "EmailAddress"})
    in
        RemoveColumns
```

12. Right-click the **Employees** query and choose **Duplicate**
13. Rename the query **Countries**
14. Edit the **Countries** query to be the following (replacing the **Source** line with the instance of your SQL Server):

```
let
    Source = Sql.Database("localhost\MSSQLSERVERDEV",
"AdventureWorksDW2019"),
    dbo_DimEmployee = Source{[Schema="dbo",Item="DimEmployee"]}[Data],
    ExpandSalesTerritory = Table.ExpandRecordColumn(
        dbo_DimEmployee, "DimSalesTerritory",
        {"SalesTerritoryCountry"}, {"SalesTerritoryCountry"}),
    RemoveColumns = Table.SelectColumns(
        ExpandSalesTerritory,{"SalesTerritoryCountry"}),
    RemoveDups = Table.Distinct(RemoveColumns)
in
    RemoveDups
```

15. Click **Close & Apply** from the ribbon of the **Home** tab
16. Switch to **Model** view and create a relationship between the **SalesTerritoryCountry** columns of the **Sales Territories** and **Countries** tables
17. Create a relationship between the **SalesTerritoryKey** columns of the **Sales Territories** and **Internet Sales** tables
18. Create a relationship between the **SalesTerritoryCountry** columns of the **Countries** and **Employees** tables
19. Save your work

How to Build Dynamic Security Models for DirectQuery

To implement this recipe, perform the following:

1. In the **Model** view, open the properties for the **Countries** to **Employees** relationship, and set the **Cross filter direction** to **Both**
2. Check the checkbox for both **Assume referential integrity** and **Apply security filter** in both directions and then click **OK**

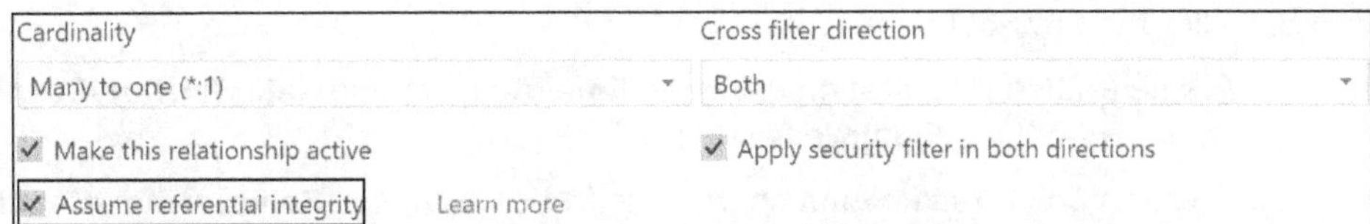

Figure 8.15: Bidirectional relationship between the Countries and Employees tables

3. The model should now look the same as that shown in *Figure 8.16*

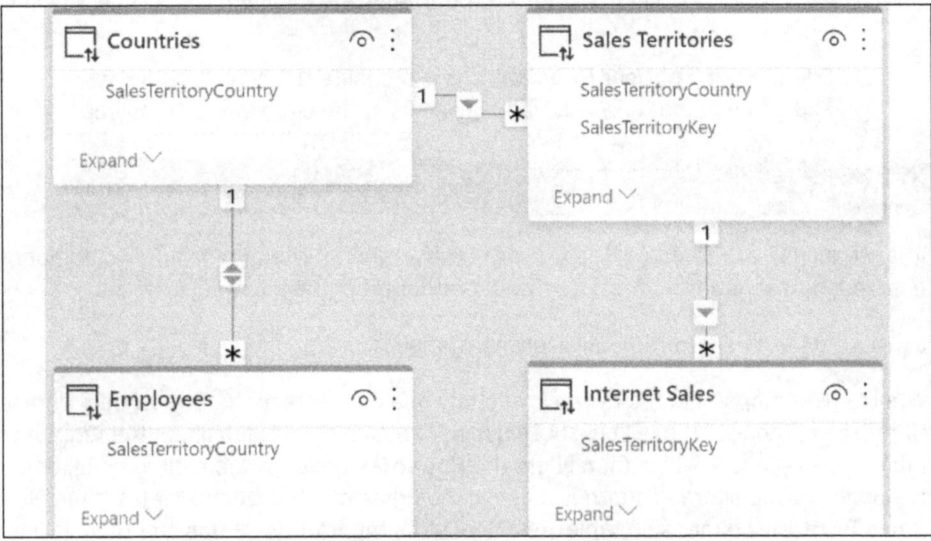

Figure 8.16: Dynamic user security relationships

4. Create the following measure, **Current User Principal Name**:

```
Current User Principal Name = "david8@adventure-works.com"
```

5. Click **Manage roles** in the ribbon of the **Modeling** tab
6. Click **Create**, and name the role **Current User**, with a table filter DAX expression on the **Employees** table of the following code:

```
[EmailAddress] = [Current User Principal Name]
```

7. *Figure 8.17* shows this DAX formula entered into Power BI Desktop's interface for creating RLS roles

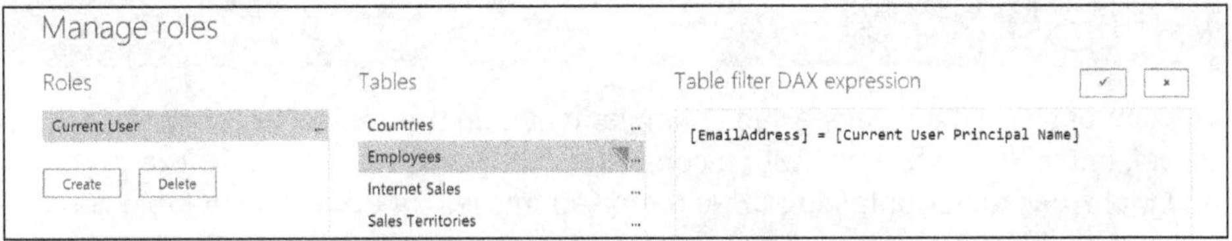

Figure 8.17: DAX table filter expression applied to the EmailAddress column of the Employees table

8. Click the **Save** button
9. Create a Table visualization using the **EmailAddress** and **SalesTerritoryCountry** columns from the **Employees** table
10. Create a **Clustered column chart** visualization using the **SalesTerritoryCountry** column from the **Countries** table as the **Axis**, and the **SalesAmount** column (sum) from the **Internet Sales** table as **Values**
11. Click **View as** in the ribbon of the **Modeling** tab, choose **Current User**, and click the **OK** button to see that only the **United States** column is shown in the clustered column chart
12. Edit the **Current User Principal Name** measure to be `lynn0@adventure-works.com` and observe that only **Australia** is shown in the clustered column chart

How it works

In a production environment, the **Current User Principal Name** measure would not be hardcoded to an email address, but would rather be of the following formula:

```
Current User Principal Name = USERPRINCIPALNAME()
```

When a user mapped to the dynamic security role connects to the DirectQuery dataset, their UPN is computed via the `USERPRINCIPALNAME` function. This value filters the **Employees** table to a single row, which then filters the **Countries** table via the bidirectional, one-to-many relationship. The filtered countries, such as Australia and the United States, then filter the **Sales Territories** dimension table. As a final step, the **Internet Sales** fact table is filtered by the **Sales Territories** table, and thus all **Internet Sales** measures and aggregations reflect the given **SalesTerritoryCountry** of the employee.

Note that the **Countries** table, which contains only the distinct country values, is necessary, since the **Sales Territories** table contains many regions for the same country, and all relationships must have a side that identifies each row of a table.

Ensure that **Apply security filter in both directions** is selected for the bidirectional (both) cross-filter relationship between the **Countries** and **Employees** tables. In addition, the **Assume referential integrity** setting causes the DirectQuery data model to send inner join SQL queries to the source database and this—of course—significantly improves performance with larger models.

There's more

The approach from this recipe can be implemented in the same way for an Import mode model, and can also be used with a consolidated security role table. For example, instead of an **Employees** table containing UPNs (email addresses), a **Permissions** table could be loaded to the model containing the names of each RLS role and the columns to secure.

For each role, a simple security filter could be applied that references the name of the role. As in this recipe, **Bridge** tables containing the unique values of the secured columns could be created, and security filters would flow across relationships from the **Permissions** table to the **Dimension** and **Fact** tables via the **Bridge** table(s).

Security Role	Sales Country	Product Category
European Bike	France	Bikes
European Bike	United Kingdom	Bikes
European Bike	Germany	Bikes
USA Non Bikes	United States	Accessories
USA Non Bikes	United States	Clothing
USA Non Bikes	United States	Components

Figure 8.18: RLS permissions table

Given the performance advantage of relationship filtering (including bidirectional relationship filtering), as well as the avoidance of relatively complex DAX, there could be value for organizations to follow this approach to dynamic security for both Import and DirectQuery models.

See also

- Row-level security (RLS) with Power BI: `https://bit.ly/3nhx3zW`
- Row-level security (RLS) guidance in Power BI Desktop: `https://bit.ly/3tUH3kY`

Displaying the Current Filter Context

DAX measures can be created to dynamically display the current filter context to report users. These measures can detect filters, retrieve values, and apply conditional logic to the filters applied to both slicer visuals and report- and page-level filters. With the filter context as a visual aid, users consuming or interacting with Power BI reports can focus on the data visualizations to obtain insights more quickly and with greater confidence. In addition, such measures can be useful when designing RLS scenarios as a check that the correct information is being filtered by the RLS rules.

In this recipe, DAX measures are created to detect and display the filter selections applied to a specific column, either on the report canvas itself or as a report- or page-level filter. An additional example displays the values of a column that are "remaining," given the filters applied to the column directly and indirectly via other filters.

Getting ready

To prepare for this recipe, follow these steps:

1. Open a Power BI Desktop file locally and access the **Power Query Editor** by clicking on **Transform Data** in the ribbon of the **Home** tab
2. Create a query named **AdWorksDW**, similar to the following:

```
let
    Source = Sql.Database("localhost\MSSQLSERVERDEV",
"AdventureWorksDW2019")
in
    Source
```

3. Disable load on the **AdWorksDW** query and place it into a **Data Sources** query group
4. Right-click the **AdWorksDW** query and choose **Reference**
5. Rename the query **Sales Territories**, choose the **DimSalesTerritory** table, and move to the **Other Queries** query group
6. Create a **Products** query using the following code:

```
let
    Source = AdWorksDW,
    Navigation = Source{[Schema="dbo",Item="DimProduct"]}[Data],
    Subcategory =
        Table.ExpandRecordColumn(
            Navigation, "DimProductSubcategory",
            {"EnglishProductSubcategoryName", "DimProductCategory"},
            {"Product Subcategory", "DimProductCategory"}
        ),
    Category =
        Table.ExpandRecordColumn(
            Subcategory, "DimProductCategory",
            {"EnglishProductCategoryName"}, {"Product Category"}
        )
in
   Category
```

7. Move the **Sales Territories** and **Products** queries to the **Other Queries** query group
8. Select **Close & Apply** from the ribbon of the **Home** tab
9. Save your work

How to do it

To implement this recipe, perform the following:

1. Create a DAX measure for **Regions Selected**:

```
Regions Selected =
    VAR Selected =
        FILTERS('Sales Territories'[SalesTerritoryRegion])
    VAR String = "Regions Selected: " &
        CONCATENATEX(
            Selected,[SalesTerritoryRegion],", ",[SalesTerritoryRegion])
    VAR StringLength = LEN(String)
    VAR NumOf = COUNTROWS(Selected)
RETURN
    SWITCH(TRUE(),
        NOT(ISFILTERED('Sales Territories'[SalesTerritoryRegion])),
            "No Regions Selected",
        StringLength < 45, String,
        NumOf & " Regions Selected" )
```

2. Create a DAX measure for **Categories Selected**:

```
Categories Selected =
    VAR Selected =
        FILTERS('Products'[Product Category])
    VAR String = "Categories Selected: " &
        CONCATENATEX(
            Selected,[Product Category],", ",[Product Category])
    VAR StringLength = LEN(String)
    VAR NumOf = COUNTROWS(Selected)
RETURN
    SWITCH(TRUE(),
        NOT(ISFILTERED('Sales Territories'[SalesTerritoryRegion])),
            "No Categories Selected",
        StringLength < 45, String,
        NumOf & " Categories Selected" )
```

3. Add a **Card** or **Multi-row card** visualization for each measure created

4. Add slicer visualizations for the **SalesTerritoryRegion** column in the **Sales Territories** table and the **Product Category** column in the **Products** table

Regions Selected: Australia, Canada, Germany

Categories Selected: Bikes, Components

SalesTerritoryRegion
Australia
Canada
Central
France
Germany
NA
Northeast
Northwest
Southeast
Southwest
United Kingdom

Product Category
(Blank)
Accessories
Bikes
Clothing
Components

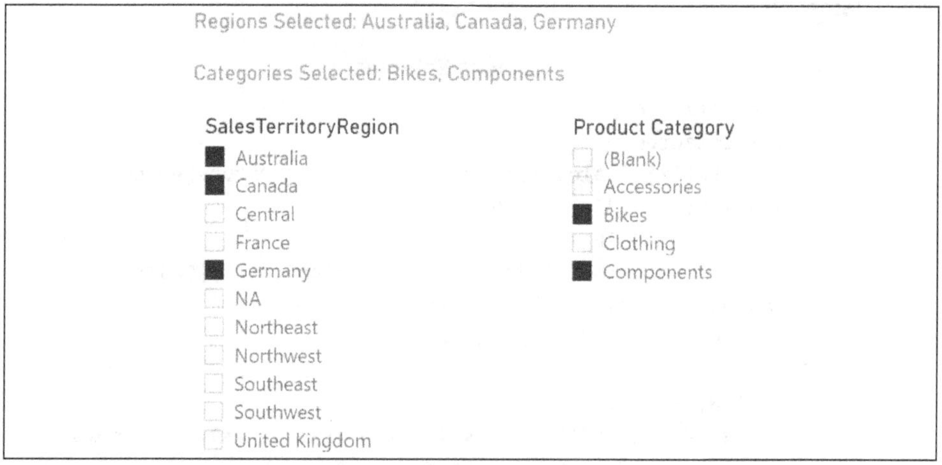

Figure 8.19: Two Multi-row Card visuals displaying the filter context from two Slicer visuals

How it works

In both measures, four DAX variables and a `SWITCH` function are used to support three separate conditions. When no filters are applied, the message **No Regions Selected** or No Categories Selected is returned. When many regions/categories are selected, resulting in a long text string (over 45 characters in this example), a short message is returned advising of the number of regions/categories selected. Otherwise, an ordered, comma-separated list of the selected region/category values is returned.

The `FILTERS` function returns a table of the values that are directly applied as filters to a column. The third parameter to `CONCATENATEX` is optional, but drives the sort order of the text values returned, and thus is recommended to aid the user when accessing the report by placing the values returned in a logical sorting order versus unsorted. As per *Figure 8.19*, the values are sorted alphabetically.

In this example, a separate measure was created for the **Product Category** column in the **Products** table, and both columns are being filtered by slicer visuals. The two measures displayed in the multi-row Card visuals will also reflect filters applied via report- and page-level filters. For example, if there were no selections on the **Product Category** slicer, or if this slicer was removed completely, the categories-selected measure would still detect and display product category filters from page- and report-level filters.

You should plan ahead when creating multiple similar measures. Name variables in such a way that DAX code can be reused between multiple measures, and ensure that the variables' names still make sense within the context of each measure's code.

There's more

1. Create a DAX measure that identifies the remaining **SalesTerritoryRegion** values, given all other filters are applied:

```
Regions Remaining =
    VAR Remaining = DISTINCT('Sales Territories'[SalesTerritoryRegion])
    VAR String = "Regions Remaining: " &
        CONCATENATEX(
            Remaining,[SalesTerritoryRegion],", ",[SalesTerritoryRegion])
    VAR StringLength = LEN(String)
    VAR NumOf = COUNTROWS(Remaining)
RETURN
    SWITCH(TRUE(),
        NOT(ISCROSSFILTERED('Sales Territories')),
            "No Sales Territories Filters",
        StringLength < 55, String,
        NumOf & " Regions Remaining")
```

2. Create a DAX measure that identifies the remaining **Product Subcategories** values, given all other filters are applied:

```
Subcategories Remaining =
    VAR Remaining = DISTINCT('Products'[Product Subcategory])
    VAR String = "Subcategories Remaining: " &
        CONCATENATEX(
            Remaining,[Product Subcategory],", ",[Product Subcategory])
    VAR StringLength = LEN(String)
    VAR NumOf = COUNTROWS(Remaining)
RETURN
    SWITCH(TRUE(),
        NOT(ISCROSSFILTERED('Sales Territories')),
            "No Products Filters",
        StringLength < 55, String,
        NumOf & " Subcategories Remaining")
```

The `DISTINCT` function replaces the `FILTERS` function used in the earlier example to return the unique values still active despite filters on other columns. The `ISCROSSFILTERED` function replaces the `ISFILTERED` function used in the earlier example to test if any column from the **Sales Territories** dimension table is being used as a filter.

Test the new measure by applying filters on columns that would reduce the available or remaining values, as shown in *Figure 8.20*.

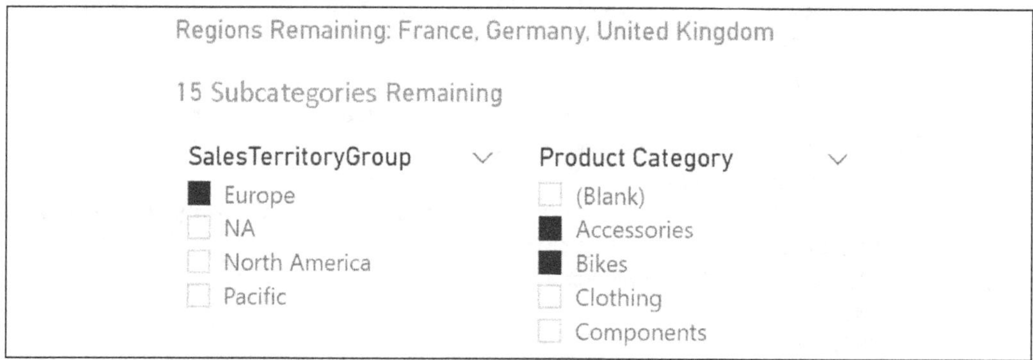

Figure 8.20: Regions Remaining and Subcategories Remaining measures

The **SalesTerritoryRegion** and **Product Subcategory** columns are impacted by filters applied to the **SalesTerritoryGroup** and **Product Category** columns, respectively. Given the number of characters in the text string of 15 product subcategories, only the number remaining is displayed.

Note that these remaining expressions will return the same string values as the first example, when filters are applied directly on the given column. For example, if the **Northwest** and **Northeast** regions were selected on a sales territory region slicer, these would be the only two regions remaining. The techniques applied in these two examples can be blended or enriched further, such as by associating a numeric measure with each dimension value returned by the delimited string.

See also

- DAX `FILTERS` function: `https://bit.ly/3aAVTFB`
- DAX `CONCATENATEX` function: `https://bit.ly/3sVmvHQ`
- DAX `ISCROSSFILTERED` function: `https://bit.ly/3vo13gr`

Avoiding Manual User Clicks

A common scenario in BI projects is the need to customize a core set of reports and dashboards to better align with the responsibilities and analytical needs of specific roles or users within a larger team or organizational function. A given business user should, ideally, have immediate and default visibility to relevant data without the need to interact with or modify content, such as applying filter selections.

Power BI's extensive self-service capabilities are sometimes a solution—or part of it—to this need, and additional role-specific, IT-supported reports and dashboards are another realistic option.

A third option, and the one that is the subject of this recipe, is to embed user-based dynamic filtering logic into DAX measures. With this approach, a single or small group of reports and dashboards can be leveraged across multiple levels of an organization, thus avoiding the need for new report development.

Getting ready

To prepare for this recipe, follow these steps:

1. Open a Power BI Desktop file locally and access the **Power Query Editor** by clicking on **Transform Data** in the ribbon of the **Home** tab
2. Create a query named **AdWorksDW**, similar to the following:

```
let
    Source = Sql.Database("localhost\MSSQLSERVERDEV",
"AdventureWorksDW2019")
in
    Source
```

3. Disable load on the **AdWorksDW** query and place into a **Data Sources** query group
4. Right-click the **AdWorksDW** query and choose **Reference**
5. Rename the query **Internet Sales** and choose the **FactInternetSales** table
6. Repeat steps *4* and *5* for a query named **Sales Territories** that points to the **DimSalesTerritory** table, and a query named **Customers** that points to the **DimCustomers** table
7. Edit the **Customers** query to expand the **DimGeography** column:

```
let
    Source = AdWorksDW,
    dbo_DimCustomer = Source{[Schema="dbo",Item="DimCustomer"]}[Data],
    ExpandGeography = Table.ExpandRecordColumn(
        dbo_DimCustomer, "DimGeography",
        {"City", "StateProvinceName", "EnglishCountryRegionName",
"PostalCode"},
        {"City", "StateProvinceName", "EnglishCountryRegionName",
"PostalCode"})
in
    ExpandGeography
```

8. Move the **Internet Sales** query to a query group called **Facts**, and the **Sales Territories** and **Customers** queries to a query group called **Dimensions**
9. Create an **Enter Data** query named **Sales User Roles** in the **Dimensions** query group with the following information:

EmailAddress	SalesTerritoryKey	UserRole
`david8@adventure-works.com`	2	`Country`
`linda3@adventure-works.com`	4	`Region`
`pamela0@adventure-works.com`	6	`Group`

10. In the **Other Queries** group, create a **Blank** query called **Calculations**
11. Select **Close & Apply** from the ribbon of the **Home** tab
12. Create a relationship between the **SalesTerritoryKey** columns of the **Sales Territories** and **Internet Sales** tables
13. Create a relationship between the **SalesTerritoryKey** columns of the **Sales Territories** and **Sales User Roles** tables
14. Create a relationship between the **CustomerKey** columns of the **Internet Sales** and **Customers** tables
15. Set the **Data category** for the **Postal Code** column in the **Customers** table to **Postal Code**
16. Save your work

The model should now look the same as that shown in *Figure 8.21*.

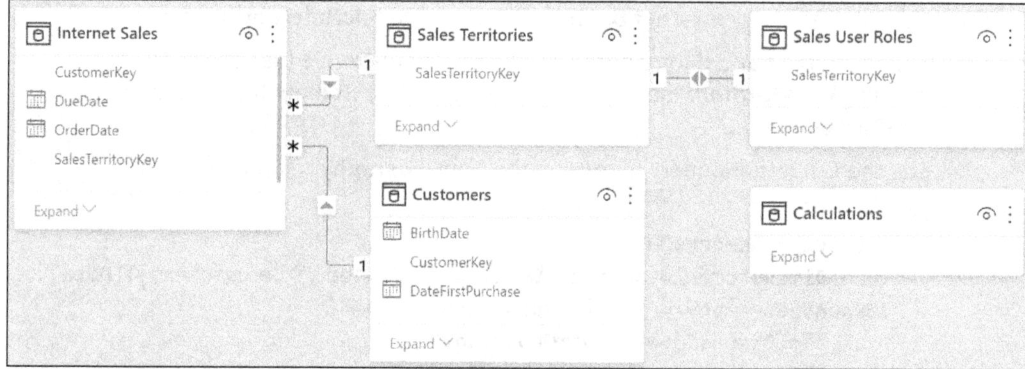

Figure 8.21: The model for this recipe

How to Avoid Manual User Clicks

To implement this recipe, use the following steps:

1. Create the following DAX measures in the **Calculations** table:

```
User Principal Name = "david8@adventure-works.com"

User Sales Territory Key = LOOKUPVALUE('Sales User
Roles'[SalesTerritoryKey],
    'Sales User Roles'[EmailAddress],[User Principal Name])

User Sales Role =
    VAR RoleLookup = LOOKUPVALUE('Sales User Roles'[UserRole],
        'Sales User Roles'[EmailAddress],[User Principal Name])
RETURN IF(ISBLANK(RoleLookup),"Role Not Found",RoleLookup)

User Sales Group = IF([User Sales Role] = "Role Not Found",
    "Role Not Found", LOOKUPVALUE('Sales Territories'[SalesTerritoryGrou
p],
        'Sales Territories'[SalesTerritoryKey],[User Sales Territory
Key]))

User Sales Country = IF([User Sales Role] = "Role Not Found",
    "Role Not Found", LOOKUPVALUE('Sales Territories'[SalesTerritoryCoun
try],
    'Sales Territories'[SalesTerritoryKey],[User Sales Territory Key]))

User Sales Region = IF([User Sales Role] = "Role Not Found",
    "Role Not Found", LOOKUPVALUE('Sales Territories'[SalesTerritoryRegi
on],
    'Sales Territories'[SalesTerritoryKey],[User Sales Territory Key]))
```

2. Create two DAX measures in the **Calculations** table to detect the filter context of the **Sales Territories** table, and to filter the **Internet Sales** table as appropriate:

```
Sales Territory Detection = IF(ISCROSSFILTERED('Sales Territories'),
    "Filters Applied", "No Filters")

Internet Sales Amount = SWITCH(TRUE(),
    [Sales Territory Detection] = "Filters Applied" ||
        [User Sales Role] = "Role Not Found",SUM('Internet
Sales'[SalesAmount]),
        [User Sales Role] = "Group",
```

```
            CALCULATE(SUM('Internet Sales'[SalesAmount]),
            FILTER(ALL('Sales Territories'),
                'Sales Territories'[SalesTerritoryGroup] = [User Sales
Group])),
        [User Sales Role] = "Country",
            CALCULATE(SUM('Internet Sales'[SalesAmount]),
            FILTER(ALL('Sales Territories'),
                'Sales Territories'[SalesTerritoryCountry] =
                    [User Sales Country])),
        [User Sales Role] = "Region",
            CALCULATE(SUM('Internet Sales'[SalesAmount]),
            FILTER(ALL('Sales Territories'),
                'Sales Territories'[SalesTerritoryRegion] =
                    [User Sales Region])) )
```

3. Create a standard report with the new measure and the **Sales Territory** table to test or demonstrate the logic

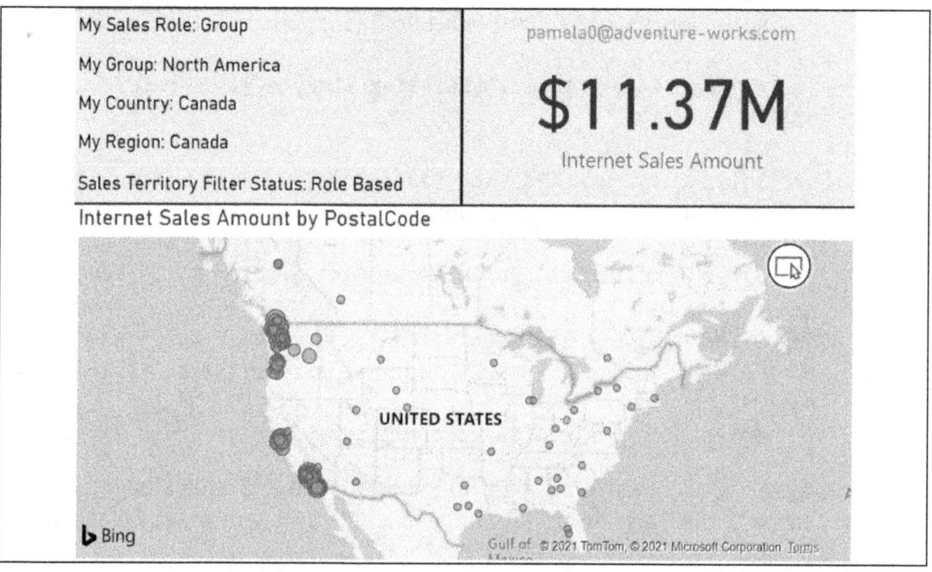

Figure 8.22: Default filter context for the user Pamela, a group role member for North America

4. Change the **User Principal Name** measure to test the three different roles

How it works

In a production environment, the **User Principal Name** measure would not be hardcoded to an email address, but would rather be of the following formula:

```
User Principal Name = USERPRINCIPALNAME()
```

In addition, a production implementation would store the **Sales User Roles** table in the SQL data warehouse instead of using an **Enter Data** query.

The measures in this recipe build on one another, culminating in the **Internet Sales Amount** measure. The purpose of these measures is to provide a specific default filter context to apply to a measure (**Internet Sales Amount**). A country role member, for example, should see data filtered by his or her country by default when opening the report. However, conditional logic can also allow for user filter selections to be applied, allowing for additional visibility as an option as well.

The **Sales Territory Detection** measure is fundamental to this approach. If no columns on the **Sales Territories** table have been filtered, such as via slicers, then the sales measure should default to a specific filter context based on the user. If filter selections have been made on **Sales Territories** columns, then these selections should be used by the measure.

The **Internet Sales Amount** measure defaults to summing the **SalesAmount** column in the **Internet Sales** table if the current user is not found in the **Sales User Roles** table. If a role is identified for the user and no filters have been applied on the **Sales Territories** table, a filter at the user's role level (**Group**, **Country**, or **Region**) and the specific dimension member is applied.

There's more

The five DAX measures exposed in the top-left card visual of the sample reports are defined as follows:

```
User Role Status = "My Sales Role: " & [User Sales Role]

Sales Group Status = "My Group: " & [User Sales Group]

Sales Country Status = "My Country: " & [User Sales Country]

Sales Region Status = "My Region: " & [User Sales Region]

Filter Status = VAR Prefix = "Sales Territory Filter Status: "
RETURN IF([Sales Territory Detection] = "No Filters",
    Prefix & "Role Based",Prefix & "User Defined")
```

See also

- DAX `LOOKUPVALUE` function: `https://bit.ly/3gdjZKl`

Conclusion

This chapter contains detailed examples of building and deploying dynamic, user-based security for both import and DirectQuery datasets as well as examples of dynamic filter context functionality to enhance the user experience. Data security where users or groups of users are prevented from viewing a portion of a dataset is often a top requirement in Power BI deployments and security implementations can range from simple to complex. Given the variety of use cases and the importance of this feature to securely share a dataset across stakeholders, it is important to understand the process and techniques available for developing, testing, and operationalizing data security roles.

9

Applying Advanced Analytics and Custom Visuals

Power BI Desktop's standard report authoring tools provide a robust foundation for the development of rich BI and analytical content. Custom visualizations developed by Microsoft and third parties further supplement these capabilities with their own unique features and can be integrated with standard visuals in Power BI reports and dashboards. Additionally, geospatial analysis features such as the ArcGIS maps visual for Power BI, custom dimension groupings, and animation and annotation options further aid in the extraction of meaning from data and also support sharing these insights with others.

Power BI Desktop also includes advanced analytics features reflecting modern data science tools and algorithms, including clustering, forecasting, and support for custom R and Python scripts and visuals. For example, an analytics pane is available to enrich visuals with additional metrics, such as a trend line, and the Quick Insights feature empowers report authors to rapidly analyze specific questions and generate new visualizations.

This chapter contains a broad mix of recipes highlighting many of the latest and most popular custom visualization and advanced analytics features of Power BI. This includes top custom visuals such as bullet charts, the ArcGIS maps visual for Power BI, and data storytelling via animation and annotation. Additionally, examples are provided on leveraging Power BI datasets and the DAX, R, and Python languages to embed custom statistical analyses and visualizations, respectively.

In this chapter, we will cover the following recipes:

- Incorporating Advanced Analytics
- Enriching Content with Custom Visuals and Quick Insights
- Creating Geospatial Mapping with ArcGIS Maps
- Democratizing Artificial Intelligence
- Building Animation and Storytelling
- Embedding Statistical Analyses
- Grouping and Binning
- Detecting and Analyzing Clusters
- Forecasting and Anomaly Detection
- Using R and Python Visuals

Technical Requirements

The following are required to complete the recipes in this chapter:

- Power BI Desktop
- SQL Server with the **AdventureWorksDW2019** database installed. This database and instructions for installing it are available here: `http://bit.ly/2OVQfG7`
- Files for this chapter and can be downloaded from the following GitHub repository: `https://github.com/PacktPublishing/Microsoft-Power-BI-Cookbook-Second-Edition`

Incorporating Advanced Analytics

The standard line, scatter, column, and bar chart visualization types available in Power BI Desktop, which generally represent the majority of Power BI report content, given their advantages in visual comprehension, can be further enhanced via a dedicated analytics pane. Similar to visual-level filters, the Power BI analytics pane creates measures scoped to the specific visual, such as trend lines, constant lines, percentile lines, min, max, and average. This additional logic provides greater context to the visual and avoids the need to author complex or visual-specific DAX measures.

> *"This pane is our home for all of our analytics features and you'll be able to use this to augment your charts with any kind of additional analytics that you need."*
>
> *- Amanda Cofsky Rivera, Power BI Program Manager*

This recipe includes two examples of leveraging the analytics pane in Power BI Desktop to raise the analytical value of chart visuals: one for a clustered column chart and another for a line chart. The predictive forecasting feature built into the analytics pane is described in the *Forecasting and Anomaly Detection* recipe later in this chapter.

Getting ready

To prepare for this recipe, follow these steps:

1. Open a new file in Power BI Desktop
2. Click **Transform data** from the ribbon of the **Home** tab
3. In the **Power Query Editor**, create a new query called `Internet Sales` that imports the **FactInternetSales** table in the **AdventureWorksDW2019** database
4. Click **Close & Apply** from the ribbon of the **Home** tab

How to Incorporate Advanced Analytics

To implement this recipe, use the following steps:

1. In the **Report** view, create a clustered column chart visualization using the **OrderDate** column of the **Internet Sales** table as the **Axis** and the **average of the UnitPrice** column as **Values**
2. In the **Axis** field well of the **Visualizations** pane, select the dropdown under the **OrderDate** column and switch from **Date Hierarchy** to **OrderDate**

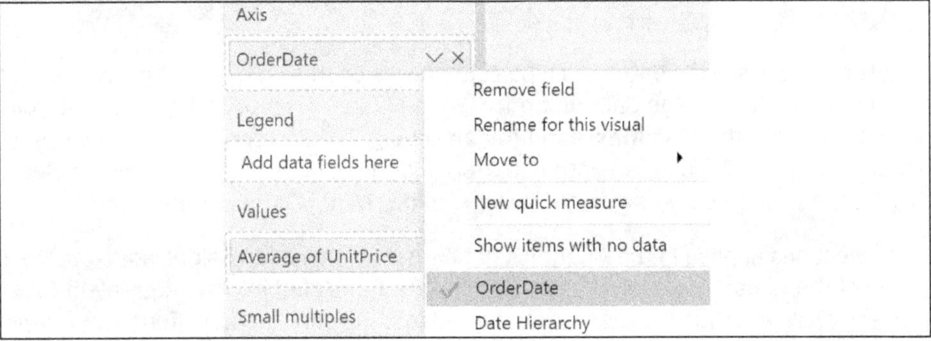

Figure 9.1: The automatic Date Hierarchy when a date column is added to a visual

3. Use the **Filters** pane to only display values from **1/1/2013** to **4/1/2013**
4. In the **Visualizations** pane, click on the **Analytics** pane (the magnifying glass icon)
5. Open the **Trend Line** card, click **Add**, and apply the **Color** black, a **Dashed** line **Style**, and **Transparency** of **0%**

6. Add **Min**, **Max**, and **Median** lines to the visual from the respective card in the **Analytics** pane
7. Set the names of these lines, **Min:**, **Max:**, and **Median:**, respectively, along with the **Color** black, **Transparency** of **0%**, and line **Style** of **Solid**
8. For each **Min**, **Max**, and **Median** line, toggle **Data label** to **On** and set **Text** to **Name and value**
9. Format the colors of the columns to contrast with the analytics lines

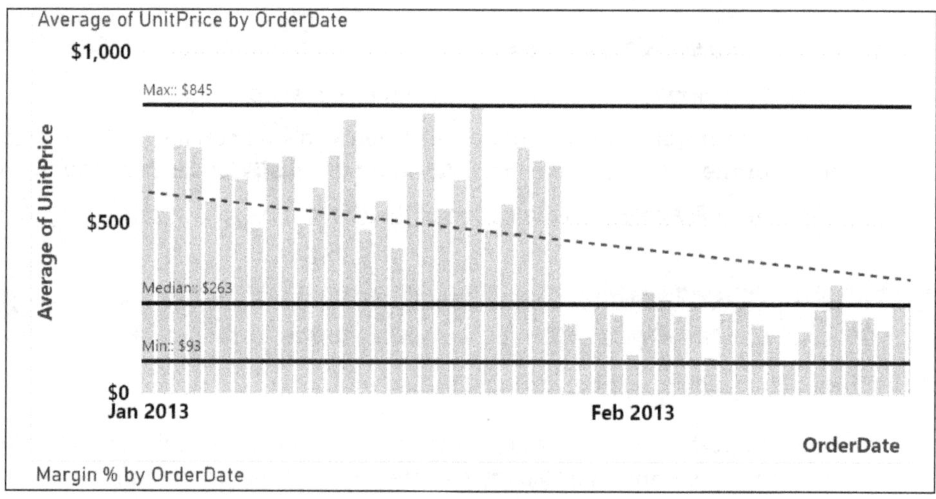

Figure 9.2: Clustered column chart with 4 dynamic lines from the analytics pane: Trend, Min, Max, and Median

How it works...

In this example, since a date data type column was used as the axis, the trend line calls out the decline in the average daily unit prices in the first quarter of 2013. Given the volume of individual dates, the **Min**, **Max**, and **Median** lines give the user quick takeaways, such as the median daily unit price for an entire quarter, and the option to further analyze sales activity on February 11, when daily unit prices reached a low (**Min**) of $93 per unit.

The selections applied in the **Analytics** pane result in new expressions added to the DAX query of the visual. The analytics calculations are translated into the equivalent DAX expressions (i.e., `MINX`, `AVERAGEX`) and passed into the `GROUPBY` table function. Running a SQL Server Profiler trace against a Power BI Desktop file and viewing the full DAX query associated with a given visual (including all filters applied) is a great way to understand advanced DAX functions and filter context. In Windows Task Manager, you can identify the **Process ID** (**PID**) associated with Power BI Desktop's `msmdsrv.exe` process. Alternatively, you can use the `TASKLIST` command from Command Prompt; run `netstat -anop tcp`, find the local port (in the **local address** column) associated with this process, and pass this value to SQL Server Profiler.

```
EVALUATE
  GROUPBY(
    __DSOCore,
    "MinInternett_Net_Sales", MINX(CURRENTGROUP(), [Internet_Net_Sales]),
    "MaxInternet_Net_Sales", MAXX(CURRENTGROUP(), [Ineternet_Net_Sales]),
    "AverageInternet_Net_Sales",AVERAGEX(CURRENTGROUP(), [Ineternet_Net_Sales]),
    "MinMinDate", MINX(CURRENTGROUP(), [MinDate])
  )
```

Figure 9.3: A SQL Server profile trace of a Power BI file using the Analytics pane for Min, Max, and Average

There's more...

Line charts support even more analytics features than most other visuals, including forecasting and X-axis constant lines. To see line chart analytics in action, do the following:

1. Create a measure called `Margin %` using the following formula:

```
Margin % =
    VAR __Price = SUM('Internet Sales'[SalesAmount])
    VAR __Cost = SUM('Internet Sales'[TotalProductCost])
RETURN DIVIDE(__Price - __Cost,__Price,0)
```

2. In the **Report** view, create a **Line chart** visualization using **OrderDate** (the column not the hierarchy) as the **Axis** and `Margin %` as **Values**
3. Use the **Filters** pane to only display values from `1/1/2013` to `4/1/2013`
4. In the **Analytics** pane, add a **Y-Axis Constant line** named **Target:** with a **Value** of `0.4`
5. Add an **X-Axis Constant Line** called **End of Quarter:** for `3/31/2013`
6. Add a **Min** line called **Min:** and a **Max** line called **Max:**, with a **Color** of black and a **Line style** of **Solid**
7. Add a **Percentile line** called **75% Percentile** and set **Percentile** to **75%**
8. For all lines, toggle **Data label** to **On** and set **Text** to **Name and value**
9. Add a **Forecast** of **1 Month(s)** with a **Confidence interval** of **75%** and **Seasonality** of **60 points**

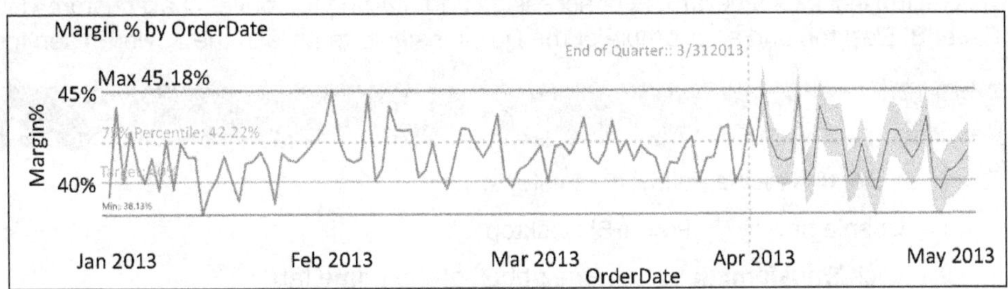

Figure 9.4: Line chart with analytics lines and forecast

In this example, 40 percent is considered a key profitability threshold, and thus a constant line helps to call out values below this level. Additionally, the percentile line set at 75 percent helps to identify the top quartile of values. The lines from the **Analytics** pane (and their formatting) provide more analytical value to users without requiring additional DAX measures for the model or cluttering the visual.

See also

- Power BI Analytics pane documentation: `http://bit.ly/2s2fA0P`
- How to trace a Power BI Desktop file: `http://bit.ly/2tYRLZg`

Enriching Content with Custom Visuals and Quick Insights

Custom visuals for Power BI can be reviewed and downloaded from AppSource to provide additional features and options beyond those supported by the standard visuals of Power BI Desktop. Over 300 custom visuals are currently available in AppSource with many of these having been developed by Microsoft to address common needs, such as the bullet, histogram, and Gantt charts. Other custom visuals available in AppSource have been developed by third parties but validated for security by Microsoft, with these visuals having unique and powerful capabilities, such as flow map network visualization and the interactive visuals developed by ZoomCharts. In addition to custom visuals, **Quick Insights** can be used in the Power BI service and in Power BI Desktop to apply advanced analytics algorithms against datasets to extract insights, such as trends or relationships, and rapidly generate new visualizations for use in reports and dashboards.

Custom visuals should only be used when they deliver a highly valuable or required functionality that is not provided by standard visuals. This is because custom visuals are often much less performant than standard visuals and are less reliable. Moreover, custom visuals are more difficult to support as report authors are less familiar with the specific options associated with custom visuals relative to standard visuals.

This recipe includes an example of accessing and utilizing the bullet chart custom visual in Power BI Desktop and an example of the Quick Insights feature in the Power BI service.

Getting ready

To prepare for this recipe, follow these steps:

1. Open a new file in Power BI Desktop
2. Click **Transform data** from the ribbon of the **Home** tab
3. In the Power Query Editor, create a new query called **Internet Sales** that imports the **FactInternetSales** table in the **AdventureWorksDW2019** database:

4. Click **Close & Apply** from the ribbon of the **Home** tab

```
    Source = Sql.Database("localhost\MSSQLSERVERDEV",
"AdventureWorksDW2019"),
    Navigation = Source{[Schema="dbo",Item="FactInternetSales"]}[Data],
    ExpandedDimSalesTerritory = Table.ExpandRecordColumn(
        Navigation, "DimSalesTerritory",
        {"SalesTerritoryCountry"}, {"SalesTerritoryCountry"})
in
    ExpandedDimSalesTerritory
```

5. In the **Visualizations** pane, click the ellipsis (**...**) and choose **Get more visuals**

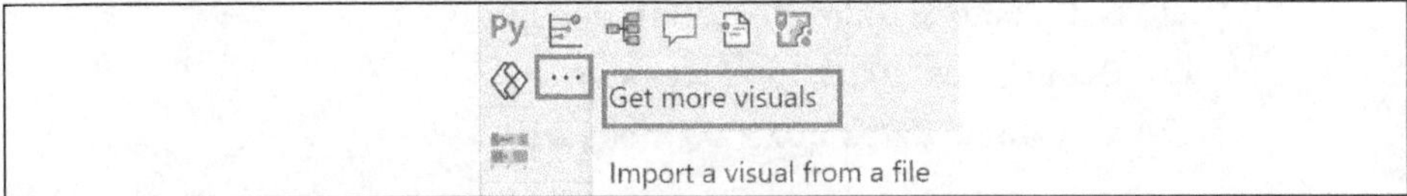

Figure 9.5: Import custom visuals from AppSource

6. Use **Search** to find the certified (blue star/checkmark icon) **Bullet Chart** visualization and click the **Add** button

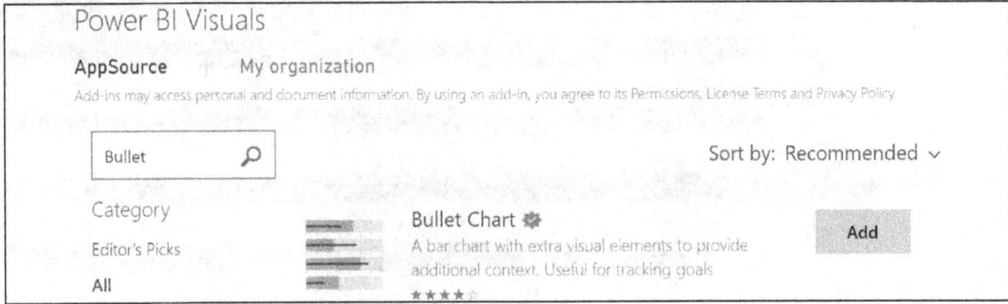

Figure 9.6: Adding a custom visual from Power BI Desktop

How to Enrich Content with Custom Visuals and Quick Insights

To implement this recipe, use the following steps:

1. Create the following measures:

```
Sales 2011 = SUMX(FILTER('Internet Sales',YEAR([OrderDate])=2011),[Sales
Amount])

Sales 2012 = SUMX(FILTER('Internet Sales',YEAR([OrderDate])=2012),[Sales
Amount])

Sales 2012 Improve = [Sales 2011] * .7

Sales 2012 Sat = [Sales 2011] * .8
```

```
Sales 2012 Good = [Sales 2011] * .9

Sales 2012 VG = [Sales 2011]
```

2. Select the Bullet Chart icon in the `Visualizations` pane to add it to the report canvas
3. Configure the visual as follows:
    - **Category: SalesTerritoryCountry column**
    - **Value: Sales 2012 measure**
    - **Needs Improvement: Sales 2012 Improve measure**
    - **Satisfactory: Sales 2012 Sat measure**
    - **Good: Sales 2012 Good measure**
    - **Very Good: Sales 2012 VG measure**

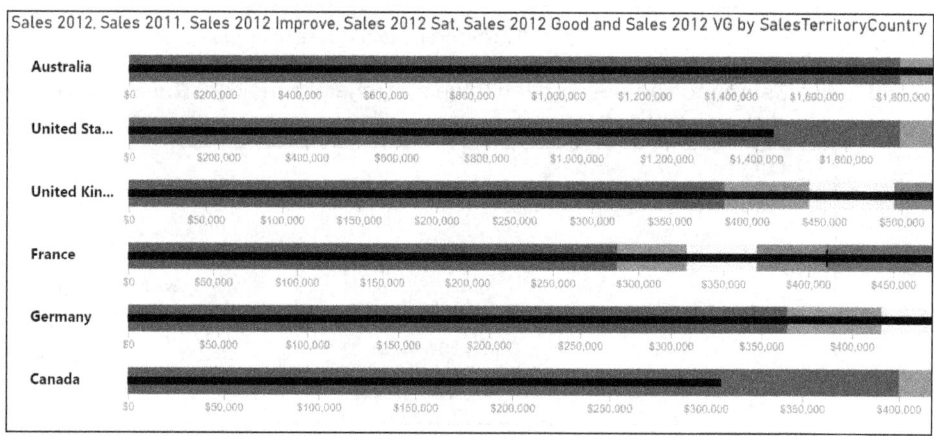

Figure 9.7: Bullet chart custom visual with data-driven ranges and threshold values

4. Publish the report to the Power BI service
5. Open the report in the Power BI service
6. Pin the bullet chart visualization to a new dashboard
7. Open the new dashboard
8. In the upper right of the pinned tile, click the ellipsis (**...**) and choose **View insights**
9. The insights engine will produce insights visuals related to the data in the dashboard tile

How it works

In this example, six DAX measures, reflecting different values relative to the target measure (**Sales 2011**), were used to drive the color thresholds and the minimum and maximum values of the bullets. Measures representing 70%, 80%, 90%, and 100% of the **Sales 2011** measure were used to drive the color categories in the bullet chart.

The bullet chart also supports manually entered target values and percentages of target values in the formatting pane. However, the data-driven approach with DAX measures is recommended, as this allows for the reuse of the calculations across other visuals, and makes it easy to adjust multiple reports when the target and threshold value logic changes.

There's more

The **Quick Insights** feature and analytics engine in the Power BI service is now available in Power BI Desktop. To see how this works, follow these steps:

1. Create a `Margin %` measure with the following code:

```
Margin % =
    VAR __Price = SUM('Internet Sales'[SalesAmount])
    VAR __Cost = SUM('Internet Sales'[TotalProductCost])
RETURN DIVIDE(__Price - __Cost,__Price,0)
```

2. Create a **Line chart** visualization with **Order Date** (hierarchy, not the column) as the **Axis** and the `Margin %` measure as the **Values**
3. Right-click the data point in the chart for **2013** and choose **Analyze** and then **Explain the decrease**

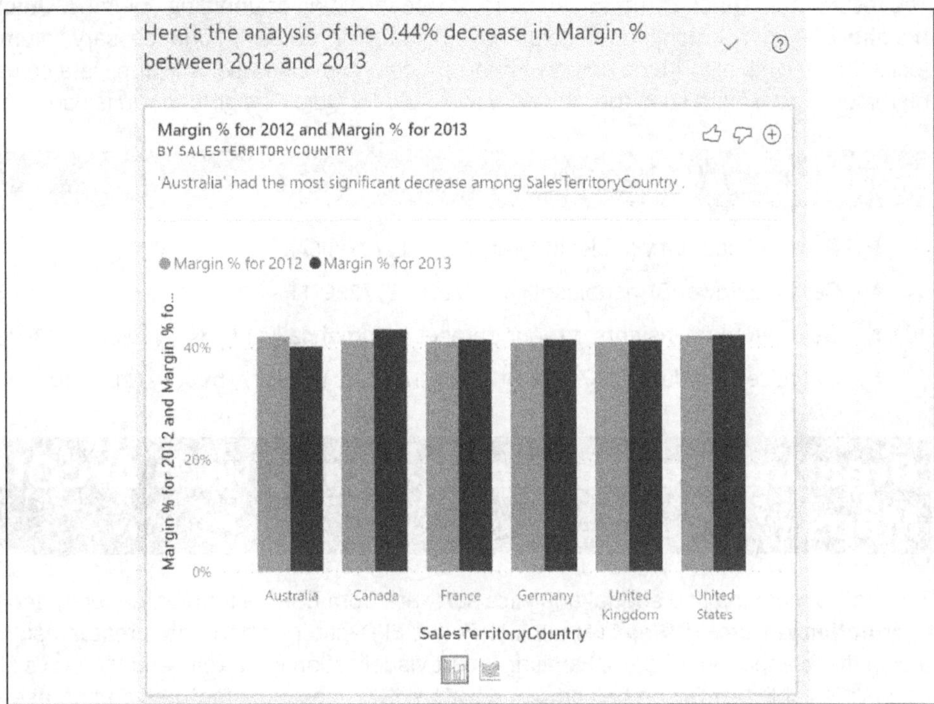

Figure 9.8: The Analyze feature in Power BI Desktop

The **Analyze** option appears when right-clicking a specific data point, enabling additional visualizations to be generated specific to the selected item, such as a date on a line chart or a dimension value on a bar chart. The generated visuals can then be added to the Power BI Desktop file and edited just like all other visuals. The **Analyze** option is the embodiment of the **Quick Insights** feature and analytics engine within Power BI Desktop.

Quick Insights can also be executed against an entire dataset in the Power BI service. To run quick insights against a dataset, click the ellipsis for the given dataset and select **Get quick insights**. The insights generated can be accessed from the same context menu via a **View Insights** option. Each insight contains a Power BI visual, the title of the insight (algorithm) applied, such as outliers and correlation, and a short description. Visuals from **View Insights** can also be pinned to new and existing dashboards.

Quick Insights applies sophisticated algorithms against datasets, including category outliers, correlation, change points in a time series, low variance, majority, seasonality in time series, and overall trends in time series. The insights engine is limited to a set duration of time to render its results.

Quick Insights visuals can be pinned to new and existing dashboards like other Power BI report and dashboard tiles. Additionally, Quick Insights can be executed against a visual that was previously generated by Quick Insights.

The results from **Quick Insights** can be improved by hiding or unhiding columns. **Quick Insights** does not search hidden columns, so hiding (or removing) unnecessary columns can focus the insights algorithms on only important columns. Likewise, any duplicate columns can be removed or hidden such that the time available for Quick Insights to run is used efficiently.

See also

- Power BI custom visuals: `https://bit.ly/3xY9GAk`
- Certified Power BI visuals: `https://bit.ly/2RETFPa`
- Generate data insights on your dataset automatically: `https://bit.ly/33qJErt`
- Optimize your data for Power BI Quick Insights: `https://bit.ly/3trWOPz`

Creating Geospatial Mapping with ArcGIS Maps

The ArcGIS mapping and spatial analytics software from ESRI, a market leader in **geographic information systems** (**GISes**), is built into Power BI Desktop to generate greater insights from the spatial component of data. Familiar report visualization field wells and the cross-filtering capabilities of Power BI can be combined with ArcGIS geospatial features and datasets, such as classification types, pins, and reference layers, to build custom, intelligent geographical visualizations into Power BI solutions.

In this recipe, a custom geographical column is created to include multiple geographical attributes (i.e., `Street Address`, `City`, and `State`) to support accurate geocoding by the ArcGIS service. The ArcGIS visualization in Power BI Desktop is then used to plot customer addresses into a **Cluster** theme map visualization with supporting **Pins** and **Infographics**.

Getting ready

To prepare for this recipe, follow these steps:

1. In the Power BI service, click on **Settings** (the gear icon) in the top right and enable ArcGIS maps on the **General** tab. This requires administrative access to the Power BI service.

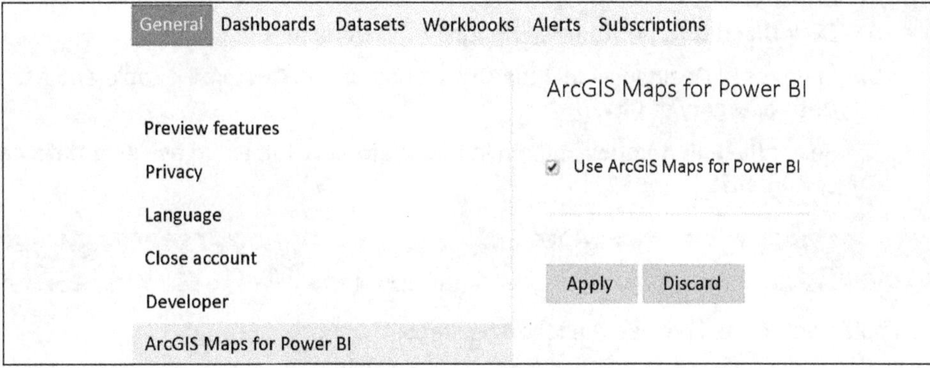

Figure 9.9: General settings dialog in Power BI service

2. Open a new file in Power BI Desktop.
3. Click **Transform data** from the ribbon of the **Home** tab.
4. In the Power Query Editor, create a new query called **Customers** using the following code (editing the **Source** line):

```
let
    Source = Sql.Database("localhost\MSSQLSERVERDEV",
"AdventureWorksDW2019"),
    dbo_DimCustomer = Source{[Schema="dbo",Item="DimCustomer"]}[Data],
    ExpandGeography = Table.ExpandRecordColumn(dbo_DimCustomer,
"DimGeography",
        {"City", "StateProvinceCode", "EnglishCountryRegionName",
"PostalCode",
            "DimSalesTerritory"},
        {"City", "StateProvinceCode", "EnglishCountryRegionName",
"PostalCode",
            "DimSalesTerritory"}),
    ExpandSalesTerritory = Table.ExpandRecordColumn(ExpandGeography,
        "DimSalesTerritory", {"SalesTerritoryRegion"},
```

```
{"SalesTerritoryRegion"}),
    DupCity = Table.DuplicateColumn(ExpandSalesTerritory, "City",
"City1"),
    DupZip = Table.DuplicateColumn(DupCity, "PostalCode", "Zip"),
    Address = Table.CombineColumns(DupZip,
        {"AddressLine1", "City1", "StateProvinceCode"},
        Combiner.CombineTextByDelimiter(", ", QuoteStyle.
None),"Address"),
    FullAddress = Table.CombineColumns(Address,{"Address", "Zip"},
        Combiner.CombineTextByDelimiter(" ", QuoteStyle.None),"Full
Address")
in
    FullAddress
```

5. Click **Close & Apply** from the ribbon of the **Home** tab.
6. In Power BI Desktop, select the **City** column in the **Customers** table and assign a **Data category** of **City**.
7. Select the **Full Address** column in the **Customers** table and assign a **Data category** of **Address**.

How to Create Geospatial Mapping with ArcGIS Maps

To implement this recipe, use the following steps:

1. Apply a page-level filter using the **SalesTerritoryRegion** column in the **Customers** table, and select **Southwest** only
2. In the **Visualizations** pane, select the **ArgGIS Maps for Power BI** visualization and then expand the visualization's size to the entire page
3. From the **Customers** table, add the **Full Address** column for **Location**, the **CustomerKey** column for **Size**, and the **YearlyIncome** column for **Color**
4. In the **Format** pane, expand **Location type** and choose **United States**

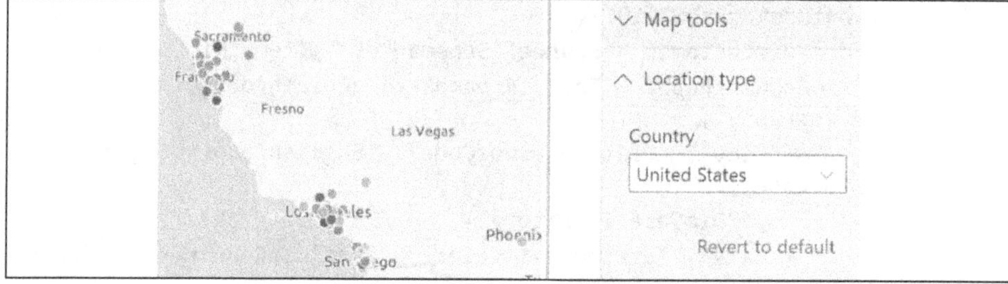

Figure 9.10: Setting the ArcGIS Location type

5. In the upper left of the ArcGIS map visualization, select **Expand map tools**

6. Click the **Layer list** icon and then the vertical ellipsis next to **Full Address** and choose **Symbology**

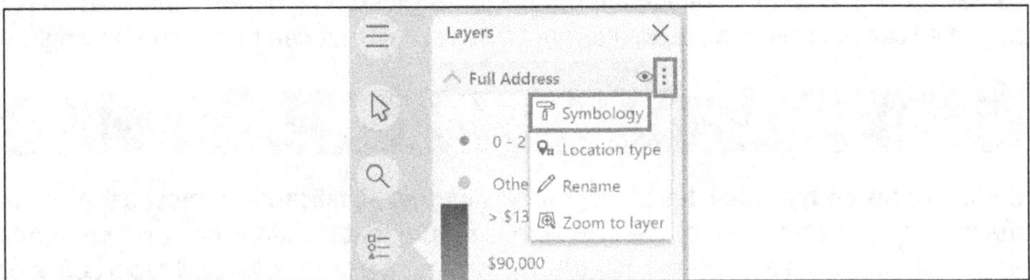

Figure 9.11: Change the Symbology of the map layer

7. Scroll down and choose **Clustering**
8. In **Map tools**, click **Analysis tools** (the wrench icon) and then **Reference layer**
9. Click **Add** under **2020 USA Per Capita Income**
10. Close the **Reference layer** dialog, click **Analysis tools** again, and this time choose **Infographics**
11. Add infographics for **Average household** size and **Median Disposable Income by Age**
12. In **Map tools**, click on the **Search** icon (the magnifying glass), type `sherman`, and choose **Sherman Oaks, CA, USA** to add a pin on the map
13. In **Map tools**, click **Analysis tools** (the wrench icon) and choose **Drive time**
14. Select the pin, enter `10` for the **Distance** for the radius, and select **OK**

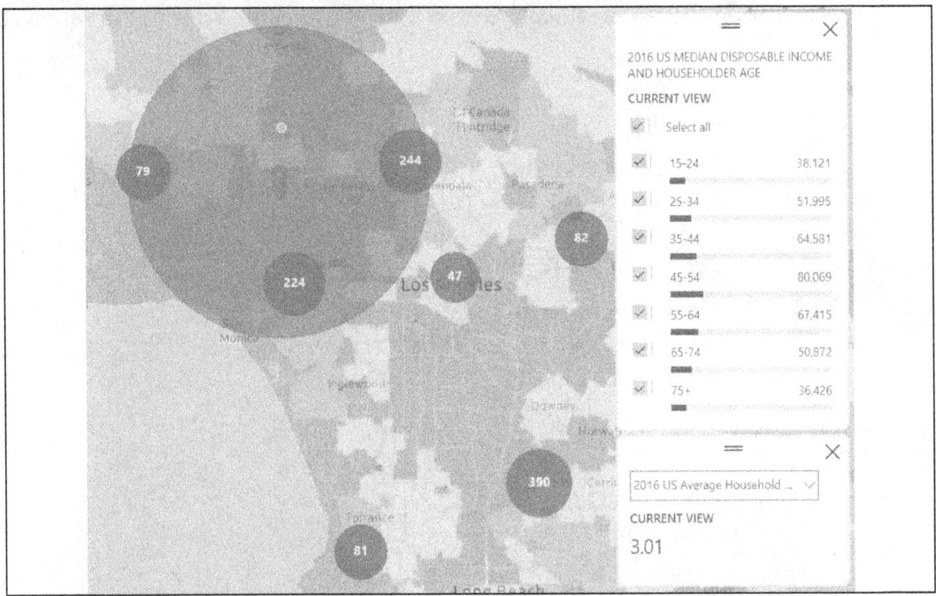

Figure 9.12: Formatted cluster theme map with a pin, analytic layer, drive time radius, and two infographics

The visual is fully interactive; the clusters and the infographic numbers all update dynamically as the zoom of the visual is changed and as different geographic areas are navigated to, such as San Francisco, CA. A common alternative to the clustering theme is the heat map, and the dark-gray canvas base map is an alternative base map that can help visualize bright colors.

How it works

Setting **Location type** provides a geographic hint that significantly improves the accuracy of the plotted points returned by the ESRI service. Note that locations can also be represented as boundaries, such as states or postal codes. Almost all the advanced report development features provided by ArcGIS are exposed in the Power BI visualization.

If **latitude** and **longitude** columns are already available for the dimension to be mapped, then these columns should be used in the ArcGIS visual instead of the **Location** field well. Providing latitude and longitude source data significantly improves performance, as it eliminates the need for ESRI to compute these values.

There's more

A powerful analytical capability of ArcGIS for Power BI is its ability to set the classification algorithm. To see how this works, do the following:

1. Make a duplicate of **Page 1** by right-clicking **Page 1** and choosing **Duplicate page**
2. In **Map tools**, change the **Symbology** of **Full Address** to **Color**
3. Scroll down to the **Classification type** area and experiment with the various options

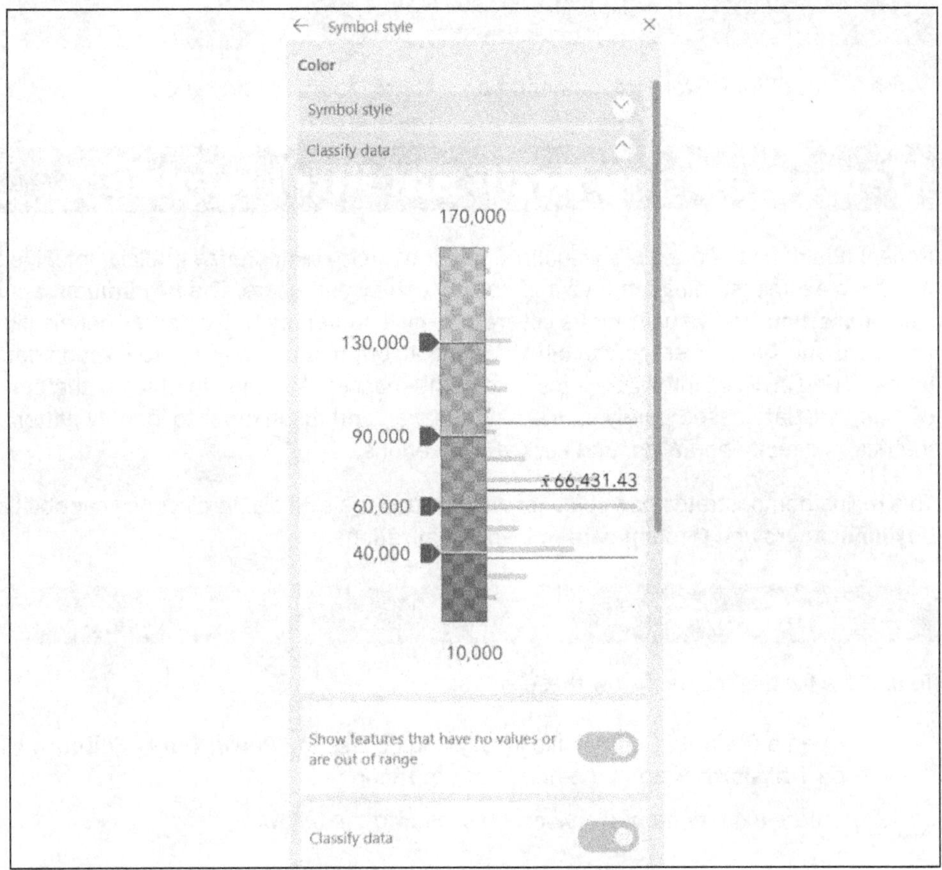

Figure 9.13: ArcGIS classification options

See also

- ArcGIS for Power BI documentation: `https://bit.ly/3vtMckC`

Democratizing Artificial Intelligence

Recent additions to Power BI's visualization library help democratize artificial intelligence by making machine learning intuitive and easy to use by end users. The **Key influencers** and **Decomposition tree** visualizations covered in this chapter, as well as other visuals like **Smart narrative** and **Q&A**, leverage machine learning algorithms to analyze visualization data in real time to bring artificial intelligence insights to the masses. Machine learning is the process of analyzing data based purely on mathematical algorithms in order to identify patterns, key metrics, clusters, anomalies, and key categorizations.

This recipe demonstrates how to configure and use the artificial intelligence capabilities of the **Key influencers** and **Decomposition tree** visualizations.

Getting ready

To prepare for this recipe, follow these steps:

1. Open a Power BI Desktop file locally and access the **Power Query Editor** by clicking on **Transform Data** in the ribbon of the **Home** tab
2. Create a query named `AdWorksDW` similar to the following:

```
let
    Source = Sql.Database("localhost\MSSQLSERVERDEV",
"AdventureWorksDW2019")
in
    Source
```

3. Disable load on the `AdWorksDW` query and place it into a **Data Sources** query group
4. Right-click the `AdWorksDW` query and choose **Reference**
5. Rename the query **Internet Sales** and choose the **FactInternetSales** table
6. Repeat *steps 4* and *5*, creating a **Dates** query that points to the **DimDates** table, and a **Sales Territories** query that points to the **DimSalesTerritory** table
7. Create a **Customers** query using the following code:

```
let
    Source = AdWorksDW,
    dbo_DimCustomer = Source{[Schema="dbo",Item="DimCustomer"]}[Data],
    ExpandGeography = Table.ExpandRecordColumn(dbo_DimCustomer,
"DimGeography",
```

```
            {"City", "StateProvinceCode", "EnglishCountryRegionName",
"PostalCode",
                "DimSalesTerritory"},
            {"City", "StateProvinceCode", "EnglishCountryRegionName",
"PostalCode",
                "DimSalesTerritory"}),
        ExpandSalesTerritory = Table.ExpandRecordColumn(ExpandGeography,
            "DimSalesTerritory", {"SalesTerritoryRegion"},
{"SalesTerritoryRegion"}),
        DupCity = Table.DuplicateColumn(ExpandSalesTerritory, "City",
"City1"),
        DupZip = Table.DuplicateColumn(DupCity, "PostalCode", "Zip"),
        Address = Table.CombineColumns(DupZip,
            {"AddressLine1", "City1", "StateProvinceCode"},
            Combiner.CombineTextByDelimiter(", ", QuoteStyle.
None),"Address"),
        FullAddress = Table.CombineColumns(Address,{"Address", "Zip"},
            Combiner.CombineTextByDelimiter(" ", QuoteStyle.None),"Full
Address")
in
        FullAddress
```

8. Create a **Products** query using the following code:

```
let
    Source = AdWorksDW,
    Navigation = Source{[Schema="dbo",Item="DimProduct"]}[Data],
    Subcategory =
        Table.ExpandRecordColumn(
            Navigation, "DimProductSubcategory",
            {"EnglishProductSubcategoryName", "DimProductCategory"},
            {"Product Subcategory", "DimProductCategory"}
        ),
    Category =
        Table.ExpandRecordColumn(
            Subcategory, "DimProductCategory",
            {"EnglishProductCategoryName"}, {"Product Category"}
        )
in
    Category
```

9. Move the **Internet Sales** query to a **Facts** query group and the **Sales Territories**, **Dates**, **Customers**, and **Products** queries to a **Dimensions** query group
10. Choose **Close & Apply** from the ribbon of the **Home** tab

11. Switch to the **Model** view and create a relationship between the **SalesTerritoryKey** columns in the **Internet Sales** and **Sales Territories** tables
12. Create a relationship between the **ProductKey** columns in the **Internet Sales** and **Products** tables
13. Create a relationship between the **DateKey** column in the **Dates** table and the **OrderDateKey** column in the **Internet Sales** table
14. Create a relationship between the **CustomerKey** columns in the **Internet Sales** and **Customers** tables
15. Save your work

How to Democratize Artificial Intelligence

To implement this recipe, use the following steps:

1. In the **Report** view, create a **Key influencers** visualization, placing the **SalesAmount** column from the **Internet Sales** table in the **Analyze** field well, and the following columns in the **Explain by** field well:
    - The **SalesTerritoryCountry** column from the **Sales Territories** table
    - The **SalesTerritoryGroup** column from the **Sales Territories** table
    - The **SalesTerritoryRegion** column from the **Sales Territories** table
    - The **Product Category** column from the **Products** table
    - The **Product Subcategory** column from the **Products** table
    - The **City** column from the **Customers** table

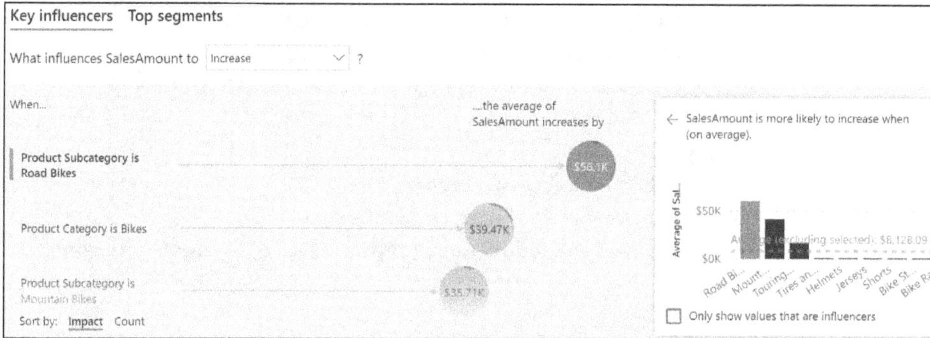

Figure 9.14: Key influencers visualization

2. Click on the different **When** items to view visuals related to the influencers

3. Click on the **Top segments** tab to view the different segments identified
4. Click on a segment of interest to view additional information and visualizations

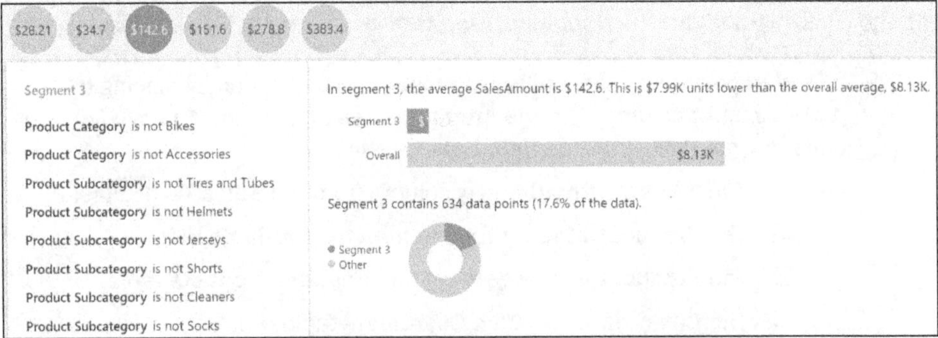

Figure 9.15: Segment detail in the Key influencers visualization

How it works

The **Key influencers** visual uses machine learning algorithms to analyze the data added to the visual and extract insights based upon these algorithms. Different visuals and insights are created depending on whether the metric has categorical or continuous key influencers. Using an unsummarized numeric field in the **Analyze** field well allows **Analysis** in the **Format** pane to be changed to either **Categorical** or **Continuous**. Using a measure or an aggregated column forces a **Continuous** analysis. Measures can be used as either the metric to be analyzed or as a key influencer (**Explain by**).

Counts can be activated in the **Analysis** section of the **Format** pane. Counts are useful for determining whether key influencers have a large impact but only represent a small portion of the total data. Enabling counts creates a ring around the key influencer circles that represents the percentage of data rows in which the key influencer appears. A ring around the entire circle means that 100% of the data contains the key influencer.

The **Top segments** tab analyzes the data in order to find clusters of similar data points. Again, machine learning clustering algorithms are used in order to find and extract these segments from the underlying data used in the visualization.

The **Key influencers** visualization has certain limitations, primarily related to the data sources supported and where the visual can be displayed. For example, the Key influencers visual does not support DirectQuery or live connections to Azure Analysis Services or SQL Server Analysis Services. In addition, the Key influencers visualization is not supported when using **Publish to web** or embedding in SharePoint Online.

There's more

Another recently added, advanced visualization is the **Decomposition tree**. To understand how to configure and use the **Decomposition tree** visualization, follow these steps:

1. In the **Report** view, create a **Key influencers** visualization by placing the **SalesAmount** column from the **Internet Sales** table in the **Analyze** field well, and the following columns in the **Explain by** field well:
    - The **SalesTerritoryCountry** column from the **Sales Territories** table
    - The **Product Category** column from the **Products** table
    - The **Product Subcategory** column from the **Products** table
    - The **City** column from the **Customers** table
    - The **CalendarYear** column from the **Dates** table
2. Click the **+** icon at the end of the **SalesAmount** bar and choose **High value**

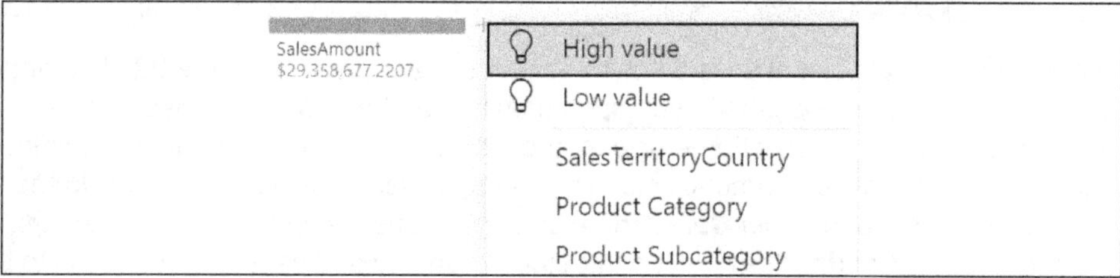

Figure 9.16: Decomposition tree expansion

3. Repeat this procedure until the tree is fully expanded, as shown in *Figure 9.17*

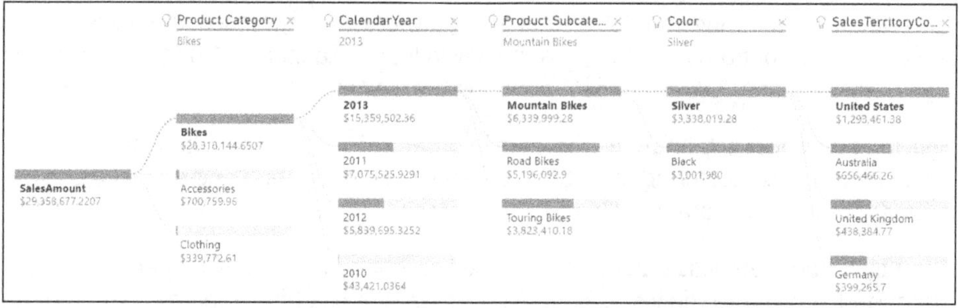

Figure 9.17: Fully expanded Decomposition tree visualization

Selecting **High value** or **Low value** when expanding the decomposition tree leverages artificial intelligence machine learning algorithms to expand the tree, to return either the highest or lowest values of the measure being analyzed, respectively. The **Decomposition tree** visualization is a powerful and flexible tool for end users to explore and analyze their data, as users can explore the **Explain by** categories in any order, or allow the machine learning algorithms to guide their analysis.

See also

- Key influencers visualizations tutorial: `https://bit.ly/3h414Cn`
- Decomposition tree: `https://bit.ly/2PC9ZiR`

Building Animation and Storytelling

Business teams and analysts are commonly responsible for sharing or "walking through" business results, trends, and the findings from their analyses with other stakeholders, such as senior management. To support the message delivery process most effectively, Power BI provides built-in animation capabilities for the standard scatter chart and ArcGIS map visualization types. Additionally, core and custom visuals, such as the pulse chart, further aid the storytelling process by embedding user-defined annotations into the visual and providing full playback control over the animation.

> *"We're bringing storytelling into Power BI. We're making Power BI into the PowerPoint for data."*
>
> *– Amir Netz, Microsoft Technical Fellow*

This recipe includes examples for preparing the standard **Scatter chart** visualization for animation, leveraging the date animation feature of the **ArcGIS Maps for Power BI** visual. Details on the **Bookmarks** pane, as well as the **Smart narrative** and other storytelling custom visuals, are also included.

Getting ready

To prepare for this recipe, follow these steps:

1. Open a Power BI Desktop file locally and access the **Power Query Editor** by clicking on **Transform Data** in the ribbon of the **Home** tab
2. Create a query named `AdWorksDW` similar to the following:

```
let
    Source = Sql.Database("localhost\MSSQLSERVERDEV",
"AdventureWorksDW2019")
in
    Source
```

3. Disable load on the `AdWorksDW` query and place this query into a **Data Sources** query group
4. Right-click the `AdWorksDW` query and choose **Reference**

5. Rename the query **Internet Sales** and choose the **FactInternetSales** table
6. Repeat *steps 4* and *5*, creating a **Dates** query that points to the **DimDates** table, and a **Sales Territories** query that points to the **DimSalesTerritory** table
7. Create a **Customers** query using the following code:

```
let
    Source = AdWorksDW,
    dbo_DimCustomer = Source{[Schema="dbo",Item="DimCustomer"]}[Data],
    ExpandGeography = Table.ExpandRecordColumn(dbo_DimCustomer,
"DimGeography",
        {"City", "StateProvinceCode", "EnglishCountryRegionName",
"PostalCode",
            "DimSalesTerritory"},
        {"City", "StateProvinceCode", "EnglishCountryRegionName",
"PostalCode",
            "DimSalesTerritory"}),
    ExpandSalesTerritory = Table.ExpandRecordColumn(ExpandGeography,
        "DimSalesTerritory", {"SalesTerritoryRegion"},
{"SalesTerritoryRegion"}),
    DupCity = Table.DuplicateColumn(ExpandSalesTerritory, "City",
"City1"),
    DupZip = Table.DuplicateColumn(DupCity, "PostalCode", "Zip"),
    Address = Table.CombineColumns(DupZip,
        {"AddressLine1", "City1", "StateProvinceCode"},
        Combiner.CombineTextByDelimiter(", ", QuoteStyle.
None),"Address"),
    FullAddress = Table.CombineColumns(Address,{"Address", "Zip"},
        Combiner.CombineTextByDelimiter(" ", QuoteStyle.None),"Full
Address")
in
    FullAddress
```

8. Create a **Products** query using the following code:

```
let
    Source = AdWorksDW,
    Navigation = Source{[Schema="dbo",Item="DimProduct"]}[Data],
    Subcategory =
        Table.ExpandRecordColumn(
            Navigation, "DimProductSubcategory",
            {"EnglishProductSubcategoryName", "DimProductCategory"},
            {"Product Subcategory", "DimProductCategory"}
        ),
    Category =
        Table.ExpandRecordColumn(
            Subcategory, "DimProductCategory",
```

```
            {"EnglishProductCategoryName"}, {"Product Category"}
        )
in
    Category
```

9. Move the **Internet Sales** query to a **Facts** query group, and the **Sales Territories**, **Dates**, **Customers**, and **Products** queries to a **Dimensions** query group
10. Select **Close & Apply** from the ribbon of the **Home** tab
11. In Power BI Desktop, select the **City** column in the **Customers** table and assign a **Data category** of **City**
12. Select the **Full Address** column in the **Customers** table and assign a **Data category** of **Address**
13. Switch to the **Model** view and create a relationship between the **SalesTerritoryKey** columns in the **Internet Sales** and **Sales Territories** tables
14. Create a relationship between the **ProductKey** columns in the **Internet Sales** and **Products** tables
15. Create a relationship between the **DateKey** column in the **Dates** table and the **OrderDateKey** column in the **Internet Sales** table
16. Create a relationship between the **CustomerKey** columns in the **Internet Sales** and **Customers** tables
17. Save your work

How to Build Animation and Storytelling

To implement this recipe, use the following steps:

1. In the **Report** view, apply a report- or page-level filter for the **SalesTerritoryGroup** column in the **SalesTerritories** table to the value **Europe**
2. Create a **Scatter** chart visualization using the **SalesTerritoryCountry** column from the **SalesTerritories** table for **Details**, the **CustomerKey** column (count) from the **Internet Sales** table for the **X Axis**, and the **SalesAmount** (sum) for the **Y Axis**
3. In the **Format** pane, expand the **Shapes** card, set the **Size** to **100**, and also toggle **Fill point**, **Category labels**, and **Color by category** to **On**
4. Create two new columns in the **Dates** table using the following formulas:

   ```
   YearMonth = [CalendarYear] & "-" & LEFT([EnglishMonthName],3)
   YearMonthSort = [CalendarYear]*100 + [MonthNumberOfYear]
   ```

5. Set **Sort by column** for the **YearMonth** column to the **YearMonthSort** column

6. Drag the **YearMonth** column into the **Play Axis** field well of the scatter chart visualization
7. Click on one or more of the circles to display their paths and test the animation capabilities by clicking on the play button to the left of the time axis

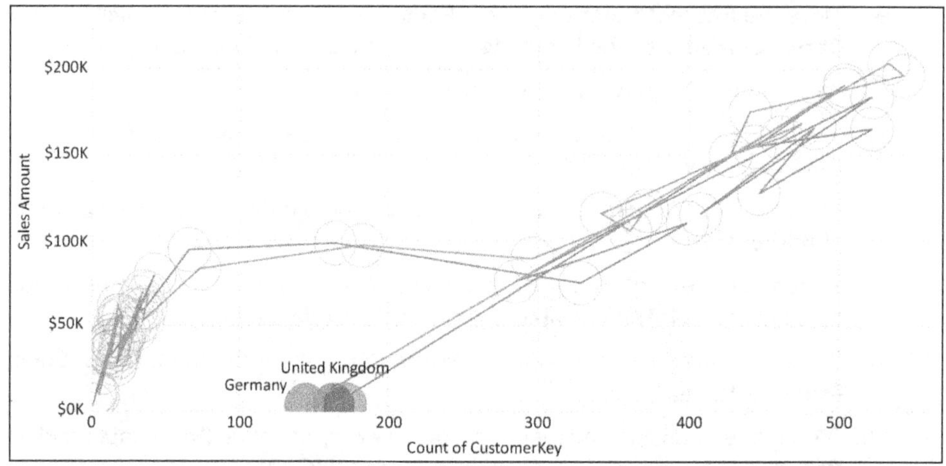

Figure 9.18: Scatter chart animation and tracing

8. Add a new page and add an ArcGIS map visualization to the page
9. Apply a page-level filter using the **SalesTerritoryRegion** column in the **Customers** table and select only **Southwest**
10. From the **Customers** table, add the **Full Address** column for **Location**, the **CustomerKey** column for **Size**, and the **YearlyIncome** column for **Color**
11. In the **Format** pane, expand **Location type** and choose **United States**
12. In the upper left of the ArcGIS map visualization, select **Expand map tools**
13. Click the **Layer list** icon and then the vertical ellipsis next to **Full Address** and choose **Symbology**
14. Scroll down and choose **Heat map**

15. Add the **FullDateAlternateKey** column from the **Dates** table to the **Time** field well

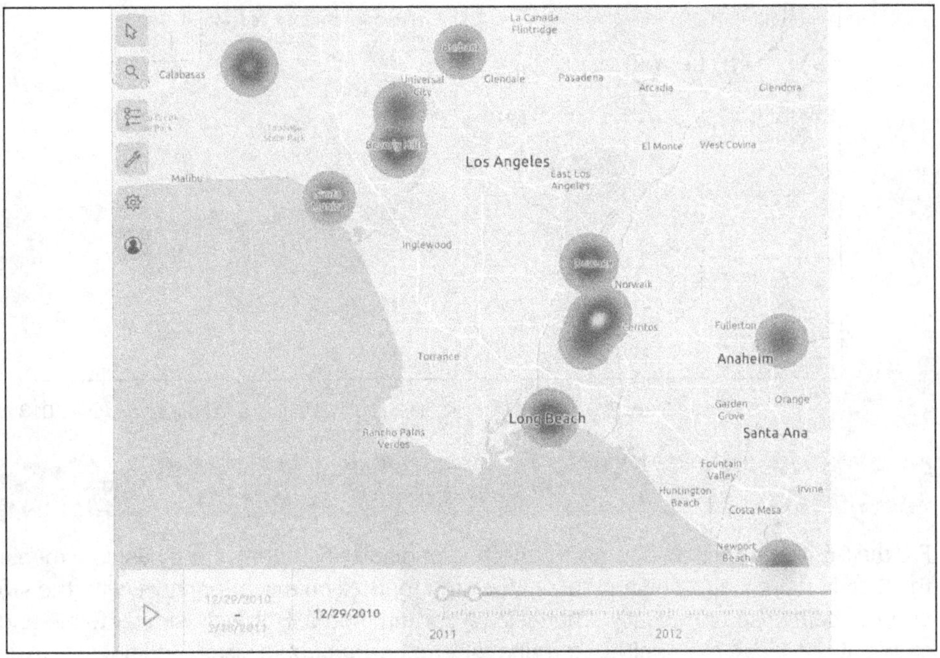

Figure 9.19: ArcGIS map for the Power BI visual using the heat map theme and the timeline

16. Add a new page and use the **Filters** pane to add a page filter using the **CalendarYears** column from the **Dates** table for the years **2011**, **2012**, and **2013**
17. In the **Visualizations** pane, click the ellipsis (...) and choose **Get more visuals**
18. Search for, find, and add the **Play Axis (Dynamic Slicer)** visualization
19. Create a **Clustered** column chart visualization with the **YearMonth** column from the **Dates** table as the **Axis**, and the **SalesAmount** column (sum) as the **Values**
20. Create a **Clustered** bar chart visualization with the **SalesTerritoryCountry** column from the **Sales Territories** table as the **Axis**, and the **SalesAmount** column (sum) as the **Values**
21. Add the **Play Axis** visualization and use the **YearMonth** column from the **Dates** table as the **Field**

22. Click the play button on the **Play Axis** visualization

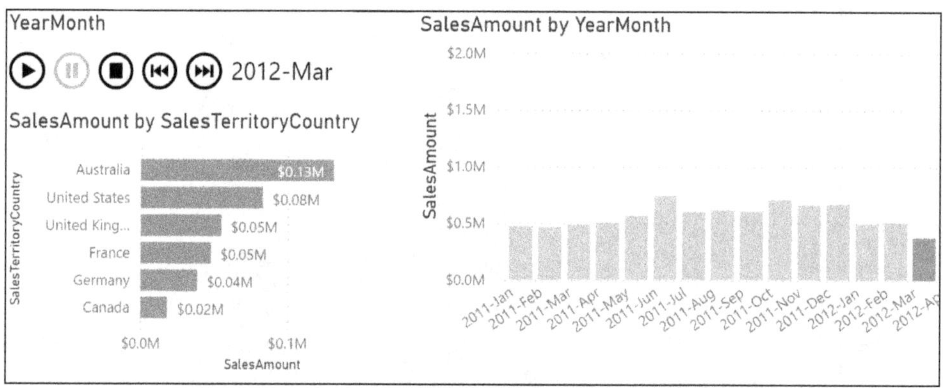

Figure 9.20: Play Axis custom visual filtering two charts and paused on June 2013

How it works

For the **Scatter chart**, an alternative method of displaying bubbles is by using a measure for the **Size** field well, applying a measure/column for **Size** on a scatter chart, with the size of the bubbles being used to visually emphasize a certain metric. However, similar to pie and donut charts, it is difficult to visually determine differences in bubble sizes. Additionally, even a small number of dimension items, such as product categories, can lead to a cluttered visualization when presented as a bubble chart.

In the **Scatter chart** example, multiple items can be selected or unselected by holding down the *Ctrl* key and clicking a bubble from a separate series. When selected, the scatter chart highlights the path of the given item (or items) up to the currently selected or filtered point on the **Play Axis**. Playing and pausing the **Play Axis** and selecting the dimension(s) of the scatter chart makes it easy for presenters to address a significant outlier or a point in time at which a relevant trend began.

Microsoft has also created the **Enhanced Scatter** custom visual, which supports a background image URL, such as a business location or diagram, and images for the individually plotted categories. However, this visual does not include a **Play Axis** or any visual animation like the standard scatter chart used in this recipe. The **Enhanced Scatter** visualization is available in AppSource.

For the ArcGIS visualization, the column used for the **Time** field well must be of the date or the date/time data type, such as an individual calendar date or a week ending date. Text and numeric data type columns, such as calendar year, are not supported. The timeline at the bottom of the visual can be used to play through each individual date value, or a custom time interval can be set by modifying the start and end points of the timeline.

For instance, a date interval representing four weeks could be set at the beginning of the timeline, and clicking the play icon would sequentially display each interval. The forward and backward icons can be used to quickly navigate to different time periods or intervals.

Finally, the Play Axis visualization adds animation capabilities to visualizations that have no native animation features. The Play Axis visualization works by taking advantage of the native cross-filtering and cross-highlighting capabilities of Power BI. The Play Axis visualization is best used in combination with column charts, bar charts, and other charts that allow for the **Highlight** visual interaction.

There's more

Bookmarks enable the saving of specific report states, including filter context and the visibility of specific items on the report canvas. This can be particularly useful with animated visuals in order to skip to the most interesting parts of the animation. The **Bookmarks** pane can be accessed in the ribbon of the **View** tab while in the **Report** view. Use the **Add** button to create bookmarks. Use the **View** button to easily page through bookmarks like a slideshow.

Figure 9.21: Bookmarks pane in Power BI Desktop

The **Selection** pane, also available in the ribbon of the **View** tab, can be used with bookmarks to set the visibility of visuals for a bookmark. Playing through bookmarks in Power BI reports resembles Microsoft PowerPoint presentations (in presentation mode) that leverage animation. Additionally, bookmarks can be linked with other objects in the report, such as images, making it possible to create an intuitive navigation experience across report pages.

Microsoft is also adding narrative and storytelling visuals to Power BI. The **Smart narrative** visual has been added to Power BI Desktop. To see how Smart narrative works, follow these steps:

1. Create a new page and add a **Clustered** column chart visualization to the page using the **CalendarYear** column from the **Dates** table as the **Axis**, and the **SalesAmount** column from the **Internet Sales** table as the **Values**
2. Copy and paste this visual

3. With the copy of the visual selected, click the **Smart narrative** visual in the **Visualizations** tab

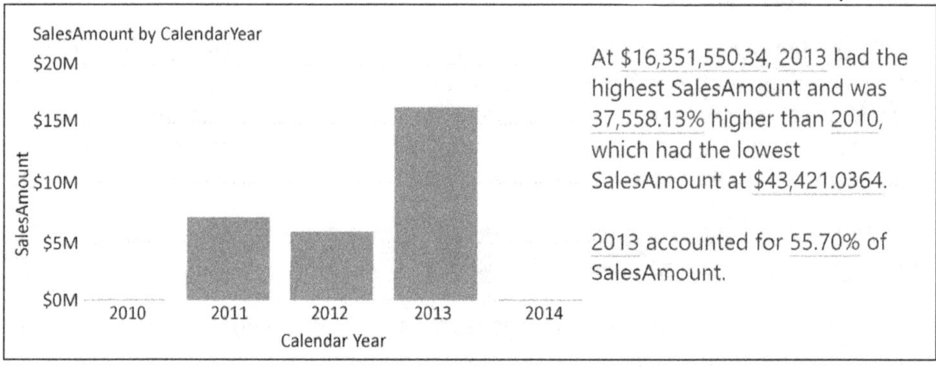

Figure 9.22: The same data presented as both a clustered column chart and Smart narrative visual

The Smart narrative visualization analyzes the data and creates a natural language narrative of the data presented in the visualization. Additional custom visuals focused on integrating explanatory text or annotations with data from the data model include the Add Intelligent Narratives for BI visual, the Enlighten Data Story visual, and Timeline Storyteller.

See also

- Scatter, bubble, and dot plot charts in Power BI: `https://bit.ly/3u38toZ`
- Use bookmarks in Power BI Desktop to share insights and build stories: `https://bit.ly/2QK3ACS`
- Smart narratives tutorial: `https://bit.ly/3e57xuM`

Embedding Statistical Analyses

Statistical analysis beyond basic aggregations is typically implemented outside of business intelligence semantic models by data scientists and data science applications. When possible, however, it is much more efficient to leverage existing data models, Power BI skills, and the features used for other Power BI reports and dashboards—such as the **Analytics** pane described earlier in this chapter.

In this recipe, the data points supporting a linear regression model are created from an existing Power BI data model. This model is then analyzed and described via DAX measures, with values such as slope, Y-intercept, and the Z-score for residuals. Finally, a rich report page is constructed to visualize the strength and accuracy of the regression model and to detect outliers.

Getting ready

To prepare for this recipe, follow these steps:

1. Open a Power BI Desktop file locally and access the **Power Query Editor** by clicking on **Transform Data** in the ribbon of the **Home** tab
2. Create a query named **AdWorksDW** similar to the following:

```
let
    Source = Sql.Database("localhost\MSSQLSERVERDEV",
"AdventureWorksDW2019")
in
    Source
```

3. Disable load on the **AdWorksDW** query and place it into a **Data Sources** query group
4. Right-click the **AdWorksDW** query and choose **Reference**
5. Rename the query **Internet Sales** and choose the **FactInternetSales** table
6. Repeat *steps 4* and *5*, creating a **Dates** query that points to the **DimDates** table
7. Move the **Internet Sales** query to a **Facts** query group, and the **Dates** query to a **Dimensions** query group
8. Choose **Close & Apply** from the ribbon of the **Home** tab
9. Switch to the **Model** view and create a relationship between the **DateKey** column in the **Dates** table and the **OrderDateKey** column in the **Internet Sales** table
10. Create two new columns in the **Dates** table using the following formulas:

```
YearMonth = [CalendarYear] & "-" & LEFT([EnglishMonthName],3)
YearMonthSort = [CalendarYear]*100 + [MonthNumberOfYear]
```

11. Set the **Sort by column** for the **YearMonth** column to the **YearMonthSort** column
12. Save your work

How to Embed Statistical Analyses

To implement this recipe, use the following steps:

1. In the **Report** view, click **New table** from the ribbon of the **Modeling** tab and use the following code:

```
MktSalesRegression =
    FILTER(
        SUMMARIZECOLUMNS(
```

```
                'Dates'[YearMonth],
                'Dates'[YearMonthSort],
                CALCULATETABLE('Dates',
                    'Dates'[FullDateAlternateKey] >= DATE(2011,1,1) &&
                    'Dates'[FullDateAlternateKey] <= DATE(2013,12,31)),
                "Marketing Amount",
                        VAR __MonthNum = MAX('Dates'[MonthNumberOfYear])
                        VAR __Value = SUM('Internet Sales'[SalesAmount])
                    RETURN SWITCH(__MonthNum,
                        1,__Value*.8,
                        2,__Value*.8,
                        3,__Value*.8,
                        4,__Value*.8,
                        5,__Value*.8,
                        6,__Value*1,
                        7,__Value*.8,
                        8,__Value*.8,
                        9,__Value*.6,
                        10,__Value*.8,
                        11,__Value*.8,
                        12,__Value*.8),
                "Internet Sales", SUM('Internet Sales'[SalesAmount])
            ),
            NOT(ISBLANK([Internet Sales]) || ISBLANK([Marketing Amount]))
        )
```

2. Create measures for the correlation coefficient, slope, y-intercept, and coefficient of determination (R squared):

```
MktSalesCorrelNum = SUMX(MktSalesRegression,
    (   (MktSalesRegression[Marketing Amount] -
            AVERAGE(MktSalesRegression[Marketing Amount]) ) *
        ( MktSalesRegression[Internet Sales] -
            AVERAGE(MktSalesRegression[Internet Sales]) )
    ) )

MktSalesCorrelDenomX = SUMX(MktSalesRegression,
    (   MktSalesRegression[Marketing Amount] -
        AVERAGE(MktSalesRegression[Marketing Amount]) )^2 )

MktSalesCorrelDenomY = SUMX(MktSalesRegression,
    (   MktSalesRegression[Internet Sales] -
        AVERAGE(MktSalesRegression[Internet Sales]) )^2 )

Mkt-Sales Correl = DIVIDE([MktSalesCorrelNum],
    SQRT([MktSalesCorrelDenomX]*[MktSalesCorrelDenomY]) )
```

```
Mkt-Sales R Squared = [Mkt-Sales Correl]^2

MktSalesSlope = DIVIDE([MktSalesCorrelNum],[MktSalesCorrelDenomX])

MktSales Intercept = AVERAGE(MktSalesRegression[Internet Sales]) -
    ( [MktSalesSlope]*AVERAGE(MktSalesRegression[Marketing Amount]) )
```

3. Click **New table** from the ribbon of the **Modeling** tab and use the following code:

```
Residuals =
    VAR Intercept = [MktSales Intercept]
    VAR Slope = [MktSalesSlope]
RETURN
    ADDCOLUMNS(MktSalesRegression,"Y Intercept",Intercept,"Slope",Slope,
    "Predicted Internet Sales", ([Marketing Amount]*Slope) + Intercept,
    "Residual",[Internet Sales] - (([Marketing Amount]*Slope) +
Intercept))
```

4. Create the following measures:

```
Residuals Amount = SUM(Residuals[Residual])

Residuals Average = CALCULATE(AVERAGE(Residuals[Residual]),ALL(Residua
ls))

Residuals Sample Std Dev = CALCULATE(STDEV.S(Residuals[Residual]),ALL(Re
siduals))

Residuals Z Score = DIVIDE([Residuals Amount] - [Residuals
Average],[Residuals Sample Std Dev])

Regression Line Message = "Regression Line: Y= " &
FORMAT([MktSalesSlope],"#,###") & "X" & "+" & FORMAT([MktSales
Intercept],"#,###")

Last Month Internet Sales =
    VAR __LastMonth = MAX('Residuals'[YearMonthSort])
RETURN
    LOOKUPVALUE('Residuals'[Internet Sales],[YearMonthSort],__LastMonth)

Last Month Predicted Internet Sales =
    VAR __LastMonth = MAX('Residuals'[YearMonthSort])
RETURN
    LOOKUPVALUE('Residuals'[Predicted Internet Sales],[YearMonthSort],__
LastMonth)
```

5. From the **Report** view, create card visuals to display the **Last Month Internet Sales, Last Month Predicted Internet Sales, Mkt-Sales Correl, Mkt-Sales R Squared,** and **Regression Line Message** measures
6. Create a scatter chart visualization using the **Marketing Amount** column (sum) from the **MktSalesRegression** table as the **X Axis**, the **Internet Sales** column (sum) from the **MktSalesRegression** table as the **Y Axis**, and the **YearMonth** column from the **MktSalesRegression** table as **Details**
7. Add a **Trend** line from the **Analytics** pane
8. Create a second scatter chart visualization using the **Predicted Internet Sales** column (sum) from the **Residuals** table as the **X Axis**, the **Residuals Z Score** column (sum) from the **Residuals** table as the **Y Axis**, and the **YearMonth** column from the **Residuals** table as **Details**

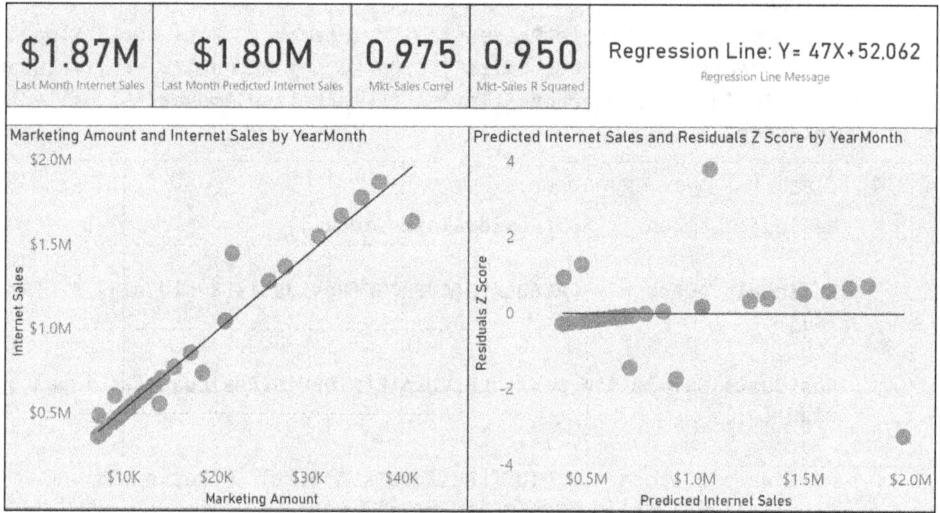

Figure 9.23: Regression report page

With this report design, the user can instantly perceive the strength of the relationship via the **Marketing Amount and Internet Sales by YearMonth** scatter chart and the high values for the correlation and R squared cards shown in *Figure 9.23*. The **Predicted Internet Sales and Residuals Z Score by YearMonth** scatter chart helps to identify the months with relatively large variations.

How it works

In this example, we have obviously engineered a monthly marketing spend metric to have a high correlation with internet sales. Had we used the actual **Sales and Marketing** expenditure numbers from the general ledger (**FactFinance**) fact table, we would have found no correlation at all.

Simple (single-variable) regression models are often insufficient to estimate Y values accurately, but many of the concepts and techniques used in this recipe are applicable to more complex, multiple linear regression models.

The main correlation calculations deal with data in the **MktSalesRegression** table. This table creates rows with corresponding data between the two metrics we wish to correlate. The `SUMMARIZECOLUMNS` function groups the table at the monthly grain, and the `FILTER` function removes any rows (months) that do not have both internet sales and marketing values. It is crucial to the calculations that the data does not contain gaps in any one time series. The `CALCULATETABLE` function passes a filtered date table to `SUMMARIZECOLUMNS` in order to exclude certain months. The **Marketing Amount** and **Internet Sales** columns are the two measures we wish to find or not find a correlation between. Note that to attempt a correlation between different measures, only the **Marketing Amount** and **Internet Sales** expressions need to be changed—all other measures and DAX calculations can remain the same.

A new SQL view could be developed in the source system to meet the regression table requirements and, as another alternative, M queries within the dataset could leverage the existing general ledger, internet sales, and date queries. However, small DAX tables such as this example (with 36 rows) are a good option for supporting custom or advanced analysis and functionality.

The correlation coefficient is split into three separate intermediate measures (**MktSalesCorrelNum**, **MktSalesCorrelDenomX**, and **MktSalesCorrelDenomY**) and these measures are referenced in the **Mkt-Sales Correl** measure. With the correlation and its components defined in the model, the slope (**MktSalesSlope**) measure can leverage the same numerator measure, **MktSalesCorrelNum**, and the **MktSalesCorrelDenomX** measure as well. Finally, we can compute the y-intercept for the regression, **MktSales Intercept**.

We now have all of the components for the equation of our line, $y = mx + b$, where m is the slope and b is the y-intercept. This formula is what allows us to compute the **Predicted Internet Sales** in our **Residuals** table. The **Predicted Internet Sales** column in the **Residuals** table implements the equation of a line ($y = mx + b$) by referencing the **Marketing Amount** column (x), the slope (**MktSalesSlope**), and the y-intercept (**MktSales Intercept**). Finally, the **Residual** column is computed to subtract the predicted sales value from the observed (actual) value in the **Internet Sales** column.

A Z-score is computed for each residual data point (a month) to determine if the variation (or "miss") between the predicted and observed values is large relative to other data points. To support the visualization, a measure returns a text string containing the equation of the regression model's line. Additionally, two measures are created to display actual and predicted internet sales for the last month in the analysis.

The two calculated tables in this recipe, **MktSalesRegression** and **Residuals**, do not have any relationships to other tables in the model. Refreshing the source tables (queries) of the two DAX tables also refreshes the calculated tables.

There's more

The created DAX measures in this recipe correspond to the `CORREL`, `SLOPE`, and `INTERCEPT` functions in Microsoft Excel. The documentation for these Excel functions provides the following formulas:

The formula for the `CORREL` function, for a sample (Pearson's Correlation Coefficient):

$$Correl\ (X,Y) = \frac{\sum(x-\bar{x})(y-\bar{y})}{\sqrt{\sum(x-\bar{x})^2(y-\bar{y})^2}}$$

The standard formula for finding the slope of a line:

$$b = \frac{\sum(x-\bar{x})(y-\bar{y})}{\sum(x-\bar{x})}$$

The standard formula for finding a y-intercept:

$$a = \bar{y} - b\bar{x}$$

Correlation coefficients can range from -1 to 1. A positive correlation between two metrics means that as one measure goes up or down, the other metric also goes up or down. There are also inverse correlations represented by negative numbers, where the two metrics are inversely correlated, meaning that when one metric goes up, the other metric goes down, and vice versa. Values close to 1 or -1 indicate that the two metrics have a strong correlation and directly affect one another. Values closer to 0 indicate that the two metrics are not related to one another.

The R squared value, or the coefficient of determination, is simply the square of the correlation coefficient. R squared values fall between 0 and 1 since the square of a negative number is positive. An R squared value of 1 indicates that the movements of one metric are 100% explained by the movements in the comparison metric, while a value of 0 indicates that there is no relation between the two metrics. R squared values between .85 and 1 are considered "high," meaning that the two metrics are closely linked, while anything below .7 is considered weak or of relatively little influence.

It is important to consider that time series data often exhibits seasonality, meaning that the numbers are artificially higher or lower than they would otherwise be due to, for example, quarterly influences. Think retail sales and holidays in the fourth calendar quarter like Thanksgiving and Christmas. When data exhibits seasonality, it is critically important that the metric's values are de-seasonalized before performing the correlation.

Another consideration is leading and lagging indicators. Leading indicators mean that the values in one time series are related to another, but there is an offset of some number of weeks or months. In other words, one metric may go up and correspond to the other metric going up, but there is a period of time or delay before the second metric reflects the movement of the first metric.

Finding leading indicators can be extremely valuable in business, as they provide a predictive metric upon which a business can make decisions and act based upon expected future behavior. To find leading indicators, the values in the correlation analysis must be offset from one another by the appropriate number of time periods. This generally leads to the correlation calculations taking place at various time period offsets in order to determine if one indicator leads or lags another.

See also

- Slope and intercept equation descriptions: `http://bit.ly/2tdzrgA`
- De-Seasonalized Correlation Coefficient: `https://bit.ly/2SeTSsp`

Grouping and Binning

Grouping and binning in Power BI creates group columns that can then be utilized like other columns in the model to simplify report visualizations and self-service analysis, given their reduced granularity. Additionally, groups can be managed and edited in Power BI Desktop, providing a flexible option for dataset owners to respond quickly to changing requirements or preferences.

This recipe provides examples for using grouping and binning functionality within Power BI Desktop.

Getting ready

To prepare for this recipe, follow these steps:

1. Open a Power BI Desktop file locally and access the **Power Query Editor** by clicking on **Transform Data** in the ribbon of the **Home** tab
2. Create a query named `AdWorksDW` similar to the following:

```
let
    Source = Sql.Database("localhost\MSSQLSERVERDEV",
"AdventureWorksDW2019")
in
    Source
```

3. Disable load on the `AdWorksDW` query and place it into a **Data Sources** query group
4. Right-click the `AdWorksDW` query and choose **Reference**
5. Rename the query **Internet Sales** and choose the **FactInternetSales** table

6. Repeat *steps 4* and *5*, creating a **Dates** query that points to the **DimDates** table, and a **Customers** query that points to the **DimCustomer** table
7. Move the **Internet Sales** query to a Facts query group and the **Dates** and **Customers** queries to a **Dimensions** query group
8. Select **Close & Apply** from the ribbon of the **Home** tab
9. Switch to the **Model** view and create a relationship between the **DateKey** column in the **Dates** table and the **OrderDateKey** column in the **Internet Sales** table
10. Create a relationship between the **CustomerKey** columns in the **Customers** table and the **Internet Sales** table
11. Save your work

How to Perform Grouping and Binning

To implement this recipe, carry out the following steps:

1. Right-click the **DateFirstPurchased** column in the **Customers** table and choose **New Group**
2. Set the **Name** to **Customer First Purchase Calendar Quarter**, the **Bin size** to **3**, choose **Months** from the dropdown, and click **OK**

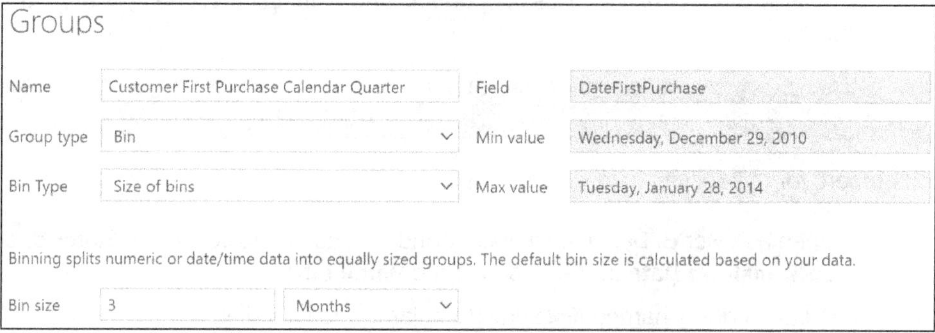

Figure 9.24: Groups dialog for the First Purchase Date column with a Bin size of 3 Months

3. Create a **Matrix** visual that analyzes the sales of these quarterly customer bins using the newly created **Customer First Purchase Calendar Quarter** column in the **Customer** table for **Rows**, the **CalendarYear** column from the **Dates** table for **Columns**, and the **SalesAmount** column (sum) from the **Internet Sales** table as **Values**
4. Optionally, add conditional formatting to the **SalesAmount** column in the **Values** field well by clicking the down arrow to the right of the column name and selecting **Conditional formatting** and then **Data bars**

Customer First Purchase Calendar Quarter	2010	2011	2012	2013	2014	Total
January 2014					$26,089	$26,089
October 2013				$2,064,938	$3,907	$2,068,846
July 2013				$1,201,124	$4,391	$1,205,515
April 2013				$1,537,392	$4,975	$1,542,367
January 2013				$1,087,279	$6,332	$1,093,611
October 2012			$1,620,094	$1,631,978		$3,252,072
July 2012			$1,461,896	$1,581,699		$3,043,595
April 2012			$1,320,543	$1,465,738		$2,786,281
January 2012			$1,378,995	$1,419,521		$2,798,516
October 2011		$2,038,185	$3,485	$1,404,207		$3,445,877
July 2011		$1,814,388	$16,952	$1,132,372		$2,963,712
April 2011		$1,801,595	$22,953	$955,837		$2,780,385
January 2011		$1,421,357	$17,567	$835,667		$2,274,591
October 2010	$43,421			$33,798		$77,219

Figure 9.25: Customer First Purchase Calendar Quarter grouping used in Matrix Visual

How it works

By grouping the customers into quarterly bins, the new grouping column (**Customer First Purchase Calendar Quarter**) has only 14 unique values and can be used in report visualizations. In this analysis, it is clear that sales in 2017 are being driven by customers that first purchased in the first and second quarters of 2013 (January 2013, April 2013). Interestingly, customers that first purchased in 2011 were large buyers in 2015, but then generally disappeared in 2016, and returned in 2017.

There's more

In this example, the goal is to group (bin) customers based on the number of days since their last purchase. To see how this works, perform the following:

1. Create the following measure to define **Today**:

   ```
   Today = DATE(2014,1,28)
   ```

2. Create the following columns in the **Customers** table:

   ```
   Last Order Date = CALCuLATE(MAX('Internet Sales'[OrderDate]))

   Days Since Last Purchase = ([Today] - [Last Order Date]) * 1
   ```

3. Create a numerical grouping based on the **Days Since Last Purchase** column to help analyze this data

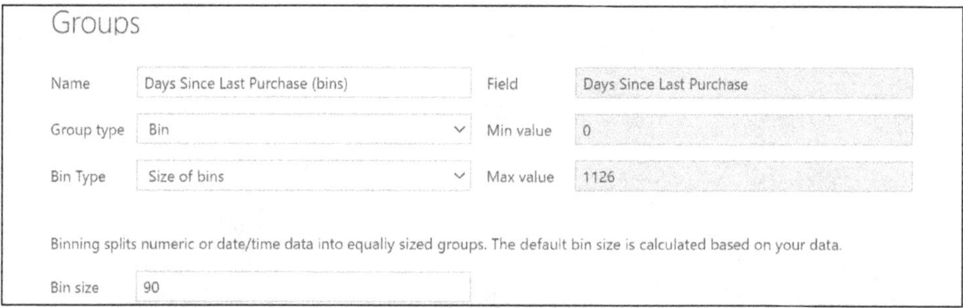
Groups

Name	Days Since Last Purchase (bins)	Field	Days Since Last Purchase
Group type	Bin	Min value	0
Bin Type	Size of bins	Max value	1126

Binning splits numeric or date/time data into equally sized groups. The default bin size is calculated based on your data.

Bin size	90

Figure 9.26: Grouping created based on the Days Since Last Purchase column

4. Create a **Clustered** bar chart to display the information graphically using the newly created **Days Since Last Purchase (bins)** column in the **Customers** table as the **Axis**, and the **SalesAmount** column from the **Internet Sales** table as **Values**

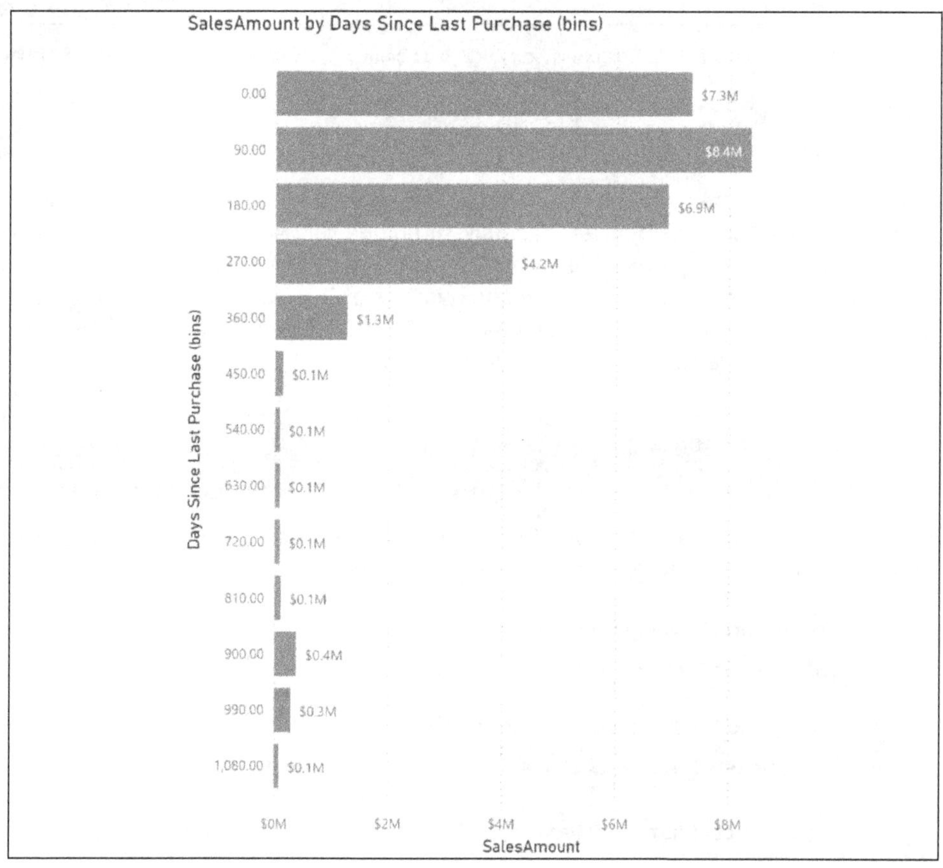

Figure 9.27: Clustered bar chart of internet sales by the 90 Days Since Last Purchase grouping

The new grouping column (**90 Days Since Last Purchase**) helps determine that $15.7 M of total historical internet sales is comprised of customers that have purchased within the past 180 days ($7.3 M for the 0 to 90 group and $8.4 M for the 90 to 180 group).

As groupings are effectively calculated columns within the data model and are not visible to source systems, the logic of grouping columns should eventually be migrated to new columns in a source data warehouse. Groups can be very helpful for proof-of-concept scenarios and short-term solutions, but as per other recipes, data transformation processes should be limited in Power BI Desktop to keep the dataset as manageable and scalable as possible. If a data warehouse option is not available, M query transformations can be used, rather than DAX calculated columns.

See also

- Use grouping and binning in Power BI Desktop: `https://bit.ly/3xHnMpG`

Detecting and Analyzing Clusters

Clustering is a data mining and machine learning technique used to group (cluster) the items of one dimension based on the values of one or more measures. Given the number of distinct dimension items, such as products or customers, and the number of measures describing those items, clustering is a powerful method of exploring data to discover relationships not easily detected with standard reporting and analysis techniques. Power BI Desktop provides built-in support for the creation of clusters and allows these clusters to be managed, revised, and used in Power BI reports like other columns in the data model.

In this recipe, a customer cluster is created based on the sales amount, the count of orders, and the count of days since the last purchase. DAX measures are created to support this analysis, and a **Scatter Chart** visual is created to further analyze the clusters.

Getting ready

To prepare for this recipe, follow these steps:

1. Open a Power BI Desktop file locally and access the **Power Query Editor** by clicking on **Transform Data** in the ribbon of the **Home** tab
2. Create a query named `AdWorksDW` similar to the following:

```
let
    Source = Sql.Database("localhost\MSSQLSERVERDEV",
"AdventureWorksDW2019")
in
    Source
```

3. Disable load on the `AdWorksDW` query and place it into a **Data Sources** query group
4. Right-click the `AdWorksDW` query and choose **Reference**
5. Rename the query **Internet Sales** and choose the **FactInternetSales** table
6. Repeat *steps 4* and 5, creating a **Dates** query that points to the **DimDates** table, a **Customers** query that points to the **DimCustomer** table, and a **Sales Territories** query that points to the **DimSalesTerritory** table
7. Create a **Products** query using the following code:

```
let
    Source = AdWorksDW,
    Navigation = Source{[Schema="dbo",Item="DimProduct"]}[Data],
    Subcategory =
        Table.ExpandRecordColumn(
            Navigation, "DimProductSubcategory",
            {"EnglishProductSubcategoryName", "DimProductCategory"},
            {"Product Subcategory", "DimProductCategory"}
        ),
    Category =
        Table.ExpandRecordColumn(
            Subcategory, "DimProductCategory",
            {"EnglishProductCategoryName"}, {"Product Category"}
        )
in
   Category
```

8. Move the **Internet Sales** query to a **Facts** query group, and the **Dates**, **Customers**, and **Products** queries to a **Dimensions** query group
9. In the **Other Queries** group, create a blank query called **Calculations**
10. Select **Close & Apply** from the ribbon of the **Home** tab
11. Switch to the **Model** view and create a relationship between the **DateKey** column in the **Dates** table, and the **OrderDateKey** in the **Internet Sales** table
12. Create a relationship between the **CustomerKey** columns in the **Customers** table and the **Internet Sales** table
13. Create a relationship between the **ProductKey** columns in the **Products** table and the **Internet Sales** table
14. Create a relationship between the **SalesTerritoryKey** columns in the **Sales Territories** table and the **Internet Sales** table
15. Save your work

How to Detect and Analyze Clusters

To implement this recipe, use the following steps:

1. Create the following measures in the **Calculations** table:

```
Today = DATE(2014,1,28)

Internet Gross Sales = SUM('Internet Sales'[SalesAmount])

Internet Sales Discounts = SUM('Internet Sales'[DiscountAmount])

Internet Net Sales = [Internet Gross Sales] - [Internet Sales Discounts]

Internet Sales Orders = DISTINCTCOUNT('Internet Sales'[SalesOrderNumber])

Last Purchase Date = LASTNONBLANK('Dates'[FullDateAlternateKey],[Intern
et Net Sales])

Days Since Last Purchase = DATEDIFF([Last Purchase Date],[Today],DAY)
```

2. In the **Report** view, create a **Table** visualization using the **CustomerAlternateKey** column from the **Customers** table and the **Internet Net Sales**, **Internet Sales Orders**, and **Days Since Last Purchase** measures
3. Select the **table** visualization, click the ellipsis (**...**), and choose **Automatically find clusters**
4. In the **Clusters** dialog, **Name** the cluster **Customers** (**RFM**), enter a **Description** of **Clusters for All CustomerAlternateKey, Internet Net Sales, Internet Sales Orders, Days Since Last Purchase**, and then click **OK**

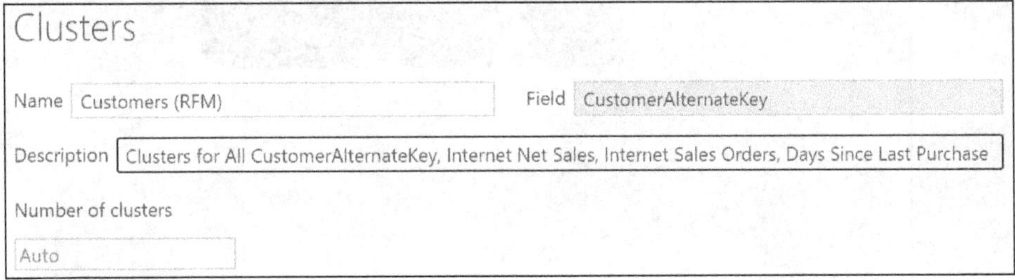

Figure 9.28: Clusters dialog

5. Create three additional measures in the **Calculations** table to help describe the clusters created:

```
Average Customer Sales =
AVERAGEX(DISTINCT(Customers[CustomerAlternateKey]),[Internet Net Sales])
```

```
Average Customer Orders =
AVERAGEX(DISTINCT(Customers[CustomerAlternateKey]),[Internet Sales
Orders])

Average Days Since Last Purchase =
AVERAGEX(DISTINCT(Customers[CustomerAlternateKey]),[Days Since Last
Purchase])
```

6. Create a simple **Table** visualization using the three measures created plus the **Customers** (**RFM**) column and **CustomerAlternateKey** (count) from the **Customers** table, as well as the **Internet Net Sales** measure

Customers (RFM)	Internet Net Sales	Count of CustomerAlternateKey	Average Customer Sales	Average Customer Orders	Average Days Since Last Purchase
Cluster1	$7,856,813	14072	$558	1.29	175
Cluster2	$1,201,140	410	$2,930	1.00	852
Cluster3	$20,300,724	4002	$5,073	2.28	172
Total	**$29,358,677**	**18484**	**$1,588**	**1.50**	**189**

Figure 9.29: Average Customer Measures used with the Customers (RFM) clusters

7. On a new page, create a Scatter chart with the **Average Days Since Last Purchase** measure as the **X Axis**, the **Average Customer Sales** measure as the **Y Axis**, and the **Customers (RFM)** column from the **Customers** table as **Legend**

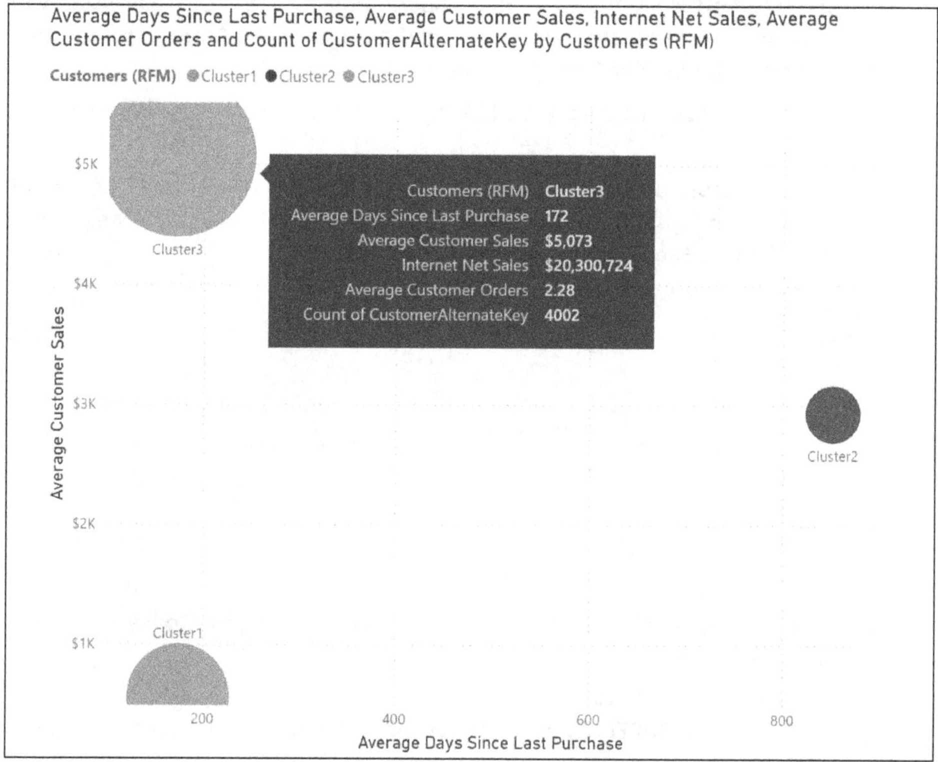

Figure 9.30: Clusters visualized in a scatter chart by Internet Net Sales and Days Since Last Purchase

A potential use case or action based on these clusters is to focus marketing efforts on converting the **Cluster1** customers, who have purchased recently, to higher-value **Cluster3** customers. Also, **Cluster2** customers may have already committed to a new bike supplier or, more optimistically, may have purchased a bike two to three years ago, and may not be aware of what bike-related accessories and clothing are available.

How it works

Feature engineering is a common practice in data science, in which new columns are added to a dataset to produce more accurate models. The new columns often contain built-in logic, and features (columns) are added, removed, and modified iteratively based on the models produced. Identify measures that add the most value to the algorithm by representing the dimensions in different ways. The three measures used to support the clustering in this example follow the RFM technique, identifying the recency, frequency, and monetary (value) of the customer's purchase history. Adding measures (feature engineering) that cover each component of RFM is useful for various marketing and customer attrition analyses.

Following the RFM technique, the **Days Since Last Purchase** measure identifies the recency, **Internet Sales Orders** measures the frequency, and **Internet Net Sales** measures the monetary value. The **Last Purchase Date** measure is an intermediary measure created to support the **Days Since Last Purchase** measure. **Days Since Last Purchase** uses the **Last Purchase Date** measure and a **Today** measure as parameter inputs to the DATEDIFF function. In a production scenario, the **Today** measure would use the TODAY function instead of a hard-coded DATE.

Three clusters were created in this example. These clusters are represented by a column added to the **Customers** table of the data model with the name provided in the **Clusters** dialog, **Customers (RFM)**. The cluster column is identified in the **Fields** list with two overlapping square shapes, and an **Edit clusters** option is available by either right-clicking the column or selecting the ellipsis next to the column.

For the analysis measures, **Average Customer Sales**, **Average Customer Orders**, and **Average Days Since Last Purchase**, the **AVERAGEX** function is used to iterate over the unique customer keys provided by the **DISTINCT** function to compute the customer-specific value (sales, orders, and days since purchase) and then return the average of the measures from each cluster.

The Power BI clustering feature uses the K-Means algorithm to determine the optimal number of clusters to create. Currently, a cluster is limited to 15 measures and one dimension; an error message is returned if these limits are exceeded.

There's more

In addition to the standard Power BI clustering from this recipe, additional custom visuals for clustering are available in the AppStore, including **Clustering** and **Clustering with Outliers**. Both these custom visuals are built with the R statistical programming language.

Like the table visual from the example, clusters can also be automatically created from a Scatter chart visual. These clusters are limited to two input measures (X and Y) but the clusters are automatically added to the **Details** field. To see how this works, do the following:

1. On a new page, create a Scatter chart visualization using the **Internet Net Sales** measure as the **X Axis**, the **Internet Sales Orders** measure as the **Y Axis**, and the **EnglishProductName** column from the **Products** table as **Details**
2. Select the scatter chart visualization, click the ellipsis (**...**), and choose **Automatically find clusters**

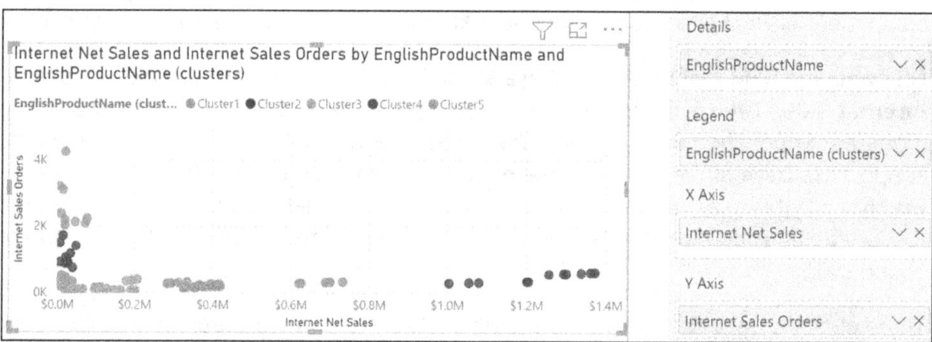

Figure 9.31: Clusters automatically added to the legend of a Scatter chart

See also

- Apply clustering techniques: `https://bit.ly/3gVwKK3`

Forecasting and Anomaly Detection

Standard Power BI report and dashboard visualizations are great tools to support descriptive and diagnostic analytics of historical or real-time data, but ultimately organizations need predictive and prescriptive analytics to help guide decisions involving future outcomes. Power BI Desktop provides a time series forecasting tool with built-in predictive modeling capabilities that enables report authors to quickly create custom forecasts, evaluate the accuracy of these forecasts, and build intuitive visualizations that blend actual or historical data with the forecast.

This recipe contains two complete forecasting examples. The first example builds a monthly forecast for the next three months utilizing an automatic date hierarchy. The second example builds a weekly forecast of the next eight weeks and evaluates the forecast's accuracy when applied to recent data. Finally, an example of using anomaly detection is provided.

Getting ready

To prepare for this recipe, follow these steps:

1. Open a Power BI Desktop file locally and ensure that the **Auto Date/Time** setting in the **Current File Data Load** options is enabled (through **File | Options and settings | Options**)
2. Access the **Power Query Editor** by clicking on **Transform Data** in the ribbon of the **Home** tab
3. Create a query named `AdWorksDW` similar to the following:

```
let
    Source = Sql.Database("localhost\MSSQLSERVERDEV",
"AdventureWorksDW2019")
in
    Source
```

4. Disable load on the `AdWorksDW` query and place it into a **Data Sources** query group
5. Right-click the `AdWorksDW` query and choose **Reference**
6. Rename the query **Internet Sales** and choose the **FactInternetSales** table
7. Repeat *steps 4* and *5*, creating a **Dates** query that points to the **DimDates** table
8. Move the **Internet Sales** query to a **Facts** query group and the **Dates** query to a **Dimensions** query group
9. In the **Other Queries** group, create a blank query called **Calculations**
10. Select **Close & Apply** from the ribbon of the **Home** tab
11. Switch to the **Model** view and create a relationship between the **DateKey** column in the **Dates** table, and the **OrderDateKey** column in the **Internet Sales** table
12. Save your work

How to Perform Forecasting and Anomaly Detection

To implement this recipe, carry out the following steps:

1. Create the following measures in the **Calculations** table:

```
Today = DATE(2014,1,28)

Internet Gross Sales = SUM('Internet Sales'[SalesAmount])

Internet Sales Discounts = SUM('Internet Sales'[DiscountAmount])

Internet Net Sales = [Internet Gross Sales] - [Internet Sales Discounts]
```

2. In the **Report** view, create a Line chart visualization using **FullDateAlternateKey** from the **Dates** table as the **Axis**, and the **Internet Net Sales** measure as the **Values**
3. With the visualization selected, click on the **Expand all down one level in the hierarchy** button twice to navigate to the monthly grain

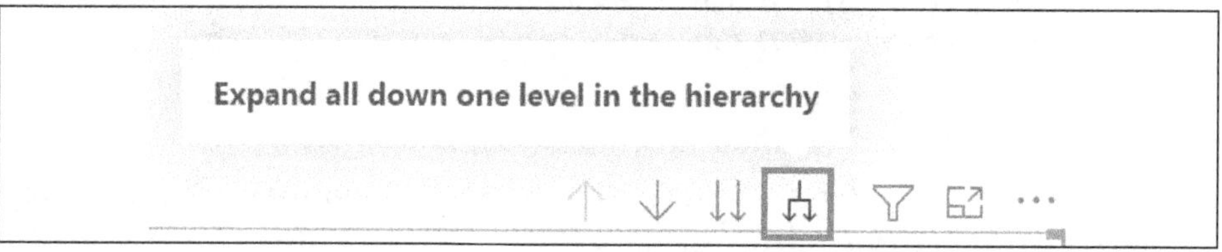

Figure 9.32: Expand all down used to display the line chart visual by month

4. With the line chart selected, open the **Analytics** pane, expand **Forecast**, and click **Add**
5. Enter **3** for **Forecast** length, **1** for **Ignore last**, and **12** for **Seasonality**

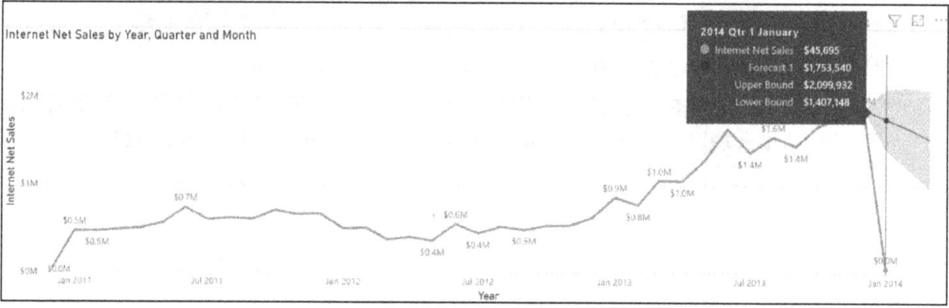

Figure 9.33: Monthly forecast with three forecast points and excluding the most current month

6. Create new columns in the **Dates** table with the following code:

```
Sequential =
    VAR __Date = 'Dates'[FullDateAlternateKey]
    VAR __Year = YEAR(__Date)
    VAR __Calendar = ADDCOLUMNS(ALL('Dates'),
            "__Year", YEAR('Dates'[FullDateAlternateKey]),
            "__WeekNum", WEEKNUM('Dates'[FullDateAlternateKey]))
    VAR __FirstYear = MINX(__Calendar,[__Year])
    VAR __WeekNum = MAXX(FILTER(__Calendar,
        [FullDateAlternateKey] = __Date), [__WeekNum])
    VAR __MaxWeeks = GROUPBY(__Calendar, [__Year],
        "__MaxWeek", MAXX(CURRENTGROUP(), [__WeekNum]))
    VAR __Start = SUMX(FILTER(__MaxWeeks, [__Year]<__Year), [__MaxWeek])
    VAR __Calendar1 = ADDCOLUMNS(__Calendar,
            "__MaxWeek",
            MAXX(FILTER(__Calendar, [__Year] =
                EARLIER([__Year])),[__WeekNum]))
    VAR __SubtractTable = GROUPBY(FILTER(__Calendar1,
            [__Year] < __Year && [__WeekNum] = [__MaxWeek]), [__Year],
            "__NumWeekDays", COUNTX(CURRENTGROUP(),[FullDateAlternateK
ey]))
    VAR __Subtract = COUNTROWS(FILTER(__SubtractTable, [__
NumWeekDays]<7))
    VAR __Sequential = IF(__Year=__FirstYear,
        __WeekNum,
        __Start + __WeekNum - __Subtract)
RETURN __Sequential

Week Ending Date =
    VAR __CurrentWeek = [Sequential]
RETURN
    MAXX(FILTER(ALL('Dates'),[Sequential] = __CurrentWeek),
        [FullDateAlternateKey])


IsCurrentWeek =
    VAR __CurrentWeek =
        LOOKUPVALUE('Dates'[Sequential],'Dates'[FullDateAlternateKey],[T
oday])
RETURN
    IF([Sequential] = __CurrentWeek,1,0)
```

7. In the **Report** view, create another **Line chart** visualization using **Week Ending Date** (not the hierarchy) from the **Dates** table as the **Axis**, and the **Internet Net Sales** measure as the **Values**
8. With the visualization selected, use the **Filters** pane and add the **IsCurrentWeek** column to the filters for the visualization, and exclude values of **1**
9. With the line chart selected, open the **Analytics** pane, expand **Forecast**, and click **Add**
10. Enter **8** for **Forecast** length, **5** for **Ignore last**, and **52** for **Seasonality**

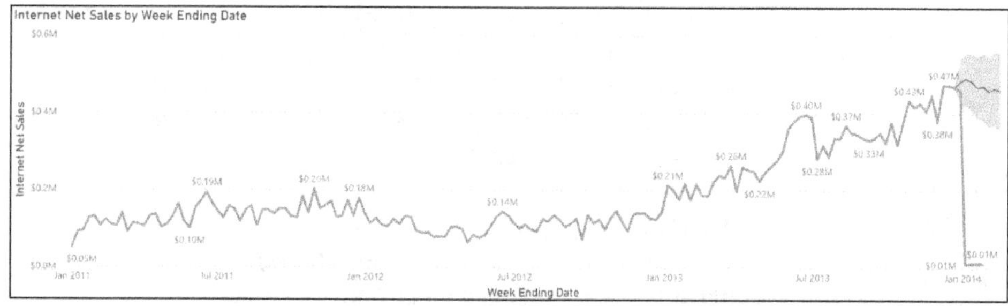

Figure 9.34: Weekly sales trend and three-week forecast, which excludes the prior 5 completed weeks

How it works

The Power BI Forecast tool uses the exponential smoothing time series predictive algorithm. This method is widely used in multiple domains and helps to suppress outlier values while efficiently capturing trends. The forecast tool is currently only available to the **Line chart** visual, and only one measure (line) on this visual is allowed. The x-axis value needs to have a date or date/time data type or be a uniformly increasing whole number and a minimum of six date points are required.

The Forecast tool in Power BI includes an **Ignore last** feature, which allows the exclusion of incomplete periods (months, weeks, and days) from the forecast. However, for common additive measures, such as **Sales Amount**, not filtering out the current period often significantly detracts from the usability of the visual, given the steep decline represented by the current (incomplete) period. Dynamically updated date columns, such as **IsCurrentWeek**, generally resolve this issue.

In the first line chart, by default, a forecast of the chosen measure is created for 10 points (months) in the future with a 95 percent **Confidence interval**. The forecast automatically determines the step (monthly grain) and also determines a seasonality factor to apply to the forecast. In this example, no filters have been applied to the report, and thus the current month, which is incomplete, is initially being used by the forecast. By setting **Ignore last** to **1** point we exclude the most current, incomplete month.

The forecast now includes a forecasted value for the current (incomplete) month. Applying the **Seasonality** variable at its known grain (12 per year) overrides the default seasonality factor.

When the seasonality (points per cycle) is known, it is recommended to apply this value manually to improve accuracy. Hovering over a forecast data point exposes both the forecast and the upper and lower boundary values, given the 95 percent confidence interval.

In the second example, the last completed **Week Ending Date** is 1/25/14. Therefore, given **5** points to ignore, this point and the four previous weeks are excluded from the forecasting algorithm, such that the forecast can only use the weeks ending on 12/21/13 and earlier to generate its projections. Three additional forecast points (8 (Forecast Length) – 5 (Ignore Last)) are computed for the weeks ending on 2/1/14, 2/8/14, and 2/15/14.

There's more

In addition to the forecasting feature, the line chart visualization also now includes an anomaly detection feature. To see how this works, do the following:

1. Ensure that the **Anomaly detection** feature is activated in the **Preview** features by selecting **File** | **Options and settings** | **Options**, and then **Preview** features
2. Copy the **Week Ending Date** line chart to a new page
3. Remove **Forecast** in the **Analytics** pane
4. Expand **Find anomalies** and choose **Add**

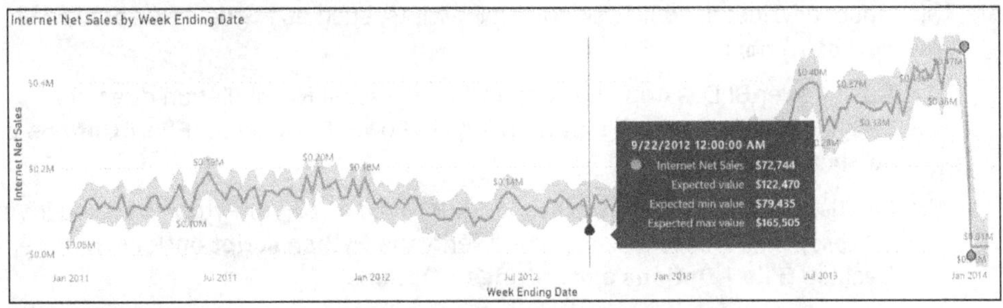

Figure 9.35: Find anomalies

The default **Sensitivity** is 70 percent. Increasing the **Sensitivity** identifies more anomalies.

See also

- Data Forecasting and Analytics with Power BI Desktop: `https://bit.ly/3xFWakx`
- Anomaly detection tutorial: `https://bit.ly/3t6NAIc`

Using R and Python Visuals

The R and Python programming languages, including their powerful and extensible features in data processing, advanced analytics, and visualization, are deeply integrated with Power BI. R and Python scripts can be used as a data source for a Power BI dataset, as a data transformation and shaping process within M queries, and as their own visualization type within Power BI reports and dashboards. Like standard Power BI visuals, R and Python script visuals directly leverage the relationships defined in the data model and can be dynamically filtered via other visuals, such as slicers.

In this recipe, two histogram visualizations are created in Power BI Desktop with R scripts: one with R's standard distribution base graphics, and another with the popular `ggplot2` visualization package. Additionally, a Python visual example is included.

Getting ready

To prepare for this recipe, follow these steps:

1. Download and install the R engine on the local machine using either of the following:
    - `https://cran.r-project.org/bin/windows/base/`
    - `https://aka.ms/rclient/`
2. Install the `ggplot2` package for R via the following command: `install.packages("ggplot2")`.
3. Optionally, install an IDE for editing R scripts, such as RStudio (`https://www.rstudio.com/`).
4. Open Power BI Desktop and confirm that the local R installation directory path is reflected in the **R script** options in Power BI Desktop (**File** | **Options and settings** | **Options**).
5. Similarly, install Python from `http://www.python.org` or Python bundled in Anaconda (`https://www.anaconda.com/`) and verify the **Python script options** in Power BI Desktop (**File** | **Options and settings** | **Options**).

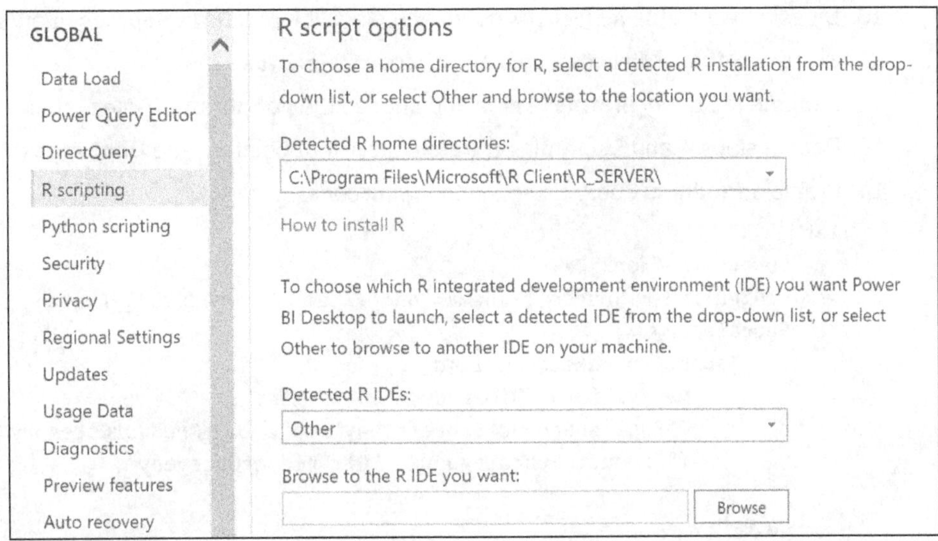

Figure 9.36: R script options in Power BI Desktop

The **Detected R IDEs** and **Detected Python IDEs** dropdowns can be used to choose between multiple installed IDEs. If R and Python script visuals have not been used in Power BI Desktop, an **Enable script visuals** prompt will appear. Click **Enable**.

6. Install matplotlib for Python using the following command: `python -m pip install matplotlib`.
7. Install pandas for Python using the following command: `python -m pip install pandas`.
8. Access the **Power Query Editor** by clicking on **Transform Data** in the ribbon of the **Home** tab.
9. Create a query named `AdWorksDW` similar to the following:

```
let
    Source = Sql.Database("localhost\MSSQLSERVERDEV",
"AdventureWorksDW2019")
in
    Source
```

10. Disable load on the `AdWorksDW` query and place it into a **Data Sources** query group.
11. Right-click the `AdWorksDW` query and choose **Reference**.
12. Rename the query **Internet Sales** and choose the **FactInternetSales** table.
13. Repeat *steps 4* and *5*, creating a **Dates** query that points to the **DimDates** table.
14. Create a **Products** query using the following code:

```
let
    Source = AdWorksDW,
    Navigation = Source{[Schema="dbo",Item="DimProduct"]}[Data],
    Subcategory =
        Table.ExpandRecordColumn(
            Navigation, "DimProductSubcategory",
            {"EnglishProductSubcategoryName", "DimProductCategory"},
            {"Product Subcategory", "DimProductCategory"}
        ),
    Category =
        Table.ExpandRecordColumn(
            Subcategory, "DimProductCategory",
            {"EnglishProductCategoryName", "ProductCategoryKey"},
            {"Product Category", "ProductCategoryKey"}
        )
in
   Category
```

15. Move the **Internet Sales** query to a **Facts** query group and the **Dates** and **Products** queries to a **Dimensions** query group.
16. In the **Other Queries** group, create a blank query called **Calculations**.
17. Select **Close & Apply** from the ribbon of the **Home** tab.
18. Switch to the **Model** view and create a relationship between the **DateKey** column in the **Dates** table, and the **OrderDateKey** column in the **Internet Sales** table.
19. Create a relationship between the **ProductKey** columns in the **Products** table and the **Internet Sales** table.
20. Save your work.

How to Use R and Python Visuals

To implement this recipe, use the following steps:

1. Create the following measures in the **Calculations** table:

```
Internet Gross Sales = SUM('Internet Sales'[SalesAmount])

Internet Sales Discounts = SUM('Internet Sales'[DiscountAmount])

Internet Net Sales = [Internet Gross Sales] - [Internet Sales Discounts]
```

2. In the **Report** view, use the **Filters** pane to add a filter for the **CalendarYear** column from the **Dates** table, and select **2013** only
3. Add an R script visual from the **Visualizations** pane, and add the **ProductKey** and **ListPrice** columns from the **Products** table, the **CalendarYear** column from the **Dates** table, and the **Internet Net Sales** measure to the **Values** field well
4. Enter the following R script into the R script editor and click the **Run script** icon:

```
par(bg = "#E6E6E6")
hist(dataset$'ListPrice', breaks = seq(from=0, to = 2500, by = 500), col
= "#2C95FF",
main = "Current Year Online Sales List Price Distribution", cex.main =
1.75, cex.axis = 1.2, cex.lab = 1.4, ylab = "Count of Products", xlab
= "Product List Price Bins", las = 1, labels = TRUE, border = "black",
ylim=c(0,50))
```

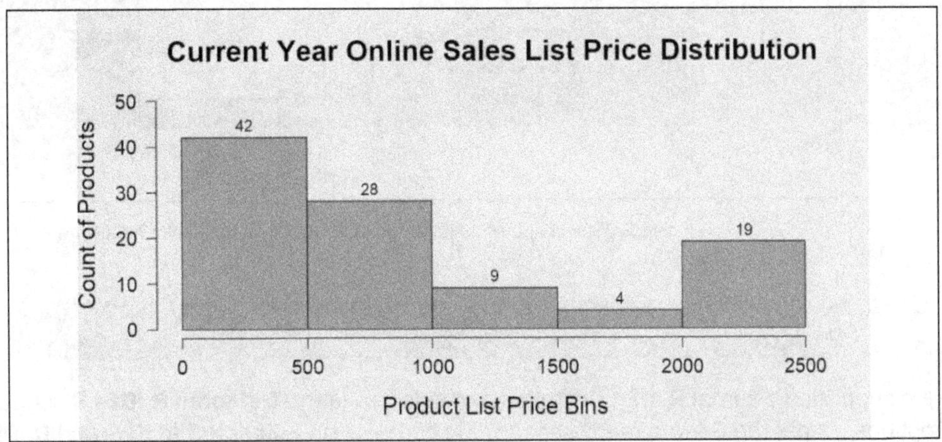

Figure 9.37: R script visual rendered in Power BI via Base Graphics

5. Copy and paste the R script visual on the same page

6. Select the pasted R script visual and change the code to the following:

```
prices <- as.numeric(as.character(dataset$'ListPrice'))
breakpoints <- seq(from=0, to = 2500, by = 500)
library("ggplot2")
ggplot(dataset, aes(x = prices)) + geom_histogram(breaks = breakpoints,
fill = "#2C95FF", color = "black") + xlab("Product List Price Bins")
+ ylab("Count of Products") + ggtitle("Current Year Online Sales List
Price Distribution") + stat_bin(breaks = breakpoints, geom="text",
aes(label=..count..), vjust = -1) + coord_cartesian(ylim=c(0,50)) +
theme(text = element_text(size = 16)) + theme(plot.title = element_
text(hjust = .5))
```

7. The result of this code change is shown in *Figure 9.38*

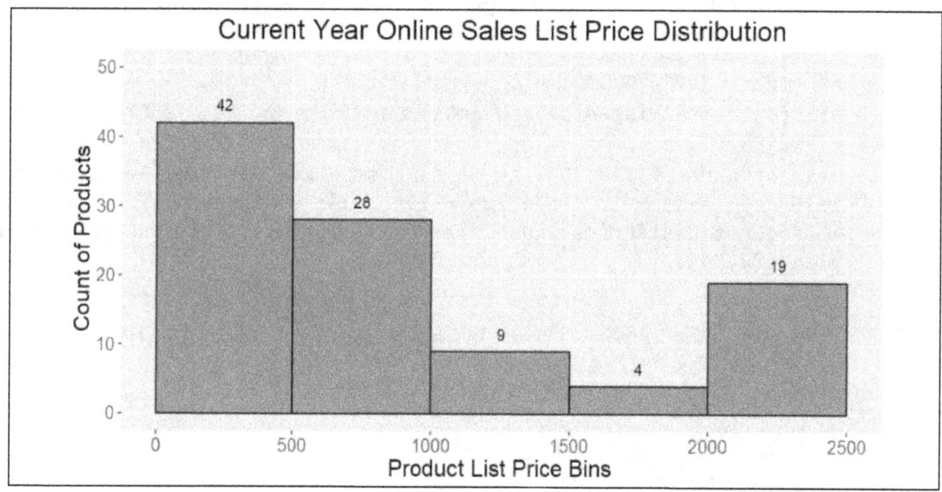

Figure 9.38: R script visual rendered in Power BI via the ggplot2 package

How it works

If a supported external R IDE is installed and selected in the **Detected R IDEs** R scripting options, as per the *Getting ready* section, you can click on **Edit script in External R IDE** (the up arrow icon). This will launch the IDE application (such as RStudio) and export the data frame from Power BI Desktop. Common features of R scripting IDEs, such as IntelliSense and Variable History, are helpful (if not essential) for developing complex R script visuals.

The requirement for both visualizations in this recipe is to display the distribution of the product list prices that have been sold online in the current calendar year. The first example uses the standard `hist()` function with R's base graphics and the second example uses the `ggplot()` function provided by the `ggplot2` package for R.

The light gray background color is set via the `par()` function, and arguments to the `hist()` function define the x- and y-axes, the text strings for the titles, data labels, font sizes, and the light blue color of the bars. The `seq()` function is used to configure the x-axis intervals (bins) with a width or bin size of $500, and a maximum price of $2,500.

`ggplot2`'s `geom_histogram()` requires a continuous variable, and thus the **List Price** column is converted to a numeric data type in the `prices` variable. The vector expression (`seq()`) used for the x-axis (bins by 500 to 2,500) in the prior example is used as the parameter to the **breaks** argument of `geom_histogram()` and `stat_bin()`. Likewise, the expression for the y-axis in the prior example is reused, but passed as a parameter to the `coord_cartesian()` function. The `qplot()` function, short for quick plot, is also available in the `ggplot2` package, and can result in the faster development of relatively complex visualizations with less code—often in just one line.

The R script editor in Power BI Desktop automatically creates a data frame and removes duplicate rows based on the columns loaded to the **Values** field well.

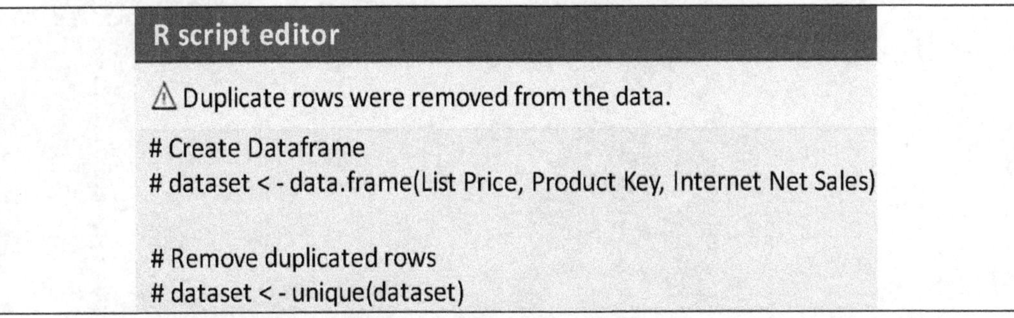

Figure 9.39: Power BI Desktop R script editor data frame and duplicate removal

In this example, in which the intent is to count individual products (including those with the same list price), it is necessary to add a separate column in the data frame (the **product key** column) that makes each row of the data frame unique. In other scenarios, the `Table.AddIndexColumn()` M function could be used to create uniqueness.

Including the **Internet Net Sales** measure in the R script visuals data frame allows the visual to be filtered by the **Date** dimension columns and other dimension tables on the report page.

By default, the products without any sales, given this filter context, will not be included in the data frame, as per the requirements of this recipe. The **show items with no data** option for the **Product Key** column in the **Values** field well can be used if the products without sales are to be included in this visualization.

The R script data source connector is available in the **Other** category of the **Get Data** dialog. A **Run R Script** command icon is available in the **Transform** window of the Query Editor. Many custom visuals built with R are already available in AppSource, and as of July 2017, R custom visuals can include interactive features, such as selection and zoom.

There's more

Python can also be used to create visuals. To see how this is done, perform the following:

1. Create a new page and use the **Filters** pane to add a filter for the **CalendarYear** column from the **Dates** table, and select **2013** only
2. Create a Python visual and add the **Product Category** column from the **Products** table, and the **Internet Net Sales** measure to the **Values** field well
3. Use the following code for the Python visual, and click the **Run script** icon:

```
import matplotlib.pyplot as plt
dataset.plot(kind='bar',x='Product Category',y='Internet Net Sales')
plt.show()
```

4. This code change results in the visual shown in *Figure 9.40*

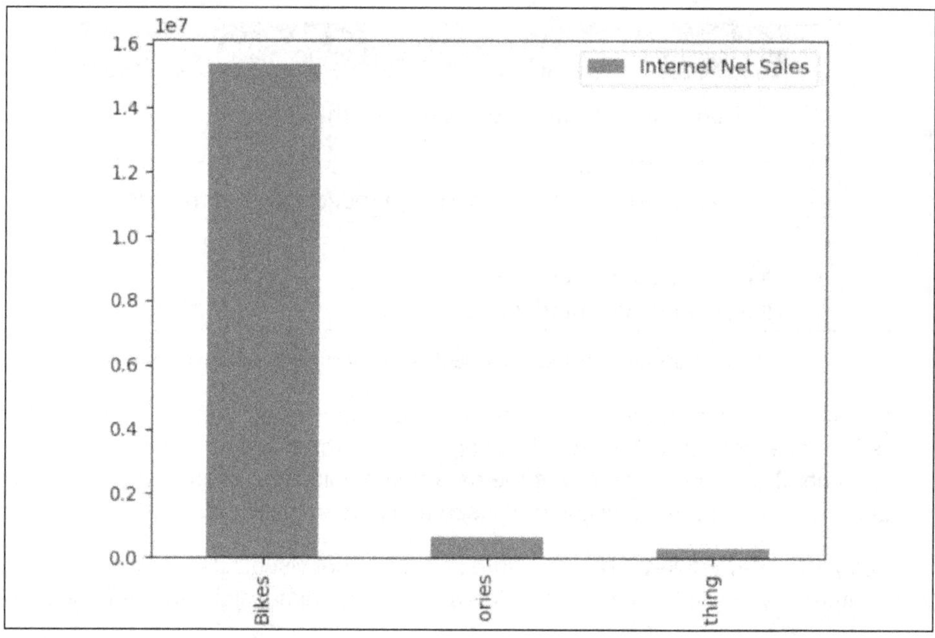

Figure 9.40: Default Python histogram

See also

- Install Microsoft R Client on Windows: `https://bit.ly/3aYfDDl`
- Create Power BI visuals using R: `https://bit.ly/3aWN4pP`

- R Script Visual Showcase for Power BI: `https://community.powerbi.com/t5/R-Script-Showcase/bd-p/RVisuals`
- Run Python Scripts in Power BI Desktop: `https://bit.ly/2QNtDcl`
- Create Power BI visuals using Python in Power BI Desktop: `https://bit.ly/3aUfVve`

Conclusion

This chapter contained a broad mix of recipes highlighting many of the latest and most popular custom visualizations and advanced analytics features of Power BI. This included custom visuals, the ArcGIS map visual, and data storytelling via animation and annotation. Additionally, examples were provided of leveraging Power BI datasets, and the DAX, R, and Python languages to embed custom statistical analyses and visualizations.

10

Administering and Monitoring Power BI

In addition to solutions targeting business processes and entities, such as sales and customers, Power BI can also serve as a platform for system monitoring and administration. Diverse system telemetry and diagnostic data sources such as logs from Azure services, performance monitor counters, and events can be integrated into Power BI datasets to deliver robust visibility to system health, activity, and performance. Although there are several dedicated monitoring tools available, such as Operations Manager in Microsoft System Center, building a custom solution with Power BI provides full flexibility and control over all layers of the solution, while leveraging relevant Power BI features, including data-driven alerts, email notifications and subscriptions, and Power BI mobile. Additionally, as more organizations adopt and deploy Power BI, existing licenses and experience can significantly reduce the costs of developing and maintaining these solutions.

This chapter's recipes highlight the most common and impactful administration data sources, including Windows Performance Monitor, SQL Server Query Store, on-premises data gateways, the MSDB system database, and Extended Events. Power BI solutions built on top of these sources proactively assess usage trends and resource bottlenecks, and deliver the detailed analysis necessary to identify root causes. Additionally, the metadata of existing Power BI and SSAS data models exposed via **dynamic management views** (**DMVs**), such as measure and relationship definitions and resource consumption, can be integrated to provide a simplified reference or documentation asset for both BI and business teams. Erin Stellato, principal consultant from SQL skills and Microsoft Data Platform MVP, has contributed to several of these recipes, including references to the setup and utilization of relational database monitoring and administrative data sources.

In this chapter, we will cover the following recipes:

- Creating a centralized IT monitoring solution with Power BI
- Constructing a monitoring, visualization, and analysis layer
- Importing and visualizing dynamic management view (DMV) data
- Increasing DBA productivity
- Providing documentation
- Analyzing SSAS tabular databases and gateways
- Analyzing Extended Events
- Visualizing log file data
- Leveraging the Power BI PowerShell Module

Technical requirements

- Power BI Desktop.
- SQL Server with the **AdventureWorksDW2019** database installed. This database and instructions for installing it are available here: `http://bit.ly/2OVQfG7`.
- Files for this chapter can be downloaded from the following GitHub repository: `https://github.com/PacktPublishing/Microsoft-Power-BI-Cookbook-Second-Edition`.

Creating a centralized IT monitoring solution with Power BI

Power BI's rich data connectivity and transformation capabilities are very well suited for the integration needs of system and database administrators. A collection of log files containing performance monitor counter statistics can be retrieved from a file directory (or multiple directories), consolidated, and further enhanced to support reporting. Additional sources, such as snapshots of performance and configuration data stored in a dedicated administrator database, can also be included in a scheduled data refresh process, and the inclusion of existing BI dimension tables, such as date and time, further simplifies the overall monitoring solution.

In this recipe, a set of Windows Performance Monitor counter files containing statistics on CPU, memory, and more are integrated with administrative data stored in a SQL Server database, including query wait statistics and instance configuration values.

Getting ready

To prepare for this recipe, follow these steps:

1. Identify the administrative stakeholders familiar with the current state of monitoring and the top priorities of the solution, such as "How is performance today?" and/or "Has a configuration changed?"
2. Sharpen the meaning of these questions to identify the required data sources, including performance counters and system views
3. Create a dedicated database named **Admin** in SQL Server that will exclusively store system and administrative data
4. Use Windows Performance Monitor to design and schedule a new data collector set containing the following performance monitor counters:
    - `\Memory\Available Mbytes`
    - `\PhysicalDisk(_Total)\Avg. Disk sec/Read`
    - `\PhysicalDisk(_Total)\Avg. Disk sec/Write`
    - `\Processor(_Total)\% Processor Time`
    - `\SQL Server:Buffer Manager\Page life expectancy`
    - `\SQL Server:SQL Statistics\Batch Requests/sec`

Performance Monitor defaults to `.blg` log files, but Power BI can only consolidate files in text, CSV, and Excel format, so set **Log format** to **Comma separated**. Windows Performance Monitor is well documented and understood by most administrators. Best practices and automation via PowerShell are outside the scope of this recipe.

How to create a centralized IT monitoring solution

To implement this recipe, perform the following steps:

1. Open a Power BI Desktop file locally and access **Power Query Editor** by clicking on **Transform Data** in the ribbon of the **Home** tab.
2. Create query parameters called **SQLServer**, **AdventureWorksDB**, and **AdminDB**, and set their values to your SQL Server instance, **AdventureWorksDW2019** and **Admin**, respectively.
3. Create a query named **AdWorksDW**:

```
let
    Source = Sql.Database(SQLServer, AdventureWorksDB)
in
    Source
```

4. Create a query named **AdminDB**:

```
let
    Source = Sql.Database(SQLServer, AdminDB)
in
    Source
```

5. Disable load on the **AdWorksDW** and **Admin** queries, and place both queries into a **Data Sources** query group.
6. Create a **Parameters** query group.
7. In the **Parameters** query group, create a parameter called **CounterHistoryDays** and assign a value of **7** or **30** to limit the number of days retrieved.
8. In the **Parameters** query group, create a parameter called **PerformanceCountersFolder** and set the value equal to the location of the performance counter log files.
9. Create a query called **Performance Counters** in the **Other Queries** query group to retrieve the performance counter log files:

```
let
    CurrentDate = DateTime.Date(DateTime.LocalNow()),
    EarliestDate = Date.AddDays(CurrentDate,-CounterHistoryDays),
    SourceFolder = Folder.Files(PerformanceCountersFolder),
    ReportFiles = Table.SelectRows(SourceFolder, each [Extension] =
".csv" and
        DateTime.Date([Date modified]) >= EarliestDate)
in
    ReportFiles
```

10. Click on the double arrows pointed down on the **Content** column to combine the files remaining into one query. In the **Combine Files** dialog, click **OK**.
11. In the **Transform File from Performance Counters** query group, edit the **Transform Sample File** query:

```
let
    Source = Csv.Document(Parameter1,[Delimiter=",",
        Columns=8, Encoding=1252, QuoteStyle=QuoteStyle.None]),
    PromoteHeaders = Table.PromoteHeaders(Source,
[PromoteAllScalars=true]),
    ParsedDate = Table.AddColumn(PromoteHeaders, "Date",
        each Date.From(DateTimeZone.From(
            [#"(PDH-CSV 4.0) (Eastern Daylight Time)(240)"])), type
date),
    ParsedTime = Table.AddColumn(ParsedDate, "Time",
        each Time.From(DateTimeZone.From(
            [#"(PDH-CSV 4.0) (Eastern Daylight Time)(240)"])), type
time),
    RemoveColumns = Table.RemoveColumns(ParsedTime,
```

```
        {"(PDH-CSV 4.0) (Eastern Daylight Time)(240)"}),
    RenameColumns = Table.RenameColumns(RemoveColumns,
        {{"Memory\Available MBytes", "AvailableMemoryMB"},
        {"Buffer Manager\Page life expectancy", "PageLifeExpectancy"},
        {"SQL Statistics\Batch Requests/sec", "BatchRequestsPerSec"},
        {"PhysicalDisk(_Total)\Avg. Disk sec/Read",
"AvgDiskSecPerRead"},
        {"PhysicalDisk(_Total)\Avg. Disk sec/Write",
"AvgDiskSecPerWrite"},
        {"Processor(_Total)\% Processor Time", "ProcessorTime%"}}),
    HourText = Table.AddColumn(RenameColumns, "TextHour", each
        if Time.Hour([Time]) < 10 then "0" & Text.From(Time.
Hour([Time])) else
        Text.From(Time.Hour([Time])), type text),
    MinText = Table.AddColumn(HourText, "TextMin", each
        if Time.Minute([Time]) < 10 then "0" &
             Text.From(Time.Minute([Time])) else
             Text.From(Time.Minute([Time])), type text),
    SecText = Table.AddColumn(MinText, "TextSec", each
        if Number.RoundDown(Time.Second([Time]),0) < 10 or
            Number.RoundUp(Time.Second([Time]),0) < 10 then "0" &
            Text.From(Number.RoundDown(Time.Second([Time]),0))
        else Text.From(Number.RoundDown(Time.Second([Time]),0)), type
text),
    SecondCol = Table.AddColumn(SecText,"SecondOfDay",
        each [TextHour] & [TextMin] & [TextSec], type text),
    RemoveOtherColumns = Table.SelectColumns(SecondCol,
        {"AvailableMemoryMB", "PageLifeExpectancy",
"BatchRequestsPerSec",
        "AvgDiskSecPerRead", "AvgDiskSecPerWrite", "ProcessorTime%",
        "Date", "Time", "SecondOfDay"})
in
    RemoveOtherColumns
```

12. On the **Performance Counters** query, remove the automatically added **Changed Type** query step and replace this with your own manually set types:

```
    TypeChanges = Table.TransformColumnTypes(PreviousStep,
        {{"AvailableMemoryMB", Int64.Type}, {"PageLifeExpectancy",
Int64.Type},
        {"BatchRequestsPerSec", type number},
        {"AvgDiskSecPerRead", type number},
        {"AvgDiskSecPerWrite", type number}, {"ProcessorTime%", type
number},
        {"Date", type date}, {"Time", type time}, {"SecondOfDay", type
text}})
```

13. In the **Other Queries** group, create a blank query called **Calculations**.
14. Select **Close & Apply** from the ribbon of the **Home** tab.
15. Create a **Dates** table using the following DAX code:

```
Dates =
    VAR __Today = TODAY()
RETURN
    CALENDAR(DATE(YEAR(__Today)-1,1,1),DATE(YEAR(__Today)+1,12,31))
```

16. Create a **Time** table:

```
Time =
    VAR __hrs = SELECTCOLUMNS(GENERATESERIES(1,23,1),"Hour",[Value])
    VAR __mins = SELECTCOLUMNS(GENERATESERIES(0,59,1),"Minutes",[Value])
    VAR __secs = SELECTCOLUMNS(GENERATESERIES(0,59,1),"Seconds",[Value])
    VAR __hoursMinutes = GENERATEALL(__hrs, __mins)
    VAR __hoursMinutesSeconds = GENERATEALL(__hoursMinutes,__secs)
    VAR __final = ADDCOLUMNS(ADDCOLUMNS(__hoursMinutesSeconds,
            "Time", TIMEVALUE(FORMAT([Hour],"00") & ":" &
                FORMAT([Minutes],"00") & ":" & FORMAT([Seconds],"00"))),
            "SecondOfDay", FORMAT([Hour],"00") & FORMAT([Minutes],"00")
&
                FORMAT([Seconds],"00"))
RETURN __final
```

17. Change the **Data type** of the **Date** column in the **Dates** table to **Date**.
18. Change the **Data type** of the **SecondOfDay** column in the **Time** table to **Text**.
19. In the **Model** view, create a relationship between the **Date** columns in the **Dates** table and the **Performance Counters** table.
20. Create a relationship between the **SecondOfDay** columns in the **Time** table and the **Performance Counters** table.
21. Save your work.

How it works...

The scheduled data collector set will automatically generate a subdirectory for each new file output. The Power BI M query references the root directory (or parent), and all supported file formats in subdirectories of this query are available for retrieval. Depending on the volume of counters, their time interval (that is, 15 seconds), and the schedule and duration of the collector set, a significant volume of files can accumulate.

If the source `DateTime` column is already rounded to whole seconds, such as SQL Server `datetime2(0)`, then a **Time** column created via the `DateTime.Time` M function can be used for the relationship to the **Time** dimension table.

Casting SQL Server datetime data type columns to `datetime2(0)` in the SQL view used to import to Power BI is recommended in order to avoid additional rounding logic implemented in a Power BI query. In the case of Performance Monitor Counter log files, the `DateTime` column is not rounded to the whole second, and therefore, rounding logic is applied within the M query to create a six-character text column. The concatenated `SecondOfDay` column is used for the relationship with the **Time** dimension table.

In this example, the **Time** dimension table has 86,400 rows, or 1 row for every second of a day. The detail at this granularity can be helpful in troubleshooting and deeper analysis, but a time dimension at the minute grain with only 1,440 rows may be sufficient. Whether in seconds or minutes, a **Time** dimension table is especially recommended for filtering multiple fact tables in the same report and for providing useful groupings, such as the 7 A.M. to 9 A.M. timeframe.

There's more...

Additional performance data can be added to the model; SQL performance metrics, including wait statistics and the instance configuration data store. Tables can be created in the **Admin** database, such as **WaitStats** and **ConfigData**, with columns that correspond to the `sys.dm_os_wait_stats` and `sys.configurations` system views, respectively. Essentially, these tables contain snapshots of performance or configuration data, just as performance counters represent point-in-time values at the intervals chosen. Maintaining these data collection processes enables tools such as Power BI to generate insights and drive appropriate responses. Refer to the following sources for further information:

- The setup of the wait statistics data store and the capture of wait statistics are described by Erin Stellato in the following blog post: `https://sqlperformance.com/2015/10/sql-performance/proactive-sql-server-health-checks-5`
- The setup of the instance configuration data store and the capture of these values are also described by Erin Stellato in this blog post: `https://sqlperformance.com/2015/02/system-configuration/proactive-sql-server-health-checks-3`

SQL views should be created in the admin database for both `Wait Stats` and the `Config Data` tables. Each view should apply report-friendly column aliases and `WHERE` clauses to only import the timeframes required. The `value` and `value_in_use` columns in the `sys.configurations` view and table to be created in the **Admin** database are stored in a `sql_variant` data type. The view used to import this data to Power BI casts these columns as an **Integer** data type and casts the datetime **CaptureDate** column to `datetime2(0)`, to round this column to seconds.

Import the two views for **WaitStats** and **ConfigData** into the Power BI model and build the appropriate relationships as required. Additional inputs, such as SQL Server Agent and backup log files, can also be integrated to aid administrators in assessing the causes and impacts of changes in available resources, workloads, and system configurations.

See also

- Combine binaries in Power BI Desktop: `http://bit.ly/2oL2nM4`

Constructing a monitoring, visualization, and analysis layer

Monitoring and administration tools, such as Performance Monitor, SQL Server Activity Monitor, Query Store, and Extended Events, include their own graphical interfaces for viewing and analyzing their own specific datasets. However, these features are limited relative to the data exploration and visualization capabilities provided by dedicated BI tools, such as Power BI. Additionally, as per the first recipe of this chapter, system and database administrators require an integrated view over distinct data sources with a common and flexible visual surface. The ability to define logic on top of monitoring source data, along with the "anywhere" availability of Power BI content and its data alert and advanced analytics features, further enhances the value of integrated monitoring datasets.

In this recipe, the monitoring dataset created in the first recipe of this chapter is leveraged to develop reporting content that addresses top stakeholder priorities, such as "How is the performance today?" and "Has any configuration value changed?" A report visualization specific to SQL Server Query Store is included in the *There's more...* section.

Getting ready

To prepare for this recipe, follow these steps:

1. Obtain guidance from stakeholders and subject matter experts (SMEs) on performance baselines and threshold values. For example, should the metric "available memory" be compared to the last 7, 30, or more days? Are there good (green), satisfactory (yellow), and problem (red) values associated with wait statistics measures or CPU time?
2. Complete the first recipe in this chapter, *Creating a centralized IT monitoring solution with Power BI*.

How to construct a monitoring visualization and analysis layer

To implement this recipe, perform the following steps:

1. In the **Calculations** table, create simple DAX measures (`AVERAGE`, `MIN`, and `MAX`) for the performance counters, and date intelligence measures to support a comparison of performance monitoring counters against prior time periods or baselines:

```
Available Memory MB (Today) = CALCULATE([Available Memory (MB)],
    FILTER(ALL('Dates'),'Dates'[Date] = [Today]))

Batch Requests per Sec (Yesterday) = CALCULATE([Batch Requests Per Sec],
    FILTER(ALL('Dates'),'Dates'[Date] = [Yesterday]))

Min Available Memory MB (Today) = CALCULATE([Min Available Memory (MB)],
    FILTER(ALL('Dates'),'Dates'[Date] = [Today]),ALL('Time'))
```

2. Create an **Hour Time** column in the **Time** table to enable slicer selection:

```
Hour Time = TIMEVALUE(FORMAT('Time'[Hour],"00") & ":00")
```

3. Create a report page based on the performance monitor counters that addresses top visibility needs, such as "How is performance today?" and "How close are we to resource thresholds?".

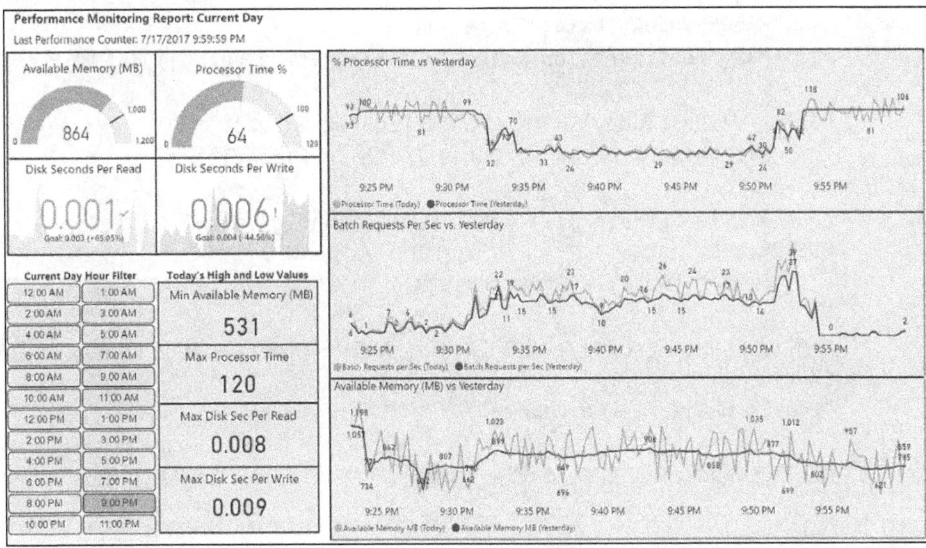

Figure 10.1: Performance Monitoring Report page leveraging Windows Performance Monitor counters

How it works...

The two gauge visuals and the KPI visuals are used to display the highest priority counters relative to predefined thresholds or baselines. For example, **Disk Seconds Per Read** is highlighted in green, given the lower value than the goal of .003; **Disk Seconds Per Write** is highlighted in red due to the higher value than the goal of .004. All four visuals respect the hour filter control (a custom Chiclet slicer) from the lower left, and a **Minute of Day Time** data type column from the **Time** dimension table is used for the KPI visual's **Trend axis.**

A **Today's High and Low Values** group of Card visuals ignores the **Time** filter selection (for example, 9:00 P.M. from the slicer), but applies the current date filter. CPU (% processor), batch requests per second, and available memory are plotted against the prior day values in the line charts in this example. Seven- and 30-day average measures are commonly used for the performance baseline.

There's more...

Report visualizations can also be created for the wait statistics and configuration values, if implemented from the previous recipe. To see how this works, perform the following steps:

1. Create DAX measures to identify database instance configuration changes:

```
Config Value = IF(AND(HASONEVALUE('Configuration
Values'[ConfigurationID]),
     HASONEVALUE('Dates'[Date])),
     MAX('Configuration Values'[Configuration Value]),BLANK())

Config Value (Today) = CALCULATE([Config Value],
     FILTER(ALL('Dates'),'Dates'[Date] = [Today]))

Config Value (Yesterday) = CALCULATE([Config Value],
FILTER(ALL('Dates'),
     'Dates'[Date] = [Yesterday]))

Config Change (Today) = IF([Config Value (Today)] <> [Config Value
(Yesterday)],
"Config Change", "No Change")

Config Changes = IF([Config Value] = [Prior Day Config],0,1)
```

Performance Monitoring Report: Instance Configuration

Last Configuration Capture Date: 7/15/2017

Current Day Configuration Changes

Configuration Name	Config Value (Today)	Config Value (Yesterday)
cost threshold for parallelism	70	100
max server memory (MB)	64,688	53,248

Prior 30 Days Configuration Changes

Configuration Name	Date	Config Value	Prior Day Config
cost threshold for parallelism	7/12/2017	100	5
max degree of parallelism	7/12/2017	0	8
Agent XPs	6/16/2017	1	
blocked process threshold (s)	6/16/2017	5	

Figure 10.2: Instance Configuration Report page: Current day and trailing 30-day history of changes

2. The **Current Day Configuration Changes** table visual uses a visual-level filter on the **Config Change (Today)** measure such that only changed configurations (for the current day) are displayed. The **Prior 30 Days Configuration Changes** table visual uses two visual-level filters. One filter is applied to the **Date** column from the **Dates** dimension table and uses the relative date filtering feature to retrieve the past 30 days but excludes the current day; the other filter condition is applied against the **Config Changes** measure for values of 1.
3. Create similar DAX measures for the **Wait Statistics** table, such as the current-day average wait in seconds.
4. On a new page, compare the average of the current day's wait statistics capture data against a prior date:

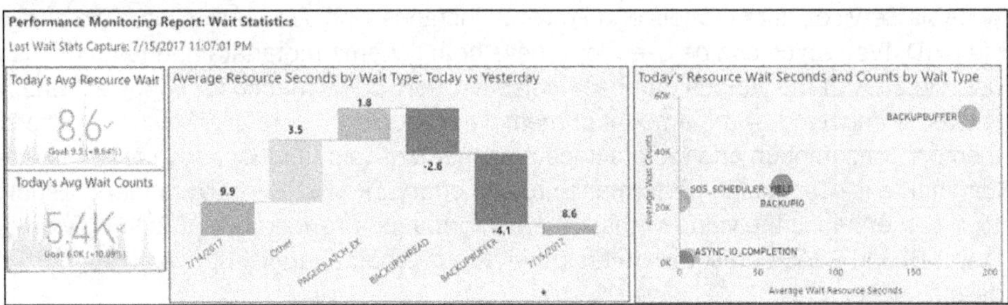

Figure 10.3: Wait Statistics report sample: KPIs, Waterfall, and Scatter Chart visuals

> *"Wait statistics are probably the single best way to start troubleshooting a SQL Server performance issue. SQL Server knows why execution is being stalled (in other words, why threads are having to wait), so using this information to identify bottlenecks and avenues for further investigation can dramatically reduce the time it takes to diagnose the cause of workload degradation."*
>
> *—Paul Randal, CEO of SQLskills, Microsoft Data Platform MVP*

In this limited sample of a wait statistics report, relative date filtering is applied at the page level to only include the past 30 days; thus, the 30-day trend is displayed in the background of the two KPI visuals. Relative date filters are also applied at the visual level to the waterfall and scatter charts to include only the last 2 days and the current day, respectively. The breakdown field well of the Waterfall chart is used to automatically identify the largest drivers of the change in wait seconds (wait types) from the prior day to the current day.

A high-level wait statistics report can be used as a quick starting point of analysis to identify bottlenecks in a system. Additionally, with mature and predictable baseline data in place, the report can be used to troubleshoot performance degradation issues. For example, a sudden spike in `PAGEIOLATCH_EX` waits may indicate a missing index issue, related database schema, or code change.

See also

- SQL Server Wait Types library: `https://www.sqlskills.com/help/waits/`.

Importing and visualizing dynamic management view (DMV) data

Analysis Services data models and Power BI instances include many dynamic management views (DMVs), which can be used to retrieve both schema metadata and resource usage associated with the various database objects. Query performance for imported data models is directly impacted by the amount of memory consumed. Therefore, having visibility to memory consumption and factors impacting memory consumption, such as compression and cardinality, is essential in performance tuning efforts. Power BI integration and visualization tools can enhance the value of the system information provided by DMVs to provide owners of Power BI and SSAS datasets with an intuitive, sustainable reporting layer in support of these assets.

In this recipe, M queries are created to retrieve and transform DMV information from a Power BI dataset. Essential relationships, measures, and report visuals are then built to support memory usage analysis.

Getting ready

To prepare for this recipe, follow these steps:

1. Open the Power BI Desktop file containing the dataset to be analyzed. This file must remain open during data retrieval.
2. Open DAX Studio from **External Tools**.
3. Retrieve the server name and port associated with the running Power BI Desktop file from the bottom right of the DAX Studio status bar; an example would be `localhost:56514`.
4. In DAX Studio, in the upper-left corner under **Metadata**, right-click the database ID and choose **Copy Database ID**.
5. Open a new Power BI Desktop file and click on **Transform data** in the ribbon of the **Home** tab to open the **Power Query Editor** window.
6. Create two parameters, **Server** and **Database**, and apply the values retrieved from DAX Studio as the current values:

Figure 10.4: Query Parameters with values for the local Power BI model

How to import and visualize DMV data

To implement this recipe, perform the following steps:

1. Create a **Segments** query:

```
let Source = AnalysisServices.Database
(Server, Database,[Query="Select * From $SYSTEM.DISCOVER_STORAGE_TABLE_
COLUMN_SEGMENTS"]),
    Segments = Table.AddColumn(Source, "Structure Type", each
        if Text.Range([TABLE_ID],1,1) <> "$" then "Data"
        else if Text.Start([TABLE_ID],2) = "H$" then "Column Hierarchy"
        else if Text.Start([TABLE_ID],2) = "U$" then "User Hierarchy"
        else if Text.Start([TABLE_ID],2) = "R$" then "Relationship"
        else "unknown", type text),
    RenameTable = Table.RenameColumns(Segments,{{"DIMENSION_NAME",
"Table"}}),
    KeyColumn = Table.AddColumn(RenameTable, "ColumnKey", each [Table] &
"-" & [COLUMN_ID], type text)
in KeyColumn
```

2. Create a **Columns** query:

```
let Source = AnalysisServices.Database
(Server, Database,[Query="Select * From $SYSTEM.DISCOVER_STORAGE_TABLE_
COLUMNS"]),
    BasicData = Table.SelectRows(Source, each ([COLUMN_TYPE] = "BASIC_
DATA")),
    RenameTable = Table.RenameColumns(BasicData,{{"DIMENSION_NAME",
"Table"},{"ATTRIBUTE_NAME","Column"}}),
    KeyColumn = Table.AddColumn(RenameTable, "ColumnKey", each [Table] &
"-" & [COLUMN_ID], type text),
    DateRetrieved = Table.AddColumn(KeyColumn, "Date Retrieved", each
DateTime.Date(DateTime.LocalNow()), type date)
in DateRetrieved
```

3. Create a blank query called **Calculations**
4. Click **Close & Apply** in the ribbon of the **Home** tab
5. In **Model** view, create a relationship between the **ColumnKey** columns in the **Segments** and **Columns** tables
6. Create the following DAX measures:

```
BytesPerMB = 1048576

Segment Size (MB) = DIVIDE(SUM(Segments[USED_SIZE]),[BytesPerMB])

Dictionary Size (MB) = DIVIDE(SUM('Columns'[DICTIONARY_
SIZE]),[BytesPerMB])

Data Size (MB) =
    CALCULATE([Segment Size (MB)],Segments[Structure Type] = "Data")

Column Hierarchies Size (MB) =
    CALCULATE([Segment Size (MB)],Segments[Structure Type] = "Column
Hierarchy")

User Hierarchy Size (MB) =
    CALCULATE([Segment Size (MB)],Segments[Structure Type] = "User
Hierarchy")

Relationship Size (MB) =
    CALCULATE([Segment Size (MB)],Segments[Structure Type] =
"Relationship")

Total Column Size (MB) = [Data Size (MB)] + [Dictionary Size (MB)]

Total Size (MB) = [Column Hierarchies Size (MB)] + [Relationship Size
```

```
(MB)] +
    [User Hierarchy Size (MB)] + [Dictionary Size (MB)] + [Data Size
(MB)]

Last Refresh Message = VAR RefreshDate = MAX('Columns'[Date Retrieved])
    RETURN "Last Refreshed: " & RefreshDate
```

7. Create a Power BI report page based on the retrieved and modeled DMV data, as seen in *Figure 10.5:*

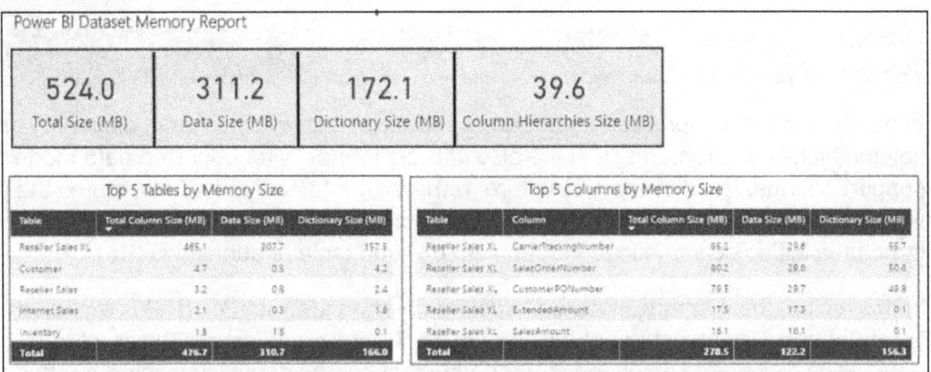

Figure 10.5: Summary Memory report of the Power BI dataset

How it works...

For the **Segments** query, the **Server** and **Database** parameters, along with a SQL statement against the `DISCOVER_STORAGE_TABLE_COLUMN_SEGMENTS` DMV, are used to extract and access memory usage data from the running Power BI Desktop file (which contains an analysis services instance). The conditional column, **Structure Type**, is added to identify the memory structure represented by each row, and a concatenated column, **ColumnKey**, is created to support a relationship with the **Columns** table.

For the **Columns** query, the `DISCOVER_STORAGE_TABLE_COLUMNS` DMV is filtered based on the **Column_Type** column and a concatenated column, **ColumnKey**, is created for the relationship with the **Segments** table. Additionally, a dynamic **Date Retrieved** column is added to support the reporting layer.

The memory columns for both source DMVs are in terms of bytes. **Megabytes** (**MB**) are more intuitive and presentable given that they have fewer digits; thus, the **BytesPerMB** measure (which is hardcoded to 1,048,576) is used to `DIVIDE` the `SUM` of the **USER_SIZE** and **DICTIONARY_SIZE** columns. The **Structure Type** column created in the **Segments** query is used to support different components of overall memory usage, and two total measures are created for summary-level reports.

Card visuals are used to display overall memory usage; two table visuals with top *N* visual-level filters provide additional details. In this example, the **Reseller Sales XL** table is by far the largest table in the model, and specifically, the **CarrierTrackingNumber**, **SalesOrderNumber**, and **CustomerPONumber** columns of this table are consuming the most memory. Clicking on a table name in the **Top 5 Tables** visual cross-filters the **Top 5 Columns** visual.

More DMVs and logic can be added to build a more robust template report for use across Power BI projects. Note that the **Server** and **Database** parameters will need to be updated when a PBIX file being analyzed has been closed and reopened.

There's more...

In addition to the compressed data memory structures for each column, dictionary and column hierarchy structures (**H$**) are also created internally for imported data models to support queries. The dictionary structure, retrieved via the columns DMV, stores the unique values of a column, and so it is larger for high-cardinality columns. Two additional memory structures include user-defined hierarchies (**U$**) and table relationships (**R$**).

In this recipe, the memory allocated to column hierarchy structures (**H$**) is excluded from the **Total Column Size** measure but included in the **Total Size** measure. This is intended to focus analysis on the larger components of memory that can be directly impacted by revisions to the data model. Likewise, the memory used for relationships and user-defined hierarchies is small relative to the data and dictionary size of the model's columns.

Basic performance tuning of imported data models largely focuses on minimizing high-cardinality columns and relationships to reduce the memory scanned. More advanced tuning, generally reserved for SSAS models, involves the partitioning of tables, segment sizes, and optimizing the sort order used by the engine during compression. Only the sort order is available to Power BI datasets.

The Vertipaq Analyzer utilizes DMVs to collect information on datasets and is now integrated into DAX Studio under the **Advanced** menu as well as in Tabular Editor 3. Using the Vertipaq Analyzer is a quicker and easier way to analyze the memory size, cardinality, and other aspects of your data model versus writing your own queries against the DMVs.

See also

- Kasper de Jonge has published a blog on building an SSAS memory report with Power BI: `http://bit.ly/2tDumgk`.
- SQL BI's Vertipaq Analyzer Excel file: `http://bit.ly/2sTTuSO`.
- **Dynamic Management Views** (**DMVs**) in Analysis Services: `https://bit.ly/33etDoc`.

- Vertipaq Analyzer script for Tabular Editor 2: `https://bit.ly/2YA97zv`

Increasing DBA productivity

SQL Server Query Store is a monitoring feature available to all editions of SQL Server 2016 and later—it significantly simplifies and expedites query tuning and troubleshooting. The Query Store database provides aggregated metrics regarding query executions, query plans, and wait statistics to enable visibility to performance trends and usage patterns.

> *"Query Store is a fantastic flight data recorder for your execution plans. It will help you troubleshoot parameter sniffing issues, connection settings issues, plan regressions, bad stats, and much more."*
>
> *—Brent Ozar, Author and Microsoft-Certified Master in SQL Server*

Query Store includes a graphical interface of charts and user controls, and its schema lends itself to custom T-SQL queries such as *10 longest-running queries in the past hour*. While these are great features and sufficient for certain scenarios, administrators often have to make trade-offs between the flexibility of T-SQL and the graphical controls provided by Query Store. In this recipe, simple T-SQL statements are passed from Power BI to SQL Server Query Store in order to identify and analyze recent performance issues, as well as the performance of a specific stored procedure.

Getting ready

To prepare for this recipe, follow these steps:

1. Enable Query Store in the latest version of **SQL Server Management Studio** (**SSMS**), either via the **Database Properties** dialog in the Object Explorer interface (right-click on the database and choose **Properties**) or via the following T-SQL statement:

   ```
   ALTER DATABASE AdventureWorksDW2019 SET QUERY_STORE = ON;
   ```
2. Configure Query Store settings, such as **Statistics Collection Intervals**, **Retention**, and **Max Size (MB)** according to your requirements.

In this example, the performance of individual queries will be aggregated or summarized into 5-minute time frames. Smaller collection time intervals provide greater details, but also require more storage and collection resources. For maximum detail with no grouping of queries, an Extended Events session can be scheduled. Refer to the *Analyzing Extended Events* recipe later in this chapter for more details.

How to increase DBA productivity

To implement this recipe, perform the following steps:

1. Build and test the T-SQL statements to retrieve the required Query Store statistics:

```
SELECT
[rs].[avg_duration], [rs].[avg_logical_io_reads], [qst].[query_text_id],
[qsq].[query_id],
[qst].[query_sql_text], CASE WHEN [qsq].[object_id] = 0
       THEN N'Ad-hoc' ELSE OBJECT_NAME([qsq].[object_id])
       END AS [ObjectName],
[qsp].[plan_id], GETUTCDATE() AS CurrentUTCTime,
[rs].[last_execution_time],
       CAST((DATEADD(MINUTE,
              -(DATEDIFF(MINUTE, GETDATE(), GETUTCDATE())),
              [rs].[last_execution_time])) AS datetime2(0))
       AS LocalLastExecutionTime
FROM
       [sys].[query_store_query] [qsq]
       JOIN [sys].[query_store_query_text] [qst] ON
              [qsq].[query_text_id] = [qst].[query_text_id]
       JOIN [sys].[query_store_plan] [qsp] ON
              [qsq].[query_id] = [qsp].[query_id]
       JOIN [sys].[query_store_runtime_stats] [rs] ON
       [qsp].[plan_id] = [rs].[plan_id]
WHERE [rs].[last_execution_time] > DATEADD(hour, -8, GETUTCDATE())
```

2. Create an additional T-SQL statement containing similar performance-related columns, filtered to a specific stored procedure that also retrieves the collection interval times:

```
SELECT * FROM
[sys].[query_store_query] [qsq]
JOIN [sys].[query_store_query_text] [qst] ON
       [qsq].[query_text_id] = [qst].[query_text_id]
JOIN [sys].[query_store_plan] [qsp]  ON
       [qsq].[query_id] = [qsp].[query_id]
JOIN [sys].[query_store_runtime_stats] [rs] ON
       [qsp].[plan_id] = [rs].[plan_id]
JOIN [sys].[query_store_runtime_stats_interval] [rsi] ON
       [rs].[runtime_stats_interval_id] = [rsi].[runtime_stats_interval_
id]
WHERE [qsq].[object_id] = OBJECT_ID(N'Sales.usp_GetFullProductInfo')
```

3. Create a view and a parameterized stored procedure in SQL Server for the two **Query Store** queries, without the `WHERE` clause filter—this condition will be driven by the Power BI parameter.
4. Design the SQL Server stored procedures to include a `WHERE` clause with a parameter that will be passed from Power BI, such as the following:

```
CREATE PROCEDURE [Website].[QueryStoreProc]
@QSProcedure nvarchar(55)
AS ......
WHERE [qsq].[object_id] = OBJECT_ID(@QSProcedure)
```

5. Open a Power BI Desktop file locally and add server and database parameters for the Query Store database.
6. Create a new query, **AdWorksDW**, with the `Sql.Database` function that references these two parameters.
7. Create a parameter, **HoursInPast**, with a data type of decimal number and a **QueryStoreProcedure** text parameter.
8. Create a new M query, **Query Store DurationIO**, that retrieves the I/O and duration statistics for all queries and uses the **HoursInPast** parameter:

```
let
    Source = AdWorksDW,
    SQLView = Source{[Schema="Website", Item="QueryStoreDurationIO"]}
[Data],
    ParamFilter = Table.SelectRows(SQLView, each
        [LocalLastExecutionTime] >=
            (DateTime.LocalNow() - #duration(0,HoursInPast,0,0))),
    ExecutionDate = Table.AddColumn(ParamFilter,
        "Last Execution Date",
        each DateTime.Date([LocalLastExecutionTime]), type date),
    ExecutionTime = Table.AddColumn(ExecutionDate,
        "Time", each DateTime.Time([LocalLastExecutionTime]), type time)
in ExecutionTime
```

9. Create a new M query, **Query Store Procedure**:

```
let
    Source = AdWorksDW,
    Procedure = Value.NativeQuery(Source,
        "EXECUTE Website.QueryStoreProc @QSProcedure = "
        & "'" & QueryStoreProcedure & "'"),
    InsertedDate = Table.AddColumn(Procedure, "Date",
        each DateTime.Date([end_time]), type date),
    InsertedTime = Table.AddColumn(InsertedDate, "Time",
        each DateTime.Time([end_time]), type time)
in InsertedTime
```

10. Create a blank query called **Calculations**.
11. Click **Close & Apply** from the ribbon of the **Home** tab.
12. Create a **Dates** table using the following DAX code:

```
Dates =
    VAR __Today = TODAY()
RETURN
    CALENDAR(DATE(YEAR(__Today)-1,1,1),DATE(YEAR(__Today)+1,12,31))
```

13. Create a **Time** table:

```
Time =
    VAR __hrs = SELECTCOLUMNS(GENERATESERIES(1,23,1),"Hour",[Value])
    VAR __mins = SELECTCOLUMNS(GENERATESERIES(0,59,1),"Minutes",[Value])
    VAR __secs = SELECTCOLUMNS(GENERATESERIES(0,59,1),"Seconds",[Value])
    VAR __hoursMinutes = GENERATEALL(__hrs, __mins)
    VAR __hoursMinutesSeconds = GENERATEALL(__hoursMinutes,__secs)
    VAR __final = ADDCOLUMNS(ADDCOLUMNS(__hoursMinutesSeconds,
            "Time", TIMEVALUE(FORMAT([Hour],"00") & ":" &
                FORMAT([Minutes],"00") & ":" & FORMAT([Seconds],"00"))),
            "SecondOfDay", FORMAT([Hour],"00") & FORMAT([Minutes],"00")
&
                FORMAT([Seconds],"00"))
RETURN __final
```

14. Change the **Data type** of the **Date** column in the **Dates** table to **Date**.
15. Change the **Data type** of the **SecondOfDay** column in the **Time** table to **Text**.
16. In the **Model** view, create relationships between the **Query Store DurationIO** and **Query Store Procedure** tables with the **Dates** and **Time** tables.
17. Add DAX measures to the **Calculations** table:

```
Average CPU Time (QS Proc) = AVERAGE('Query Store Procedure'[avg_cpu_
time])

Average Duration (QS Proc) = AVERAGE('Query Store Procedure'[avg_
duration])

Average Logical IO Reads (QS Proc) =
    AVERAGE('Query Store Procedure'[avg_logical_io_reads])
```

18. Create dedicated report pages for the two Query Store tables leveraging the measures and relationships:

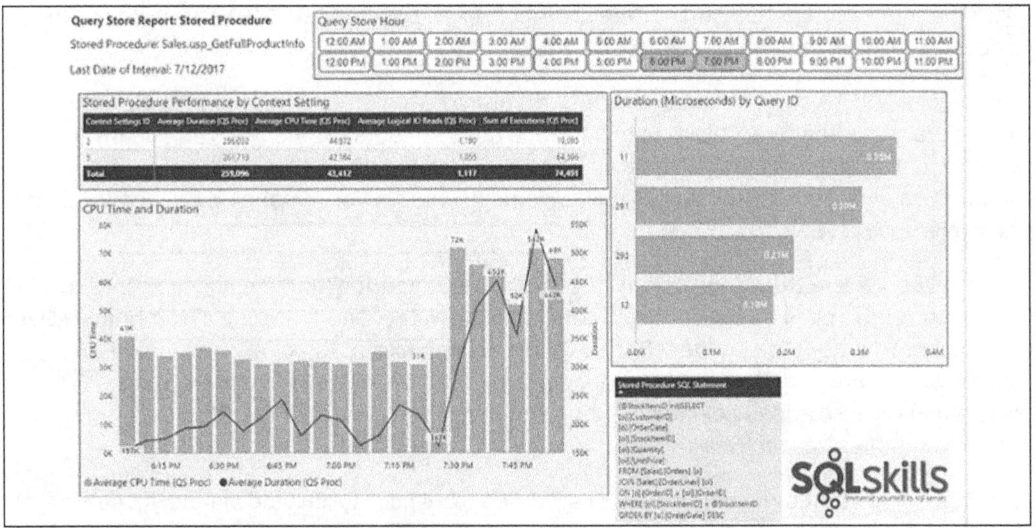

Figure 10.6: Query Store Sample report page - Stored Procedure

The **Query Store Stored Procedure** report page breaks out measures of performance by **Context Settings ID** and individual **Query ID**. A combination chart displays the trend of CPU and duration performance across the intervals; the SQL statement associated with the procedure is displayed via a table visual. Additionally, a custom Chiclet slicer is used to give the user simple filtering control for the hourly time frames.

How it works...

SQL Server Query Store collects compile and runtime information related to the queries and query plans of a database. This persisted data is made available for analysis via three separate data stores:

- A plan store containing query execution plan information
- A runtime stats store of execution statistics
- A wait stats store of query wait statistics

These three data stores can be queried in SQL Server 2016 or later via the following system views: `sys.query_store_plan`, `sys.query_store_runtime_stats`, and `sys.query_store_wait_stats`.

The first T-SQL query retrieves the average duration and logical I/O reads of the Query Store intervals collected over the previous 8 hours, as well as the SQL statement itself and the **Query ID**. A parameter can be set for the number of hours to retrieve in Power BI, and thus the SQL view created for retrieving this data does not require a `WHERE` clause. Power BI will dynamically build a T-SQL statement with a `WHERE` clause filter containing the parameter via Query Folding.

Note that the **LocalLastExecutionTime** column is cast to a `datetime2(0)` data type to provide a date value, rounded to the nearest second.

The second T-SQL query demonstrates how to return Query Store statistics for a stored procedure, since the Query Store user interface does not support the analyzing of any activity specific to a stored procedure. Administrators often require visibility to both the specific timeframes and the overall performance to pinpoint when a performance issue occurred, and its significance relative to a baseline.

For the **Query Store DurationIO** query, the **LocalLastExecutionTime** column is filtered by the `DateTime` value that is based on the current local `DateTime`, and the value in the **HoursInPast** parameter. You may click on **View Native Query** to confirm that the query was folded to the server. A **Date** and **Time** column are added via the `DateTime.Date` and `DateTime.Time` M functions. These added columns will be used in relationships with the **Date** and **Time** dimension tables, respectively.

The SQL Server stored procedure `Website.QueryStoreProc` is executed via the `Value.NativeQuery` function and the Power BI parameter **QueryStoreProcedure** is passed into the concatenated text string. **Date** and **Time** columns are also added to support relationships with the **Date** and **Time** dimension tables. Like the **Query Store DurationIO** query, the `end_time` in the stored procedure is of the `datetime2(0)` data type, such that **Time** columns created via `DateTime.Time` will be rounded off to the nearest second.

There's more...

Individual SQL query statements can also be retrieved from Query Store and Extended Events. The top *N* visual-level filter can be applied to a table visual based on an `Avg Duration` measure, as seen in *Figure 10.7*:

SQL Query	Avg Duration (QS DIO)	Avg Logical IO Reads (QS DIO)
select top 4096 [_].[avg_duration], [_].[avg_logical_io_reads], [_].[query_text.io], [_].[query_id], [_].[query_sql_text], [_].[ObjectName], [_].[plan_id], [_].[CurrentUTCTime], [_].[last_execution_time], [_].[LocalLastExecutionTime] from [Website].[QueryStoreDurationIO] as [_] where [_].[LocalLastExecutionTime] >= convert(datetime2,'2021-09-07' 04:48:40.6340493	1.85	7927
select top 4096 [_].[avg_duration] as [avg_duration]	1.85	7884
Total	**3.70**	**15811**

Figure 10.7: A Table Visual filtered for the top 10 SQL Query values based on the Duration measure

See also

- Monitoring performance by using the Query Store: `http://bit.ly/2s9Cx5r`

Providing documentation

As data models grow and change to support new business processes and logic, access to current documentation becomes imperative. Visibility to basic metadata, such as the relationships of the model, columns of the tables, and the filtering logic built into measures, can significantly aid business teams in utilizing Power BI datasets. Additionally, business intelligence and IT professionals who may be new to a specific model or unfamiliar with a component of the model can benefit greatly from direct access to technical metadata, such as data source parameters, SQL and M queries, and the configured security roles.

In this recipe, several **dynamic management views** (**DMVs**) related to the schema of a Power BI dataset are accessed and integrated into a Power BI report. A template is then created with parameters, enabling standard documentation reports across multiple Power BI datasets.

Getting ready

To prepare for this recipe, follow these steps:

1. Open the Power BI Desktop file containing the dataset to be analyzed. This file must remain open during data retrieval.
2. Open DAX Studio from **External Tools**.
3. Retrieve the server name and port associated with the running Power BI Desktop file from the bottom right of the DAX Studio status bar, such as **localhost:56514**.
4. In DAX Studio, near the upper-left corner under **Metadata**, right-click the database ID and choose **Copy Database ID**.
5. Open a new Power BI Desktop file and click on **Transform data** in the ribbon of the **Home** tab to open the **Power Query Editor** window.
6. Create two parameters, **Server** and **Database**, and apply the values retrieved from DAX Studio as the current values.

How to provide documentation

To implement this recipe, perform the following steps:

1. Create a new blank M query called **TablesDMV** that retrieves the `TMSCHEMA_TABLES` DMV via the **Server** and **Database** parameters:

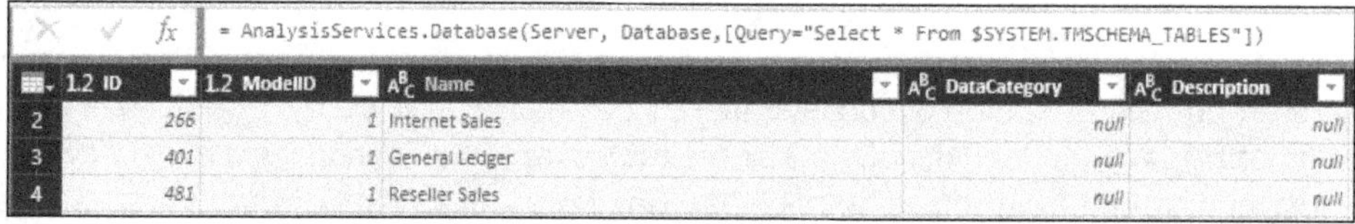

```
= AnalysisServices.Database(Server, Database,[Query="Select * From $SYSTEM.TMSCHEMA_TABLES"])
```

	ID	ModelID	Name	DataCategory	Description
2	266	1	Internet Sales	null	null
3	401	1	General Ledger	null	null
4	481	1	Reseller Sales	null	null

Figure 10.8: Table metadata of the running Power BI Desktop file

2. Duplicate the **TablesDMV** query to retrieve the following five schema DMVs as well:
   - `SYSTEM.TMSCHEMA_COLUMNS`
   - `SYSTEM.TMSCHEMA_MEASURES`
   - `SYSTEM.TMSCHEMA_ROLES`
   - `SYSTEM.TMSCHEMA_TABLE_PERMISSIONS`
   - `SYSTEM.TMSCHEMA_RELATIONSHIPS:`

3. Name the queries according to their source, and organize these and their parameters into their own folders:

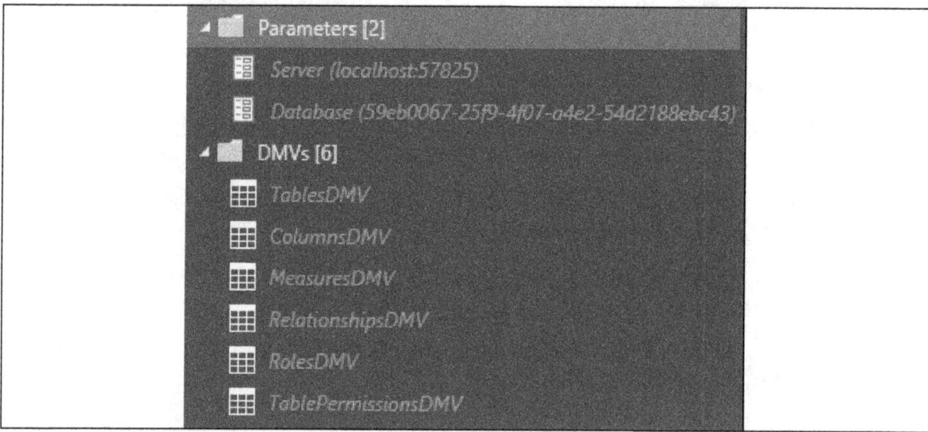

Figure 10.9: Parameters and DMV queries used to support model documentation

4. Create a third query group named **Documentation** and a new blank query named **Columns**:

```
let
    Tables = TablesDMV, Columns = ColumnsDMV,
    Join = Table.NestedJoin(Columns,{"TableID"},Tables,{"ID"},
```

```
        "TableColumns",JoinKind.LeftOuter),
    TableExpand = Table.ExpandTableColumn(Join,"TableColumns",
        {"Name"},{"Table"}),
    DataType = Table.AddColumn(TableExpand, "Data Type", each
        if [ExplicitDataType] = 2 then "Text" else
        if [ExplicitDataType] = 6 then "Whole Number" else
        if [ExplicitDataType] = 8 then "Decimal Number" else
        if [ExplicitDataType] = 9 then "Date" else
        if [ExplicitDataType] = 10 then "Fixed Decimal Number" else
"Other",
            type text),
    ColumnType = Table.AddColumn(DataType, "Column Type", each
        if [Type] = 1 then "Standard" else
        if [Type] = 2 then "Calculated" else "Other", type text),
    Filter = Table.SelectRows(ColumnType, each
            not Text.StartsWith([ExplicitName], "RowNumber")
            and not Text.StartsWith([Table],"LocalDate")
            and not Text.StartsWith([Table], "DateTableTemplate")),
    Rename = Table.RenameColumns(Filter,
        {{"ExplicitName","Column"}, {"DataCategory", "Data Category"},
        {"IsHidden", "Is Hidden"}, {"FormatString", "Column Format"}})
in Rename
```

5. Create a new blank query named **Relationships** and identify the tables and columns for each relationship:

```
let
    Relationships = RelationshipsDMV,
    Tables = TablesDMV, Columns = ColumnsDMV,
    FromTableJoin = Table.NestedJoin(Relationships,
        {"FromTableID"}, Tables, {"ID"},"FromTableCols",JoinKind.Inner),
    FromTable = Table.ExpandTableColumn(FromTableJoin,
        "FromTableCols",{"Name"},{"From Table"}),
    ToTableJoin = Table.NestedJoin(FromTable,
        {"ToTableID"},Tables,{"ID"},"ToTableCols",JoinKind.Inner),
    ToTable = Table.ExpandTableColumn(ToTableJoin,"ToTableCols",
        {"Name"},{"To Table"}),
    FilterDateTbls = Table.SelectRows(ToTable,
        each not Text.StartsWith([To Table],"LocalDateTable")),
    FromColumnJoin = Table.NestedJoin(FilterDateTbls,
        {"FromColumnID"},Columns,{"ID"},"FromColumnCols",JoinKind.
Inner),
    FromColumn = Table.ExpandTableColumn(FromColumnJoin,"FromColumnCo
ls",
        {"ExplicitName"},{"From Column"}),
```

```
    ToColumnJoin = Table.NestedJoin(FromColumn,
        {"ToColumnID"},Columns,{"ID"},"ToColumnCols",JoinKind.Inner),
    ToColumn = Table.ExpandTableColumn(ToColumnJoin,"ToColumnCols",
        {"ExplicitName"},{"To Column"}),
    CrossFiltering = Table.AddColumn(ToColumn, "Cross Filtering",
        each if [CrossFilteringBehavior] = 1 then "Single Direction"
            else "Bidirectional", type text),
    Rename = Table.RenameColumns(CrossFiltering,{{"ID","Relationship
ID"}})
in Rename
```

6. Create a simple query called **Metrics** based on the **MeasuresDMV** query that adds the table name via a join to the **TablesDMV** query
7. Add a query called **Security Roles** that joins the **RolesDMV** query with the **TablePermissionsDMV** query and the **TablesDMV** query, such that the name of the security role, the filter condition, and the table of the filter condition are included in the query
8. Click **Close & Apply** from the ribbon of the **Home** tab
9. In **Report** view, create the following four report pages:
    - ❑ Columns
    - ❑ Relationships
    - ❑ Measures
    - ❑ Security
10. Use table visuals to expose the most important columns from each integrated M query on each page:

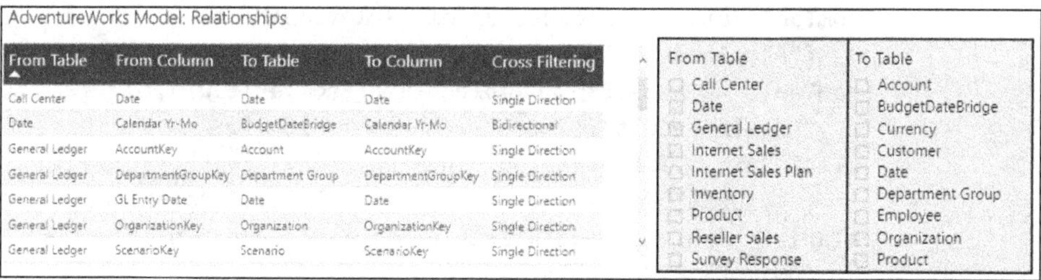

Figure 10.10: Relationships metadata report page

The alternating rows Matrix style is useful for simple table lists such as metadata documentation. For larger, more complex models, slicer visuals give users the ability to quickly answer their own questions about the model such as "Which tables are related to internet sales?" or "Which measures are hidden from the Fields list?":

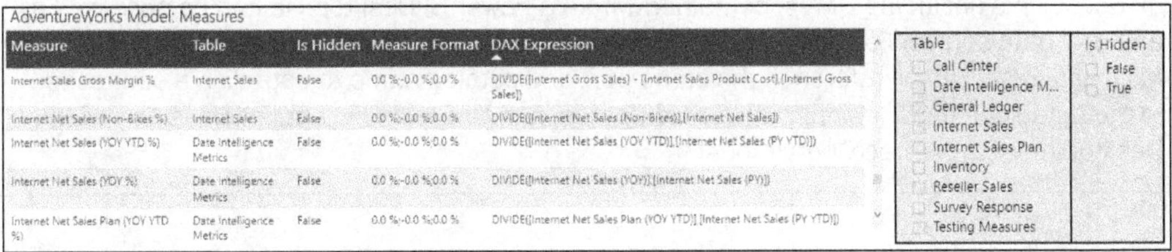

Figure 10.11: Measures metadata report page

Table and matrix visuals support word wrap for both headers and individual values. For table visuals exposing the **DAX Expression** column and other long columns such as SQL statements, enable **Word wrap** in the **Values** card of the formatting pane.

1. With the report pages complete, save the Power BI Desktop file and publish the report to the Power BI service.
2. In Desktop, click on **File**, and then on **Export**, to save a Power BI template file (`.pbit`).
3. Test the template by retrieving the port and catalog name for a separate dataset and opening the template:

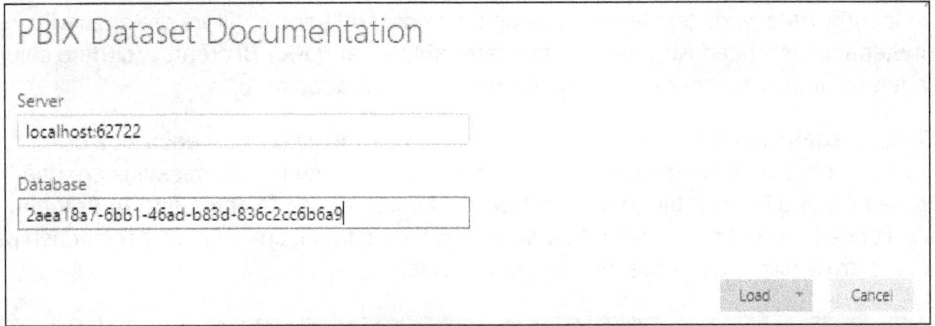

Figure 10.12: Opening the template (.pbit) file to generate documentation on a separate Power BI dataset

With the target dataset open, the queries will prompt for authorization, but will then load the report pages.

How it works...

When used as a dataset rather than a report with a live connection, an open Power BI Desktop file includes an instance of SQL Server Analysis Services (SSAS). Therefore, all data model objects (including DMVs) contained within a Power BI Desktop file can be accessed as an SSAS data source. For example, SQL Server Profiler, SQL Server Management Studio, and Microsoft Excel can all reference the same port and catalog name to establish a connection to the data source. Additionally, the same approach in this recipe is applicable to Power BI Desktop models in DirectQuery mode:

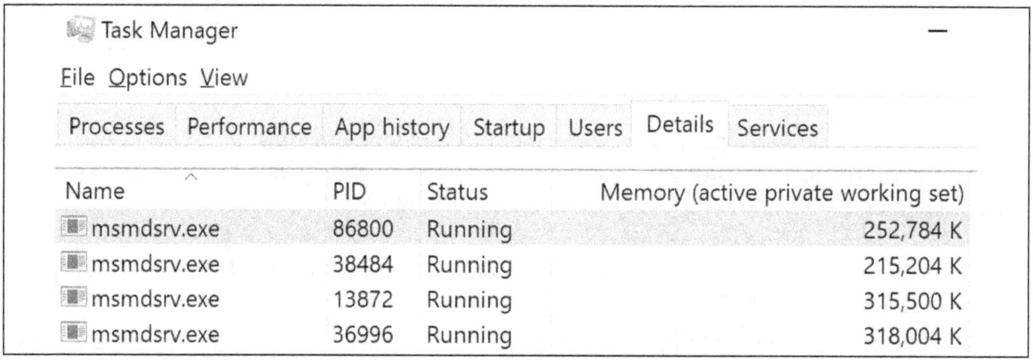

Task Manager

File Options View

Processes | Performance | App history | Startup | Users | Details | Services

Name	PID	Status	Memory (active private working set)
msmdsrv.exe	86800	Running	252,784 K
msmdsrv.exe	38484	Running	215,204 K
msmdsrv.exe	13872	Running	315,500 K
msmdsrv.exe	36996	Running	318,004 K

Figure 10.13: Windows Task Manager: SQL Server Analysis Services processes associated with open PBIX datasets

The **Columns** query joins the **Columns** and **Tables** DMV queries and creates two new columns to identify data types and any calculated columns. Additionally, filters are applied to remove metadata associated with the internal date tables that Power BI creates for date columns, and a few columns are renamed to support the documentation reports.

The **Relationships** DMV contains the Table and Column ID keys for each side of every relationship defined in the model. Therefore, four separate join expressions are used to retrieve the **From Table** and **From Column** as well as the **To Table** and **To Column**. Additionally, a column is added to identify any bidirectional cross-filtering relationships, and filters are applied to remove internal date tables.

There's more...

For SSAS tabular documentation, additional DMVs such as `TMSCHEMA_KPIS` and `TMSCHEMA_PERSPECTIVES` may be utilized, along with more details on the display folders of columns and measures, the descriptions entered by model authors for various objects, and partitions. It's possible that metadata currently specific to SSAS, such as perspectives and KPIs, will also be utilized by Power BI datasets in the future.

See also

- *Four Different Ways to Find Your Power BI Local Port Number*: `https://bit.ly/3uiV01d`
- *Dynamic Management Views (DMVs) in Analysis Services*: `https://bit.ly/33etDoc`

Analyzing SSAS tabular databases and gateways

A Microsoft on-premises data gateway enables specific cloud services, including Power BI, Azure Analysis Services, Power Apps, and Power Automate, to securely connect to on-premises data sources. In the context of Power BI, these connections support both the scheduled refresh of imported datasets stored in Power BI, as well as DirectQuery and Live Connection datasets, in which only report queries and their results are exchanged between Power BI and the on-premises source. As the availability and performance of the gateway are critical for any Power BI and other supported cloud service deployment requiring on-premises data, regular monitoring of both the gateway service and its host server(s) is recommended.

In this recipe, performance monitor counters specific to the on-premises data gateway and SQL Server Analysis Services are integrated into a single Power BI dataset. This source data is dynamically retrieved and enhanced via M queries, and sample report visualizations are created to support monitoring and analysis.

Getting ready

To prepare for this recipe, follow these steps:

1. For the initial deployment or planning phases, review the available documentation, tips, and best practices on both SSAS tabular and the on-premises data gateway, including the recommended hardware and network configuration.

   SSAS tabular servers should have 2.5x the RAM of their compressed in-memory databases, and outbound port 443 should be opened to run the on-premises data gateway in the default HTTPS mode (ports 9350-9353 if TCP mode). Despite sufficient hardware, the design and complexity of data models, M queries, and DAX measures can significantly impact resource usage and performance. See *Chapter 11, Enhancing and Optimizing Existing Power BI Solutions,* for more details.

2. Identify a secure network location directory to store the performance counter file. This path could use a common network drive and the parent folder of other monitoring log files.

3. Use Windows Performance Monitor to design and schedule a new data collector set that contains the following performance monitor counters:
    - \MSOLAP:Memory\Memory Limit Hard KB
    - \MSOLAP:Memory\Memory Limit High KB
    - \MSOLAP:Memory\Memory Limit Low KB
    - \MSOLAP:Memory\Memory Limit Vertipaq KB
    - \MSOLAP:Memory\Memory Usage KB

Performance Monitor defaults to `.blg` log files, but Power BI can only consolidate files in text, CSV, and Excel format, so set **Log format** to **Comma separated**. Windows Performance Monitor is well documented and understood by most administrators. Best practices and automation via PowerShell are outside the scope of this recipe.

How to analyze SSAS tabular models and gateways

To implement this recipe, perform the following steps:

1. Open a new Power BI Desktop file to be used for both the SSAS tabular and on-premises data gateway counters.
2. Create data source parameters for the **Server**, **Database**, and the number of days of history (**CounterHistoryDays**) to retrieve.
3. Define a query, **AdWorksDW**, that exposes the database objects (tables and views).
4. Create a new query called **SSAS Memory** that selects the parent folder location of the SSAS tabular performance counters, and follow the same steps of importing performance monitor counter files described in the *Creating a centralized IT monitoring solution with Power BI* recipe earlier in this chapter.
5. Click **Close & Apply** from the ribbon of the **Home** tab.
6. Create a **Dates** table using the following DAX code:

```
Dates =
    VAR __Today = TODAY()
RETURN
    CALENDAR(DATE(YEAR(__Today)-1,1,1),DATE(YEAR(__Today)+1,12,31))
```

7. Create a **Time** table:

```
Time =
    VAR __hrs = SELECTCOLUMNS(GENERATESERIES(1,23,1),"Hour",[Value])
```

```
    VAR __mins = SELECTCOLUMNS(GENERATESERIES(0,59,1),"Minutes",[Value])
    VAR __secs = SELECTCOLUMNS(GENERATESERIES(0,59,1),"Seconds",[Value])
    VAR __hoursMinutes = GENERATEALL(__hrs, __mins)
    VAR __hoursMinutesSeconds = GENERATEALL(__hoursMinutes,__secs)
    VAR __final = ADDCOLUMNS(ADDCOLUMNS(__hoursMinutesSeconds,
            "Time", TIMEVALUE(FORMAT([Hour],"00") & ":" &
                FORMAT([Minutes],"00") & ":" & FORMAT([Seconds],"00"))),
            "SecondOfDay", FORMAT([Hour],"00") & FORMAT([Minutes],"00")
&
                FORMAT([Seconds],"00"))
RETURN __final
```

8. Change the **Data type** of the **Date** column in the **Dates** table to **Date**.
9. Change the **Data type** of the **SecondOfDay** column in the **Time** table to **Text**.
10. In the **Model** view, create a relationship between the **Date** columns in the **Dates** table and the **SSAS Memory** table.
11. Create a relationship between the **SecondOfDay** columns in the **Time** table and the **SSAS Memory** table.
12. Create DAX measures to support reporting and analysis, such as the following:

```
KB to GB Conversion = 1048576

Avg Memory Limit Hard (GB) =
     DIVIDE(AVERAGE('SSAS Memory'[Memory Limit Hard KB]),[KB to GB
Conversion])

Avg Memory Usage GB (Today) =
     CALCULATE([Avg Memory Usage (GB)],
          FILTER(ALL('Date'),'Date'[Date] = [Current Date]))

Max Memory Usage GB (Today) =
     CALCULATE([Max Memory Usage (GB)],
          FILTER(ALL('Date'),'Date'[Date] = [Current Date]))

Max Memory GB (Today, All Time) =
     CALCULATE([Max Memory Usage GB (Today)],ALL('Time'))
```

13. Create an SSAS tabular memory report leveraging the consolidated counter files, model relationships, and measures:

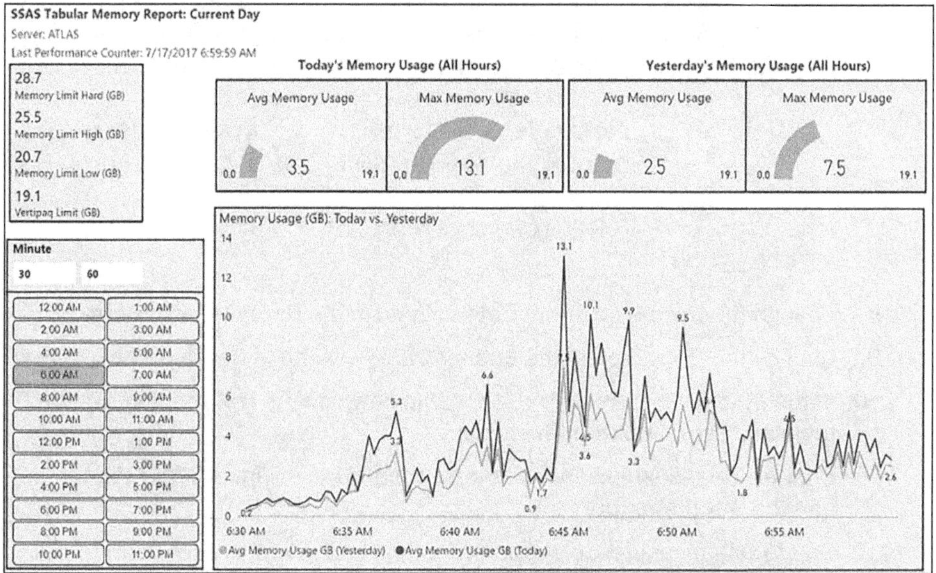

Figure 10.14: SQL Server Analysis Services server properties - memory properties

How it works...

SSAS Tabular requires memory during processing operations to load new data, in addition to the memory used for existing data. Additionally, temporary memory structures are sometimes created to resolve certain queries. These three components comprise the 2.5x RAM recommendation (2x for current and new data and .5x for temporary structures).

As the memory required by the SSAS instance exceeds certain memory limits or thresholds, given the amount of RAM available to the server and the memory properties defined in analysis server properties, SSAS takes various actions, ranging from clearing out low-priority memory caches (`LowMemoryLimit`) to aggressively terminating user sessions (`HardMemoryLimit`). A reference to SSAS memory property documentation is included in the *See also* section.

The DAX measures convert the memory counter values from KB to GB and make it easy to compare the current day versus the prior day in different filter contexts. For example, the **Avg Memory Usage GB (Today)** measure is filtered to the current date but will respect user or report filter selections on the **Time** dimension table. The **Max Memory GB (Today, All Time)** measure, however, will ignore both **Dates** and **Time** filter selections to always show the highest memory usage value for the current day.

Significant spikes in memory usage may indicate sub-optimal DAX measures or inefficient report queries that require large, temporary memory structures. BI teams would want to ensure that memory usage does exceed the memory limits identified by the counters, to avoid performance degradation. Increases in the SSAS memory limit property settings, or simply more overall RAM for the SSAS server, are two options to avoid memory shortages.

There's more...

Scheduled refreshes of imported datasets to Power BI can require significant resources at the time of refresh, based on the size of the dataset and whether its M queries can be folded to the data source as SQL statements. For example, if an M function that doesn't have an equivalent expression in the source Oracle database is used, the M engine in the gateway will be used to execute the logic, such as filter, sort, and aggregate.

DirectQuery and SSAS live connections are less resource-heavy, however, as only queries and query result data are transferred across the gateway. Despite this, it is important to consider the fact that these connections generate a high frequency of queries based on the number of concurrent users, their usage or interaction with the published reports, the type and volume of visualizations, and whether **row-level security** (**RLS**) roles have been configured.

Performance reports can also be created for Power BI gateways. To understand how this is done, perform the following steps:

1. Create and schedule a new performance monitor data collector set containing the on-premises data gateway counters:

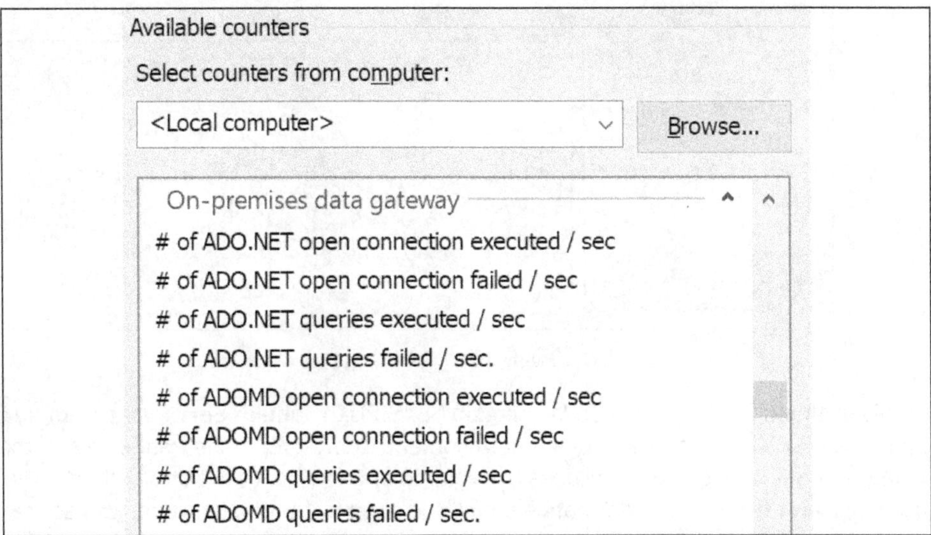

Figure 10.15: On-premises data gateway performance counters

2. In the same Power BI Desktop file containing the SSAS counters, create an additional query to the parent folder of the gateway counter files and apply the same M query transformations to filter the files imported, adjust data types, rename columns, and add **Date** and **Time** columns to support relationships to the **Dates** and **Time** dimension tables
3. Build basic aggregation measures against the different gateway counter columns
4. Build additional DAX measures that apply or remove filter contexts from the **Dates** and **Time** tables, following the same expression patterns as the **SSAS Memory** DAX measures
5. Design a dedicated gateway report page for the gateway performance counters:

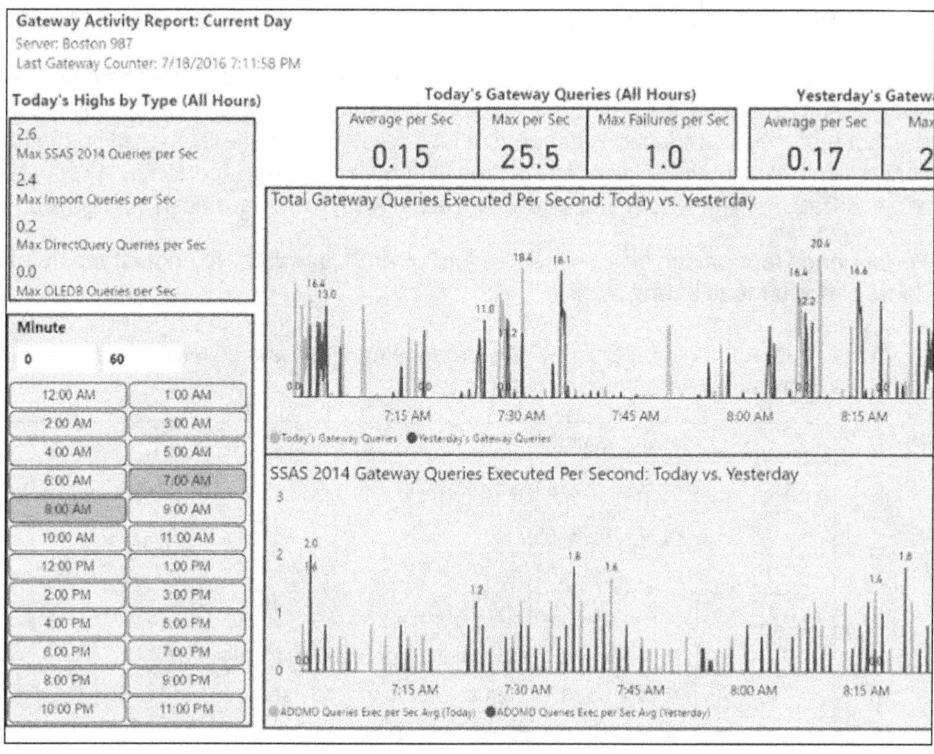

Figure 10.16: Gateway performance report

In this example, the organization is using an SSAS 2014 Tabular Server as a primary data source for Power BI report and dashboard content. Therefore, measures based on the ADOMD gateway counters are used to expose the volume of this workload (bottom chart). The **# of all queries executed / sec** performance counter is used by the top chart, as well as the average and maximum card visuals above the line chart. Though less common, the organization also uses this gateway to support certain import refreshes of Power BI datasets (Mashup counters) and DirectQuery datasets (ADO.NET counters).

Card, gauge, and standard KPI visuals pinned as tiles to dashboards can drive data alerts and email notifications. In the context of this recipe, memory usage in excess of the Vertipaq and other memory limits could warrant a data alert. Likewise, a high number of query failures, or an unexpected query type activity reported by the gateway counters, could also drive a data alert. For example, if a particular gateway is intended to be dedicated to Import (Mashup) workloads, the counters shouldn't report query activity for ADO.NET (DirectQuery) or OLEDB connections.

It should be noted that the on-premises data gateway supports logging via the **Diagnostics** tab of the management application. Detailed logging can be enabled by toggling the **Additional logging** option on although this should only be used when troubleshooting and not left on permanently as this considerably increases the number and size of log files. The gateway logs can be exported on the same **Diagnostics** tab.

See also

- *Guidance for Deploying a Data Gateway for Power BI*: `http://bit.ly/2t8hk9i`
- *SQL Server Analysis Services Memory Properties*: `http://bit.ly/2vuY1I2`
- *Monitor and optimize on-premises data gateway performance*: `https://bit.ly/3nffIJQ`

Analyzing Extended Events

Extended Events is a highly configurable and lightweight performance monitoring system available to both the SQL Server relational database engine and Analysis Services. A vast library of events is available to specific sessions, which can be saved, scheduled, and then analyzed to support performance tuning, troubleshooting, and general monitoring. However, similar to other monitoring tools (such as Windows Performance Monitor and SQL Server Query Store), the Extended Events graphical interface lacks the rich analytical capabilities and flexibility of reporting tools such as Power BI.

In this recipe, the output of an Extended Events session containing query execution statistics is retrieved in a dedicated Power BI event analysis report file. The 1.4 million rows of event data from this file are enhanced during the import process, and report visualizations are developed to call out the most meaningful trends and measures, as well as support further self-service analysis.

Getting ready

To prepare for this recipe, follow these steps:

1. Identify the events associated with the top monitoring and troubleshooting use cases

2. Create separate extended event sessions tailored to these use cases with filters to exclude irrelevant or redundant data

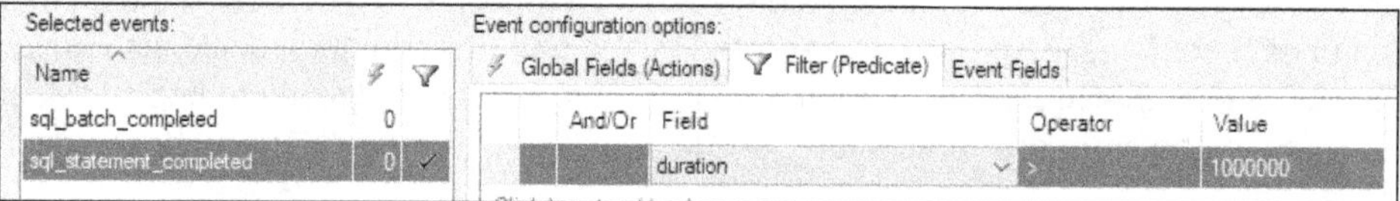

Figure 10.17: An Extended Events session with two events and a filter

3. Determine the data storage target for the session(s), such as an **event file**, and the location of this file
4. Optionally, configure settings such as **Event retention mode** and **Max memory size** and/or optionally configure a SQL Agent job to start and stop the event session

How to analyze Extended Events

To implement this recipe, perform the following steps:

1. Obtain access to the Extended Events target XEL target file and open it from **SQL Server Management Studio** (**SSMS**), or open it directly from Windows Explorer in a distinct instance of SSMS.
2. With the XEL file open in SSMS, click on the **Extended Events** tab on the toolbar and select **Export to** at the bottom.
3. Choose the **CSV File** option, enter a filename describing the session, and select a network path common to Extended Events and, potentially, other performance and administrative log files:

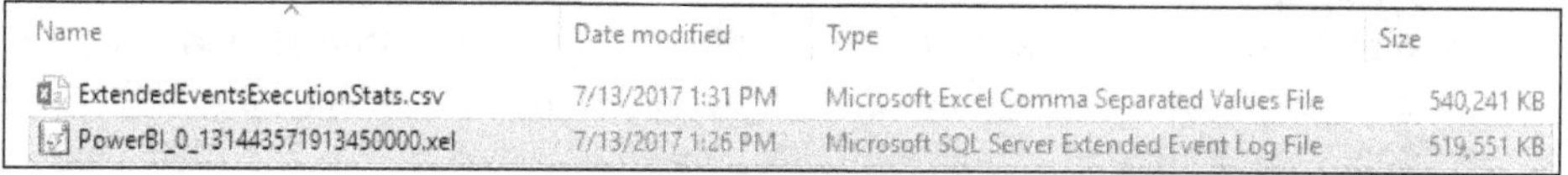

Figure 10.18: An Extended Events session target XEL file and its export as a CSV file

4. Open a Power BI Desktop file that already contains **Dates** and **Time** tables, or create these tables using the same process as described in the *Creating a centralized IT monitoring solution with Power BI* recipe earlier in this chapter
5. Click **Transform data** from the ribbon of the **Home** tab to open **Power Query Editor**
6. Create a parameter for the directory folder path of the event session files and a parameter for the session filename

7. Open a blank query that concatenates the two parameters into a full file path. Name this query **XEventsSession**:

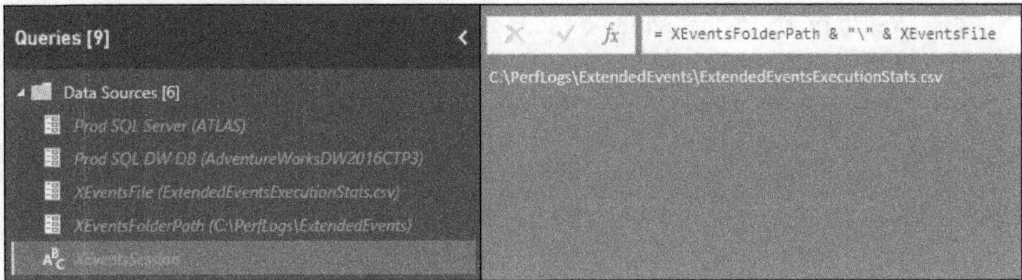

Figure 10.19: Query Editor view with the Data Sources parameter and XEventsSession query

8. Create a query that uses the text/CSV data connector, and replace the file path with the **XEventsSession** query
9. Promote the top row as the column headers and convert the data types via the `Table.TransformColumnTypes` function
10. Add a **Date** column based on the **Timestamp** column of the source file:

```
let
    Source = Csv.Document(File.Contents(XEventsSession),
        [Delimiter=",", Columns=31, Encoding=65001,QuoteStyle=QuoteSty
le.None]),
    PromotedHeaders = Table.PromoteHeaders(Source,
[PromoteAllScalars=true]),
    ChangeTypes = Table.TransformColumnTypes(PromotedHeaders,
        {{"timestamp", type datetime}, {"duration", Int64.Type}}),
    DateColumn = Table.AddColumn(RenameColumns, "Timestamp Date",
        each DateTime.Date([timestamp]), type date)
in
    DateColumn
```

11. Add a **Time** column and a **SecondOfDay** column to support a relationship with the **Time** dimension table

    See the *Creating a centralized IT monitoring solution with Power BI* recipe earlier in this chapter for the **SecondOfDay** column logic and syntax. Like the Performance Monitor Counter data in that example, the timestamp from the Extended Events session is not at the seconds grain, and so adding a time column via the `DateTime.Time` M function is not sufficient to support a model relationship with the **Time** dimension table

12. Name this query **Execution Stats**; disable the load of the **XEventsSession** query

13. Create a blank query called **Calculations**
14. Click **Close & Apply** from the ribbon of the **Home** tab
15. Create many-to-one, single-direction relationships from **Execution Stats** to the **Dates** and **Time** tables
16. Develop and format simple DAX measures to support common aggregations of Extended Events fact columns, such as the average, minimum, and maximum of query duration, CPU time, and logical reads and writes:

```
Average CPU Time = AVERAGE('Execution Stats'[cpu_time])

Max Duration = MAX('Execution Stats'[duration])

Minimum Logical Reads = MIN('Execution Stats'[logical_reads])
```

17. Create a report to visualize the data, like the one shown in *Figure 10.20*:

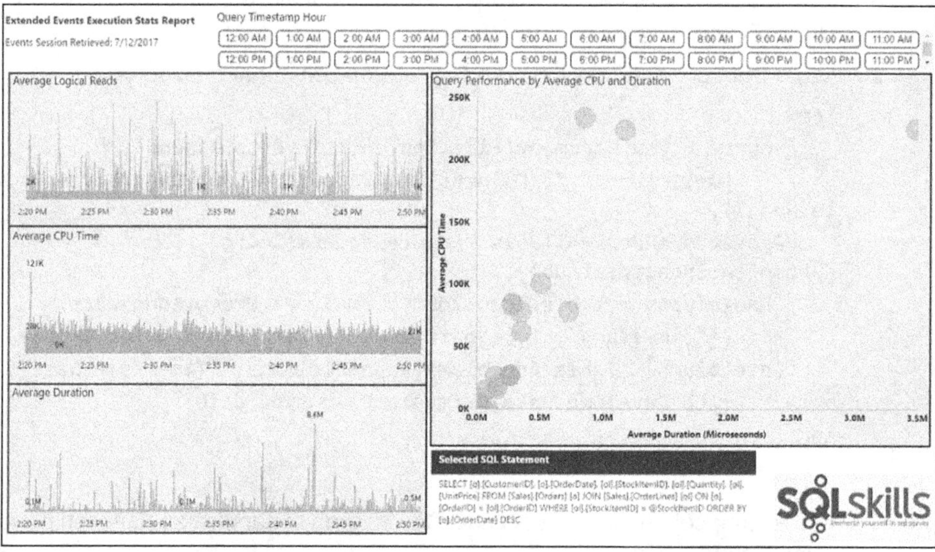

Figure 10.20: Extended Events Execution Stats Report page

In this example, 3 line charts highlight spikes in logical reads, CPU time, and query duration that occurred during the 30-minute Extended Events session. The scatter chart plots individual query_hash values by duration and CPU time and uses the Tooltip to expose the individual SQL statement represented. A table visual with word wrapping is used to display the SQL statement associated with the user's selection as well. Refer to the *How it works...* section for more details on the sample report visual.

How it works...

By design, Extended Events sessions cannot be written to tables within SQL Server. Additional options for capturing and analyzing event session data are available, such as the **histogram** and **pair matching** targets. Data can also be viewed live via **Watch Live Data**; the CSV and table export options expose this data to tools such as Power BI.

Note that if the events file was exported to a table in SQL Server, the Power BI dataset could be configured for DirectQuery mode. Avoiding the import to Power BI via DirectQuery could be a useful or even a necessary design choice if large and/or multiple event session files are needed in the same Power BI dataset. The dedicated **Admin** database described in the first recipe of this chapter could store the Extended Events data, and essential **Dates** and **Time** tables could be imported into this same server and database, thereby permitting DirectQuery mode.

There's more...

SQL Server Profiler is supported in SQL Server 2016, but is now a deprecated feature for the relational database engine; Extended Events is its long-term replacement. Profiler is not a deprecated feature for Analysis Services, although a graphical interface to Extended Events is a new feature in SSAS 2016, and several new SSAS trace events are exclusively available via Extended Events. Regardless of the database engine (relational or analytical), Extended Events is more efficient and flexible than SQL Server Profiler, thus allowing for more nuanced event data collection with less impact on production workloads. Events associated with new SQL Server features are exclusive to Extended Events.

Additional standard event sessions, such as blocking and deadlocking sessions, could be integrated into the Power BI dataset, similar to the consolidated dataset and visualization layer described earlier in this chapter. As the solution matures, custom groupings of events and/or bins of numerical columns could be embedded in the dataset to simplify analysis further.

In Azure, Azure Log Analytics can be used to monitor activities of virtual machines and other resources running in Azure. Kusto queries can be written to extract log events from this data. These Kusto queries can then be exported to **Power Query (M)** using the **Export** menu. These **Power Query (M)** queries can then be pasted into a blank query in Power BI to extract the same data and include in a model.

See also

- *Quickstart: Extended Events in SQL Server*: `https://bit.ly/2Ss8pRN`
- *XEvents overview—SQL Server*: `https://bit.ly/2QJmfPj`
- *Log Analytics tutorial - Azure Monitor*: `https://bit.ly/3hn3NGn`

Visualizing log file data

Log files containing SQL Server Agent job history and the Power BI usage activities stored in the Office 365 audit log and Power BI activity log can also be integrated into the Power BI monitoring solution described earlier in this chapter. For example, SQL Agent job data can reveal important trends, such as the performance of a nightly job used to load a data warehouse and the duration and reliability of individual steps within these jobs. Likewise, detailed reporting and, optionally, alerts based on user activities in the Power BI service, such as deleting a dashboard, enable BI and IT administrators to better manage and govern Power BI deployments.

In this recipe, transformations are applied to the structure of the Power BI audit log to convert the audit data stored in JSON format and adjust for local time reporting. Additionally, an advanced T-SQL query is used to access the job history data in SQL Server Agent system tables, and to prepare this data for visualization in Power BI. While this recipe covers the Office 365 audit log, similar information can be obtained using the Power BI activity log. Refer to the *See also* section of this recipe for more information on the Power BI activity log.

Getting ready

To prepare for this recipe, follow these steps:

1. In the Power BI Admin portal, select **Tenant Settings** and enable audit logging:

Audit and usage settings

◢ Create audit logs for internal activity auditing and compliance

Enabled for the entire organization

Users in the organization can use auditing to monitor actions taken in Power BI by other users in the organization.

Enabled

Figure 10.21: Power BI audit logging enabled

2. Make sure that you are an Office 365 Global Administrator, or otherwise have permissions enabled to access the Office 365 audit logs
3. Run a **PowerShell** session as **Administrator**
4. Set your execution policy:

```
Set-ExecutionPolicy RemoteSigned
```

5. Run the following command to install the Exchange Online Management module:

```
Install-Module ExchangeOnlineManagement
```

6. Connect to Microsoft Exchange Online (where <UPN> is your Office 365 email address):

```
Connect-ExchangeOnline -UserPrincipalName <UPN>
```

7. Make sure that you are able to run PowerShell remotely (where <UPN> is your Office 365 email address):

```
Set-User -Identity <UPN> -RemotePowerShellEnabled $true
```

8. Verify audit log access:

```
Search-UnifiedAuditLog -StartDate 5/1/2021 -EndDate 5/4/2021 -RecordType
PowerBI -ResultSize 1000 | Format-Table | More
```

9. Export the audit log to a CSV file:

```
Search-UnifiedAuditLog -StartDate $startDt -EndDate $endDt -RecordType
PowerBI | Export-Csv $csvFile
```

10. Create a view in the **Admin** SQL Server database (described in the *Creating a centralized IT monitoring solution with Power BI* recipe earlier in this chapter) that queries the `dbo.sysjobhistory` and `dbo.sysjobs` tables in the `msdb` database:

```
CREATE VIEW vFact_AgentJobHistory AS SELECT
 [h].[server] as [Server], [j].[name] AS [Job Name],
CASE [j].[enabled] WHEN 0 THEN 'Disabled' WHEN 1 THEN 'Enabled' END AS
[Job Status]
, [j].[date_created] as [Date Created], [j].[date_modified] as [Date
Modified]
, [j].[description] as [Job Description], [h].[step_id] AS [Step ID],
[h].[step_name] AS [Step Name]
, CAST(STR([h].[run_date],8, 0) AS date) AS [Run Date]
, CAST(STUFF(STUFF(RIGHT('000000' + CAST ( [h].[run_time] AS VARCHAR(6 )
) ,6),5,0,':'),3,0,':') as time(0)) AS [Run Time]
, (([run_duration]/10000*3600 + ([run_duration]/100)%100*60 + [run_
duration]%100 + 31 ) / 60)
    AS [Run Duration Minutes]
, CASE [h].[run_status] WHEN 0 THEN 'Failed' WHEN 1 THEN 'Succeeded'
WHEN 2 THEN 'Retry'
WHEN 3 THEN 'Cancelled' WHEN 4 THEN 'In Progress' END AS [Execution
Status],
[h].[message] AS [Message Generated]
FROM [msdb].[dbo].[sysjobhistory] [h] INNER JOIN [msdb].[dbo].[sysjobs]
[j] ON [h].[job_id] = [j].[job_id]
```

How to visualize log file data

To implement this recipe, perform the following steps:

1. In Power BI Desktop, create parameters for the file path and filename; local time zone offsets to UTC

2. Create a blank query called **PBIAuditLog** that returns the full file path based on the parameters; disable the load:

Figure 10.22: PBIAuditLog file path query and other parameters in Query Editor

3. Create a new query called **O365PBIAuditLog**:

```
let
    Source = Csv.Document(File.Contents(PBIAuditLog),
        [Delimiter=",", Columns=13, Encoding=65001,
QuoteStyle=QuoteStyle.Csv]),
    RemoveTopRows = Table.Skip(Source,1),
    PromoteHeaders = Table.PromoteHeaders(RemoveTopRows,
[PromoteAllScalars=true]),
    ApplyDateType = Table.TransformColumnTypes(PromoteHeaders,
        {{"CreationDate", type datetime}}),
    AddCreationDateColumn = Table.AddColumn(ApplyDateType,
        "CreationDateOnly", each DateTime.Date([CreationDate]), type
date),
    AddLocalTime = Table.AddColumn(AddCreationDateColumn,"LocalCreationD
ate",
        each [CreationDate] + #duration(0,USEasternDSTOffset,0,0)),
    AddLocalCreationDateColumn = Table.AddColumn(AddLocalTime,
        "LocalCreationDateOnly", each DateTime.Date([LocalCreationDate]),
type date),
    ParseJSON = Table.TransformColumns(AddLocalCreationDateColumn,
        {{"AuditData", Json.Document}})
in
    ParseJSON
```

4. Add steps to expand the **Audit** column and set the appropriate data types for the expanded columns

5. Create or reuse **Server** and **Database** parameters to create a query called **SQLAgentHistory** that retrieves the agent data:

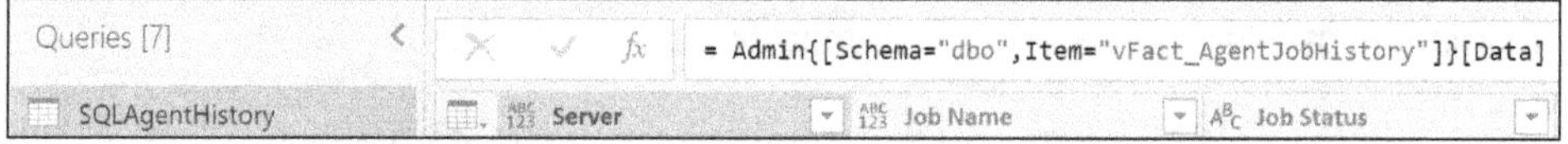

Figure 10.23: SQL Server Agent History view exposed in the "AdminProd" query

6. Click **Close & Apply** from the ribbon of the **Home** tab
7. Create a **Dates** table using the following DAX code:

```
Dates =
    VAR __Today = TODAY()
RETURN
    CALENDAR(DATE(YEAR(__Today)-1,1,1),DATE(YEAR(__Today)+1,12,31))
```

8. Create a **Time** table:

```
Time =
    VAR __hrs = SELECTCOLUMNS(GENERATESERIES(1,23,1),"Hour",[Value])
    VAR __mins = SELECTCOLUMNS(GENERATESERIES(0,59,1),"Minutes",[Value])
    VAR __secs = SELECTCOLUMNS(GENERATESERIES(0,59,1),"Seconds",[Value])
    VAR __hoursMinutes = GENERATEALL(__hrs, __mins)
    VAR __hoursMinutesSeconds = GENERATEALL(__hoursMinutes,__secs)
    VAR __final = ADDCOLUMNS(ADDCOLUMNS(__hoursMinutesSeconds,
        "Time", TIMEVALUE(FORMAT([Hour],"00") & ":" &
            FORMAT([Minutes],"00") & ":" & FORMAT([Seconds],"00"))),
        "SecondOfDay", FORMAT([Hour],"00") & FORMAT([Minutes],"00")
&
            FORMAT([Seconds],"00"))
RETURN __final
```

9. Change the **Data type** of the **Date** column in the **Dates** table to **Date**
10. Change the **Data type** of the **SecondOfDay** column in the **Time** table to **Text**
11. In the **Model** view, create relationships between the **Dates** and **Time** tables and the **O365PBIAuditLog** and **SQLAgentHistory** tables
12. Create DAX measures and report visuals to break out agent jobs by their steps and duration over time
13. Create report pages to visualize the data:

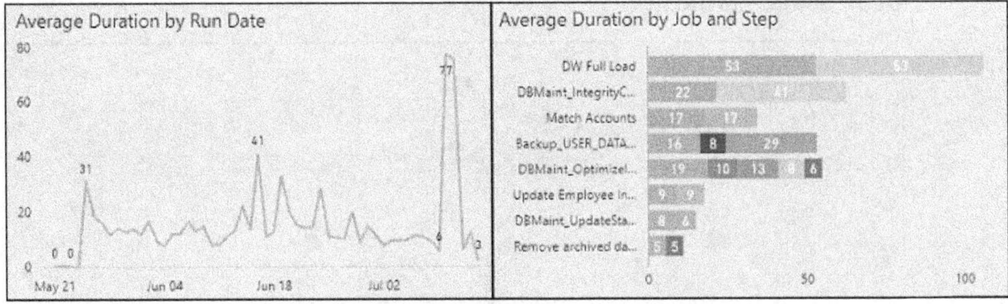

Figure 10.24: SQL Server Agent History visuals—Average Duration by Run Date and Job and Step

How it works...

The `Search-UnifiedAuditLog` cmdlet for PowerShell is used to access Power BI data from the Office 365 audit log. Variables for the full CSV file path and start and end date can be defined, evaluated, and passed as parameters to the `Search-UnifiedAuditLog` cmdlet. Refer to the *See also* section of this recipe for additional information.

Over 20 SQL Server Agent system tables are available in the `dbo` schema of the `msdb` database. In the view created in the *Getting ready* section of this recipe, the `run_date` and `run_time` columns are stored as integers by SQL Server and are thus converted to date and time data types, respectively. The `run_duration` column is stored as an integer in the `HHMMSS` format and is converted to minutes. The `run_status` column is replaced with an **Execution Status** column to display a user-friendly value, such as **succeeded**, and likewise a **Job Status** column is created from the enabled source column to display disabled versus enabled values.

For the SQL Agent report in this recipe, a stacked bar chart is used to display the individual steps comprising each job; hovering over the bars displays details specific to the job step. User selections on the bar chart filter the line chart, enabling easy access to the recent performance of any job step. Analyzing SQL Agent job history in Power BI is vastly easier and more flexible than the Job Activity Monitor and Log File Viewer interfaces in SQL Server Management Studio.

There's more...

The Power BI service provides free usage reporting for dashboards and published reports. These usage reports can be easily extended to analyze activity for all reports and dashboards contained in an app workspace using the following steps:

1. Open the app workspace in the Power BI service and select the vertical ellipses for a report or dashboard; choose **View usage metrics report** (usage metrics can also be accessed with the report or dashboard open via the toolbar ellipses (...) and selecting **Open usage metrics**):

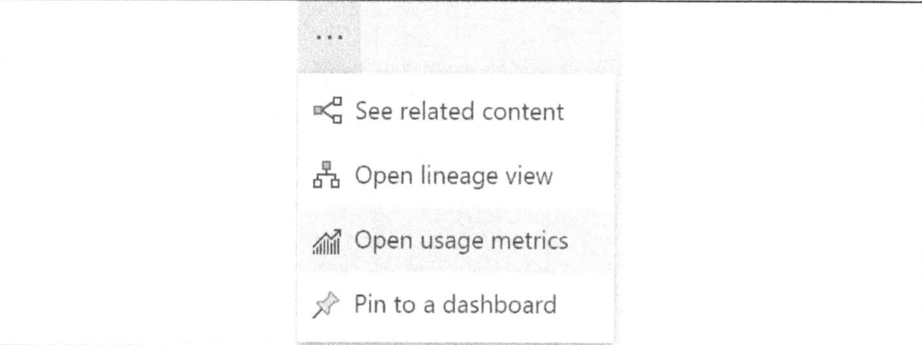

Figure 10.25: Usage metrics report

2. With the usage metrics report open, click on **File** | **Save as** to add a new report to the app workspace:

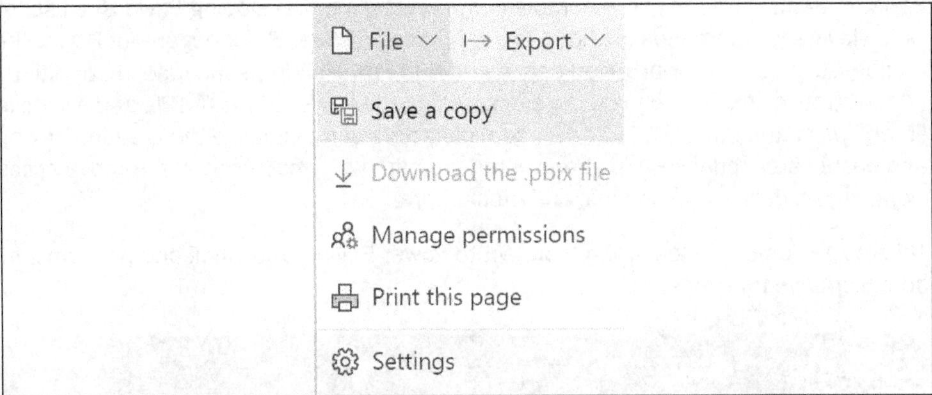

Figure 10.26: Save as to create a dataset of usage metrics for the workspace

3. Open the new report and simply remove the report-level filter such that all reports and dashboards are included:

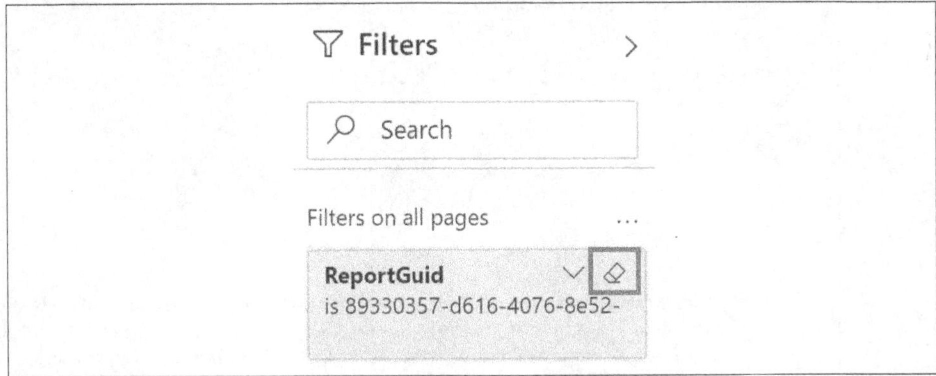

Figure 10.27: Usage metrics report

Note that individual users are included in the dataset and default report, making it easy to identify who is or isn't accessing content.

See also

- *SQL Server Agent Table documentation*: `http://bit.ly/2v7kWdc`
- *Monitor usage metrics in the new workspace experience*: `https://bit.ly/2SrjylV`
- *Track user activities in Power BI*: `https://bit.ly/3raDXZD`

Leveraging the Power BI PowerShell Module

Power BI administrators can automate common tasks by developing PowerShell scripts which leverage commands included in the Microsoft Power BI Management PowerShell module such as Get-PowerBIWorkspace and Add-PowerBIWorkspaceUser. In addition, custom administrative solutions can be developed using the Power BI REST APIs and .NET client library. Using the Power BI REST API, administrators can automate the creation of workspaces and dashboards, publish workspace content, share workspace content, remove access to workspaces, delete workspaces, and much more.

This recipe demonstrates how to connect to Power BI via PowerShell and perform simple administrative functions.

Getting ready

To prepare for this recipe, follow these steps:

1. Enable Power BI APIs in **Tenant settings** of the Power BI service:

   ◢ Allow service principals to use Power BI APIs

   Enabled for the entire organization

   Web apps registered in Azure Active Directory (Azure AD) will use an assigned service principal to access Power BI APIs without a signed in user. To allow an app to use service principal authentication its service principal must be included in an allowed security group. Learn more

    Enabled

   Service principals can use APIs to access tenant-level features controlled by Power BI service admins and enabled for the entire organization or for security groups they're included in. You can control access of service principals by creating dedicated security groups for them and using these groups in any Power BI tenant level-settings. Learn more

   Figure 10.28: Power BI APIs tenant settings in the Power BI service

2. Make sure that you are a Power BI Administrator or otherwise have permissions for Power BI
3. Run a **PowerShell** session as **Administrator**
4. Set your execution policy:

   ```
   Set-ExecutionPolicy RemoteSigned
   ```

5. Run the following command to install the Exchange Online Management module:

   ```
   Install-Module MicrosoftPowerBIMgmt -Force
   ```

6. Connect to Power BI:

```
Login-PowerBI
```

7. Verify access:

```
Get-PowerBIWorkspace | Format-Table
```

How to leverage the Power BI PowerShell Module

To implement this recipe, perform the following steps:

1. In PowerShell, get a list of all new workspaces, including personal workspaces, and export this as a CSV file:

```
Get-PowerBIWorkspace -Scope Organization -All | Export-Csv c:\temp\
workspaces.csv
```

2. Get a list of all workspaces, including classic workspaces, but excluding personal workspaces, and export this to a CSV file:

```
Get-PowerBIWorkspace -All | Export-Csv c:\temp\workspaces2.csv
```

3. Get a list of all workspace users for all new workspaces:

```
Get-PowerBIWorkspace -Scope Organization -Include All -All |
ForEach-Object {
$Workspace = $_.name
$WorkspaceId = $_.Id
foreach ($User in $_.Users) {
[PSCustomObject]@{
Workspace = $Workspace
Id = $WorkspaceId
Role = $User.accessright
User = $user.Identifier}}} | Export-Csv "c:\temp\workspaceusers.csv"
-NoTypeInformation
```

4. Create a query called **Workspaces2** and disable the load:

```
let
    Source = Csv.Document(File.Contents("C:\temp\workspaces2.csv"),
        [Delimiter=",", Columns=15, Encoding=1252,
QuoteStyle=QuoteStyle.None]),
    RemoveRows = Table.Skip(Source,1),
    Headers = Table.PromoteHeaders(RemoveRows, [PromoteAllScalars=true]),
    ChangeTypes = Table.TransformColumnTypes(Headers,{{"Id", type text},
        {"Name", type text}, {"IsReadOnly", type logical},
        {"IsOnDedicatedCapacity", type logical}, {"CapacityId", type
text},
        {"Description", type text}, {"Type", type text}, {"State", type
text},
```

```
        {"IsOrphaned", type logical}, {"Users", type text},
        {"Reports", type text}, {"Dashboards", type text},
        {"Datasets", type text}, {"Dataflows", type text},
        {"Workbooks", type text}})
in ChangeTypes
```

5. Create a query called **Workspaces**:

```
let
    Source = Csv.Document(File.Contents("C:\temp\workspaces.csv"),
        [Delimiter=",", Columns=15, Encoding=1252,
QuoteStyle=QuoteStyle.None]),
    RemoveRows = Table.Skip(Source,1),
    Headers = Table.PromoteHeaders(RemoveRows, [PromoteAllScalars=true]),
    ChangeTypes = Table.TransformColumnTypes(Headers,{{"Id", type text},
        {"Name", type text}, {"IsReadOnly", type logical},
        {"IsOnDedicatedCapacity", type logical}, {"CapacityId", type
text},
        {"Description", type text}, {"Type", type text}, {"State", type
text},
        {"IsOrphaned", type logical}, {"Users", type text},
        {"Reports", type text}, {"Dashboards", type text},
        {"Datasets", type text}, {"Dataflows", type text},
        {"Workbooks", type text}}),
    AppendQuery = Table.Combine({ChangeTypes, Workspaces2}),
    RemoveDups = Table.Distinct(AppendQuery, {"Id"})
in
    RemoveDups
```

6. Create a query called **WorkspaceUsers**:

```
let
    Source = Csv.Document(File.Contents("c:\temp\workspaceusers.csv"),
        [Delimiter=",", Columns=4, Encoding=1252, QuoteStyle=QuoteStyle.
None]),
    Headers = Table.PromoteHeaders(Source, [PromoteAllScalars=true]),
    ChangeType = Table.TransformColumnTypes(Headers,
        {{"Workspace", type text}, {"Id", type text},
        {"Role", type text}, {"User", type text}})
in ChangeType
```

7. Optionally, create export files for Reports, Dashboards, Datasets, Dataflows, and Workbooks within each workspace, similar to the following:

```
Get-PowerBIWorkspace -Scope Organization -Include All -All |
ForEach-Object {
$Workspace = $_.name
$WorkspaceId = $_.Id
```

```
foreach ($Report in $_.Reports) {
[PSCustomObject]@{
Workspace = $Workspace
Id = $WorkspaceId
ReportID = $Report.Id
Report = $Report.Name}}} | Export-Csv "c:\temp\wsreports.csv"
-NoTypeInformation
```

8. Click **Close & Apply** from the ribbon of the **Home** tab.
9. Create a relationship between the **ID** columns in the **Workspaces** and **WorkspaceUsers** tables.
10. Optionally, create additional relationships between the **ID** columns in the **Workspaces** table and other tables for Reports, Dashboards, Datasets, Dataflows, and Workbooks.
11. Create a measure to concatenate the users:

```
Users = CONCATENATEX('WorkspaceUsers',[User],", ")
```

12. Create a matrix visualization using the **Name** column from the **Workspaces** table as **Rows**, the **Role** column from the **WorkspaceUsers** table as **Column**, and the **Users** measure as **Values**.

How it works...

Classic Power BI workspaces have less functionality than newer ones. With Classic workspaces, the list of user permissions cannot be retrieved through the Power BI API because access is granted through Office 365 groups. In addition, `PSCustomObject` is not included in cmdlet calls that support classic workspaces. As a Power BI Admin, you can upgrade workspaces by accessing the Power BI **Admin portal** and selecting **Workspaces**. In the **Workspaces** listed, select one or more workspaces, and then click **Upgrade** from the toolbar.

With the matrix visualization created in this recipe, it is easy to find classic workspaces by clicking on the dropdown for the **Name** column in the **Rows** field and selecting **Show items with no data**. Non-orphaned workspaces with no users listed, such as **Admin**, **Contributor**, **Member**, or **Viewer**, are almost certainly classic workspaces that should be upgraded.

There's more...

There are many PowerShell cmdlets available for Power BI, including the following:

1. Get a list of all deleted workspaces:

```
Get-PowerBIWorkspace -Scope Organization -Deleted -All
```

2. Restore a workspace:

```
Restore-PowerBIWorkspace -Id "<Workspace GUID>" -RestoredName
"<Workspace Name>" -AdminEmailAddress "<Admin UPN>"
```

3. Find orphaned workspaces:

```
Get-PowerBIWorkspace -Scope Organization -Orphaned -All
```

4. To resolve an orphaned workspace issue:

```
Add-PowerBIWorkspaceUser -Scope Organization -Id <Workspace ID>
-UserPrincipalName '<User UPN>' -AccessRight Admin
```

5. Get Power BI Activity Log events:

```
$events = Get-PowerBIActivityEvent -StartDateTime '2021-07-14T00:00:00'
-EndDateTime '2021-07-14T23:59:59' -ActivityType 'ViewDashboard' |
ConvertFrom-Json
$events.Count
$events[0]
```

Not all Power BI REST API calls have corresponding PowerShell cmdlets. However, this does not mean that these REST API calls cannot still be used from PowerShell. The Power BI cmdlets for PowerShell include the general `Invoke-PowerBIRestMethod` method. This method allows the calling of any Power BI REST API call, such as in this example, which creates a JSON file with all workspaces, including associated users, reports, dashboards, datasets, and workbooks:

```
Invoke-PowerBIRestMethod -Url 'https://api.powerbi.com/v1.0/myorg/admin/
Groups?$top=5000&$expand=users,reports,dashboards,datasets,workbooks' -Method
Get > c:\temp\workspaces.json
```

This method uses the same credentials as set by the `Login-PowerBI`, `Login-PowerBIServiceAccount`, or `Connect-PowerBIServiceAccount` calls. To use the authenticated session outside of PowerShell, use the following command:

```
Get-PowerBIAccessToken -AsString
```

See also

- PowerShell cmdlets, REST APIs, and .NET client libraries for administrators: `https://bit.ly/3vDJ5qc`
- Power BI REST APIs: `https://bit.ly/3eR7OR6`
- Power BI Cmdlets reference: `https://bit.ly/3h1ShR2`
- Track user activities in Power BI: `https://bit.ly/3raDXZD`

Conclusion

This chapter's recipes highlighted the most common and impactful administration data sources, including Windows Performance Monitor, SQL Server Query Store, the on-premises data gateway, the MSDB system database, and Extended Events. Power BI solutions built on top of these sources proactively assess usage trends and resource bottlenecks, while delivering the detailed analysis necessary to identify root causes. Additionally, this chapter covered the metadata of existing Power BI and SSAS data models exposed via **dynamic management views** (**DMVs**), such as measure and relationship definitions and resource consumption.

11

Enhancing and Optimizing Existing Power BI Solutions

Power BI projects often begin by focusing on specific functional requirements, such as a set of dashboards and reports for a given business area and team. With relatively narrow requirements and small datasets, sufficient performance and reliability is often achievable without design and code enhancements to the data retrieval, model, and reporting layers. Additionally, Power BI Premium capacity and in certain cases Analysis Services resources provide viable options to enhance the scalability of a dataset.

For larger Power BI projects—particularly when the options of Power BI Premium and Analysis Services are not available—it becomes important to identify opportunities to improve report query performance and to more efficiently use system resources to store and refresh the dataset.

Additionally, the data import process can often be made more resilient and less resource intensive. Furthermore, the application of standard coding syntax, variables, and comments in both Power Query (M) and DAX expressions further improves the sustainability of Power BI datasets.

This chapter's recipes contain top data modeling, DAX measure, and M query patterns to enhance the performance, scalability, and reliability of Power BI datasets. This includes performance tuning examples of both data models and measures, error handling and query folding examples of M queries, and supporting details on the DAX and M query engines.

In this chapter, we will cover the following recipes:

- Enhancing Data Model Scalability and Usability
- Improving DAX Measure Performance
- Pushing Query Processing Back to Source Systems
- Strengthening Data Import and Integration Processes
- Isolating and Documenting DAX Expressions
- Improving Data Load Speeds with Incremental Refresh

Technical Requirements

The following are required to complete the recipes in this chapter:

- Power BI Desktop
- SQL Server with the `AdventureWorksDW2019` database installed. This database and instructions for installing are available here: `http://bit.ly/2OVQfG7`
- Files for this chapter and can be downloaded from the following GitHub repository: `https://github.com/PacktPublishing/Microsoft-Power-BI-Cookbook-Second-Edition`

Enhancing Data Model Scalability and Usability

The performance of all Power BI reports is impacted by the design of the data model. The DAX queries executed upon accessing a report and when dynamically updating report visuals in interactive, self-service user sessions all rely on the relationships defined in the model and optimizations applied to the model's tables. For in-memory models, the cardinality of the columns imported and the compression of these columns contribute to the size of the dataset and query duration. For DirectQuery data models, the referential integrity of the source tables and the optimization of the relational source largely drive query performance.

This recipe includes three optimization processes, all focused on a Reseller Sales fact table with 11.7 million rows. The first example leverages the DMVs and Power BI memory report created in *Chapter 10, Administering and Monitoring Power BI*, to identify and address the most expensive columns. The second example splits a dimension table into two smaller tables, and the final example applies a custom sort order to the imported fact table to optimize the compression of a column commonly used by reports.

Getting ready

To prepare for this recipe, follow these steps:

1. Obtain a sharp definition of the goal of the optimization or the problem being resolved. For example, is the intent to reduce the size of the overall dataset such that more data can be loaded while remaining under 1 GB? Alternatively, is the goal to make the dataset easier to manage and less error prone during refresh, or is it to improve the query performance experienced with Power BI reports?
2. Document the current state or baseline, such as query duration, to evaluate the effectiveness of the modifications.

Performance optimization is a broad area in Power BI, as many components are involved, including the data sources, data access queries, data models, and DAX measure calculations. Performance is also significantly impacted by the design of reports and dashboards with more dense, unfiltered, and complex report pages and visuals consuming more resources. Additionally, despite efficiency in all of these areas, sufficient hardware must be provisioned to support the given processing and analytical query workloads, such as the server(s) for the on-premises data gateway and Power BI Premium capacity.

The good news is that it is usually not difficult to align a particular issue, such as an excessively large dataset or a slow query, with at least one of its main contributing factors, and there are often simple modifications that can deliver noticeable improvements. Additionally, there are many tools available to analyze and monitor the different components of Power BI as described in *Chapter 10, Administering and Monitoring Power BI* and there are free features in the Power BI service, such as **Usage Metrics Reports** and **View related**, that can be of further assistance in isolating issues.

This recipe relies on previous recipes, specifically:

- *Importing and Visualizing Dynamics Management View (DMV) Data in Chapter 10, Administering and Monitoring Power BI*
- *Selecting and Renaming Columns* in *Chapter 2, Accessing and Retrieving Data*

How to do it...

To implement this recipe, do the following:

1. Retrieve and analyze the memory consumed by the columns of the largest fact table or tables. The `DISCOVER_STORAGE_TABLE_COLUMN_SEGMENTS` DMV used in the previous chapter's *Importing and visualizing dynamic management view (DMV) data* recipe provides this detail.
2. As per the *Selecting and Renaming Columns* recipe of *Chapter 2, Accessing and Retrieving Data*, identify expensive columns that may not be needed in the dataset or that can be rounded to lower precision, split as separate columns, or expressed via simple measures.

For import mode models, an expensive column is one with many unique values (high cardinality), such as the **Order Number** columns used as examples in *Chapter 2, Accessing and Retrieving Data*. Likewise, a **DateTime** column with multiple time values per date will consume more memory than two separate **Date** and **Time** columns. Preferably, only the **Date** column or only the **Date** and **Time** columns should be imported, rather than the **DateTime** column.

Also, per the *Selecting and Renaming Columns* recipe, DAX measures that execute simple arithmetic against low-cardinality columns, such as **Unit Price** and **Quantity**, can eliminate the need to import more expensive derived columns such as **Sales Amount** and **Sales Amount with Taxes**. Furthermore, though counter-intuitive, the `SUMX` measure with arithmetic across multiple columns often outperforms the simple `SUM` measure.

3. Identify columns that are stored as decimal number data types with a high scale (number of digits to the right of the decimal point). If this level of precision is not required, consider rounding off these columns in the SQL view or via the M import query to reduce the cardinality (unique values) and thus improve compression. If a (19,4) column will provide sufficient size and precision, apply the fixed decimal number type in the model.
4. Replace any DAX calculated columns on large fact tables since imported columns achieve much better compression than calculated columns. Calculated columns on fact tables can often be addressed with DAX measures without sacrificing performance but if DAX measures are not an option, move the column's logic to the SQL view or M query of the fact table, or within the data source itself. If the M query is revised, ensure that the logic is folded to the source system.
5. Remove or replace DAX calculated columns on any large dimension tables as well by moving this logic to the data retrieval process or leveraging the source system.

   Look for calculated columns with a `RELATED` or `LOOKUPVALUE` function, which, like an Excel `VLOOKUP` function, simply retrieves column values from a table on the one side of a many-to-one relationship with a fact table. Business users often utilize the `RELATED` and `LOOKUPVALUE` functions to flatten or de-normalize a fact table as they would in standard Excel worksheets, but this duplication is rarely necessary in Power BI, and calculated columns are not compressed like standard imported columns. Additionally, look to migrate the logic of calculated column expressions, such as calculated dates, differences in dates, and derived numerical columns, into DAX measures.
6. In this example, the current state of the dataset is 334 MB of compressed disk space (the size of the PBIX file converted from KB) and 674 MB of total memory per the memory report introduced in *Chapter 10, Administering and Monitoring Power BI*.

Following the steps outlined, several quick wins are identified on the **Reseller Sales** fact table (11.7M rows), including the following:

- Only the last four characters of the **CarrierTrackingNumber** are needed for analysis.
- The **Order Date**, **Ship Date**, and **Due Date** columns in `YYYYMMDD` format can be removed, as they are redundant with the date data types for these columns, and only the date data types are used for relationships.
- Four calculated columns can be removed (**Days between Due Date**, **Order Days**, **Reseller**, and **Product Name**) as a `DATEDIFF` DAX measure, and existing dimension columns can be used instead.
- The **Sales Amount**, **Extended Amount**, and **Total Product Cost** columns can be removed, as simple DAX measures can compute their values.

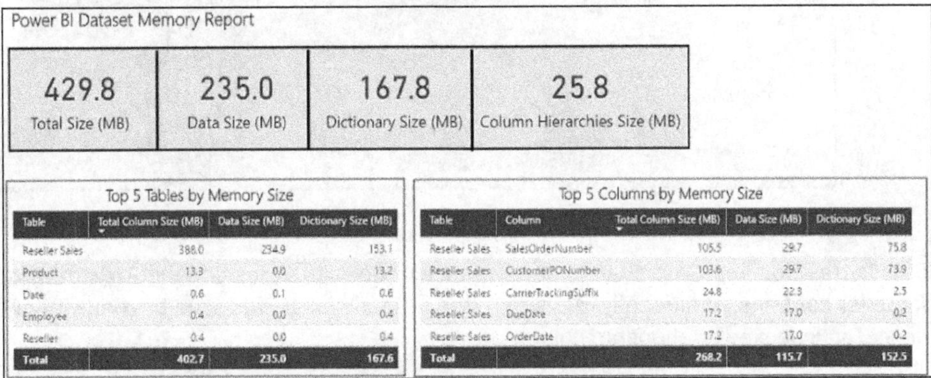

Power BI Dataset Memory Report

429.8	235.0	167.8	25.8
Total Size (MB)	Data Size (MB)	Dictionary Size (MB)	Column Hierarchies Size (MB)

Top 5 Tables by Memory Size

Table	Total Column Size (MB)	Data Size (MB)	Dictionary Size (MB)
Reseller Sales	388.0	234.9	153.1
Product	13.3	0.0	13.2
Date	0.6	0.1	0.6
Employee	0.4	0.0	0.4
Reseller	0.4	0.0	0.4
Total	**402.7**	**235.0**	**167.6**

Top 5 Columns by Memory Size

Table	Column	Total Column Size (MB)	Data Size (MB)	Dictionary Size (MB)
Reseller Sales	SalesOrderNumber	105.5	29.7	75.8
Reseller Sales	CustomerPONumber	103.6	29.7	73.9
Reseller Sales	CarrierTrackingSuffix	24.8	22.3	2.5
Reseller Sales	DueDate	17.2	17.0	0.2
Reseller Sales	OrderDate	17.2	17.0	0.2
Total		**268.2**	**115.7**	**152.5**

Figure 11.1: Power BI Dataset Memory Report refreshed with a revised SQL view for Reseller Sales

After making the revisions, the dataset is now 429 MB in memory and the **Power BI Desktop file** (**PBIX**) is 221 MB on disk, representing 33%+ savings in memory and disk space.

Large-dimension tables (approximately 1 million+ rows), with their high-cardinality relationships to fact tables, are a major performance bottleneck with Power BI and SSAS Tabular import models. Consider the following dimension table with attributes describing both resellers and promotions:

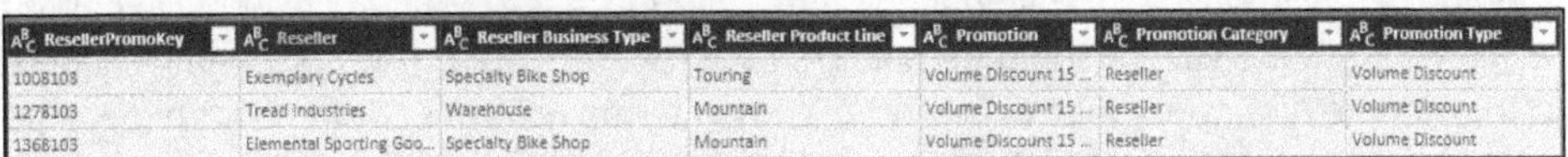

ResellerPromoKey	Reseller	Reseller Business Type	Reseller Product Line	Promotion	Promotion Category	Promotion Type
1008103	Exemplary Cycles	Specialty Bike Shop	Touring	Volume Discount 15 ...	Reseller	Volume Discount
1278103	Tread Industries	Warehouse	Mountain	Volume Discount 15 ...	Reseller	Volume Discount
1368103	Elemental Sporting Goo...	Specialty Bike Shop	Mountain	Volume Discount 15 ...	Reseller	Volume Discount

Figure 11.2: Reseller promotion dimension table

7. The consolidated table contains 10,520 rows and the relationship column on the **Reseller Sales** table is 19.4 MB in size.

Column	Total Column Size (MB)	Data Size (MB)	Dictionary Size (MB)	VERTIPAQ_STATE
CarrierTrackingSuffix	23.9	22.3	1.6	COMPLETED
ResellerPromoKey	19.4	19.2	0.2	COMPLETED
OrderDate	16.7	16.5	0.2	COMPLETED

Figure 11.3: Reseller promo key, approximately 20 MB in size

8. We can split (normalize) this table into smaller **Reseller** (701 rows) and **Promotion** (16 rows) dimension tables and drop the consolidated **Reseller Promotion** dimension table and the expensive `ResellerPromoKey` column on the fact table.

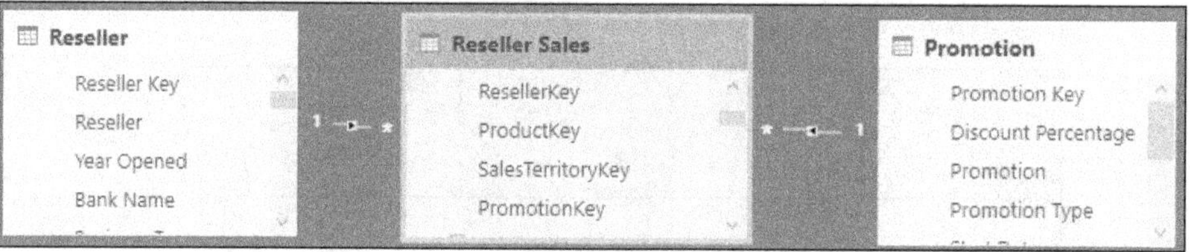

Figure 11.4: Reseller and Promotion Tables Replace Consolidated Reseller Promotion

Smaller relationships improve the performance of queries accessing the **Promotion** and **Reseller** columns. Additionally, the size of the dataset will be reduced by removing the `ResellerPromoKey` relationship column.

In this particular example, the row counts are small enough that little impact is observed, but consider splitting large dimension tables over 200,000 rows into smaller tables (lower granularity) as query workloads increase. For example, a 1 million-row customer table could possibly be split into two tables for the data model based only on common query patterns such as customer regions or geographies.

How it works...

Remember that DAX queries executed against import mode models access and scan the memory associated with individual columns. Therefore, several very expensive columns with millions of unique values could be present on a fact table but may not negatively impact the performance of a query that does not reference these columns. Removing these expensive columns or replacing them with less expensive columns reduces the overall size of the dataset but you should not expect query performance to improve.

When data is loaded into a Power BI Desktop model (import mode), the VertiPaq storage engine applies compression algorithms to each column to reduce the memory and thus improve performance.

VertiPaq first stores all unique values of a column (either via value encoding or hash encoding), and then, more importantly, applies **run-length encoding** (**RLE**) to store a repeated value only once for a set of contiguous rows in which it appears. Therefore, columns with few unique values, such as month names, are highly compressed, while primary key and GUID columns are not compressed at all.

The data models in Power BI Desktop (and Power Pivot for Excel) are stored in column segments of 1 million rows. For example, a 20 million-row sales fact table will contain approximately 20 distinct segments. If the data required of report queries is spread across all 20 segments, then more resources (and a longer duration) are required to access each segment and consolidate these results to resolve the query. However, if the segments are ordered by date or perhaps by a given dimension (for example, **StoreID**) and a report query contains a filter that uses this order, such as fiscal year or store region, then only a subset of the segments is queried.

As a simple example, assume a 20 million-row fact table is ordered by date when importing to Power BI and each calendar year represents 1 million rows. A report query that is filtered on only 2 years will therefore need to access only two of the 20 column segments as the other 18 segments contain dates outside the scope of the query.

Vertipaq Analyzer is now integrated into DAX Studio under the **Advanced** menu as well as in Tabular Editor 3. Vertipaq Analyzer is an easy way to quickly identify the columns consuming the most memory. This and the Best Practice Analyzer in Tabular Editor are two of the most common and easy-to-use tools to analyze the health of a Power BI dataset.

There's more...

While analyzing the data model and making optimizations is important, optimizations can also be made within the Power Query Editor. For example, avoid loading tables that are only used for data retrieval/transformation logic, such as staging queries, to a data model. Even if hidden from the **Fields** list, these tables consume processing and storage resources like all other tables of the model and add unnecessary complexity. Right-click on these queries in the Power Query Editor and disable **Enable load** to remove the table from the data model. Keep in mind that data models with many M queries, whether loaded or not, can overwhelm the available threads/resources of the source system during a refresh as all queries are submitted simultaneously.

Also, identify tables that rarely change and consider disabling the default **Include in report refresh** property (by right-clicking the query in the Power Query Editor). The table can still be loaded to the data model and thus be available for relationships and DAX measures, but its source query will no longer be executed with each refresh. Typical candidates for this include an annual budget or plan table that is only updated once a year, a `Currency` table, and possibly a geographic or demographic table.

Finally, Power BI applies sophisticated algorithms during the import process to determine the sort order that maximizes compression. However, the chosen sort order might not align with the top performance priorities of the model. For example, it may be more important to improve query performance for reports accessing a certain column, such as **StoreID** or **Date** (via relationships to dimension tables), rather than minimizing the size of the overall dataset. Ordering the imported data by these priority columns maximizes their compression while potentially reducing the compression applied to other columns. To demonstrate this, consider the following:

1. Identify the column (or columns) to order by and note the current memory. In this example, the **OrderDate** column is 16.7 MB.

Table	Column	Total Column Size (MB)	Data Size (MB)	Dictionary Size (MB)
Reseller Sales	CarrierTrackingSuffix	24.8	22.3	2.5
Reseller Sales	OrderDate	16.7	16.5	0.2

Figure 11.5: OrderDate column of 16.5 MB in Data Size (without sort)

2. Add an expression to the fact table M query that uses the `Table.Sort` function to order by the **OrderDate** column.

```
let
    Source = AdWorksDW,
    ResellerSales = Source{[Schema="BI",Item = "vFactResellerSalesXL"]}
[Data],
    OrderDateSort = Table.Sort(ResellerSales,{{"OrderDate", Order.
Descending}})
in
    OrderDateSort
```

3. Right-click on the last step in the **Power Query Editor** and click on **View Native Query** to ensure the sorting was folded to the source.
4. If **View Native Query** is grayed out, consider moving the sort step to the first transformation step in the preceding code. Upon refreshing the **Reseller Sales** fact table, the data size of **OrderDate** is reduced by 36% to 10.6 MB.

Table	Column	Total Column Size (MB)	Data Size (MB)	Dictionary Size (MB)
Reseller Sales	CarrierTrackingSuffix	24.8	22.3	2.5
Reseller Sales	ResellerKey	13.4	13.4	0.0
Reseller Sales	ProductKey	12.6	12.6	0.0
Reseller Sales	OrderDate	10.8	10.6	0.2

Figure 11.6: Improved compression for the OrderDate column due to the sort order of the Import query

5. Determine whether any other columns, particularly relationship columns such as **ProductKey**, increased in size.
6. Optionally (though it is recommended), evaluate top or common DAX queries for performance changes.

Specifying an `Order By` clause in the import to Power BI exposes the given column to maximum RLE compression given the cardinality of the column. In many scenarios, optimizing the compression on the active relationship date column via sorting offers the best overall performance advantage. However, depending on the structure and distribution of reports and users, ordering by a different fact table column such as **ProductKey** or **StoreID** could be the best choice. DAX Studio makes it relatively easy to test the performance of queries against many different model designs.

Passing the Order By operation back to the source (via query folding) is generally good for the refresh process and certainly good for the on-premises data gateway. However, with large fact tables (10 million+ rows) this can require large amounts of source system resources.

See also

- Best practice rules to improve your model's performance: `https://bit.ly/3xPgDn4`
- Best practice rules for Tabular Editor: `https://bit.ly/3l5325w`
- Vertipaq Analyzer script for Tabular Editor 2: `https://bit.ly/2YA97zv`

Improving DAX Measure Performance

Just as specific columns and relationships can be optimized for performance per the prior recipe, frequently used DAX measures can also be targeted for performance improvements. Existing DAX measures may contain inefficient data access methods that generate additional, unnecessary queries or that largely execute in a single CPU thread. Revising measures to better leverage the multi-threaded storage engine and to avoid or reduce unnecessary queries and iterations can deliver significant performance improvements without invasive, structural modifications to the model.

In this recipe, DAX queries executed by Power BI visuals are captured and analyzed using the Performance Analyzer feature of Power BI Desktop. The first example highlights a common misuse of the `FILTER` function for basic measures. In the second example, two alternative approaches to implementing an `OR` filter condition across separate tables are described relative to a common but less efficient approach. Additional details of the DAX query engine, using DAX variables to improve performance, and DAX as a query language, are also covered.

Getting ready

To prepare for this recipe, follow these steps:

1. Open the Power BI Desktop file containing the data model and measures to be analyzed
2. Select **DAX Studio** from the ribbon of the **External Tools** tab
3. If necessary, build a sample report page that aligns with a poorly performing report or a common report layout
4. In Power BI Desktop, select **Performance analyzer** from the ribbon of the **View** tab

How to do it...

To implement this recipe, use the following steps:

1. In the **Performance analyzer** pane, select **Start recording**.
2. Make a selection on one of the Power BI Desktop report visuals and observe the DAX queries in **Performance analyzer**. In this case, the measure under study is the `Gross_Sales_Warehouse` measure defined as follows:

```
Gross_Sales_Warehouse = CALCULATE([Reseller Gross Sales], FILTER('Resell
er','Reseller'[Business Type] = "Warehouse"))
```

3. Expand the visual in **Performance analyzer** containing the desired measure and choose **Copy query**:

```
DEFINE
 VAR __DS0FilterTable = FILTER(KEEPFILTERS(VALUES('Date'[Calendar
Year])),
      OR('Date'[Calendar Year] = 2016, 'Date'[Calendar Year] = 2017))
 VAR __DS0FilterTable2 = FILTER(KEEPFILTERS(VALUES('Product'[Product
Category])),
     'Product'[Product Category] = "Bikes")
 VAR __DS0FilterTable3 = FILTER(KEEPFILTERS(VALUES('Promotion'[Promotion
Type])),
      OR(OR(OR('Promotion'[Promotion Type] = "Excess Inventory",
      'Promotion'[Promotion Type] = "New Product"),'Promotion'[Promotion
Type] = "No Discount"),
      'Promotion'[Promotion Type] = "Volume Discount"))
 EVALUATE
   TOPN(1001,SUMMARIZECOLUMNS('Reseller'[Reseller],__DS0FilterTable,__
DS0FilterTable2,__DS0FilterTable3,
       "Gross_Sales_Warehouse", 'Reseller Sales'[Gross Sales
Warehouse]),
     [Gross_Sales_Warehouse],0,'Reseller'[Reseller],1)
```

In this case, the `FILTER` function does not operate on the results of an `ALL` function like with date intelligence patterns. The `TOPN` function accepts the table from `SUMMARIZECOLUMNS`, which groups by individual Reseller companies and their associated gross sales warehouse values:

1. In DAX Studio, enable **Server Timings** and **Query Plan** on the top toolbar
2. With the DAX Studio trace running, click on **Run** or the *F5* key and note the performance in the **Server Timings** window
3. Click on **Clear Cache** and execute the query again to obtain a baseline average for the duration, SE queries (storage engine), and SE %
4. In Power BI Desktop, create a new measure that avoids the `FILTER` function:

```
Gross Sales Warehouse Rev = CALCULATE([Reseller Gross Sales],
'Reseller'[Business Type] = "Warehouse")
```

Within the DAX query engine, the **Gross Sales Warehouse Rev** measure is expressed as the following:

```
CALCULATE([Reseller Gross Sales],FILTER(ALL('Reseller'[Business
Type]),'Reseller'[Business Type] = "Warehouse"))
```

Some BI organizations may adopt standards that require the longer, more explicit version and avoid "syntax sugar."

Return to DAX Studio and replace the existing references to the current measure with the name of the measure:

```
EVALUATE
 TOPN(1001,SUMMARIZECOLUMNS('Reseller'[Reseller],__DS0FilterTable,__
DS0FilterTable2,__DS0FilterTable3,
 "Gross Sales Warehouse Rev", [Gross Sales Warehouse Rev]),[Gross Sales
Warehouse Rev],0,
'Reseller'[Reseller],1)
```

With the cache cleared, execute the query with the revised measure. Create a revised average based on 4-5 separate query executions:

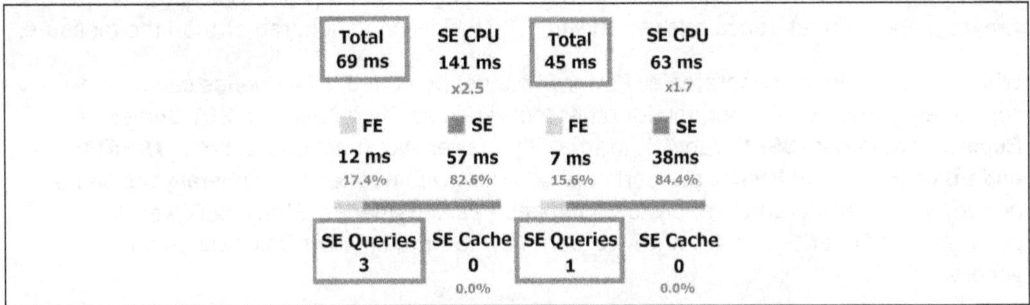

Figure 11.7: Server timings of the baseline query with original measure versus revised measure in DAX Studio

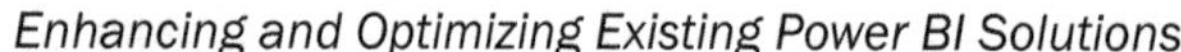

The baseline query executed 35% faster (**69 ms** to **45 ms**) with the revised measure and only needed **1 SE** query.

How it works...

The reason the first measure is slower is that with the `FILTER` on **Reseller**, the filter selections on slicer visuals of the report (**Date**, **Product**, and **Promotion**) have to be respected before the filter on warehouse is executed. For example, the **Reseller** dimension table will be filtered to only include resellers with bike category sales in 2016-2017 and of certain promotions before the **Warehouse** filter is applied. This requires additional scans of the fact table and is thus less efficient.

DAX queries from Power BI report visuals are resolved by the DAX formula engine and the DAX storage engine. The storage engine is the in-memory columnar compressed database for import mode models (also known as VertiPaq) and is the relational database for DirectQuery models. In either mode, the formula engine is responsible for generating query plans and can execute all DAX functions, including complex expression logic, though it is limited to a single thread and no cache.

The formula engine sends requests to the storage engine and if the storage engine does not have the requested data in an existing data cache, the storage engine utilizes multiple threads to access segments of data (1 thread per segment, 1 million rows per segment) from the data model. The storage engine executes a simple join, grouping, filter, and aggregations, including distinct count, to make requested data caches available to the formula engine. Given this architecture, a fundamental DAX and Power BI model design practice is to maximize the allocation of queries to the storage engine and minimize the size of data caches operated on by the formula engine.

Given the performance advantage of reducing storage, engine requests also consider the use of variables. While the primary benefit of DAX variables is improved readability, variables can also reduce the number of queries associated with a measure (and hence its execution duration) since variables are evaluated only once and can be reused multiple times in an expression. Look for DAX measures with multiple branches of `IF` or `SWITCH` conditions that reference the same calculation or measure multiple times. For these measures, consider declaring a variable that simply references the existing measure (`VAR MyVariable = [Sales Amount]`) and then reference this variable in each logical condition, rather than the measure.

While the DAX queries generated by Power BI cannot be edited, DAX queries can be completely authored from scratch for other tools such as the datasets in **SQL Server Reporting Services** (**SSRS**) reports. Many of the newer DAX functions, such as **TREATAS and SUMMARIZECOLUMNS**, are particularly helpful with queries and generally the same performance considerations apply to both measures and queries. Studying Power BI-generated DAX queries is a great way to learn how to write efficient DAX queries and DAX in general.

There's more...

Another example of where a DAX measure can be optimized is in this example where a measure must be filtered by an `OR` condition on two columns from separate tables. A `FILTER` function cannot be avoided in this scenario like in the prior example, since multiple columns must be referenced in the same expression (the `OR` condition). The current measure is defined as follows:

```
Reseller Gross Sales (Filter OR) =
CALCULATE([Reseller Gross Sales], FILTER('Reseller Sales',
RELATED('Product'[Product Subcategory]) = "Mountain Bikes" ||
RELATED('Reseller'[Reseller Country]) IN {"United States", "Australia"}))
```

A `FILTER` is applied on the fact table and separate `RELATED` functions are used to implement the required `OR` logic. To see how this measure can be optimized, consider the following:

1. Just like in the previous example, capture a sample DAX query generated in Power BI Desktop from the **Performance analyzer** pane
2. Test and analyze the query in DAX Studio to establish a baseline for the current measure
3. Now create two separate alternative measures—one with `SUMMARIZE` and another with `CROSSJOIN`:

   ```
   Reseller Gross Sales (Summarize OR) =
   CALCULATE([Reseller Gross Sales], FILTER(
   SUMMARIZE('Reseller Sales','Product'[Product Subcategory],'Reseller'[Res
   eller Country]),     'Product'[Product Subcategory] = "Mountain Bikes" ||
   'Reseller'[Reseller Country] IN {"United States", "Australia"}))

   Reseller Gross Sales (Crossjoin OR) =
   CALCULATE([Reseller Gross Sales], FILTER(
   CROSSJOIN(ALL('Product'[Product Subcategory]),ALL(Reseller[Resell
   er Country])), 'Product'[Product Subcategory] = "Mountain Bikes" ||
   'Reseller'[Reseller Country] IN {"United States", "Australia"}))
   ```

4. In Power BI Desktop, confirm that the new measures produce the same results as the current measure
5. In DAX Studio, replace the references to the (filter `OR`) measure with references to the new measures

6. Repeat the process of executing multiple queries with the cache cleared and documenting the performance to establish baselines for all three versions of the measure

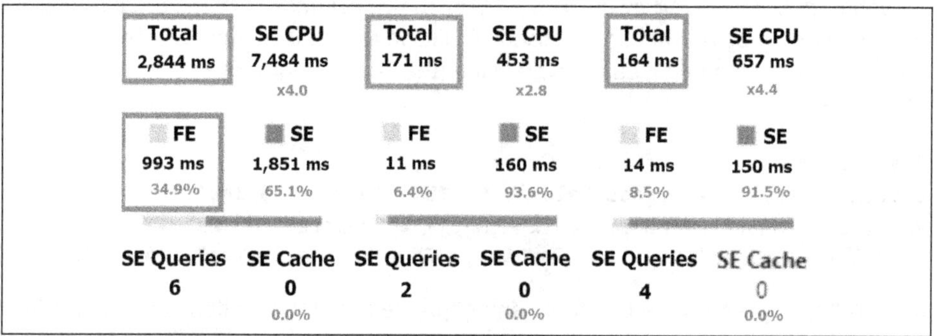

Figure 11.8: Server timings of the baseline query (filter OR) measure versus the two new measures in DAX Studio

Both new measures were 16.7X faster than the current state (2,844 to 170 ms) and were over 90% executed in the **storage engine** (**SE**). In this scenario, the `CROSSJOIN` approach was slightly faster than `SUMMARIZE` but this comparison would vary based on the cardinality of the columns involved. The larger point from this example is the danger associated with implementing logic that's not supported by the storage engine within the expression parameter of iterating functions like `FILTER` and `SUMX`. This is especially true when the table parameter to these functions has many rows such as the 11.7 million-row **Reseller Sales** fact table used in this recipe.

Note that the `ALL` function can be used to produce the table parameter if both columns are from the same table, such as `ALL('Product'[Product Category],'Product'[Product Color])`. `ALL` cannot directly access columns from separate tables.

At a high level, always think about the size of the table being filtered and look for simple filter conditions and single columns that can be used to reduce the size of this table. For example, replace the table parameter of functions like `SUMX` and `FILTER` with a `CALCULATETABLE` function that implements simple, efficient filter conditions. More complex expressions that cannot be handled by the storage engine can then operate against this smaller table. Similarly, consider (and test) nesting filter conditions such that the most selective, efficient filter condition is applied first (the inner `FILTER`, the outer `CALCULATE`):

```
CALCULATE(
  CALCULATE(<param1>, <param2>
) //outer calculate

FILTER(
  FILTER(<param1>,<param2>), // inner FILTER
  <param2>
)
```

See also

- Use Performance analyzer to examine report element performance in Power BI Desktop: `https://bit.ly/3eWXdEb`

Pushing Query Processing Back to Source Systems

During the scheduled refresh of datasets retrieving from on-premises sources, any query transformations not executed by the source system will require local resources of the **M** (**Mashup**) engine of the on-premises data gateway server. With larger datasets, and potentially with other scheduled refreshes occurring on the same gateway server at the same time, it becomes important to design M queries that take full advantage of source system resources via query folding. Although transformations against some sources such as files will always require local resources, in many scenarios M queries can be modified to help the engine generate an equivalent SQL statement and thus minimize local resource consumption.

In this recipe, a process and list of items is provided to identify queries not currently folding and the potential causes. Additionally, a query based on an existing SQL statement is redesigned with M expressions to allow query folding.

Getting ready

To prepare for this recipe, follow these steps:

1. Identify the dataset to evaluate for query folding
2. Use gateway server memory performance counter data to establish a baseline of the resources currently used to perform refreshes as these counters should be impacted by any changes

Also, establish a baseline for query performance using the new **Diagnostic tools** within Power Query Editor's **Tools** tab.

The dataset to be optimized will generally be a large PBIX file (100 MB+) published to the Power BI service with a scheduled refresh configured to use an on-premises data gateway and that queries a relational database (SQL, Oracle) as the primary source. If the large PBIX file is retrieving from a file or a collection of files within a folder, revisions are certainly possible, such as filtering out files based on their modified date relative to the current date, however, query folding is not an option for file sources.

How to do it...

The following steps outline the general query folding analysis process:

1. Open the Power BI Desktop file used as the published dataset with scheduled refreshes of on-premises data.
2. Click on **Edit Queries** from the ribbon of the **Home** tab to open the Power Query Editor.
3. Starting with the largest queries (the fact tables), right-click on the final step exposed in the **Query Settings** window.

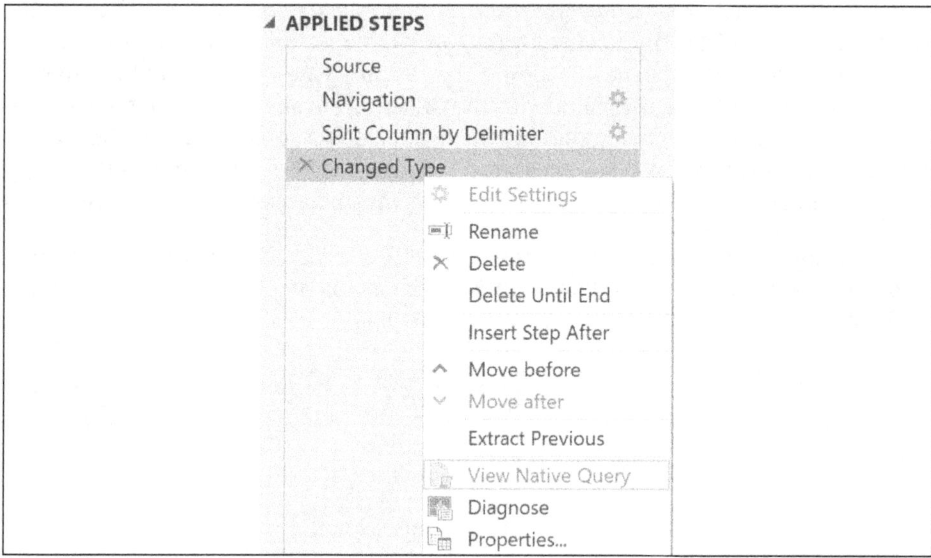

Figure 11.9: View Native Query disabled for final query step

If the **View Native Query** option is disabled, then the local M engine is performing at least this final step. If **View Native Query** is not disabled, you can optionally view the SQL statement as per prior recipes.

4. Check the previous steps to determine which steps, if any, were folded, and thus the step that caused the query to use local resources. Once a step (M variable expression) in a query uses local resources all subsequent steps in the query will also use local resources.
5. Identify the cause of the local operation, such as a specific M function not supported by the source system.

6. Consider revising the source database object, the M expressions, and data source privacy levels to enable query folding.

As an example of performing this process, consider the following case, where a business analyst has used a SQL statement and the Query Editor to construct a customer query:

```
let
    Source = Sql.Database("ATLAS", "AdventureWorksDW2016CTP3",
[Query="Select CustomerKey,FirstName,LastName,BirthDate,MaritalStatus,YearlyIncome From dbo.DimCustomer"]),
    ChangedType = Table.TransformColumnTypes(Source,{{"BirthDate", type date}, {"YearlyIncome", Int64.Type}}),
    ReplacedValue = Table.ReplaceValue(ChangedType,"M","Married",Replacer.ReplaceText,{"MaritalStatus"}),
    ReplacedValue1 = Table.ReplaceValue(ReplacedValue,"S","Single",Replacer.ReplaceText,{"MaritalStatus"}),
    MergedColumns = Table.CombineColumns(ReplacedValue1,{"FirstName", "LastName"},Combiner.CombineTextByDelimiter(" ", QuoteStyle.None),"Customer Name"),
    RenamedColumns = Table.RenameColumns(MergedColumns,{{"MaritalStatus", "Marital Status"}, {"YearlyIncome", "Yearly Income"}, {"BirthDate", "Date of Birth"}})
in RenamedColumns
```

Figure 11.10: Customer query based on native SQL statement and M transformations

In this scenario, the SQL statement is against the base customer table in the data warehouse (not the view) and the subsequent transformations applied against the query results all use local gateway server resources during each refresh process since the first step executes a native SQL query. The existing SQL view (**vDim_Customer**) contains the **Customer Name** column, eliminating the need for the merge operation, though the **Marital Status** column is not transformed into the longer **Married** or **Single** string as per the analyst's transformations. The query can be modified to perform better by taking advantage of query folding as follows:

1. Create a new M query that uses parameters for the server and database and that uses the customer SQL view:

   ```
   let Source = AdWorksProd,
   Customer = AdWorksProd{[Schema = "BI", Item = "vDim_Customer"]}[Data],
   SelectColumns = Table.SelectColumns(Customer,{"Customer Key", "Customer
   Name", "Date of Birth",
   "Marital Status", "Annual Income"}),
   MarriageStatus = Table.AddColumn(SelectColumns, "M Status", each if
   [Marital Status] = "M" then "Married" else "Single", type text),
   RemovedColumns = Table.RemoveColumns(MarriageStatus,{"Marital Status"}),
   RenamedColumns = Table.RenameColumns(RemovedColumns,{{"M Status",
   "Marital Status"},
   {"Annual Income", "Yearly Income"}})
   in RenamedColumns
   ```

   The existing SQL view, **vDim_Customer**, is leveraged and the **Marital Status** conditional logic is built within a `Table.AddColumn` expression. The few remaining steps simply select, remove, and rename columns and are all transformations that can be folded back to SQL Server.

2. Right-click on the final step of the new, revised query and ensure that **View Native Query** is enabled.

```
Native Query

select [_].[CustomerKey] as [CustomerKey],
    [_].[FirstName] as [FirstName],
    [_].[LastName] as [LastName],
    [_].[BirthDate] as [BirthDate],
    [_].[YearlyIncome] as [YearlyIncome],
    case
        when [_].[MaritalStatus] = 'M' and [_].[MaritalStatus] is not null
        then 'Married'
        else 'Single'
    end as [Marital Status]
from
(
    select [CustomerKey],
        [FirstName],
        [LastName],
        [BirthDate],
        [MaritalStatus],
        [YearlyIncome]
```

Figure 11.11: Native query (folded) based on the revised M query for Customers

The new query returns the same results but is now folded back to SQL Server rather than using local resources. The `if...then...else` M expression was folded into a `CASE` expression for SQL Server to execute.

How it works...

Query folding is impacted by the transformations supported by the source system, internal proprietary M engine logic, privacy levels assigned to data sources, the use of native database queries (SQL statements), and the use of custom M functions and logic. For example, even if query folding is appropriate from a performance standpoint such as using a server in a join operation with a local file, folding will not occur if the local file is configured as a private data source.

As per the query folding redesign example in this recipe, if the first step or **Source** step of the query is a native SQL statement, consider revising the M query steps to help the M engine form a SQL query (fold the M query). Any M transformation applied on top of a native SQL database query (via `Value.NativeQuery`) will not be folded to the source system. If native SQL queries are used, such as the stored procedure calls, the recommendation is to embed all query steps and transformations in the native SQL query itself. If this is not possible, embed the most resource-intensive operations in the stored procedure and pass filtering parameters from Power BI to the stored procedure to reduce the workload on the local M engine.

If there are required transformations or logic that are not supported by the source system for query folding, the recommendation is to move these steps to the very end of the query. For example, allow SQL Server to execute the filter, the derived columns, and other simple steps via query folding, and only then apply the complex steps locally on top of the SQL query result set.

Several common M functions are not supported by most relational database sources, such as `Table.Distinct`, which removes duplicate rows from tables, and `Table.RemoveRowsWithErrors`, which removes rows with errors from tables. If data sources are merged in the query, check their privacy settings (**Data source settings** | **Edit Permissions...**) to ensure that privacy is configured to allow folding, such as from an organizational source to a different organizational source.

In general, the following operations are not supported by query folding:

- Changing column data types
- Adding index columns
- Merging or appending queries from different sources
- Adding custom columns using Power Query functions that have no equivalent function in the data source

There's more...

For large models with many queries and large tables, consider disabling the default parallel loading of tables in **File** | **Options** | **Options and settings** | **CURRENT FILE** as many queries executed simultaneously may overwhelm source system resources and cause the refresh process to fail.

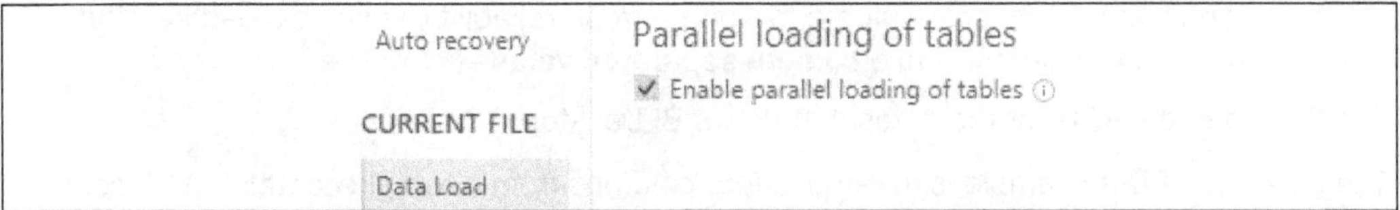

Figure 11.12: Parallel loading of tables – CURRENT FILE setting

Just because a query is folded into a SQL statement, it does not mean there are no possible performance issues. For example, the query might be selecting more columns than needed by the data model or might be executing outer join queries when the database schema supports inner joins. Visibility of these queries can inform changes to the BI architecture and M queries.

Owners of the relational database system or data warehouse can take note of Power BI's folded SQL queries via tools like **Extended Events**. For example, database administrators or BI team members could revise existing SQL views, table indexes, and more based upon the information gathered. Likewise, the Power BI query author could be informed of better or preferred methods of accessing the same data such as joining on different columns.

See also

- Power Query query folding: `https://bit.ly/3jB5wrx`
- Optimize Power Query when expanding table columns: `https://bit.ly/3trdKFA`

Strengthening Data Import and Integration Processes

Many Power BI datasets must be created without the benefit of a data warehouse or even a relational database source system. These datasets, which often transform and merge less structured and governed data sources such as text and Excel files, generally require more complex M queries to prepare the data for analysis. The combination of greater M query complexity and periodic structural changes and data quality issues in these sources can lead to refresh failures and challenges in supporting the dataset. Additionally, as M queries are sometimes initially created exclusively via the Query Editor interface, the actual M code generated may contain unexpected logic that can lead to incorrect results and unnecessary dependencies on source data.

This recipe includes practical examples of increasing the reliability and manageability of data import processes including data source consolidation, error handling and comments, and accounting for missing or changed source columns.

Getting ready

To prepare for this recipe, follow these steps:

1. Identify the dataset to evaluate for data refresh reliability, such as a dataset that imports information from a **comma-separated values** (**CSV**) File
2. Open the PBIX for the dataset in Power BI Desktop

The objective of this example is to retrieve four columns from a text file containing 30 columns describing customers.

How to do it...

To implement this recipe, use the following steps:

1. Connect to the file with the text/CSV connector and replace the hardcoded path with a query created from parameters:

```
let Source = Csv.Document(File.Contents(CustomerTextFile),[Delimiter="
", Columns=30, Encoding=1252, QuoteStyle=QuoteStyle.None]),
PromotedHeaders = Table.PromoteHeaders(Source, [PromoteAllScalars=true])
in PromotedHeaders
```

2. Delete the default `Columns` parameter of the `Csv.Document` function (`Columns=30`)
3. Use a `Table.SelectColumns` function to select the four columns needed and specify the optional `MissingField.UseNull` parameter
4. Finally, set the data types for each of the four columns:

```
let Source = Csv.Document(File.Contents(CustomerTextFile),
        [Delimiter=" ", Encoding=1252, QuoteStyle=QuoteStyle.None]),
PromoteHeaders = Table.PromoteHeaders(Source, [PromoteAllScalars=true]),
SelectColumns = Table.SelectColumns(PromoteHeaders,
        {"CustomerKey", "CustomerAlternateKey", "EmailAddress",
"BirthDate"},  MissingField.UseNull),
TypeChanges = Table.TransformColumnTypes(SelectColumns,
        {{"CustomerKey", Int64.Type}, {"CustomerAlternateKey", type
text}, {"BirthDate", type date}})
in TypeChanges
```

How it works...

With these changes, the query has access to all columns of the source file (not just 30) but only creates dependencies on the four columns needed. Most importantly, the `MissingField.UseNull` option protects the query from failing if one of the four columns is renamed or removed from the source file. With the `MissingField.UseNull` option, if one of the four columns selected is removed or renamed, a null value is substituted thus avoiding query failure.

CustomerKey	CustomerAlternateKey	EmailAddress	BirthDate
11000	AW00011000	jon24@adventure-works.com	null
11001	AW00011001	eugene10@adventure-works.com	null
11002	AW00011002	ruben35@adventure-works.com	null

Figure 11.13: Four columns selected from the text file despite the BirthDate column removed from the source

A `MissingField.Ignore` option is also available to retrieve only the columns found in `Table.SelectColumns`.

Be sure to avoid the automatic data type changes applied by default to unstructured sources. If enabled, this will effectively create a hardcoded dependency to each of the columns in the source. Likewise, for all other transformations, try to limit or avoid explicitly referencing column names and always favor selecting required columns rather than removing unnecessary columns. The columns explicitly selected are less likely to be changed or removed in the future and removing columns creates a risk that new columns added to the source will be loaded to the data model.

There's more...

In addition to improvements in reliability, one can also use **Query Diagnostics**, available in the **Tools** ribbon of the Power Query Editor, to analyze query performance. There are also methods for improving the overall maintainability of Power Query code. Two such methods are comments and data source management.

As with all coding languages, comments can be used to improve the overall maintainability of M code, as in the example below:

```
/* This query joins the Product query to the Product Subcategory query.
   The product subcategory column 'EnglishProductSubcategoryName' is renamed
'Product Subcategory' */
let ProductToProductSubCatJoin =
try
// Nested outer join based on Subcategory Surrogate Key
Table.NestedJoin(Product,{"ProductSubcategoryKey"},#"Product Subcategory",{"
ProductSubcategoryKey"},"ProductSubCatColumns",JoinKind.LeftOuter) otherwise
Product,
AddProductSubCatColumn =
try
// Will return nulls if EnglishProductSubcategoryName is renamed or missing in
Product Subcategory query
Table.ExpandTableColumn(ProductToProductSubCatJoin, "ProductSubCatColumns",{"Eng
lishProductSubcategoryName"}, {"Product Subcategory"}) otherwise Product
in AddProductSubCatColumn
```

Comments are used in both multi-line and single-line formats to help explain the logic. Multi-line comments begin with `/*` and end with `*/` while single-line comments are preceded by the `//` characters. Variable names (that is, `AddProductSubCatColumn`) are in proper casing with no spaces so as to avoid unnecessary double quotes and to further describe the process.

Another method of increasing the maintainability of Power Query code is through proper data source management. Consider a PBIX file that includes 10 queries access three different data sources are hardcoded into each query. In this example, 10 queries use three separate sources (SQL Server, an Excel file, and an MS Access database file). Any change to the data source paths or connection information would require changing up to 10 different queries. To see how this can be resolved, consider the following:

1. Open the Power BI Desktop file and identify the data sources being accessed by all queries
2. The **Data source settings** dialog from the **Transform data** dropdown in the ribbon of the **Home** tab in **Report** view will expose current file sources
3. For greater detail, open the **Power Query Editor** and click on **Query Dependencies** from the ribbon of the **View** tab

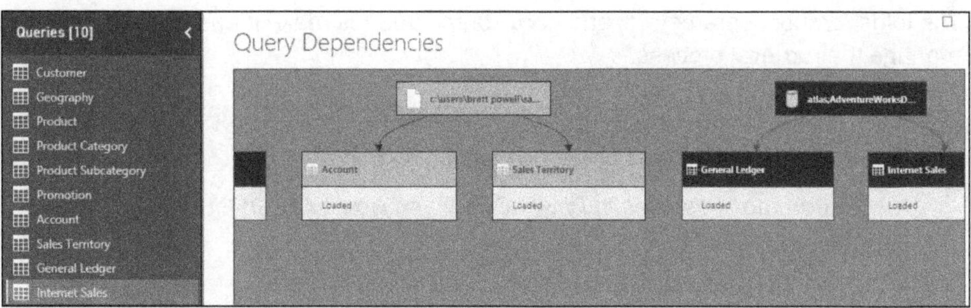

Figure 11.14: Query Dependencies view of 10 queries

4. Create the following folder groups in the queries window: **Parameters**, **Data Source Queries**, **Dimensions**, and **Facts**
5. Create six text parameters to abstract the file name, file path, server, and database names from the three sources
6. Develop three data source queries from individual blank queries that reference these parameters:

```
= Sql.Database(#"SQL Server AdWorks Server", #"SQL Server AdWorks DB")
= #"MS Access AdWorks Path" & "\" & #"MS Access AdWorks DB" & ".accdb"
= #"MS Excel Ad Works Path" & "\" & #"MS Excel Ad Works File" & ".xlsx"
```

7. Assign names to these queries such as **MS Access Ad Works Connection** and disable their load to the data model
8. Finally, modify each of the 10 queries to reference one of the three data source queries such as the following:

```
let Source = Access.Database(File.Contents(#"MS Access Ad Works
Connection"), [CreateNavigationProperties=true]),
Customer = Source{[Schema="",Item="DimCustomer"]}[Data]
in Customer
```

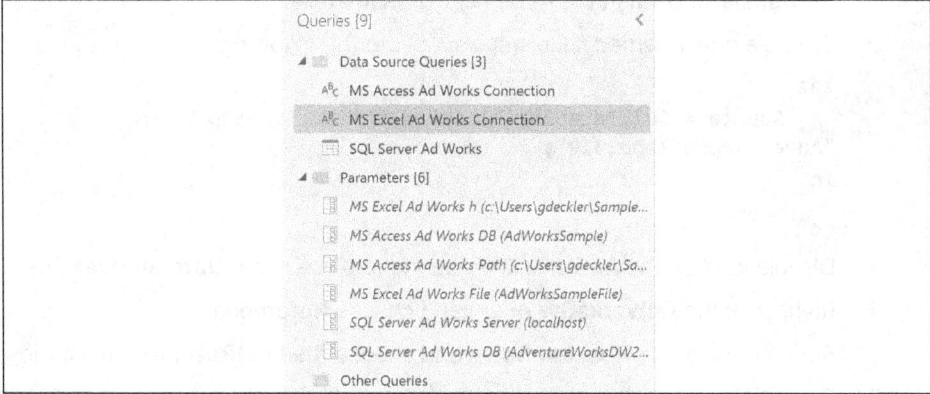

Figure 11.15: Consolidated and parameterized data sources organized in the Power Query Editor

The folder groups, parameters, and data source queries make it easier to understand and manage the retrieval process.

See also

- *10 Common Mistakes in Power Query and How to Avoid Pitfalls* by Gil Raviv: `http://bit.ly/2uW6c33`
- *Query Diagnostics*: `https://bit.ly/2YBEmKv`

Isolating and Documenting DAX Expressions

Isolating expressions into independent and interchangeable DAX measures or as variables within measures is recommended to simplify development and ownership of the dataset. Independent measures can be hidden from the **Fields** list yet contain core business definitions and efficient filtering logic to drive the results and performance of many other measures in the model. Although scoped to each measure, DAX variables provide a self-documenting coding style and, unlike scalar-valued measures, also support table values thus allowing for even greater modularity.

In this recipe, DAX variables, measures, and comments are used in different examples that demonstrate best practices around the creation and use of DAX expressions.

Getting ready

To prepare for this recipe, follow these steps:

1. Open a Power BI Desktop file locally and access the **Power Query Editor** by clicking on **Transform Data** in the ribbon of the **Home** tab
2. Create a query named `AdWorksDW` similar to the following:

```
let
    Source = Sql.Database("localhost\MSSQLSERVERDEV",
"AdventureWorksDW2019")
in
    Source
```

3. Disable load on the **AdWorksDW** query and place it in a **Data Sources** query group
4. Right-click the **AdWorksDW** query and choose **Reference**
5. Rename the query **Reseller Sales** and choose the **FactResellerSales** table
6. Repeat *steps 4* and *5* to create a **Resellers** table that chooses the **DimReseller** table and a **Dates** query that chooses the **DimDate** table.

7. Move the **Reseller Sales** query to a **Facts** query group and the **Resellers** and **Dates** queries to a **Dimensions** query group
8. In the **Other Queries** query group, create a blank query called **Calculations**
9. Choose **Close & Apply** from the ribbon of the **Home** tab
10. Save your work

How to do it...

To implement this recipe, use the following steps:

1. Create the following base measures in the **Calculations** table:

```
Reseller Gross Sales = SUM('Reseller Sales'[SalesAmount])

Reseller Discount Amount = SUM('Reseller Sales'[DiscountAmount])
```

2. Create a **Reseller Margin** % measure in the **Calculations** table:

```
Reseller Margin % =
/*
Net Sales = Gross sales net of discounts that have shipped
Product Cost = Product standard cost of all ordered products
(including not shipped). A Date of 12/31/2099 used for
unshipped sales order lines since 1/1/2015
*/
    VAR ShippedSales = CALCULATETABLE('Reseller Sales',
        'Reseller Sales'[ShipDate] <> DATEVALUE("12/31/2099"))
    VAR NetSalesShipped = CALCULATE([Reseller Gross Sales] -
        [Reseller Discount Amount],ShippedSales)
    VAR ProductCost = SUMX('Reseller Sales',
        'Reseller Sales'[OrderQuantity] *
        'Reseller Sales'[ProductStandardCost])
RETURN
    DIVIDE(NetSalesShipped - ProductCost,NetSalesShipped)
```

3. Create a **Reseller Gross Sales (Custom)** measure in the **Calculations** table:

```
Reseller Gross Sales (Custom) =
    VAR CurrentDate = MAX('Dates'[FullDateAlternateKey])
    VAR ResellerTypes = CALCULATETABLE('Resellers',
        Resellers[BusinessType] = "Warehouse")
    VAR DateHistory = --Trailing 10 Days
    FILTER(ALL('Dates'),'Dates'[FullDateAlternateKey] <= CurrentDate &&
        'Dates'[FullDateAlternateKey] >= CurrentDate - 10)
RETURN
    CALCULATE([Reseller Gross Sales],ResellerTypes,DateHistory)
```

How it works...

The **Reseller Margin %** measure includes three lines of comments to describe the business definitions of the measure's components. Comments can also be added per line via the -- and // characters and Power BI applies green color coding to this text. Embedding comments is recommended for both complex measures with multiple components and simple measures, which form the foundation of many other measures.

The **ShippedSales** variable filters the **Reseller Sales** fact table to exclude the unshipped sales order lines and this table is used as a filter parameter in the **NetSalesShipped** variable. The existing **Reseller Gross Sales** and **Reseller Discount Amount** measures are referenced, but the **ProductCost** variable is explicitly defined against the **Reseller Sales** fact table (shipped or not). Though significantly longer than alternative DAX expressions for the same calculation, the use of variables and comments eliminates (or reduces) the need to review other measures to understand the logic and source columns.

For the **Reseller Gross Sales (Custom)** measure, variables are declared for each of the tables to be filtered and a comment (**Trailing 10 Days**) is inserted to help explain the **DateHistory** variable. The variables are invoked as filter parameters to `CALCULATE`, and so the **Reseller Gross Sales** measure reflects this modified filter context. The same functional result can be achieved by defining all the filtering logic within `CALCULATE`, but this would make the expression less readable and thus more difficult to support.

There's more...

DAX Formatter can be used within DAX Studio to align parentheses with their associated functions. Long, complex DAX measures can be copied from Power BI Desktop into DAX Studio to be formatted. To use DAX Studio to format queries, open DAX Studio, copy and paste the query from Power BI Desktop into the main window, and then click on **Format Query** in DAX Studio. Copy and paste the query from DAX Studio and replace the expression in Power BI Desktop with the formatted expression.

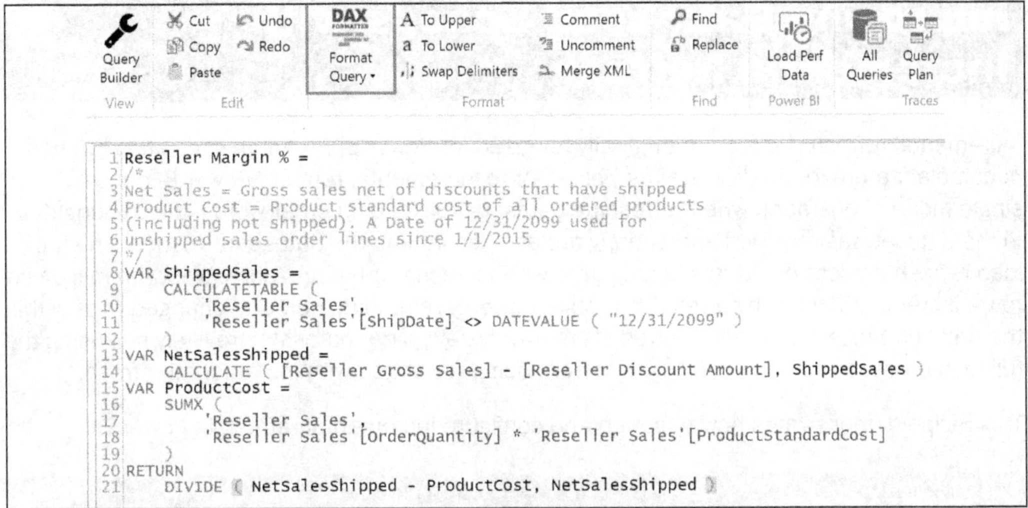

Figure 11.16: DAX Formatter in DAX Studio used to format a year-to-date measure

DAX authoring in Power BI Desktop also supports parentheses highlighting, but DAX Formatter isolates functions to individual lines and indents inner function parameters. Without the function isolation and indentation provided by DAX Formatter, complex expressions are often wide and difficult to interpret or troubleshoot.

See also

- Improve Power BI Performance by Optimizing DAX: `https://bit.ly/3uqUs4x`

Improving Data Load Speeds with Incremental Refresh

Incremental refresh is a feature originally released for Power BI Premium capacities but has become a feature for Pro licenses as well. Prior to incremental refresh, Power BI only had a single mode of operation when refreshing datasets, full load. In other words, the existing data in the dataset was removed and entirely replaced each time the dataset refreshed. The full load refresh process could take a long time when dealing with large fact tables with millions of rows. Incremental refresh solves this problem by only refreshing new and changed data within the dataset. Since incremental refresh is relatively new, older datasets are likely still using the full load process and thus might benefit from being retrofitted with incremental refresh.

This recipe demonstrates how to set up and configure incremental refresh in Power BI.

Getting ready

To prepare for this recipe, follow these steps:

1. Open a Power BI Desktop file locally and access the **Power Query Editor** by clicking on **Transform Data** in the ribbon of the **Home** tab
2. Create a query named `AdWorksDW` similar to the following:

```
let
    Source = Sql.Database("localhost\MSSQLSERVERDEV",
"AdventureWorksDW2019")
in
    Source
```

3. Disable load on the `AdWorksDW` query and place it in a **Data Sources** query group
4. Right-click the `AdWorksDW` query and choose **Reference**
5. Rename the query **Reseller Sales** and choose the **FactResellerSales** table
6. Move the **Reseller Sales** query to a **Facts** query
7. In the **Other Queries** query group, create a blank query called **Calculations**
8. Choose **Close & Apply** from the ribbon of the **Home** tab
9. Save your work

How to do it...

To implement this recipe, use the following steps:

1. In Power BI Desktop, click the **Data** view and sort the **OrderDate** column in the **Reseller Sales** table in descending order by right-clicking the column in the main table window (not the **Fields** list) and choosing **Sort descending**
2. Note the last date, **11/29/2013 12:00:00 AM**
3. Sort the **OrderDate** column in ascending order and note the first date, **12/29/2010 12:00:00 AM**
4. In **Report** view, click **Transform data** in the ribbon of the **Home** tab
5. In the Power Query Editor, click **Manage parameters** in the ribbon of the **Home** tab
6. Click **New**, provide a **Name** of **RangeStart**, a **Type** of **Date/Time**, and a **Current Value** of **12/28/2010 12:00:00 AM** (one day less than the minimum value)
7. Click **New** to create another parameter with a **Name** of **RangeEnd**, a **Type** of **Date/Time**, and a **Current Value** of **11/28/2013 12:00:00 AM** (one day less than the maximum value)
8. Move **RangeStart** and **RangeEnd** to a **Parameters** query group
9. Select the **Resellers Sales** query
10. In the **OrderDate** column header, select the drop-down button and choose **Date/Time Filters** and then **Custom Filter...**
11. Fill in the **Filter Rows** dialog as follows:

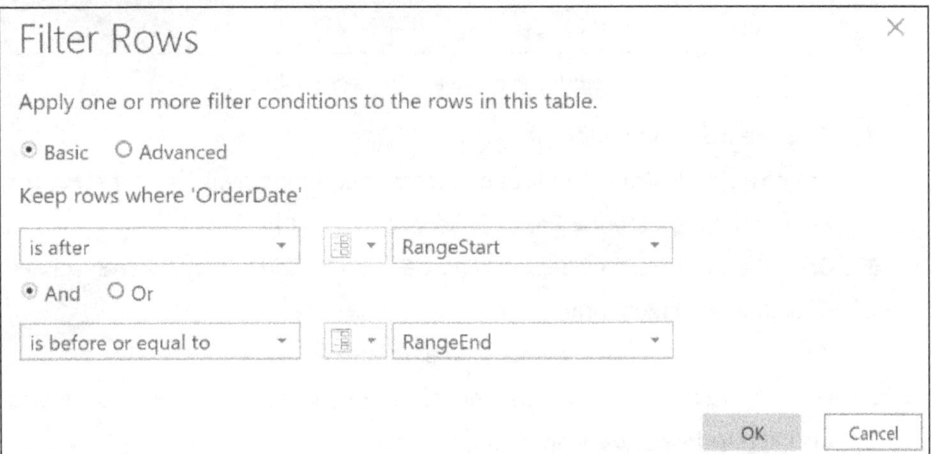

Figure 11.17: Configuring filters for incremental refresh

12. Click **Close & Apply**
13. In **Data** view, sort the **OrderDate** column in descending order and note that rows for **11/29/2013 12:00:00 AM** are not present
14. While still in **Data** view, right-click the **Reseller Sales** table and select **Incremental refresh**
15. In the **Incremental refresh** dialog, toggle **Incremental refresh** to **On** for the **Reseller Sales** table and set **Store rows...** to **30 Years** and **Refresh rows...** to **3 Days**, as shown in the following image:

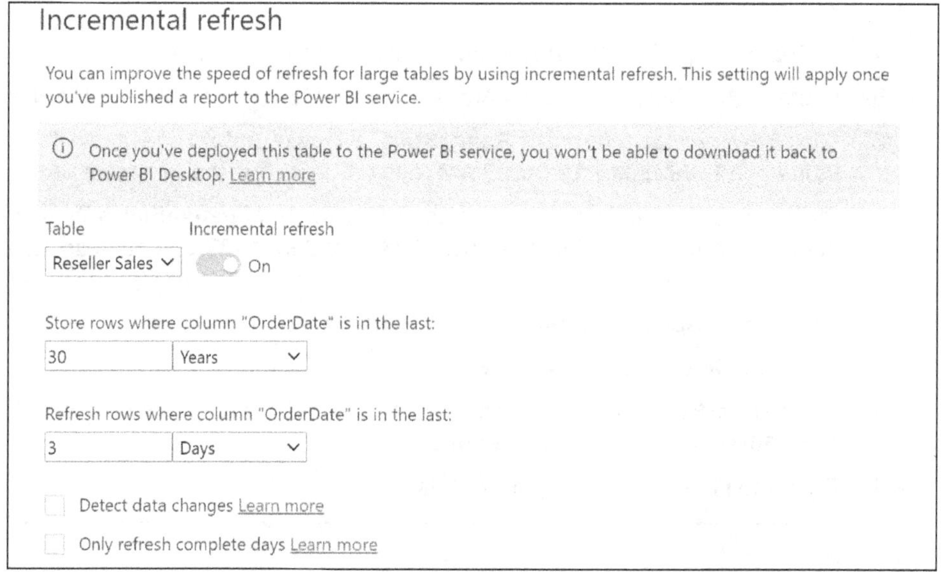

Figure 11.18: Incremental refresh dialog settings

16. Click the **Apply all** button
17. Create a simple Card visualization for the report that displays the **Latest OrderDate**
18. Publish the report to the Power BI service
19. Open the workspace where the report was published in the Power BI service
20. Open the **Settings** for the dataset
21. If necessary, add the data source to any gateway cluster
22. Open the workspace where the report was published in the Power BI service
23. Click the **Refresh now** icon for the dataset
24. Open the **Settings** for the dataset and investigate the **Refresh history**
25. Wait for the dataset to refresh and then open the report to verify that the **Latest OrderDate** is now **11/29/2013 12:00:00 AM**

How it works...

Incremental refresh uses the reserved parameter names **RangeStart** and **RangeEnd** in executing incremental refresh. While initially set during the configuration of incremental refresh, these parameters are thereafter updated by the Power BI service to determine which rows within the dataset to refresh incrementally.

When configuring the filter rows for incremental refresh, it is important that the two conditions for **RangeStart** and **RangeEnd** do not both include an equal to (=) clause as this may result in duplicate data. Only configure one of the conditions to include an equal to (=) clause in order to avoid such circumstances.

Upon first refreshing the data in the service, Power BI refreshes the entire dataset per the **Store rows where column is in the last** setting in the **Incremental refresh** dialog. In other words, during the first refresh of a dataset configured for incremental refresh, the refresh process functions like a full reload of all of the data. All rows within the store period are included in the dataset unless other filters apply. Subsequent refreshes only refresh the new data per the **Refresh rows where column is in the last** setting.

It is important to remember that once incremental refresh is configured, the Power BI file can no longer be exported from the service. Thus, it is imperative that the original Power BI desktop file be preserved in the event that changes need to be made.

There's more...

There are two optional incremental refresh settings in the **Incremental refresh** dialog. These optional settings are the following:

- Detect data changes
- Only refresh complete days

The **Detect data changes** setting can be used to further optimize the data refreshed by incremental refresh. A column of type **Date/Time** must be used for this setting and this column should not be the same column used for the **RangeStart** and **RangeEnd** parameters. The Power BI service evaluates the maximum value of this column when refreshing and if the value has not changed since the previous refresh then no data is refreshed within the dataset.

The **Only refresh complete days** setting is used to prevent partial days from being included in data refreshes. For example, in the event that the refresh operation detects that a day is incomplete, such as a scheduled refresh at 4 AM, then that day's data is not included in the refresh operation. This can be useful for organizations that only want complete daily information in their datasets for reporting purposes.

See also

- Incremental refresh in Power BI: `https://bit.ly/3f3DSkM`
- Incremental refresh for datasets in Power BI: `https://bit.ly/3w10oSv`

Conclusion

This chapter's recipes contained top data modeling, DAX measure, and M query patterns to enhance the performance, scalability, and reliability of Power BI datasets. This included performance tuning examples of both data models and measures, error handling, and query folding examples of M queries in addition to supporting details on the DAX and M query engines. The next chapter is all about deploying and distributing Power BI content using the Power BI service, Teams, and mobile devices.

12

Deploying and Distributing Power BI Content

Thus far, much of this book has focused on the individual BI professional working with Power BI to create data models, reports, dashboards, and other BI and system assets. However, BI is all about providing insights and information to the business. Thus, for any BI project to be successful, the data and insights created must be shared and distributed throughout the organization.

This chapter contains detailed examples and considerations for deploying and distributing Power BI content via the Power BI service and Power BI mobile application. This includes the creation and configuration of app workspaces and apps, procuring and assigning Power BI premium capacities, configuring data sources and refresh schedules, and deriving greater value from the Power BI mobile application. Additionally, topics such as staging deployments across development and production environments, as well as multi-node premium capacity deployments, are covered.

In this chapter, we will cover the following recipes:

- Preparing for Content Creation and Collaboration
- Managing Content between Environments
- Sharing Content with Colleagues
- Configuring Workspaces
- Configuring On-Premises Gateway Data Connections
- Publishing Apps

- Publishing Reports to the Public Internet
- Enabling the Mobile Experience
- Distributing Content with Teams

At the end of this chapter, you will be well informed about how to deploy and distribute your Power BI content.

Technical Requirements

The following are required to complete the recipes in this chapter:

- Power BI Desktop.
- SQL Server with the `AdventureWorksDW2019` database installed. This database and instructions for installing it are available here: `http://bit.ly/2OVQfG7`.
- Files for this chapter and can be downloaded from the following GitHub repository: `https://github.com/PacktPublishing/Microsoft-Power-BI-Cookbook-Second-Edition`

Preparing for Content Creation and Collaboration

Power BI collaboration environments can take many forms, ranging from a small group of Power BI Pro users creating and sharing content with each other in a single app workspace to large-scale corporate BI scenarios characterized by many read-only users accessing Power BI premium capacity resources via Power BI apps. Given the cost advantages of the capacity-based pricing model Power BI Premium provides, as well as the enhanced performance and scalability features it delivers, it is important to properly provision and manage these resources.

This recipe provides two processes fundamental to the overall purpose of this chapter: deploying and distributing Power BI content. The first process highlights several critical questions and issues in planning and managing a Power BI deployment. The second process details the provisioning of Power BI Premium dedicated capacity resources and the allocation of those resources to specific deployment workloads via app workspaces.

Getting ready

There are five main licensing mechanisms for Power BI

- Power BI Free

- Power BI Pro
- Dedicated capacity (Embedded, Premium)
- Premium Per User
- On-premises (Power BI Report Server)

Power BI Free provides extremely limited sharing and distribution features (Publish to web) while Power BI Pro and Premium Per User require every user that creates or consumes Power BI content to be licensed. Dedicated capacities such as Embedded and Premium allow free users to consume content published to embedded or premium dedicated capacity workspaces. On-premises implementations are licensed via Power BI Report Server, a superset of SQL Server Reporting Services (SSRS).

It is essential to carefully review the licensing and features associated with each deployment option. For example, many of the features in the Power BI service such as dashboards and Q&A (natural language queries) are not available in on-premises Power BI Report Server. Likewise, certain Power BI Premium SKUs are exclusive to embedding Power BI into applications. For a more complete treatment of Power BI licensing options, see the *See also* section of this recipe.

How to do it...

To implement this recipe, do the following:

1. Determine how Power BI content (datasets, reports, and dashboards) will be deployed and consumed by users.
   - Will content be deployed to the Power BI service and accessed via apps and Power BI mobile apps?
   - Will content be deployed to the Power BI service but embedded into business applications?
   - Will content be deployed to the Power BI report server on-premises and accessed via the reporting services web portal as well as the Power BI mobile app?

   For hybrid deployments, such as using both the Power BI service and embedding, or using the Power BI service and Power BI Report Server, estimate the resources required for each of these workloads and evaluate both a consolidated licensing model and separate, dedicated licenses. For example, if 16 virtual cores are provisioned with a Power BI premium P2 SKU, 16 separate cores are also available for licensing Power BI Report Server on-premises. Such consolidated licensing may be more advantageous than licensing Power BI Report Server separately and paying for additional Power BI Pro licenses.

2. Identify or estimate the Power BI Pro and Power BI Free users based on their roles and needs in the organization.
    - ❑ Will the user create and publish content (Power BI Pro)?
    - ❑ Will the user only consume content and optionally create content for their personal use (Power BI Free)?

   Connecting to published datasets via Analyze in Excel and Power BI service Live Connections are Power BI Pro features and are thus not available to Power BI Free users even if the dataset is assigned to a Power BI Premium capacity. However, a Power BI Free user can still view and subscribe to reports and dashboards in Premium capacities, and can also export content to CSVs and PowerPoint.

3. For larger deployments with many read-only users, estimate the Power BI Premium resources required.
    - ❑ Use the Power BI Dedicated Capacity Load Assessment Tool referenced in the *See also* section as a starting point.
    - ❑ Plan how deployment workloads will be allocated across premium capacity nodes.
    - ❑ Will a given workload (or perhaps a business function) have its own capacity, or will a single, larger capacity support multiple or all workloads or teams?

   If Power BI datasets in import mode will serve as the primary data storage option supporting reports and dashboards, consider their memory usage relative to the memory available per Power BI Premium SKU. For example, 25 GB of RAM is currently available in a P1 capacity node, and this may be insufficient for larger dataset (model) sizes stored in the service with a scheduled refresh. Like SSAS tabular models, 2.5X of memory should be provisioned to support both processing and refreshing, queries, and temporary memory structures created during queries.

4. Evaluate and plan data modeling tools (datasets).
    - ❑ Will Power BI Desktop be used for both data modeling and report development or will Analysis Services be used for data modeling and Power BI Desktop only used for reporting?
    - ❑ What will the storage mode of these new semantic models be (Import, DirectQuery, Composite) and what are the implications for required memory? For example, aggregations are exclusively available with Power BI Premium and thus significantly less memory would need to be provisioned if aggregations are used correctly.
    - ❑ Are changes to a relational data source or infrastructure necessary to support performance?

   In some scenarios, the relational data source must be revised or enhanced to support sufficient DirectQuery performance. These enhancements vary based on the source but may include indexes (such as Columnstore indexes in SQL Server), greater compute and memory resources, denormalization, and referential integrity.

If SSAS is being used on-premises as the source for Power BI (via the on-premises data gateway), it may be beneficial to utilize Azure ExpressRoute to create a private connection to the Azure data center of the Power BI tenant.

5. Plan for scaling and migrating Power BI projects as adoption and needs change and identify key points of the project lifecycle and the capabilities needed to migrate and scale as needs change.

   Examples of this include adding separate Power BI Premium capacity nodes (scale out), larger capacity nodes (scale up), migrating a Power BI Desktop dataset to SSAS or Azure Analysis Services, staging deployments across Dev, Test, and Production Power BI workspaces and apps, moving workspaces into and out of premium capacities, and transferring ownership of content across teams, such as from a business team to a corporate BI team.

6. Assign roles and responsibilities to Power BI team members.
   - ❑ Dataset authors, including source connectivity, retrieval queries, data modeling, and measuring development
   - ❑ Report authors, including dashboards, mobile-optimized reports and dashboards, and apps
   - ❑ Administrators, including the on-premise data gateway, premium capacities, and tenant settings

7. Target skills and knowledge specific to these team roles.
   - ❑ Dataset authors should learn the fundamentals of DAX, M, and data modeling for Power BI and SSAS.
   - ❑ Report authors should know or learn about visualization standards, interactivity and filtering, and custom visuals.
   - ❑ Administrators should study monitoring tools and data available for on-premises gateway monitoring, workspaces, premium capacities, the Office 365 audit log, and the Power BI activity log.

   Report authors, who are often business analysts outside of IT or BI organizations, should regularly review new and recent report features released in the Power BI monthly updates.

8. Build collaboration processes across teams.
   - ❑ Dataset authors should collaborate with the owners and subject matter experts of data sources. For example, any changes to data source schemas or resources should be communicated.
   - ❑ Report authors should have access to dataset documentation and collaborate with dataset authors. For example, metrics or dimensions not available for new reports should be communicated. Any standards such as a corporate Power BI report theme or fonts should be documented.

- ❑ Administrators should collaborate with the Office 365 global admin, data governance, and security teams. For example, administrators should confirm that Power BI tenant settings align with organizational policies. Additionally, administrators can request or procure security groups to manage Power BI.
- ❑ Plan for common support scenarios, new project requests, and requests for enhancements. For example, create a process for automatically assigning Power BI licenses and security group memberships. Additionally, plan for questions or issues from consumers of Power BI content.

Successful Power BI deployments of any significant scale require planning, team and cross-team collaboration, business processes, active management, and targeted skills and resources. The steps in this recipe only identify several of the fundamental topics—the actual process is always specific to an organization and its deployment goals, policies, and available skills and resources.

There's more...

Power BI Premium was introduced to support large-scale deployments of Power BI for enterprises. Power BI Premium is, at its core, a pool of dedicated hardware resources for a given organization to configure and utilize according to their own use cases and policies. Although other legacy Microsoft BI technologies such as Analysis Services and Reporting Services will continue to be supported, all new features and capabilities, such as composite models and aggregations, are exclusively available to Power BI Premium customers. Additionally, Power BI Premium capacity enables new scenarios including embedding content in applications and using a combination of both the Power BI public cloud service and an on-premises deployment of the Power BI Report Server. Perhaps most importantly for large deployments, Power BI Premium avoids the need to purchase licenses for each user since read-only users can access Power BI Premium content without a pro license. Additionally, as a managed cloud service, resources can be aligned with the changing needs of an organization via simple scale-up and scale-out options.

> *"In many cases Power BI Premium was built to address the challenges of deploying Power BI at scale where you have larger data models that have grown over time and when you have more users that are accessing the content."*
>
> *- Adam Wilson, Power BI group program manager*

In this example, workspaces specific to functional areas in an organization are associated with two separate Power BI Premium capacity nodes.

An additional workspace and the **My Workspace** associated with all accounts (Power BI Free and Pro) are included in a shared capacity--the multi-tenancy environment of the Power BI Service. The process for provisioning and configuring such an environment is as follows:

1. A Microsoft 365 global admin or billing admin purchases the required Pro and Free licenses in the **Microsoft 365 admin center**.
2. These licenses are assigned to users according to the roles determined in the planning stage earlier.

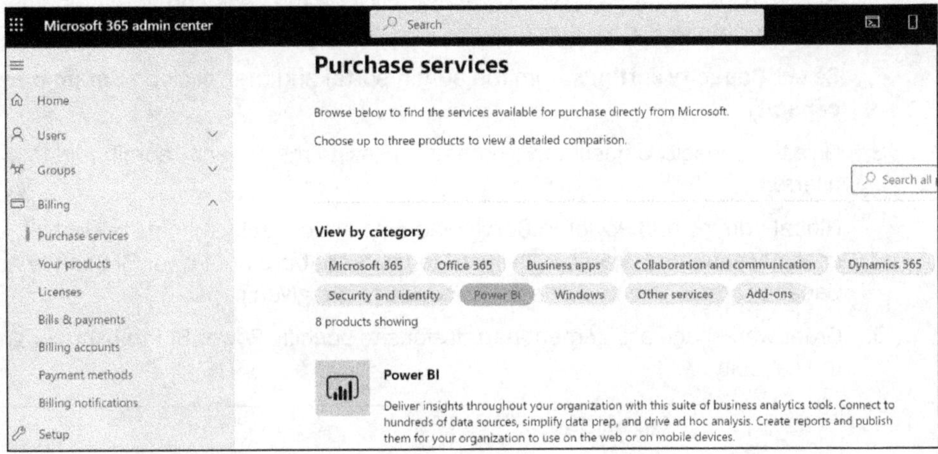

Figure 12.1: Microsoft 365 admin center – Purchase services

3. Purchase a Power BI Premium P2 capacity node by scrolling down, clicking the **Details** button under the **Power BI Premium P2** heading, and then clicking the **Buy** button.

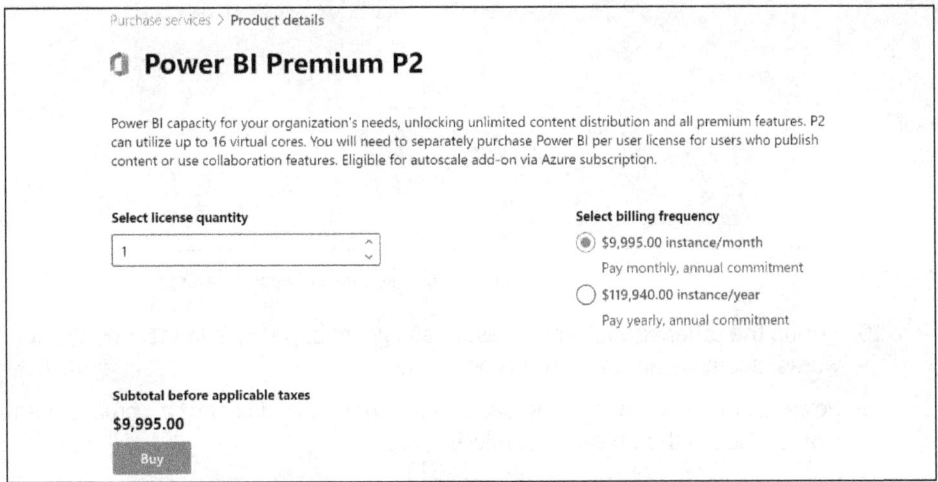

Figure 12.2: Purchasing a Power BI Premium P2 capacity

4. Purchase a Power BI Premium P3 capacity.
5. Confirm that the new Power BI Premium subscriptions appear in the **Your products** window along with any purchased Power BI Pro and Power BI Free licenses.
6. The Microsoft 365 global admin or Power BI Service Administrator opens the Power BI admin portal. In the Power BI service, click on the gear icon at the top right and select **Admin Portal**.
7. Select **Capacity settings** from the admin portal and then click on **Set up new capacity**.
8. Give the capacity a descriptive name and assign the capacity admin role to a user or users.

   Global admins and Power BI Service Admins are capacity admins by default, but the capacity admin role can be assigned to users that are not Power BI Service Admins. Capacity admin role privileges are specific to the given capacity.
9. Grant workspace assignment permissions to specific Power BI Pro users or groups for the capacity.

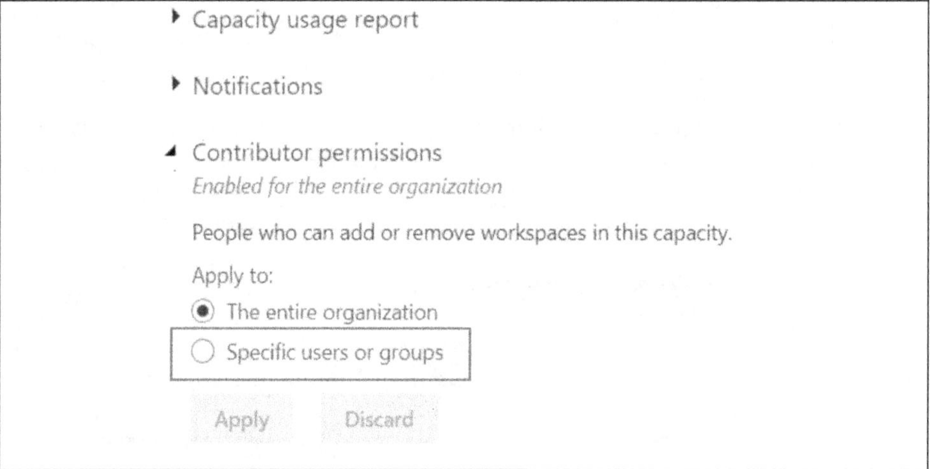

Figure 12.3: User permissions in Capacity settings

10. Set up the other capacity purchased, assign its capacity admins, and grant its workspace assignment permissions.
11. Power BI Pro users with workspace assignment permissions can create premium workspaces in the Power BI service.

In the Power BI admin portal, capacity admins can assign or remove workspaces from premium capacity, as well as whitelisting users such that all of a given user's workspaces are assigned to premium capacity.

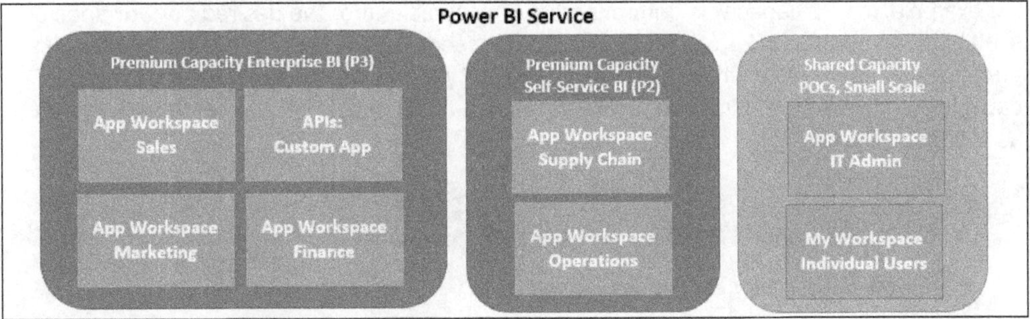

Figure 12.4: Power BI Premium capacity assigned to workspaces

In this example, three workspaces (sales, marketing, and finance) are assigned to a Power BI Premium Capacity named **Enterprise BI (P3)**. Additionally, this capacity also supports the embedded reporting needs of a custom application. The larger P3 (32 cores, 100 GB RAM) capacity was chosen given the higher volume of query traffic for these workspaces, as well as the need for larger dataset sizes.

Supply chain and operations workspaces were assigned to a P2 capacity. In this case, though less of a workload than the P3 capacity, these groups still need to share content with many free users. Finally, a workspace for a small group of IT users (IT Admin) with Power BI Pro licenses is maintained in Shared Capacity. This workspace did not require Power BI Premium, given minimal needs for distribution to free users and given smaller datasets with relatively infrequent refresh schedules.

Scaling out Power BI Premium involves distributing provisioned capacity (v-cores) across multiple capacities. For example, the 32 v-cores purchased as part of a P3 capacity node could optionally be split into three separate capacities: two P1 capacities of 8 v-cores each and one P2 capacity of 16 v-cores (*8 + 8 + 16 = 32*). This ability to distribute v-cores across distinct premium capacities is referred to as *v-core pooling*.

In-place scaling of Premium capacities involves purchasing an additional capacity node in the Microsoft 365 admin center as per the recipe, then adjusting the capacity size of a given premium capacity to reflect the additional cores:

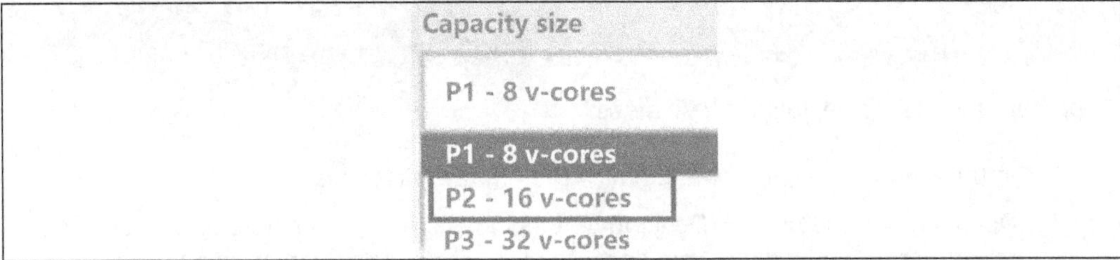

Figure 12.5: Available v-cores for a capacity in the Power BI admin portal

For example, if a P1 capacity is determined to be insufficient for the desired performance or scalability, an additional P1 capacity can be purchased. At this point, with two P1 capacities purchased at 8 v-cores each, a P2 capacity size (16 v-cores) can be set for the original capacity in the Power BI admin portal. This makes it quick and easy to incrementally scale up as requirements change.

See also

- Power BI Licensing in Pictures: `https://bit.ly/2R4xYYN`
- What is Microsoft Power BI Premium?: `https://bit.ly/3eyrpq8`
- Planning a Power BI enterprise deployment whitepaper: `http://bit.ly/2wBGPRJ`
- Capacity and SKUs in Power BI embedded analytics: `https://bit.ly/2REM437`
- Capacity planning: `https://bit.ly/3tG66aR`

Managing Content between Environments

Corporate BI and IT teams familiar with project lifecycles, source control systems, and managing development, testing, and production environments should look to apply these processes to Power BI deployments as well. Power BI Desktop does not natively interface with standard source control systems such as Azure DevOps. However, Power BI files can be stored in SharePoint Online Team site and OneDrive for Business to provide visibility to version history, synchronization between local device and the cloud service, restore capabilities, and more. In the Power BI service, separate development, test, and production workspaces and their corresponding apps can be created to support a staged deployment. Utilizing these tools and features enables Power BI teams to efficiently manage their workflows and to deliver consistent, quality content to users.

This recipe contains a recipe for deploying content using Power BI Deployment Pipelines, which is a Premium feature. Alternative methods for those without Premium are included in the *There's more* section.

Getting ready

To prepare for this recipe, follow these steps:

1. In the Power BI Service, create a new Premium workspace.
2. Open a report in Power BI Desktop that includes query parameters and **Publish** the report to the Premium workspace created in Step 1. The query parameters should be set to **Text**.

Again, this recipe requires a Power BI Premium capacity.

How to do it...

Creating and using Power BI Deployment Pipelines is relatively easy. To create and use a pipeline follow these steps:

1. In the Power BI Service, choose **Deployment pipelines** from the left navigation pane.
2. Choose **Create a pipeline**.
3. Provide a **Pipeline name** and click the **Create** button.
4. Click the **Assign a workspace** button.
5. Choose the Premium workspace created in Step 1, assign the deployment stage for the workspace of **Development** and click the **Assign** button.

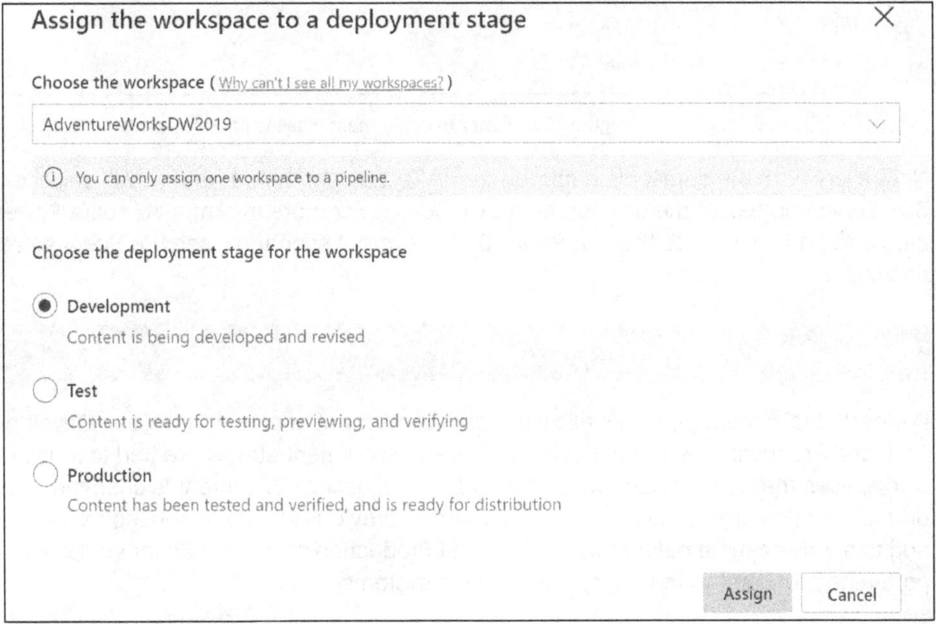

Figure 12.6: Assign a workspace to a deployment pipeline

6. Under the **Development** stage, click the **Deploy to test** button. This creates a new workspace and deploys the content in **Development** to this workspace.

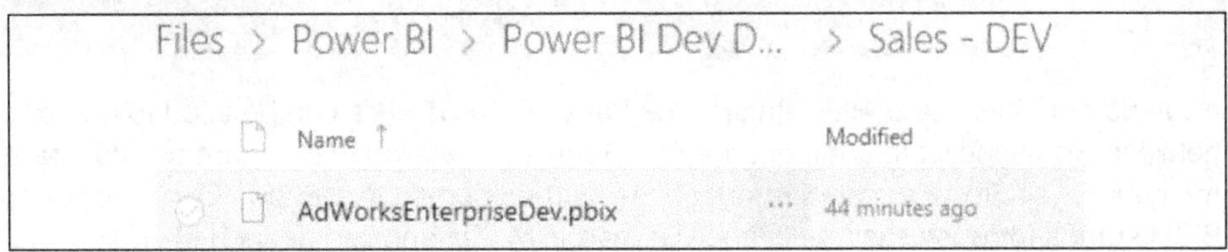

Figure 12.7: Power BI deployment pipeline

7. Once the content is deployed to **Test**, click the lightning bolt icon in the **Test** stage header.
8. Click on the dataset under the **Datasets** heading.
9. Expand **Parameter rules** and click the **Add rule** button.
10. Under the **For this parameter heading**, choose a parameter.
11. Under the **Apply this value**, edit the parameter and click the **Save** button.

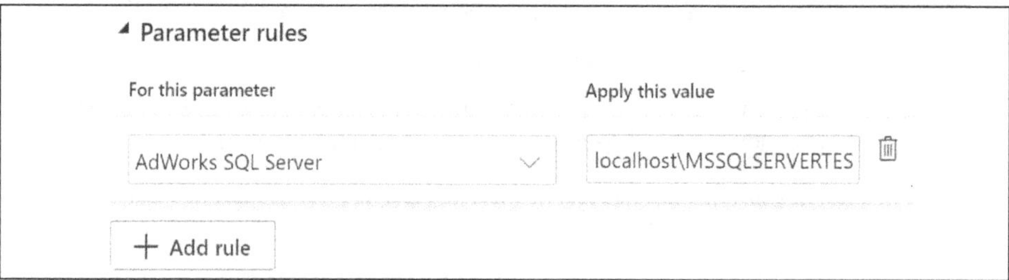

Figure 12.8: Power BI deployment pipeline parameter rule

Now, every time the dataset is deployed to the Test stage, the parameter will point to the test SQL Server instead of the development SQL Server. For more information about Power BI pipelines and how to use them in Power BI deployment scenarios, see the *See also* section of this recipe.

How it works...

Power BI deployment pipelines allow the easy movement of content between Development, Test, and Production deployment stages. These deployment stages are tied to individual workspaces that are created automatically by the pipeline. As content is changed within the different stages, that content can be deployed to previous stages or subsequent stages. In addition, rules can be defined within Test and Production stages that change data sources or parameters to point to the appropriate source systems.

The Development stage is designed to be the working area for report development. The Test stage is where developed content can be shared with business users for user acceptance testing. Finally, the Production stage is where the final product is presented to the business.

There's more...

If you do not have Power BI Premium, the Power BI REST API's can be used to deploy content between workspaces. In addition, the ALM Toolkit allows you to compare two compare and merge Analysis Services tabular models using the open-source BISM Normalizer toolset. BISM stands for Business Intelligence Semantic Model and is a defined Microsoft model for reporting, analytics, scorecards, and dashboards.

BISM includes three layers, the **Data model layer** (tabular and multi-dimensional), **Business logic and queries layer** (DAX and MDX), and the **Data access layer** (ROLAP, MOLAP, Vertipaq, and DirectQuery). The ALM Toolkit uses the BISM foundation to generate a comparison of Analysis Services models and can then merge the changes in one model with another model. For more information about the ALM Toolkit and how to use it in deployment scenarios, see the *See also* section of this recipe.

Finally, Maik van der Gaag developed a free set of tasks for Azure DevOps Pipelines called **Power BI Actions**. This set of tasks allows common deployment actions to be automated via Azure DevOps Pipelines, allowing the creation of a continuous integration, continuous development (CICD) process for Power BI deployments. For more information about the CICD with Azure DevOps and how to use it in Power BI deployment scenarios, see the *See also* section of this recipe.

See also

- Power BI REST API reference for Report operations: `http://bit.ly/2v8ifKg`
- ALM Toolkit documentation: `https://bit.ly/3f95ODQ`
- AzureDevOps: CICD for PowerBI Reports: `https://bit.ly/3hfrHnM`
- Introduction to deployment pipelines: : `https://bit.ly/3uxzMrT`

Sharing Content with Colleagues

Power BI apps are the recommended content distribution method for large corporate BI deployments, but for small teams and informal collaboration scenarios, sharing dashboards and reports provides a simple alternative. By sharing a dashboard, the recipient obtains read access to the dashboard, the reports supporting the dashboards tiles, and immediate visibility of any changes in the dashboard. Additionally, dashboards and reports can be shared with Power BI Pro users external to an organization via security groups and distribution lists, and Power BI Pro users can leverage **Analyze in Excel** as well as the Power BI mobile apps to access the shared data. Moreover, Power BI Free users can consume dashboards and reports shared with them from Power BI Premium capacity.

In this recipe, a Power BI dashboard is shared with a colleague as well as a contact in an external organization. Guidance on configuring and managing shared dashboards and additional considerations is included throughout the recipe and the *How it works...* and *There's more...* sections.

Getting ready

Confirm that both the owner of the dashboard and the recipient(s) or consumers have Power BI Pro licenses. If the recipient(s) does not have a Power BI Pro license, check if the dashboard is contained in a workspace that has been assigned to premium capacity. Either Pro licenses or Premium capacity are required to share the dashboard. A Power BI Pro user cannot share a dashboard hosted in Power BI shared capacity with a Power BI free user.

Enable the external sharing feature in the Power BI Admin Portal, either for the organization or specific security groups. The owner of a shared dashboard can allow recipients to reshare a dashboard but any dashboards shared with external users cannot be shared. Additionally, user access to the dashboard and the ability to reshare can be removed by the dashboard owner. Unlike the **Publish to web** feature described later in this chapter, external sharing can be limited to specific security groups or excluded from specific security groups.

In this example, Jennifer from the BI team is responsible for sharing a dashboard with Brett from the Canada sales team and another person, Jack, from outside the organization. Brett will need the ability to share the dashboard with a few members of his team.

How to do it...

To implement this recipe, do the following:

1. Create a dedicated workspace in the Power BI service.
2. Set the privacy level of the workspace to allow members to edit content and add team members to the workspace.
3. Create a security role in Power BI Desktop for the **Canada sales team**.
4. Publish the Power BI Desktop file to the workspace and add members or security groups to the **Canada sales team** role.

   By using security roles, an existing Power BI Sales dataset containing sales for other countries can be used for the dashboard. Brett will be allowed to share the dashboard, but RLS will prevent him and those mapped to the security role via security groups from viewing sales data for other countries. See *Chapter 8, Implementing Dynamic User-Based Visibility in Power BI*, for details on configuring RLS.
5. Create new Power BI Desktop report files with live connections to the published dataset in the workspace.
6. Build essential visualizations in each file and publish these reports.
7. In the Power BI service, create a new dashboard, **Canada Sales Dashboard**, and pin visuals from reports, and adjust the layout.

8. Click on **Share** from the **Canada Sales Dashboard** in the workspace of the Power BI service.

Figure 12.9: Sharing the Canada Sales dashboard

9. Add Brett, the external user, and optionally a message on the **Share dashboard** form.

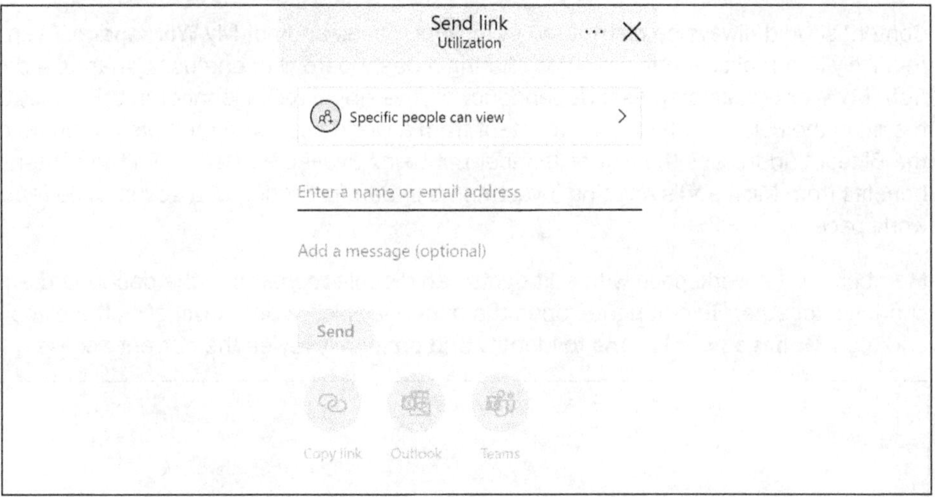

Figure 12.10: Share dashboard form in the Power BI service

Power BI will detect and attempt to auto-complete as email addresses are entered in the Grant access to input box. Additionally, though sharing dashboards is sometimes referred to as peer-to-peer sharing, a list of email addresses can be pasted in, and all common group entities are supported, including distribution lists, security groups, and Office 365 groups. Per the image, a warning will appear if a user external to the organization is entered.

10. In this example, leave the **Allow recipients to share this dashboard** option enabled below the message. Click on **Grant Access.**

If left enabled on the share form, recipients will receive an email notification as well as a notification in Power BI.

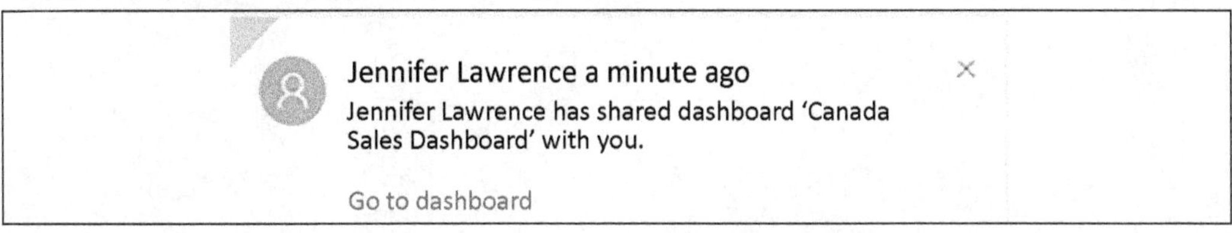

Figure 12.11: Notification center in the Power BI service of the dashboard recipient

For the recipient, the dashboard appears in the **Shared with me** tab. If enabled by the dashboard owner (and if the user is internal to the organization), the option to reshare the dashboard with others is enabled. The user will be able to favorite the dashboard, access it from the Power BI mobile app, and interact with the content, such as filtering selections, but cannot edit the report or dashboard.

How it works...

Content should always be distributed from workspaces and not **My Workspace**. Even in relatively informal scenarios such as sharing a dashboard with one user, sharing a dashboard from **My Workspace** creates a dependency on the single user (Jennifer in this case) to maintain the content. Sharing the content from a workspace with multiple members of the BI team addresses the risk of Jennifer not being available to maintain the content and benefits from Microsoft's ongoing investments in administration and governance features for workspaces.

Members of the workspace with edit rights can disable reshares of the dashboard and stop sharing altogether. To edit rights, open the dashboard, click on **Share**, click the ellipsis (**...**), and then **Manage permissions** to identify and optionally revise the current access.

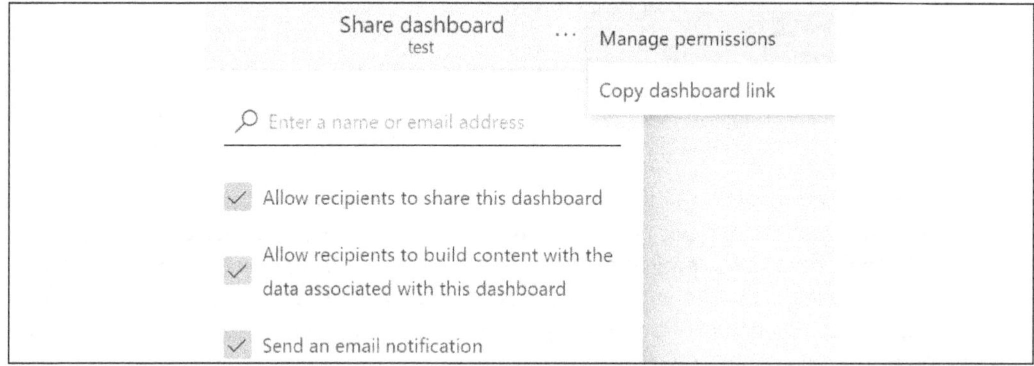

Figure 12.12: Share dashboard, Manage permissions

In the **Manage permissions** pane, click **Advanced** at the bottom and then click on the **Direct access** tab. Here you can add users, edit permissions and remove access as shown in *Figure 12.13*.

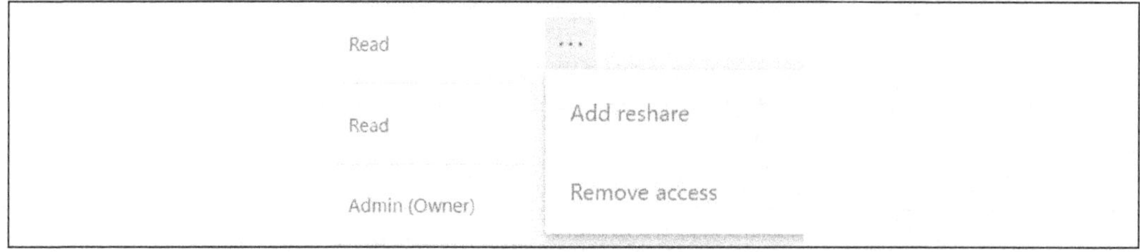

Figure 12.13: Sharing and access options

There's more...

Sharing reports in the Power BI service operates identically as sharing dashboards in terms of the user interface. The only difference is that the process starts on a report page in the service rather than a dashboard.

Datasets can also be shared by providing read access to the dataset specifically. This is done by clicking the three vertical dots next to a dataset either in the left-hand navigation pane or when viewing the **Datasets + dataflows** pane of a workspace.

See also

- Share Power BI reports and dashboards with coworkers and others: `https://bit.ly/3f99llw`
- Ways to collaborate and share in Power BI: `https://bit.ly/3tylUMv`

Configuring Workspaces

Workspaces (formerly App workspaces) are shared areas in the Power BI service for Power BI Pro users to develop content. The datasets, reports, and dashboards contained within workspaces can be published as a Power BI app for distribution to groups of users. Additionally, workspaces can be assigned to Power BI Premium capacities of dedicated hardware to enable all users, regardless of license, to consume the published app and to provide consistent performance and greater scalability. Furthermore, workspaces retain a one-to-one mapping to published apps, enabling members and administrators of workspaces to stage and test iterations prior to publishing updates to apps.

Understanding the history of workspaces is beneficial when reading various historical documentation on the subject. When Power BI was first released, the service included the concept of workspaces. However, these workspaces were tied to Office 365 groups and had various limitations. Microsoft released an update to group workspaces and named these new workspaces. Traditional workspaces were labeled **Classic workspaces**. Today, all new workspaces are workspaces and are now known simply as **workspaces** since Classic workspaces have been all but phased out. While this may all seem a bit Istanbul, not Constantinople, just understand that when reading blog posts and other information that refers to workspaces, that this simply means the modern workspace experience in the Power BI service.

In this recipe, a workspace is created and configured. Within the recipe and in the supporting sections, all primary considerations are identified, including the scope or contents of workspaces and the assignment of workspaces to premium capacity.

Getting ready

To prepare for this recipe, follow these steps:

1. Confirm that Power BI Pro licenses are available to administrators and members of the workspace.
2. Ensure that the workspace aligns with the policy or standard of the organization for Power BI content distribution.
3. If premium capacity has been provisioned but not bulk assigned to all workspaces of an organization, determine if the new workspace will be hosted in a premium capacity.
4. If Premium capacity has been provisioned and authorized for the new workspace, evaluate the current utilization of premium capacity, and determine if the expected workload of datasets and user queries from the new app deployment will require a larger or separate capacity. In addition, confirm that the workspace administrator has workspace assignment permission, or assign this permission in the Power BI admin portal per the first step in *How to do it...*.
5. Retrieve your Power BI tenant's UTC offset by clicking the question mark (?) icon in the upper-right corner of the Power BI service and choose **About Power BI**. The UTC offset is shown in *Figure 12.14*, in this case -0400:

Figure 14: UTC offset of Power BI tenant

6. Retrieve the Premium capacity ID from the **Capacity settings** of the admin portal in the Power BI service.
7. While in **Capacity settings**, click the gear icon under **Actions** for the desired capacity and note the **CAPACITY ID**.
8. From a workspace in the Power BI service, select **Get data** from the lower-left corner of the screen.
9. In the **Services** section, click the **Get** button.
10. Search for **Premium** and choose the **Premium Gen2 Capacity Utilization Metrics** app.

11. On the **AppSource** page for the template app, click the **Get It Now** button as shown in *Figure 12.15*:

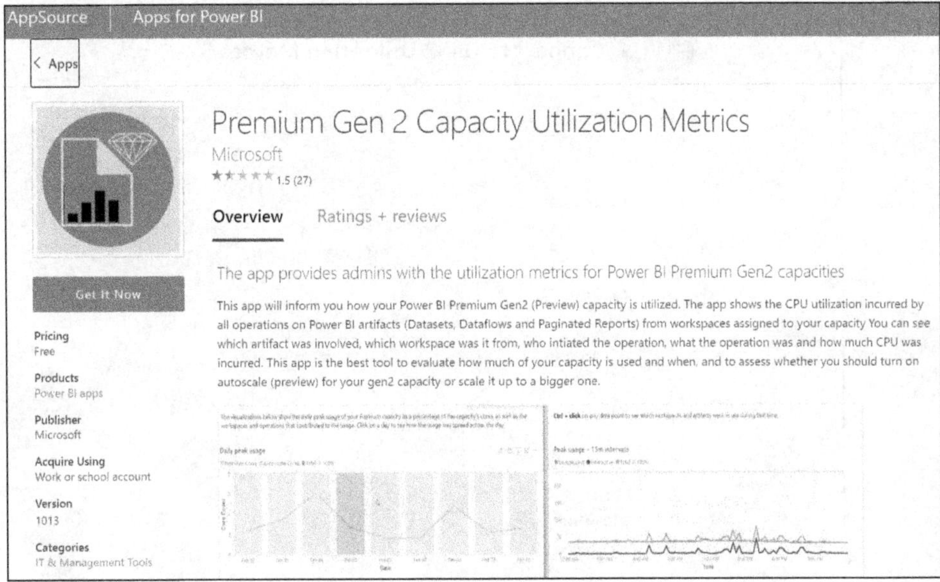

Figure 12.15: Premium Gen2 Capacity Utilization Metrics App in AppSource

12. Fill in the contact information, accept the terms and conditions, and click the **Continue** button.
13. Click the radio button for **Install to a new workspace**, provide a workspace name, and then click the **Install** button to install the app.

This completes the steps to prepare for this recipe.

How to do it...

To implement this recipe, do the following:

1. Open the new workspace and choose **Apps** from the navigation pane in the Power BI service.
2. Click on the **Gen2 Utilization Metrics** app.
3. At the top of the screen, click on **Connect your data** as shown in *Figure 12.16* below:

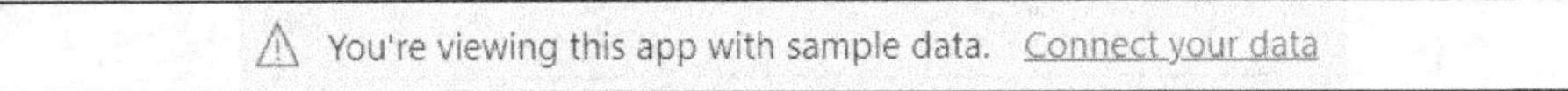

Figure 12.16: Gen2 Utilization Metrics prompt to Connect your data

4. Enter the **CapacityId** and other information requested by the app and click the **Next** button.

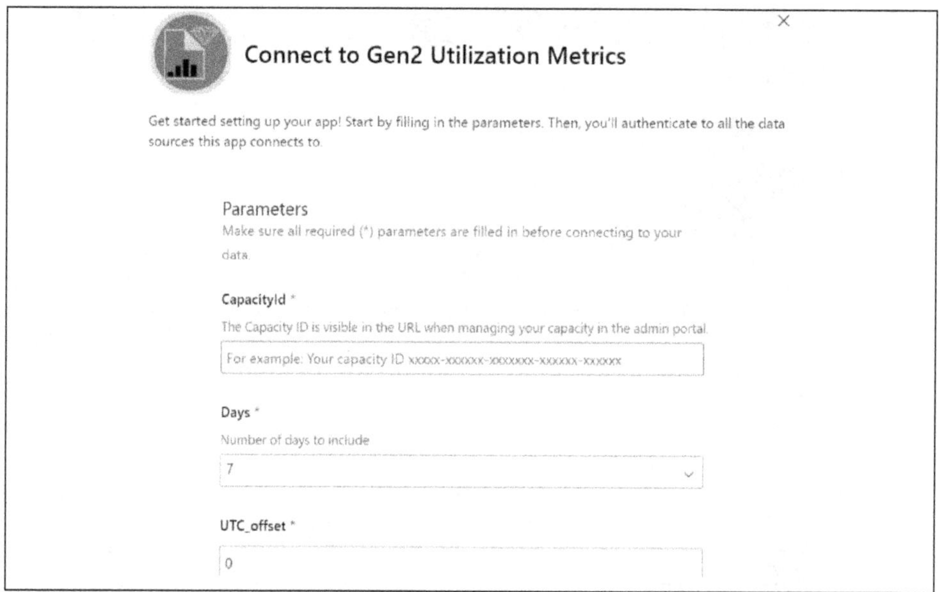

Figure 12.17: Connect to Gen2 Utilization Metrics

5. On the next screen, choose **Sign in and connect** and sign in to the Power BI service.
6. View the recent performance of the capacity via the usage measurements for CPU, memory, and queries.
7. Assuming that the capacity metrics are in order, exit the app by clicking the **Go back** link in the lower-left corner of the app.
8. Click on the arrow next to **Workspaces** and then click on **Create a workspace**.

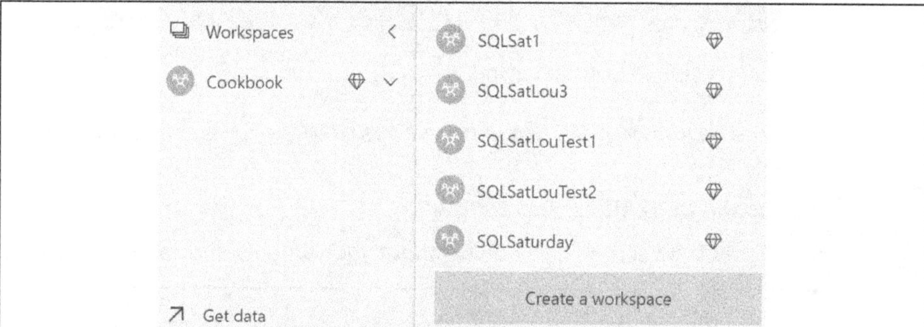

Figure 12.18: Create a workspace in the Power BI service

Workspaces assigned to premium capacity are identified with a diamond icon in the Power BI service.

9. Provide a workspace name, expand the **Advanced** section, choose a **License mode** of **Premium per capacity** and select a capacity.

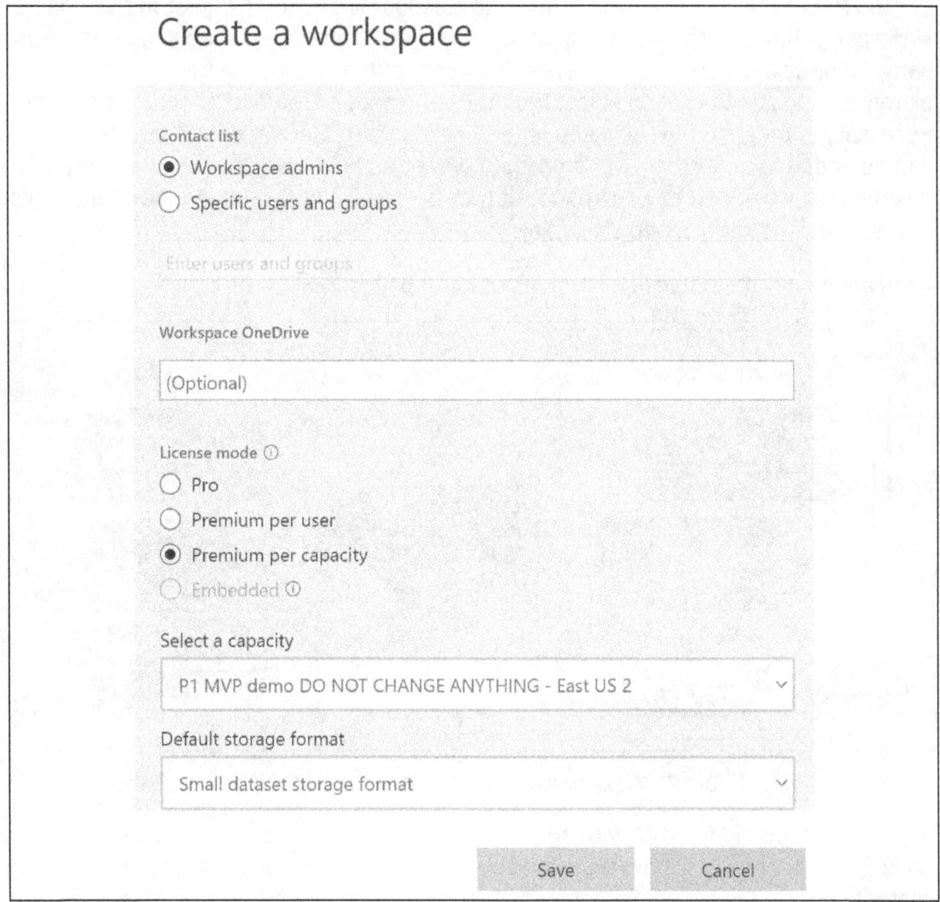

Figure 12.19: Creating a Premium workspace

10. Click the **Save** button to create the workspace.
11. In the workspace, click the **Access** link in the header to add workspace members.

Workspace members can now publish datasets and reports and create dashboards to distribute via an app. Technically it is possible to add members to a view-only group and assign developers to the role of workspace admin such that they can edit content. This method of collaboration is not recommended, as the view-only members will have immediate visibility of all changes, as with sharing dashboards. Published apps from workspaces provide for staging deployments and are the recommended solution for distributing content to read-only members.

How it works...

Per the *Preparing for Content Creation and Collaboration* recipe earlier in this chapter, workspaces have a one-to-one mapping to apps and can have a wide scope (for example, sales), a narrow scope such as a specific dashboard, or a balance between these two extremes, such as European sales. If broad workspaces are used, then it may not be necessary to create a new workspace for a particular project or dashboard as new content can be added to an existing workspace. However, as an increasing volume of reports and dashboards are added to workspaces, it may be beneficial to consider new, more focused workspaces and revisions to the policy.

Apps are simply the published versions of workspaces.

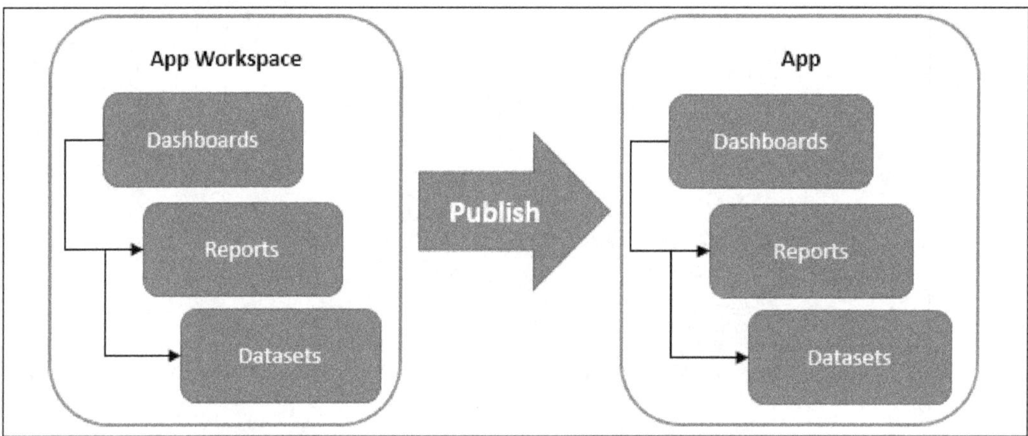

Figure 12.20: Workspaces: one-to-one relationship with published apps

Users consume and interact with apps. Content is created and managed in workspaces. Consumers of apps only have visibility of published versions of apps, not the workspace content. Per the *Preparing for Content Creation and Collaboration* and *Managing Content between Environments* recipes in this chapter, not all content from a workspace has to be included in the published app.

There's more...

Office 365 Global Admins and Power BI Admins are Capacity Admins of Power BI Premium capacities by default. These admins can assign users as Capacity Admins per capacity during the initial setup of the capacity and later via **Admin permissions** within the **Capacity settings** of a capacity in the Power BI admin portal. Capacity Admins have administrative control over the given capacity but must also be granted assignment permissions in the **Contributor permissions** setting to assign workspaces to premium capacities if the capacity admin will also be responsible for associating a workspace to premium capacity.

See also

- Manage Power BI Premium: `http://bit.ly/2vq8WHe`
- Monitor Power BI Premium capacities: `https://bit.ly/3xZqp6f`

Configuring On-Premises Gateway Data Connections

The promise of leveraging the Power BI service and mobile application to provide access to a rich set of integrated dashboards and reports across all devices requires thoughtful configuration of both the data sources and the datasets which use those sources. For many organizations, the primary business intelligence data sources are hosted on-premises, and thus, unless Power BI reports are exclusively deployed to on-premises Power BI Report Server, the on-premises data gateway is needed to securely facilitate the transfer of queries and data between the Power BI service and on-premises systems. Additionally, the datasets which typically support many reports and dashboards must be configured to utilize an on-premises data gateway for either a scheduled refresh to import data into Power BI or to support DirectQuery and Live Connection queries generated from Power BI.

This recipe contains two examples of configuring data sources and scheduled refreshes for published datasets. The first example configures two on-premises data sources (SQL Server and Excel) for an import mode Power BI dataset and schedules a daily refresh. The second example configures a separate on-premise SQL Server database for a DirectQuery Power BI dataset and sets a 15-minute dashboard tile refresh schedule.

Getting ready

To prepare for this recipe, follow these steps:

1. Download, install, and configure the on-premises data gateway as per *Creating an On-Premises Data Gateway* in *Chapter 1, Configuring Power BI Tools*.
2. Become an administrator of the on-premises data gateway.

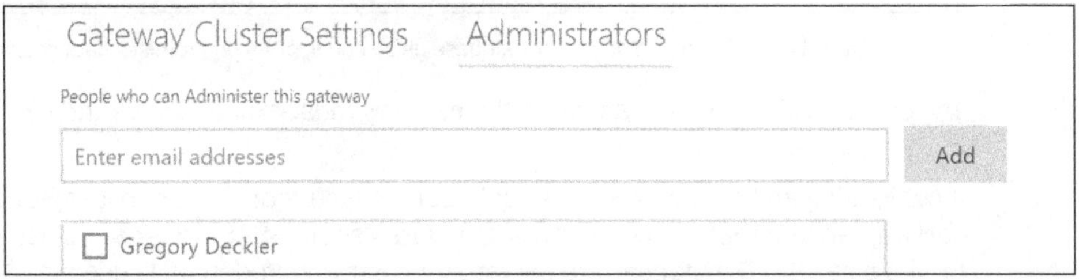

Figure 12.21: Administrators of an on-premises data gateway

It is strongly recommended to have at least two administrators for each gateway installed to provide redundancy and backup of administrative functions.

How to do it...

In this example, an import mode dataset has been created with Power BI Desktop to retrieve from two on-premises data sources, a SQL Server database and an Excel file. To implement this recipe, do the following:

1. Identify the server name and database name used in the Power BI Desktop file.
2. Identify the full path of the Excel file.
3. In the Power BI service, click on the gear icon in the top-right corner and select **Manage Gateways**.
4. From the **Manage Gateways** interface, click on **ADD DATA SOURCE** and choose **SQL Server**.
5. Provide an intuitive source name that won't conflict with other sources and enter the server and database names.

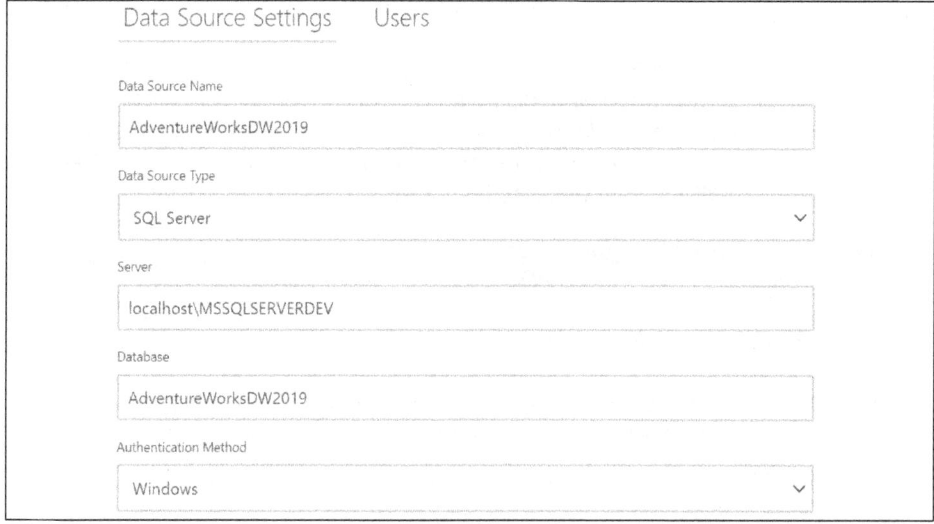

Figure 12.22: Adding a SQL Server database as a source for an on-premises data gateway

The server and database names for the gateway must exactly match the names used in the Power BI dataset.

If configuring an SSAS data source (data source type = analysis services) for a gateway, ensure that the credentials used are also an SSAS server administrator for the given SSAS instance. The server administrator credential is used in establishing the connection but each time a user interacts with the SSAS data source from Power BI, their UPN (user principal name) is passed to the server via the

`EffectiveUserName` connection property. This allows RLS roles defined in the SSAS database to be applied to Power BI users.

6. Under **Advanced Settings**, check that the source uses the appropriate privacy level, such as organizational or private.
7. Click on **Add** and then, via the **Users** tab, add users authorized to use this gateway for this data source.

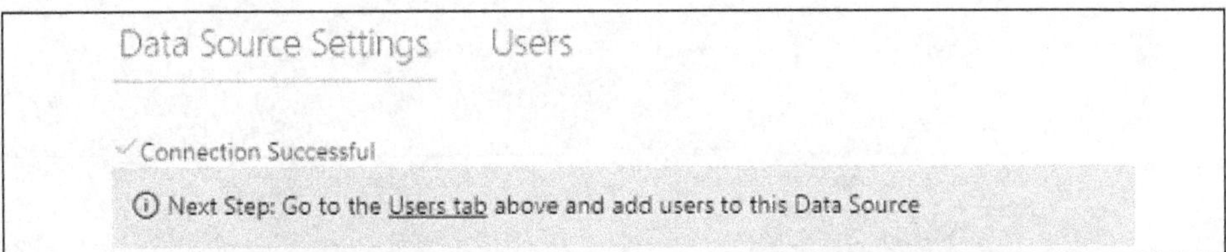

Figure 12.23: Successful setup of a data source for the on-premises data gateway

8. Add an additional data source for the Excel file using the file data source type.
9. Like the SQL Server data source, authorize users for this gateway and this data source via the **Users** page.
10. Publish the import mode Power BI Desktop file (dataset) to a workspace in the Power BI service.
11. Access the workspace and from the **Datasets + dataflows** list, click on the **Schedule refresh** icon for the dataset.

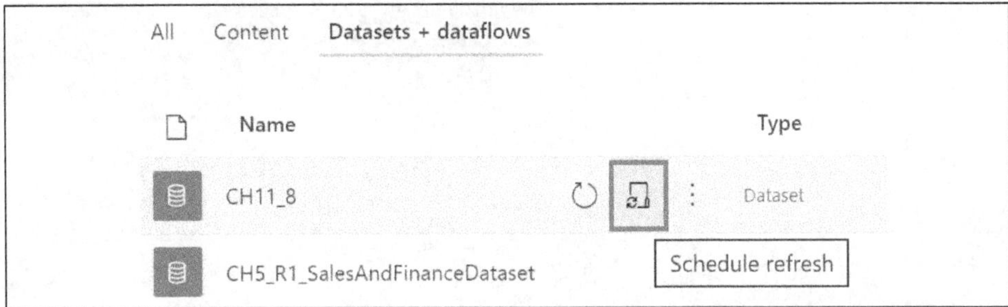

Figure 12.24: Actions available to a published dataset in the Power BI service

12. Expand the **Gateway connection** section.

    The gateway will appear as an option for data refresh if the following three criteria are met:

    - The user is listed on the **Users** page of the data source(s) within the gateway
    - The server and database names configured in the Power BI Service for the gateway match the names used in the Power BI Desktop file
    - Each data source used by the dataset is configured as a data source for the gateway

13. In the **Data sources included in this dataset** section, use the **Maps to** dropdown to select the configured gateway data source connection.

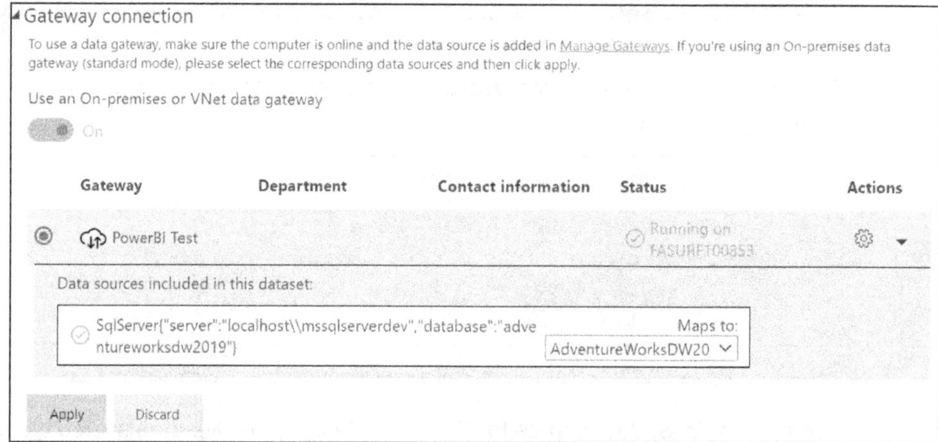

Figure 12.25: Associating the data source with the Power BI gateway data connection

14. Click the **Apply** button to connect the data source to the gateway.
15. Now expand the **Scheduled refresh** section.
16. Click the **Add another time** link to add a scheduled time for the refresh to occur.
17. Once you've finished adding refresh times, click the **Apply** button.

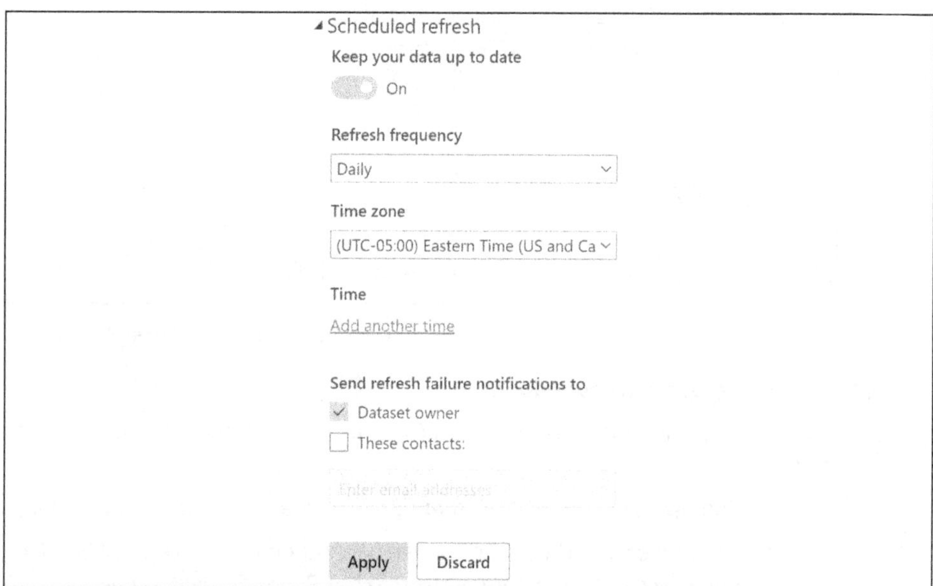

Figure 12.26: Scheduled refresh of the dataset

Your dataset is now scheduled to refresh.

How it works...

For shared capacities, there is no guarantee that scheduled refreshes will occur at the exact time they are scheduled, such as 5:00 AM in this example. The actual refresh may take place as long as 20-30 minutes after the time scheduled in the Power BI service.

Data caches used by dashboard tiles are updated after refresh operations for import mode datasets (or manually). The Power BI service also caches data for report visuals and updates these caches as datasets are refreshed. Dashboard tiles can be refreshed manually in the Power BI service via the **Refresh visuals** menu item (top-right, circular arrow icon). Likewise, reports can be manually refreshed from the Power BI service, but this is only relevant for DirectQuery and SSAS live connections; this does *not* initiate a refresh for an import mode dataset.

Import mode datasets can be refreshed via the schedule in the Power BI service or via the REST API. Power BI data refresh APIs allow BI teams to trigger refresh operations in the Power BI service programmatically.

For example, a step can be added to an existing nightly (or more frequent) data warehouse or ETL process that initiates the refresh of a Power BI dataset that uses this data source. This allows dashboards and reports in the Power BI service to reflect the latest successful refresh of the data source(s) as soon as possible. In other words, the gap or lag between the source system refresh and the Power BI dataset scheduled refresh can be reduced to the amount of time needed to refresh the dataset in the Power BI service.

To trigger a refresh for a dataset in the Power BI service, simply make the following HTTP request:

```
POST https://api.powerbi.com/v1.0/myorg/groups/{group_id}/datasets/{dataset_id}/
refreshes
```

See the documentation on Power BI REST API authentication and the Power BI REST API reference in the *See also* section of this recipe.

There's more...

In this example, a Power BI Desktop file (dataset) in DirectQuery mode based on a separate on-premise SQL Server database must be deployed to the Power BI service. The intent is for the dashboards based on this dataset to be as current as possible. To implement this recipe, do the following:

1. Like the import mode dataset, add the SQL Server database as a data source to the gateway.
2. Assign user(s) to this data source and gateway.

3. Publish the DirectQuery Power BI Desktop file (dataset) to an App Workspace in the Power BI service.

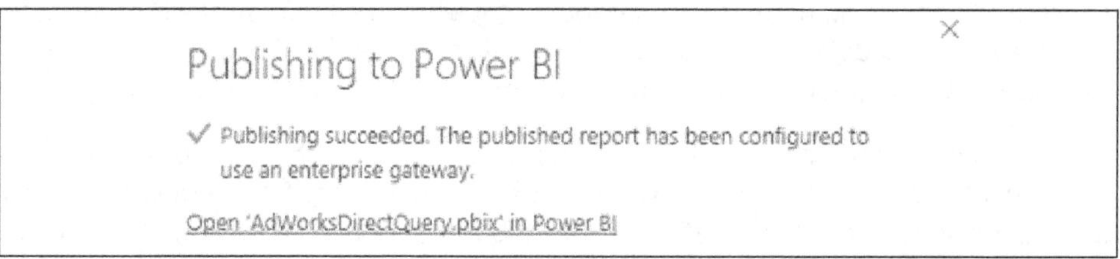

Figure 12.27: Publishing a DirectQuery dataset from Power BI Desktop

Power BI automatically configures the dataset to use a gateway by matching the data sources configured in the PBIX file and the sources configured in the Power BI service for the gateway. The user must also be listed for the gateway.

4. Access the workspace in the Power BI service and from the datasets list, click on **Settings** via the ellipsis (**...**).
5. Modify the scheduled cache refresh frequency from 1 hour to 15 minutes.

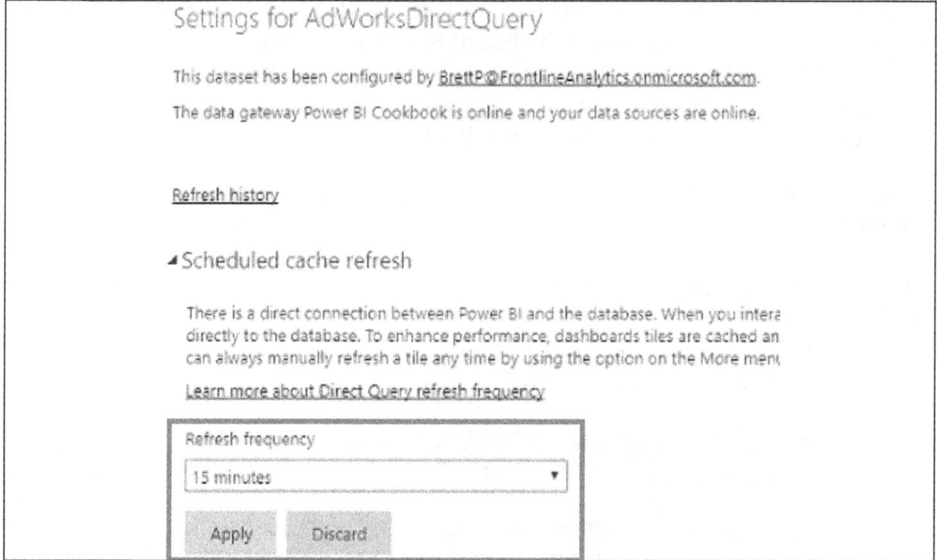

Figure 12.28: DirectQuery dataset settings

By default, the dashboard tiles are refreshed each hour for DirectQuery and Live Connection datasets. In this process, queries are sent by the Power BI service through the gateway to the dataset sources. In this scenario, the organization is comfortable with the more frequent queries, but in other scenarios simply a daily or even a weekly dashboard refresh would be sufficient to avoid adding workload to the data source.

See also

- Power BI REST API Datasets – Refresh Dataset: `https://bit.ly/3xWvE6J`
- Add or remove a gateway data source: `https://bit.ly/3f7GvSG`
- How to configure a Power BI report scheduled refresh: `https://bit.ly/3evfZU7`

Publishing Apps

Apps in Power BI are collections of related dashboards and reports from a single workspace focused on a given subject area. Apps are the recommended distribution method for larger solutions involving several distinct reporting artifacts and targeting groups of end users who only need read access.

In this recipe, we demonstrate how to create and publish an app in the Power BI service.

Getting ready

To prepare for this recipe, complete the first recipe *Building a Dashboard* in *Chapter 5, Working in the Service*.

How to do it...

To implement this recipe, use the following steps:

1. In the Power BI service, select a workspace, such as the workspace containing the **North American Sales** dashboard created in *Chapter 5, Working in the Service, Building a Dashboard*.
2. Toggle datasets to **No** and all other items to **Yes** in the **Include in app** column.

Figure 12.29: Workspace contents

3. Click the **Create app** button.
4. On the **Setup** tab, edit the **App name** and enter a **Description**. You can upload a custom **App logo** and set the **App theme color** and **Contact Information** as well.

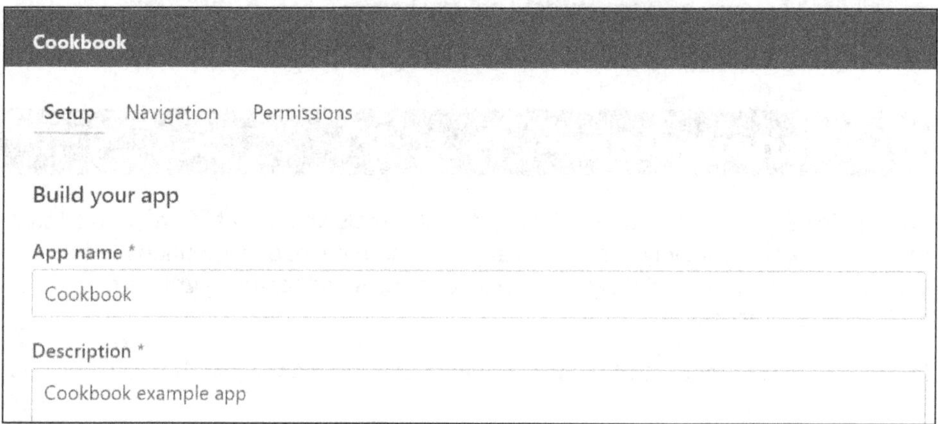

Figure 12.30: App Setup tab

5. Click the **Navigation** tab.
6. Use the **New** dropdown and choose **Section**.
7. Select the **New section** and change the **Name** to **North America**.
8. Create three additional sections for **Global Sales Reports**, **Customers**, and **Supporting Materials**.
9. Move report element links into sections by clicking on the item in the **Navigation** pane and selecting a section from the **Section** dropdown.

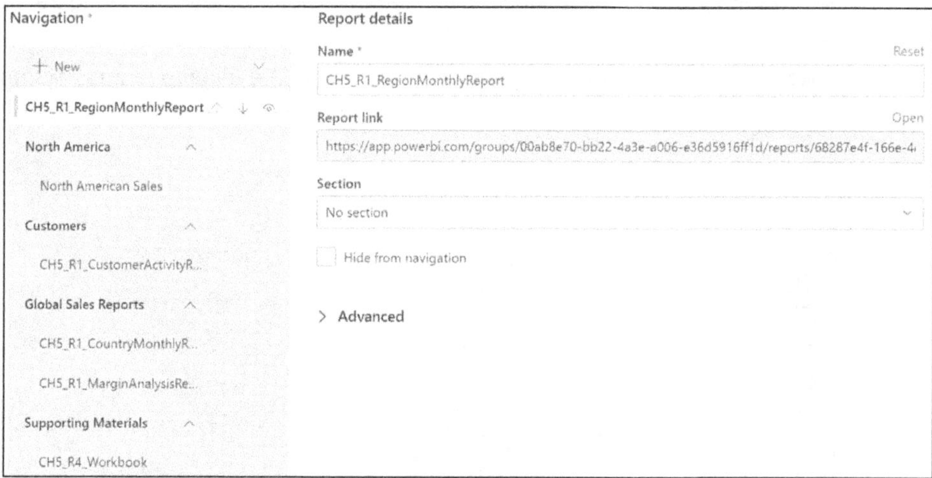

Figure 12.31: App Navigation tab

10. Select the **Permissions** tab.
11. Add specific individuals or groups to have access to the app and set the permissions. It is recommended that you uncheck the settings under the **Allow everyone who has app access to** heading and instead control permissions at the dataset level. In addition, it is generally recommended to check the checkbox for **Install this app automatically** under the **Installation** heading.

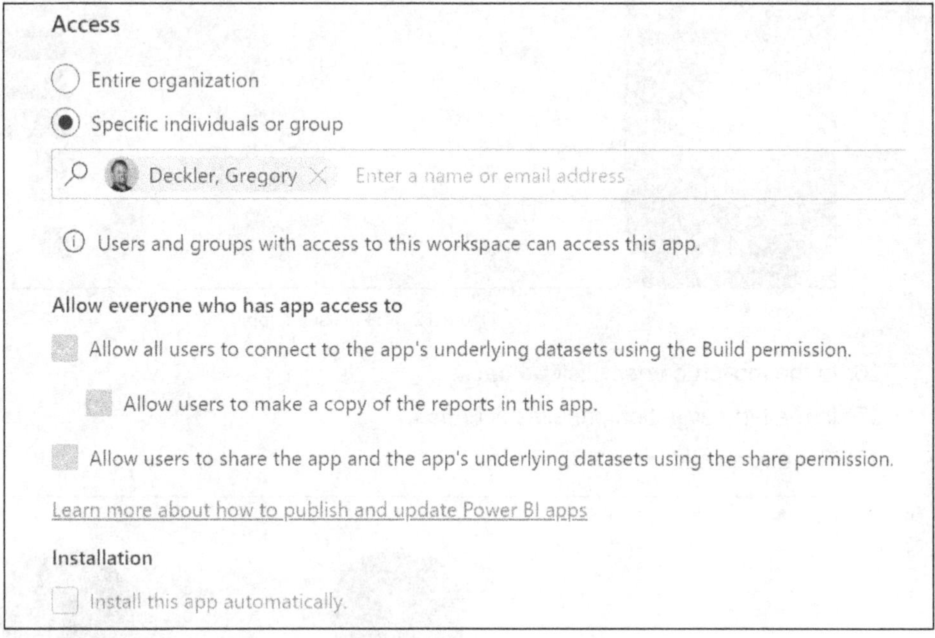

Figure 12.32: App Permissions tab

12. Click the **Publish app** button in the lower-right corner.
13. A popup with the name of the app will appear. Click the **Publish** button.
14. In the **Successfully published** dialog, click the **Go to app** button.

Figure 12.33: App successfully published

15. The app will look similar to the following:

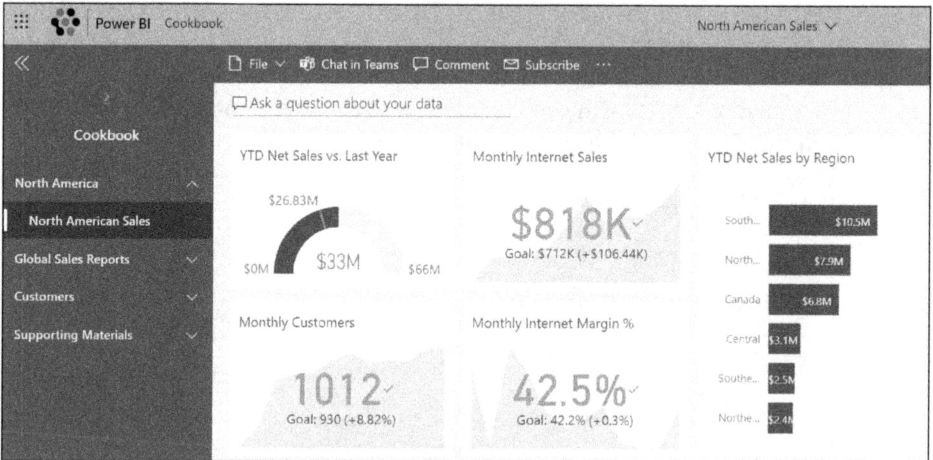

Figure 12.34: Published app

16. In the top-left corner, click **Go back**.
17. In the left navigation pane, select **Apps**.
18. The app should be listed.

Figure 12.35: Apps

You have now built your first app!

How it works...

Apps are a content type in the Power BI service that allows multiple dashboards, reports, and workbooks to be shared and accessed in a single place. Apps are limited to a single app per workspace and while apps can contain links to content outside of the workspace, those links will not function as part of the app but rather simply transport the user to the external dashboard, report, or web address.

Even with these limitations, apps are advantageous when it comes to sharing multiple content items at the same time when the designer does not want to give business users permissions to the entire workspace. Business users benefit by having a single link for all of the content included in the app.

There's more...

Once an app is published, it can be modified. This is done from the workspace by clicking the **Update app** button in the upper-right corner where the **Publish app** button was located. The tabs for configuring the app are the same as when publishing, except the **Permissions** tab now includes a **Links** area:

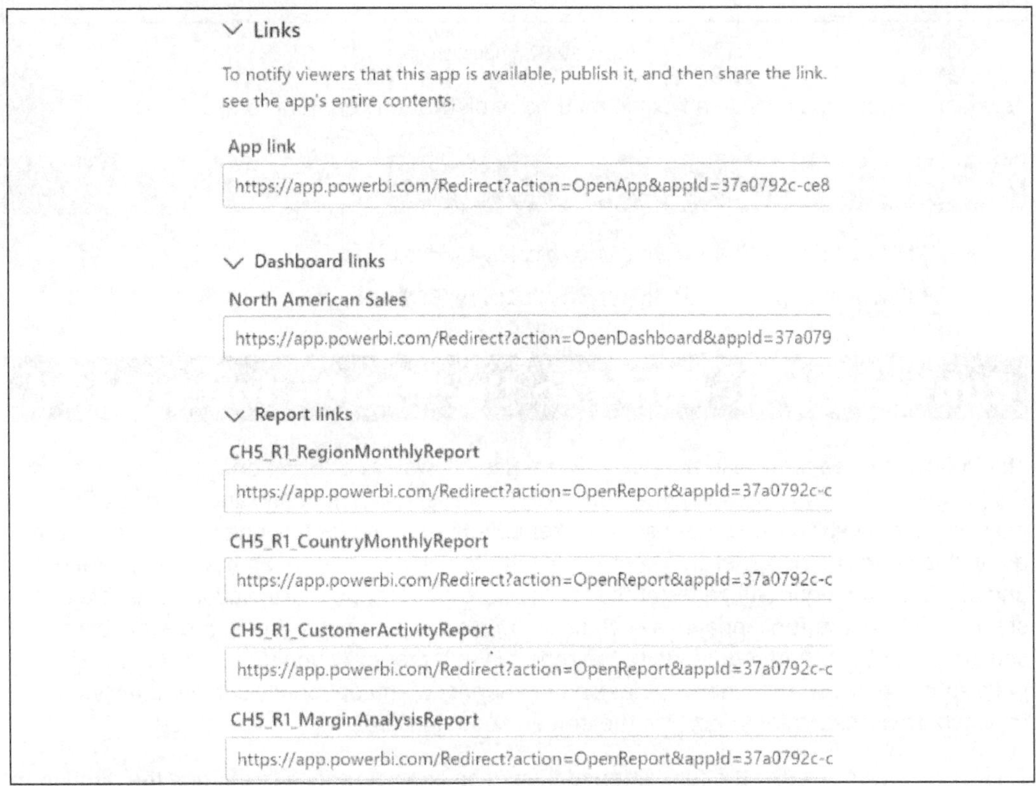

Figure 12.36: Links area on the app's Permissions tab

The settings for the app on all three tabs can be edited and then, once complete, simply click the **Update app** button in the lower-right corner where the **Publish app** button was located originally.

Apps can also be unpublished. This is also done from the workspace by using the ellipsis (**...**) and then selecting **Unpublish App**.

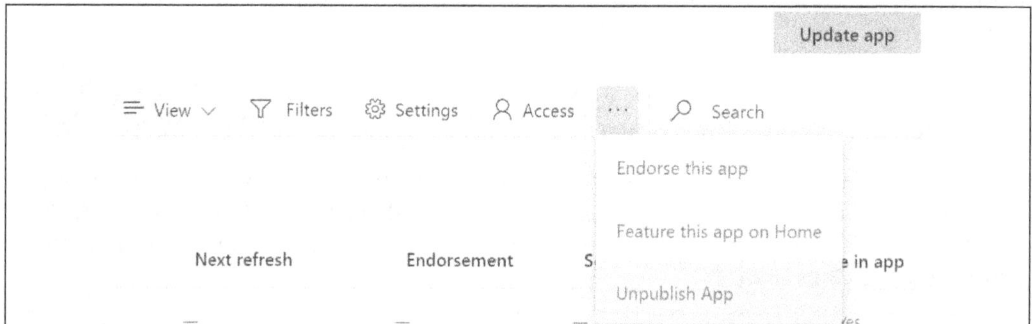

Figure 12.37: Unpublish App

As you can see, apps provide a flexible method of distributing content to users.

See also

- What is a Power BI app?: `https://bit.ly/3fMYsI5`
- Publish an app in Power BI: `https://bit.ly/39NWl2S`

Publishing Reports to the Public Internet

The **Publish to web** feature in the Power BI service allows Power BI reports to be shared with the general public by embedding the report within websites, blog posts, and sharing URL links. If the **publish to web** tenant setting is enabled and if a user has edit rights to a report, an embed code can be generated containing both the HTML code for embedding the report and a URL to the report. All pages of the report, including any supported custom visuals and standard interactive functionalities such as filtering and cross highlighting, are available to consumers of the report. Additionally, the report is automatically updated to reflect refreshes of its source dataset and embed codes can be managed and optionally deleted if necessary, to eliminate access to the report via the embed code and URL.

This recipe walks through the fundamental steps and considerations in utilizing the **publish to web** feature.

Getting ready

To prepare for this recipe, follow these steps:

1. In the Power BI service, click on the gear icon in the upper-right corner and select **Admin portal**.

2. In the Admin portal, click **Tenant settings**.
3. Under **Export and sharing settings**, find and expand **Publish to web**.
4. Enable **Publish to web** if disabled.

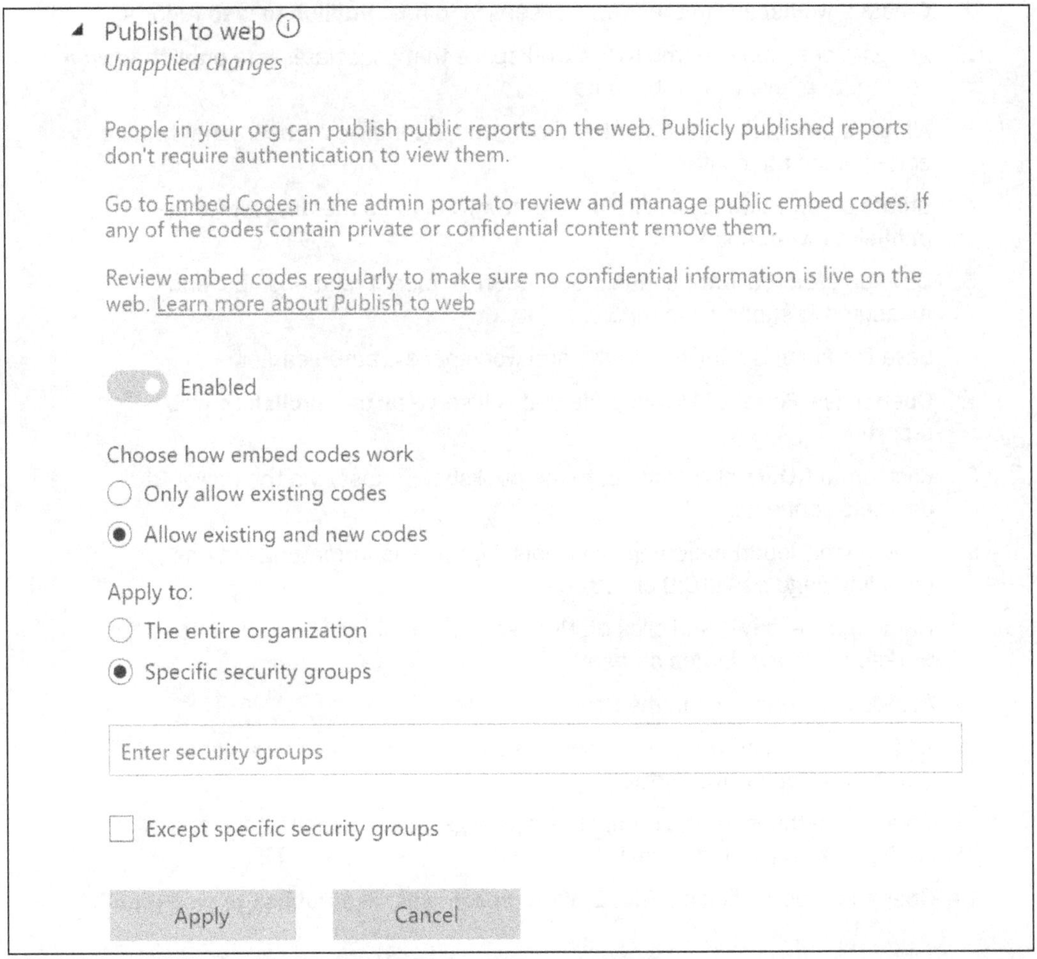

Figure 12.38: Publish to web setting within the tenant settings of the Power BI admin portal

The **publish to web** feature can be either enabled or disabled for all users in the organization, enabled for specific security groups, or disabled for specific security groups. Given the real security risk posed by **Publish to web**, it is highly recommended to keep this setting disabled unless the business requires this capability, and even then to limit the feature to specific security groups.

How to do it...

To implement this recipe, use the following steps:

1. Create a workspace in the Power BI service to host **Publish to web** reports.
2. Assign a descriptive name to the workspace that associates it to **publish to web** content or publicly available data.
3. Allow members to edit content and only add the individual users that require edit rights to the content.
4. Create a new Power BI Desktop file that will serve as the dataset for the **publish to web** report.
5. Develop essential data connections, queries, model relationships, and measures to support the report.
6. Save the file and publish it to the app workspace created earlier.
7. Open a new Power BI Desktop file that will serve as the **publish to web** report.
8. Click on **Get Data** and connect to the published dataset via the Power BI datasets connector.
9. Develop the report including all visuals, layout, and formatting options, including page size (16:9 or 4:3).
10. Name the file, save, and click on **Publish**. The report will be published to the workspace of the source dataset.
11. Access the workspace in the Power BI service.
12. Add any new on-premises data sources to the on-premises data gateway in the manage gateways portal.
13. Open the settings for the dataset, assign a gateway (if applicable), and configure a scheduled refresh.
14. Open the report, click on **File, Embed report**, and then **Publish to web (public)**.

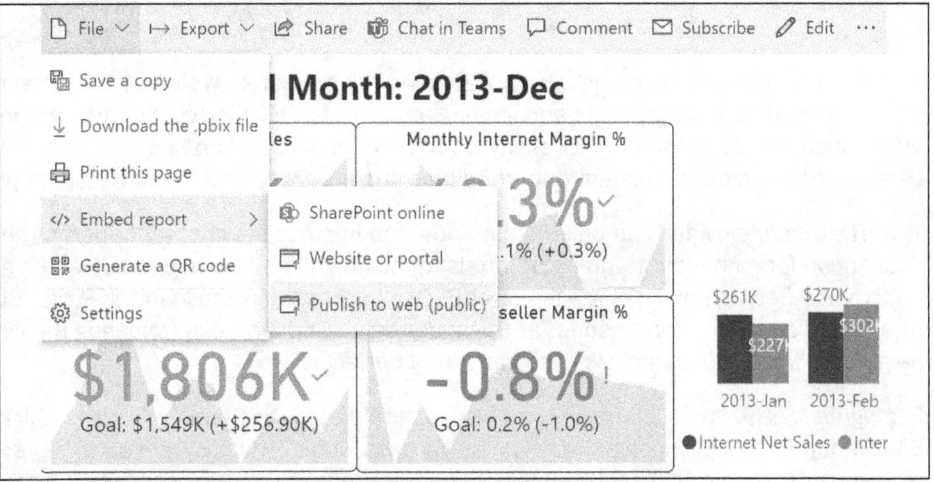

Figure 12.39: The Publish to web option for a report in the Power BI service

15. Click on **Create embed code** and then **Publish**.
16. A **Success**! dialog is displayed allowing you to copy the embed codes for the report.

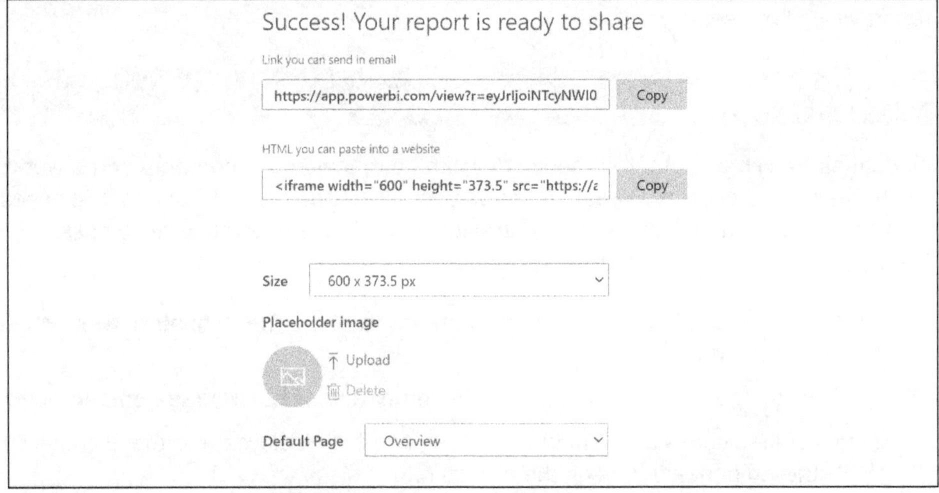

Figure 12.40: Successful Publish to web

You are now ready to share the **Publish to web** URL or use the HTML code in your own website.

How it works...

A separate workspace is not technically necessary for **publish to web**, but this isolation is recommended for manageability and limiting the risk of publishing confidential or proprietary information. Similarly, Premium capacity is not required but could be appropriate for larger datasets or when more frequent data refreshes and consistent performance are important.

The HTML code provided can be edited manually to improve the fit of the report on the destination for embedding. Adding 56 pixels to the height dimension can adjust the size of the bottom bar. Setting the page size in Power BI Desktop, the view mode in the Power BI service (the **View** icon in the report header at the upper right), and manually adjusting the iFrame height and width values may be necessary for a perfect fit.

Per *Figure 12.39*, Power BI reports can also be embedded in SharePoint Online. Clicking on **SharePoint Online** provides a URL that can be used with a Power BI web part in SharePoint online. Users accessing the SharePoint online page must also have access to the report in the Power BI service.

Power BI caches the report definition and the results of the queries required to view the report as users view the report. Given the cache, it can take approximately one hour before changes to the report definition or the impact of dataset refreshes are reflected in the version of the report viewed by users.

There's more...

All **Publish to web** and other embed codes can be managed by members of the workspace where the embed code was created. In addition, all embed codes from all workspaces can be managed by administrators in a central location. To see how this is accomplished, do the following:

1. In the Power BI service, open the workspace where the **Publish to web** embed code was created.
2. Click the gear icon in the upper-right corner and select **Manage embed codes**.
3. All embed codes created for the workspace are displayed and these codes can be retrieved or deleted using the ellipsis (**...**).

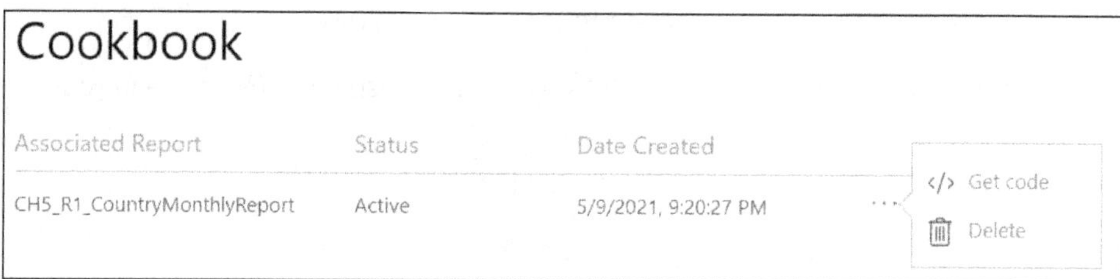

Figure 12.41: Manage embed codes interface for a workspace

4. Now click on the gear icon again and choose **Admin portal**.
5. In the admin portal, select **Embed Codes**.
6. All embed codes for all workspaces are displayed and the three vertical dots allow the reports to be viewed or the embed code deleted.

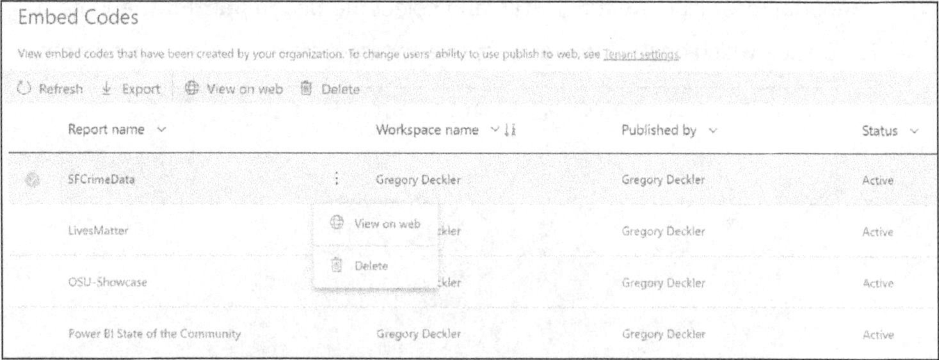

Figure 12.42: Manage embed codes in the admin portal

A **Status** of **Not Supported** indicates that one of the few unsupported features has been used by the report, such as RLS, SSAS tabular on premises, R visuals, or ArcGIS Maps for Power BI.

See also

- Publish to web from Power BI: `https://bit.ly/3bezKxq`

Enabling the Mobile Experience

Power BI mobile apps have been designed to align closely with the user experience and feature set available in the Power BI service. This provides a simple, familiar navigation experience for users and allows BI and IT teams to leverage existing Power BI assets and knowledge to enhance the mobile experience in their organization.

This recipe contains two processes to take advantage of Power BI's mobile capabilities. The first process helps identify "quick win" opportunities that require limited BI/IT investment to better utilize basic Power BI mobile features. The second process identifies somewhat less common yet powerful and emerging use cases for Power BI mobile applications.

Getting ready

To prepare for this recipe, follow these steps:

1. Identify the most highly used dashboards and reports by opening the Power BI admin portal (gear icon: **Admin portal**) and select the **Usage metrics** menu item.
2. Decide which dashboards and reports to target for mobile enhancements.

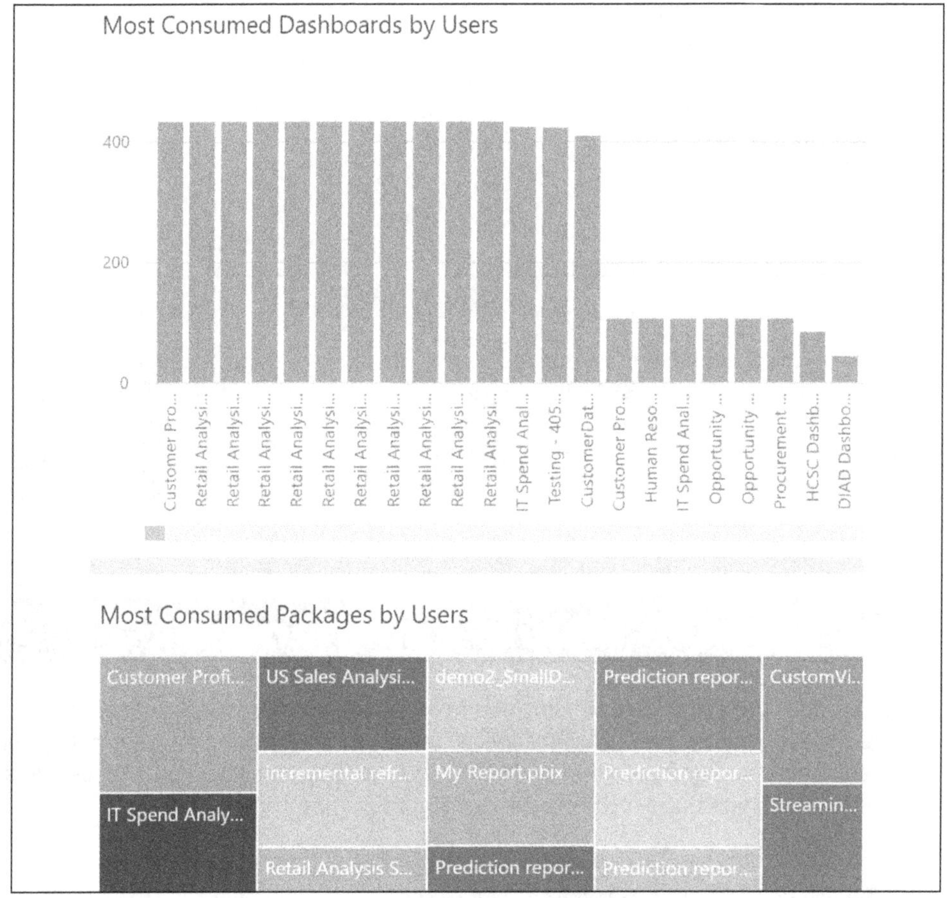

Figure 12.43: Usage metrics in the Power BI admin portal

The most consumed dashboards and packages visuals provide a summary of consumption or usage by count of users. For much more granular analysis of usage, the Microsoft 365 audit log for Power BI events can be imported and analyzed per *Chapter 10, Administering and Monitoring Power BI*. Additionally, usage metrics reports specific to individual dashboards and reports are now available in the Power BI service in the ellipsis (**...**) menu. Though scoped to a specific item, these reports also indicate the split between web and mobile usage.

How to do it...

To implement this recipe, use the following steps:

1. Optimize a Power BI dashboard for mobile consumption by opening the dashboard and switching to **Mobile view**.

Figure 12.44: Switching to Mobile view for a dashboard in the Power BI service

2. Unpin image, text, and less mobile-friendly or relevant tiles from the Mobile view.
3. Resize and organize KPIs and essential visuals at the top of the **Mobile view**.

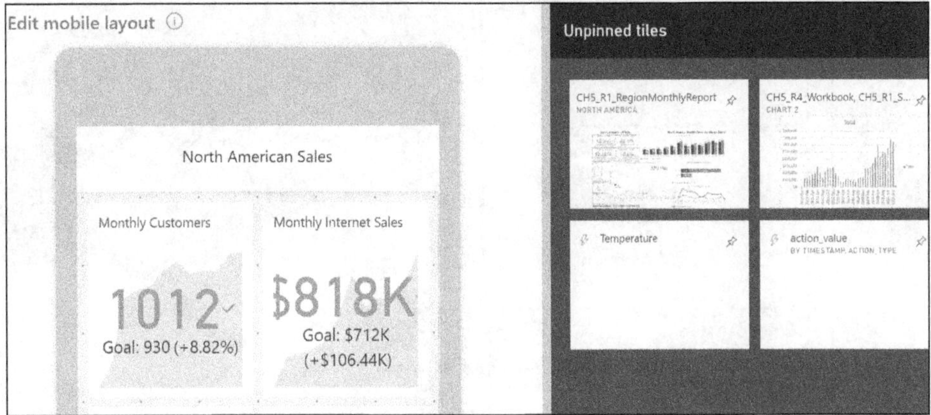

Figure 12.45: Customizing the Mobile view of a dashboard in the Power BI service

4. Open the PBIX file for a report.
5. Choose **Mobile layout** in the ribbon of the **View** tab of the most important report pages and design the custom mobile layout of the page. See *Chapter 4, Authoring Power BI Reports*, for details on this process.
6. Publish the updated Power BI report to a workspace in the Power BI service and re-pin any dashboard tiles.
7. Test the mobile-optimized dashboards and reports from mobile devices.
8. Publish updates from Power BI workspaces to Power BI apps containing these mobile enhancements.

9. Check that **Favorites** are being used for dashboards and for apps by mobile users.
10. Demonstrate the process of configuring a data alert with a notification on a dashboard tile in the Power BI mobile app.

Figure 12.46: Notifications of data alerts appear outside the mobile app

11. Demonstrate the annotate and share feature and related scenarios to mobile users.

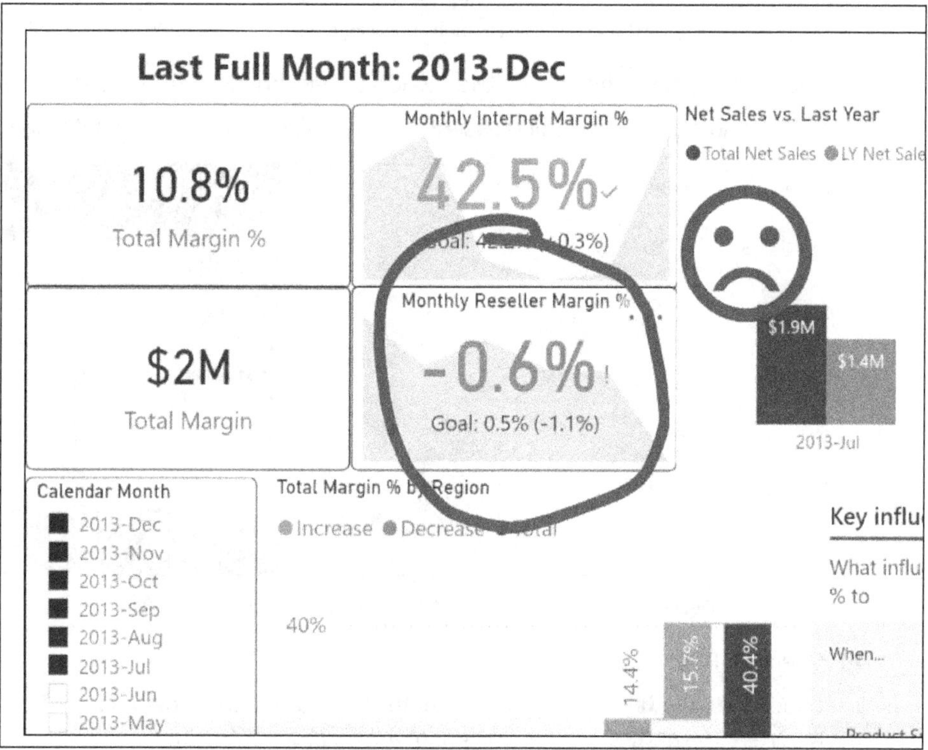

Figure 12.47: Annotation added to a Power BI report in Power BI mobile and shared via email

In this example, a report accessed in Power BI Mobile is lightly annotated, and a short message is shared with a colleague, requesting further analysis. A link to the report annotated is built into the shared email enabling the recipient to immediately act on the message and optionally share an annotated response that addresses the request.

12. Use the Windows 10 Power BI app in meetings and presentations.

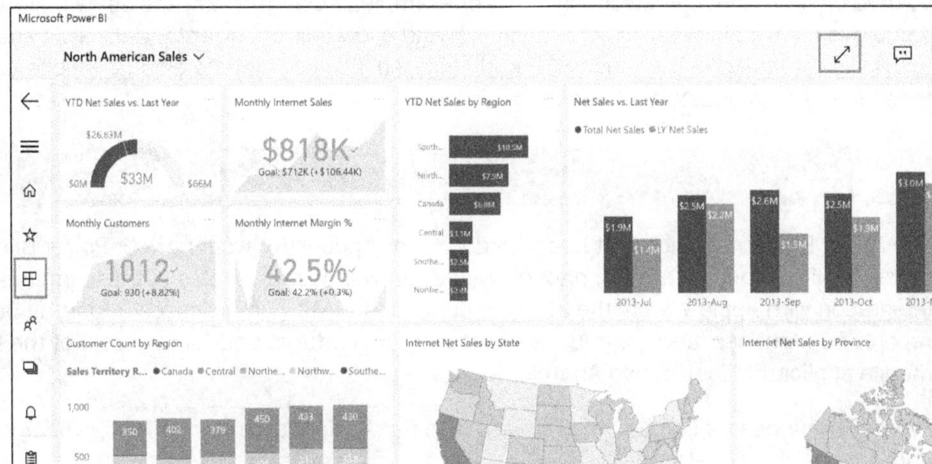

Figure 12.48: Windows 10 Power BI app

The Windows 10 Power BI app supports touch-enabled devices, annotations, and easy navigation controls.

13. Optimize datasets for Q&A. See the recipe *Preparing for Q&A* in *Chapter 5*, *Working in the Service*, for more details.

14. Test common questions and provide users with examples and keywords to better use the feature.

Building and optimizing mobile experiences can greatly aid in the adoption of Power BI.

How it works...

Only the owner of the dashboard will have the option to customize the Mobile view in the Power BI service. As per *Chapter 4*, *Authoring Power BI Reports*, the mobile layout for report pages is implemented within Power BI Desktop files. Therefore, any Power BI Pro user with access to the workspace of the report in the Power BI service and the source PBIX file(s) could optimize these reports for mobile consumption.

By enabling the Responsive Visuals property for Cartesian visuals such as the column, bar, and line charts, these visuals will be optimized to display their most important elements as their size is reduced. This effectively makes it realistic to use these more dense visuals in the mobile layout for reports and mobile view for dashboards. However, it still may make sense to prioritize KPI, card, and gauge visuals in mobile layouts, given the limited space.

Data alerts configured by users are only visible to those users, and there are no limits on the volume of alerts that can be configured. For example, a user may want to set two alerts for the same dashboard tile to advise of both a high and a low value. Currently, data alert and favorite activity is not stored in the Office 365 audit logs, so it's necessary to engage mobile users on these features to understand adoption levels.

There's more...

The Power BI team at Microsoft has provided many options for working with Power BI on mobile devices such as tablets, phones, and even watches. Examples of these options include integration with Apple Watch, the ability to connect and view on-premises Reporting Services reports from phones, and continuous updates to the features and functionality of the Power BI mobile application for iOS and Android devices.

Power BI dashboards can be synchronized with the Apple Watch via the Power BI for iOS application.

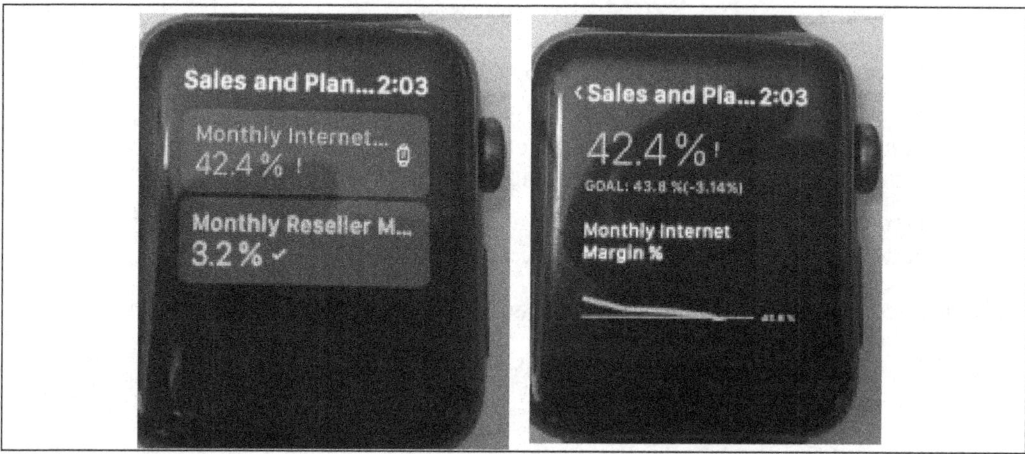

Figure 12.49: Index Screen (left) and the In-Focus Tile (right) of the Power BI mobile app on the Apple Watch

Simply open a dashboard in Power BI for iOS, click on the ellipsis (**...**) and then click on **Sync with watch**. Only card and KPI tiles are supported, but Apple Watch faces can be configured to display one of the Power BI tiles.

SSRS reports can be accessed and viewed from the Power BI mobile apps by tapping your profile image icon in the upper-left corner of the app and then **Connect to server**.

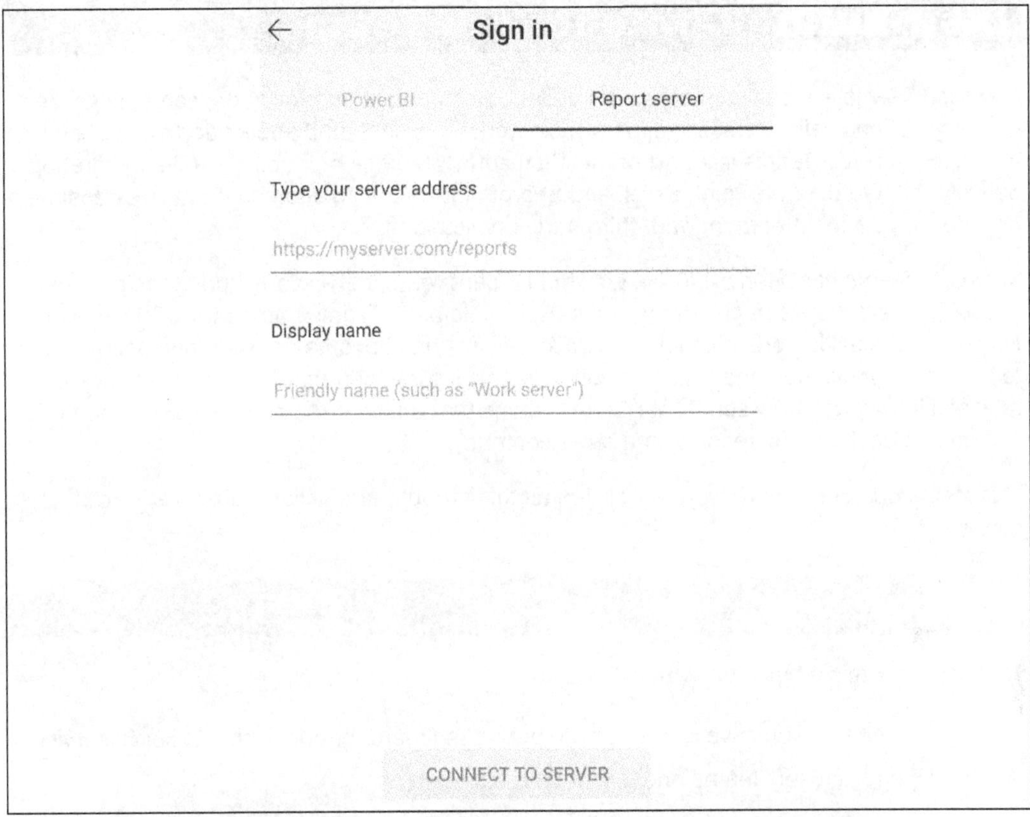

Figure 12.50: Navigation menu in Power BI Mobile with connection to a report server

As you can see, Power BI has wide support for a variety of different mobile devices.

See also

- Microsoft Power BI on the Apple App Store: `https://apple.co/2R6kaNs`
- Power BI mobile apps documentation: `https://bit.ly/33wKWB3`
- View on-premises report server reports and KPIs in Power BI Mobile: `http://bit.ly/2noIloX`

Distributing Content with Teams

Microsoft Teams is a unified platform for collaboration and communication, combining video meetings, phone calls, file storage, persistent workplace chat, and application integration into a unified interface. Teams is a part of the Microsoft 365 office productivity suite, integrating natively with Word, PowerPoint, Excel, and SharePoint Online. In addition, feature extensions provide support for integrating with third-party applications.

Microsoft Teams has seen explosive growth in recent years, particularly during the pandemic in 2020. In fact, between March and June 2020, Microsoft Teams had nearly 900% growth. For over half a million organizations, Microsoft Teams has become an essential tool used daily to drive communication and collaboration. It is no surprise then that Microsoft has recently released integration between Power BI and Teams that enables Teams to act as a distribution channel for dashboards, reports, and other content.

This recipe demonstrates how to utilize Teams to distribute and collaborate on Power BI content.

Getting ready

To prepare for this recipe, follow these steps:

1. Ensure that you have published a report, dashboard, or app to the Power BI service.
2. Open Microsoft Teams and join or create a team.

You are now prepared to complete this recipe.

How to do it...

To implement this recipe, use the following steps:

1. Within Teams, select **Teams** in the navigation pane and then select a channel within a team.
2. In the team's header area (tabs), select the plus icon (**+**) to **Add a tab**.

Figure 12.51: Add a tab in Microsoft Teams

3. Within the **Add a tab** dialog, search for *power bi* and select the Power BI app.

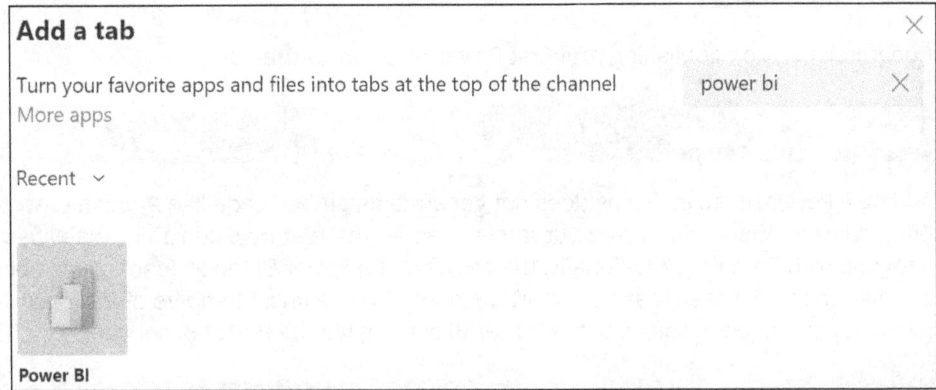

Figure 12.52: Add a Power BI tab in Microsoft Teams

4. In the Power BI dialog, select a dashboard or report from **Workspaces**, **Apps**, or **Shared with me**.

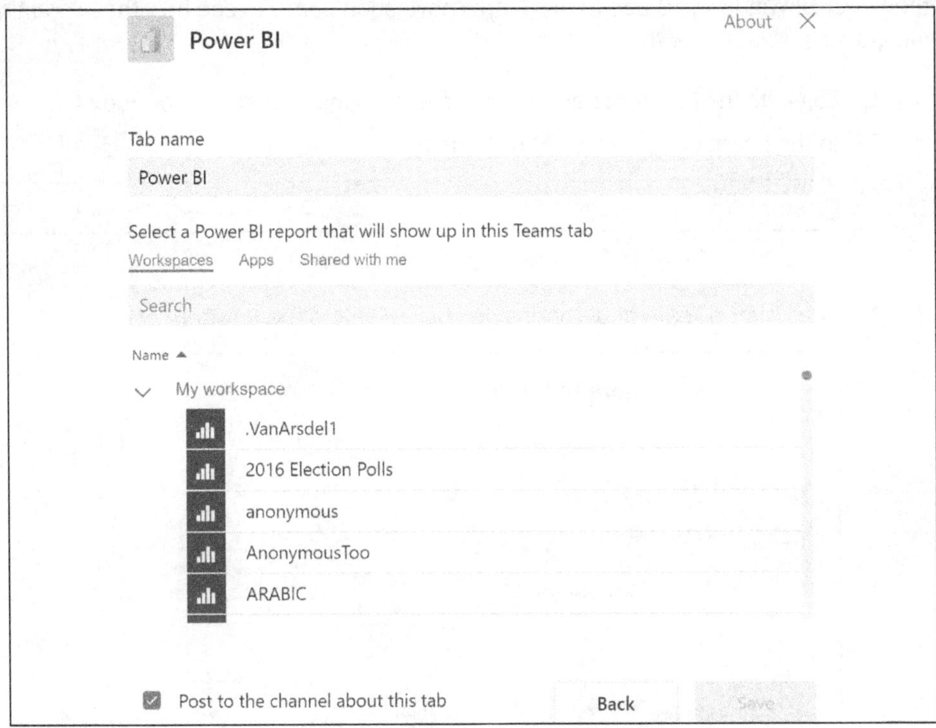

Figure 12.53: Adding Power BI content to Teams

5. Click the **Save** button.
6. The report or dashboard name is added as a tab for the team.

7. If **Post to the channel about this tab** is checked, a post appears in the **Posts** tab of the **General** channel.

Congratulations on publishing your first Power BI report to Teams!

How it works...

Adding a Power BI tab in Teams does not generate an embed code like **Publish to web** or embedding in SharePoint online but rather uses Teams' feature extension capabilities to integrate with Power BI. Additionally, the creation of a Power BI tab in Teams does not grant permissions to the dashboard or report distributed via Teams. Members of the given Team must be granted permissions to the Power BI content via the Power BI service.

There's more...

Adding Power BI tabs to teams within Microsoft Teams is not the only way that Power BI is integrated with Microsoft Teams. Two additional integrations exist, **Chat in Teams** and pinning the Power BI Windows 10 app to the Teams navigation pane. To see how these additional integrations work, follow these steps:

1. Log in to the Power BI service and open a dashboard, report, or app.
2. In the header bar, click **Chat in Teams**.

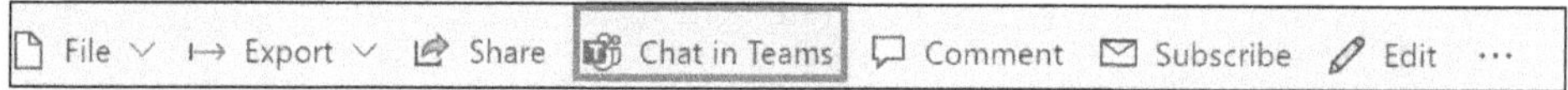

Figure 12.54: Chat in Teams

3. Search for a Team or a Channel to share a link to the Power BI content.

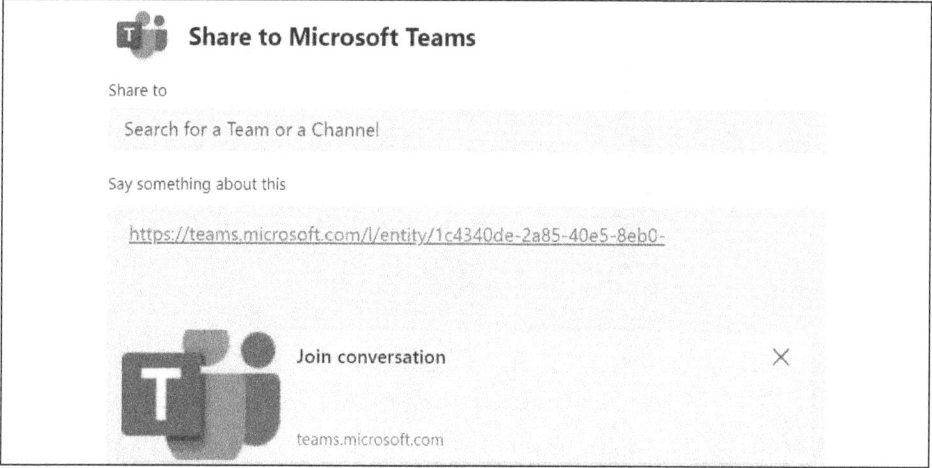

Figure 12.55: Share to Microsoft Teams

4. Click the **Share** button.
5. A post containing a link to the Power BI content is posted to the **Posts** tab of the selected team and channel.

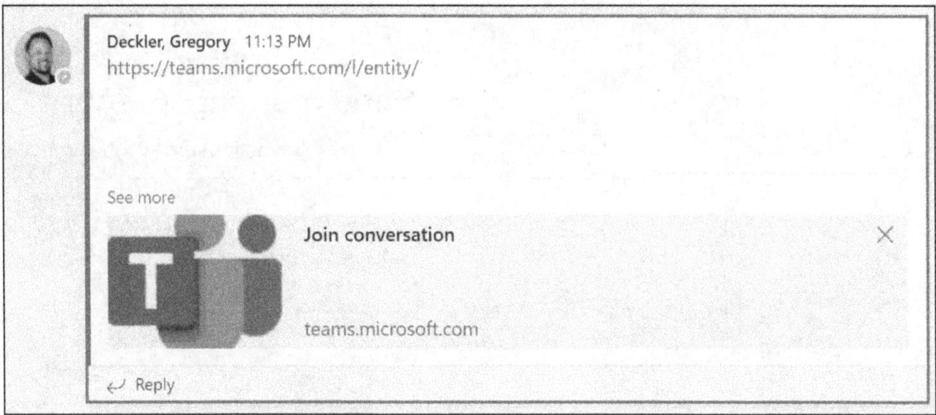

Figure 12.56: Power BI report link shared to Teams Posts tab

6. In Teams, select the ellipsis (...) from the navigation pane and search for *power bi*.

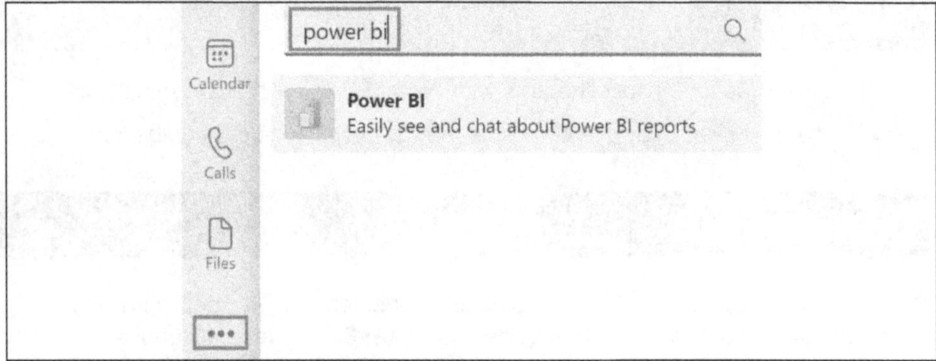

Figure 12.57: Adding the Power BI app in Teams

7. Select the Power BI app and then click the **Add** button.

8. The Power BI app is now pinned to the Teams navigation bar.

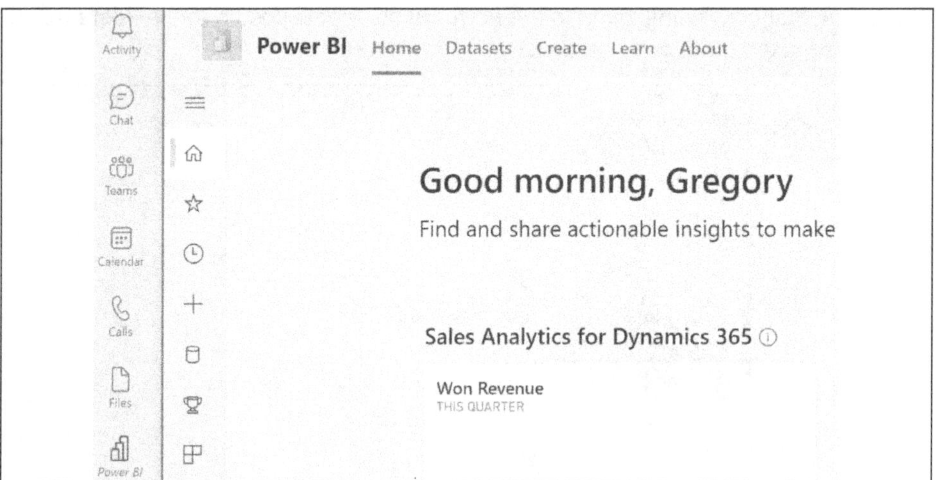

Figure 12.58: The Power BI app in Teams

As you can see, there are many integration points between Power BI and Teams.

See Also

- Collaborate in Microsoft Teams with Power BI: `https://bit.ly/2QYrXgl`
- Add the Power BI app to Microsoft Teams: `https://bit.ly/2RD8ly8`

Conclusion

This chapter contained detailed examples and considerations for deploying and distributing Power BI content via the Power BI service and Power BI mobile applications. This included the creation and configuration of app workspaces and apps, procuring and assigning Power BI Premium capacities, configuring data sources and refresh schedules, and deriving greater value from Power BI mobile applications. Additionally, processes and sample architectures were shared, describing staged deployments across development and production environments and multi-node premium capacity deployments.

In the next chapter, we will explore integrating Power BI with other applications, including SQL Server Reporting Services, Excel, PowerPoint, Azure Analysis Services, Dataverse, Dynamics 365, and more!

13

Integrating Power BI with Other Applications

Power BI tools and services including Power BI Desktop, the Power BI web service, and Power BI mobile applications form a modern, robust business intelligence and analytics platform by themselves. Power BI Premium further extends the scalability and deployment options of Power BI solutions, enabling organizations to deliver Power BI content to large groups of users via apps in the Power BI service, embedded within custom applications, the on-premises Power BI Report Server, or some combination of these distribution options.

However, many organizations either already have extensive self-service and corporate BI assets and skills in other tools, such as Excel, Analysis Services (Azure Analysis Services (AAS) or SQL Server Analysis Services (SSAS)), and SQL Server Reporting Services (SSRS), or are interested in utilizing the unique features of these tools as part of their Power BI solutions. As one example, an organization may choose to keep many existing Excel reports in Excel rather than convert them to Power BI reports given the unique features of Excel such as cube formulas. Similarly, some organizations may continue to use an existing AAS resource for semantic models rather than migrate these models to Power BI Premium for some time due to significant reporting dependencies on these models. Moreover, given the many additional features and benefits of Power BI datasets, organizations with legacy Excel-based Data Models (formerly Power Pivot) may choose to migrate these assets to Power BI.

The recipes in this chapter highlight powerful integration points between Power BI, SSRS, Analysis Services, Excel, PowerPoint, Power Apps, and Power Automate. In this chapter, we will cover the following recipes:

- Integrating SSRS and Excel
- Migrating from Power Pivot for Excel to Power BI

- Accessing and Analyzing Power BI Datasets in Excel
- Building Power BI Reports into PowerPoint Presentations
- Connecting to Azure Analysis Services
- Integrating with Power Automate and Power Apps
- Leveraging Dataverse and Dynamics 365
- Connecting Dynamics 365 Finance and Operations and the Power Platform

At the end of this chapter you will have a firm understanding of how Power BI works and integrates with other Microsoft technologies.

Technical Requirements

The following are required to complete the recipes in this chapter:

- Power BI Desktop
- Excel
- Visual Studio
- SQL Server with the **AdventureWorksDW2019** database installed. This database and instructions for installing it are available here: `http://bit.ly/2OVQfG7`
- Files for this chapter can be downloaded from the following GitHub repository: `https://github.com/PacktPublishing/Microsoft-Power-BI-Cookbook-Second-Edition`

Integrating SSRS and Excel

Power BI Desktop is the primary report authoring tool for content published to the Power BI service as well as for Power BI report visuals embedded in custom applications. However, for many organizations a significant portion of existing or legacy reporting workloads built with SSRS and Excel must be maintained. In many cases, existing SSRS and Excel reports can be converted to modern Power BI reports and dashboards but Power BI is not intended as a full replacement for all the features and use cases for these other tools. In addition to supporting paginated reports (aka SSRS reports) via Power BI Premium and data refresh of Excel reports built against Power BI datasets, the Power BI service offers further methods of integrating content from Excel and SSRS into Power BI. Additionally, given the common database engine and DAX language of Power BI, Power Pivot for Excel, and Analysis Services, BI teams can take full control of reports rendered in SSRS and Excel by authoring custom DAX queries.

This recipe contains two examples of authoring and publishing content from SSRS and Excel to Power BI.

Getting ready

To prepare for this recipe, follow these steps:

1. If necessary, download, install, and configure Microsoft SSRS: `https://bit.ly/3yfdTjk`.
2. Ensure that SSRS is configured for Power BI integration:

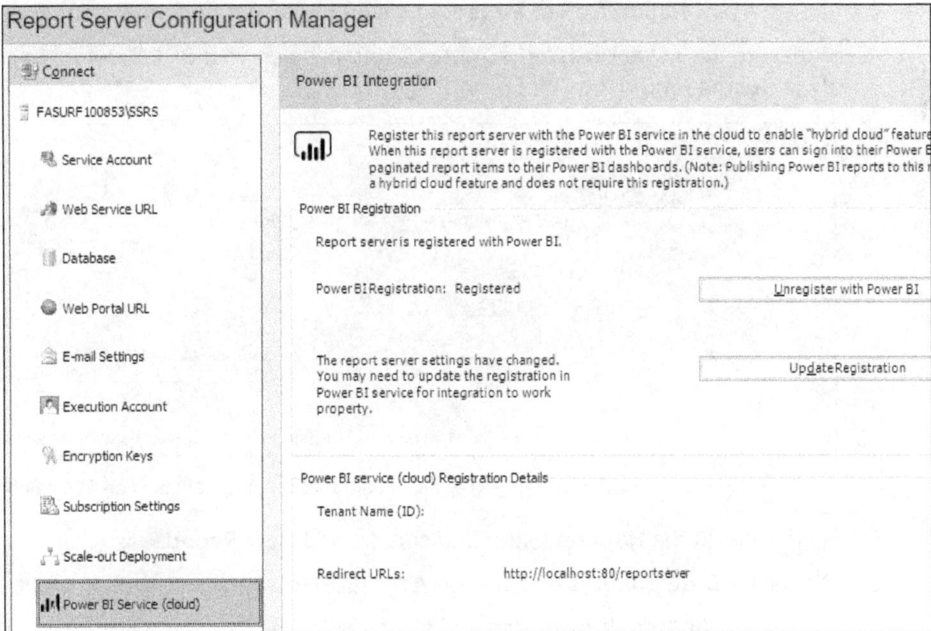

Figure 13.1: Report Server Configuration Manager—Power BI Integration

3. The **Power BI Integration** menu item is at the bottom of the list and includes the Power BI tenant name (ID). You must have configured the web service URL and web portal URL to configure this setting.
4. Ensure that you have Visual Studio installed and verify that in Visual Studio you have **SQL Server Data Tools** installed, the **Workload** for **Data storage and processing**, and the **Extension** for **Microsoft Reporting Services Projects**. Install the appropriate items as necessary in Visual Studio. To understand how to install Visual Studio, use this link: `https://bit.ly/389eozC`.

You are now ready to complete the steps for this recipe.

How to do it...

To implement this recipe, do the following:

1. Create or identify a workspace in the Power BI service to host the report content.
2. Create or identify the dashboards in this workspace that will display the report content.
3. Create a new **Report Server Project** in Visual Studio or open an existing one.
4. Configure the **AdventureWorksDW2019** database on your **SQL Server** as a **Shared Data Source** for the project:

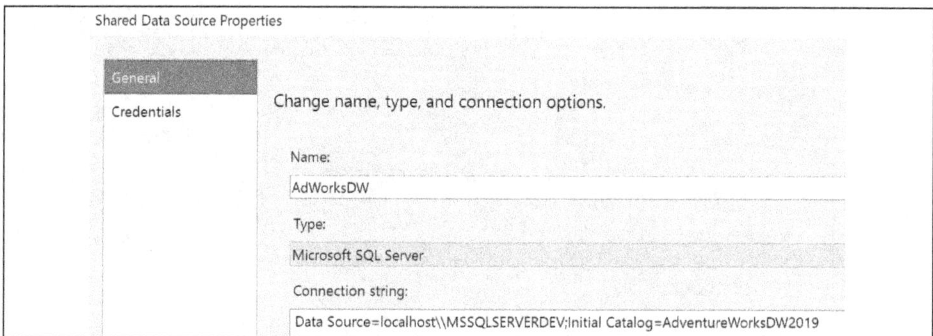

Figure 13.2: Report Server Project –shared data source Configuration for an SQL database

5. Right-click on the **Reports** folder and choose **Add New Report**.
6. Right-click **Data Sources** and choose **Add Data Source...**.
7. Choose the **Shared data source** option, select the **Shared Data Source** created in Step 4, and press the **Next>** button.
8. Build your own query or use the following query:

```
SELECT
  vProducts.ProductKey AS [vProducts ProductKey]
  ,vProducts.EnglishProductSubcategoryName
  ,vProducts.EnglishProductName
  ,vProducts.DaysToManufacture
  ,vProducts.Color
  ,FactInternetSales.ProductKey AS [FactInternetSales ProductKey]
  ,FactInternetSales.OrderQuantity
  ,FactInternetSales.UnitPrice
  ,FactInternetSales.DiscountAmount
  ,FactInternetSales.SalesAmount
  ,FactInternetSales.TaxAmt
  ,FactInternetSales.Freight
```

```
    ,vProducts.EnglishProductCategoryName
    ,FactInternetSales.OrderDate
  FROM
    vProducts
    INNER JOIN FactInternetSales
      ON vProducts.ProductKey = FactInternetSales.ProductKey
```

9. Click the **OK** button to exit **Query Designer** and then click the **Next>** button.
10. Choose **Tabular** and click the **Next>** button.
11. Click the **Finish>>** button.
12. Click the **Finish** button.
13. Remove the table created in the central design panel (design surface).
14. Use the dataset to create SSRS report visuals for pinning. Charts, gauge panels, maps, and images can be pinned from SSRS to Power BI dashboards.
15. Deploy the SSRS report to a report folder in the SSRS portal and confirm that it renders properly:

Figure 13.3: Pin SSRS report visual to Power BI Dashboard

16. Click on the Power BI icon and then click on the chart in the report you wish to pin.
17. Choose the **Workspace**, the **Dashboard**, and the **Frequency of updates**:

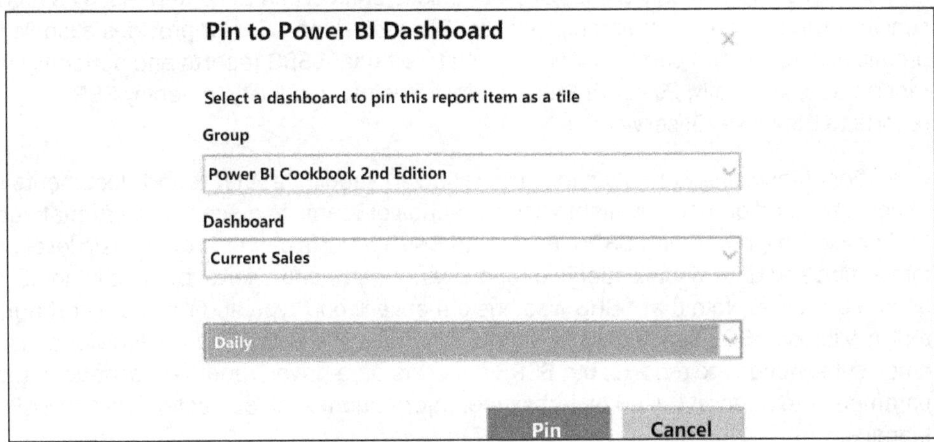

Figure 13.4: Pin to Power BI from SSRS

18. Click the **Pin** button.
19. In the SSRS portal, click on the gear icon and select **My subscriptions** to confirm the **Power BI Dashboard** subscription:

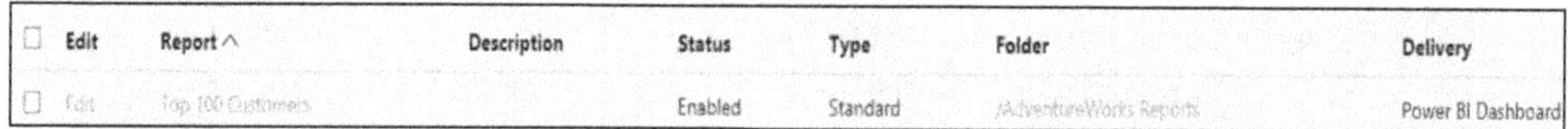

Figure 13.5: My subscriptions in SSRS

20. In the Power BI service, adjust the size, position, and optionally the title and subtitle of the dashboard tile.
21. Click on the dashboard tile to test that the URL opens the report in the SSRS portal. Set the link to open in a separate tab.

This recipe is now complete.

How it works...

Microsoft has been clear that Power BI and SSRS are designed for unique BI workloads and scenarios and organizations can choose the tool that is best suited for their given projects, as well as using multiple report authoring tools within the same solution and overall BI deployment. Power BI is designed for a modern, interactive, and rich data exploration experience.

SSRS, now included with Power BI Report Server, continues to deliver robust enterprise reporting capabilities with updated paginated report objects suited for operational reporting and distribution features such as subscriptions.

In certain reporting scenarios, a paginated or "classic" report with a fully configured page and report layout defined in a Visual Studio SSRS project is appropriate. Additionally, for organizations that can only deploy BI on-premises or if certain BI content such as highly sensitive reports must remain on-premises, Power BI Report Server provides a single on-premises solution and portal to include both traditional SSRS reports and optionally Power BI reports as well. Finally, Power BI Premium includes the capability to deploy SSRS paginated reports to the Power BI service.

Operational reporting workloads in which relatively simple, tabular report documents need to be distributed or made available across groups or teams in a specific file format such as PDF or Excel align well with SSRS. Paginated SSRS reports can provide a basic level of user interaction and data visualization via report parameters and charts, but this is not its strength or core use case. Note that SSRS also has a mobile report type and mobile report authoring tool in Microsoft SQL Server Mobile Report Publisher. Power BI supports individual user email subscriptions to reports, but SSRS supports data-driven report subscriptions that apply parameters to a report based on subscriber information, such as Eastern Region or Sales Managers.

Future improvements to Power BI's report and dashboard subscription capabilities along with greater control over tabular and matrix visuals and Power BI Premium-dedicated hardware may position Power BI to assume a greater share of reporting workloads traditionally handled by SSRS.

There's more...

In addition to building integrations with SSRS, Microsoft has also integrated another popular BI tool, Excel, with Power BI. To demonstrate Excel's integration with Power BI, do the following:

1. Confirm that the Excel reporting content uses the Excel Data Model as its data source. Only workbooks with data models can be configured for a scheduled refresh in the Power BI service. For details on how to build an Excel report using the Excel Data Model, use this link: `https://bit.ly/3j9AYOB`.
2. Identify the data source used by the Excel Data Model and add this source to the on-premises data gateway if necessary.
3. Develop and test DAX queries in DAX Studio to be used as the datasets and tables in Excel.
4. Open the Excel workbook containing the Data Model.
5. From the **Data** tab, click on **Existing Connections** and select one of the queries used to load the data model. Choose one of the smaller dimension table queries, such as `Currency`:

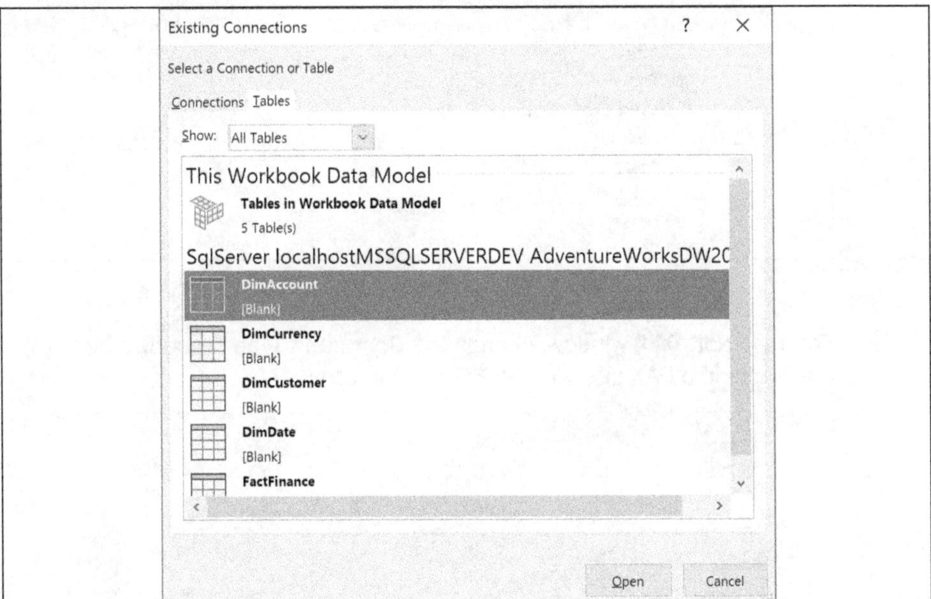

Figure 13.6: Existing Connections—M Queries used to load the Data Model

6. Click on **Open** in the **Existing Connections** menu and then select **Table** from the **Import Data** dialog:

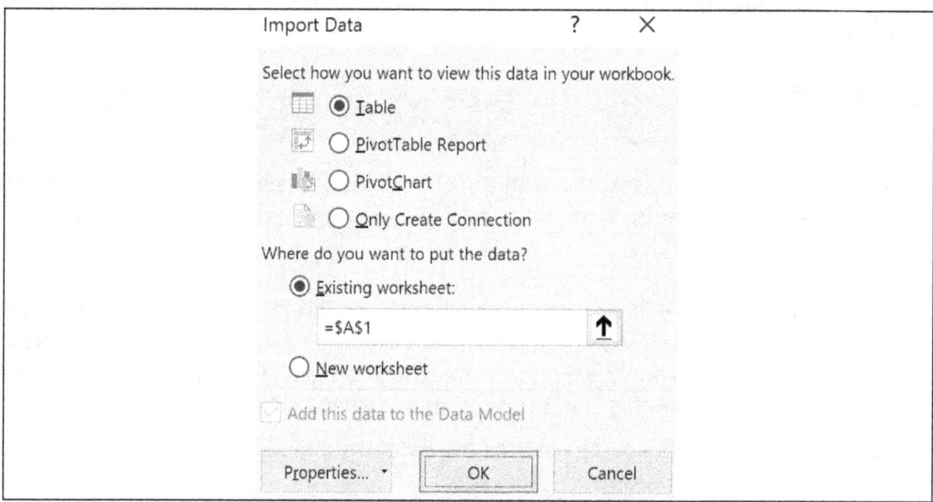

Figure 13.7: Import Data: The Table option

7. An Excel table reflecting the chosen query will be loaded to a worksheet.
8. Right-click on any cell inside the imported table, and from the **Table** options, select **Edit DAX...**:

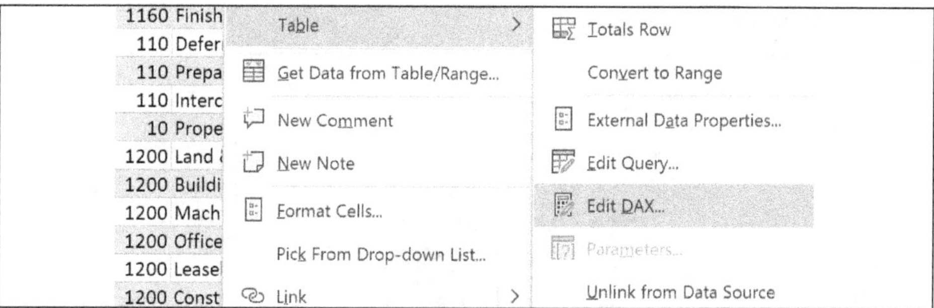

Figure 13.8: Excel table options—Edit DAX...

9. From the **Edit DAX** window, change the **Command Type** dropdown from **Table** to **DAX** and paste in a DAX query in the **Expression** area:

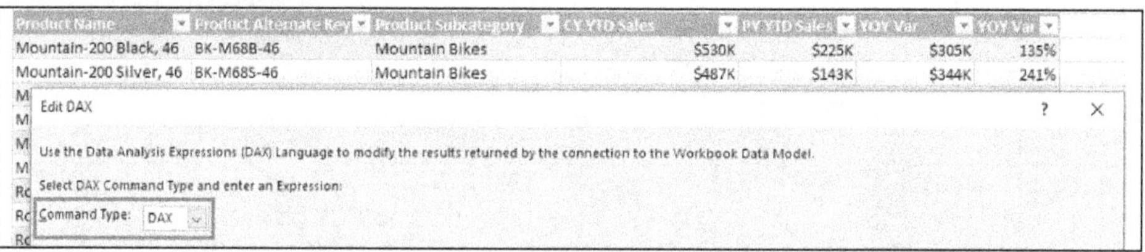

Figure 13.9: DAX query to retrieve the top 15 products based on current year to date sales

10. Press the **OK** button.
11. Choose **File** and then **Publish** from the Excel ribbon.
12. In the **Publish** dialog, choose the workspace and then click the **Upload** button:

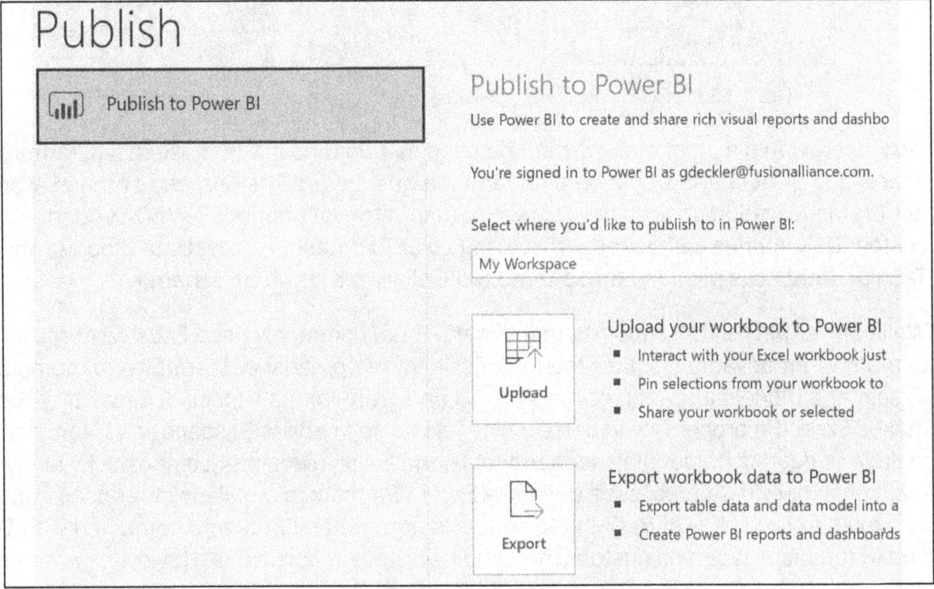

Figure 13.10: Uploading the Excel Data Model to the Power BI workspace

13. Open the Power BI service and navigate to the workspace containing the published Excel workbook.
14. From the **Workbooks** menu of the workspace, select the three vertical dots and then choose **Schedule refresh**.
15. Associate the data source with a data gateway, click on **Apply**, and then schedule a data refresh:

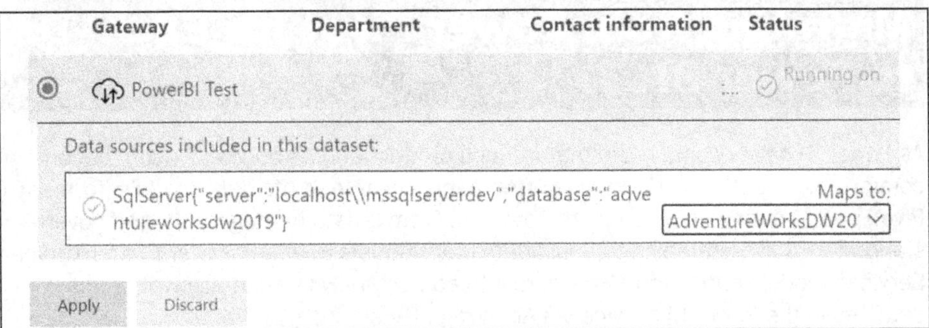

Figure 13.11: Gateway configuration for the workbook

16. Select the workbook to open the report. Select the entire table and then click on **Pin**.

17. On the **Pin to Dashboard** dialog, choose the dashboard and click on the **Pin** button:

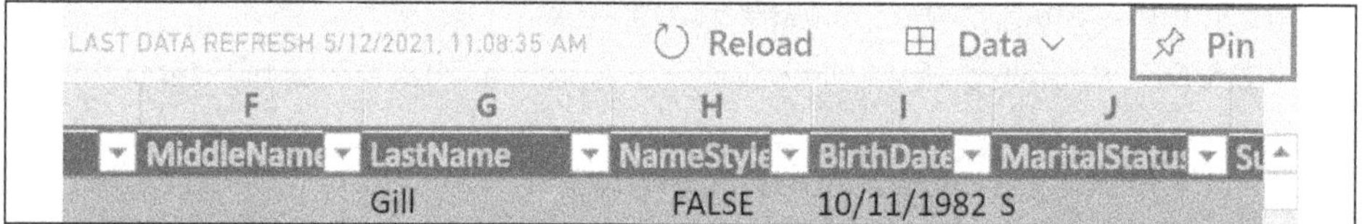

Figure 13.12: Excel table in the published workbook selected—Pin to Dashboard is in the top right

Very rarely would a plain table of data be used in a dashboard. In most cases, formatted Excel charts and pivot charts would be pinned to the dashboard. The purpose of these examples is not the visualization choices but rather the data retrieval methods with DAX queries. Note that custom DAX queries can be reused across Power BI datasets, Excel Data Models, and SSAS Tabular databases provided these three tools align to a common schema.

While Power BI Desktop supports many of the most commonly used Excel features in addition to many other advantages, the free-form flexibility of spreadsheet formulas for complex "what-if" scenario modeling across many variables and granular (cell-specific) formatting controls makes Excel the proper tool in certain small-scale self-service BI scenarios. Examples of this include budgeting or planning scenario tools and break-even or price sensitivity analyses. In addition, legacy data processes driven by Excel VBA macros are likely other good candidates to remain in Excel. Power BI Desktop supports parameter inputs and combined with DAX and M functions it can be customized to deliver these report types. However, parameters are not supported in the Power BI service and Power BI Desktop lacks the inherent flexibility of spreadsheet formulas and custom cell-level formatting and conditional logic.

See also

- SQL Server Reporting Services Integration with Power BI: `https://bit.ly/3y6LN9J`
- Publish to Power BI from Microsoft Excel: `https://bit.ly/3bnDa0l`

Migrating from Power Pivot for Excel Data to Power BI

As Power BI has become more mature as a product and as business users become more comfortable with the platform, it is often beneficial to migrate data models (formerly Power Pivot) and M queries from Excel to Power BI. From a data management and governance standpoint, it is preferable to consolidate data models to either Power BI and/or Analysis Services models and to limit Excel's role to ad hoc analysis such as pivot tables connected to datasets in the Power BI service via Analyze in Excel.

In this brief recipe a data model and its source M queries contained in an Excel workbook are migrated to a Power BI dataset via the Import Excel Workbook to Power BI Desktop migration feature. Additional details on the workbook content imported and other options and considerations for Excel-to-Power BI migrations are included in the *How it works...* and *There's more...* sections.

Getting ready

Analyze the Excel workbook to identify the components that can be imported to Power BI Desktop. For example, a table or range of data in an Excel worksheet will not be imported but tables in the Excel data model will be imported. Similarly, Power View report sheets in Excel and their visuals will be migrated but standard Excel charts, pivot tables, and worksheet formulas and formatting will not be migrated.

In some scenarios it may be necessary to revise the Excel workbook to establish a data source connection and query that will be migrated. Additionally, it may be necessary to re-create Excel-specific report visualizations such as pivot tables and charts with Power BI Desktop report authoring visuals. Excel workbooks that contain a high level of customization such as VBA macros and complex Excel formula logic may require significant modifications to the Excel workbook or to the Power BI Desktop model or some combination of both to support a migration.

How to do it...

To implement this recipe, do the following:

1. Save or download the latest Excel workbook
2. Open a new Power BI Desktop (PBIX) file
3. From **Report View**, click **File** | **Import** | **Power Query, Power Pivot, Power View**

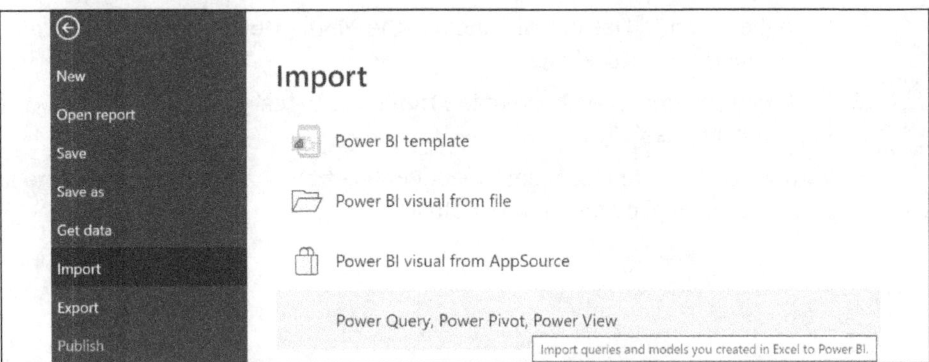

Figure 13.13: Import queries and models created in Excel to Power BI

4. Select the Excel file and click the **Open** button

5. A warning message appears advising that not all contents of the workbook are included in the import:

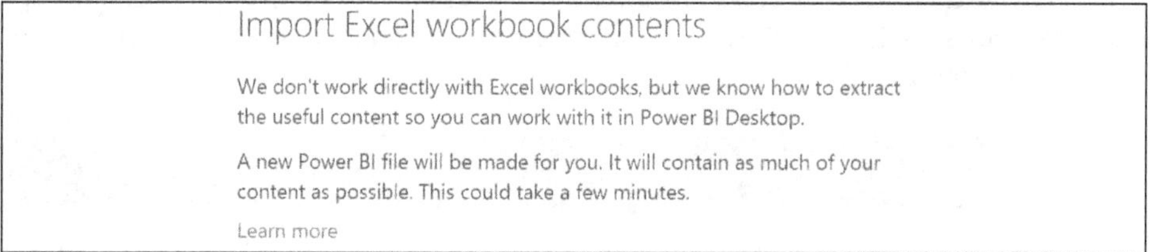

Figure 13.14: Import warning when importing an Excel file to Power BI

6. Click the **Start** button
7. A migration completion message will appear that breaks out the different items completed:

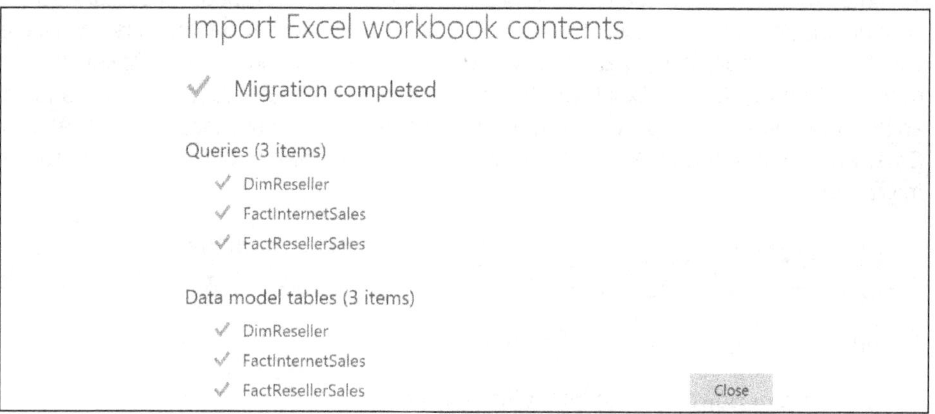

Figure 13.15: Import Excel Model to Power BI Desktop Migration completed

8. Click the **Close button**
9. Save the Power BI Desktop file and use the **Model view** to confirm all relationships were imported successfully
10. Click **Refresh** from the ribbon of the **Home** tab to test that all *M* queries were imported successfully
11. With essential testing complete, click **Publish** from the ribbon of the **Home** tab and choose a workspace for the new dataset

Your new Power BI dataset is now available in the Power BI service. You can even create new live connection reports against this dataset if desired.

How it works...

The migration may take a few minutes depending on the size of the data model imported. Power BI Desktop imports M queries, data model tables, DAX measures and KPIs, and any power view for Excel sheets.

Workbooks with significant dependencies on items that do not import, such as Excel formulas, standard Excel tables (not model tables), worksheet range data, standard Excel charts, and conditional formatting, may need to remain supported in some capacity. For example, a minimum amount of data could be imported to Excel's data model to continue to drive Excel-based reports and this workbook could be uploaded to the Power BI service and refreshed.

Power BI table and matrix visuals include the most important features of Excel pivot tables such as rich conditional formatting options, displaying multiple measures on rows, drill up/down hierarchies on rows and columns, controls for subtotals visibility, a stepped or staggered layout, percentage of row/column/totals, and more. These enhancements, along with the powerful cross highlighting capabilities exclusive to Power BI reports, make it feasible and advantageous to migrate most Excel pivot table-based reports to Power BI.

For example, if the Power Pivot for Excel workbook contained several worksheets of pivot tables, pivot charts, and standard Excel charts, new Power BI reports containing the same metrics and attributes can be developed as alternatives. With both the data model and the reports completely migrated to Power BI, the Excel workbook can be removed from the Power BI service or any other refresh and distribution process.

There's more...

If certain Excel-specific content is needed despite the migration, the Power Pivot for Excel data model can be uploaded to the same workspace and a refresh schedule can be configured on this workbook in the Power BI service. This can be accomplished by choosing **File** and then **Publish** from the Excel ribbon. Once the file is published to a workspace in the Power BI service, the Power Pivot dataset appears in the workspace's **Datasets** while the Excel workbook appears in the workspace's **Workbooks**.

Workbooks can also be added to the Power BI service by using the **Get Data** link in the lower-left corner of the service and then choosing **Files**:

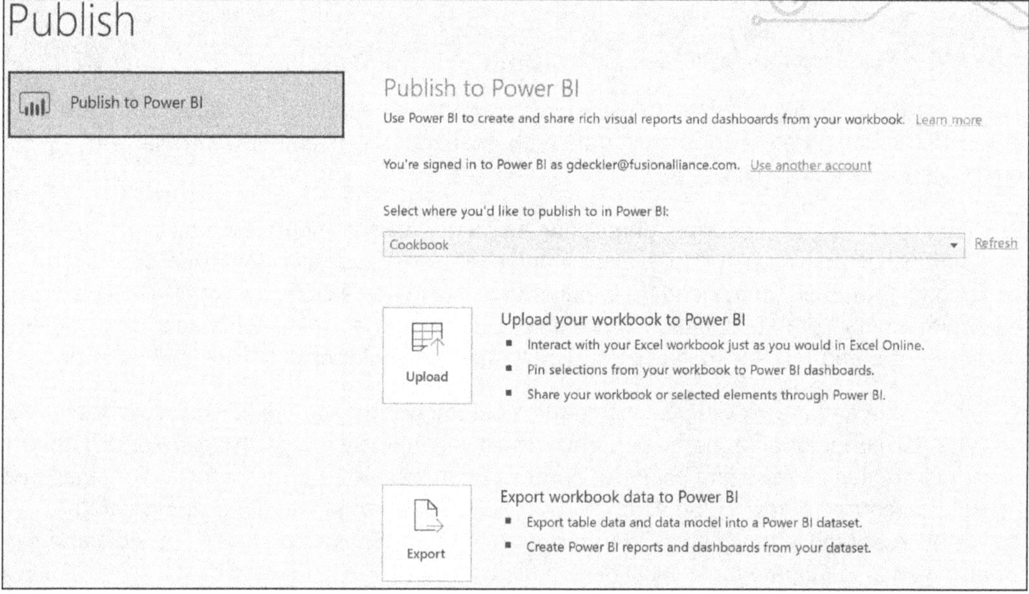

Figure 13.16: Publish Excel workbook with Data Model to Power BI–upload

The **Export** option in Excel is equivalent to the import migration process to Power BI Desktop from this recipe except that the new dataset is already published to a workspace in the Power BI service. This approach to migration is not recommended, however, as you lose the ability to download the PBIX file of the created dataset from the Power BI service. Importing to Power BI Desktop first, per this recipe, maintains this option.

See also

- Import Excel workbooks into Power BI Desktop: `https://bit.ly/3eI4gBG`

Accessing and Analyzing Power BI Datasets in Excel

With a centralized and potentially certified Power BI dataset hosted in the Power BI service, Excel users with both Free and Pro licenses can take full advantage of Excel's familiar interface as well as advanced features and use cases such as cube formulas and custom DAX queries.

Although these Excel reports, like SSRS paginated reports, are only a supplement to the Power BI reports and dashboards in the Power BI service, they are often useful for scorecard layouts with custom formatting and many measures and columns.

In this scenario, an experienced Excel user with deep business knowledge can leverage the performance, scale, and automatic refresh of the published Power BI dataset to create custom, fully formatted Excel reports. Additionally, the Excel report author has the flexibility to apply report-scoped logic on top of the dataset using familiar techniques and these customizations can inform BI teams or dataset owners of existing gaps or needed enhancements.

This recipe contains two examples of accessing and analyzing Power BI datasets in Excel. The first example uses cube formulas and Excel slicers to produce an interactive template report. The second example passes a custom DAX query to the Power BI dataset to support an Excel map. Additional details on cube functions in Excel and new Excel visuals are included in the supporting sections.

Getting ready

To prepare for this recipe, follow these steps:

1. Ensure that the user has a Power BI Pro license.
2. Confirm that the Power BI Pro user has access to the workspace containing the Power BI report and dataset.
3. Choose a report to use for the analysis. For example, if you have completed the recipes in *Chapter 5, Working in the Service* **CH5_R1_CountryMonthlyReport** is a good choice. You can download the PBIX for this report from GitHub and publish it to the Power BI service.

You are now ready to complete this recipe.

How to do it...

To implement this recipe, do the following:

1. Open the chosen report in the Power BI service
2. In the header/ribbon for the report, choose **Export** and then **Analyze in Excel**
3. Open the Excel file downloaded from the Power BI service

4. Click on the pivot table and add measures and columns from the dataset:

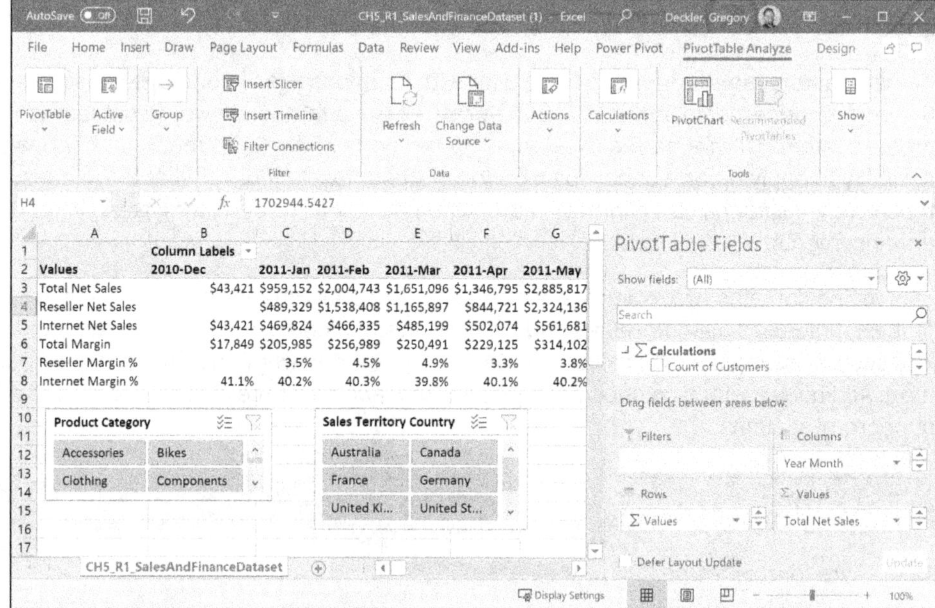

Figure 13.17: Excel Pivot Table with two Slicers based on the Power BI dataset

5. Select a cell within the pivot table
6. Select the **OLAP Tools** dropdown from the **PivotTable Analyze** tab and click on **Convert to Formulas:**

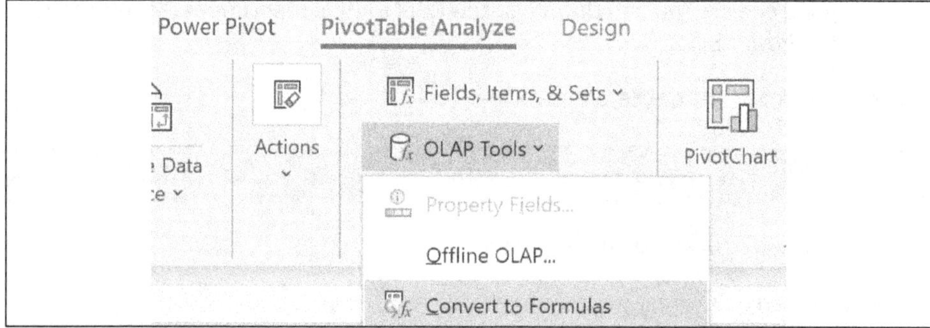

Figure 13.18: Convert to Formulas Option in the PivotTable Analyze Tab of Excel

How it works...

The pivot table is converted to Excel formulas such as the following:

```
=CUBEVALUE("pbiazure://api.powerbi.com <id> Model",$A3,C$2, Slicer_Sales_
Territory_Hierarchy)
```

In this example, the workbook cell **C3** references the **Total Net Sales** measure in cell **A3** and the **2011-Jan** dimension value in cell **C2**. Note that the two Excel slicer visuals remain connected to each `CUBEVALUE` formula cell and thus can be used for filtering the report. The calendar months (e.g. `2011-Jan`) are converted to `CUBEMEMBER` functions with a hard-coded reference to a specific value. These formulas must be maintained and/or updated by the Excel report author:

```
=CUBEMEMBER("pbiazure://api.powerbi.com <id> Model","[Dates].[Year
Month].&[2011-Jan]")
```

The Excel report author(s) can quickly learn to customize the cube formulas such as applying different filters and to support changes to the report, including new metrics (rows) and attribute values (columns).

The `CUBEVALUE` and `CUBEMEMBER` functions are the most common cube functions but several others can be used as well, such as `CUBESETCOUNT`. The **Formulas** interface in Excel provides information on the arguments for each function. In more advanced scenarios, **Named Ranges** can be assigned to cube formulas and optionally other formulas in the report, and then passed into cube formulas as parameters:

```
=CUBEMEMBER(strConn,"[PeriodStart].[Period Start].["&SPUser&"]")
```

In this example, `strConn` is a **Named Range** in Excel containing the name of the data connection to the Power BI dataset. `PeriodStart` is a column in a disconnected and hidden `PeriodStart` table in the data model and `SPUser` is a named range reflecting a business user's selection on a classic combo box form control in Excel. A separate `CUBEVALUE` function can reference this `CUBEMEMBER` function such that user selections in simple Excel controls can be passed via cube functions to the source dataset and reflected in the report.

There's more...

Once Analyze in Excel has created the connection between the Power BI dataset and Excel, this connection can be used to create additional report elements. To see how this is done, do the following:

1. In the same Excel workbook opened locally, create a **New sheet**.
2. Select **Existing Connections** from the ribbon of the **Data** tab.

3. In the **Existing Connections** dialog, select the Power BI connection and select the **Open** button.
4. In the **Import Data** dialog, choose **PivotTable Report** and then select the **OK** button.
5. Create a simple pivot table report with one measure and one attribute such as **Internet Net Sales** by **Product Category**.

Row Labels	Internet Net Sales
Accessories	$700,760
Bikes	$28,318,145
Clothing	$339,773
Grand Total	**$29,358,677**

Figure 13.19: Excel pivot table based on the Power BI service dataset

6. Double-click on one of the measure cells such as **$339,773** to execute a "drill-through" query. All columns of the underlying **Internet Sales** fact table will be retrieved filtered by the **Clothing** category.

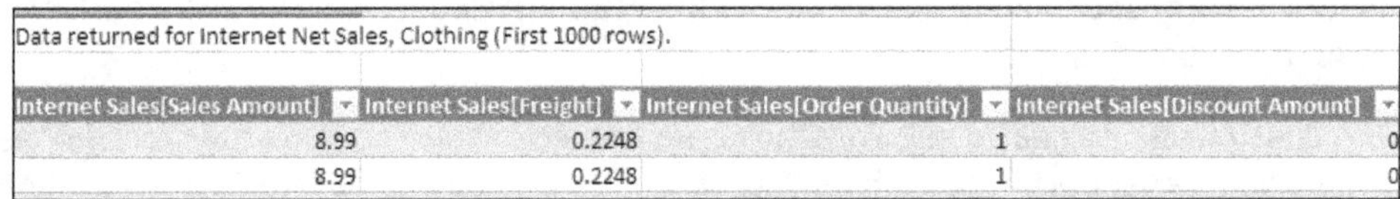

Data returned for Internet Net Sales, Clothing (First 1000 rows).

Internet Sales[Sales Amount]	Internet Sales[Freight]	Internet Sales[Order Quantity]	Internet Sales[Discount Amount]
8.99	0.2248	1	0
8.99	0.2248	1	0

Figure 13.20: Excel table result from drill through

7. Select a cell in the Excel table and right-click and choose **Table** and then **Edit Query...**.

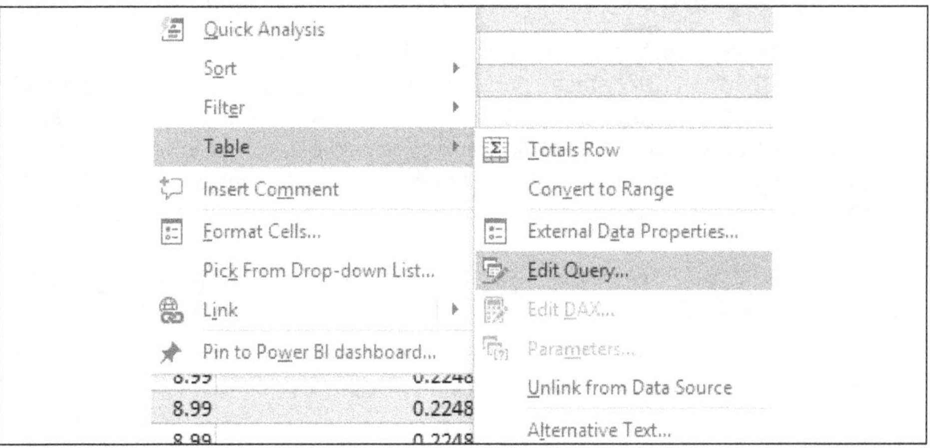

Figure 13.21: Excel Table Options

8. In the **Command Text** area, enter (or paste) a custom DAX query and click on **OK**.

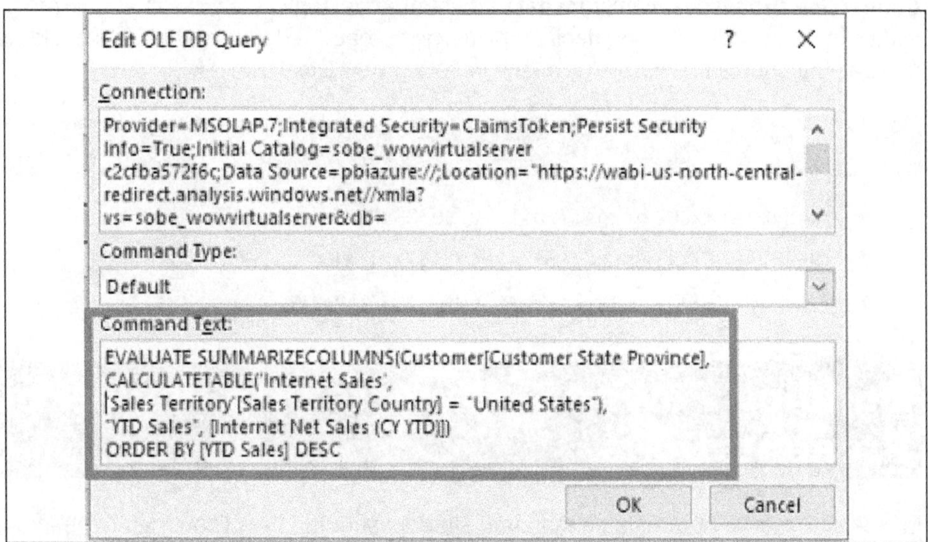

Figure 13.22: DAX Query pasted from DAX Studio into the Command Text area of the Edit OLE DB Query dialog

9. If the query is valid, the Excel table will update to return the columns specified in the query.
10. Visuals, such as a map visual, can use this table (DAX query) as their data source.

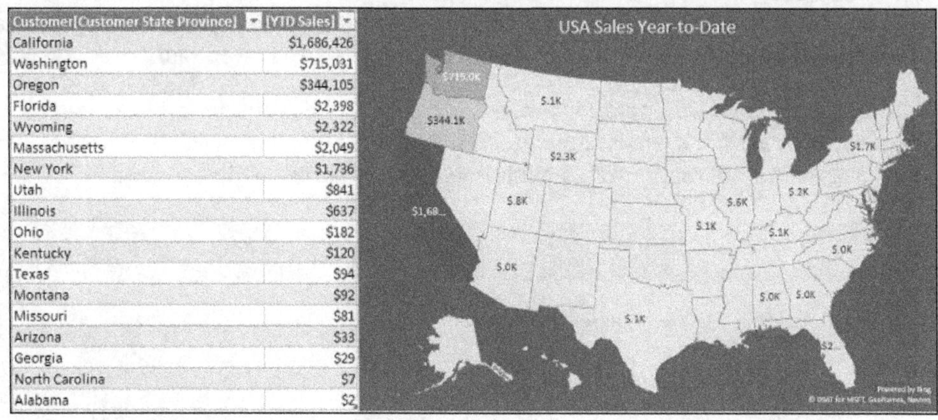

Customer[Customer State Province]	[YTD Sales]
California	$1,686,426
Washington	$715,031
Oregon	$344,105
Florida	$2,398
Wyoming	$2,322
Massachusetts	$2,049
New York	$1,736
Utah	$841
Illinois	$637
Ohio	$182
Kentucky	$120
Texas	$94
Montana	$92
Missouri	$81
Arizona	$33
Georgia	$29
North Carolina	$7
Alabama	$2

Figure 13.23: Excel table results from the DAX query (left) and Excel maps visual (right)

The number of rows to retrieve can be adjusted in the **OLAP Drill Through** property in **Connection Properties**. A custom data label format is applied to the visual to express the values in thousands with one decimal place. Note that the default pivot table could not be used as the source for this visual or several other new Excel visuals.

See also

- Analyze in Excel: `https://bit.ly/3bIMSeM`
- CUBEVALUE function: `https://bit.ly/3DfftUA`
- CUBEMEMBER function: `https://bit.ly/3AXr1Kq`

Building Power BI Reports into PowerPoint Presentations

Microsoft PowerPoint remains a standard slide presentation application and the integration of data analyses and visualizations from external tools is very commonly an essential component of effective presentation decks. In response to the volume of customer requests, the Power BI service supports the ability to export Power BI reports as PowerPoint files. Each page of the Power BI report is converted into an independent PowerPoint slide and the Power BI service creates a title page based on the report and relevant metadata, such as the last refreshed date. There are certain current limitations, such as the static nature of the exported file and the visuals supported, but the feature is available to all Power BI users to streamline the creation of presentation slides. However, even deeper integration is planned for the future, including the ability to embed dynamic Power BI reports into PowerPoint.

This recipe contains a preparation process to better leverage the Export to PowerPoint feature and to avoid current limitations. Additionally, a sample process is described of a user exporting a Power BI report from a published app and accessing the content in PowerPoint.

Getting ready

To prepare for this recipe, follow these steps:

1. Log in to the Power BI service.
2. Click the gear icon in the upper-right corner and choose **Admin portal**.
3. Click on **Tenant settings**.

4. Under **Export and sharing**, enable the **Export reports as PowerPoint presentations or PDF documents** feature in the Power BI admin portal:

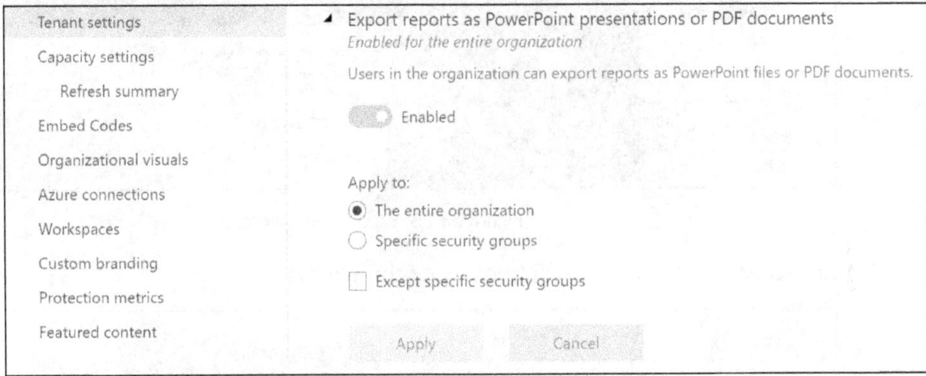

Figure 13.24: Tenant settings in the Power BI admin portal

   As per the preceding screenshot, the Power BI admin or Office 365 global admin can also limit the feature to specific security groups.

5. Identify the Power BI report that will serve as the source of the PowerPoint to be created and its dataset.
6. If the report contains many pages, count the number of report pages. Currently reports with over 15 pages cannot be exported.
7. Determine whether any report visuals are not supported, including R visuals and custom visuals that have not been certified.
8. Check whether any background images are used in the report visuals or if any custom page sizes have been set. It is best to avoid both background images and custom page sizes.
9. Based on previous steps and initial tests of the export, either apply revisions to the existing report or create a separate report (using the current report as a starting point) that will be dedicated to PowerPoint.

You are now ready to complete the steps for this recipe.

How to do it...

To implement this recipe, do the following:

1. Open the report in the Power BI service.

2. From the report header, choose **Export** and then **PowerPoint**.

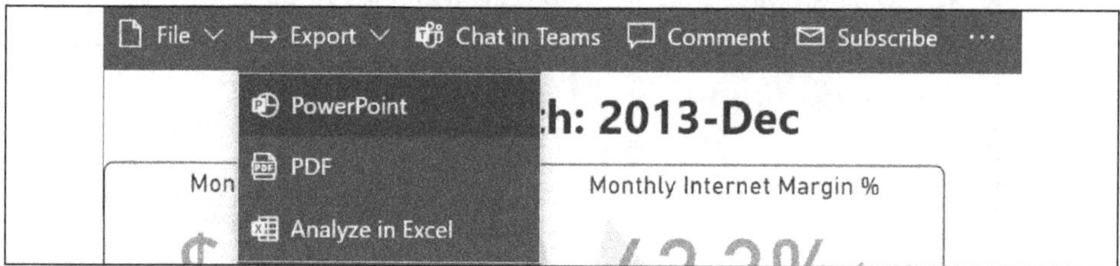

Figure 13.25: Export to PowerPoint

3. An **Export** dialog provides options, click the **Export** button.

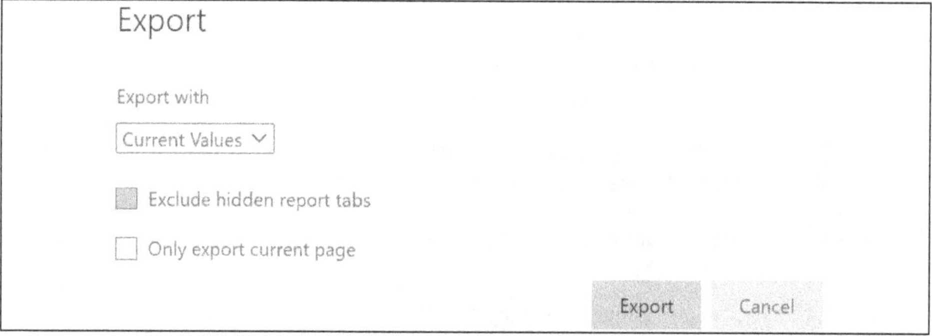

Figure 13.26: Export options for PowerPoint

4. A message will indicate that the export is in progress and may take a few minutes.
5. Open the PowerPoint file and make additional adjustments as needed in PowerPoint.

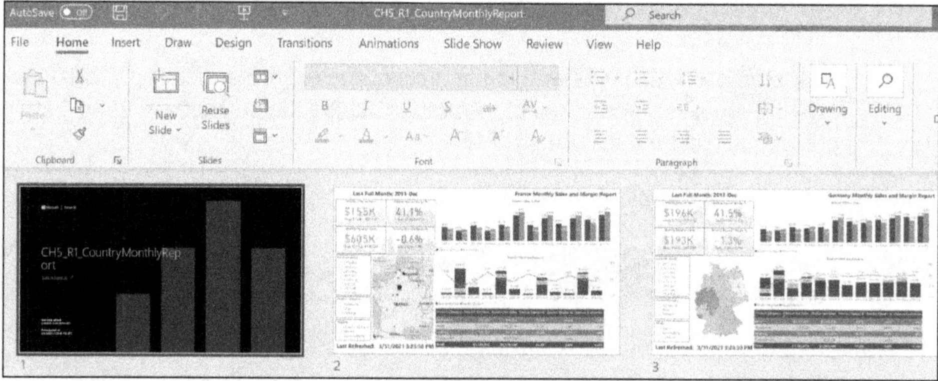

Figure 13.27: An exported Power BI report in Slide Sorter view of Microsoft PowerPoint

As you can see, exporting to PowerPoint is quite easy!

How it works...

Depending on the browser and its download settings, either the file is downloaded to a specific path or the browser displays a message for saving or opening the PowerPoint file. A title page is generated automatically by the export process, containing the name of the report and a link to the report in the Power BI service. The title page also includes a last data refresh and a downloaded at date and time value. Each report page is converted into a slide that contains a high-quality, rendered image of the report page. Any **Alt Text** specified for visuals is included in the **Notes** for each page.

Similar to other planning and precautions with highly visible content such as executive dashboards, it is important to obtain knowledge and confidence in the data sources, refresh process, data quality, and ownership. For example, if the source dataset retrieves from multiple sources including ad hoc Excel files and has a history of refresh failures then the report might not be a good candidate for a PowerPoint presentation. A report based on an IT-managed Analysis Services model that has already been validated and has a clear owner would be a better choice.

Background images will be cropped with a chart's bounding area and thus it is recommended to remove or avoid background images. Additionally, the exported report pages always result in standard 16:9 PowerPoint slide sizes and thus custom or non-standard page sizes should also be avoided. Shapes such as rectangles and lines to provide custom groupings, borders, and background colors for visuals may also need to be removed for proper PowerPoint rendering. Finally, non-certified visuals, R visuals, and Python visuals should be avoided in reports where exporting to PowerPoint is used.

There's more...

The Power BI service supports exporting reports to PowerPoint or PDF as well as to an image file through the Power BI REST API. In addition, paginated reports can be exported to the following additional formats:

- MHTML
- Microsoft Word
- XML

A third-party add-in is available for integrating Power BI tiles from the Power BI service into Microsoft Office documents called Power BI Tiles and is available in AppSource: `https://bit.ly/3w2sUmq`. The offering from DevScope includes an automated Office-to-Power BI refresh process and supports Word, Outlook, and PowerPoint.

See also

- Export entire reports to PowerPoint: `https://bit.ly/3tIaPZl`
- Power BI tiles: `http://www.powerbitiles.com/`

Connecting to Azure Analysis Services

Power BI Premium is now a superset of Analysis Services and powerful new features such as composite models and aggregations are exclusive to Power BI Premium. Nonetheless, it wasn't long ago in which Azure Analysis Services (AAS) was Microsoft's flagship semantic modeling tool and thus many organizations' production BI workloads currently leverage AAS models as the source for Power BI and other report types.

Given the additional features and product roadmap of Power BI Premium, deep compatibility between AAS and Power Premium, as well as a straight forward migration path, many AAS (and SSAS) models will eventually be re-deployed to Power BI Premium. Nonetheless, Azure Analysis Services will remain a fully supported and common cloud service that BI developers should be familiar with.

> *"I think it is fair to say that we're the only vendor that can claim a strong presence in self-service business intelligence with Power BI and corporate business intelligence, which is typically owned and managed by IT, with Analysis Services."*
>
> *- Christian Wade, Senior Program Manager*

In this recipe, an Azure Analysis Services server is created and a Power BI Desktop file is imported to this server. The migrated model is then opened in SQL Server Data Tools for Visual Studio as an Analysis Services project.

Getting ready

To prepare for this recipe, follow these steps:

1. Obtain an MS Azure subscription.
2. Identify the location of your Power BI service tenant by clicking on the question mark in the top-right menu and selecting **About Power BI**.

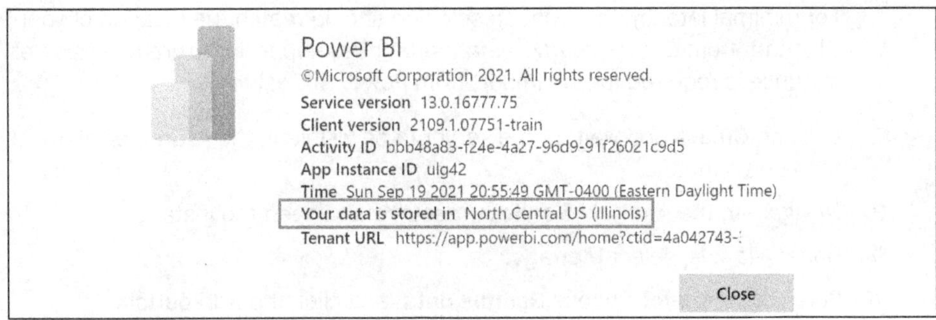

Figure 13.28: Power BI service tenant location

Note that a tenant can be thought of like an apartment in an apartment building. The Power BI service in Microsoft Azure is akin to the building, providing the foundation, plumbing, and other common facilities. However, each resident within the Power BI service has their own private living area (tenant).

3. Log in to the Microsoft Azure portal, `https://portal.azure.com`.
4. Choose **Create a resource**.
5. Search for **Analysis Services** and select **Create**.
6. Create an Azure Analysis Services server by filling in the required fields:

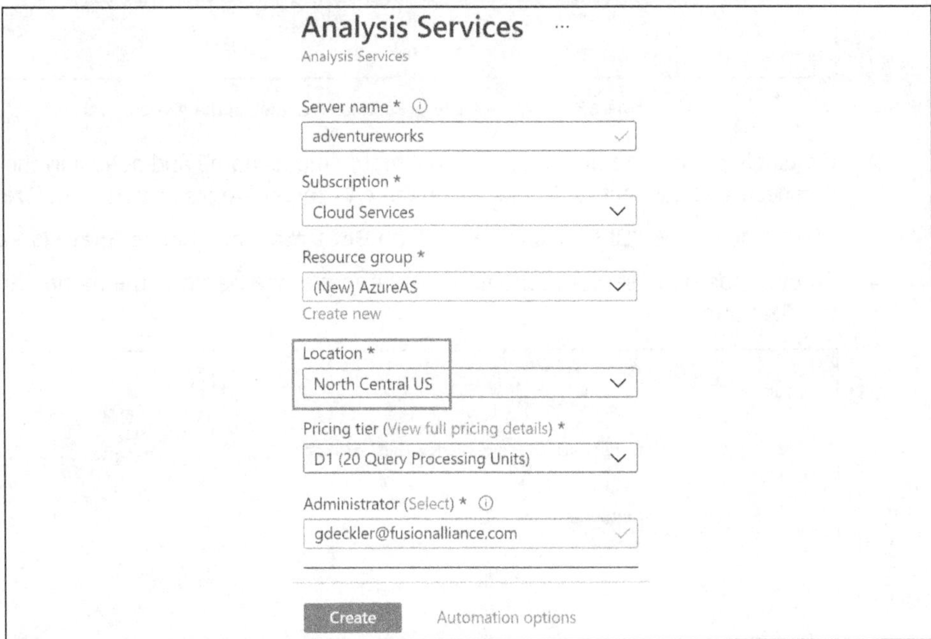

Figure 13.29: Create an Azure Analysis Services Server

For minimal latency, the location selected should match the location of your Power BI tenant from *Getting ready*. A standard or developer tier Azure Analysis Services instance is required for the import from Power BI Desktop.

7. Click on **Create** and wait for the server to be visible in the Azure portal (usually less than one minute).
8. Navigate to the **Analysis Services** resource and open the instance.
9. Under **Models**, select **Manage**.
10. Select **New Model**, choose **Sample data**, and click the **Add** button.

A new model called **adventureworks** will be added to your Analysis Services instance.

How to do it...

To implement this recipe, do the following:

1. With the Analysis Services resource open, click **Overview** and obtain the **Server name**.

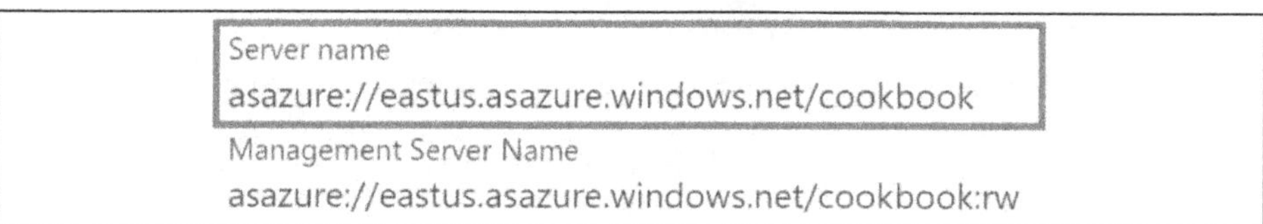

Figure 13.30: Azure Analysis Services resource in the Azure portal

2. If multiple models are on the server, confirm the model name and optionally the perspective to connect to. All models on the AAS server are also listed in the Azure portal.
3. Open a new Power BI Desktop file, click on **Get Data**, and choose **Analysis Services**.
4. Enter or paste the server name and the database (the name of the model) and press the **OK** button:

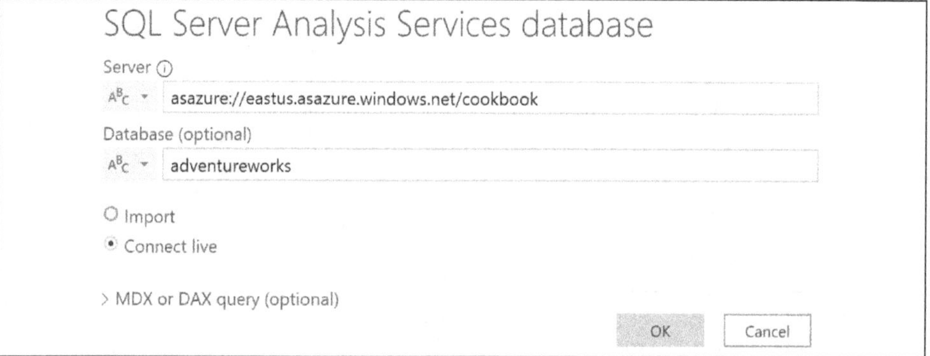

Figure 13.31: Azure Analysis Services data source configuration in Power BI Desktop

5. Authenticate using a **Microsoft account**.
6. Create a Power BI report and publish it to a workspace in the Power BI service.

As you can see, connecting to an Analysis Services database is quite simple and straightforward.

How it works...

Connect live is the default option and this should represent the vast majority if not all connections as data has already been imported to (or connected from, in the case of SSAS DirectQuery models) the Azure Analysis Services database. Importing data to Power BI Desktop would require its own refresh process, but in certain rare scenarios, a DAX query can retrieve from the AAS database and then optionally merge or integrate this data with other data sources in Power BI Desktop.

Just like Power BI Desktop reports with live connections to datasets in the Power BI service, the report author can also create DAX measures specific to the given report with live connections to Analysis Services. This feature enables report authors familiar with DAX to address the unique metric requirements of a report. If the same report-level measures are being remade across multiple reports, the BI/IT team responsible for the Analysis Services model can consider implementing this logic into the model.

Azure Analysis Services instances are priced per hour according to **QPUs** (**Query Processing Units**) and memory. One virtual core is approximately equal to 20 QPUs. For example, an S4 instance with 400 QPUs has roughly 20 virtual cores and 100 GB of RAM:

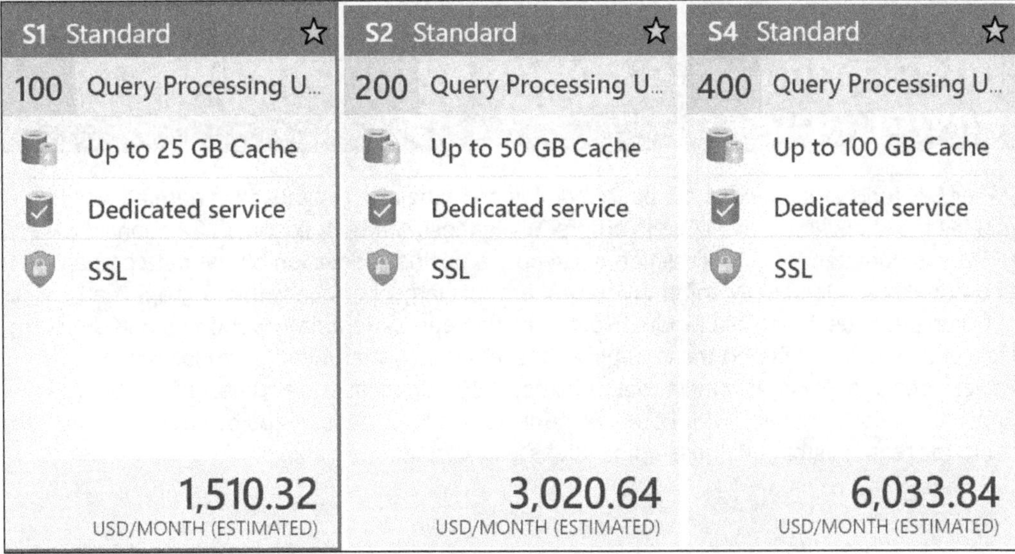

Figure 13.32: Azure Analysis Services instance pricing

Azure Analysis Services servers can be paused, and no charges are incurred while servers are paused. Additionally, the pricing tier of a server can be moved up or down a service tier such as from S1 to S3 or vice versa. A server can also be upgraded from lower service tiers such as from development to standard, but servers cannot be downgraded from higher service tiers.

There's more...

Given that Power BI and Analysis Services Tabular share the same database engine and because Azure Analysis Services eliminates the query latency and infrastructure costs of communication between the Power BI service and on-premises servers via the on-premises data gateway, organizations may consider migrating their Power BI and SSAS models to Azure Analysis Services. As one example, the data source for a model such as Teradata can remain on-premises but the scheduled or triggered model refresh process of model tables and table partitions would update the Azure-hosted model through the on-premises data gateway. In addition to the other cost and flexibility advantages of the Azure Analysis Services **Platform-as-a-Service** (**PaaS**) offering, Power BI Premium capacities can enable all business users to access the Power BI reports and dashboards built on top of Azure Analysis Services models. Once migrated to Azure Analysis Services, the tabular model can be accessed as the source for a Power BI report.

See also

- Azure Analysis Services: `https://azure.microsoft.com/en-us/services/analysis-services/`
- Client libraries for connection to Azure Analysis Services: `http://bit.ly/2vzLAvO`

Integrating with Power Automate and Power Apps

Power BI's tools and services are built to derive meaning and insights from data as well as making those insights accessible to others. While these are both essential functions, Power BI itself is not intended to take action or execute a business decision on the data it analyzes and visualizes. Additionally, information workers regularly interface with many applications or services and thus, to remain productive, there is a need to automate workflows and embed logic between Power BI and these applications in order to streamline business processes. Power Apps and Power Automate, both Microsoft 365 applications and part of the Business Application Platform along with Power BI, serve to address these needs by enabling business users to create custom business applications and workflow processes.

In this recipe a Power Automate workflow is created to support a streaming dataset in the Power BI service. Specifically, the Power Automate workflow is configured to read from an on-premises SQL Server table every two minutes and push this data into Power BI to provide near real-time visibility and support for data-driven alerts and notifications.

Getting ready

To prepare for this recipe, follow these steps:

1. Open **SQL Server Management Studio (SSMS)**, connect to the local SQL database containing the **AdventureWorksdW2019** database, and familiarize yourself with the **Columns** of the **dbo.FactSurveyResponse** table:

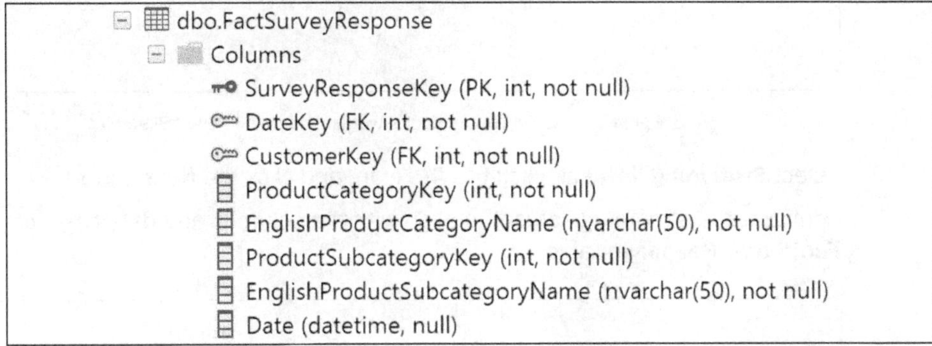

Figure 13.33: dbo.FactSurveyResponse columns in the AdventureWorksDW2019 database

2. Ensure that you have a data gateway running that is compatible with Power Automate. See *Chapter 1, Configuring Power BI Tools* for installation instructions.

In this recipe, an on-premises data gateway is used to support a Power BI streaming dataset from an on-premises SQL Server database table via Power Automate. Per previous chapters the same gateway that supports Power BI refresh processes and live connections or DirectQuery models can also be used for Power Apps and Power Automate. Depending on the workloads generated by these different activities and applications, and based on gateway resource monitoring, it may be necessary to isolate Power Apps and Power Automate to a dedicated on-premises gateway or, in the future, add a server to a high-availability gateway cluster.

How to do it...

To implement this recipe, do the following:

1. Open a workspace in the Power BI service and click on the **New** button in the top menu bar.

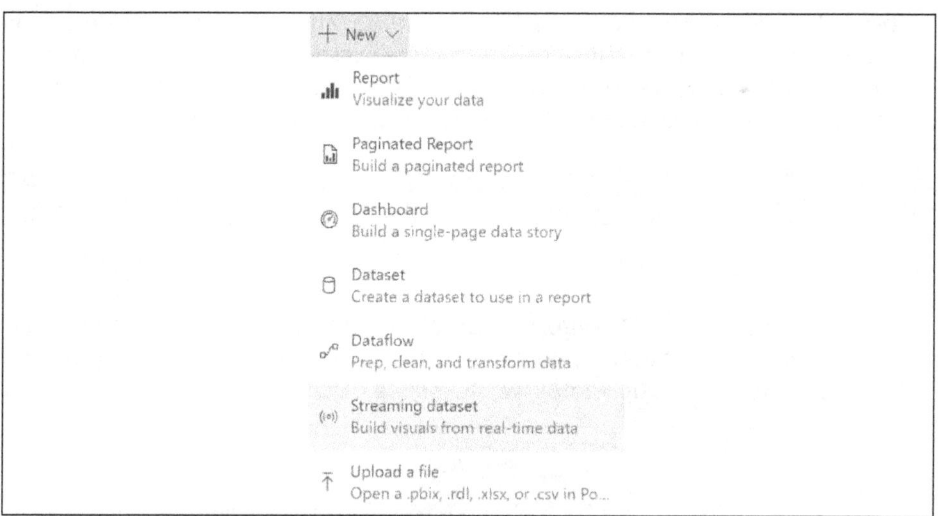

Figure 13.34: New options for a workspace in the Power BI service

2. Select **Streaming dataset**, click the **API** icon, and click the **Next** button.
3. Configure the streaming dataset to align with the columns and data types of the **FactSurveyResponse** table.

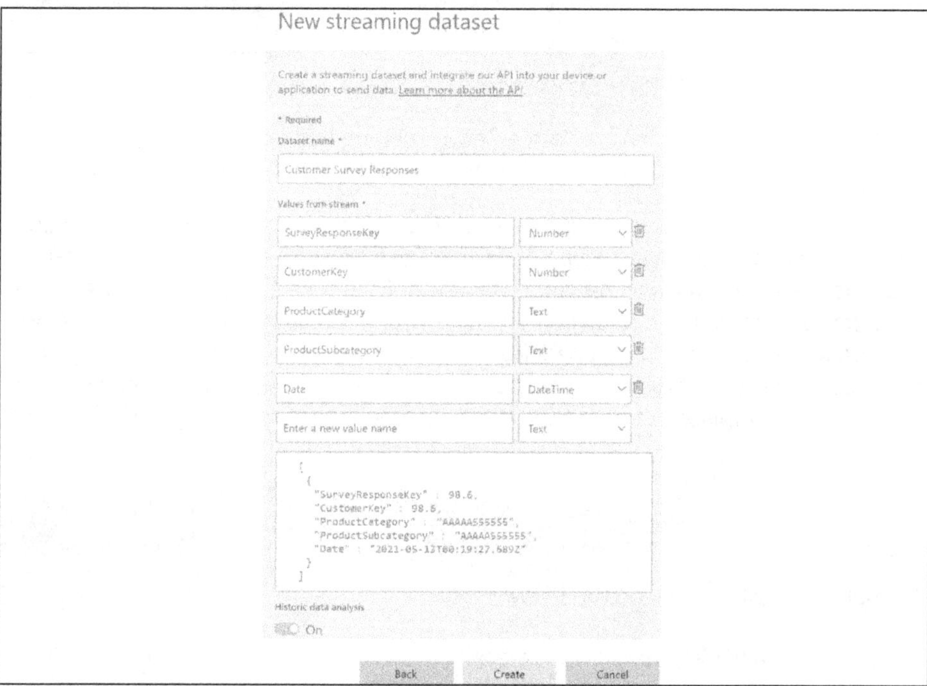

Figure 13.35: Streaming dataset configuration

4. Enter a **Dataset name**, enable the **Historic data analysis** setting, and click the **Create button**.
5. Copy the **Push URL** value and click the **Done** button.
6. Log in to Power Automate in Microsoft 365: `https://flow.microsoft.com`.
7. In the left navigation pane, click **Create**.
8. In the **Start from blank** area, click **Scheduled cloud flow**.
9. Provide a **Flow name**, set the workflow to **Repeat every 5 Minute**, and then click the **Create** button.

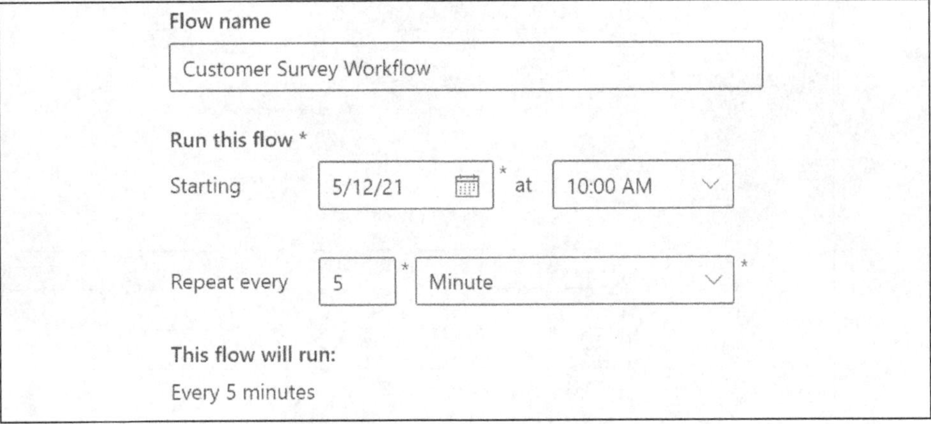

Figure 13.36: Creating a Power Automate workflow

10. On the design screen, click **New step**.
11. Search for SQL Server and in **Actions** choose **Get rows (V2)**.

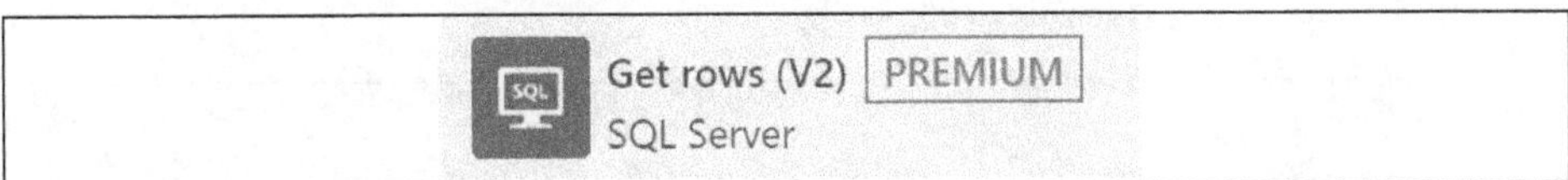

Figure 13.37: Get rows SQL Server action in Power Automate

12. Enter in the connection information for the SQL Server and then click the **Create** button. For the gateway to appear, the connection information must match a data source configured on the gateway.

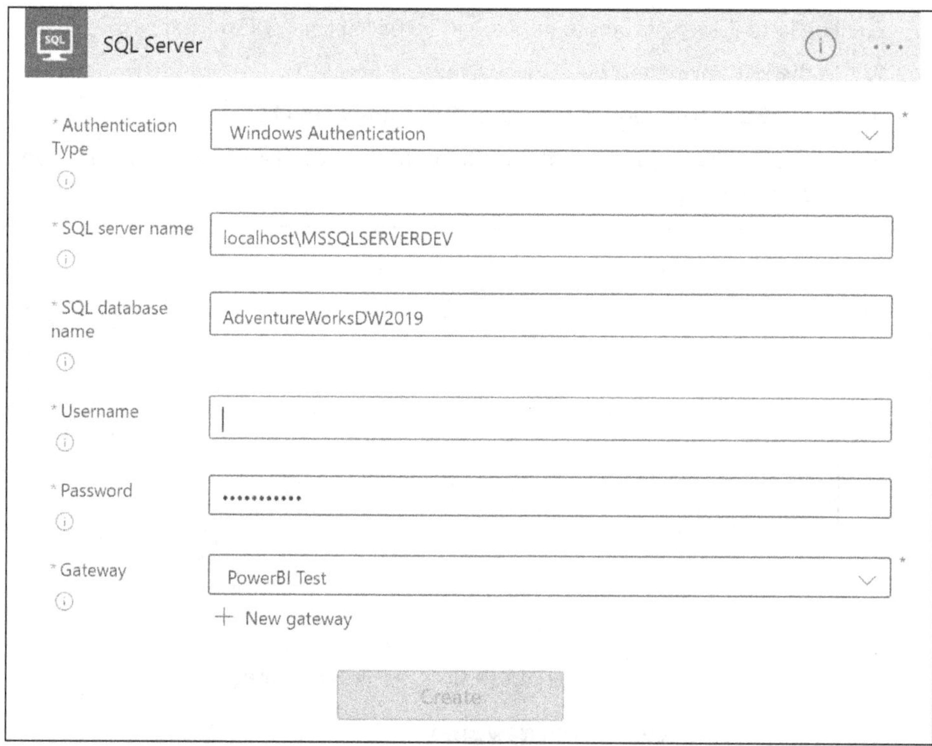

Figure 13.38: SQL Server connection information in Power Automate

13. Configure the **Get rows (V2)** step:

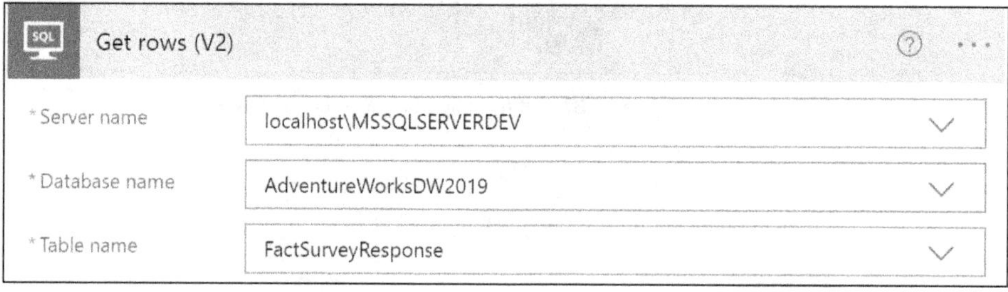

Figure 13.39: Configuration of the SQL Server Get rows (V2) step in Power Automate

14. Click the **New step** button.
15. Search for **Power BI** and choose **Add rows to a dataset (Preview)**.
16. Configure the **Add rows to a dataset (Preview)** step for the **Workspace** and **Dataset** created previously.

17. Choose **RealTimeData** as the **Table** and configure the columns for the dataset.

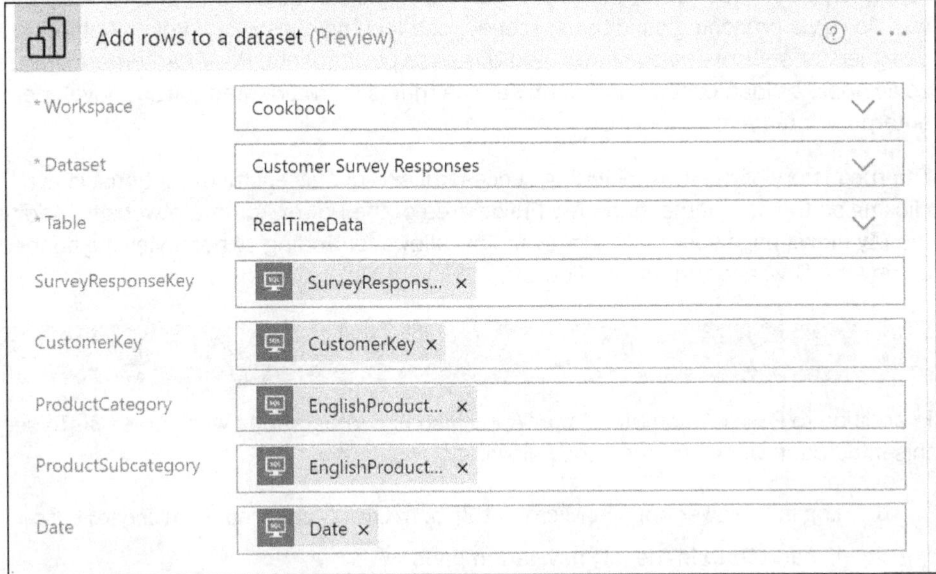

Figure 13.40: Configuration of the Add rows to a dataset step in Power Automate

18. Click the **Save** button when complete.
19. Click on **My flows** and **Run** the workflow.
20. Monitor the flow by clicking on the **Flow Runs Page** link and waiting for the flow to complete.
21. Open a new Power BI Desktop file.
22. Click **Get data** and choose **Power BI datasets**.
23. Select the **Customer Survey Responses** dataset and click the **Create** button.
24. Create a simple visual that counts the rows in the dataset.

In a production scenario, this recipe would need to be modified such that each run of the Power Automate flow does not duplicate the rows already present in the Power BI dataset.

How it works...

When historical data analysis is enabled for a streaming dataset in the Power BI service, the dataset created is both a streaming dataset and a push dataset. As a push dataset, a database and table for the dataset are created in the Power BI service allowing Power BI report visuals and functionality to be created from this table. Without historical data analysis enabled (the default), the dataset is only a streaming dataset. Power BI temporarily caches the data but there is no underlying database, and thus the only method for visualizing this data is via a real-time streaming dashboard tile.

Power Automate flows are conceptually similar to the control flow interface for **SQL Server Integration Services (SSIS)** packages. Complex logic can be added to Power Automate workflows via branching conditions, scopes, and looping constructs. Power Automate is designed for self-service scenarios and business power users. Power Automate utilizes Azure Logic Apps, a cloud-based integration service that is more oriented toward developers and enterprise integration scenarios.

The run history of the flow, including successful and unsuccessful executions, is available by clicking on the flow name in the **My Flows** area of the Power Automate website. Additionally, the **My Flows** page specific to the given flow allows for adding owners, viewing connections, editing the flow, and turning the flow off.

There's more...

In addition to Power Automate, Power Apps also has integrations with Power BI. To see how this integration works, perform the following steps:

1. Log in to Power Apps in Microsoft 365: `https://powerapps.microsoft.com`
2. Expand **Data** in the left navigation pane
3. Select **Tables**
4. Select the **Data** dropdown and choose **Get data** and then **Get data** again

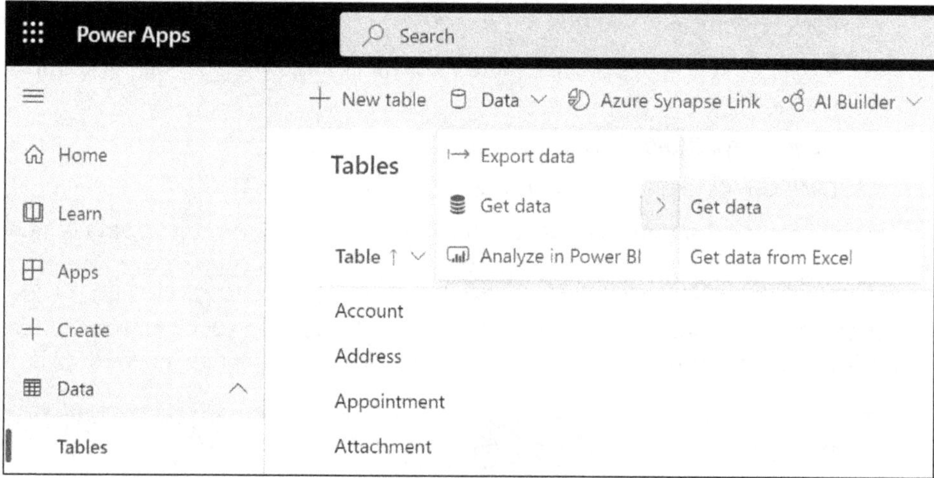

Figure 13.41: Getting data

5. Choose **Power Platform dataflows**
6. For **Connection**, choose **Create new connection** and authenticate
7. Click the **Next** button

8. Choose a table from a dataflow and click **Next**

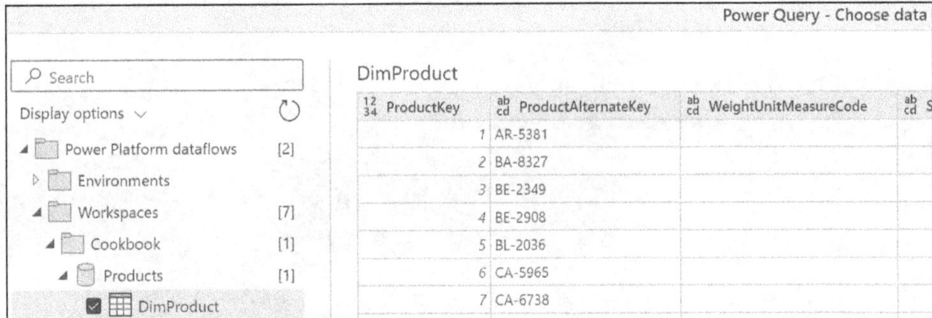

Figure 13.42: Choosing a dataflow table

9. Click the **Next** button
10. Choose **Load to new table** and click the **Next** button

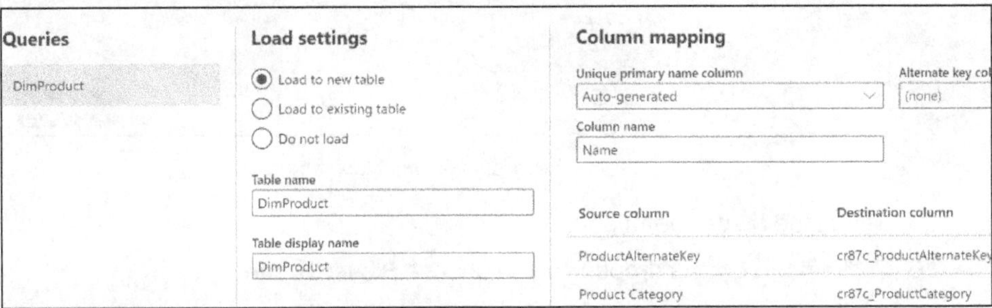

Figure 13.43: Load as a new table

11. Select whether to refresh manually or automatically and click the **Publish** button
12. Back on the **Tables** screen, in the left navigation pane, click **Create**
13. Choose **Canvas app from blank**

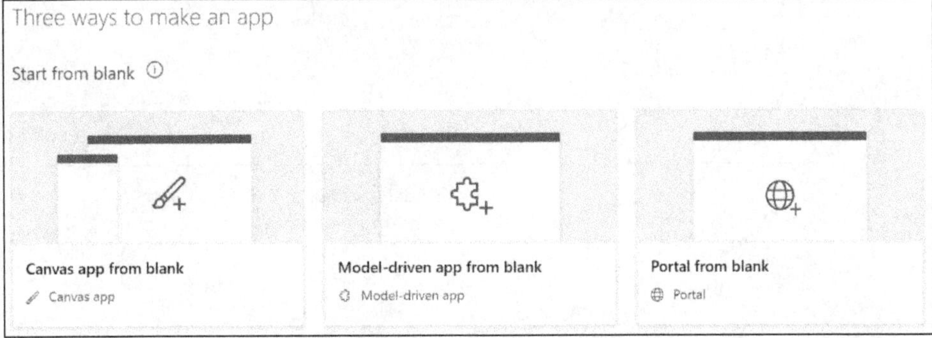

Figure 13.44: Three ways to create a Power app

14. Provide an **App name** and then click the **Create** button

Figure 13.45: Create app from blank

15. Select the **Insert** menu option
16. Click on the **Charts** dropdown and choose **Power BI tile**

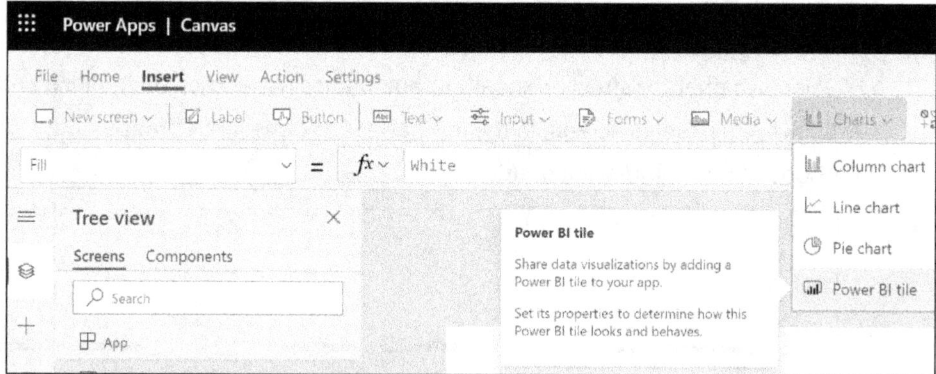

Figure 13.46: Insert Power BI tile

17. Choose a **Workspace**, **Dashboard**, and **Tile** from the Power BI service

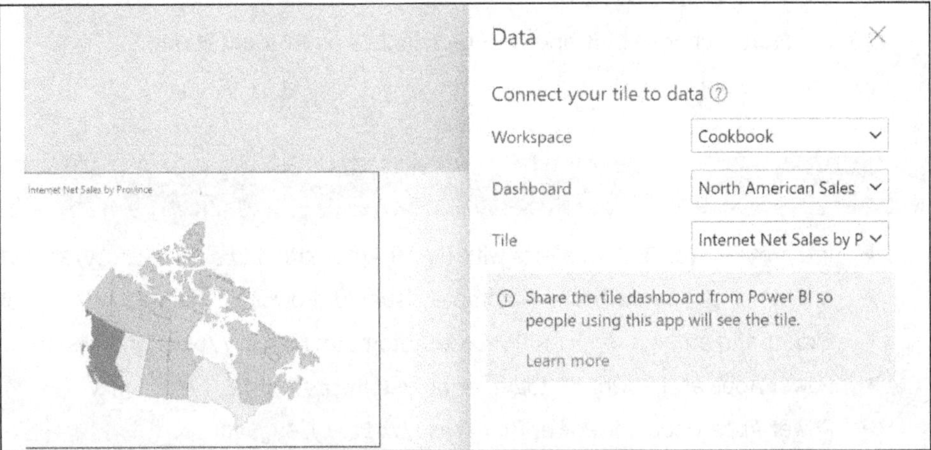

Figure 13.47: Choosing a dashboard tile

18. From the **Home** menu, select **New screen** and choose **List**

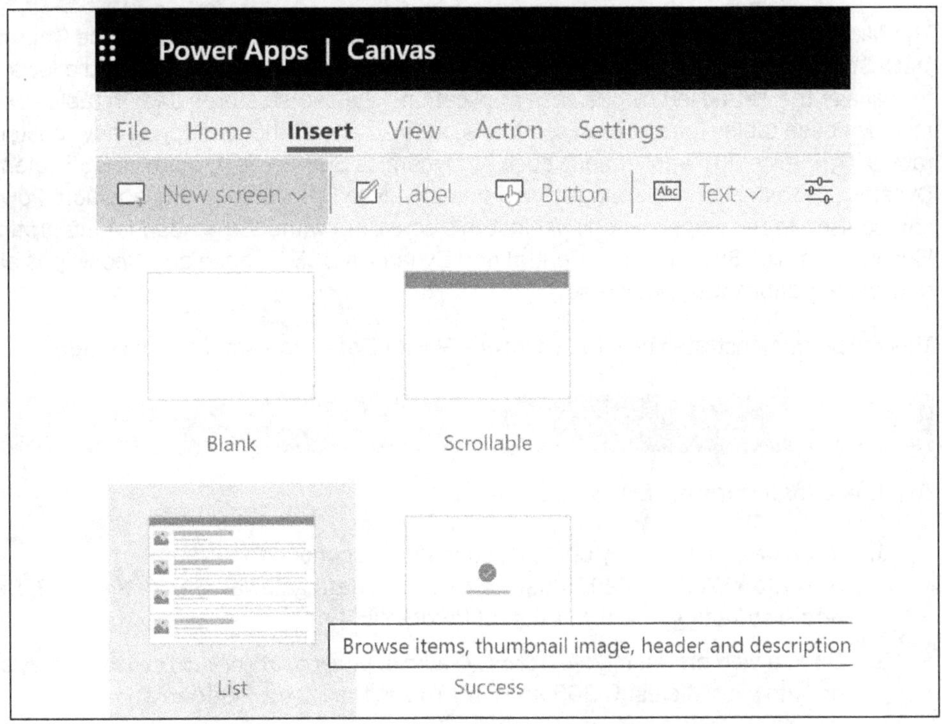

Figure 13.48: Creating a new List screen

19. Select a list item and edit the **Data** source to choose the table created previously (in this case, **DimProduct**)
20. For **Fields**, choose **Edit** and change **Title2** to be **Product Name**
21. Save the app

See also

- Integrate Power BI data alerts with Power Automate: `https://bit.ly/3tHLv5R`
- Announcing the new Power Automate visual for Power BI: `https://bit.ly/3vY9C1J`
- Export and email a report with Power Automate: `https://bit.ly/3fc8eBT`
- Power Apps and Power BI, together at last: `https://bit.ly/2QbQHkC`
- Power Apps visual for Power BI: `https://bit.ly/3yg5a0n`

Leveraging Dataverse and Dynamics 365

The Microsoft Power Platform includes Dataverse, what was formerly called the **Common Data Service (CDS)**. Dataverse stores business data securely in the cloud and allows you to manage the data used by business applications. Dataverse stores data in tables and includes base tables for common scenarios but also allows the creation of new, custom tables. Dynamics 365 applications such as Dynamics 365 Sales, Dynamics 365 Talent, and Dynamics 365 Customer Service store data natively in Dataverse and in addition, Power Apps can be used to build applications against this core data without the need for integration. Finally, Dynamics 365 Business Central and Dynamics 365 Finance and Operations also have native integrations with Dataverse.

This recipe demonstrates how to use Power BI with Dataverse and Dynamics 365.

Getting ready

To prepare for this recipe, follow these steps:

1. If you have not already done so, configure a connection to your **AdventureWorksDW2019** database in your data gateway. See *Chapter 12, Deploying and Distributing Power BI Content* for details.
2. Open a web browser, go to `https://admin.powerplatform.microsoft.com`, and log on with your Microsoft 365 account. This is the Power Platform admin center.
3. In the left-hand navigation pane, click on **Environments**.

4. In the ribbon area, click **+ New**. This opens a **New environment** pane on the right-hand side of the page.

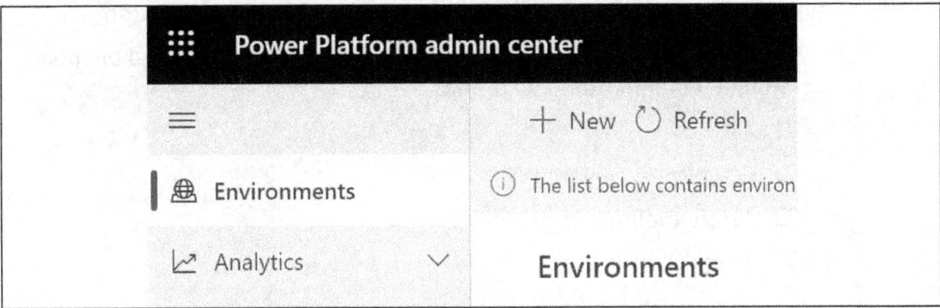

Figure 13.49: Power Platform admin center

5. In the **New environment** pane, enter a **Name** for the environment, choose a **Type** (either **Production**, **Sandbox**, or **Trial**), and choose a **Region**. Additionally, toggle **Create a database for this environment** to **Yes** and click the **Next** button at the bottom of the pane.
6. Choose a **Language** and **Currency**. Provide a **URL** if desired.
7. Toggle **Enable Dynamics 365 apps** to **Yes**.
8. Click the dropdown for **Automatically deploy these apps** and check all the boxes.
9. Click the **Save** button at the bottom of the pane.
10. Click the environment and note the **Environment URL**.

You are now ready to complete this recipe.

How to do it...

To implement this recipe, use the following steps:

1. Navigate to `https://powerapps.com` and switch to the new environment created in *Getting ready*. The current environment is located in the upper-right corner.
2. In the left-hand navigation, expand **Data** and click **Dataflows**.
3. Click on the **Create a dataflow** button and choose **Start from blank**.
4. Provide a **Name** for your dataflow like **Customers** and click the **Create** button.
5. Choose **SQL Server database**.
6. Enter the connection information for your on-premises **AdventureWorksDW2019** database.

7. Choose your gateway from the dropdown for **On-premises data gateway**.
8. Enter your authentication information and click the **Next** button.
9. Select the **DimCustomer** table and click the **Transform data** button.
10. Expand the **DimGeography** column for the following columns and uncheck **Use original column name as prefix**:
    - City
    - StateProvinceName
    - EnglishCountryRegionName
    - PostalCode
11. Click the **Next** button.
12. Select **Load to existing table** and choose **Contact** as the **Table display name**.
13. Create the following mappings:
    - `City = Address1_City`
    - `EnglishCountryRegionName = Address1_Country`
    - `AddressLine1 = Address1_Line1`
    - `AddressLine2 = Address1_Line2`
    - `PostalCode = Address1_PostalCode`
    - `StateProvinceName = Address1_StateOrProvince`
    - `Phone = Address1_Telephone1`
    - `YearlyIncome = AnnualIncome`
    - `BirthDate = BirthDate`
    - `FirstName = FirstName`
    - `Title = JobTitle`
    - `LastName = LastName`
    - `TotalChildren = NumberOfChildren`
    - `Phone = Telephone1`
14. With all other columns set to **(none)**, click the **Next** button.
15. Leave the default for **Refresh manually** and click the **Create** button.
16. A refresh will start automatically, allow the refresh to complete.
17. Create a new Power BI Desktop file
18. Choose **Get data** and then **Dataverse**.
19. Enter the **Environment URL** from *Step 10* of *Getting started*.

20. Sign in and click the **Connect** button.
21. Choose **Contact** in the **Navigator** and click the **Load button**.
22. Create a simple report visual to display the contacts loaded into the **Dataverse** environment:

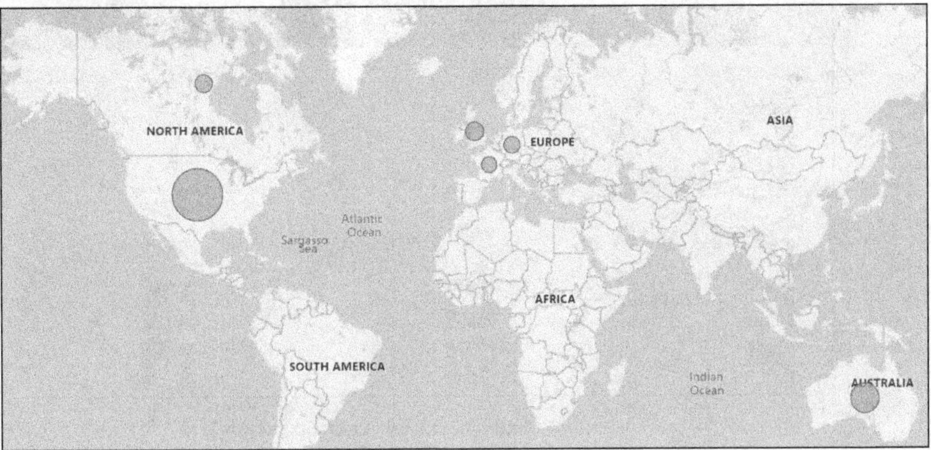

Figure 13.50: Customers in the Dataverse environment

Figure 13.50 shows customer locations loaded into the Dataverse.

How it works...

Power Apps dataflows use the same Power Query technology used by Power BI. These dataflows can ingest data from many different sources, including on-premises sources via the data gateway and cloud-based sources as well. Once data is imported into Dataverse, this data can be accessed by Power BI either via Import or DirectQuery.

It is important to point out that Power Apps and Power Automate can also natively access data stored in a Dataverse environment.

There's more...

In addition to the Dataverse, Power BI has native integration with Dynamics 365 applications, allowing Power BI dashboards to be displayed within Dynamics 365 applications. To demonstrate this functionality, do the following:

1. Open the Power Platform admin center, `https://admin.powerplatform.microsoft.com`
2. In the left-hand navigation pane, click on **Environments**
3. Click on the environment created in this recipe

4. Click on the link for the **Environment URL** to open the environment
5. Select the gear icon in the upper-right corner and choose **Advanced Settings**
6. From the **Settings** dropdown in the upper left, select **Administration**:

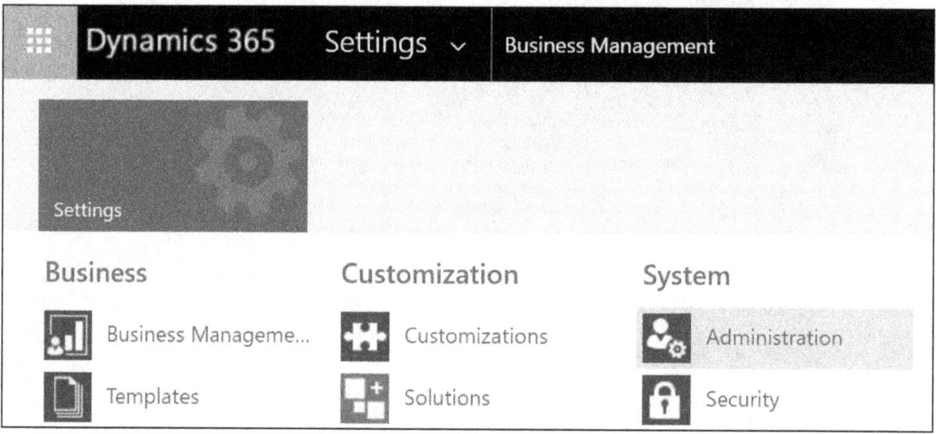

Figure 13.51: Dynamics 365 settings

7. Select **System Settings**
8. Click the **Reporting** tab and set **Allow Power BI visualization embedding** to **Yes**
9. Click the **OK** button
10. Open the Sales Hub app for the environment and click on **Dashboards**
11. Select **New** and then **Power BI Dashboard**
12. Sign in to Power BI if necessary
13. Select a **Workspace** and a **Dashboard** and click the **Save** button
14. Select New and then **Dynamics 365 Dashboard**
15. Choose a layout and then click the **Create** button
16. Click the **Add a Power BI tile to the dashboard** icon:

Figure 13.52: Add a Power BI tile to the dashboard icon in Dynamics 365

17. Choose a **Workspace**, a **Dashboard**, and a **Tile** and then click the **OK** button
18. Provide a **Name** for the dashboard and click **Save** and then click **Close**

Power BI dashboards and tiles continue to exhibit their link behavior to the underlying report. Clicking on a report tile opens the underlying report and this report is interactive, meaning that clicking on visuals will cross filter other visuals in the report exactly the same as if viewing the report in the Power BI service.

See also

- Administer Power Platform: `https://bit.ly/3bqaKTQ`
- Create and use dataflows in Power Apps: `https://bit.ly/3eP6tLL`

Connecting Dynamics 365 Finance and Operations and the Power Platform

Power BI is part of Microsoft's Power Platform family of products. The Power Platform includes Power BI, Power Apps, Power Automate, and Power Virtual Agents. However, the Power Platform is also part of a larger family of products, Microsoft Business Applications. Microsoft Business Applications are applications built around Dynamics 365 for Sales, Dynamics 365 Business Central, and Dynamics 365 Finance and Operations. Microsoft actually breaks down Business Applications into the following:

- Microsoft Power Platform
- Customer Service
- Field Service
- Finance
- Marketing
- Operations
- Commerce
- Human Resources
- Sales

However, note that Customer Service, Field Service, Marketing, Commerce, Human Resources, and Sales are all built around the Microsoft **customer relationship management (CRM)** system, which used to be called Microsoft CRM. The extensible Microsoft CRM system, sometimes called XRM, is actually the heart of Dataverse. The Finance and Operations applications refer to the **enterprise resource planning (ERP)** applications, either Dynamics 365 Finance and Operations or Dynamics 365 Business Central. Note that Dynamics 365 Finance and Operations is built from Dynamics **AX (Axapta)** and Dynamics 365 Business Central is built from Dynamics **NAV (Navision)**. Dynamics **GP (Great Plains)** did not make the transition to the cloud.

The Power Platform admin center provides a central location that is built for integrating the various products in the Microsoft Business Applications portfolio. This also includes powerful data integration features that allow administrators to integrate data from many different environments into Dataverse environments. Similar to dataflows, these data integration projects facilitate central control of data management policies and the flow of business information.

This recipe demonstrates how to use the Power Platform admin center to create a data integration project that synchronizes Dynamics 365 Finance and Operations data with a Dataverse environment and then builds a Power BI report from that data.

Getting ready

To prepare for this recipe, follow these steps:

1. Open a web browser, go to `https://admin.powerplatform.microsoft.com`, and log on with your Microsoft 365 account. This is the Power Platform admin center.
2. In the left-hand navigation pane, click on **Environments**.
3. In the ribbon area, click **+ New**. This opens a **New environment** pane on the right-hand side of the page.
4. In the **New environment** pane, enter a **Name** for the environment, choose a **Type** (either **Production**, **Sandbox**, or **Trial**), and choose a **Region**. Additionally, toggle **Create a database for this environment** to **Yes** and click the **Next** button at the bottom of the pane.
5. Choose a **Language** and **Currency**. Provide a **URL** if desired.
6. Toggle **Enable Dynamics 365 apps** to **Yes**.
7. Click the dropdown for **Automatically deploy these apps** and check all the boxes.
8. Click the **Save** button at the bottom of the pane.
9. Click the environment and note the **Environment URL**.
10. Click the **Environment URL** to open the environment.
11. Click the gear icon in the upper-right corner and select **Advanced Settings**.
12. Click **Settings** and then **Security**.
13. Select **Teams**.
14. Check the box next to the default team and select **MANAGE ROLES**.
15. Check the box for **System Administrator** and click the **OK** button.

How to do it...

To implement this recipe, use the following steps:

1. Navigate to `https://powerapps.com` and switch to the new environment created in *Getting ready*. The current environment is located in the upper-right corner.
2. Expand **Data** and choose **Connections**.
3. Click **New connection**.
4. Search for **Dynamics** and add a **Fin & Ops Apps (Dynamics 365)** connection.
5. Repeat *Steps 3* and *4* to add a **Dataverse** connection and a **Dynamics 365 (deprecated)** connection.
6. Under the **Data** heading, now choose **Tables**.
7. Switch to the **All** view and search for *warehouse*.
8. Click the **Warehouse** table.
9. Click **Add column**.
10. Add a **City** text column.
11. Click **Save Table** in the lower-right corner.
12. Navigate to the Power Platform admin center.
13. Click on **Data integration**.
14. Click **New connection set**.
15. Provide a descriptive value for **Connection set name**.
16. For the **First app connection**, choose your **Finance and Operations apps** connection created previously and select the correct environment.
17. For the **Second app connection**, choose **Dynamics 365 for Sales** and select the environment created in this recipe. Note that at the time of writing, **Dynamics 365 for Sales** is the correct connection type. The legacy **Common Data Service** connection type does not work and the new **Dataverse** connection type does not appear in the list of available applications. In the future, the **Dataverse** connection type will likely be the correct choice.
18. Select the correct organization, such as **USMF** for **Finance and Operations apps**, and the environment name for the **Dynamics 365 for Sales** organization.
19. Click the **Save** button.
20. Click **New project**.
21. Provide a **Project name** such as **Warehouse Sync**.
22. Click **Choose an existing connection set** and select the connection set created previously.

23. Click **Choose template**, select the **Warehouses (Fin and Ops to Field Service)** template, and click the **OK** button.
24. Select the organization pair under **Organizations** and click the **Create** button.
25. Click the **Warehouse Sync** project.
26. Click **Refresh tables**.
27. Under the **Map** column, click the **>** icon.
28. Delete any mappings with a **Destination** of **None**.
29. Click **Add mapping**.
30. Add a mapping from **PRIMARYADDRESSCITY** to the **City** column created previously.

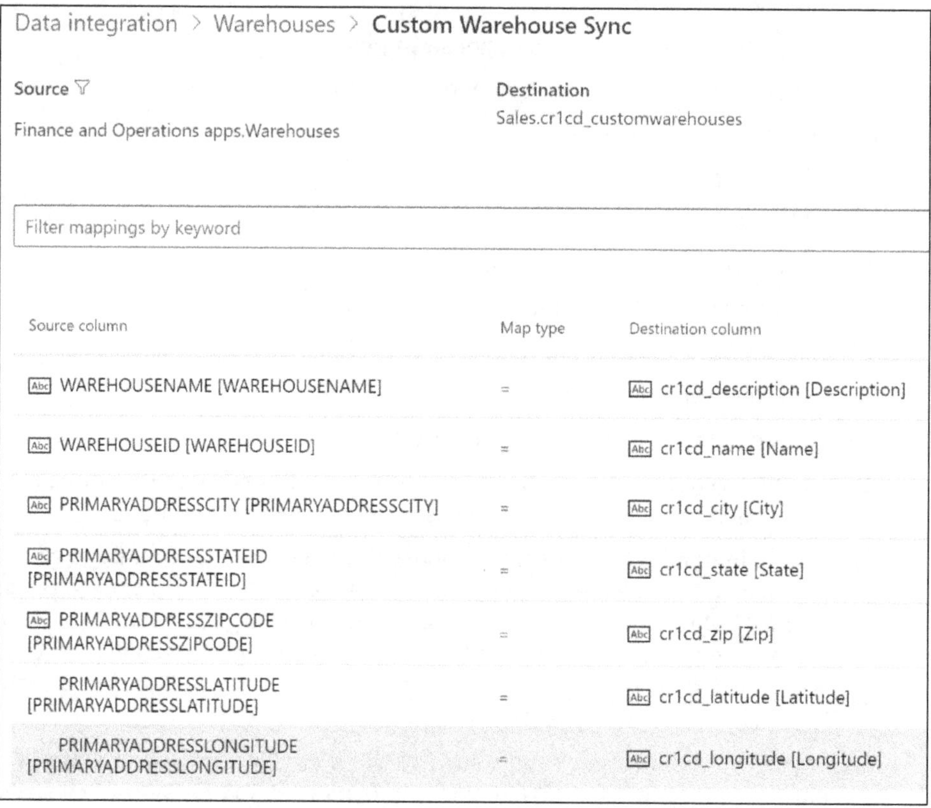

Figure 13.53: Warehouse sync sources and destinations

31. Click **Save**.
32. Click the project name in the breadcrumb.
33. Click **Run project**.

34. Click the **Execution history** tab and wait for the synchronization to complete. There should be 31 **Upserts**.
35. Create a new Power BI Desktop file.
36. Choose **Get data** and then **Dataverse**.
37. Enter the **Environment URL** from *Step 9* of *Getting started*.
38. Sign in and click the **Connect** button.
39. Choose **msdyn_warehouse** in the **Navigator** and click the **Load** button.
40. Create a simple report visual to display the warehouses loaded into the **Dataverse** environment.
41. Save and publish the report to the Power BI service.
42. Open the report in the Power BI service and pin the report visual to a dashboard:

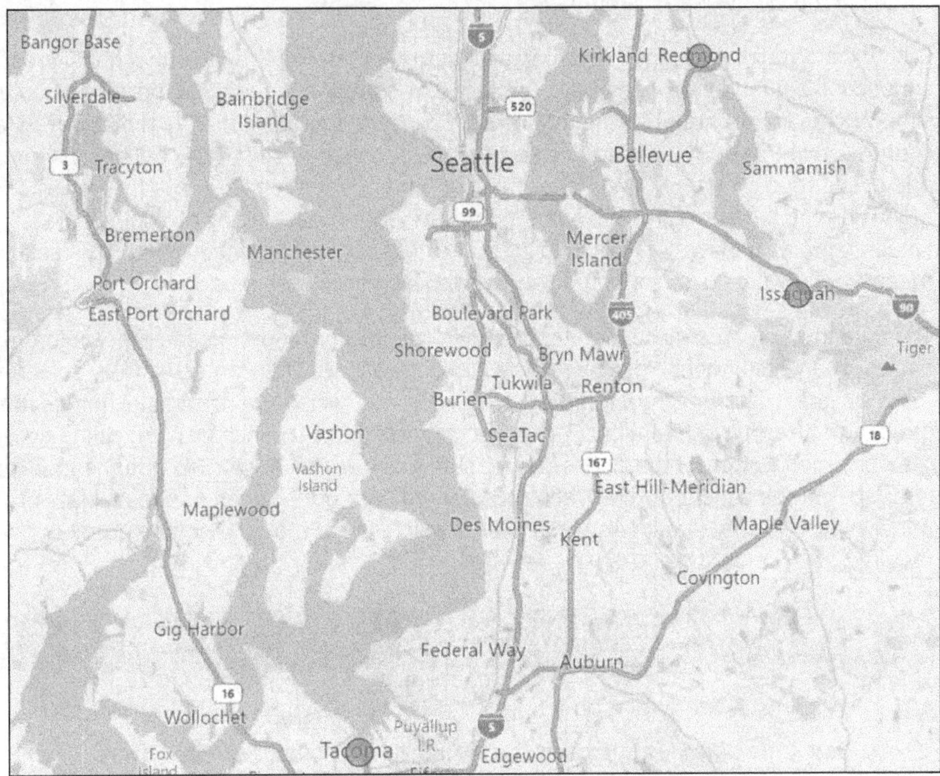

Figure 13.54: Warehouses in the Dataverse environment

Figure 13.54 shows the location of warehouses from Dynamics 365 Finance and Operations loaded into Dataverse.

How it works...

While provisioning the environment, you are given the option to either create a database or not. You might choose to not create a database if the environment is to be used solely for Power Apps and Power Automate development with source data coming from somewhere other than the Dataverse environment. By creating the Dataverse environment with a database and checking the box to **Deploy Dynamics 365 apps** to **Yes**, additional tables are added to the environment to support the chosen applications.

It is important that you set the role for the default team to **System Administrator** or **System Customizer**. By default, the team created as part of the provisioning process has no rights within the system while the user that created the environment is given the **System Administrator** role, among others. However, the synchronization performed by the connection sets, projects, and tasks currently uses the team permissions, not the user permissions, when writing to the Dataverse environment.

Creating a data integration project consists of three tasks, creating connections, creating a connection set, and finally creating a project that contains the tasks to perform. A connection simply holds the authentication credentials for a data source, similar to defining a data source connection in Power BI (data source settings). A connection set simply defines a source and destination system. Unlike Power BI where the destination is always the Power BI data model, data integration projects can synchronize data between any two source systems. Finally, a project defines the tasks to be performed during data integration. The tasks hold the mappings between columns in the source and destination systems.

The data integration projects created in the Power Platform admin center leverage the same Power Query technology as Power BI and dataflows. This can be seen by selecting the task in the data integration project created in this recipe and then selecting **Advanced query and filtering**. The familiar Power Query editor interface is shown, including access to the **Advanced Editor** for the direct insertion of M code. This **Advanced query and filtering** interface can be used to further refine the source data query, such as the removal of unnecessary columns, to improve the overall efficiency of the data source query or perform required transformations.

See also

- Administer Power Platform: `https://bit.ly/3bqaKTQ`
- Integrate data into Microsoft Dataverse: `https://bit.ly/3bpQykV`

Conclusion

This chapter highlighted powerful integration points between Power BI, SSRS, Analysis Services, Excel, PowerPoint, Power Apps, Power Automate, Dataverse, and Dynamics 365. This included connecting Power BI to Analysis Services, leveraging DAX as a query language to support custom reports in Excel, pinning reporting service visuals to Power BI dashboards, and utilizing cube formulas to build templates or scorecard report layouts. Additionally, an example was provided of designing an automated workflow with Power Automate to push data from a relational database to a streaming dataset in the Power BI service, thus delivering real-time visibility to source data changes via common Power BI visualization and data alert capabilities.

Packt>

packt.com

Subscribe to our online digital library for full access to over 7,000 books and videos, as well as industry leading tools to help you plan your personal development and advance your career. For more information, please visit our website.

Why subscribe?

- Spend less time learning and more time coding with practical eBooks and Videos from over 4,000 industry professionals
- Learn better with Skill Plans built especially for you
- Get a free eBook or video every month
- Fully searchable for easy access to vital information
- Copy and paste, print, and bookmark content

Did you know that Packt offers eBook versions of every book published, with PDF and ePub files available? You can upgrade to the eBook version at `www.Packt.com` and as a print book customer, you are entitled to a discount on the eBook copy. Get in touch with us at `customercare@packtpub.com` for more details.

At `www.Packt.com`, you can also read a collection of free technical articles, sign up for a range of free newsletters, and receive exclusive discounts and offers on Packt books and eBooks.

Other Book You May Enjoy

If you enjoyed this book, you may be interested in these other books by Packt:

Microsoft Power BI Quick Start Guide. – Second Edition

Devin Knight

Mitchell Pearson

Bradley Schacht

Erin Ostrowsky

ISBN: 978-1-80056-157-1

- Connect to data sources using import and DirectQuery options
- Use Query Editor for data transformation and data cleansing processes, including writing M and R scripts and dataflows to do the same in the cloud

- Design optimized data models by designing relationships and DAX calculations
- Design effective reports with built-in and custom visuals
- Adopt Power BI Desktop and Service to implement row-level security
- Administer a Power BI cloud tenant for your organization
- Use built-in AI capabilities to enhance Power BI data transformation techniques
- Deploy your Power BI desktop files into the Power BI Report Server

Packt is searching for authors like you

If you're interested in becoming an author for Packt, please visit `authors.packtpub.com` and apply today. We have worked with thousands of developers and tech professionals, just like you, to help them share their insight with the global tech community. You can make a general application, apply for a specific hot topic that we are recruiting an author for, or submit your own idea.

Share Your Thoughts

Now you've finished *Microsoft Power BI Cookbook, Second Edition*, we'd love to hear your thoughts! Scan the QR code below to go straight to the Amazon review page for this book and share your feedback or leave a review on the site that you purchased it from.

`https://packt.link/r/1801813043`

Your review is important to us and the tech community and will help us make sure we're delivering excellent quality content.

Index

A

B

E

F

G

H

I

P

Q

R

S

T

U

V

W

Download a free PDF copy of this book

Thanks for purchasing this book!

Do you like to read on the go but are unable to carry your print books everywhere? Is your eBook purchase not compatible with the device of your choice?

Don't worry, now with every Packt book you get a DRM-free PDF version of that book at no cost.

Read anywhere, any place, on any device. Search, copy, and paste code from your favorite technical books directly into your application.

The perks don't stop there, you can get exclusive access to discounts, newsletters, and great free content in your inbox daily

Follow these simple steps to get the benefits:

1. Scan the QR code or visit the link below

`https://packt.link/free-ebook/9781801813044`

2. Submit your proof of purchase
3. That's it! We'll send your free PDF and other benefits to your email directly

Printed in the USA
CPSIA information can be obtained
at www.ICGtesting.com
JSHW061116240823
47065JS00009B/199